Masterpieces of Contemporary Jurisprudents in China

Gathering the best Chinese legal scholars in different legal fields, this series collects the most representative academic monographs selected and renewed by authors themselves, showing the world updates and development of legal research in China for a more active academic controversy. Through a living publication, this series can provide a full view of legal theoretical research in China to all English readers, and also could be a reliable and effective reference for foreign jurists that specialise in different fields to search answers about China.

Mingkai Zhang

The Fundamental Issues upon Criminal Law Theories

Translated by Sun Lin, Jiang Su, Bao Han, Yue Lei, and Zheng Daxuan

Springer

法律出版社
LAW PRESS · CHINA

Mingkai Zhang
School of Law
Tsinghua University
Beijing, Beijing, China

ISSN 2523-3025 ISSN 2523-3033 (electronic)
Masterpieces of Contemporary Jurisprudents in China
ISBN 978-981-95-1275-1 ISBN 978-981-95-1276-8 (eBook)
https://doi.org/10.1007/978-981-95-1276-8

Jointly published with Law Press China
The print edition is not for sale in China (Mainland). Customers from China (Mainland) please order the print book from: Law Press China.

Originally published by Law Press, China, 2017

Translation from the Chinese Simplified language edition: "犯罪论的基本问题" by Mingkai Zhang, © Law Press · China 2017. Published by Law Press · China. All Rights Reserved.

Sponsored by Chinese Fund for the Humanities and Social Sciences (本书由中华社会科学 基金资助).

This Springer imprint is published by the registered company Springer Nature Singapore Pte Ltd.
The registered company address is: 152 Beach Road, #21-01/04 Gateway East, Singapore 189721, Singapore

Preface (For the Translated English Version)

This book is a collection of articles published by Professor Mingkai Zhang, who is no doubt one of the most influential scholars in criminal law research in China, and currently is the Vice President of Chinese Association of Criminal Law, Vice President of China Association of Police Law, the member of Advisory Committee of the Supreme People's Procuratorate of the People's Republic of China, the special invited researcher of the Association of International Criminal Law of RENMIN University of China, the member of guiding group of Doctoral Program of Criminal Law of Peking University, the adjunct professor of National Judges College, the adjunct professor of National Prosecutors College of P.R.C, the director and professor of the Zhongnan University of Economics and Law, the visiting research of the University of Tokyo, the visiting research professor of Tokyo Metropolitan University, the advanced visiting scholar of University of Bonn, the associated dean of School of Law of Tsinghua University, the Deputy Director of the eighth Prosecutor's Office of the Supreme People's Procuratorate of the People's Republic of China, Vice President of the People's Procuratorate of Xicheng District of Beijing Municipality.

As a matter of fact, the translation is a huge task. During this process, we met a lot of obstacles in finding corresponding names, expressions in different theoretical milieu, because some of them have been quoted frequently in theoretical research for years, and the expression somehow is quite different with the original ones, we have made great effort to contact the scholars and overseas students to ensure we could do our best in translation. Hereby, we'd like to express our thanks to Ms. Wang Mengjia, Ms. Yang Hua, and Ms. Zhao Rong as assistants in our translating, and several other scholars and overseas students in Germany and Japan who gave us valuable advice.

Howsoever, we can't help reckoning some of the omission and error will still be in the final version, we are expecting with great gratitude for our audience to give us feedbacks with no hesitation.

Beijing, China — The translators

Contents

1 **The Pillars of the Theoretical System of Crime** 1
1.1 The Cause and Defect of Unification of Objectivity and Subjectivity in Theoretical System of Crime 1
1.2 Reasons of Constructing Theoretical System of Crime Based on Wrongdoing and Culpability 8
1.3 The Obstacles of Theoretical System of Crime Based on Wrongdoing and Culpability 25
References 30

2 **Criminal Omission Through Creation of Dangerous Situations** 33
2.1 Theoretical Prerequisite of *Ingerenz* 34
2.2 Basic Nature of *Ingerenz* 37
2.3 Specific Contents of *Ingerenz* 52
2.4 Action Scope of *Ingerenz* 60
References 66

3 **Causation and Objective Attribution** 69
3.1 The Formation of the Theory of Objective Attribution 70
3.2 The Theoretical Positioning of Objective Attribution 79
3.3 The Evaluation of the Theory of Objective Attribution 85
3.4 The Reference of the Theory of Objective Attribution 97
References 106

4 **Theory of Wrongdoing from the Perspective of Behavioral Utilitarianism** 109
4.1 The Basic Premise 109
4.2 The Basic Theory 114
4.3 General Conclusion 141
References 143

5 Basic Nature of Defense by Accident 145
5.1 The Theory of Accomplishment of *Handlungsunwert* 147
5.2 The Theory of Attempt of *Handlungsunwert* 156
5.3 The Theory of Attempt of *Erfolgsunwert* 167
5.4 The Dualism of *Erfolgsunwert* 172
5.5 The Theory of Innocence of *Erfolgsunwert* 174
References 178

6 Basic Legal Principles of Risk Assumption 181
6.1 General Theory of Risk Assumption 181
6.2 Involvement in Self-Endangerment 191
6.3 Endangerment by the Third Party Based on Consensus 199
References 216

7 How to Dealing with Specific Method Mistake 219
7.1 The Scope of Method Mistakes 220
7.2 The Relation Between the Theory of Mistake and the Theory of Intention 223
7.3 The Doctrines of Concrete Accord 226
7.4 Theory of Behavior Planning 234
7.5 The Doctrines of Legally Prescribed 237
7.6 Conclusion 245
References 246

8 Jurisprudence of Reasonableness 249
8.1 Basic Issues of Reasonableness 249
8.2 Multiple Meanings of Reasonableness 253
8.3 The Overall Fate of Reasonableness 262
8.4 Specific Issues of Reasonableness 268
8.5 Conclusion 277
References 278

9 The Legal Nature of Abandonment of Crime 281
9.1 Statement of Problems 281
9.2 Path of Japanese Doctrines 283
9.3 Path of German Doctrines 295
9.4 The Basic Position of this Article 299
References 307

10 The Identification of Joint Crime 311
10.1 Defects of Traditional Methods 311
10.2 Focus on Wrongdoing 320
10.3 Center on the Perpetrator 328

10.4 Oriented by Causality 336
10.5 Brief Conclusion 347
References........ 348

11 Legal Concurrence and Ideal Concurrence 351
11.1 Necessity of Distinction........ 351
11.2 Formal Standard........ 354
11.3 Identity of Legal Interests 360
11.4 The Inclusiveness of Wrongdoing 368
11.5 Brief Conclusion 386
References........ 388

Chapter 1
The Pillars of the Theoretical System of Crime

*The original title is "Building the Theory of Crime on the Basis of Wrongdoing and Culpability", published in *Modern Law Science*, 2009, Vol. 6.

Currently, the discussion upon the theoretical system of crime seems a little bit formalized, which lacks the view of what the core or the pillar shall be, and is usually about the theories of how to define the crime (whether a legal provision or a theoretical concept), what elements are in a crime, and what sequence the elements shall be in. This thesis is aimed to explain that the theoretic system of crime should be established on the base of wrongdoing and culpability.

1.1 The Cause and Defect of Unification of Objectivity and Subjectivity in Theoretical System of Crime

It is generally held that "objectivity" and "subjectivity" have established China's traditional system of crime. In other words, the definition of crime is the combination of criminal object, objective aspect, subject and subjective aspect (referred to as the quadripartite system); the theory of criminal law further develops the object and objective aspect into "objectivity", the subject and subjective aspect into "subjectivity"; the unification of objectivity and subjectivity then occupies the basic position in its features, even becomes the core of China's theoretical system of crime.

The following reasons can explain that situation in China:

Firstly, influenced by the Soviet theory of criminal law, the theoretical system of crime pillared by objectivity and subjectivity in China were formed.

Soviet theory of criminal law gives more emphasis to the unification of subjective and objective elements, while due to ideological reasons, there were some misunderstandings and improper criticism to German theory of criminal law. For example, although Feuerbach didn't put culpability but only acts and objective

M. Zhang, *The Fundamental Issues upon Criminal Law Theories*, Masterpieces of Contemporary Jurisprudents in China,
https://doi.org/10.1007/978-981-95-1276-8_1

elements into elements, he had never ignored the significance of guilt (culpability). C.C.Stübel believed that there was no connection between guilt, capacity for culpability and elements. A. H. Trainin argued that Feuerbach and C.C.Stübel "arbitrarily partitioned the unified definition of crime", so he further emphasized that guilt, capacity for culpability and so forth shall be included in elements.[1] Moreover, A. H. Trainin brought up the theory that the behavioral criminal law suggested by the old school "is organically connected with the specific trend of the whole bourgeois-democratic system"; while in new school's theory, it "refers to punishing the accused in accordance with his/her social class and turns the imprisonment to the proles' exclusive punishment in fact." He further brought forward that "the long-term entangled quarrels, which are among bourgeois criminal jurists over the question of whether the 'act' or 'the actor' is more important, contribute to the illusion that nothing else but two elements mentioned above have the effect of influencing the judgment of the crime and further influencing the type and methods of penalty. On the contrary, "in the socialist system of criminal law, the deep thought about the actor does not or cannot mean the separation of 'actor' and 'act', nor does it mean the underestimation of the objective aspect of the crime. Socialist criminal law doesn't build on the basis of separation or the opposition of subjective and objective elements. Instead, it is on the dialectical evaluation of the actor and his act as a whole."[2] It can be demonstrated from the statement of A. H. Trainin that the reasons for emphasizing the unification of objectivity and subjectivity are to distinguish the socialist theory of criminal law from bourgeois theory of criminal law. However, it's still not clear whether the unification of objectivity and subjectivity brought up by A.H. Trainin refers to the unification of punishment base (ground) and object, or that of elements constituting the crime.

"The period from 1949 to 1953 has witnessed the establishment of the criminal law of People's Republic of China. Negating Old government's criminal law while taking almost verbatim from Soviet's criminal law were the main features of this period."[3] Therefore, China's criminal law text book in 1950's pointed out that "a criminal act is the unification of objective and subjective elements of one's social harmful act. Subjectivity (intention or negligence) reveals in objectivity. That is to say, one's act can be regarded as criminal act only when the social harmfulness posed (or may be posed) by it. Without showing a criminal intention or negligence, or the objective harm not posed by the intention or negligence, one's act cannot be treated as criminal offence... The definition of crime is always the unification of

---

[1] \[苏\]A.H.特拉伊宁:《犯罪构成的一般学说》，薛秉忠等译，中国人民大学出版社1958年版，第15页。A.H.Трайнин, trans. Xue Binzhong.(1958) *General Theories of Crime*, China Renmin University Press, 15.

[2] \[苏\]A.H.特拉伊宁:《犯罪构成的一般学说》，薛秉忠等译，中国人民大学出版社1958年版，第18、27、46页。A.H.Трайнин, trans. Xue Binzhong.(1958) *General Theories of Crime*, China Renmin University Press, 18, 27, 46.

[3] 高铭暄主编:《新中国刑法科学简史》，中国人民公安大学出版社1993年版，第8页。Gao Mingxuan ed.(1993) *Brief History of Criminal Law in People's Republic of China*, Press of People's Public Security University of China, 8.

necessary objective and subjective elements of a crime."[4] As the new theoretical system of crime cannot be completed in a short time, the original one has to be abided by even after China's Reform and Opening-up. In this sense, quadripartite system based on subjectivity and objectivity as its pillars has its own historical inevitability.

Secondly, because of the historical lessons of the "Cultural Revolution", unification of subjectivity and objectivity has become the guiding principle of creating the theory of crime to avoid the objective attribution and subjective attribution in China.

As a matter of fact, a great deal of objective and subjective attributions existed during the "Cultural Revolution". In order to eliminate those, the unification of subjectivity and objectivity has been required. For example, the earlier text book regarding unification of subjectivity and objectivity as one of the criminal law principles pointed out that "Human thoughts dominate human behavior, while human behaviors reflect human thoughts. Based on this dialectical materialism principle, China's criminal law goes on following the unification of subjectivity and objectivity in determining the crime and the culpability. That is to say, subjective attribution and objective attribution shall not be adopted, but to take a one-sided approach. The former only takes one's subjectivity, psychology and *mens rea* into consideration and the latter only considers the objective damage, regardless of whether there is subjective intention and negligence. Obviously, subjective attribution and objective attribution will lead to the separation of actor's thinking and act, and inevitably give rise to wrongful pursuit of criminal culpability, confusion of crime and non-crime as well as violation of socialist legal principles. The unification of subjective and objective, on the other side, brings forward that the premise of determining a crime and pursuing criminal culpability is that the actor must objectively conduct the social harmful act and has the intention or negligence of conducting the criminal act and getting certain result. No crime shall be determined and no criminal culpability shall be pursued without any of the two elements above."[5] Clearly, as the guiding principle of constructing theoretical system of crime, the unification of subjectivity and objectivity is aimed to eliminate the phenomena of objective attribution and subjective attribution. In this sense, the principle is of practical significance in convicting and sentencing.

Thirdly, conceiving the social harmfulness as the crime nature and emphasizing the social harmfulness consist of objective and subjective elements can contribute to maintaining the quadripartite system based on objectivity and subjectivity.

---

[4] 中央政法干部学校刑法教研室编著:《中华人民共和国刑法总则讲义》，法律出版社1957年版，第74~75页。Political Science and Law Cadres Institution of the CPC Central Committee ed.(1957) *Handouts of General Rules of Criminal Law in People's Republic of China*, Law Press,74–75.

[5] 中央政法干部学校刑法教研室编著:《中华人民共和国刑法总则讲义》，法律出版社1957年版，第74~75页。Political Science and Law Cadres Institution of the CPC Central Committee ed.(1957) *Handouts of General Rules of Criminal Law in People's Republic of China*, Law Press,74–75.

Influenced by Soviet theories of criminal law, China's counterpart theory has regarded social harmfulness as the crime nature since the last 1950's. It also holds that the inner structure of social harmfulness is the combination or unification of objective and subjective elements. For example, the criminal law text book of 1950's pointed out: "the social harmfulness of act is the most essential feature of a crime". Three closely related aspects have determined the social harmfulness degree: "the nature of act", "the damage and its range" and "the actor's subjective aspect". In other words, "the degree of social harmfulness of distinguishing crime and non-crime is a result of combined and unified thinking of the three aspects. So, the degree of social harmfulness is determined by all objective and subject aspects of the act."[6] In China, after the Reform and Opening-up, the most popular theory of criminal law still holds the view that the social harmfulness consists of the objective elements and the subjective elements. For example, some book says: "social harmfulness of an act is the basic feature of the crime." Thus, what indeed determines the degree of social harmfulness? The answer might be: A.the object of the offence: what kind of social relationship has been violated by the act… B.means, consequence, time and location of the act… C.the condition and subjective element of the actor."[7] In summary, the degree of social harmfulness has been determined by four elements, or, by objective danger and subjective viciousness.

The social harmfulness is the nature of crime, and what committees a crime is the manifestation of crime concept or the legal form of the social harmfulness, of which the degree of harmfulness is determined by the combination and unification of subjectivity and objectivity. Thus, it is a must to view the definition of crime as the unification of subjectivity and objectivity, which therefore becomes the pillar of the theoretical system of crime.

Fourthly, some misunderstandings about the theoretical system of crime in Germany and Japan also play a part in maintaining the system based on the pillar of objectivity and subjectivity.

Chinese scholars got to know the theories of criminal law after the Reform and Opening-up. Unfortunately, some misunderstandings emerged during that period. In Germany and Japan, the prevalent theoretical system of crime featured by conformity of elements, liability (*Rechtswidrigkeit*) and condemnable (*Verantwortlichkeit*) is misunderstood by lots of Soviet and Chinese scholars, who regarded the elements of crime as the same as that of their domestic systems. In their view, the system of classic criminal theory separated the objective and subjective elements of a crime, thus subject elements shall be admitted into the elements. For example, Soviet

[6] 中央政法干部学校刑法教研室编著:《中华人民共和国刑法总则讲义》，法律出版社1957年版，第56、61、63~64页。Political Science and Law Cadres Institution of the CPC Central Committee ed.(1957) *Handouts of General Rules of Criminal Law in People's Republic of China,* Law Press,56, 61, 63–64.

[7] 中央政法干部学校刑法教研室编著:《中华人民共和国刑法总则讲义》，法律出版社1957年版，第56、61、63~64页。Political Science and Law Cadres Institution of the CPC Central Committee ed.(1957) *Handouts of General Rules of Criminal Law in People's Republic of China,* Law Press,56, 61, 63–64.

scholars pointed out: "Each criminal act is the unification of objective and subjective elements of certain social harmful act. To dialectically understand the unification is the base of correctly understanding the definition of crime in Socialist criminal law."[8] Some Chinese scholars also observed: "The theory upon the definition of crime proposed by Berlinguer, the pioneer of modern theory of the definition of crime, advocates that only objective elements shall be included in elements, while the subjective elements, including intention or negligence and so on, shall be totally excluded from the the definition of crime. It is such a one-sided and incorrect theory and therefore criticized or reformed by some scholars. On the contrary, in Chinese theory of criminal law, the elements shall contain all the necessary objective and subjective elements that will determine a crime. It is an organic and unified integral being blending a series of objective and subjective elements. It directly reflects the basic principle of the integration of subjectivity and objectivity and shows *Chinese Criminal Law*'s opposing attitude to both of the objective and subjective attribution."[9]

In fact, classical theoretical system of crime deemed capacity for culpability, intention and negligence as parts of the elements of culpability, rather than elements of crime. However, it is not the same thing with objective attribution. The definition of crime refers to all the elements which committees a crime in China, while in Germany and Japan, the element of crime is merely one of the elements to determine a crime. Obviously, the reason why the unification of subjectivity and objectivity has been attached great importance in China is that as the only ground for determining a crime, the element of crime has been interpreted as the same as the criminal elements in Germany and Japan, or required to have the same function with the latter.

When the element of crime has been regarded as all the factors to determine a crime, it is not wrong to require the existence of subjectivity and objectivity. In this case, merely taking subjective element or objective element into consideration will inevitably lead to objective or subjective attribution. However, it is far from enough to regard the objectivity and subjectivity as the pillar of crime.

Firstly, the connotations of subjectivity and objectivity vary from different occasions. Therefore, the real meanings shall be made clear in constructing the theoretical system of crime. To begin with, in traditional quadripartite system, act is an objective element while intention and negligence are subjective elements from the perspective of practical structure; criminal object is an objective element in the

[8]\[苏\]契希克瓦节主编:《苏维埃刑法总则》，中央人民政府法制委员会编译室、中国人民大学刑法教研室译，法律出版社1955年版，第206页。Чхиквадзе, trans. Translation Office of the Legislative Affairs Commission of the CPC Central Committee & Criminal Law Teaching and Researching Office of China Renmin University(1955) *Course of Soviet Criminal Law,* Law Press, 206.

[9]\[苏\]契希克瓦节主编:《苏维埃刑法总则》，中央人民政府法制委员会编译室、中国人民大学刑法教研室译，法律出版社1955年版，第206页。Чхиквадзе, trans. Translation Office of the Legislative Affairs Commission of the CPC Central Committee & Criminal Law Teaching and Researching Office of China Renmin University(1955) *Course of Soviet Criminal Law,* Law Press, 206.

sense of ontology; however, it is uncertain to classify the age of responsibility and capacity for culpability as "subjective element" for those don't belong to the inner mind. Therefore, traditional system is not an ideal way of classification. Moreover, in the traditional system, social harmfulness cannot be determined by objective and subjective elements separately, but it can be determined by the unification of them. Therefore, the respective function and meaning of the objective and subjective elements cannot be identified. "When we try to build the system of criminal law, the question of whether or not to apply descriptive or normative language has been raised. To put it in another way, the question is, whether the elements of building a system of criminal law are the facts that can be judged or described."[10] The author preferred to construct the theoretical system of crime from the perspective of value and purpose. If "objectivity" refers to the outward objects, and "subjectivity" to the inner mind, the discussion about the two elements still halts at the level of description.[11] However, "the descriptive distinction between outward objects and inner mind can only been made with relation to evaluation. In other words, the distinction only makes sense with respect to its legal importance. Therefore, distinguishing the objective and subjective elements from the very beginning is of no enlightening significance and cannot be treated as testing method; on the contrary, classifying the objective facts as wrongdoing and classifying subjective facts as culpability are very important."[12]

Secondly, if the unification and integration of objectivity and subjectivity being the sole requirement, it cannot explain the relationship between objectivity and subjectivity, nor can it guarantee the determination of crime from objectivity to subjectivity. Deeming subjectivity and objectivity as the only elements of a crime, is just like deeming oxygen and hydrogen as elements of water, hence it doesn't matter which element shall be prior. Therefore, the theoretical system of crime by the sequence of subjectivity to objectivity has come into being (crime subject, subjective aspect of a crime, objective aspect of a crime, crime object). This system emphasizes the idea that "it is the intention or negligence that determines the specific criminal act of the actor", and leads to the determination of a crime with the

---

[10]\[德\]许迺曼:"刑法体系思想导论", 载许玉秀、陈志辉合编:《不移不惑献身法与正义——许迺曼教授刑法事法论文选辑》, 台北春风煦日论坛2006年版, 第293页。Bernd Schünemann, *Criminal Law System's Manifesto*, as cited in Chen Zhihui, ed., *Unbestechlich und unbeirrbar im dienst von recht unechtigkeit: abhandlungen zur gesamten strafrechtswissenschaft von BERND SCHUNEMANN*, Taiwan: taedp.org.tw, 2006:293.

[11]There exists the same question to generalize conditions of crime establishment into actus reus and mens rea in the Anglo - American theory of criminal law.

[12]\[德\]许迺曼:"区分不法与罪责的功能", 载许玉秀、陈志辉合编:《不移不惑献身法与正义——许迺曼教授刑法事法论文选辑》, 台北春风煦日论坛2006年版, 第424页。Bernd Schünemann, *Distinguishing the Illegality and Culpability*, as cited in Chen Zhihui, ed., *Unbestechlich und unbeirrbar im dienst von recht unechtigkeit: abhandlungen zur gesamten strafrechtswissenschaft von BERND SCHUNEMANN*, Taiwan: taedp.org.tw, 2006:424.

Schunemann also points out: it is hasty and wrong to classify subjective aspects in the infringement of legal interests and objective aspects into culpability, because there are objective elements of responsibility and subjective elements of violation (ibid.).

sequence of subjectivity to objectivity. The most forceful way to illustrate such theory is that, it has taken the theory of abstract danger, even the theory of subjective danger in distinguishing the incapable crime and attempted crime.

Thirdly, regarding the objectivity and subjectivity as the crime pillar makes it difficult to limit the scale of punishment in some cases. That is because the quadripartite system asserts that the social harmfulness, or to say, consists of objective harmfulness and subjective viciousness, is the nature of crime. Therefore, as long as the social harmfulness reaches a serious level, it shall be considered to be a crime. Objective harmfulness and subjective viciousness have positively provided grounds for crime in the quadripartite system, thus the crime cannot be easily determined and limited. In fact, the requirement of subjective element is to solve the problem of subjective attribution, that is, to ascribe the act and consequence to the actor after the nature and consequence of the one's act are objectively determined. Therefore, although elements like capacity for culpability, intention, and negligence and so on can provide basis for possibility of punishment, they also play key roles in limiting the establishment of crime. For example, A broke into one's house and took the world-famous painting as an ordinary painting. Under the quadripartite system, A had the intention and he objectively committed the burglary, thus there was a unification of subjectivity and objectivity, so he shall be responsible to the extremely large amount of money. However, it is not appropriate. The right way is to consider the objective value of the stolen property first, then to find out whether the actor has the idea of the value of the property. If the actor objectively steals the property of extremely large value, but his recognition is at a lower value, then he shall only be responsible to the latter. On the contrary, if A had stolen the ordinary paintings for the world-famous paintings, under the quadripartite system, A shall be deemed to be with the intent of stealing the property of extremely large value. Although A did not steal the property of extremely large value, his subjectivity and objectivity had unified in the property of extremely large value, thus A shall be punished as those who steal extremely large amounts of extreme property (attempted). However, the right way is to recognize the actor as stealing property of large amount in the aspect of wrongdoing, then to determine whether the actor should be responsible in the aspect of culpability. Then the result will be: the actor is only subject to the legal penalty of stealing property of large amount value, but not the property of extremely large value.

Fourthly, it is also doubtful whether objectivity and subjectivity separately corresponds to objective harmfulness and subjective viciousness (or subjective fault). In context of Chinese Crime Theory, we hold that the nature of crime is social harmfulness, on the other hand, the concepts of "objective harmfulness" and "subjective viciousness" are also emphasized in the theory from time to time. It is still difficult to get in line with the traditional concepts of objectivity and subjectivity to objective harmfulness and subjective viciousness. Most typically, in quadripartite system, the special identification has been classified as "subjectivity ", but clearly it has been regarded as an element of proving the objective harmfulness. It is also hard to establish the status of reasonableness (*Zumutbarkeit*) in the quadripartite system.

The author doesn't object to using the concepts the of objectivity and subjectivity. However, the understanding of the crime itself cannot stop here. The theoretical system of crime shall start with value and purpose, further reflecting the judgment of the act.

1.2 Reasons of Constructing Theoretical System of Crime Based on Wrongdoing and Culpability

"Realizing wrongdoing and culpability are the distinct elements of constructing the system of criminal law, according to Hanz Welzel, is the most significant progress made by scholars of recent two or three generations; Wilfried Küper holds that it is a great achievement and there is no going back; additionally, in Spanish law, Santiago Mir Puig asserts that this progress also establishes *Los dos pillars basicos*, in other words, the second pillar of crime."[13] In summary, wrongdoing should be kept strictly separated and apart from culpability in the research of criminal law.

Countries like Germany and Japan adopt the system of tripartite system, namely, conformity of elements of crime, wrongdoing and culpability.[14] In this system, "it is confusing that the object of study is how to exclude the wrongdoing, rather than how to determine the wrongdoing. However, we must realize that the conformity of elements of crime, which refers to all the features against the criminal law of an act, is concerned about the wrongdoing. As long as the act wasn't permitted by law, it is illegal. Therefore, the facts of decisive significance will be allocated to the tiers of elements and 'wrongdoing'. To some extent, the wrongdoing itself is just a result of conformity of elements of crime and a lack of ground for elimination of crime".[15] It can be seen that in tripartite system," "although the judgment of conformity of elements of crime at the first stage can be distinguished from that of crime elimination facts at the second stage, above two stages are all the judgments of wrongdoing.

---

[13]\[德\]许迺曼:"区分不法与罪责的功能"，载许玉秀、陈志辉编:《不移不惑献身法与正义——许迺曼教授刑事法论文选辑》，台北春风和煦学术基金2006年版，第416页。Bernd Schünemann, *Distinguishing the Illegality and Culpability*, as cited in Chen Zhihui, ed., *Unbestechlich und unbeirrbar im dienst von recht unechtigkeit: abhandlungen zur gesamten strafrechtswissenschaft von BERND SCHUNEMANN*, Taiwan: taedp.org.tw, 2006:416.

[14]In German's three-tier theoretical system of criminology, the elements of the second tier are called "wrongdoing"(*Rechtswidrigkeit*); and because the constitutive elements are of an illegal type, illegal constitutive definition of crime are referred to as "unlawful" (*Unrecht*). The concept of wrongdoing emphasizes the nature of the act (value judgment), is the evaluation of the object; because the behavior that conforms to the constitutive elements is the object of evaluation, the concept of unlawful includes the evaluation object of the wrongdoing and the evaluation of the object (C.Roxin,Strafrecht Allgemeiner Teil,Band, 4.Aufl.,München:C.H.Beck, 2006, S.600 f.).

[15]\[德\]冈特·施特拉腾韦特、洛塔尔·库伦:《刑法总论I——犯罪论》，杨萌译，法律出版社2006年版，第81页。GiinterStratenwerth, Lothar Kuhlen, trans. Yang Meng.(2006) *Strafrecht Allgemeiner Teil I: Die Straftat*, Law Press, 81.

Therefore, the essential judgments to criminal law can be divided into judgment of wrongdoing and of culpability from the overall situation. That's to say, the pillar of theoretical system of crime is wrongdoing and culpability."[16]

Setting the wrongdoing and culpability as the pillars of the theory of crime[17] has a well-founded basis and intrinsic rationality.

(1) Setting the wrongdoing and culpability as the pillar of the theory of crime corresponds to the distinctions between causal responsibility and moral responsibility in philosophy. Besides, it is also reasonable in the view of social psychology.

In perspective of philosophy, responsibility in broader sense can mean causal responsibility and moral responsibility. For example, one's precious vase has been broken. It is a result no matter it caused by the guest's intended act or by the owner's cat. "In this sense, the guest and the cat should be liable to the broken vase in each situation. Both of them have the casual liabilities and have played certain causal roles in breaking the vase. However, although human and animals all have the causal liabilities to certain events, only the human can take the moral liability to the result".[18] In other words, "we must distinguish the causal responsibility and moral responsibility. Both of the guest and the cat have played causal roles in breaking the vase. However, when human and nonhuman all have abilities to causally raise the result, only human will take the moral responsibility. However, when human and nonhuman all have the abilities to causally raise the result, only human will take the moral responsibility. The attitudes that apply only to human is one of the intrinsic features of being a human. We can appropriately attribute the attitudes to a human, only when she/he is able to take the moral responsibility. On the other side, we always believe that only when a human did something of her/his own free will, can we say that he/she is morally responsible for what he did".[19]

---

[16]\[日\]井田良:《刑法总论の理论构造》，成文堂2005年版，第1页。大陆与我国台湾地区的部分学者，将德语的"Schuld"(即本文所称责任)翻译为"罪责"。 Ida Makoto.(2005) *Theories of General Rules of Criminal Law*, seibundoh, 1. Some scholars in Chinese Mainland and Taiwan hold the view that the German word "Schuld" which in my theses is called culpability shall be put into the word "responsibility".

[17]In the era of principle of legality, the premise to the violation of law is the behavior meeting the constitutive definition of crime. While acts meeting the constitutive definition of crime and violating law (without grounds for elimination of crime) is unlawful. "The infringement of legal interests" in this article refers to being unlawful.

[18]\[美\]约翰·马丁·费舍、马克、拉维扎:《责任与控制》，杨绍刚译，华夏出版社2002年版，第2页。John Martin Fischer, Mark Ravizza, trans. Yang Shaogang, *Responsibility and Control*(2002), Huaxia Publishing House, 2.

[19]徐向东:《理解自由意志》，北京大学出版社2008年版，第11页。Xu Xiangdong(2008), *Understanding Free Wills*, Peking University Press, 11.

Being relative to causal responsibility, moral responsibility does not particularly need to be associated with moral right or wrong, but with responsiveness of human being. In criminal law, causal responsibility is an objective attribution problem, and moral responsibility is subjective attribution. However, this does not mean that criminal culpability is an ethical or moral responsibility.

It is also the process of determining a crime. For example, C is dead, which is a result. In judicial practice, the first thing to do is to find out the causal responsibility or the reasons that lead to the death of C, or to say, whether it is A, who is of sound mind that intended to shoot C, or it is B, who is suffering mental disorder shoot C to death. Both of A and B have the causal responsibilities to C, for their acts deprived C of his/her life. That makes the case of wrongdoing (the infringement of legal interest). However, it is still not the ground of pursuing the moral responsibility. The fact that A is able to take the moral responsibility for what he did while B cannot, so only A will be held responsible for moral responsibility. In a word, both of A and B shall take the causal responsibilities but only A shall take the moral responsibility. In this sense, the wrongdoing is about the causal responsibility and the culpability is about moral responsibility, corresponding to the causal responsibility and moral responsibility in philosophy.

In the view of social psychology, "the motion sequence expected by Finchem, Chaval and Schultz can be expressed as: result → reason-finding → responsibility → condemnation → punishment. This process is established on the following premises: (a) attribution should be distinguished from judgment of responsibility; (b) judgement of responsibility should be distinguished from condemnation; (c) attribution of responsibility should indirectly affect the punishment and other social reactions through the condemnations of the intermediary. Thus, attribution of responsibility and the consequence belong to a series of elements of the process." In other words, "The finding of the behavioral responsibility starts with the happening of an event, followed by the finding of reasons. After realizing what happened, the first step is to determine whether the event is due to personal act or the circumstance. Only the event attributes to the person, does he/she be regarded as liable."[20]

The determination of crime is also the same with the case. When certain results have been caused, the first thing to do is to figure out the attribution, or to say, whose and what acts lead to the result. It is a must to distinguish the attribution from culpability. Determining whether the actor should be responsible after the attributing the crime to him/her. If the criminal policy and necessity of preventing crimes have been taken into consideration, it is possible that the actor may not be condemned and punished by the criminal law. Therefore, setting the wrongdoing and culpability as the pillar of theory of crime, and further determining the crime from the wrongdoing to culpability are well grounded in social psychology.

(2) Setting the wrongdoing and culpability as the pillars of the theoretical system of crime is in accordance with the substantive object of the crime.

The substance of the theoretical system of crime depends on the substantive object of the crime. Then, what is the substantive object of the crime? Only the following two conditions have been satisfied can an act be regarded as a crime: First,

[20]\[美\]B.维纳:《责任推断:社会行为的理论基础》，张爱卿、郑葳等译，华东师范大学出版社2004年版，译者导言，第5、9页。Bernard Weiner, trans. Zhang Aiqing, Zheng Wei, (2004) *Judgments of responsibility: A foundation for a theory of social conduct*, Shanghai: East China Normal University Press, 5, 9.

there is a fact (wrongdoing); second, this fact can be attributed to the actor (culpability).[21]

"The wrongdoing refers to the violation of criminal legal norms (evaluation norms) in terms of its form, is also the feature and the evaluation of certain acts in nature of negativity by the criminal norms. Therefore, the wrongdoing shall be determined in accordance with the purpose of criminal law. Which means, what acts will be forbidden shall take a reference with the purpose in law. Thus, the concept of substantive wrongdoing and the understanding of the concept and essence of the wrongdoing are based on that of the tasks and purpose of criminal law."[22] Criminal law is aimed to protect the legal interest, thus acts and consequences that violating the legal interest will be banned. In other words, only acts violating or threatening the legal interests will be regarded as crimes. This infringement of legal interest is the substantive wrongdoing, and it will be forbidden by the criminal law even without intention or negligence, so criminal law will never allow the murder committed by mental patients, nor allow the robbery committed by the minors under 14 years old. Moreover, the notion that someone objectively violates the legal interests is of no social harmfulness clearly is untrue. For example, A disclosed the state's secrets to foreign organizations with no intention and negligence. His act is obviously an infringement of legal interest. One more example, B's act leads to the death of others without intention and negligence, which is certainly an infringement of legal interest. However, criminal law doesn't punish the mentioned acts is not because those acts are not violations of legal interest, but because the actors don't have *vorwerfbarkeit* to be punished.

In conclusion, "the premise that the criminal acts shall be socially harmful… is set up in the enlightenment period of modern criminal law by great effort. It appeared in the constitutions of many countries as a result of its long historical origin. Meanwhile, even being questioned and ignored, that premise has become the legal interest protecting theory for almost two centuries. As the base of discussion of teleology in crime field, the principles of social harmfulness or protection of legal interest are still indispensable."[23]

To point out, only the element of violating the legal interests is not enough to constitute a crime. A view accepted by the people is that, only when the actor can be blamed for his/her illegal act, such acts can be prescribed (determined) as a crime. Put it further, the actor can be held responsible and condemned for the illegal act

---

[21] 参见\[日\]前田雅英:《刑法总论讲义》，东京大学出版会2006年第4版，第36页以下。See Maeda Masahide.(2006) *Handouts of General Rules of Criminal Law(fourth Edition)*, University of Tokyo Press, 1–36.

[22] \[日\]山口厚:《刑法总论》，有斐阁2007年版，第101页。 Yamaguchi Atsushi.(2007) *General Rules of Criminal Law*, Yuhikaku Press, 101.

[23] \[德\]许迺曼:"刑事不法之体系"，载许玉秀、陈志辉合编:《不移不惑献身法与正义——许迺曼教授刑法事法论文选辑》，台北春风煦日论坛2006年版，第201页。Bernd Schünemann, (2006) *Illegality System of Criminal Law*, as cited in Chen Zhihui, ed., *Unbestechlich und unbeirrbar im dienst von recht unechtigkeit: abhandlungen zur gesamten strafrechtswissenschaft von BERND SCHUNEMANN*, Taiwan: taedp.org.tw, 201.

and consequences, a crime can hence come into being. This is criminal law's very function of safeguarding human rights. The premise of citizens' freedom is based on the prediction possibility, in case that citizens will be punished as long as they violated legal interest even acting with great caution, no freedom can be said to be endowed. Or to say, only when citizens, who violate legal interests intentionally or negligently, will the legal interest violated behavior be regarded as a crime. This requirement protects the prediction possibility of citizens and further protects their freedom. Therefore, *vorwerfbarkeit* (culpability) is another pillar of the crime.

> The existing law can be reorganized from two value aspects: the act is of obvious objective valueless (especially in sense of criminal law) and the actor is personally liable to the act. To push forward for sub-aspects, it can be educed that only when, firstly, the act is forbidden on any account, and secondly, unexpected in any approved forms (that is, certain legal interest has been seriously violated and the protection of criminal law to the legal interest is effective, necessary and appropriate), will the specific principle of valueless in criminal law (wrongdoing in criminal law) come into being; as to the individual crime and responsibility, the act should be avoidable on any account (the actor will be blamed), then it is necessary for the motive to be of no proper value (necessary to be punished). The fundamental basis of the system of criminal law is thus constituted by the values, that is, by the wrongdoing and culpability, which all belong to the appropriate range of valueless.[24]

Setting the wrongdoing and culpability as the pillars of crime is in accordance with the concept of crime in China. Article 13 of *Criminal Law* of China provides that: "A crime refers to an act that endangers the sovereignty, territorial integrity and security of the State, splits the State, subverts the State power of the people's democratic dictatorship and overthrows the socialist system, undermines public and economic order, violates State-owned property, property collectively owned by the working people, or property privately owned by citizens, infringes on the citizens' rights of the person, their democratic or other rights, and any other act that endangers society and is subject to punishment according to law. However, if the circumstances are obviously minor and the harm done is not serious, the act shall not be considered a crime." Although this article has always been regarded as the expression of crime features, including social harmfulness, criminal wrongdoing and subject to punishment, it still can be interpreted in a more reasonable way. Firstly, the purpose of criminal law is to protect the legal interest, therefore, the social harmful acts or acts violating legal interests are forbidden by the criminal law. Secondly, not all the social harmful acts are subject to punishment. According to the criminal law, only when the three requirements are all met, will the act be punished: (a) the social harmful acts must be categorized as elements by law, or be punished by the specific provisions of criminal law or other regulations (which prescribed punishment for the specified social harmful acts), this is the first tier of "is subject to punishment according to law"; (b) for that minor and not serious social harmfulness, in

[24]\[德\]许逎曼:"刑法体系思想导论"，载许玉秀、陈志辉合编:《不移不惑献身法与正义——许逎曼教授刑法事法论文选辑》，台北春风煦日论坛2006年版，第293页。Bernd Schünemann, (2006) *Criminal Law System's Manifesto*, as cited in Chen Zhihui, ed., *Unbestechlich und unbeirrbar im dienst von recht unechtigkeit: abhandlungen zur gesamten strafrechtswissenschaft von BERND SCHUNEMANN*, Taiwan: taedp.org.tw, 293.

accordance with Article 13 of *Criminal Law*: "if the circumstances are obviously minor and the harm done is not serious," the act shall not be punished, this is the second tier of "is subject to punishment according to law"; (c) the only existence of social harmful act is not enough to be punished by law. According to the *Criminal Law,* only when the actor has intention to the social harmful act and consequence (Article 14) or has the negligence (Article 15), and reaches the age of responsibility (Article 17) and shall bear the capacity for culpability (Article 18), and his/her act can be foreseen by the actor (Article 16), will the actor be punished by law, which makes the third tier. The first tier is determined by the purpose of protection of legal interest, showing the rationality in terms of the ordinary people (including the country and the society); the second tier is determined by the modesty of the criminal law; while the third one is the requirement of respecting people, showing the reasonableness in terms of the actor. In summary, the serious infringement of legal interest and culpability is the substance of the crime.

In conclusion, the purpose shall be the starting point when the concept of criminal law is being discussed. As the purpose of criminal law is aimed to protect the legal interest, considering the purpose first is quite reasonable to the victims (including the country, society and citizens); the reasonableness to the actor shall also be taken into consideration.[25] Thus, "the purposes of criminal law are mostly the same in the modern society. Therefore, there is no good reason to make different choices on distinguishing the wrongdoing and culpability: when we regard the purpose of criminal law as protection of legal interest, which can be realized by general prevention, reasonable retribution or special prevention by the principle of justification of crime and culpability, there must be two different views, which are (a) to develop and emphasize the view that the victim's act is valueless based on the social harmfulness, and (b) to highlight that the actor's act can be avoided, that is, *vorwerfbarkeit*."[26]

(3) Setting the wrongdoing and culpability as the pillars of the theoretical system of crime conforms with the nature and mechanism of criminal law.

Since Binding had established the theory of norms, the arguments about the system of criminal law has continually been discussed due to the controversies over the nature of criminal norms, eventually formed the confrontation, except for the following views: the criminal code, which regulates the behavior of the judge (adjudication norms), obviously implies the negative evaluation (behavior norms) of the

[25] 参见\[德\]许迺曼:"千喜年后的德国刑法学"，载许玉秀、陈志辉合编:《不移不惑献身法与正义——许迺曼教授刑法事法论文选辑》，台北春风煦日论坛2006年版，第173页。Bernd Schünemann, (2006) *German Criminal Law after the Millennium*, as cited in Chen Zhihui, ed., *Unbestechlich und unbeirrbar im dienst von recht unechtigkeit: abhandlungen zur gesamten strafrechtswissenschaft von BERND SCHUNEMANN*, Taiwan: taedp.org.tw, 173.

[26] \[德\]许迺曼:"区分不法与罪责的功能"，载许玉秀、陈志辉合编:《不移不惑献身法与正义——许迺曼教授刑法事法论文选辑》，台北春风煦日论坛2006年版，第429页。Bernd Schünemann, (2006) *Distinguishing the Illegality and Culpability*, as cited in Chen Zhihui, ed., *Unbestechlich und unbeirrbar im dienst von recht unechtigkeit: abhandlungen zur gesamten strafrechtswissenschaft von BERND SCHUNEMANN*, Taiwan: taedp.org.tw, 429.

actors' behaviors by the legislature; the legislature must give negative evaluation to the criminal act, otherwise the punishment to the criminal act is meaningless. Thus, the evaluation norms that negatively judged the actors' behavior shall precede the adjudication norms in logic; since the task of criminal law is to protect the legal interest, only when the citizens are all against the acts that violated legal interest, will the task be accomplished. Therefore, there is a norm that regulates the citizens in fact.[27]

The evaluation norms refer to evaluating the value of certain act from the perspective of criminal law, that is, whether an act is harmful is judged by the criminal norms. Therefore, the criminal norms are also the evaluation norms. The concept of determination norms is that the criminal norms order people to follow the criminal law when they performing certain acts, thus it also is called the intention determination norms. The evaluation norms precede determination norms in logic. As the evaluation norms are the absolute logical premises of the determination norms, it is unbelievable if there is no law as evaluation norms; that is because if someone wants to make a "determination" for others, he/she must know the matters be decided in advance; he/she must "evaluate" the matters in a decisive sense. The logical premises of the determination norms are also the laws being the evaluation norms and the law being the "orders of objective life". The wrongdoing is determined by the evaluation norms while the culpability is determined by the determination norms.[28]

The wrongdoing and culpability of crime just correspond to the mechanism of protection of legal interest and human right. As the purpose of criminal law is to protect the legal interests, the violations of legal interests are equal to illegal acts; and the prohibition of illegal acts means the realization of protection of legal interest. However, the criminal law can only punish the individual act that can be avoided. In other words, the actors will be punished only when they are reasonableness. Culpability is an important element to protect the individual's freedom. Punishing the responsible acts is to achieve the target of protecting human rights.

(4) Setting the wrongdoing and culpability as the pillars of the theoretical system of crime is conductive to the reasonable distinctions between justifiable cause and cause of preventive culpability.

Apart from the elements of crime, the traditional quadripartite system also discusses two legal grounds for elimination of crimes, which are justifiable defense and necessity; later, some extralegal grounds for elimination of crimes have also

---

[27]\[德\]许迺曼:"区分不法与罪责的功能"，载许玉秀、陈志辉合编:《不移不惑献身法与正义——许迺曼教授刑法事法论文选辑》，台北春风煦日论坛2006年版，第429页。Bernd Schünemann, (2006) *Distinguishing the Illegality and Culpability*, as cited in Chen Zhihui, ed., *Unbestechlich und unbeirrbar im dienst von recht unechtigkeit: abhandlungen zur gesamten strafrechtswissenschaft von BERND SCHUNEMANN*, Taiwan: taedp.org.tw, 429.

[28]\[德\]许迺曼:"区分不法与罪责的功能"，载许玉秀、陈志辉合编:《不移不惑献身法与正义——许迺曼教授刑法事法论文选辑》，台北春风煦日论坛2006年版，第429页。Bernd Schünemann, (2006) *Distinguishing the Illegality and Culpability*, as cited in Chen Zhihui, ed., *Unbestechlich und unbeirrbar im dienst von recht unechtigkeit: abhandlungen zur gesamten strafrechtswissenschaft von BERND SCHUNEMANN*, Taiwan: taedp.org.tw, 429.

been discussed. However, the important distinction between justifiable cause and cause of preventive culpability has never been made. The reason why the distinction is so important is that the killing upon justifiable defense is totally different in nature from the killing committed by the insane. The former is justified and will not be forbidden and negatively evaluated by the criminal law, while the latter is on the contrary. Therefore, acts of justifiable defense and necessity cannot be conducted in the former situation, but can be conducted against the insane (if justifiable defense cannot be applied, the necessity can be conducted). For another example, people who kill others for justifiable defense shouldn't be required to not act for justifiable defense afterwards; but people who kill others by accident will be asked not to do the same thing again.

Moreover, there are great differences between justifiable cause and cause of preventive culpability. For example, *German Criminal Law* has divided the necessities into necessity as justifiable cause (Article 34) and cause of preventive culpability (Article 35). The connotation of the former is that in order to ensure the actor against the present risks to his/her and others' lives, bodies, freedom and property, and the legal interest being harmed is smaller than that being protected by law, the act will be permitted by the law and thus eliminating the wrongdoing. The latter refers to that when the legal interest harmed is no less than the legal interest protected, although the purpose of the act is to protect himself/herself, the relatives or others who closely related to the actor from present dangers, the act will still be regarded as illegal, and, the responsibility of the actor will be excluded from the culpability for there is no *zumutbarkeit*. Clearly, as to the necessary limits, the justifiable cause are different from that of cause of preventive culpability.

In criminal law, all grounds for elimination of crimes can only be divided into justifiable cause and cause of preventive culpability. That is to say, acts described in the specific provisions of criminal law (acts meet elements of crime) can only be negated as crimes from the perspectives of eliminating either the wrongdoing or the culpability. Even in common law system, where tripartite system has not been adopted, the substantive reasons upon defense (counterargument) have been divided into that for good cause (justifiable cause) and for exemption (cause of preventive culpability). "In common law, the homicide acts can be divided into defense for justification and for forgiveness. Some homicide acts, such as the executioner enforcing the judgments, is the defense for justification. Other acts of killing are entire forgiven defense, if the accident leading others' death isn't caused by the ignorance that shall be punished by law, and then it is a pure defense for forgiveness... The view that the defense for justification and for forgiveness should be distinguished has become popular again in recent years. An act is justified when we express the definite approval to the act; when we are against certain acts, and it is not appropriate to regard the acts as crimes, then those acts can be forgiven."[29] Furthermore, scholars in US had summarized the advantages of making such

---

[29] \[英\]J.C.史密斯、B.霍根:《英国刑法》，李贵方等译，法律出版社2000年版，第215页。Smith, Hogan, trans. Li Guifang, (2000) *Criminal Law*, Beijing: Law Press, 215.

distinction. To distinguish the grounds for good reason and for exemption can be conductive for the criminal law to play the role of guiding people's behaviors. In another word, "people should choose the justifiable act rather than the wrongful act which can be exempted from culpability. If the system of criminal law fails to provide a clear distinction between the two behaviors and paths, people's behaviors will not be well guided." This distinction is able to "provide the unification of the theory of criminal law" and is helpful to solve the criminal culpability of the accomplices." The defense for good cause can be wildly applied while the defense for exemption only to certain individuals," and so forth.[30] Some believes that there are facts that lie between two defenses, however, this existence of certain acts doesn't mean that there is no connection between those facts with wrongdoing and culpability. It only means that people haven't figured it out whether those facts aimed to eliminate the wrongdoing or the culpability or both. To make an illustration, a victim has killed a kid who cannot understand the meaning of the act of holding a loaded pistol and is going to pull the trigger at the victim. In this case, there is a dispute about whether the killing act is a defense for good cause (justifiable defense) or a defense for exemption (necessity, without culpability), yet it doesn't mean that the defense is out of the ground for elimination of wrongdoing and culpability.[31]

Substantively speaking, the ground for elimination of crimes can only and must be divided into justifiable cause and cause of preventive culpability, thus, as the correspondence, wrongdoing and culpability shall be the pillars of crime.

(5) Setting the wrongdoing and culpability as the pillars of the theoretical system of crime can solve the problems related with justifications and exemptions.

The classic theoretical system of crime that adopts the theory upon wrongdoing in form only recognizes the facts of legal justifications (elimination of wrongdoing). It, however, seems not so appropriate. As the law cannot prescribe all justifications, hence, legal justifications are limited. Therefore, acts without wrongdoing will be treated as crimes if the legal justifications being recognized. The criminal law in China only prescribes justifiable defense and necessity, while the consent of the victim (*Einwilligung*) has not been included. Therefore, if someone has been asked to conduct the transgender surgery, the act will definitely be regarded as an assault under the ground that deny the the consent of the victim belong to the justifications, which is clearly not appropriate. On the other side, it is impossible for the legislature to include all legal justifications in a law. The criminal law is only able to

[30]\[美\]约书亚·德雷斯勒:《美国刑法精解》，王秀梅等译，北京大学出版社2009年版，第199~200页;另参见储槐植:《美国刑法》，北京大学出版社2005年版，第65~66页。Joshua Dressler, trans. Wang Xiumei, (2009) *Understanding Criminal Law*, Beijing: Peking University Press, 199–200; Also see Chu Huaizhi, (2005) *Criminal Law of America*, Beijing: Peking University Press, 65–66.

[31]参见\[美\]约书亚·德雷斯勒:《美国刑法精解》，王秀梅等译，北京大学出版社2009年版，第201页;\[日\]井田良:《讲义刑法学·总论》，有斐阁2008年版，第278页。See Joshua Dressler, trans. Wang Xiumei, (2009) *Understanding Criminal Law*, Beijing: Peking University Press, 201; Ida Makoto.(2008) *Handout of Criminal Law·General Rules*, Yuhikaku Press, 278.

establish the forbidden norms as well as the main and usual exceptions, rather than establishing all the exceptions without missing anything. Thus, the substantive theory of wrongdoing shall be recognized and the supra-law justifications shall be admitted.

However, "the number of justifications is very large, and those facts can be seen in a variety of legal fields", under which a basic principle is necessary".[32] "Anyway, only after the substantive wrongdoing has been defined as 'acts harmful for the society' and the principles upon the elimination of wrongdoing like 'means is equivalent to ends' and 'the gains overbalance the losses ' have been developed, will people start to realize the problems being ignored or unsettled by the legislators, and thus explore the solutions by the system."[33] Whether laws, criminal one and others, have provided or not, it's not appropriate to determine or deny a crime solely based on the increasing or decreasing objective elements. However, we can and shall determine whether the acts that are in accordance with the specific provisions of criminal law constitute the elimination of wrongdoing by balancing the legal interests.

It is the same with the case of exemption. Once the normative theory of culpability is adopted, there will be a clear standard for the actor to distinguish unavoidable acts (conversely, the actor cannot be expected to conduct lawfully). For instance, in China, the actor does not commit bigamy if, the actor marries to make a living due to natural disasters; or, family in distress due to the long-term missing spouse; or, the actor gets married after being trafficked; or, the actor marries another person because of compelling force, arranged marriage or escaping from marital abuse. What is the reason in this example? The traditional theory in criminal law will explain that "because the actor is forced by objective conditions with small subjective viciousness".[34] To make a further analysis, there will be more questions: firstly, this explanation itself shows the degree of subjective viciousness can be determined by the objective elements; secondly, in quadripartite system which is based on objectivity and subjectivity, is the reason why the above mentioned situations do not constitute bigamy out of the lack of objective elements or the lack of subjective elements? If the latter is true, then it is the lack of intention, or the lack of other subjective elements? This is a problem that the quadripartite system is difficult to answer; thirdly, is the reason behind the above-mentioned bigamy justified or unjustified that there is no *vorwerfbarkeit*? This is a tough one for quadripartite system to answer. However, if the theoretic system of crime is established based on

[32] Claus Roxin,Strafrecht Allgemeiner Teil,Band I, 4.Aufl.,München:C.H.Beck, 2006, S.648.

[33] \[德\]许迺曼:"刑法体系思想导论", 载许玉秀、陈志辉合编:《不移不惑献身法与正义——许迺曼教授刑法事法论文选辑》, 台北春风煦日论坛2006年版, 第272页。Bernd Schünemann, (2006) *Criminal Law System's Manifesto*, as cited in Chen Zhihui, ed., *Unbestechlich und unbeirrbar im dienst von recht unechtigkeit: abhandlungen zur gesamten strafrechtswissenschaft von BERND SCHUNEMANN*, Taiwan: taedp.org.tw, 272.

[34] 高铭暄、马克昌主编:《刑法学》, 北京大学出版社、高等教育出版社2007年版, 第552页。Gao Mingxuan & Ma Kechang ed.(2007) *Criminal Law*, Peking University Press & Higher Education Press,552.

infringement of legal interests and culpability, it can then answer the above questions clearly: first, the subjective factor is not the only one to determine the presence and the amount of culpability. *Zumutbarkeit* is both objective and regulated culpability; second, the actor does not commit bigamy due to the lack of *Zumutbarkeit*[35]; third, the above acts are wrong and unlawful. The reason of not committing bigamy is that the actor is not culpable.

In short, to build a theoretical system of crime based on wrongdoing and culpability finds justifications and exemptions without omission and equips them with reasonable identification standards.

(6) Setting the wrongdoing and culpability as the pillars of the theoretical system of crime can solve the issues arising from the establishment and the derivativeness of accomplice.

A joint crime is a crime committed by two or more persons jointly. Whether problems related to accomplice can be handled properly or not is an important standard to examine the theoretical system of crime. If the theoretical system of crime cannot deal with issues about accomplice, it thus has a serious flaw in that system. If the theoretical system of crime can properly handle complex problems related to accomplice, it indicates that the system is superior. Dividing the substance of crime into wrongdoing and culpability and further viewing joint crimes as an wrongdoing form rather than a culpability helps deal with issues about accomplice. Now let's take a case here to demonstrate: knowing that a 13-year-old A is going to kill C, B still provides a gun to A, then A uses this gun to kill C. First of all, it should be certain that it is the behavior of A and B that together caused the death of C, or B killed C through the behavior of A. Therefore, both A's and B's behaviors are illegal. However, A does not assume wrongdoing because A does not reach the age of responsibility; under an opposite situation, B bears the culpability of the accomplice.[36] It is not difficult to see that distinguishing between wrongdoing and culpability is the key to solving the issues about accomplice. For another example, a 15-year-old female A was "officially" hired as a state-owned bank staff (national staff). One of her duties is to deliver around 300,000 Yuan from a savings bank to a bank branch office by foot about five pm every day. One day, A met four fellows (all reached the age of criminal culpability), she proposed that four fellows pretend to beat her severely to take 300,000 Yuan away, and then five people would share that money. The four fellows accepted the proposal. Afterwards, A lied to the her

[35] Of course, in the case of an increasingly perfect social assistance system, the theory of expectation of possibility cannot be abused to excuse people committing bigamy.

[36] Anglo-American theory of criminal law solves this problem with the help of defenses. "V is killed by insane D with the gun provided by sane X. Even though D is acquitted for mental reasons, there is no legal reason to make X not guilty of murder because she provided help soberly. After all, a wrong act has already occurred, that is, V's death. The fact that D is exempt from criminal culpability because of brain problems cannot prevent a normal person who is helping him to commit an offense." (\[美\]约书亚·德雷斯勒:《美国刑法精解》，王秀梅等译，北京大学出版社2009年版，第200页Joshua Dressler, trans. Wang Xiumei, (2009) *Understanding Criminal Law*, Beijing: Peking University Press, 200)

working bank that 300,000 Yuan was robbed. In China's current theoretical system of crime and theory of accomplice, both age of criminal culpability and capacity for culpability are elements of crime and of joint crimes. It is impossible for A to commit a joint crime with four fellows because A does not reach the age of criminal culpability. In that case, it is insurmountably difficult to convict those four fellows. If crime is divided into wrongdoing and culpability and natural person and special identity are classified into the former's elements and age of criminal culpability and capacity for culpability are classified into the latter's elements, and then it is unrebuttable that A and four fellows have committed a joint corruption (with A as perpetrator). However, A bears no culpability for not reaching age of responsibility and the rest still commit a joint crime of corruption.

The theory of dual nature of abetting (independence and derivativeness) is the general theory in China's criminal law. Whether this theory is appropriate or not, degree of derivativeness needs to be discussed. Once using the tripartite system or bipartite system based on wrongdoing and culpability, it can help to further solve issues related to degree, while the quadripartite system cannot solve these issues. To be clear, if we agree that the perpetrator's behavior fits with objective element, then abetting issue of status crime cannot be solved. If the perpetrator is required to fit with the requirements of crime object, objective aspects and crime subject, the former problem would be solved, yet leading to another form of culpability, namely, the complicity of juvenile delinquency with adults' involvements (especially as aiding criminal).

(7) Setting the wrongdoing and culpability as the pillars of the theoretical system of crime is in line with the purpose of penalty.

Penalty is not just about retribution. "Penalty is a correctional method, and also a method of forming a motive which partly prevents the perpetrator from repeating his behavior (correction) and prevents others from doing the same behavior (threat)... Therefore, the question of culpability is: who should be punished in a given situation? Who should be regarded as a real perpetrator?... We do not blame a person with mentally illness simply because he was not intended to do so. Attempting to influence him/her by promise or threat is futile, since his/her troubled mind cannot respond to such an impact because of the disorder of his normal mechanism. We do not try to motivate him, but we try hard to treat and cure him (in a metaphor way, we are responsible for his illness and try to eliminate the cause). When a person is forced to do something, we will not accuse him, but accuse the man who threatens him. The reason is obvious: if we were able to stop the person who had threatened him, the behavior could be prevented; the threatener was the one we had to influence in order to prevent the same behavior in the future."[37]

[37]\[德\]莫里茨·石里克:"人何时应该负责任"，载徐向东编:《自由意志与道德责任》，江苏人民出版社2006年版，第59~60页。Friedrich Albert Moritz Schlick, (2006) *Lebensweisheit*, as cited in Xu Xiangdong ed., *Free Will and Moral Responsibility*, Nanjing: Jiangsu People's Publishing House, 59–60.

What does penalty prevent? It prevents the infringement of legal interests rather than evil thoughts. How can we prevent crimes? Crimes can be prevented only if the perpetrator is likely to engage in criminal activity. If the perpetrator feels no choice but to commit an offense, imposing a penalty is impossible to prevent a crime. As a result, "criminal law protects legal interests only when the receiver of criminal rules (*Normadressaten*) has a motive. If the person is impossible to act alternatively (*Möglichkeit zum Andershandeln*), criminal law then loses its efficacy."[38] In other words, "when the pressure of purpose upon the perpetrator (*motivationsdruck)* is too much, *zumutbarkeit* of a lawful behavior does not exist. Moreover, if under the same circumstances, even the average public cannot meet the anticipation of acting legally, from the perspective of penalty's defending effect both in general and in particular, no penalty shall be inflicted."[39]

It is noticeable that what and how to prevent is just corresponding to wrongdoing and culpability. In order to achieve the purpose of penalty, the pillar of theoretical system of crime hence shall be wrongdoing and culpability.

(8) Setting the wrongdoing and culpability as the pillars of the theoretical system of crime is conducive to the implementation and improvement of system of security measures.

In order to prevent one committing a crime again, security measures are necessary, it refers to the sanctions posed by judicial or administrative authorities as the replacement of or supplement to penalty and improvement, educational and protective measures to protect or correct actors. Security measures are declared by judiciary authorities and applied to persons. The prerequisite for the application of security measures is that the perpetrator has committed the offenses prohibited by criminal law. In other words, the penalty applies to wrongdoing with culpability, while security measures apply to wrongdoing. Obviously, only by distinguishing the wrongdoing and culpability, it can help to implement and improve system of security measures.

China's system of security measure is not perfect yet, for the existing measures, the precondition of behavior is the wrongdoing rather than the culpability of the perpetrator. Example 1: Can the following provision of article 64 of *Criminal Law* be applied to persons without capacity for criminal culpability?: "All money and property illegally obtained by a criminal shall be recovered, or compensation shall be or covered; the lawful property of the victim shall be returned without delay;

---

[38]\[德\]许迺曼:"刑法罪责理论的现状"，载许玉秀、陈志辉合编:《不移不惑献身法与正义——许迺曼教授刑法事法论文选辑》，台北春风煦日论坛2006年版，第573页。Bernd Schünemann, (2006) *The Current Situation of Criminal Law Guilt Theory*, as cited in Chen Zhihui, ed., *Unbestechlich und unbeirrbar im dienst von recht unechtigkeit: abhandlungen zur gesamten strafrechtswissenschaft von BERND SCHUNEMANN*, Taiwan: taedp.org.tw, 573.

[39]\[德\]许迺曼:"罪责原则在预防刑法中的功能"，载许玉秀、陈志辉编:《不移不惑献身法与正义——许迺曼教授刑事法论文选辑》，台北春风和煦学术基金2006年版，第606页。Bernd Schünemann, (2006) *Functions of Culpability in Preventing Crimes,* as cited in Chen Zhihui, ed., *Unbestechlich und unbeirrbar im dienst von recht unechtigkeit: abhandlungen zur gesamten strafrechtswissenschaft von BERND SCHUNEMANN*, Taiwan: taedp.org.tw, 606.

and contrabands and possessions of the criminal that are used in the commission of the crime shall be confiscated". The traditional quadripartite system only has one interpretation of crime and criminals, the above-mentioned provisions cannot be applied to those without capacity for criminal culpability. According to Article 64 of the *Criminal Law*, drugs and obscene articles held by mentally ill persons cannot be confiscated; controlled knives in the killing of other people used by those who do not reach the age of responsibility shall not be confiscated. This is obviously improper. According to the theoretical system of crime with wrongdoing and culpability as the pillar, the property stolen and robbed by those without capacity for criminal culpability are illegal. Their behavior of killing and injury is still illegal, during which they also make themselves some criminals, thus Article 64 of the *Criminal Law* shall be applied to them reasonably. Example 2: The fourth paragraph of Article 17 of the *Criminal Law* provides: "If a person is not given criminal punishment because he has not reached the age of 16, the patriarch of his family or his guardian shall be ordered to discipline him. When necessary, he may be taken in by the government for rehabilitation." The first paragraph of Article18 provides: "If a mental patient causes harmful consequences at a time when he is unable to recognize or control his own conduct, upon verification and confirmation through legal procedure, he shall not bear criminal culpability, but his family members or guardian shall be ordered to keep him under strict watch and control and arrange for his medical treatment. When necessary, the government may compel him to receive medical treatment." These two provisions show that, although people under the age of criminal culpability and mental patients without capacity for criminal culpability will not be punished, they may carry out security measures when they implement an offense that complies with the elements specified in the specific provisions of the *Criminal Law*. Obviously, only to distinguish between wrongdoing and culpability, it is conducive to the implementation of the above provisions.

With the development of security measures, it will be imposed on people whose behavior is unlawful even though he or she lacks culpability; but for those who do not commit illegal acts, security measures cannot be imposed. Therefore, the tripartite system and bipartite system distinguishing between justifiable cause and cause of preventive culpability meets the needs of security measures.

(9) Setting the wrongdoing and culpability as the pillars of the theoretical system of crime helps to clarify the foundation of giving a severer or lesser or mitigated punishment or exempting from punishment.

In quadripartite system with objectivity and subjectivity as the pillar, it is hard to make the foundation of giving a severer or lesser or mitigated punishment or exempting from punishment clear and definite. It is because the impossibility of giving a severer or a lesser punishment cannot judge by the decrease or increase in objective elements and subjective elements. That in turn leads to the arbitrariness of sentencing standard. For example, in Xu Ting's case,[40] the majority advocate a mitigated punishment. But its basis (such as faulty victims and modest restraining in criminal law, etc.) is not so persuasive. It is worth mentioning that, to make a death sentence with or without a suspension term, the current reasoning basis are among whether the conflict is caused by civil disputes, whether the victim has fault and its fault degree as well as whether the defendant's family has compensated for the victim (family members), which obviously deviate from the justification of the penalty.

"'Why' the penalty is the ground and the degree of justification"[41] In other words, the ground of justification of penalty is exactly that of sentencing. According to the general theory of criminal law, the justification of penalty comes from the justice of retribution and the justification of its purpose. Article 5 of China's *Criminal Law* provides: "The degree of punishment shall be commensurate with the crime committed and the criminal culpability to be borne by the offender." Firstly, if we search for the ground of justification from the crime committed itself, then the "crime" and the "criminal culpability" can be interpreted respectively as the degree of infringement of law, namely wrongdoing, and *vorwerfbarkeit*, namely culpability. Accordingly, the degree of penalty should be consistent with the wrongdoing and culpability caused by criminals. On the contrary, wrongdoing and culpability are the pillars of crime. Secondly, if the necessity of crime prevention is taken into account, then the provisions of article 5 of the *Criminal Law* on the principle of principal of suiting punishment to crime demand that the degree of penalty should equate with crime and the possibility of re-committing a crime. The former is what retributive punishment demands while the latter is what the purposive punishment demands. Both the starting point and destination are to maximize the positive function of the penalty, to achieve the purpose of justice and crime prevention. Because the penalty must be compatible with the severity of the crime, it can prevent the heavier penalties for the pursuit of crime prevention; because the penalty must equate with the possibility of re-committing a crime, "the severity of the punishment should only be absolutely necessary to achieve its goals",[42] so unnecessary penalties can be prevented in order to pursue retribution.

From the mentioned analysis, we can clarify that sentencing should be based on the following aspects: the seriousness of wrongdoing, the degree of culpability and the necessity of crime prevention; the first two are from the crime itself; the third is

[40] At 10:00 pm on April 21, 2006, the defendant Xu Ting came to a bank located in Tianhe District, Huangpu Road, withdrawing through ATM. Xu found that the bank account only detained 1 Yuan when withdrawing 1000 Yuan; so, Xu Ting continuously withdrew 54,000 Yuan. That night, Xu Ting came back to the residence, telling the companion Mr. Guo. The two then came back to that ATM to withdraw money repeatedly. After investigation, Xu Ting has drawn a total of 175,000 Yuan; Mr. Guo withdrew 18,000 Yuan. Afterwards, the two ran off with the money.

[41] \[日\]平野龙一:《刑法总论I》，有斐阁1972年版，第27页。 Hirano Ryuuichi.(1972) *General Rules of Criminal Law I*, Yuhikaku Press, 27.

[42] \[英\]吉米·边沁:《立法理论——刑法典原理》，李贵方等译，中国人民公安大学出版社1993年版，第78页。Jeremy Bentham, trans. Li Guifang, (1993) *The theory of legislation*, Press of People's Public Security University of China, 78.

to locate a reason beyond crime itself. Therefore, setting the wrongdoing and culpability as the pillar of crime makes the basis for sentencing clear and definite.

(10) Setting the wrongdoing and culpability as the pillars of the theoretical system of crime helps to clarify the concepts such as "crime" and "committing a crime" provided in criminal law.

In Germany, Japan and other countries, where the wrongdoing and culpability are the pillar of theoretical system of crime, scholars often discuss the nature of crime and the essence of wrongdoing as the same problem. Some scholars discuss the theory of infringement of legal interests and the theory of norm violation at the same time under the topic "the theory of wrongdoing"[43]; meanwhile, in the discussion of "the essence of crime", some scholars introduce the theory of infringement of legal interests and the theory of norm violation.[44] This means that the essence of wrongdoing is the nature of the crime, which thus indicates that the wrongdoing is a crime to some extent.

In general, a crime refers to the behavior meeting all elements of the crime, that is, a crime is a behavior with wrongdoing and culpability. However, the essence of crime is the infringement of legal interests. In this sense, as long as a behavior violates legal interests, it possesses the essence of crime. In China, the "crime" and "committing a crime" specified in many provisions only mean the wrongdoing meets the subjective elements. For example, the first paragraph in Article 115 of *Criminal Law* provides: "Whoever commits arson, breaches a dike, causes explosion, spreads poison or inflicts serious injury or death on people or causes heavy losses of public or private property by other dangerous means, shall be sentenced to fixed-term imprisonment in excess of 10 years, life imprisonment or death." The second paragraph provides: "Whoever negligently commits the crime mentioned in the preceding paragraph shall be sentenced to fixed-term imprisonment in excess of three years but not exceeding seven years; if the circumstances are minor, he shall be sentenced to fixed-term imprisonment not exceeding three years or criminal detention." Obviously, "the crime mentioned in the preceding paragraph" in second paragraph refers to acts (committing arson, breaching a dike and other acts causing heavy losses of public or private property and endangering public security) fulfilling the subjective elements and natures specified in the first paragraph; but it does not require the behavior imposed are out of intention as provided in paragraph 1. If "crime" must be in full compliance with all crime requirements, then it is impossible to understand Article 115 (2) of the *Criminal Law*. In other words, if "crime" refers to the behavior fully meets subjective and objective elements of crime, then paragraph 2 of Article 115 can only be interpreted as: "Whoever negligently commits the crime mentioned in the preceding paragraph shall be sentenced to fixed-term imprisonment in excess of 3 years but not exceeding 7 years." which is not

[43]\[日\]前田雅英:《刑法总论讲义》，东京大学出版会2006年版，第48页以下。Maeda Masahide.(2006) *Handouts of General Rules of Criminal Law*, University of Tokyo Press, 1–48.

[44]\[日\]木村光江:《刑法》，东京大学出版会1997年版，第21页。Kimura Mitsue.(1997) *Criminal Law*, University of Tokyo Press, 21.

proper. The third paragraph in Article 20 provides: "If an Acts in defense against an on-going assault, murder, robbery, rape, kidnap or any other crime of violence that seriously endangers his personal safety, thus causing injury or death to the perpetrator of the unlawful act, it is not undue defense, and he shall not bear criminal culpability." Since the justified behavior will not yield to the unjustified behavior, when necessary, the justifiable defense is allowed in the case where the on-going unlawful infringement is caused by any person no matter whether he reaches the legal age or has the capacity for culpability. Thus, the "violent crime" in the above-mentioned clause is not limited to the case where the unlawful infringement is done by the person who does reach the legal age and have the capacity for culpability, which means, for those under the age of 14 who conduct murder, robbery, rape and any other crime of violence seriously endangering personal safety, the justifiable defense is allowed. This also shows that murder, robbery, rape and other acts committed by people who do not reach the legal age are part of the "violent crime" stipulated in Article 20.

In addition, criminal law also made the provisions such as "whoever commits the crime of theft, fraud or forcible seizure of money or property", "knowingly... to a criminal", "a person he knows to be guilty", "illegally acquired goods" and so forth. Even the scholars who insist on the quadripartite system cannot but admit that "these 'crimes' can only logically refer to the objective behaviors: under the German system, according with the elements of crime and the wrongdoing (such as, 13-year-olds commits a crime of theft.) In German, this will not be a problem at all (children can commit a 'crime'). However, under the Chinese theoretical system of crime, it is difficult to justify in this context: there is a conflict among legal rules, the theoretical system and the system of discourse, leaving the defendant the space to quibble and embarrassing the prosecution at the same time. This is a technically difficult problem for the Chinese system (it can only be done but hard to say so)."[45] "It can only be done" means that we only adopt the tripartite system in China; yet what can and should be done clashes with the quadripartite system, it is inappropriate to say so.

On balance, there exists sufficient basis and internal rationality in the theoretical system of crime with wrongdoing and culpability as the pillar. It is true that the system of crime with objectivity and subjectivity as the pillar is not necessarily completely antagonistic to the theoretical system of crime with wrongdoing and culpability as the pillar. However, at least the subjective and objective elements in China's current quadripartite system are not completely corresponding to the wrongdoing and culpability. For example, there are both wrongdoing (such as special status) and culpability (such as capacity for culpability) in the subject of crime. Another example, *zumutbarkeit* is the normative evaluation based on objective situations relating to culpability rather than a subjective issue. What is more, the criminal purpose is an inner thought, when it comes to the objective and subjective

[45]冯亚东、邓君韬:"德国犯罪论体系对中国之启示"，载《国家检察官学院学报》2009年第1期。Feng Yadong & Deng Juntao, (2009) *An Inspiration to China from German Criminology System*, as cited in *Journal of National Prosecutors College*, No.1.

division, it must be subjective; while it needs further discussion to determine whether the criminal purpose is an element of wrongdoing or culpability, or parts of them in accordance with the division between wrongdoing and culpability. Perhaps some fall in the former category, some in the latter. More importantly, the understanding of the substance of crime cannot remain in the concept of objectivity and subjectivity. In China, the current situation that "concepts of crime are evaluative while the definition of crime is descriptive" is yet ideal, because the concept of crime and theoretical system of crime should directly reflect the evaluation. In other words, while building a theoretical system of crime, we must firstly clarify what is prohibited by criminal law, what behavior will be subject to negative evaluation of criminal law (wrongdoing), and secondly clarify that on what conditions can be blamed to the actor (culpability). After the elements of wrongdoing are defined, that of culpability can be determined (for example, if we adopt *Handlungsunwert*, then the intention is an element of wrongdoing, instead of that of culpability). Therefore, "the future of the system of criminal law is all about not to distinguish its connotation rather than the structural and technical distinction between the elements and wrongdoing."[46]

1.3 The Obstacles of Theoretical System of Crime Based on Wrongdoing and Culpability

It cannot be denied that in China, there may be language or expressive obstacles to theoretical system of crime with wrongdoing and culpability as the pillars. This is because China's criminal law has used the concept of wrongdoing and culpability in another sense so far. However, this kind of language or expressive obstacles shall not prevent to build a theoretical system of crime with wrongdoing and culpability as the pillar.

(1) Wrongdoing

As mentioned earlier, in the traditional quadripartite system, the (criminal) wrongdoing is equivalent to a crime. The behavior which does not meet the four elements is not (criminal) wrongdoing, vice versa. So, it will be difficult to accept that (criminal) wrongdoing is a crime, some scholars thus opposed the introduction of the tripartite system with wrongdoing and culpability as pillars.

Some scholar pointed out: "In China's long-standing legal environment and jurisprudence context, if the behavior is 'wrongdoing' (basically a synonym for 'unlawful'), the actor is bound to certain legal responsibility (namely, law-breakers

[46]\[德\]许迺曼:"刑法体系思想导论"，载许玉秀、陈志辉合编:《不移不惑献身法与正义——许迺曼教授刑法事法论文选辑》，台北春风煦日论坛2006年版，第296页。Bernd Schünemann, (2006) *Criminal Law System's Manifesto*, as cited in Chen Zhihui, ed., *Unbestechlich und unbeirrbar im dienst von recht unechtigkeit: abhandlungen zur gesamten strafrechtswissenschaft von BERND SCHUNEMANN*, Taiwan: taedp.org.tw, 296.

must be prosecuted). In Chinese context, to adjudicate the nature of the behavior already contains the judgment of the basic condition of the subject of act. There is no need to accuse a mental patient or a child of 'wrongdoing', just as there is no need to blame a monkey who scratched a man no matter how emotional we are. How to evaluate things in life is not important (since knowledge is often plural and constantly changing), while legal definition must be cautious and accurate. Accusing a child of 'wrongdoing' or 'crime' is not conducive not only to education and prevention, but also to increase misunderstanding and confusion."[47] But in my point of view, this argument is not the reason which holds back to build a theoretical system of crime with wrongdoing and culpability as the pillar.

Firstly, in China, "wrongdoing" has different meanings. "Wrongdoing is not equal to the crime" is also an often-mentioned statement; even in other branches of law, wrongdoing may also refer to the objective aspect without *vorwerfbarkeit*. For example, even if the actor has no subjective fault in infringement of the traffic rules, this behavior also considered as wrongdoing. Therefore, the different meaning of the concept of wrongdoing cannot be the reason to hold back the theoretical system of crime with wrongdoing and culpability as the pillar. Plus, "wrongdoing" has multiple meanings, which is include in the "law-breakers must be prosecuted" and as one of elements of definition of crime "wrongdoing", indeed bear different meanings. Moreover, the meaning of "prosecuted" in the "law-breakers must be prosecuted" deserves further studying. "Law-breakers must be prosecuted" may be understood that the actor must be affixed legal responsibility; it may also be understood as 'wrongdoing must be investigated' and the case will be dealt with separately.[48]

Secondly, the issues whether a child has killed or infringed upon the life of others, or, whether he can be accused (condemned) by law, are completely different; we cannot deny the fact that monkey scratched people on the ground that the monkey cannot be blamed; and we cannot deny the fact that people were scratched by the monkeys only because monkeys cannot be accused. In other words, confirming that certain acts violate legal interest only indicates that the mentioned acts are banned by criminal law. Therefore, they are unjustified and that does not mean the actors must be punished. Obviously, the above view mixes the wrongdoing and culpability.

Thirdly, "wrongdoing" and "unlawful" in criminal law are not identical to the concept of "crime". To be clear, the first paragraph of Article 20 provides: "An act

---

[47] 冯亚东、邓君韬:"德国犯罪论体系对中国之启示"，载《国家检察官学院学报》2009年第1期。Feng Yadong & Deng Juntao, (2009) *An Inspiration to China from German Criminology System*, as cited in *Journal of National Prosecutors College*, No.1.

[48] In the morning of August 11, 2009, the author had to take an unlicensed car near the Central Television Tower in Beijing. The driver drove in the wrong direction for ten meters away. The author immediately asked the driver: "Are you not afraid of the police?" The driver said: "Now the police are in Chang'an Avenue (The most significant political avenue in China). Besides, breaking the law is different from committing a crime. I just break the law, and criticizing is enough. Penalty is for people who have committed a crime only."

that a person commits to stop an unlawful infringement in order to prevent the interests of the State and the public, or his own or other person's rights of the person, property or other rights from being infringed upon by the on-going infringement, thus harming the perpetrator, is justifiable defense, and he shall not bear criminal culpability". The above wrongdoing include not only the general offense, but also purely objective unlawful infringements, thus it does not equal to crime. In addition, when it comes "to "the amount of illegal gains is relatively large" in criminal law provisions, the expression of "illegal" is not necessarily equivalent to "crime".

Fourthly, even for general people, regarding objective wrongdoing as crime is also a common phenomenon. For instance, an under-14 adolescence caused death to somebody then was hidden by his parents who were worried for the arrest of their child by the judiciary, which happens all the time. This shows that the parents take an objective wrongdoing as a crime and understand their child's behavior breaks law. In addition, there are news saying like "the crime age assumes the low age tendency" and "a 12-years old child committed a crime" and so on, which also takes objective wrongdoing as crime. Since there is no obstacle for ordinary people to understand wrongdoing only from the view of infringement of legal interest, to say nothing for criminal law scholars and judicial staff.

Some scholar who opposes the theoretical system of crime with wrongdoing and culpability as the pillar also points out that "if it is recognized that the violation by a child or a mentally ill is 'wrongdoing' or 'unlawful' or a crime, then it is justifiable to act in justifiable defense against it on the grounds that the conditions of justifiable defense can be fully consistent. So, there will be an adverse effect to protection of the rights and interests of the person without capacity for culpability. In this regard, different circumstances should be treated separately: (a) if the sufferer knows that the infringer has capacity for culpability, he can only implement necessity, which means, the last choice is to injury the infringer. The sufferer can carry out defense if he does not know the infringer does not have the capacity. In the latter case, it is feasible to see the mentioned behavior as justifiable defense from the actor's point of view (all elements of justifiable defense are satisfied). In consideration of praising virtue and punishing vice by law, after all, the damage was done to the actor who has no capacity for culpability, there is no need to affirm that positively. Hence, according to subjective aspects of crime in criminal law, the behavior can be subject to decriminalization (because the defender does not know harm results).Therefore, there is no necessity to determine the nature of the behavior of the defender as justifiable defense (as to determine the nature positively, it should be regarded as a general sense of "defensive behavior" that can be considered as exemptions).[49]

According to this view, the unlawful infringement by people without capacity for culpability is not "wrongdoing infringement" when the victim is capable of eluding and when the defender knows that is not "wrongdoing infringement"; reversely, the occasion is "wrongdoing infringement". If this being true, there is no standard for

[49] 冯亚东、邓君韬:"德国犯罪论体系对中国之启示"，载《国家检察官学院学报》2009年第1期。Feng Yadong & Deng Juntao, (2009) *An Inspiration to China from German Criminology System*, as cited in *Journal of National Prosecutors College*, No.1.

determining "wrongdoing infringement"; it is hard to agree that the existence of unlawful infringement is decided by whether can be eluded by the victim and whether the third party realize that the actor has no capacity for culpability. Additionally, in case that the actor without capacity for culpability while the victim knows the infringement but cannot elude, what will be the standard for the determination? In accordance with the tripartite system or bipartite system based on wrongdoing and culpability, intentional homicide committed by a 13 years old person as wrongdoing and justifiable defense against it is feasible. The above point of view mixes the wrongdoing and culpability. However, in order to solve the defense against children and mental patients, "'defensive behavior' with exemption" must be admitted. This shows that the distinction between wrongdoing and culpability is very necessary.

In short, it is necessary and feasible to use the concept of "wrongdoing" in the substantive sense of infringement of legal interests indicating that criminal law prohibits the infringement of legal interest.

(2) Culpability

There are more than 20 terms of "criminal culpability" in China's criminal law. In the late 1980s and early 1990s, the academics of China's criminal law comprehended the concept of criminal culpability in the sense of the legal consequences of the crime and the legal responsibility that should be borne by the crime. So, will the criminal culpability in the sense of the *vorwerfbarkeit* as the pillar of the theoretical system of crime lead to the confusion? The author holds a negative answer.

Firstly, the concept of criminal culpability has different meanings even in foreign countries with theoretical system of crime with wrongdoing and culpability as the pillar. There are "Schuld" and "culpability" in the sense of *vorwerfbarkeit* and "Verantwortlichkeit" and "criminal culpability" in Germany and Japan, the latter "refers to guilty, instead of the responsibility in above sense, which considered to be be punished and called as criminal culpability".[50] This shows that Germany's "Schuld", Japan's "culpability" are equivalent to "offence" in China's criminal law (differing from fault in the sense of theory of guilty mind); and Germany's "Schuld" and Japan's "culpability" are equivalent to "criminal culpability" in China referring to the legal consequences of the crime.

Secondly, as a matter of fact, the concept of culpability in the sense of *vorwerfbarkeit* do exist China's theory of criminal law. The concept of "capacity for culpability" and "age of criminal culpability" are the demonstrations in the sense of *vorwerfbarkeit*, rather than the criminal consequences. Killing committed by a person without capacity for culpability is illegal, yet not constituting a crime rather than constituting a crime without bearing the criminal culpability. In other words, it is inappropriate to discuss the "criminal culpability" in the sense of age of criminal

---

[50]\[日\]大塚仁:《刑法概说(总论)》，有斐阁2008年版，第437页。Otsuka Hitoshi.(2008) *Overview of Criminal Law*, Yuhikaku Press, 437.

culpability and capacity for culpability are not the same as that of criminal consequence.[51]

Thirdly, considering criminal culpability as the intermediary or link between crime and penalty also raises questions. Obviously, there is no need for intermediary or link. The intermediary between crime and penalty is not required in both common law countries and civil law countries. The provisions of the criminal law in international community (including China) on the crime and statutory punishment also indicate that there is no need for link between crime and penalty. Similarly, it is quite difficult or even impossible to make purely criminal culpability as the intermediary or a link between crime and penalty substantial. Playing the role of a bridge, it is difficult for a link to have real significance. More importantly, if the criminal culpability is seen as an intermediary between the crime and penalty, the system of *crime- criminal culpability - penalty* will be formed and ignore the other legal consequences of the crime, such as non-penalty punishment and simply conviction. To say the least, even if considering criminal culpability as the intermediary between crime and penalty, it does not prevent culpability in the sense of *vorwerfbarkeit* as the pillar of crime and the basic elements.

Fourthly, the translation from the German word "Schuld" into "责任(responsibility)" in Chinese may not be proper; it would seem more appropriate to translate the word "Schuld" into Chinese as "罪过" (origninally means sin in Chinese; of course, this term does not the superordinate concept of intention and negligence, but *vorwerfbarkeit*).[52] Conventionally, we also do not need to translate "Schuld" in Germany as well as "culpability" in Japan into "罪过(sin)", as long as understand the meaning and make a distinction between the former concepts and "criminal culpability" in China's theory of criminal law. In other words, this concept in China is still used in the sense of the legal consequences of the crime. Even criminal culpability is discussed in the theory of crime part of textbooks, yet criminal culpability is not seen as a constitutive definition of crime. In this case, "mens rea" which is equivalent to Schuld and "责任(responsibility)" is supposed to be studied in theory of crime rather than "criminal culpability" as legal consequences.

All in all, the term "culpability" does not only have one meaning. Even if considering criminal culpability as criminal legal consequences or as an intermediary between crime and penalty, it does not prevent culpability in the sense of *vorwerfbarkeit* as one of the pillars of crime.

In addition, in the context of China, it is also important to note that "the substance of crime refers to the objective danger and subjective viciousness. The evaluation of objective danger is to see if there is infringement of legal interests and the judgment of whether the subject has subjective viciousness is to see if there is a *vorwerfbarkeit*". In this sense, as long as there are substantive evaluation standard

[51] 参见张明楷:《刑法学》(上)，法律出版社1999年版，第164页以下。See Zhang Mingkai, (1999) *Criminal Law 1*, Law Press China, 1–164.

[52] 参见张明楷:"犯罪论体系的思考"，载《政法论丛》2003年第6期。See Zhang Mingkai, (2003) *Thinking about the System of the Theory of Crime*, as cited in *Journal of Political Science and Law*, No.6.

of the objective danger and subjective viciousness, and quadripartite system can be slightly modified according to the former standards.[53] However, it is appropriate to build a theoretical system of crime with wrongdoing and culpability as the pillars upon considering followings: (a) the conceptes like objective danger and subjective viciousness are not of full equivalence to wrongdoing and culpability; (b) there is no progressive relationship between the objective danger and subjective viciousness but can be comprehensive evaluated; (c) there are some specific borrowed theories in China's criminal theory that is difficult to be discussed leaving the concept of wrongdoing and culpability aside; and (d) with a view of the convenience of international academic exchanges.[54]

References

A.H.Трайнин, trans. Xue Binzhong. (1958). *General Theories of Crime*, China Renmin University Press, 15, 18, 27, 46.

Bernard Weiner, trans. Zhang Aiqing, Zheng Wei. (2004). *Judgments of Responsibility: A Foundation for a Theory of Social Conduct,* East China Normal University Press, 5, 9.

Bernd Schünemann. (2006). Criminal Law System's Manifesto, in Chen Zhihui (ed.), Unbestechlich und unbeirrbar im dienst von recht unechtigkeit: abhandlungen zur gesamten strafrechtswissenschaft von BERND SCHUNEMANN, Taiwan: taedp.org.tw, 272, 293, 296.

Bernd Schünemann. (2006). *Distinguishing the Illegality and Culpability,* in Chen Zhihui (ed.), Unbestechlich und unbeirrbar im dienst von recht unechtigkeit: abhandlungen zur gesamten strafrechtswissenschaft von BERND SCHUNEMANN, Taiwan: taedp.org.tw, 416, 424, 429.

Bernd Schünemann. (2006). *Functions of Culpability in Preventing Crimes*, in Chen Zhihui (ed.), Unbestechlich und unbeirrbar im dienst von recht unechtigkeit: abhandlungen zur gesamten strafrechtswissenschaft von BERND SCHUNEMANN, Taiwan: taedp.org.tw, 606.

Bernd Schünemann. (2006). *German Criminal Law after the Millennium*, in Chen Zhihui (ed.), Unbestechlich und unbeirrbar im dienst von recht unechtigkeit: abhandlungen zur gesamten strafrechtswissenschaft von BERND SCHUNEMANN, Taiwan: taedp.org.tw, 173.

Bernd Schünemann. (2006). *Illegality System of Criminal Law*, in Chen Zhihui (ed.), Unbestechlich und unbeirrbar im dienst von recht unechtigkeit: abhandlungen zur gesamten strafrechtswissenschaft von BERND SCHUNEMANN, Taiwan: taedp.org.tw, 201.

Bernd Schünemann. (2006). *The Current Situation of Criminal Law Guilt Theory*, in Chen Zhihui (ed.), Unbestechlich und unbeirrbar im dienst von recht unechtigkeit: abhandlungen zur gesamten strafrechtswissenschaft von BERND SCHUNEMANN, Taiwan: taedp.org.tw, 573.

Chu Huaizhi. (2005). *Criminal Law of America*, Beijing: Peking University Press, 65–66.

Claus Roxin. (2006). *Strafrecht Allgemeiner Teil*, Band I, 4. Aufl., München: C.H. Beck, 648.

Feng Yadong & Deng Juntao. (2009). *An Inspiration to China from German Criminology System*, in Journal of National Prosecutors College, No.1.

[53] 参见黎宏:"我国犯罪构成体系不必重构", 载《法学研究》2006年第1期。See Li Hong, (2006) *Current System of Constitution of Crime Does Not Have to Be Restructured*, as cited in *Chinese Journal of Law*, No.1.

[54] Unfortunately, Chinese academics have not proposed theories which can provide as references to German and Japan counterparts (as we all know, seeing the social harm as the nature of crime and adopting the four-requirement theoretical system of criminology did not derive from China), hence, we cannot expect they could learn from us right now.

Friedrich Albert Moritz Schlick. (2006). Lebensweisheit, in Xu Xiangdong (ed.), *Free Will and Moral Responsibility*, Jiangsu People's Publishing House, 59–60.
Gao Mingxuan ed. (1993). *Brief History of Criminal Law in People's Republic of China*, Press of People's Public Security University of China, 8.
Gao Mingxuan & Ma Kechang ed. (2007). *Criminal Law*, Peking University Press & Higher Education Press, 552.
Giunter Stratenwerth, Lothar Kuhlen, trans. Yang Meng. (2006). *Strafrecht Allgemeiner Teil* I: Die Straftat, Law Press, 81.
Hirano Ryuuichi. (1972). *General Rules of Criminal Law I*, Yuhikaku Press, 27.
Ida Makoto. (2005). *Theories of General Rules of Criminal Law*, Seibundoh, 1.
Ida Makoto. (2008). *Handout of Criminal Law·General Rules*, Yuhikaku Press, 278.
Jeremy Bentham, trans. Li Guifang. (1993). *The Theory of Legislation*, Press of People's Public Security University of China, 78.
John Martin Fischer, Mark Ravizza, trans. Yang Shaogang. (2002). *Responsibility and Control*, Huaxia Publishing House, 2.
Joshua Dressler, trans. Wang Xiumei. (2009). *Understanding Criminal Law*, Beijing: Peking University Press, 199–201.
Kimura Mitsue. (1997). *Criminal Law*, University of Tokyo Press, 21.
Li Hong. (2006). *Current System of Constitution of Crime Does Not Have to Be Restructured*, in Chinese Journal of Law, No.1.
Maeda Masahide. (2006). *Handouts of General Rules of Criminal Law*, University of Tokyo Press, 1–48.
Otsuka Hitoshi. (2008). *Overview of Criminal Law*, Yuhikaku Press, 437.
Political Science and Law Cadres Institution of the CPC Central Committee ed. (1957). *Handouts of General Rules of Criminal Law in People's Republic of China*, Law Press, 56, 61, 63–64, 74–75.
Smith, Hogan, trans. Li Guifang. (2000). *Criminal Law*, Beijing: Law Press, 215.
Xu Xiangdong. (2008). *Understanding Free Wills*, Peking University Press, 11.
Yamaguchi Atsushi. (2007). *General Rules of Criminal Law*, Yuhikaku Press, 101.
Zhang Mingkai. (1999). *Criminal Law 1*, Law Press China, 1–164.
Zhang Mingkai. (2003). *Thinking about the System of the Theory of Crime*, in Journal of Political Science and Law, No.6.
Чхиквадзе, trans. Translation Office of the Legislative Affairs Commission of the CPC Central Committee & Criminal Law Teaching and Researching Office of China Renmin University. (1955). *Course of Soviet Criminal Law*, Law Press, 206.

Chapter 2
Criminal Omission Through Creation of Dangerous Situations

The theory of criminal law has classified criminal omission into omission crime and commission by omission. As for the omission crime, the criminal law not only expressly prescribes the actor/perpetrator, but also defines the criminal omission as a constitutive element. Therefore, the certainly omission crime is completely in accordance with the principle of *nulla poena sine lege*. However, as it's known, the recognition of the certainly commission by omission may run against the above principle.[1]

To make sure the punishments to commission by omission are in conformity with the principle of *nulla poena sine lege*, criminal legislation, criminal theories, and the precedents in German, Austria, Japan and other civil law systems have regarded the legal duties upon *Garantenstellung* as one of the elements of the commission by omission. That is to say, the person subject of legal duties to prevent the consequences from happening is *Garantenstellung* and such obligation is the legal duties. Therefore, according to theory of criminal law, the first thing is to identify

*The original title is "Criminal Omission through ***Ingerenz***", published in ***Chinese Journal of Law***, 2011, Vol.6.

[1] Both the scholars from civil law system and common law system all hold the view that punishing commission by omission is against the doctrine of *nulla poena sine lege*. For example, in Japan, some scholars believe that the commission by omission violates the doctrine of *nulla poena sine lege*, therefore bringing out the idea that the so called act of intentional homicide could only be identified as crime of abandonment of responsible protector.(参见日浅田和茂:《刑法总论》，成文堂2007年补正版，第150、162页 Asada Kazushige.(2007) *General Theory of Criminal Law (Supplementary Edition)*, Seibundo Publishing Co, 150, 162). In America, "even though there are other reasons for punishing the criminal omission, a few scholars still criticize it as for violating the doctrine of *nulla poena sine lege*"(美约书亚·德雷斯勒:《美国刑法精解》，王秀梅等译，北京大学出版社2009年版，第95页Joshua Dressler, trans. Wang Xiumei, (2009) *Understanding Criminal Law*, Beijing: Peking University Press, 95).

M. Zhang, *The Fundamental Issues upon Criminal Law Theories*, Masterpieces of Contemporary Jurisprudents in China,
https://doi.org/10.1007/978-981-95-1276-8_2

the person subject of legal duties to prevent the consequences, or in other words, to identify the source of the special duty (as the basis of legal duties).

The basis of legal duties has experienced the evolutionary process from the formality deontology to the substantial deontology. The reason for that is since the criminal law principle based on liberalism observes that certain acts should not be punished as long as the acts were not conducted actively, thus, only when the substantive basis exists, can the penalty be imposed to deter or compel people to observe legal duties of *Garantenstellung*. Therefore, the legal duties of *Garantenstellung* should be understood from a substantial perspective. However, there are still unresolved problems, among which the issue of *Ingerenz* (creation of dangerous situations) is most controversial.

This article first illustrates the theoretical prerequisite of *Ingerenz*, and then demonstrates that *Ingerenz* can be the basis (essential nature) for the occurrence of legal duties. It also discusses the specific content and finally explains the scope of function.

2.1 Theoretical Prerequisite of *Ingerenz*

As for the source of legal duties, China's theory of criminal law has always taken the formality deontology. The earlier criminal law text books had adopted the trichotomy of formality theory, that is, the legal duties come from the regulations of other laws, professional (or business) acts and *Ingerenz*.[2] The recent criminal law text books have adopted the theory of four-branch formality by bearing legal duties (such as contract) as the source.[3]

We have to admit that the formality deontology is not only theoretically defective, but also leads to an unreasonable scope of *Garantenstellung* in judicial practice.

(1) According to the theory of four-branch formality, as long as the actor has legal duties, he is *Garantenstellung* and will be punished by the criminal law if the duty has not been performed. However, this point of view cannot answer the following question: An act, which is against other laws, cannot be directly regarded as a crime, since it is so, why should the violation of other laws in the way of criminal omission can be directly determined as a crime? Moreover, why does the breach of contract can be directly convicted by criminal law rather than be handled in conformity with the contract law?[4]

[2] 参见高铭暄主编:《刑法学》，法律出版社1982年版，第121~122页。See Gao Mingxuan ed. (1982) *Criminal Law*, Law Press, 121–122.

[3] 参见高铭暄、马克昌主编:《刑法学》，北京大学出版社、高等教育出版社2010年版，第74~76页；陈兴良:《规范刑法学》(上册)，中国人民大学出版社2008年版，第122~123页。Gao Mingxuan & Ma Kechang eds. (2010) *Criminal Law*, Peking University Press & Higher Education Press, 74–76; Chen Xingliang. (2008) *Normative Criminal Law 1*, China Renmin University Press, 122–123.

[4] 参见日山口厚:《刑法总论》，有斐阁2007年版，第81页。Yamaguchi Atsushi.(2007) *General Rules of Criminal Law*, Yuhikaku Press, 81.

(2) The theory of four-branch formality has deemed the duty stipulated by other laws as the primary source of legal duties (it intends to explain that the legal duties is not moral obligation). But in some occasions, the actor will not be incriminated even though he doesn't fulfill the duties of other laws. For example, Article 5 of *Fire Prevention Law of China's Republic of China*: "All units and individuals have the obligation to...report fire alarms." Article 44: "All individuals should report fire alarms where a fire has broken out." However, an ordinary citizen shall not be convicted as the criminal of arson or any other crimes even if he has not report fire alarms.[5] Therefore, the theory of four-branch formality is self- contradictory.
(3) The theory of four-branch formality cannot provide reasonable grounds for certain acts that should be punished. For example, a 7 year -old girl took the initiative to propose the indecency with an adult male A when he was at home alone, and A didn't refuse it. It may not be proper to count A had performed legal duties, but it even more inappropriate if A is acquitted.[6] However, according to the theory of four-branch formality, A is not *Garantenstellung* for there is no basis of legal duties. This conclusion is hard to be accepted. For another example, B, who was responsible for raising the infant of others by contract, intentionally provided the child with no food hence caused the death of the child. In this case, even though the contract was void or exceeded the agreed term, B should be punished as the criminal omission. However, according to the theory above, no source of performing legal duties exists in the case.

Severer problems will emerge if we comprehend *Ingerenz* in view of formality. The outstanding manifestation of the problem is that the punishment to the criminal omission is improperly expanded. For example, a man tried to break up with his girlfriend, who disagreed and claimed to commit a suicide yet the man had made his mind for breaking up. Then the woman attempted suicide in front of the man, who neither stopped her, nor took her to the hospital. The prior judicial practice usually considered the man's act as a criminal omission due to *Ingerenz*.[7] However, both falling in love and breakup are common and normal acts with no danger. Regarding

[5] In America, "A person who bears the legal responsibility to report the fire has failed to report, negligently or recklessly leading to the result of death, will be accused of crime of homicide in certain forms."(美约书亚·德雷斯勒:《美国刑法精解》，王秀梅等译，北京大学出版社2009年版，第95页Joshua Dressler, trans. Wang Xiumei, (2009) *Understanding Criminal Law*, Beijing: Peking University Press, 95)But it is not the case in China and it is hard to say a common citizen who discovered a fire shall be the legal duty to report it.

[6] Scholars of England have pointed out that: "even the 'act' can be performed by omission sometimes, for example, someone may be convicted of crime of gross indecency for passively accepting the child's behavior"(J.C.史密斯、B.霍根:《英国刑法》，李贵方等译，法律出版社2000年版，第56页Smith, Hogan, trans. Li Guifang, (2000) *Criminal Law*, Beijing: Law Press, 56.)

[7] 参见岳耀勇:"见死不救罪责难逃"，载《检察日报》2000年5月9日；柴文斌、王辉:"听任女友寻短见见死不救被判刑"，载《法制日报》2000年12月2日。See Yue Yao Yong: "Failure to Rescue Cannot Escape Criminal Liability," as cited in *Procuratorate Daily*, 9 May 2000; Chai Wen Bin & Wang Hui. "Sentenced for Allowing Girlfriend to Commit Suicide by Failing to Rescue," as cited in *Legal Daily*, 2 December 2000.

those acts shall bearing *Ingerenz* and making the actors bear the criminal culpability of anything resulted mean that each and every move of citizen will make themself bear legal duty, which is obviously contrary to the basic criminal law principle of protecting the freedom of citizens.

Germany and Japan once adopted the theory of formality deontology.[8] However, due to the obvious defects of the theory, Germany and Japan had long started to explore the substantive source of legal duty.[9] The dominating opinion in Germany nowadays is to divide the legal duties into the duty of protecting vulnerable (helpless) legal interests and the duty to supervising the sources of danger.[10] This theory of functional duality had also been supported by some Japanese scholars. For example, Professor Yamanaka Keiichi further classified the duty of protection into normative basis, institutional or arbitrary basis, and functional basis, and he also classified the *Aufsichtspflicht* (duty to supervising) into the duty to supervise the management of dangerous objects, the duty to supervise the third party and the duty to prevent result happen of the actor who brings the danger.[11] Since the theory of functional duality has distinct trace of formality deontology (the manifestation of it is to classify all kinds of sources of legal duty), parts of the scholars in Germany and Japan had tried to find a substantive basis for legal duties so that to adopt a single standard. German Professor Schünemann in later chapter brought up the theory of *Herrschaft über den Grund des Erfolges* (control over the ground of the infringement of legal interest) and got the support of Japanese Professor Yamaguchi Atsushi. The main content of this theory is that the actor has the legal duties only when he controls over the cause leading to the effect. Controlling over the ground of the infringement of legal interest can be divided into the source of danger and the fragility of legal interest.[12]

However, a substantive judgment of whether the actor controls the source of danger and whether the actor controls over the vulnerable legal interests will be lack of clarity without restrictions in form, and thereby leading to unreasonable

---

[8] The former and formality theory of legal duty of German holds that, the sources of duty to act are the law, contract and dangerous *Ingerenz*, and further adding the closed relationship of life(Vgl.,H. Jescheck/T.Weigend, *Lehrbuch des Strafrechts: Allgemeiner Teil*, 5.Aufl.,Duncker & Humblot, 1996,S.621). The Japanese theory holds that, the grounds of the duty to act are decrees, contract, custom or principles (including *Ingerenzs*). 参见日团藤重光:《刑法纲要总论》，创文社1990年版，第149页；日大塚仁:《刑法概说(总论)》，有斐阁2008年版，第153页。See Dandou Shigemitsu.(1990) *General Outline of Criminal Law*, Kodansha Publishing Co, 149; Otsuka Hitoshi.(2008) *Overview of Criminal Law*, Yuhikaku Press, 153.

[9] America has adopted the theory of formality legal duty so far(参见美约书亚·德雷斯勒:《美国刑法精解》，王秀梅等译，北京大学出版社2009年版，第96页以下Joshua Dressler, trans. Wang Xiumei, (2009) *Understanding Criminal Law*, Beijing: Peking University Press, 1–96).

[10] Vgl.,H.Jescheck/T.Weigend, *Lehrbuch des Strafrechts: Allgemeiner Teil*, 5.Aufl.,Duncker & Humblot, 1996,S.621ff；德约翰内斯·韦塞尔斯:《德国刑法总论》，李昌珂译，法律出版社2008年版，第433页。Johannes Wessels, trans. Li Changke, (2008) *Strafrecht Allgemeiner Teil*, Law Press, 433.

[11] 参见日山中敬一:《刑法总论》，成文堂2008年版，第234~237页。See Yamanaka Keiichi. (2008) *General Theory of Criminal Law*, Seibundo Publishing Co, 234–237.

[12] 参见日山口厚:《刑法总论》，有斐阁2007年版，第89页。Yamaguchi Atsushi.(2007) *General Theory of Criminal Law*, Yuhikaku Press, 89.

enlargement or reduction of the punishment scope from time to time. The distinct problem is how to determine whether the actor controls over the fragility of legal interests or not. For example, A found an abandoned infant when he went hunting in the field. No third party was present at that time and the baby's life was totally depended on A who could also easily protect this vulnerable legal interest. Therefore, can we identify A's controls over protecting the vulnerable legal interest?If the answer is yes, then as long as A didn't rescue the infant, he would be convicted as criminal omission. This result, however, will turns a person into a criminal due to certain accidental facts (if A hadn't gone hunting or passed by, there would be no crime), and there would be no prediction possibility for the citizens. If the answer is no, how to come up with the theory that A had no control over this vulnerable legal interest, which completely relied on A at that time? Thus, even if controlling over the cause of the effect can be divided into the the source of danger and the fragility of legal interest, the specific standard for identifying "control" shall be further clarified. Or to say, it is necessary to formally determine whether the actor should undertake the legal duties according to the principle of social division of labor. The formality duty is designed to clarify the obligations of individuals, so as to achieve the stability of the law. In other words, when the substantive investigation is being conducted, "the basis of legal duties shall not be neglected. Otherwise, the obligation of *Garantenstellung* will be infinitely enlarged. Therefore, the combination of formal inspection and substantive inspection shall be sought".[13]

Since *Ingerenz* was originally regarded as a kind of formality legal duty (*Garantenstellung* was the person who had carried out *Ingerenz*), so long as being substantially defined, certain *Ingerenz* would be the basis of legal duties.

2.2 Basic Nature of *Ingerenz*

Scholars in Germany, Japan and China Taiwan have brought out the totally opposed theories about *Ingerenz* in the process of exploring the substantive legal duty.

One of the theories is that only *Ingerenz* could be the source of legal duties, which holds that there is a structural difference between the criminal omission and *Begehungsdelikte*: the latter has the causative potency, while former makes use of the existed causal process only and doesn't have the causative potency in nature. In order to eliminate the differences and make the criminal omission equivalent with the *Begehungsdelikte* in constitutive elements, there is a requirement that "the subject of criminal omission should establish the causality that leads to the infringement of legal interests in the first place." Thus, to be the basis of criminal commission, those who imposed culpability upon omission must conduct *Ingerenz* based on intention or negligence, and that is enough.[14]

---

[13] H.Jescheck/T.Weigend, *Lehrbuch des Strafrechts: Allgemeiner Teil*, 5.Aufl.,Duncker & Humblot, 1996,S.621.

[14] 日日高义博:《不作为犯的理论》，王树平译，中国人民公安大学出版社1992年版，第111页。Hidaka Yoshihiro, trans. Wang Shuping.(1992) *The Theory of Inauthentic Omission*,

According to this point of view, a driver who deliberately fled after a crash had constituted an intentional homicide of omission, and, people who deliberately escaped from the fire scene had constituted the arson of omission. The biggest advantage of this theory is that the scope of criminal omission can be clearly defined based on the judgments of the facts. However, it is still questionable. Firstly, it negates the causative potency of criminal omission. Therefore, there will be no criminal omission if the result is caused by *Ingerenz*. In other words, the punishment objects of criminal omission should be the omission and its consequence, rather than *Ingerenz*. Secondly, this theory improperly narrowed the scope of criminal omission. For example, it denies the criminal omission in the case of being protection. Hence, a mother who didn't feed her baby and leading the baby dead didn't constitute the crime of homicide, and, the doctor on duty that offered without help to the patient who was terminally ill and died thereafter also didn't constitute the criminal omission.[15] However, this conclusion is clearly not proper. At last, this theory improperly narrowed down the punishment scope of criminal omission by defining *Ingerenz* as the act with intention or negligence.

The opposite view totally denies that *Ingerenz* may bring legal duties.

Germany Professor Schünemann insists to build a unitary system of perpetrator based on the controlling the cause of the effect. According to him, the whole system is based on the upper concept of "controlling the cause of the effect" and then two situations should be distinguished: the first is the controlling over the crime in the case of *Begehungsdelikte*, the second is controlling over some certain social fields in the case of status crime in *Garantenstellung*. However, *Ingerenz* cannot compare with the role of other *Garantenstellung* based on a typical relationship upon controlling, that is, there is no prior control over the source of infringement (the danger) or vulnerable legal interests, so the person who conducts *Ingerenz* is not in the position of *Garantenstellung*.[16] According to Professor Schünemann, only when the actor has a normal control over the danger or the vulnerable legal interest in advance, does the legal duties exists. This view, in fact, is a more substantive conclusion and requirement to the theory of functional dualism. As is known, the Paragraph 1 of Article 13 of *German Criminal Law* provides: "The actor doesn't have to prevent the consequence, as one of the constitutive elements, from occurring. The actor shall be punishable only when required by the law to prevent the result from

People's Public Security University of China Press, 111.

[15]参见日西田典之:《共犯理论の展开》，成文堂2010年版，第175~176页。See Nishida Noriyuki.(2010) *Development of Complicity Theory*, Seibundo Publishing Co, 175–176.

[16]参见德许迺曼:"德国不作为犯法理的现况"，载许玉秀、陈志辉编:《不移不惑献身法与正义——许迺曼教授刑事法论文选辑》，春风煦日学术基金2006年版，第667、656、641页。Bernd Schünemann, (2006) *The current legal situation regarding omissions in German criminal law,* as cited in Chen Zhihui, ed., *Unbestechlich und unbeirrbar im dienst von recht unechtigkeit: abhandlungen zur gesamten strafrechtswissenschaft von BERND SCHUNEMANN*, Taiwan: taedp.org.tw, 607, 656, 641.

occurring and such omission is equivalent to the act in constitutive elements."[17] Professor Schünemann, clearly, is intended to illustrate that both the criminal omission and *Begehungsdelikte* play the roles in controlling over the infringement of legal interest, and further conforming the equivalence of criminal omission and *Begehungsdelikte*.

There are no provisions similar to the Paragraph 1, Article 13 of *German Criminal Law* in China's criminal law. Since the same article of criminal law has applied to the intentional homicide of *Begehungsdelikte* and criminal omission, only when the criminal omission leading to somebody's death is indeed in conformity with the constitutive elements of "intentional homicide", hence it can be identified as intentional homicide. In other words, in China, the requirement that *Begehungsdelikte* and criminal omission should be equivalent to each other only means that the criminal omission must conform to the constitutive elements of criminal law. In the case of *Begehungsdelikte*, killing, as the way of act, is the cause of people's death, and the actor controls over the infringement. Therefore, the determination of intentional homicide of criminal omission also requires the actor to control over the cause of death. In this regard, to define the substantive legal duty as the controlling the infringement is legitimate and desirable. The problem is that whether the actor controls over the cause when he performs *Ingerenz* without preventing the occurrence of damaging result. This article holds an affirmative answer.

The process of infringement of legal interest upon *Begehungsdelikte* shows following: the creation of dangers (the act creates dangers leading to others' death) → the increase of dangers (possibility for others' death increases) → the realization of damaging result (others' death). On the one hand, this process shall be required. On the other hand, it also requires the actor to be in the position of preventing dangers while he doesn't prevent them.[18] According to the theory of functional duality in Germany, the processes of infringement of legal interest leading by criminal omission can be divided into two categories: First, legal interest turns vulnerable (or in helpless condition) due to certain reasons (man-made or legal subject's own reason, etc.), further the danger has been created→the danger increased→the damaging result has been realized. In this process, when the vulnerable legal interest relies on a specific person, his protection to legal interest is a substantive legal duty. When the specific person is bound in formality legal duty at the same time, he will be the *Garantenstellung*. Second, the danger created by the dangerous resources→the danger increased→the damaging result has been realized. During this process, only when the source of danger has been cut off, can the damaging result been prevented. And it is a substantive legal duties to cut off the source of danger. The person who has a duty to supervise (control over) the source of danger and has the formality

[17] 《德国刑法典》，冯军译，中国政法大学出版社2000年版，第10页。 *German Criminal Code*, trans. Feng Jun. (2000) China University of Political Science and Law Press, 10.

[18] 参见日山口厚:《刑法总论》，有斐阁2007年版，第80页Yamaguchi Atsushi.(2007) *General Rules of Criminal Law*, Yuhikaku Press, 80.; C.Roxin, *Strafrecht Allgemeiner Teil*, Band II, C.H.Beck, 2003,S.683 f.

legal duty in the meantime shall be *Garantenstellung*.[19] Certainly, the distinctions between two categories above are not absolute, but maybe intersect.[20]

When the legal interest becomes vulnerable and needs to be protected due to *Ingerenz*, the danger would be realized if no effective measures have been taken. In this sense, *Ingerenz* produces the duty of protection. Following comparisons may be made in this regard: first, it can be compared with the duty of protection arising from kinship. Even the theory of *Herrschaft über den Grund des Erfolges* has been adopted, the parents' duty of protecting their minor children will still be affirmed.[21] For example, A accidentally hurts the minor X, and X's parent B has a duty to help. It is true that A doesn't have to fulfill his duty to help when B offers. However, if B can't or doesn't perform his duty to help or B has requested A to offer help (a very common phenomenon), there is no reason to believe that A has no duty to help. Second, it can be compared with volunteer acceptance of danger. In a free society, when a person chooses to protect the vulnerable legal interests based on his free will, his *Garantenstellung* shall be affirmed.[22] For example, a man who voluntarily takes home an infant is obligated to bring up the infant. Since the person who voluntarily prevents the danger created by others will be imposed with the legal duties, the one who creates danger by himself shall subject to even more legal duties. Third, it can be compared with *Begehungsdelikte* that creating dangers. The order of law requires all people not to create dangers that threatening others' legal interests, thus there is no reason to believe that after a man creating this kind of danger, it is not necessary for him to prevent the danger from being a damaging result.[23] Clearly, only by affirming that *Ingerenz* is the source of legal duties, can we maintain a harmonious relationship between legal duties and criminal omission.

Howsoever, when *Ingerenz* has become a source of danger, if the danger will grow without positive measures being taken, it will be a damaging result. In this sense, *Ingerenz* produces the duty of safety. First of all, it is undeniable that the social division of labor is necessary in the modern complex society. The setting of supervisor for dangerous source in advance is also the identification of protector to vulnerable legal interest. However, compared with *Garantenstellung* who has the prior control over the source of danger, the person brought dangers to legal interests before should be more treated as *Garantenstellung*. Second, the person who conducts *Ingerenz* shall be the most suitable and easiest one to prevent the occurrence of damaging result. For example, it will be much more suitable and easier for the

[19] 参见日山口厚:《新判例から见た刑法》，有斐阁2008年版，第41~42页。See Yamaguchi Atsushi.(2008) *Criminal Law as Seen from New Judicial Precedents*, Yuhikaku Press, 41–42.

[20] 参见德约翰内斯·韦塞尔斯:《德国刑法总论》，李昌珂译，法律出版社2008年版，第433页。See Johannes Wessels, trans. Li Changke, (2008) *Strafrecht Allgemeiner Teil*, Law Press, 433.

[21] 参见日山口厚:《刑法总论》，有斐阁2007年版，第89~90页。Yamaguchi Atsushi.(2007) *General Rules of Criminal Law*, Yuhikaku Press, 89–90.

[22] 参见日岛田聡一郎:"不作为犯"，载《法学教室》2002年第8号。See Shimada Souichirou. (2002) "Omission" as cited in Hogaku Kyoshitsu, No. 8.

[23] Vgl.,C.Roxin, *Strafrecht Allgemeiner Teil*, Band II, C.H.Beck, 2003, S.762 f.

person who plants the explosive to prevent the accident from occurring, the one who detentes others shall be the most suitable and convenient one to release others, the driver who hits the passenger shall be the most suitable and easiest one to prevent the dangers from occurring by taking effective measures. Controlling the dangers resulting from the actor's *Ingerenz* is both the requirement of social division of labor and the requirement of protection of legal interest.

Obviously, the controlling over the source of danger or the vulnerable legal interests is not subject to prior normal dominance. In other words, whether the actor controls over the source of danger or vulnerable legal interests in advance should not be determined only by objective facts, but also by a normative examination according to the principle of social division of labor. "If one creates a danger that threatens the legal interests of others, the commandment of 'the danger should be ruled out (or controlled)' will also be derived from the universal prohibition of 'no violations of others' rights."[24] In a free society, the citizens have the freedom to act. However, on the one hand, citizens can not infringe on the legal benefits of others, otherwise they will bear the corresponding legal consequences. On the other hand, when the acts of citizens bring danger to legal interests, it is necessary to prevent the danger from being realized, which is the general trust principle of the society. If no one has to prevent the dangers created by him, such dangers could only be prevented by other citizens, who thereby have no freedom at all, otherwise, the dangers will be realized and legal interests cannot be protected. Moreover, as the society is getting complicated, scientific and highly technical, it is impossible for the individuals to subjectively control over the society, which is like a giant black box. In the meantime, the potential danger of personal acts is also increasing rapidly, and no one can predict the instant danger and disaster that they will face.[25] The outburst of danger is an important characteristic of modern society. What's more, any legal interest will turns vulnerable at any time. In such social background, limiting the source of legal duties to the prior and normal controlling over the source of danger or vulnerable legal interest is not only restricted, but also opposed to the social typicality.[26]

[24] 蔡圣伟:《刑法问题研究(一)》，元照出版有限公司2008年版，第230页。Cai Sheng Wei (2008) *Research on Criminal Law Issues* (1), Angle Publishing Co., Ltd., 230.

[25] 参见日井田良:"刑事立法の活性化とそのゆくえ"，载《法律时报》第75卷(2003年)第2号。See Ida Makoto.(2003) "Activation of criminal legislation and its future" as cited in *Law Times*, Vol. 75, No.2.

[26] It shall also be noticed that, scholars of criminal law in German deny that *Ingerenz* can be the source of criminal omission and will not be assumed as innocent. As it will be described later, the Article 323(c) of *German Criminal Law* has provided the crime of non-salvation in danger. However, even so, there exists the problem of imbalanced punishment. Therefore, Professor Schünemann has advocated the aggregated offense: "Actor causes dangers or has special duty to prevent danger, but is not responsible for preventing them as described in the first paragraph, shall be sentenced to…(aggregated)…"(参见德许迺曼:"德国不作为犯法理的现况"，载许玉秀、陈志辉编:《不移不惑献身法与正义——许迺曼教授刑事法论文选辑》，春风煦日学术基金2006年版，第642~643页Bernd Schünemann, (2006) *The current legal situation regarding omissions in German criminal law,* as cited in Chen Zhihui, ed., *Unbestechlich und unbeirrbar im dienst von recht unechtigkeit: abhandlungen zur gesamten strafrechtswissenschaft von BERND SCHUNEMANN*, Taiwan: taedp.org.tw, 642–643). The criminal law in China has no provisions

Professor Yamaguchi Atsushi believes that the controlling over the cause of infringement of legal interest is the substantive ground for producing the legal duties. He pointed out: "In the case of creating or increasing the danger by *Ingerenz*, the acts themselves cannot be deemed as the cause for conforming the cause of infringement of legal interest. It must be noted that, in the stage that possibly create or increase dangers, even if controlling over the source of danger of *Garantenstellung* can be regarded as the source of legal duties, the actor shall not be deemed as the cause of dominating the effect when unreasonable measures had been taken afterwards and create dangers thereby. For example, when a motor vehicle is about to rush to pedestrians, the driver is required to take reasonable measures, such as stepping on the brakes (the controlling over the source of danger). However, as long as the accident happens and other people get hurt thereby, the driver will have no control over the cause of the damaging result (In this situation, the driver is the same as others who has no business with the accident)."[27] It is reasonable to believe that the driver who makes the crash has no controlling over the cause of the injury that already arose. But, if the offender who created the accident has been regarded as having no legal duties to the development from injury to death (the danger of death), just like the third unrelated party, then the victim's life will get no protection when the accident is unexpected and there is no police present. Moreover, no one will be responsible for the victim's death. This conclusion is hard to be accepted. On the other hand, Professor Yamaguchi Atsushi admitted that the person who manufactures dangerous products will control over the cause of the infringement if he learns the dangers of the products afterwards, and therefore has the duty of recalling.[28] However, compared with the manufacture of dangerous products, the risk caused by traffic accidents is more urgent. It is paradoxical to admit the former's dominance but deny the latter's controlling over the cause of the infringement. In fact, "in the case that the driver carelessly hits the pedestrian, the actor, who starts the causal process, is in the same space with the victim and most likely to offer help. Therefore, he shall help the victim. Or to say, although the actor doesn't start the causal process on purpose, he has the opportunity to change the causality and hence has the controlling over facts as well as the duty to rescuing the victim."[29] Moreover, Professor Yamaguchi Atsushi believes that the controlling over the fragility of legal interest is generally judged by the actor's acceptance to the protection of legal interests.[30]

---

similar to Article 323(c) in *German Criminal Law*. If *Ingerenz* has been denied as source of duty to act, the legal interests will not be properly protected.

[27] 日山口厚:《刑法总论》，有斐阁2007年版，第91~92页。Yamaguchi Atsushi.(2007) *General Rules of Criminal Law*, Yuhikaku Press, 91–92.

[28] 参见日山口厚:《刑法总论》，有斐阁2007年版，第90页。See Yamaguchi Atsushi.(2007) *General Rules of Criminal Law*, Yuhikaku Press, 90.

[29] 许玉秀:《当代刑法思潮》，中国民主法制出版社2005年版，第690页。Xu Yu Xiu. (2005) *Contemporary Trends in Criminal Law Thought*, China Democracy and Legal System Publishing House, 690.

[30] 参见日山口厚:《刑法总论》，有斐阁2007年版，第90页。See Yamaguchi Atsushi.(2007) *General Rules of Criminal Law*, Yuhikaku Press, 90.

However, this point of view only takes the principle of liberalism into consideration while ignoring the principle of social division of labor.

Japanese Professor Nishida Noriyuki believes that only when the actor controls over the process of infringement concretely and realistically, the omission will constitute the criminal omission. It can be divided into two types: (a) the actor, at his own will, gets in or sets an situation in which he can exclusively control the process of infringement. Thereby, the actor is bound to the legal duties; and (b) although it is not the actor's own will, he is actually in the position that controls over the process of infringement, or to say, on the dominant occasion. In this situation, as the actor has no intention to control, the normative element that "as long as the actor shall act" shall be taken into consideration. "However, it is proper to exclude *Ingerenz* from the sources of legal duties on such an occasion. That is because (a) *Ingerenz* can be punished as the negligent crime or consequential aggregated offense in most cases. Therefore, it will be unreasonable if *Ingerenz* has been convicted of a more serious crime and be double punished; and (b) the controlling over the occasion, as the factual prerequisite of the legal duties, changes with the specific situations like escaping after causing a traffic accident or the fire scene, and further affects the constitution of the crime. As a result, the stand of the actor of criminal omission, who has been temporarily and accidentally put in such occasion, is so unstable that the stability of the law will be harmed thereby. For those reasons, the normative elements of this type of omission shall be defined as the situations that continually imposed protection and management duties based on the identity or social status, such as parents and children, the owner, the tenant and the manager of the building."[31]

However, first, as it will discuss later, it is not appropriate and will have loopholes to punish *Ingerenz* as to the negligent crime or consequential aggregated offense. When an actor is not responsible for his *Ingerenz*, he can neither be punished with the negligent crime nor with consequential aggregated offense. Second, it is not a double punishment to make *Ingerenz* the source of duty of omission. For one thing, it is not a negative legal judgment to affirm that certain *Ingerenz* may lead to the production of actor's legal duties. Even if it is regarded as a negative judgment of *Ingerenz*, the affirmation still will not directly lead to the negative legal consequences. For another, there is no double punishment will be inflicted even though *Ingerenz* has constituted a crime and the failure to fulfill the duty created by *Ingerenz* has constituted another crime. For example, A negligently sets some objects on fire that could be easily extinguished, but A intends not to do so. In this regard, A's act can only be identified as the criminal omission of arson, rather than the crime of negligently causing a fire and the crime of arson. It is even be more impossible to inflict the combined punishment. Even if *Ingerenz* and the omission in the latter stage have violated different legal interests and thus being punished jointly, the punishments are the respective evaluations of the former and

[31] 日西田典之:《共犯理论の展开》，成文堂2010年版，第180页。Nishida Noriyuki.(2010) *Development of Complicity Theory*, Seibundo Publishing Co, 180.

the latter, while there is still no double punishment. Third, the legal duties produced by *Ingerenz* is of no arbitrariness and contingency, therefore, the stability of the law will not be damaged. It is true that *Ingerenz* may also be accidental, but when the actor knows or should know that *Ingerenz* creates danger to the legal interests, the actor's legal duties has come into being. It doesn't vary from person to person, time to time and place to place. Moreover, taking *Ingerenz* as a source of legal duty is the easiest for the nation to accept. And it is right and proper to require the creator of danger to be the protector of legal interests. Furthermore, even if *Ingerenz* is contingent in some occasions, it doesn't mean that taking *Ingerenz* as the legal duties will affect the stability of the law. For example, the occurrence of danger is always contingent, but no one will regard asking for police's help as a threat to the stability of the law. That is because the police's duty to help in the situation of contingent danger is already determined. It shows that the contingency of danger has no influence on the law's stability. For the same reason, the actor may create a danger by accident, but it is a constant rule that the person who creates the danger should prevent the occurrence of the damaging result, and it will not affect the stability of the law. Actually, it is the judgment of *Ingerenz* that may have an influence on the stability of the law. Therefore, if the explicit standard have been described for *Ingerenz*, the stability of the law will not be influenced. Fourth, the view of Professor Nishida Noriyuki will lead to unfairness. For example, the defendant A finds that the candles ignited in the shrine of his house has fell down and is likely to catch a fire, but to get the insurance, A just leaves and closes the door and let the fire break out. While working in the company, B has found that the charcoal fire under the desk caused by his gross negligence has burned the table and the paperwork. To avoid being discovered, B did not extinguishes the fire, which at that time was easily to put out, nor did B tell the staff on duty, and then B just run away. The whole building was burnt down thereby. Professor Nishida Noriyuki holds that A's act has constituted the arson of omission while B's act does not. The reason is that, A is the supervisor of the building while B is not.[32] However, it is hard to be accepted. Compared with the supervisor of the building, the person who violates the regulations and uses charcoal fire should be more responsible for extinguishing the fire.

Professor Xu Yuxiu, the scholar of China Taiwan, is also against the theory that taking *Ingerenz* as the source of duty of omission.[33] She has divided *Ingerenz* and omission into different types and puts forward the solutions accordingly. But her solutions are questionable according to the author.

(1) Where *Ingerenz* is an intentional act while the subsequent behavior is an intentional act of omission or omission of negligence, and by which the legal inter-

[32] 参见日西田典之:《共犯理论の展开》，成文堂2010年版，第170、180页。See Nishida Noriyuki.(2010) *Development of Complicity Theory*, Seibundo Publishing Co, 170, 180.

[33] 许玉秀:《当代刑法思潮》，中国民主法制出版社2005年版，第673页以下。Xu Yu Xiu. (2005) *Contemporary Trends in Criminal Law Thought*, China Democracy and Legal System Publishing House, 1–673.

ests are violated are quite different, and then the acts should be punished as consequential aggregated offense. For example, a person setting fire to a building without helping the victim inside shall be convicted of the consequential aggregated offense of arson for the victim's death. It is not necessary to regard the act of fire setting as the source of duty of omission. For another example, it will be convicted of intentional injury to death if someone makes the victim to take poison (the act of injury) while forgetting to provide the person with antidote and leads to the victim's death. In this case, the prior injury should not be deemed as the source of duty of omission. However, this solution cannot solve the issues about accomplice. For example, after setting on fire A found the victim was in the building. A planned to save the victim whereas the passenger B instigated A not to do so, A took B's advice and the victim was therefore burned to death. If it is not recognized that the subsequent behavior is of independent significance, B will not be convicted as the instigator of intentional homicide.[34]

(2) Where *Ingerenz* is an intentional act while the subsequent is an intentional omission or omission of negligence, and the interests violated are the same, the actor will only be convicted of the accomplished crime of *Ingerenz*. For example, the victim had fallen into the pool when the actor was imposing murdering, the actor offered no help and led to the victim's death. Under this circumstance, the actor shall only be convicted of accomplished crime of intentional homicide based on *Ingerenz*. For another example, after deliberately detaining the victim, the actor forgot that the victim was detained, thus he will only be convicted of offense of illegal detention in accordance with *Ingerenz*. Indeed, in the latter example, it is in accordance with law to convict the actor of the accomplished crime of *Ingerenz*. However, in the former example, if the victim has been identified as being drowned to death by the forensics, it will be improper to determine that the prior killing itself is the cause of the victim's death. In other words, to ensure that the actor is responsible for the drowning of the victim, it must be affirmed that the defendant has the duty to rescue the victim who falls into the pool. That is because the consequence in criminal law is not an abstract but a concrete consequence. Whether the victim is drowned or killed are actually two different consequences, or it will be impossible to discuss the issue of causality. Moreover, the issues about accomplice will still be unsolved if the defender be punished as the accomplished crime of *Ingerenz*.

(3) Where *Ingerenz* is an act of negligence while the subsequent act is the omission of negligence, and the actor will be convicted of atypical consequential aggregated offense no matter the legal interests violated are the same or different, and *Ingerenz*, therefore, shall not be regarded as the source of legal duties. In a case that a person negligently ignited a trash bin and found a child was walking towards it, the person believed that the fire would be extinguished by itself so that he didn't stop the child, who was thereafter burned to death. In another case, someone negligently pushed others into the pool and was under the illu-

[34] The act of A violates crime of arson as well as crime of intentional homicide.

sion that the victim was good at swimming so that no help was offered, but the victim was drowned to death afterwards. However, in the former case, although it is not improper to convict the actor of so-called atypical consequential aggregated offense, the issues about accomplice will still not be solved. In the latter case, if it is to be determined as the crime of negligent homicide (drowned to death), the omission in the latter stage leading to the victim's death shall be confirmed. Otherwise, it will be difficult to deal with the case that somebody negligently pushed others into the pool but provided no help with intention knowing that the victim can't swim at all and resulted in the victim's death. Most importantly, the atypical consequential aggregated offense doesn't exist in the specific provisions of criminal law. Crime of negligent homicide is a pure negligent crime, rather than a so-called atypical consequential aggregated offense.

(4) Where *Ingerenz* is an act of negligence while the subsequent act is the omission of negligence, no matter the legal interest been violated are the same or different, such problem shall be solved by legislation. In a case that a person negligently ignited a trash bin and found a child was walking towards it, the person didn't stop the child but leaving the child burned to death. Or, somebody determined to give the victim a lesson by detaining him for another half-day, even if the person locked the victim out of negligence in the first place. Professor Xu Yuxiu argued that the issue in the former case should be solved by setting up a negligent and intentional aggregated consequential offense, and for the latter case, the law should provide the crime of negligent discontinuation to reward the negligent actor for preventing the consequence. However, firstly, this methodology has its own problems. Or to say, it is not proper to turn to legislation when one's theory doesn't work. In other words, since her view is unworkable in the interpretation theory, she should admit that her interpretation is wrong and seek for another interpretation. Secondly, both setting up a negligent and intentional aggregated consequential offense and setting up a provision of crime of negligent discontinuation are not the ideal proposals for legislation. On one hand, aggregated consequential offense is the residual of consequential responsibility.[35] Rather than setting up a negligent and intentional aggregated consequential offense, it is more proper to admit that *Ingerenz* gives rise to the legal duties and the omission can be directly deemed as intentional crime. On the other hand, the accomplished crime, rather than the attempted crime, is the only form of negligent crime. Under such circumstance, how to stipulate the crime of negligent discontinuation in the law?

What's more, Professor Xu Yuxiu doesn't take the situation that conducting *Ingerenz* with no intention or negligence into consideration. Hence, her interpretation scheme is not comprehensive.

---

[35] 参见张明楷:"严格限制结果加重犯的范围与刑罚"，载《法学研究》2005年第1期。See Zhang Mingkai. (2005) "Strictly Limiting the Scope and Punishment of Aggravated Consequence Offenses," as cited in *Chines Journal of Law*, No. 1.

From the above, it is obvious that it is not appropriate to completely deny that *Ingerenz* can be the source of duty of omission. Or to say, *Ingerenz* shall be admitted to be one of the sources of duty of omission.

In fact, China's criminal law affirms that *Ingerenz* shall be the source of duty of criminal omission. According to article 133 of China's *Criminal Law*, whoever is guilty of traffic accident shall be sentenced to fixed-term imprisonment of not more than 3 years or criminal detention. Whoever runs away from the spot after he has caused a traffic accident or is involved in other especially flagrant circumstances shall be sentenced to fixed-term imprisonment of not less than 3 years but not more than 7 years. Identifying the behavior of escaping as a ground for increasing the prescribed punishment is to urge the actor to help the victims in the circumstance of traffic accident. The actor endangering others' lives with *Ingerenz* (including the act that constituted the crime of traffic accident) had created himself bear the legal duties. The failure to perform such duty will definitely become the ground of increasing the prescribed punishment of legal penalty.[36]

Admitting that *Ingerenz* can be the source of legal duties will also solve the problems facing by the judicial practice.

For example, on November 10, 2000, *Interpretations of Certain Specific Issues concerning the Application of Law in the Trial of Criminal Cases involving Traffic Accidents* enacted by the Supreme People's Court provides: "The supervisor of the workplace, the owner, contractor or the passenger of the motor vehicle instigates the person who causes the traffic accident to escape shall be punished as the accomplice of offender of traffic accident." It shall be believed that this interpretation is proper. However, since China's *Criminal Law* only recognizes the joint intentional offense, if the provision above will not be interpreted from the perspective of *Ingerenz*, it will be held that the negligent crime of traffic accident has included an intentional consequential aggregated offense, which is hard to be understood or accepted. As mentioned above, when the actor of a traffic accident has caused serious injury to the victim, he actually has the duty to rescue due to *Ingerenz*. The death of the victim resulting from the actor's escape is actually caused by the failure to perform the duty to rescue. At this time, the offender is the one who subjects to rescue. Whoever instigates the offender to escape is the criminal of omission that instigates the offender to conduct intentional criminal omission (basic offense, equals to the crime of abandonment). In the occasion that the omission results in the aggregated consequence of victim's death, as long as the instigator has a prediction possibility to such

[36]Article 3 of *Interpretations of Certain Specific Issues concerning the Application of Law in the Trial of Criminal Cases involving Traffic Accidents* enacted by the Supreme People's Court on November tenth provides: "Escaping after the traffic accident refers to …the act of running away for escaping criminal punishment after the traffic accident." It is not proper, however. Running away for escaping criminal punishment after committing crimes is "human nature". Therefore, the voluntary surrender has become the condition of lenient treatment. If "Escape" has been interpreted as "running way for escaping criminal punishment", the reason why the "Escape" not being provided as the promotion of prescribed punishment of other crimes will not be explained.(参见张明楷:《刑法学》，法律出版社2007年版，第543页See Zhang Mingkai, (2007) *Criminal Law*, Law Press China, 543.)

consequence, he shall be hold responsible. In summary, when the defendant has been instigated to escape and punished by the relative provision, the instigator shall also be punished by the provision of death resulting from the act of escape. As the offender is the one who has the legal duties (rescue), it should be affirmed that the inciter can only be the instigator of the escaping behavior. For the same reason, the person who helps the offender to flee will also be the aider.[37]

For another example, admitting that *Ingerenz* is the source of the legal duties is conducive to solving the issue of product recall. Nowadays, in an era of the proliferation of fake and inferior products, it is conclusive that manufacturers are required to recall dangerous products. Professor Schünemann, who denies that *Ingerenz* is the source of legal duties, also refuses to admit that manufacturers have the duty to recall dangerous products and holds the view that manufactures shall be punished in accordance with the negligent act.[38] For example, manufacturers who produce dangerous products that lead other's death shall be convicted of the crime of negligent homicide. This is not ideal, however. Firstly, when manufacturers have produced the dangerous products but have no negligence during the process of manufacturing and selling, even though the danger threatening the life and body has been found afterwards, the manufacturers will not be punished as criminals if *Ingerenz* will not be regarded as the source of legal duties, because *Ingerenz* is of no negligence. The loophole of the punishment has come into being thereby. Secondly, in China, the scope of penalty for crime of homicide and serious injury out of negligence is actually narrower than that in Germany and Japan. The most typical one in China is that, the act of manufacturing and selling fake and inferior products that result in others' serious injuries will constitute the crime of aggregated consequential offense, rather than the pure negligent crime. However, manufacturing and selling fake and inferior products is an intentional crime. Hence, as negligently manufacturing and selling fake and inferior products doesn't constitute a crime, if *Ingerenz* have not be treated as the source of legal duty, it will be difficult to obtain a conviction even though the actor has negligence in the process of manufacturing and selling the products above. Moreover, the coordination of criminal law cannot be maintained even if it is identified as crime of negligent homicide or serious injury out of negligence. Thirdly,

[37] This article doesn't advocate that the crime of traffic accident out of negligence should include the intentional consequential aggregated crime. The name of the crime may be the problem: on one hand, judicial interpretation doesn't identify crime of death causing by defender's escape as an independent crime, while treating the crime oppositely when determining the instigator as accomplice. On the other hand, the crime of traffic accident is a negligent crime and includes no joint crime, but the judicial interpretation has directly affirmed the negligent joint crime. This is the problem of judicial interpretation. If the death caused by the defender's escape has been identified as an independent crime (crime of death causing by defender's escape), and the act of escape is the basic offense (criminal omission, but it is impossible for the crime to be independently punished but to be punished as the aggregated consequence of traffic accident) and the result of death is the consequential aggregated crime (equal to the crime of death by abandonment in other countries' criminal law), the judicial interpretation will not be under debate.

[38] 参见日岩间康夫:《制造物责任と不作为犯论》，成文堂2010年版，第90页以下。See Iwama Yasuo.(2010) *Product Liability and Omission Theory*, Seibundo Publishing Co, 1–90.

someone observes that, as administrative and economic law provide that the actors shall recall the dangerous products, the failure to perform the duty of recalling constitutes a criminal omission for the obligation specified by the law has not be met. But this point of view is back to the formality deontology, and it cannot answer the question why the violation of other laws will directly constitute the crime in criminal law? It is not hard to find that, requiring manufacturers of dangerous products to perform the duty of recalling based on *Ingerenz* is the most proper way to solve the problem.

Given all that, the view that the legal duties can be produced by certain *Ingerenz* shall be affirmed. But it is undeniable that extending the range of punishment by imposing no limitation on *Ingerenz* is also improper.

The problem is how to impose the limitation. In the past, the precedents of the German imperial courts did not consider about whether *Ingerenz* was legal or illegal, responsible or irresponsible for the result. The actor had been given the legal duties even *Ingerenz* was just one of the conditions that leading to the result and therefore, it is widely recognized that the omission is punishable. But in the theory of the early nineteenth century, Stübel had brought up the thought that only when *Ingerenz* was punishable or at least illegal, could it be the basis of legal duty. The theory of criminal law in the late nineteenth century generally advocated that there should be some limitations on the legal duties basing on *Ingerenz*s. In particular, after World War II, requiring *Ingerenz* to be violation of duty had become the most powerful doctrine (the theory of violation of duty), and was also adopted by the German federal court.[39]

However, the theory of violation of duty is questionable. Firstly, regarding *Ingerenz* as the source of legal duties and further affirming the omission constitutes a crime is not taking *Ingerenz* as the basis of punishment. That being the case, there is no reason to limit *Ingerenz* as the acts that violated the legal duty. In other words, there is no reason to believe that only the act violating certain duties will creates the legal duties, since all *Ingerenz* have created dangers. Secondly, the boundary of the violation of duty is clear. Although the theory of violation of duty has many supporters in Germany, only Professor Rudolphi has given a rather specific illustration. "According to Rudolphi, the boundary of the violation of duty is co-determined by the specific provisions related to accomplice, the principle of accountability, explanation of constitutive element in specific provisions as well as the general principle of wrongdoing."[40] It is not hard to find that there is no definite standard for the violation of duty. Thirdly, regarding *Ingerenz* has violated the legal duties is to exclude the justifiable defense to a large extent. But as described later, the legal duties will also be produced when excessive dangers have been created by justifiable defense. Last, the legal duties arising from *Ingerenz* is not subject to the violation of duty according to the relative provisions of China. For example, the first half of the first

[39] 参见日岩间康夫:《制造物责任と不作为犯论》，成文堂2010年版，第90页以下。See Iwama Yasuo.(2010) *Product Liability and Omission Theory*, Seibundo Publishing Co, 1–90.

[40] 日岩间康夫:《制造物责任と不作为犯论》，成文堂2010年版，第46页。Iwama Yasuo. (2010) *Product Liability and Omission Theory*, Seibundo Publishing Co, 46.

paragraph of Article 70 of *Law of The People's Republic of China on Road Traffic Safety* provides: "If a traffic accident occurs on road, the vehicle driver shall immediately park the vehicle and protect the scene; if it causes any personal injury or death, the vehicle driver shall immediately rescue the injured, and promptly reports to the traffic policeman on duty or the traffic administrative department of the public security organ." Obviously, duty to rescuing the injured is not based on the premise that the driver violates the regulations governing traffic and transportation. Duty to rescuing the injured, on the surface, comes from the legal provisions, which, however, based on *Ingerenz* of the actor.[41]

This article holds that, the urgent danger standing before the specific legal interest protected by criminal law becomes the substantial basis for *Ingerenz* to be the source of legal duties. First, *Ingerenz* posed a danger to the specific legal interest that protected by the criminal law. The danger threatening the interests that aren't protected by the criminal law cannot be the resource of legal duties. However, as described below, it is not necessary for *Ingerenz* to be wrongdoing. For example, when the act of necessity that prevents danger has produced another danger which will violate the third party's legal interests, the actor shall bear the responsibility to rescue while the act of necessity itself is not illegal. For another example, X escaped after an attempted robbery, A, B and C chased after X in order to arrest him, X then fell into the deep water at the end of the road. The act of chasing is not illegal, but it does create danger to X's life, A, B and C's duty to rescue cannot be denied. Second, in case that as the danger is obviously increasing, the danger will immediately turns into damaging result if there is not positive actions. For example, A's *Ingerenz* has led to serious injuries of others, and may also rise the danger of death. Then A shall bear the duty to rescue at that moment. If B worked in the victim's working place and violently broke the victim's finger and left, the finger fracture will not evidently increase the danger of death, thus B's act won't be possible to constitute the crime of intentional homicide of omission. Third, the actor shall control over the reason that grows the danger to damaging result. That is, in that circumstance, the actor of *Ingerenz* shall be the most effective one to prevent the consequences from occurring. Or to say, no one else should have the priority to protect the legal interests. Otherwise, the legal interest shall be protected by others. For example, a traffic policeman was just at the sense when A hit somebody by the motor vehicle on the highway. The policeman shall be the one to take the injured man to the hospital. In addition, a third party had prevented the dangerous result out of his own will after the actor created dangers to the legal interests (e.g. C has been taken to the hospital by B and rescued after being hit by A). In this case, the actor of *Ingerenz* was not required to prevent the result. However, in this situation, it doesn't mean that A has no duty to rescue, but has lost the controlling over the reason and result due to B's voluntary act of help.

[41] In Anglo-American criminal law, a driver who causes the death of a victim by failing to render aid after hitting another person through no fault of his own is guilty of homicide.(参见美乔治·弗莱彻:《反思刑法》，邓子滨译，华夏出版社2008年版，第452页See George P, Fletcher, trans. Deng Zibin, (2008) *Rethinking Criminal Law*, Huaxia Publishing House, 452.)。

To commensurate with it, the following circumstances cannot be the sources of legal duty. First, when the act does not create or increase the danger, no legal duties will come into being. Imagine that a passenger has taken an abandoned infant along the road to the civil affair administration; a driver on the highway has taken a victim that hit by the earlier car to the gas station and left victim alone; people who had the meal together have sent the drunk one to his residence. In these cases, even the victims died without rescue, the actors shall not take the responsibilities for the act of omission. In particular, it is necessary to point out that when the victim's own decision rather than the actor's *Ingerenz* that endangered the victim, *Ingerenz* didn't create the act of legal duty. As mentioned before, the party who suggests departing will has no legal duties to the other's suicide or self-injury, even if the actor used to have intercourse with the victim, or even got her pregnant. Second, there is no legal duties although the act has created or increased the danger that is not urgent or insignificant. For example, B injured C with a sharp knife that was handed by A. Even if A was at present, there was no legal duties.[42] Third, no legal duties exists when the danger created or increased is within the victim's scope of accountability. For example, A had lent the drug paraphernalia to B, who overdosed on the drug and got injured. A should bear no culpability for intentional assault of omission.[43]

The omission led by *Ingerenz* is not merely the succession of wrongdoing of the latter. That is because in the case of criminal omission, it is not *Ingerenz*, but the omission in the latter stage that shall be punished. The simple succession of wrongdoing of *Ingerenz* is difficult to provide basis for punishing the criminal omission. Besides, *Ingerenz* that produces the legal duties doesn't take the wrongdoing as precondition. Whether omission can be evaluated as one act or not cannot be generalized.[44] In situations where the duty has caused by *Ingerenz*, the omission is the process that realizing the dangers of *Ingerenz*. If there is no such act, the damaging result will not be produced; If there is *Ingerenz* but the actor has performed the legal duties, there will be no damaging injury either. So *Ingerenz* and the omission in the latter stage are the reasons of result jointly. Thus, if the actor is not responsible for *Ingerenz* (say, with no intention or negligence), the subsequent criminal culpability of omission shall be the only thing to be pursued. On the other hand, if the actor bears the culpability for *Ingerenz*, it is necessary to further examine whether *Ingerenz* and the latter constitute one act or two, and how many legal interests have been violated, and then to determine whether it is one crime or several crimes.

---

[42] Vgl.,C.Roxin,*Strafrecht Allgemeiner Teil*, Band II, C.H.Beck, 2003, S.766.

[43] Vgl.,C.Roxin,*Strafrecht Allgemeiner Teil*, Band II, C.H.Beck, 2003, S.771.

[44] It is impossible for a criminal act to both include act and omission (e.g. crime of abuse, crime of resisting taxes).

2.3 Specific Contents of *Ingerenz*

As previously mentioned, the legal duties created by *Ingerenz* shall be the urgent danger of the specific legal interests protected by criminal law. This article may takes a further discussion about several related questions.

(1) Whether the omission can be *Ingerenz*?

This article holds that the omission can be one *Ingerenz*. For example, the owner of the house failed to notice the tiles on the roof, which might fall off and bring injuries to others, in such case the owner will bear the duty to rescue.[45] Some may argue that in this occasion, the former legal duties (the duty to supervising the dangerous resources) itself shall be the basis of rescuing the injured. But it is not the fact. The house owner shall be accountable for the injury as long as the victim injured by the falling tiles. The ground is the owner's Aufsichtspflicht (duty to supervising) to prevent the tiles from falling off. If the victim has been hurt and is in danger, saving the victim is another legal duties based on the prior omission. The duty to supervising the source of danger cannot directly lead to the owner's duty to rescuing the victims. In addition, if the former legal duties has been indicated as the basis for producing the duty to rescue, it will be more likely to draw the conclusion that the owner only has negligence rather than intent to the result, which is obviously not appropriate. Take a typical case in United States as an example. The defendant Kneller raised a pair of fierce Canary dogs. In January 2001, Kneller returned to her room on the sixth floor after walking the male dog on the roof of the apartment. When she reached the corridor of the sixth floor, the male dog suddenly broke away the dog chain and rushed towards a neighbor who was about to enter her house. In the meantime, the female dog also rushed out of Kneller's door and might also involve in the gnawing. It lasted for more than 10 min, and the victim eventually died with more than 77 wounds on her body. Kneller didn't muzzle the male dog in advance, neither asked for help nor took a weapon to subdue the dog, nor called 911 when the dog was biting the lady. The California court had overruled the conviction of negligent homicide and eventually determined the case as the crime of murder.[46] Obviously, if Kneller only failed to performed duty to supervising (failure to muzzle the male dog to prevent it from biting) and led to the victim's injury or death by the dog's sudden gnawing, she would only be convicted as the criminal of negligent homicide. This article believes that the reason that convicting Kneller of murder is that after her prior omission had created the dangers violating the legal interests, she intentionally offered no help to protect the victim's life. Thereby, it shall be admitted that omissions can also be *Ingerenz*.

---

[45] Vgl.,C.Roxin,*Strafrecht Allgemeiner Teil*, Band II,C.H.Beck, 2003,S.776.

[46] 参见刘鹏:"狗咬人，女主人被判谋杀罪"，载《检察日报》2008年9月24日。See Liu Peng. (2008) "Dog Bites Person, Female Owner Convicted of Murder," in *Procuratorate Daily*, 24 September 2008.

(2) Can the act with justifiable cause be *Ingerenz*?

In light of the theory of *Erfolgsunwert,* the act has objectively created the danger that violates legal interests, if another advantageous or at least equally important legal interest has not been protected in the same time, the act will be illegal. Hence, generally speaking, *Ingerenz* that creates the danger violating the legal interests is illegal. In another word, *Ingerenz* that can be the legal duties are usually illegal.

There will a problem when an act objectively violates the legal interest, while it can protect another superior or at least equally important legal interest at the same time. Or to say, could the act with justifiable cause (or justifications) be *Ingerenz* that produces the act of legal duty?

First of all, it can be affirmed that the actor of necessity has the legal duties for preventing the innocent person being hurt. It is also the important reason why the German theory of criminal law doesn't require *Ingerenz* to be wrongdoing, however, justifiable defense is the problem included. Fletcher, an American scholar, pointed out: "the defendant had legitimately hurt others in justifiable defense and left the victim there to die. Both the German and American criminal laws hold that, the justifiable hurt shall not bear culpability for the victim's death. But it is not always the case. Even though the injury is justifiable, there is independent reason to admit that the defender has the legal duty to prevent the injured victim from dying. The offender could be the defendant's parents or spouse, or someone that medically or psychologically depends on the defendant. As soon as the offender is incapable of attacking and the defendant is no longer in danger, other duties shall prevail to control or require the defendant to actively involve and rescue the injured person."[47] Professor Lin Dongmao in China Taiwan has pointed that: "The justifiable defender shall not be placed in the position of *Garantenstellung*. It is necessary for the unlawful infringer to predict the consequences of counterattack and bear the consequence on his own. No one owns the status of *Garantenstellung* as well as the duty to rescue for strangers; if the defender of justifiable defense is believed to be the *Garantenstellung* for the unlawful infringer, it is no better than admitting that the legal status of the infringer is higher than that of the stranger. Only when the act of justifiable defense exceeds the limits of necessity (excessive defense), does the defender of justifiable defense has the status of *Garantenstellung*. For example, a weak woman was battered with a baseball bat by the salesman walked way certain objects from the store, under which it was a must for the salesman to send the woman to hospital. Recognizing that the defender of justifiable defense has the status of the *Garantenstellung* will equate the justifiable defense with excessive defense, and will even treat the defender of justifiable defense as the unlawful infringer. It is unfair to the defender of justifiable defense."[48] However, this point of view is too absolute. In this article, different situations shall be analyzed in different

[47] 美乔治·弗莱彻:《反思刑法》，邓子滨译，华夏出版社2008年版，第451页。George P, Fletcher, trans. Deng Zibin, (2008) *Rethinking Criminal Law*, Huaxia Publishing House, 451.

[48] 林东茂:《刑法综览》，中国人民大学出版社2009年版，第122页。Lin Dong Mao. (2009) *Overview of Criminal Law*, China Renmin University Press, 122. The author used to agree with

ways. First, the defender of justifiable defense has no duty to rescue when the act of justifiable defense leading to the victim's death at the endangering scene. Second, if injuries caused by justifiable defense are proper and won't result in death, or to say, has no possibility to produce excessive danger, the defender of justifiable defense shall bear no duty to rescue. Third, if the justifiable defense has caused the injury (which is not excessive) and posed an urgent danger of death, the result of death will be unjustified and the defender of justifiable defense's duty to rescue shall be affirmed. What the judicial practice confronts is that when serious injuries had been caused by the defender of justifiable defense, who neither called the police nor took the unlawful infringer to the hospital but left him bleeding to death, will the defender of justifiable defense's act be recognized as excessive defense? If the answer is no, it is clearly not appropriate. If the answer is yes, the duty to save the unlawful infringer will be affirmed (the duty to prevent the result of death). Some people may hold that even if it is identified as excessive defense, only *Ingerenz* itself shall be identified as the reason of the death, while the omission in the latter stage should not be regarded as the reason leading to the undue offense. However, it actually denies the causative potency of omission and is against the fact. This article points out that, in this occasion, it shall be admitted that *Ingerenz* and the latter omission have jointly lead to the excessive defense. In sum, if the conclusion of excessive defense will be reached, the act with justifiable cause must be confirmed as *Ingerenz* producing the legal duties.

(3) Whether the negligent criminal act can be *Ingerenz*?

One of the most important reasons for recognizing the dangerous *Ingerenz* as the source of duty is that the actor may has no culpability at all when conducting *Ingerenz*. If *Ingerenz* has been held culpable, there will be less significance for *Ingerenz* to be the source of legal duty. Conversely, if no negligence exists in the process of conducting *Ingerenz*, the identification of actor's legal duties of *Ingerenz* still won't be affected. Under the circumstance, *Ingerenz* with negligence as well as the prior negligent crime will be more capable of producing legal duties.

There is an argument believes that, only the "unpunishable *Ingerenz* that creating dangers" can be the source of legal duties. Or to say, "the actor has conducted the unpunishable act that creating danger without knowing the influence of the act (limit to the cases that produce no consequence), and he still left the dangers alone after knowing them". "For example, a person negligently imprisoning others has realized the situation immediately, while he continues to keep others with intention." "In contrast, in a case that the victim was seriously injured by the negligent traffic accident, if the actor understood the fact and realized that the victim could die but still fled, if the victim' died, it should be deemed the death was arisen from the first negligent act. The act thus can hardly illustrate the mentioned argument, as there is a high possibility for the prior negligent act leading to the victim's death and

---

such idea(参见张明楷:《刑法学》，法律出版社2007年版，第145页See Zhang Mingkai. (2007) *Criminal Law*, Law Press China, 145.)。

a low *Zumutbarkeit* to save him."[49] And that's why this article doesn't agree with that argument. First, since the common negligence and even *Ingerenz* with no negligence can be the sources of duty as long as specific dangers have been created, *Ingerenz* that has already constituted the negligent crime should be more able to be the source of legal duties. Otherwise it will create unfairness. For example, if A's act without negligence had resulted in B's injury, while A didn't rescue B even though A had realized that B would die without assistance. A will be convicted as intentional homicide of omission according to this view. When it comes to act with negligence, if X negligently injured Y, after he realized that Y would die without his help, but still didn't offer any help, X will only be convicted as crime of negligent homicide, which is obviously unfair. Second, the aforesaid view has limited the situations in which the legal duties has not produced by *Ingerenz*, to the case that there is a high possibility for the punishable *Ingerenz* to result in death. However, any slightly serious injury may lead to death without any assistance. Conversely, the life may be saved with help even though the injury is quite serious. If it is believed that the omission in the latter stage will not be punished when the result can be attributed to the punishable *Ingerenz*, the scope of the omission is obviously quite narrow. Thirdly, *Zumutbarkeit* of rescue may not be reduced even if *Ingerenz* has been negligently conducted. *Zumutbarkeit* for performing the legal duty is not subject to *Ingerenz*s' *Strafbarkeit* (punishability), but depends on incidental situations.

(4) Whether the intentional criminal act can be *Ingerenz*?

Whether the intentional crime is of more wrongdoing than the negligent crime (the view of *Handlungsunwert*), or the intentional crime should take more culpability than the negligent crime (the view of *Erfolgsunwert*), it all takes an angle of the relationship between stages or tiers, rather than an antithetical angle. That is because the possibility of preventing the result from occurring is the common constitutive element of intention and negligence from the perspective of wrongdoing, and the possibility of other acts is the common prerequisite (foundation) of crime out of intention and negligence. In other words, the possibility of preventing the result from occurring is the basic concept of crime of intention and negligence. Hence, the relationship between the intention and negligence is a matter of the possibility degree of preventing the result from occurring, and the level of culpability, as well as the level of significance in the sense of punishment. Therefore, it is the relationship between tiers. As the negligent criminal act may create legal duties to act for the actor, the intentional criminal act may produce more duties to act for the actor.[50]

Indeed, when the actor had no justifiable cause but inflicted serious injuries to the victim with the intent of murder and left the victim bleeding to death, the actor, of course, would only be convicted as criminal of intentional homicide. However,

---

[49] 日山中敬一:《刑法总论》，成文堂2008年版，第236~237页。See Yamanaka Keiichi. (2008) *General Theory of Criminal Law*, Seibundo Publishing Co, 236–237.

[50] 参见张明楷:《犯罪构成体系与构成要件要素》，北京大学出版社2010年版，第259页以下。 See Zhang Mingkai. (2010) *The System of Criminal Constitution and the Elements of Constitutive Requirements*, Peking University Press, 1–259.

based on the following considerations, it shall be admitted that intentional criminal act can be *Ingerenz* that produces legal duties.

Firstly, admitting intentional criminal act can be *Ingerenz* of legal duties will help to achieve the goal of coordination of criminal law. For example, A accidentally inflicted serious injuries to the victim, but offered no help even though he knew that the victim would die without help. If other requirements (the possibility of preventing the result from occurring and the possibility of acting) have been satisfied, there is no doubt to identify A's act as intentional homicide of omission. B intentionally caused serious injuries to the victim and offered no help even though he knew the victim would die without help. And the victim eventually died. If the intentional criminal act not be identified as *Ingerenz*, then B will only be convicted of crime of intentional injury. Compared with A, however, B's act shall subject to more serious negative judgments and more severe condemnation. Therefore, only admitting that the intentional criminal act can also be *Ingerenz* that created the legal duties, will B be convicted of intentional homicide of omission. Therefore, the criminal evaluations won't be uncoordinated. The same conclusion will be drawn from the perspective of the basis of punishment of commission by omission. When the victim is confronted with the danger of death that was caused by the intentional injury, with the actor's failure to help, the conditions of intentional homicide of atypical omission will totally be satisfied. In effect, the actor's *Ingerenz* has created dangers to life, hence getting the status of *Garantenstellung* to prevent the life from danger. As long as there is a possibility to prevent the result of death, and the actor is able to prevent the danger (e.g. taking the victim to the hospital) while doesn't stop it, the actor will be determined as the criminal of intentional homicide of omission.

Secondly, admitting intentional criminal act will help to solve the problem of justifiable defense. In the case that "the actor had installed a time bomb to destroy himself along with all other passengers after boarding the airplane, others had learnt the emergency after the takeoff but were not able to find the bomb, so they violently forced the actor to take out the bomb and defuse it". In this sense "the passengers on the airplane could use any the proper (effective) method to force the actor to speak out the location of the bomb, in which it embodied the exercise of the justifiable defense. But it is the result we can get only when the omission in the latter stage shall be regarded as illegal".[51] In other words, the act of installing the time bomb has created dangers to the legal interests, thus the actor shall bear the duty of removing the bomb.The failure of doing so is illegal and passengers can hence conduct justifiable defense and force the actor to perform his legal duties (to tell where the bomb is installed or defuse the bomb). If the intentional criminal act of installing the time bomb has been hold not creating legal duties, then it will be difficult to justifiable defense for the illegal act. It may be believed that the "ongoing unlawful infringement" required by the establishment of justifiable defense does not mean that the

[51] 蔡圣伟:《刑法问题研究(一)》，元照出版有限公司2008年版，第225页。Cai Sheng Wei. (2008) *Research on Criminal Law Issues (1)*, Angle Publishing Co., Ltd., 225.

defense can be performed when the illegal act was taking place. As long as the legal interest is confronted with an urgent danger, it can be defended. Therefore, although the act of installing the bomb has stopped, the legal interests threatened by the bomb are still in urgent danger, and *Ingerenz* can thereby be defended. However, on one hand, the defense against the actor will only made him not to act any longer, while the defense in this case is to force the actor to "act" (to tell where the bomb is installed or defuse the bomb). Or to say, the actor was going to carry out his criminal plan by omission (doesn't defuse the bomb) after installing the bomb. Hence, the object of the justifiable defense is such omission, rather than *Ingerenz*.[52] Because of this, "the German literature points out that if the right of justifiable defense will be exercised against the danger above, the actor created the danger shall be given the legal duty to eliminate it in the first place before the justifiable defense against the omission (that remains the danger) has been claimed".[53] On the other hand, the limitation of defense for the criminal omission, what's more, is obviously different from that for criminal act. In the case above, it is impossible to identify the limitation of justifiable defense based on *Ingerenz* of installing the bomb. That is, the justifiable defense against the omission shall be only to the extent necessary to force the actor to perform legal duty. Therefore, the defensive behavior against the criminal act may be the way that causes others' death; but in the criminal omission, it is impossible for the defensive act to be the reason for leading others' death. Besides, the defense against the criminal act shouldn't continue as long as the act has been called a halt, while the defense against criminal omission shall stop only if the duty has been performed by the actor. In the case aforementioned, so long as the actor gave the location of the bomb, his act could not perform the defense. Therefore, it is not proper to take *Ingerenz* as the object of defense. To make the omission the target of defense, it is necessary to affirm that the intentional criminal act is *Ingerenz* that produces the legal duties.

Thirdly, admitting intentional criminal act can help to solve the problems of joint crime. For example, A injured B seriously with an intent of homicide. However, A regretted immediately and decided to call an ambulance when he saw B lying in the blood with a lot of pain. The irrelevant third party C, nevertheless, does his utmost to dissuade A from rescuing C and left C bleeding to death. In this case, if the intentional criminal act not been identified as *Ingerenz*, then C will not be convicted. As we all know, the omission is in fact a status crime, that is to say, only the person bearing the legal duties can be the perpetrator of omission. C didn't have legal duties and hence was impossible to be the perpetrator of omission. According to the principle of the theory of derivativeness of restriction, C will be convicted as instigator of omission of homicide, as long as A's act of intentional homicide has produced duty to rescue and the omission in the latter stage also constitutes homicide.[54]

---

[52] Vgl.,Kristian Kühl, *Strafrecht Allgemeiner Teil*,3.Aufl.,Verlag Vahlen,2000,S.143.

[53] 蔡圣伟:《刑法问题研究(一)》，元照出版有限公司2008年版，第226页。Cai Sheng Wei. (2008) *Research on Criminal Law Issues (1)*, Angle Publishing Co., Ltd., 226.

[54] 参见蔡圣伟:《刑法问题研究(一)》，元照出版有限公司2008年版，第223页。Cai Sheng Wei. (2008) *Research on Criminal Law Issues (1)*, Angle Publishing Co., Ltd., 223.

Admitting the intentional criminal act can be *Ingerenz* is faced with the issue that how to determine the quantity of crime.

Firstly, after admitting the intentional criminal acts as *Ingerenz*s, it should be affirmed that if the act and omission shall be evaluated as two acts violating two distinctive legal interests, for which the actor shall take the culpability, the actor should be imposed combined punishment. For example, the actor, in infringement of the provisions of the *Forestry Law*, illegally felled precious trees and caused other's head hit by the tree. The actor didn't rescue the victim although he knew or should know that the victim would die without any help. Illegally felling precious trees is the criminal act provided in Article 344 of China's *Criminal Law*. But this article doesn't provide the result of death. In other words, the act leading to other's death shall not be evaluated as crimes of illegally felling the state-protected plants. In this case, the criminal acts of illegally felling precious trees shall be deemed as the actor's *Ingerenz* liable to rescue the victim and further convict the actor of crime of illegally felling the state-protected plants as well as the intentional homicide or negligent homicide for the actor didn't offer any help.

Secondly, in many cases, although the intentional criminal act is admitted to be *Ingerenz*, only one crime will be determined. For example, intentionally injuring others in the form of act and causing danger of death would only be identified as one crime (crime of intentional homicide or intentional injury to death); for another example, the act of intentional homicide resulted in danger of death would only be convicted of intentional homicide, if no help had been offered. Identifying each of the acts above as one crime is reasonable in conclusion; but the issue is how to illustrate it. German theory of criminal law holds that in the cases above, the intentional criminal act and criminal omission are under "impure concurrence". Some scholars believe that the relation between the crimes above is the supplementary relation of legal concurrence; some hold that the latter belongs to the "co-punishable *post factum*"; and some suggest that the relation is called "singular act", that is, acting the legal duty in the former stage and the omission in the latter stage are united as a whole (singular act).[55] However, first, the laws violated by *Ingerenz* and omission in the latter stage in China are not always fixed, thus the relationship between them cannot be concluded as supplementary. Second, not all the omission in the latter stages in the latter stage could be co-punished with *Ingerenz* or be unpunished. That is because, when *Ingerenz* is less harmful than omission in the latter stage, only the latter will be determined as a crime. Third, it is not so appropriate to take *Ingerenz* in the former stage and omission in the latter stage in the latter stage as a whole. For example, A killed B intentionally but then regretted doing so and tried to call an ambulance. C instigated A not to rescue B and B eventually died. One of the purposes of admitting that an intentional criminal act can also be *Ingerenz* is to identify C as the abettor of homicide of omission. However, if A's *Ingerenz* of killing in the former stage and the omission in the

[55] 参见蔡圣伟:《刑法问题研究(一)》，元照出版有限公司2008年版，第251~252页。Cai Sheng Wei. (2008) *Research on Criminal Law Issues (1)*, Angle Publishing Co., Ltd., 251–252.

latter stage have been taken as a whole, C will not be convicted as the abettor. That is because in a crime with a single act, it is not possible for the abettor to abet others halfway.

This article holds that the identification of quantity of crime depends not only on the number and characteristics of acts, but also on the number of legal interests violated. For one thing, when legal interests violated by *Ingerenz* in the former stage and omission in the latter stage are the same, it will be reasonable to convict the defendant of one criminal charge. For example, *Ingerenz* in the former stage and omission in the latter stage shall only be recognized as one criminal charge for only one person's life has been endangered. For another, when the legal interests violated by *Ingerenz* are included in the legal interests violated by the omission in the latter stage, only the offense of felony will be identified. For example, the duty to rescue has been created after the defendant intentionally injured others; if the legal duties has not been performed and the victim died thereof, only the crime of intentional homicide will be identified if the defendant has intent to the victim's death. That is because the legal interests of body are included in the legal interests of life.

It is worthy further discussing that whether to identify A as the criminal of intentional injury (to death) or criminal of intentional homicide in case A has intentionally conducted the act of intentional injury that endangers the victim's life, but offers no help even though A is able to do so. In China, the prescribed punishments of intentional homicide and intentional injury (to death) are the same (they are only different in the sequence of punishment types). Therefore, declaring A as the criminal of intentional injury (to death) can also make the crime accord with the the principle of suiting punishment to crime. But it should be affirmed that in terms of the nature of crime, the intentional homicide is more serious than the intentional injury (to death). The coordination of the criminal law will only be achieved by identifying A's act as crime of intentional homicide. For example, in the case above, the prerequisite of identifying A's act as crime of intentional injury (to death) is that: the actor has the intent of injury as well as the prediction possibility to the result of death. However, compared A's case with the two following cases of intentional homicide of omission, the answer will be clear. One is that B's *Ingerenz* has created injury serious enough to lead to the victim's death. In this situation, the legal duties will be produced even though B has not intent of injury. If B doesn't rescue the victim and caused death, B shall be convicted of the intentional homicide of omission. Therefore, it is more reasonable to identify A, who has the intent of intentional injury, as the criminal of intentional homicide. The other is that C intentionally injured others but has no prediction possibility to the result of death. If C's act has produced the danger threatening others' life, he will be convicted of intentional homicide of omission if C provides no help to the victim. Since it is so, A shall be guiltier of crime of intentional homicide for he is capable of predicting the result of death.

2.4 Action Scope of *Ingerenz*

Theories of criminal law in Germany and Japan, as we all know, all discuss *Ingerenz* in the scope of commission by omission, holding that *Ingerenz* only plays a role in determining *Garantenstellung* of the commission by omission, rather than that of omission crime. Both the view and practice are doubtful, however.

Obviously, the idea that *Ingerenz* only plays a role in determining *Garantenstellung* of commission by omission is based on the classification of omission crime and commission by omission. Theories of criminal law of Germany, Japan, Korea and China have all divided the criminal omission into omission crime and commission by omission with no disputes. However, further researches about the standard of classification as well as its rationality shall be carried on.

Germany and Japan have applied a slightly different standard with that of Korea. The former two countries have taken the substantive standard (the theory of substantive standard) while the latter takes the formality standard (the theory of formality standard).

The dominant ideology in Germany is that the omission crime only refers to the criminal acts that failed to perform the legal duty as required. It is true that the negative judgments by the legal order shall be avoided if acts have been conducted as legally required. However, the avoidance of the illegal result has not been stipulated as the legal duty of negative actors, and the occurrence of certain results has neither been considered as the constitutive elements by legislators. For this reason, the omission crime is the counterpart of *Tätigkeitsdelikte*. In contrast, the commission by omission requires *Garantenstellung* to prevent the result, one of the constitutive elements, from occurring. *Garantenstellung* who fails to do so will be responsible for the consequence in criminal law. Therefore, the commission by omission is the counterpart of consequential offense.[56] Or to say, *Tätigkeitsdelikte* will be affirmed as long as certain acts have been conducted, while the commission by omission will be identified providing the legal duty has failed to be performed; the consequential offense will be identified if there is a certain result, as one of the constitutive elements, leading by certain acts, while the commission by omission is the crime with certain consequence leading by the unfulfillment of duty. For example, Article 323(c) of *German Criminal Law* provides: "In the event of an unfortunate accident or a public danger or an emergency, the actor, who is required and could be expected to carry out assistance, shall be sentenced to a fixed-term imprisonment of no more than one year or pecuniary punishment if the actor doesn't offer any help, especially when there is no significant danger of his own and no other important duties will be infringed."[57] It can be noticed that there is no need to ask "whether the 'consequence' can be prevented (e.g. the death of the victim) for the constitution of this

[56] Vgl.,H.Jescheck/T.Weigend, *Lehrbuch des Strafrechts: Allgemeiner Teil*, 5.Aufl.,Duncker & Humblot, 1996, S.605 f.

[57] 《德国刑法典》，冯军译，中国政法大学出版社2000年版，第195页。 *German Criminal Code*, trans. Feng Jun. (2000) China University of Political Science and Law Press, 195.

crime"; conversely, "the police officer in charge getting a reliable information that a particular major crime may occur shall prevent the crime in the state of an emergency, even at the risk of his life. Otherwise, the police officer will be punished as an aider of the criminal".[58] The former is the omission crime while the latter is the commission by omission. As the general view in German has divided the omissions based on the requirement of the results, some scholars have brought out the idea that it is not ideal to name the omissions as omission crime and commission by omission. Some of them put forward the concepts of pure criminal omission and aggregated criminal omission and some propose the concepts of main criminal omission and subordinate criminal omission, while the others advocate using the concepts of criminal omissions with consequence and without consequence.[59]

The dominant ideology in Japan and Korea holds that if the omission has been expressly provided by the criminal law as one of the constitutive elements, it is the omission crime, otherwise it is an commission by omission if the actor conduct the act in the way of omission, which is the common constitutive elements.[60] Identifying the omission as the constitutive elements refers to specifying the subject of omission and using the words like "without" "no" to describe the omission. For example, one of the manifestations of crime of abandonment of the responsible protector prescribed in Article 218 of Japan's *Criminal Law* is that: "Whoever is responsible for protection of the aged, the disabled or the patient… provides no necessary protection to their lives".[61] It provides for the subject of act and also includes the statement of omission, thus it is the omission crime. On the contrary, the homicide of omission is not provided in criminal law and therefore the actor commit homicide in the way of negative act is commission by omission.

As Germany differs from Japan in the classification standard, the omission crime in Japan, therefore, may belong to the scope of commission by omission. For example, according to Subparagraph 2 (g), Paragraph 1 of Article 315(c) of *German Criminal Law*, whoever violates the requirement of safety and doesn't keep the stopped or unmoving vehicle at an identifiable distance from other's will be convicted of a crime. In this regard, the law actually provides the subject of criminal omission and the act of the omission. According to the theory of Japan's criminal

[58] H.Jescheck/T.Weigend, *Lehrbuch des Strafrechts: Allgemeiner Teil*, 5.Aufl.,Duncker & Humblot, 1996,S.606.

[59] Vgl.,H.Jescheck/T.Weigend, *Lehrbuch des Strafrechts: Allgemeiner Teil*, 5.Aufl.,Duncker & Humblot, 1996, S.606.

[60] 参见日团藤重光:《刑法纲要总论》，创文社1990年版，第143~144页；日山口厚:《刑法总论》，有斐阁2007年版，第74页；日大谷实:《刑法讲义总论》，成文堂2010年新版，第141页；韩金日秀、徐辅鹤:《韩国刑法总论》，郑军男译，武汉大学出版社2008年版，第466页。See Dandou Shigemitsu.(1990) *General Outline of Criminal Law*, Kodansha Publishing Co, 143–144; Yamaguchi Atsushi.(2007) *General Rules of Criminal Law*, Yuhikaku Press, 74; Ohya Minoru.(2010) *General Handouts on Criminal Law(New Edition)*, Seibundo Publishing Co, 141; Kim Il-su & Seo Bo-hyuk. *General Part of Korean Criminal Law*, trans, Zheng Junnan, Wuhan University Press, 2008, 466.

[61] 《日本刑法典》，张明楷译，法律出版社2006年版，第60页。Trans. Zhang Mingkai. (2006), *Japan Criminal Code*, Law Press, 60.

law, the crime above shall belong to omission crime,[62] but it is an commission by omission in the view of German scholars for the establishment of such crime requires the existence of danger (consequence) threatening other's bodies, lives and properties of great value.

Of course, it will be alright to take different standard in categorizing the criminal omission. However, only one standard can be adopted at one time so it is impossible to jointly apply the substantive and formality standard. This article holds that the substantive classification cannot be adopted if compared with the formality classification.

Firstly, the purpose of classifying the objects is to process the sub-items differently according to certain standard. If the omission has been distinguished on the basis that whether the consequence is required as the constitutive element, then it is enough to only make the classification between *Tätigkeitsdelikte* and the consequential offense. The biggest issue, however, is that if no *Garantenstellung* (subject of act) has been explicitly defined, how to identify the *Garantenstellung*? It is the unsettled problem faced by German's substantive classification.

Secondly, according to the German scholar, the commission by omission can be subdivided into two categories: one is the crime whose subject and content of omission have all been explicitly defined while the other is the crime without subject and defined content. As described above, the crime provided by Subparagraph 2(g), Paragraph 1 of Article 315(c) is the commission by omission. However, the following act, in the view of theory of criminal law and precedent, is an commission by omission: "The driver of the vehicle that caused the accident shall take the victim to the doctor." Otherwise, he may be bound to the responsibility of homicide (BGH 7287288)."[63] However, in the circumstance that the subject and content of omission have already been explicitly defined, there is no difficulty in explaining and identifying the crime; the omission of the second category is the problem. Herein lies problem of the commission by omission. The commission by omission in the German theory of criminal law only refers to the crime with no subject and content of omission being expressly defined, or to say, is just a part of the commission by omission. It is not conductive to solving the problems by grouping the two different types of problems into one.

Thirdly, it is not proper to hold that there is no danger or damaging result taken as constitutive elements of omission crime, or to say, identification of accomplished crime above shall be still based on the consequence. The act and consequence just simply happened at the same time. Professor C.Roxin, who adopts the theory of dualism, also holds that the distinction between *Tätigkeitsdelikte* and consequential offense is meaningful only in clarifying the casual relationship (*Lehre vonder objektive zurechnung*). "Otherwise, there will be misunderstanding. On the one hand, all crimes have consequences. In the case of *Tätigkeitsdelikte*, the actor's act, as the

[62] Vgl.,H.Jescheck/T.Weigend, Lehrbuch des Strafrechts: Allgemeiner Teil, 5.Aufl.,Duncker & Humblot, 1996, S.607.

[63] Vgl.,H.Jescheck/T.Weigend, *Lehrbuch des Strafrechts: Allgemeiner Teil*, 5.Aufl.,Duncker & Humblot, 1996, S.607.

constitutive element, is the consequence per se. On the other hand, in the situation of consequential offense, the consequence that can be incriminated must be included by the act, which is one of the constitutive elements. Therefore, the discussions about separating the consequences are only of relative significance."[64]

The theory of criminal law in China, therefore, has adopted the same standard as Japan and Korea.[65] That is because there will be no doubt as to the conformity of elements of criminal omission crime. What shall be discussed by the theory of criminal law and judicial practice are the subject and content of duty, such as, who will be convicted of criminal omission for not saving the drowning child? Herein lies the issue that doesn't exist in the typical criminal commission.

The classifications in Japan, Korea and China are still in doubt, however. According to the formality standard, it is a omission crime as long as the subject and content have been explicitly defined in the specific provisions of criminal law, thus there is no need to identify the subject (*Garantenstellung*); on the contrary, when the actor acts in the way of omission to meet the requirements that usually satisfied by the way of act, it is a must for the theory of criminal law and judicial practice to determine the subjects (*Garantenstellung*). In other words, the former is a factual judgment while the latter is a normative judgment.

But it will be found that even though certain specific provisions explicitly provide the subject and contents of omission (omission crime), the judicial practice still to reach a normative determination about qualification of subjects. As discussed above, theories of criminal law have all agreed that the aforesaid crime of abandonment of responsible protector, provided in Article 218 of *Japan Criminal Law*, is a omission crime. But it still needs to make the normative judgment about the responsible protector according to the duty source of commission by omission.[66] The actor shall be identified as the responsible protector based on *Ingerenz*. "For example, the doctor left the infant alone regardless of its possibility to survive; Injecting a young girl with analeptic in a hotel room and left after the analeptic resulting in her mental disorder. Cases above all hold the defender responsible for protecting the victims based on *Ingerenzs*."[67] Similarly, the Article 261 of China's *Criminal Law* has also provided the crime of abandonment. The subject is "the person who shall support an aged person, sick person or any other person who cannot live independently";

---

[64] C.Roxin,*Strafrecht Allgemeiner Teil*,Band I,4.Aulf.,C.H.Beck, 2006.S.330.

[65] 参见高铭暄、马克昌主编:《刑法学》，北京大学出版社、高等教育出版社2010年版，第76页；陈兴良:《规范刑法学》(上册)，中国人民大学出版社2008年版，第124页；张明楷:《刑法学》，法律出版社2007年版，第140页；曲新久:《刑法学》，中国政法大学出版社2009年版，第90页；等等。See Gao Mingxuan & Ma Kechang eds. (2011) *Criminal Law*, Peking University Press & Higher Education Press, 76;Chen Xingliang. (2008) *Normative Criminal Law 1*, China Renmin University Press, 124; Zhang Mingkai. (2007) Criminal Law, Law Press China, 140; Qu Xinjiu(2009), *Criminal Law*, China University of Political Science and Law Press, 90; etc.

[66] 参见日西田典之:《刑法各论》，弘文堂2010年版，第32页以下。See Nishida Noriyuki. (2010) *Essays on Criminal Law*, Koubundou Publishers Inc., 1–32.

[67] 日大谷实:《刑法讲义各论》，成文堂2007年新版，第71~72页。Ohya Minoru.(2007) *Lectures on Criminal Law(New Edition)*, Seibundo Publishing Co, 71–72.

however, whether the actor shall be the family member of the victim, or to say, which person can be the subject of such crime, is of evident conflict.[68] The result is that the normative judgment shall still be made according to source of duty of commission by omission.

For another example, the preceding part of Article 139 of *Criminal Law* in China provides: "After the occurrence of a safety accident, the person who has the report duty does not report or falsely reports the accident condition and thus delayed the rescue, if the circumstances are serious, he shall be sentenced to a fixed-term imprisonment of no more than three years or criminal detention." It is a omission crime whose subject can only be determined according to the source of duty of commission by omission. The Article 5 of the *Interpretation on Certain Issues concerning the Specific Application of Law in Handling Criminal cases Endangering the Safety of Mine Production* promulgated by the Supreme People's Procuratorate and the Supreme People's Court on February 28th, 2007 provides that: "the 'person who has the report duty' in Paragraph 1, Article 139 of *Criminal Law* refers to the supervisor, actual controller, investigator who are responsible for the production, operation and management as well as others who have the report duty." even with such interpretation, "others who have the report duty" shall also be illustrated by normative judgment. If the dangerous *Ingerenz* is identified as the source of duty, the person whose *Ingerenz* caused the safety accident (the act has already caused relative crime of safety accident) shall be the one bound to the report duty.

Based on the analysis above, this article holds that, on the premise of adopting the standard of formality, we should classify the criminal omission into three categories by further discussing whether the judge is required to determine the *Garantenstellung* in a normative way.

Firstly, the typical omission crime. Specific Provisions of *Criminal Law* have expressly provided *Garantenstellung*s and contents of such crime, and the identification of *Garantenstellung* is only a matter of factual judgment. It is not difficult to identify the *Garantenstellung* in determining the omission crime, and also in line with the doctrine of a legally prescribed punishment for a specified crime. For example, the Article 311 of *Criminal Law* provides: "Whoever, while clearly knowing that another person has committed the crime of espionage or terrorism, extremism refuses to provide relevant information or evidence when an officer from the judicial organ asks him to do so, if the circumstances are serious, he shall be sentenced to fixed-term imprisonment of not more than three years, criminal detention or public surveillance." *Garantenstellung* of this crime is the person who clearly knowing that another person has committed the crime of espionage, or terrorism, extremism and under the investigation of judicial organ. *Garantenstellung* only needs to be judged by the facts (whether the actor knows that the above is involved in crimes above and under the investigation of judicial organ) and the content of omission is to provide no relevant information and evidence.

[68] 参见张明楷:《刑法分则的解释原理》，中国人民大学出版社2011年版，第47页以下。See Zhang Mingkai. (2011) *Principles of Interpretation for the Specific Provisions of Criminal Law*, China Renmin University Press, 1–47.

Secondly, the atypical criminal omission crime. The Specific Provisions of *Criminal Law* in China have explicitly defined *Garantenstellung* and contents of such crime, but the identification of *Garantenstellung* is a matter of normative judgment. There is no infringement of the doctrine of a legally prescribed punishment for a specified crime when identifying the atypical criminal omission crime but the identification of *Garantenstellung* is the problem. As illustrated above, the subject of crime of abandonment stipulated in Article 261 of *Criminal Law* is the one "refuses to fulfill his duty to support an aged person, minor, sick person or any other person who cannot live independently", but the specific scope of *Garantenstellung* shall be identified according to the above principle of determining *Garantenstellung* of commission by omission in a normative way. Therefore, it is the atypical criminal omission crime as classified by this article. So is the crime stipulated in one of the paragraphs of Article 139 of criminal law.

Thirdly, commission by omission. Specific Provisions of *Criminal Law* in China do not stipulate *Garantenstellung* and contents of omission, but the actor has satisfied the constitutive element in the way of omission that is usually satisfied by act. Intentional homicide of omission and arson of omission are the cases. Clearly, identifying the omission as crime is confronted with the issue of violating the doctrine of a legally prescribed punishment for a specified crime and also the problem of how to determine *Garantenstellung*. Even if the punishment of such criminal omission does not violate the doctrine above, it is still necessary to normatively define the scope of *Garantenstellung* and illustrate conditions that satisfy the constitutive element.

It is not difficult to find out that the common point of the commission by omission and atypical criminal omission crime is that both of them require the judge to identify the scope of *Garantenstellung* in a normative way. The difference is as follows: (A) whether the commission by omission violates the doctrine of a legally prescribed punishment for a specified crime is always a question, while it is not a problem as to the atypical criminal omission crime. (B) the identification of *Garantenstellung* of commission by omission will not directly subject to the words used in the specific provisions of criminal law. For example, the statements about crime of intentional homicide and arson will not directly restrict the identification of *Garantenstellung*. However, the identification of *Garantenstellung*s of atypical criminal omission crime is directly subject to the words of specific provisions, which can be clearly seen from the Article 261 of *Criminal Law*. For example, the person who is responsible for educating the young will not be the *Garantenstellung* of crime of abandonment.

Therefore, it is not proper to discuss *Ingerenz* in commission by omission. It shall be admitted that the functional scope includes not only the commission by omission, but also some of the (atypical) omission crime. In other words, *Ingerenz* can also be the source of duty in atypical criminal omission crime.

References

Asada Kazushige.(2007) *General Theory of Criminal Law* (Supplementary Edition), Seibundo Publishing Co, 150, 162
Bernd Schünemann, (2006) *The current legal situation regarding omissions in German criminal law*, as cited in Chen Zhihui, ed., Unbestechlich und unbeirrbar im dienst von recht unechtigkeit: abhandlungen zur gesamten strafrechtswissenschaft von BERND SCHUNEMANN, Taiwan: taedp.org.tw, 607, 642-643.
Cai Sheng Wei. (2008) *Research on Criminal Law Issues (1)*, Angle Publishing Co., Ltd., 223, 225, 226, 230, 251-252
Dandou Shigemitsu.(1990) *General Outline of Criminal Law,* Kodansha Publishing Co, 143-144, 149
Feng Jun, trans. (2000) *German Criminal Code,* China University of Political Science and Law Press, 10, 195
Gao Mingxuan & Ma Kechang eds. (2010) *Criminal Law,* Peking University Press & Higher Education Press, 74-76
Gao Mingxuan ed. (1982) *Criminal Law*, Law Press, 121-122
George P, Fletcher, trans. Deng Zibin, (2008) R*ethinking Criminal Law,* Huaxia Publishing House, 451, 452
H.Jescheck/T.Weigend.(1996) Lehrbuch des Strafrechts: Allgemeiner Teil, 5.Aufl., Duncker & Humblot, S. 605f, 606, 606, 607, 607, 621, 621ff
Hidaka Yoshihiro, trans. Wang Shuping.(1992) *The Theory of Inauthentic Omission*, People's Public Security University of China Press, 111
Iwama Yasuo.(2010) *Product Liability and Omission Theory*, Seibundo Publishing Co, 1-90, 46
Jescheck, H/Weigend, T., Lehrbuch des Strafrechts: Allgemeiner Teil, 5.Aufl., Duncker & Humblot, 1996, S. 621
Johannes Wessels, trans. Li Changke, (2008) *Strafrecht Allgemeiner Teil*, Law Press, 433
Joshua Dressler, trans. Wang Xiumei, (2009) *Understanding Criminal Law,* Beijing: Peking University Press, 1-96, 95, 95
Kim Il-su & Seo Bo-hyuk. *General Part of Korean Criminal Law*, trans, Zheng Junnan, Wuhan University Press, 2008, 466
Lin Dong Mao. (2009) *Overview of Criminal Law*, China Renmin University Press, 122
Liu Peng. (2008) "Dog Bites Person, Female Owner Convicted of Murder," in Procuratorate Daily, 24 September 2008
Nishida Noriyuki.(2010) D*evelopment of Complicity Theory,* Seibundo Publishing Co, 170, 175-176, 180
Nishida Noriyuki.(2010) *Essays on Criminal Law,* Koubundou Publishers Inc., 1-32
Ohya Minoru.(2007) *Lectures on Criminal Law (New Edition)*, Seibundo Publishing Co, 71-72
Ohya Minoru.(2010) *General Handouts on Criminal Law (New Edition),* Seibundo Publishing Co, 141
Otsuka Hitoshi.(2008) *Overview of Criminal Law*, Yuhikaku Press, 153
Qu Xinjiu(2009), *Criminal Law*, China University of Political Science and Law Press, 90
See Gao Mingxuan & Ma Kechang eds. (2011) *Criminal Law*, Peking University Press & Higher Education Press, 76; Chen Xingliang. (2008) *Normative Criminal Law 1*, China Renmin University Press, 124; Zhang Mingkai. (2007) Criminal Law, Law Press China, 140; etc.
See Gao Mingxuan ed. (1982) *Criminal Law*, Law Press, 121-122
See Ida Makoto.(2003) "Activation of criminal legislation and its future" as cited in Law Times, Vol. 75, No.2
See Shimada Souichirou.(2002) "Omission" as cited in Hogaku Kyoshitsu, No. 8
Smith, Hogan, trans. Li Guifang, (2000) *Criminal Law*, Beijing: Law Press, 56
Trans. Zhang Mingkai.(2006), *Japan Criminal Code*, Law Press, 60
Vgl., C.Roxin, *Strafrecht Allgemeiner Teil*, Band I, 4.Aufl., C.H.Beck, 2006, S.330
Vgl., C.Roxin, *Strafrecht Allgemeiner Teil,* Band II, C.H.Beck, 2003, S. 683f, 762f, 766, 771, 776

Vgl., H.Jescheck/T.Weigend, *Lehrbuch des Strafrechts: Allgemeiner Teil*, 5.Aufl., Duncker & Humblot, 1996, S. 605f, 606, 606, 607, 607, 621, 621ff

Xu Yu Xiu. (2005) *Contemporary Trends in Criminal Law Thought,* China Democracy and Legal System Publishing House, 1-673, 690

Yamaguchi Atsushi.(2007) *General Rules of Criminal Law*, Yuhikaku Press, 74, 80, 81, 89, 89-90, 90, 90, 91-92

Yamaguchi Atsushi.(2007) *General Theory of Criminal Law,* Yuhikaku Press, 89

Yamaguchi Atsushi.(2008) *Criminal Law* as Seen from New Judicial Precedents, Yuhikaku Press, 41-42

Yamanaka Keiichi.(2008) *General Theory of Criminal Law*, Seibundo Publishing Co, 234-237, 236-237

Yue Yao Yong: "Failure to Rescue Cannot Escape Criminal Liability," as cited in Procuratorate Daily, 9 May 2000; Chai Wen Bin & Wang Hui. "Sentenced for Allowing Girlfriend to Commit Suicide by Failing to Rescue," as cited in Legal Daily, 2 December 2000

Zhang Mingkai. (2005) "Strictly Limiting the Scope and Punishment of Aggravated Consequence Offenses," as cited in Chines Journal of Law, No. 1

Zhang Mingkai. (2007) *Criminal Law*, Law Press China, 140, 543, 145

Zhang Mingkai. (2010) *The System of Criminal Constitution and the Elements of Constitutive Requirements*, Peking University Press, 1-259

Zhang Mingkai. (2011) *Principles of Interpretation for the Specific Provisions of Criminal Law*, China Renmin University Press, 1-47

Chapter 3
Causation and Objective Attribution

*The original title is "The theory of *Lehre Vonder Objektive Zurechnung*", published in *Peking University Law Journal*, 2013, Vol. 2.

In Professor Liu Yanhong's article *Questioning and Rethinking on Objective Attribution* (*Lehre Von der Objektive Zurechnung*) in *Peking University Law Journal*, 2011, Vol. 6 (hereinafter referred to as "Liu's article"), she argued that the theory of objective attribution referred to the theory of causation, rather than the theory of the attribution. The theory of objective attribution did not simply include the content of objective attribution, but also the content of subjective attribution, that theory actually confused the relationship among conformity of elements of crime, wrongdoing and accountability, and it also weakened the function of the tripartite system of crime. Liu further argued that China's criminal jurisprudence should adopt the theory of *Adäquanz* (the theory of adequateness), while it is not necessary to introduce the theory of objective attribution. Professor Zhou Guangquan discussed this argument with Professor Liu Yanhong in his article *Methodological Significance on the Theory of Objective Attribution*, which was published in *Peking University Law Journal*, 2012, Vol. 2 (hereinafter referred to as "Zhou's article"). Zhou's article observed that the theory of *Adäquanz* had many defects in the methodology, while the theory of objective attribution had many obvious advantages, such as using multiple principles to ensure the inspection without omissions, establishing a positive judgment and reverse inspection standard, showing effect of general punishment, highlighting the hierarchy and sufficiency of evaluation, and ensuring the objectification of criminal judgment. The theory of objective attribution only emphasized that the objective judgment must be carried out first, and it didn't confuse the tripartite system. From the author's point of view, both Liu's and Zhou's articles have reasonable points, but further discussions are needed. This article intends to make a brief analysis of the theory of objective attribution, and discusses the point of views in Liu and Zhou's articles.

M. Zhang, *The Fundamental Issues upon Criminal Law Theories*, Masterpieces of Contemporary Jurisprudents in China,
https://doi.org/10.1007/978-981-95-1276-8_3

3.1 The Formation of the Theory of Objective Attribution

The formation of the theory of objective attribution has gone through a long process.

The word "attribution" and "*Zurechung*" is derived from the Latin word "*imputatio*". Since the time of S. Pufendorf (1632–1694), "*imputatio*" has made its importance in the German criminal jurisprudence. Feuerbach also used this concept and divided it into the attribution of act (subject being the free cause of a certain fact) and the attribution of culpability (the culpability of the actor for certain fact/act). The person who gave legal philosophy meaning to the concept of attribution was Hegel, according to whose view, an external fact was the work of the actor only if it was attributed to the subject or meaning.

In the later half of the nineteenth century, the thinking method of natural science was all the rage, and the theory of attribution on philosophical was replaced by the theory of causation which was originally from natural science. Therefore, the theory of *Conditio-sine-qua-non-Formel* (theory of conditional relation) had quite an important position. Since the theory of *Conditio-sine-qua-non-Formel* could retroactively lead to infinite traces (*ex post facto*), the theory of interrupting causation hence emerged. At the end of nineteenth century, the theories of individual cause, *Regreßverbot* and *Adäquanz* appeared in the criminal law theoretical field are aimed to solve the problems of *Regressus ad infinitum*.

In the wake of the twentieth century, the theory of *Regressus ad infinitum* from the perspective of standard in the limited the theory of *Conditio-sine-qua-non-Formel* began to appear. This theory first sprouted in Scandinavian countries, as in the Netherlands and Austria. In Germany, M.L.Müller developed the theory of normative danger. In the 1920s, Austrian civil law scholars put forward the theory of constraint, which was also called the theory about association of wrongdoing from the perspective of norms, and it became a powerful theory at that time. In the 1930s, Müller's analysis about the concept of danger was adopted in the theory of *Adäquanz* by K.Engisch. He distinguished the dangerousness of act (creation of danger) from the realization of danger.

In 1927, the German civil law scholar K.Larenz published *Hegels Zurechnungslehre und der Begriff der objektiven Zurechnung (Hegel's Theory of Attribution and the Concept of Objective Attribution)*, which provided the basis for the theory of *Adäquanz* from the perspective of objective attribution. In 1930, R.Honig advocated the theory of objective attribution with objective possibility as the basis of attribution. Since then, the theory of attribution has been maintained in criminal jurisprudence.

In the 1960s, German civil law jurisprudence carefully developed the theory of normative protection scope under the influence of Anglo-American law and Austrian law. According to this theory, the result can be attributed to the acts only when it is included in the protection scope of the violated norms, and the concept of danger plays an important role herein.

In the late 1960s and early 1970s, scholars such as J.Pudolphi, C.Roxin and B.Schünemann began to advocate the normative theory of protection purpose in criminal jurisprudence. This theory was integrated with the previous theories about the creation and realization of danger, all of them formed the theory of objective attribution.[1]

From the perspective of philosophy, neo-kantianism is the theoretical basis for the formation of the theory of objective attribution. W.Windelband, one of the representative scholars of neo-kantianism, distinguished the world of fact from the world of value, and the argument of fact from the argument of value. However, he argued that all of them were related to each other, i.e. the latter was superior to the former and the former belonged to the latter. Because the argument of fact was about "truth", and the argument of value also included the question of "goodness" and "beauty". He also asserted that the "truth" was related to both the recognition and evaluation of facts, thus it was the bridge between the world of fact and value and connected these two different worlds. H.Rickert denied the objective existence of "the object itself" and argued that "there was no existence without consciousness". H.Rickert also divided the world into the world of fact and the world of value. The world of fact was the world of appearance (phenomenon) or experience while the world of value was the world of man's subjective will (*noumenon*). Value is not the real existence, but the meaning of it. Some objects have value, while the object of specific value is not the same as the value itself. In the world of fact, there are many appearances which are interrelated by transcendental categories, such as causality and necessity. Appearance is also involved in the value of the world, but in this field, it is not based on these transcendental categories, but on the value norms, the will and emotion of the cognitive subject. H.Rickert pointed out that the task of philosophy was to research the worth of these values and explore their meanings, in order to integrate them into the universal teleological connection of all values. Only when the problems of values were solved could we talk about the meaning of the world. The task of natural science was to seek for the regularities. The task of social and historical science was to describe and evaluate specific social and historical events. Jurisprudence lied between natural science and historical social science, and it belonged to cultural science which was in the middle filed. As the content of cultural science, the essential method of jurisprudence should be the method of value relations.[2]

The theory of objective attribution is based on the theory of *Conditio-sine-qua-non-Formel* or the theory of *Conditio-sine-qua-non-Formel* with lawfulness. However, it is not meaningful to declare a conditional act illegal because the purpose of declaring an act illegal is to prohibit the occurrence of such an illegal act, or to prevent ordinary people from carrying out such an illegal act. One death (a fact) caused by an act doesn't mean that this act is out of norm (a value). The result which

[1] 以上参见日山中敬一:《刑法总论》，成文堂2008年版，第248页以下。See Yamanaka Keiichi.(2008) *General Theory of Criminal Law*, Seibundo Publishing Co, 1–248.

[2] 以上参见韩震主编:《西方哲学教程》，北京师范大学出版社2006年版，第301页以下；夏基松:《现代西方哲学教程》，上海人民出版社1985年版，第115页以下。See Han Zhen ed. (2006) *A Course in Western Philosophy,* Beijing Normal University Press, 1–301; Xia Ji Song (1985) *A Course in Modern Western Philosophy*, Shanghai People's Publishing House, 1–115.

has significant deviation of cause-and-effect attributed to the actor is not conducive to preventing an ordinary person from producing such result. Therefore, it is necessary to purposefully determine which act is illegal. It is not difficult to see that the theory of objective attribution is the same as the fundamental argument of neo-kantianism. As Professor C. Roxin said that "a shift from ontological to *Philosophie der Normen* (theory of norms) could be achieved simultaneously as long as people understood the lawlessness as the infringement of legal interest resulting from the creation of unpermitted dangers. Causality and purposiveness is a type of existence which is constructed from the theoretical standpoint (the narrator's notes: the standpoint of logic of object itself). From such standpoint, only which act is killing, what is destruction or injury can be determined. On the contrary, if people think from the views of this article, (the narrator's notes: the view of *Philosophie der Normen*) they can conclude that although each killing is, within the scope of the above examples, on the premise of the empirical foundation, judging an act which caused death (*Todesverursachung*) is a killing (*Ttungshandlun*) should be based on the compliance with observations or infringement of the permitted dangers."[3] In a word, in order to make the provisions of criminal law function as behavior standards, it is necessary to conduct a normative evaluation of acts, results and causation, which is the view of neo-kantianism. Professor C.Roxin also pointed out that his theory of objective attribution tried to complete the conception of neo-kantianism and developed its content in a new way.[4]

From the perspective of criminal jurisprudence, there are two basic reasons for the formation of the objective attribution. One is the perpetrating acts such as killing, injury and destruction of poverty are lack of non-constancy,[5] the other is the *Regressus ad infinitum* of the theory of *Conditio-sine-qua-non-Formel*. As is known to all, the theory of objective attribution is aimed at consequential offense. When the infringement of legal interest occurs in real life, according to the causation of natural science, people will find the act which has conditional relation with the result naturally, and think that this act is the cause of result. If the criminal law has made a constant and specific description of constitutive element and the judicial officials think that the act which caused this result does not meet the constitutive element, it can be denied that this act constitutes a crime. However, due to the lack of constancy in killing or injury, it is difficult to draw conclusions that whether the act that caused the killing and injury belongs to the criminal law when the result is manifested as injury or death of others.[6] Thus, the conditional relation is first adopted which

[3] C.Roxin, *Das strafrechtliche Unrecht im Spannungsfeld von Rechtsgliterschutz und individueller Freiheit*, ZStW 116(2004),S.931.

[4] C.Roxin,*Strafrecht Allgemeiner Teil, Band I*, 4.Aufl., C.H.Beck,2006,S.206.

[5] The crimes of homicide and injury in this article generally include crime of intentional homicide, intentional injury, negligent homicide and the crime of serious injury caused by negligence. For the convenience of expression, the following is only the examples of homicide and injury.

[6] In the past, the Anglo-American criminal law textbooks discussed causation in the homicide in the monographs. Later, the causation was discussed in the general principles of criminal law. However, when discussing the causation in the general principles of criminal law, the cases of

implies that the act that has a causality with the injuries is affirmed as homicide or injury from the perspective of ontology, then, the conclusion that whether the result is attributed to the act can be drawn through the normative evaluation. This is the theory of objective attribution.

For example, Professor C.Roxin pointed out that if A knew B was willing to suicide and still sold lethal dose of heroin to B who died after injecting. The act of A has causation with the death of B, and A's act has eventual intent. If we holds that the act of A meets the constitutive element of homicide, A must be punished. However, it is not appropriate for A to be charged with homicide. Therefore, it is necessary to apply the theory of objective attribution under which the death of B is not attributed to A.[7] "It is self-evident that the act of A in the above example belongs to the crime of participating in suicide (assisted suicide) in *Japanese Criminal Law* (Article 202). Therefore, the constitutive element of homicide (Article 199) is the intentional killing of others 'by violating the victim's will'; in addition, the consent of the victim (*Einwilligung*) obviously has the function of being the cause about preventing the conformity of elements of crime (cause of non-conformity of elements of crime) of homicide. In contrast, in Germany, where there is no provision about assisted suicide, the act of A may be interpreted as consistent with the constitutive elements of homicide."[8] It is not difficult to understand that the reasons why Professor C.Roxin thinks that there is causation between the act of A and the result of death are as follows: (A) it is based on the theory of *Conditio-sine-qua-non-Formel* (or the theory of *Conditio-sine-qua-non-Formel* with lawfulness), and (B) the act of killing is lack of constancy, so it's hard to judge which act belongs to killing and which act is not.[9] Thus, "the theory of objective attribution provides a universally valid judgment rule which is used to judge which act causes death, injury, or damage results to be homicide, injury, or damage, and which is not".[10]

Professor Urs Kindhäuser gave an example when discussing why the theory of objective attribution shall be adopted: A lent an axe to the clumsy neighbor L, but unfortunately, L hurt himself by accident when using the axe. "In the given situation, if a person wants to explain the occurrence of the result by causation, he has to consider L's possession of axe. Therefore, A lends the axe to L is one of the cause

---

homicide are usually taken as examples.(美约书亚·德雷斯勒:《美国刑法精解》，王秀梅等译，北京大学出版社2009年版，第167页以下Joshua Dressler, trans. Wang Xiumei, (2009) *Understanding Criminal Law*, Beijing: Peking University Press, 1–167.).

[7] C.Roxin,*Strafrecht Allgemeiner Teil, Band I*, 4.Aufl., C.H.Beck,2006,S.403ff.

[8] 日曾根威彦:"客观的归属论の体系论的考察"，载日冈野光雄等编:《西原春夫先生古稀祝贺论文集》(第1卷)，成文堂1998年版，第71页。Sone Takehiko.(1998) "A systematic examination of objective attribution theory", as cited in Okano Mitsuo et al., ed., *A Collection of Congratulatory Essays by Mr. Haruo Nishihara in His Seventies(Vol, 1)*, Seibundo Publishing Co, 71.

[9] For example, if B does not want to suicide, A sells heroin as a fitness drug to B. B died after the injection, and people would be sure that A's acts convicted homicide. In t the case cited by Professor C.Roxin, it can also be considered that A's act is a homicide, but whether his act convicts homicide is questionable.

[10] 德骆克信:"客观归责理论"，许玉秀译，载《政大法学评论》1994年第50期。C.Roxin, trans. Xv Yuxiu, (1994) *The theory of objective imputation*, as cited in *Chengchi Law Review*, No. 50.

of injury of L. In addition, there will be another situation where A estimates that the neighbor L is so awkward that he will hurt himself, but still deliberately lends him the axe. How to deal with this situation? Moreover, in this situation, A is impossible to quote the justifications and cause of preventive culpability, so A is likely to be punished for intentional physical assault. However, such a conclusion is difficult for people to accept."[11] Hence, it is necessary to review the damaging result should be attributed to whom. Obviously, the reason why Professor Urs Kindhäuser pointed out the necessity (an emergency to avert an immediate danger) of reviewing the result should be attributed to whom is that (A) the causality between the act of A and L's injury, which cannot be denied on the basis of the theory of *Conditio-sine-qua-non-Formel*, similarly, (B) due to the lack of constancy in the act of damage, the act of lending axe cannot be denied as a harmful act. Hence, A cannot be punished by the theory of objective attribution.

Moreover, Professor W.Frisch pushed forward this argument. He gives some examples in such regard: "The actor shot the victim, and the victim only got a wound, but unfortunately, the victim died in hospital because the influenza virus that is currently circulating". Another example is that the actor asked the victim to travel by boat, and the victim died in the wreck.. In these two cases, Professor W.Frisch points out that according to the theory of *Conditio-sine-qua-non-Formel*, "when the actor sets a necessary condition for the occurrence of the result (such as death or injury), he triggers (causes, incurs) the result. Then, according to the opinions of the majority at that time, the objective constitutive elements of homicide or injury are simultaneously realized... It is not difficult to see that this so-called the theory of *Conditio-sine-qua-non-Formel* or the theory of adequateness will draw a conclusion with a certain cause in all the previous cases. If the association between the act and result is limited in such elements, this theory can draw a conclusion that the objective constitutive elements have been realized: If there is no gunshot wound that requires treatment, the victim will not be infected in the hospital, and, if the victim is not be persuaded to travel by boat, he will not be lost in the shipwreck. This theory also applies to other cases. Similarly, even if the parents of killer could realize the objective constitutive elements when we adopted the theory in this way... Such a similarly absurd conclusion can only be avoided if we understand 'the cause of the effect' which is required in the statutes in a more rigorous sense".[12] This passage not only criticizes the theory of *Conditio-sine-qua-non-Formel*, but also explains the reasons for the formation of the theory of objective attribution. In a word, the *Regressus ad infinitum* of the theory of *Conditio-sine-qua-non-Formel* and non-constancy of perpetrating acts about killing and injury force the theory of criminal law to restrict the theory of *Conditio-sine-qua-non-Formel*, and finally the theory of objective attribution is formed.

---

[11] U. Kindhäuser, *Strafrecht Allgemeiner Teil*, 5. Aufl., Nomos,2011,S.88f.

[12] 德沃尔冈夫·弗里希:"客观的结果归责", 蔡圣伟译, 载陈兴良主编:《刑事法评论》(第30卷), 北京大学出版社2012年版, 第223~224页。Wolfgang Frisch, trans. Cai Shengwei, (2012) *Objective Result Attribution*, as cited in Chen Xingliang ed. *Criminal Law Review*, No. 30, Peking University Press, 223–224.

It should be noted that although the theory of *Conditio-sine-qua-non-Formel* has a defect in expansion of the cause,[13] it does not mean that the theory of *Conditio-sine-qua-non-Formel* (the formula of conditional relation) cannot be applied when judging the causation. The reason is that if the objective attribution is not carried out on the basis of the conditional relation or under its premise, it will be completely separated from the factual basis. And the simple normative judgment without factual basis will inevitably undermine the stability of the judgment of conformity and wrongdoing of the constitutive elements. Italian scholar Tullio Padovani points out that "the real flaw of the theory of *Conditio-sine-qua-non-Formel* is not that it expands the scope of the cause, but is the mechanism that deeply hides in itself: The premise of using 'the thinking method of exclusion' is that people must have already known the reason for the conditions in advance, that is, how these conditions work as (one of) causes. Otherwise, the theory of *Conditio-sine-qua-non-Formel* cannot work at all. For example, A died of heart attack after taking an experimental drug which was offered by B. In this case, it is clear that A's death cannot be attributed to the act of B based on 'the thinking method of exclusion' before the medicinal properties of the experimental drug have not been determined."[14] In a word, "people apply the formula of conditional relation under the premise that the answer is not self-evident".[15] However, this defect just shows that the real conditional relation is based on objective elements, and it also shows that there is a defect in the practice of abusing conditional relation regardless of the causative potency of the conditions. Therefore, it is the abuse of the theory of *Conditio-sine-qua-non-Formel* that insists the idea that the parents of killer are the cause of the death of others, and then affirms that they realize the objective constitutive elements of homicide. In a word, if the causative potency of conditions are considered, that is, whether an act has the causative potency of causing injuries, even though the formula of conditional relation is adopted, we will deny that the killer's parents are the cause for the death of others.

---

[13]The theory of *Conditio-sine-qua-non-Formel* may only refer to the conditional relation, that is, the former is the reason of the latter when the later does not exist without the former. It may also refer to the following doctrine in the criminal law: if the conditional relation is applied to the judgment of causation in the criminal law without limiting the conditions, it will have the criminal causation. Denying the latter theory of *Conditio-sine-qua-non-Formel* does not mean that the role of conditional relation is denied. It should also be noted that although the theory of *Conditio-sine-qua-non-Formel* may expand the scope of causation or "it may form an endless relationship" (Zhou's article, P. 228), it may also limit causation. For example, in the case concerning the well-known double causation and alternative sufficient conditions, the theory of *Conditio-sine-qua-non-Formel* denied the causation. All of these can illustrate that the theory of *Conditio-sine-qua-non-Formel* is not infinite. In the absence of restrictions on the perpetrating acts of killing and injury, if there is no qualification of the conditional relation, the acts of killing and injury may be more infinite.

[14]意杜里奥·帕多瓦尼:《意大利刑法学原理》(评注版)，陈忠林译评，中国人民大学出版社2004年版，第118页。Tullio Padovani, trans. Chen Zhonglin, (2004) *Principles of Italian Criminal Law (Annotated)*, China Renmin University Press,118.

[15]U. Kindhäuser, *Strafrecht Allgemeiner Teil*, 5.Aufl., Nomos, 2011,S.79.

It thus appears that, the defect may not lie in the formula of conditional relation itself, but in the lack of constancy in the perpetrating acts, such as killing, injury and so on. In other words, the reason why the theory of *Conditio-sine-qua-non-Formel* is said to expand the scope of reasons or *Regressus ad infinitum* existed is because the early theory of criminal law did not properly define the perpetrating acts. The reason for this is also that it's difficult to define or describe concretely the perpetrating acts such as killing, injury and so on. Therefore, although the classical school of criminology holds that the killer's parents meet the constitutive elements of killing, it denies the conviction of killing on the grounds of lacking intention and negligence as the element of culpability. However, the argument that the killer's parents are still illegal cannot be accepted. *Finale Handlungslehre*, which includes intention as a constitutive element, thus making the killer's parents are lack of unlawful with intention, but still does not resolve the question of whether the killer's parents are established as criminal negligent.[16] Similarly, the theory of objective attribution also does not limit the perpetrating acts, but it argues that the act which causes death or injury is homicide or injury. Under this premise, the theory of objective attribution excludes the situation that should not be attributed to the attribution. As Professor C.Roxin said that the task of attribution of the objective constitutive elements is, first of all, to outline the situation in which the act that conforms to the constitutive elements formed from the results (the periphery of the attribution possibility), such as the legally important act of killing from the cause of death.[17] Obviously, the theory of objective attribution regards the act that causes death as killing which meets the constitutive elements at the first place. And the reason for that is because the act of killing is lack of constancy. If the provisions of the criminal law give a detailed description on the constitutive elements of the act, there will not basically have the question of expanding reasons under the theory of *Conditio-sine-qua-non-Formel*. Additionally, the given examples of the theory of objective attribution are basically limited to the cases, such as injuries, destruction of property and so on. However, the defect caused by the non-constancy of the perpetrating acts cannot be attributed to the theory of *Conditio-sine-qua-non-Formel*. On the contrary, because the acts of killing and injuring lack constancy, the earlier theory of *Conditio-sine-qua-non-Formel* judged whether an act was killing or injuring by the conditional relation firstly, rather than limiting these acts firstly, and then judged whether the act has causation with the result according to the theory of *Conditio-sine-qua-non-Formel*.

Zhou's article pointed out that "if we are in favor of *Handlungsunwert*, the status of the theory of objective attribution must be affirmed. That's to say, according to the objective attribution, whether the act has value or not, it is manifested by its danger which is not permitted by norms— those acts have the subjective intention to violate legal interests. According to judgment of the act, it has the realistic possibility of violating the legal interest. In my opinion, it is hard to admit the theory of

---

[16] 参见德克罗斯·罗克辛:"德国犯罪原理的发展与现代趋势", 王世洲译, 载《法学家》2007年第1期。See Claus Roxin, trans. Wang Shizhou, (2007) *The Development and Modern Trends of Criminal Theory in Germany*, as cited in *Jurists' Review*, No.1.

[17] C.Roxin,*Strafrecht Allgemeiner Teil, Band I*, 4.Aufl., C.H.Beck,2006,S.372.

objective attribution without *Handlungsunwert*. And it is probably difficult to systematically research and develop the theory of objective attribution from the standpoint of simple theory of the infringement of legal interest. (Zhou's article, P.242)" "This may be the deep reasons why the theory of objective attribution is researched deeply in Germany rather than Japan", which this article has doubts about.

Firstly, Zhou's article interprets the acts which create unpermitted danger in criminal law as the acts with subjective intent of the infringement of legal interest. It's worth discussing. On one hand, "The practical significance of the theory of objective attribution mainly exists in negligent crimes".[18] It is difficult to accept that the actor of criminal negligence has the subjective intent of violating the legal interest. Besides, when German scholars discuss whether acts create dangers that are not permitted by criminal law, though they may apply special cognition as the materials for determining, they do not take subjective intention and intent as the materials and standard. Moreover, using special cognition as materials is actually applying particular fact of the actor as materials for determining.

Secondly, not all people who in favor of *Handlungsunwert* advocate the theory of objective attribution. For example, Schuld, a Japanese professor in favor of *Handlungsunwert* (or a dualist based on *Handlungsunwet*) adopts the causation rather than the theory of objective attribution like German scholars.[19] Moreover, he clearly points out that there is no need to abandon the concept of perpetrating acts and the theory of *Adäquanz* in the Japanese theory and replaced them with the theory of objective attribution.[20] For another example, Professor Ooya Minoru, also in favor of *Handlungsunwert*, does not agree with the theory of objective attribution, and he is against the specific content of it.[21] On the contrary, people in favor of *Erfolgsunwert* sometimes will also adopt the theory of objective attribution. They adopt them in a different degree based on the reasons of the system of crime. Professor Yamanaka keiichi did a systematic research of the objective attribution and even developed it in details,[22] but he was considered to be the person who was in favor of *Erfolgsunwert*. Professor Maeda Masahide,[23] who is uncontroversially

---

[18] C.Roxin,*Strafrecht Allgemeiner Teil, Band I*, 4.Aufl., C.H.Beck,2006,S.373.

[19] 参见日井田良:《讲义刑法学·总论》，有斐阁2008年版，第113页以下。Ida Makoto. (2008) *Handout of Criminal Law·General Rules*, Yuhikaku Press, 1–113. Of course, the theory of *Adäquanz* contains part of the theory of objective imputation. Professor Ida Makoto adopted the theory of *Adäquanz*, and also adopted the theory of objective imputation.

[20] 日井田良:《刑法总论の理论构造》，成文堂2005年版，第63页。Ida Makoto.(2005) *Theories of General Rules of Criminal Law*, seibundoh, 63.

[21] 参见日大谷实:《刑法讲义总论》，成文堂2009年新版，第216页。See Ohya Minoru. (2009) *Lectures on Criminal Law(New Edition)*, Seibundo Publishing Co, 216.

[22] 参见日山中敬一:《刑法における客观的归属の理论》，成文堂1997年版，第1页以下。See Yamanaka Keiichi.(1997) *The Theory of Objective Attribution in Criminal Law*, Seibundo Publishing Co., 1.

[23] In his discussion of *Handlungsunwert* and *Erfolgsunwert* of Japan's post-war, Professor Naito Ken pointed out that although there are differences in various details, the scholars who basically take *Erfolgsunwert* include Nakayama Kenichi, Machino Hajime, Shinya Umezaki, Muneoka Shirou, Sone Takehiko, Yamanaka Keiichi, Asada Kazushige, Horiuchi Shouzo, Nashida Noriyuki,

classified as a person in favor of *Erfolgsunwert,* has also largely adopted the theory of objective attribution.[24]

Thirdly, the emergence of the theory of objective attribution is guided by protection of legal interest. Professor C.Roxin points out that "the theory of objective attribution has been derived through certain inevitable development from the principles of protection of legal interest... If the criminal law aims to protect the interests from man-made infringement, it can only be realized by this theory: The criminal law prohibits the production of danger which threatens the legal interests, and evaluates the state of realizing such danger in the form of the infringement of legal interest breaching the prohibition provision as unlawfulness. Therefore, the act of the constitutive elements is always an act with the infringement of legal interest in the form of unpermitted danger which is realized by man-made."[25] He also added that "the criminal law is for 'the protection of assistive legal interests'. When people think about that how to protect the legal interest through the criminal law, the answer can be given by means of logic which cannot be refuted: The unpermitted risk is prohibited in order to protect the legal interest,[26] in addition, the person who caused the prohibited results by exceeding the legally permissible danger is regarded as the person who has done an accomplished act and will be sentenced. Then the author shall put the theory of objective attribution further in this article herein: When a person creates an unpermitted risk for the protection of legal interest in criminal law, and when this risk is realized in a forbidden result, he is a criminally actor with unlawfulness as long as he does not have a justified ground."[27] It is not difficult to

---

Ookoshi Yoshihisa, Maeda Masahide, Mikito Hayashi, Yamaguchi Atsushi and etc.(日内藤谦:《刑法理论の史的展开》，有斐阁2007年版，第596页Naitou Ken.(2007) *Historical Development of Criminal Theory*, Yuhikaku Press, 596.

[24]参见日前田雅英:《刑法总论讲义》，东京大学出版会2011年版，第178页以下。See Maeda Masahide.(2011) *Handouts of General Rules of Criminal Law(fourth Edition)*, University of Tokyo Press, 1–178.

[25]C.Roxin,*Das strafrechtliche Unrecht im Spannungsfeld von Rechtsgliterschutz und individueller Freiheit*, ZStW 116(2004),S.929f.

[26]In the German literature, the "*Risiko*" in unpermitted danger and the "*Gefahr*" in the potential damage offense are two different words. The author tried to understand the difference between the two words, but found that there is no difference between them. Professor Kindhäuser clearly points out that the concept of "*Risiko*" is actually the same as the concept of "*Gefahr*". (U. Kindhäuser, *Strafrecht Allgemeiner Teil*, 5.Aufl., Nomos, 2011, S.90) The author also asked Wang Gang, who was studying for a doctor degree in Germany, to ask German professors that why they use different words on dangers. Wang Gang said that with regard to the question of whether there is a difference between the unpermitted risk (*Risiko*) and danger (*Gefahr*) in the theory of objective imputation, he asked Professor who said that the two words were slightly in the daily semantics. However, there is no essential difference of the two words in the theory of objective imputation. In his point of view, the creation of unpermitted risk can also be called the creation of unpermitted danger. Therefore, this article uses the concept of risk and danger in the same sense.

[27]德克罗斯·罗克辛:"德国犯罪原理的发展与现代趋势"，王世洲译，载《法学家》2007年第1期。Claus Roxin, trans. Wang Shizhou, (2007) *The Development and Modern Trends of Criminal Theory in Germany*, as cited in *Jurists' Review*, No.1.

see that the theory of objective attribution not only does not conflict with *Erfolgsunwert*, but also comes from *Erfolgsunwert*.

Fourthly, for the reasons why the dominant ideology of *Japanese Criminal Law* did not adopt the theory of objective attribution in Germany, Japanese Professor Saeki Hitoshi made a clear statement. He says that "in Japan, the causation in criminal law not only includes the judgment of factual causation, but also includes the judgment regarding the law about whether the result can be attributed to the act. Moreover, the theory of *Adäquanz* in recent years has essentially absorbed the content of the theory of objective attribution. In spite of this, the reason why the theory of objective attribution has not become the dominant ideology is that it's different from in Germany, where the theory of *Conditio-sine-qua-non-Formel* is said to be the dominant ideology. In Japan, where the combination of perpetrating acts and the theory of *Adäquanz* is the dominant ideology, if it is judged flexibly, in essence, it is possible to absorb the judgment structure of the theory of objective attribution that includes the creation of dangers and realization of results. Instead, it is not necessary to adopt a separate judgment framework. In addition, the theory of objective attribution goes beyond the traditional category of causation. It has a wide range of contents, including the theories of negligent crime, perpetrator and accomplice, and the interpretation of the specific provisions in criminal law. It is also the reason for hesitation in adopting the theory of objective attribution."[28]

It can be seen from the above that it is difficult to affirm the rationality of *Handlungsunwert* after affirming the rationality of the theory of objective attribution.

3.2 The Theoretical Positioning of Objective Attribution

Liu's article holds that the theory of objective attribution is not the theory of constitutive element, but rather the theory of causation. Since the causation between act and result is the causation of the constitutive elements, "the theory of causation is the theory that pays attention to the conformity judgment of constitutive elements" (Liu's article, P.1219). However, the theory of objective attribution is not equated with the theory of constitutive element just because it involves the conformity of elements of crime. The theory of objective attribution "is consistent with the theory of causation in several points, such as the recognition of related risks as the content of judgment, the judgment about whether there is a adequateness between the risk of the unlawfulness and result and related final conclusion. On the contrary, as the dominant ideology, the theory of causation is actually a theory of attribution. But unfortunately, as the theory of causation, the theory of objective attribution has completely located itself from the previous theory of causation from the beginning,

[28] 日佐伯仁志:"因果关系(2)", 载《法学教室》2004年8月号(第287号)。Saeki Hitoshi.(2004) "Causal relationship (2)", as cited in *Hogaku Kyoshitsu, August (No. 287).*

in addition, it holds itself as a theory of constitutive elements, but a theory of causation." (Liu's article P.1221).

According to Zhou's article, "the theory of objective attribution is the essential theory of normative judgment, which is obviously different from the causation. Causation is a matter of the existence of fact and aims to solve a certain relationship between act and result, therefore, it is a form of judgment and evaluation of fact. The judgment of objective attribution is a judgment of attribution based on the formation of causation, which is a kind of substantive judgment." (Zhou's article, P. 232). "the theory of objective attribution is the question of the conformity of elements of crime". (Zhou's article, P. 248).

In this article, the above different viewpoints are actually the arguments about the orientation of the theory of objective attribution, which are related to whether and how China can learn from it, and it involves two relations: (A) the relationship between the (theory of) causation and the (theory of) objective attribution, and (B) the relationship between the theory of objective attribution and the theory of constitutive elements (whether the theory of objective attribution is the theory of constitutive elements).

(1) The Relationship between the Causation and the Objective Attribution

Before discussing this relationship, the meaning of the concept of causation must be clarified at the beginning.

For the concept of causation, there are two different views. One view regards causation as a physical and real relationship, and the other sees causation as a conceptual and logical relationship.[29] The concepts of causation in Liu's and Zhou's articles are not the same. The concept of causation that Liu's article puts forward is not the same as the pure conditional relation or the causation of facts, but includes the comparative evaluation of causation. In other words, Liu's article uses the concept of causation at the level of the theory of *Adäquanz*, so that the concept of causation includes normative evaluation. Therefore, Liu's article uses the concept of causation in a broad sense, which includes the factual causation and normative judgment.[30] While in Zhou's article, the causation is limited to the causation without normative judgment and fact. In other words, Zhou's article uses the concept of causation in the theory of objective attribution, so that causation becomes a simple

[29] 日山中敬一:《刑法总论》，成文堂2008年版，第251页以下。Yamanaka Keiichi.(2008) *General Theory of Criminal Law*, Seibundo Publishing Co, 1–251.

[30] Japanese theory of criminal law also uses the concept of causation in a broad sense. For example, when Professor Maeda Masahide introduced the theory of causation, he listed the theory of *Conditio-sine-qua-non-Formel*, the theory of *Adäquanz* and the theory of objective imputation(参见日前田雅英:《刑法总论讲义》，东京大学出版会2011年版，页182以下 See Maeda Masahide.(2011) *Handouts of General Rules of Criminal Law*, University of Tokyo Press, 1–182). For another example, Prof. Yamaguchi Atsushi divided the causation into three sections: an overview, causation as factual relationship, causation as the realization of danger.(参见日山口厚:《刑法总论》，有斐阁2007年版，页49以下See Yamaguchi Atsushi.(2007) *General Rules of Criminal Law*, Yuhikaku Press, 1–49). In fact, "causation as the realization of danger" is also the key content of objective imputation.

concept of fact. From this point of view, the dispute between Zhou's and Liu's article is whether the theory of objective attribution is the theory of causation. It is not a right or wrong issue, but an issue caused by the different definition of causation. This is because, as a concept indicating the constitutive elements, it may include normative evaluation. For example, if the perpetrating act is considered to be an act that meets the constitutive elements and has a risk of the infringement of legal interest, this concept includes normative evaluation. For another example, the result, as the objective constitutive elements, does not refer to any result of the act, but must be the result of the infringement of legal interest. Therefore, when A was intentionally shot at B but failed and killed a mouse, the death of the mouse could not be evaluated as a result in criminal law. The concept of causation in criminal law does not necessarily only be a simple concept of fact, but depends on the theory in which people use.

The concept of objective attribution in Germany also bears a broad and a narrow sense. The objective attribution in a broad sense contains the judgment of factual causation and the subsequent normative judgment, while the objective attribution in the narrow sense is the normative judgment on the results attribution after determining the factual causation. For example, in the Chapter 11 of Professor C.Roxin's criminal law textbook, about "The Attribution of the Objective Constitutive Elements" is divided into two parts, of which the first part is "the theory of causation", and the second part is "the further attribution on objective constitutive elements".[31] "The Attribution of the Objective Constitutive Elements", as the title of Chapter 11, is a kind of objective attribution in a broad sense. In this system, it can be argued that the factual causation is a part of the objective attribution in a broad sense. Professor C.Roxin also clearly pointed out that the attribution of objective constitutive elements must obviously be carried out through two sequential stages: (A) the theory of causation should be explained, then (B) other requirements of attribution should be discussed.[32] For another example, the criminal law textbooks of Professor H.Jescheck and Professor T.Wrigend respectively discuss the following content in "the constitutive elements about unlawfulness": the objective constitutive elements, the causation and objective attribution, the errors of intention and constitutive elements, the subjective constitutive elements. The part of "the causation and objective attribution" respectively discusses some contents: causation as a basis for accountability in criminal law and objective attribution, the determination of the causation, the limitation of the former theory about objective attribution, and the new theory of objective attribution.[33] In this system, the factual causation is not a part of objective attribution, but the premise of the objective attribution. The objective attribution mentioned above is a kind of objective attribution in a narrow sense. The chapter "The Objective Constitutive Elements of Crime" in Professor

---

[31] C.Roxin,*Strafrecht Allgemeiner Teil, Band I*, 4.Aufl., C.H.Beck,2006,S.343ff.

[32] C.Roxin,*Strafrecht Allgemeiner Teil, Band I*, 4.Aufl., C.H.Beck,2006,S. 350.

[33] H.Jescheck/T.Weigend,*Lehrbuch des Strafrechts.Allgemeiner Teil*, 5.Aufl.,Duncker & Humblot 1996,S.272ff.

Urs Kindhäuser's criminal law textbook is divided into two sections, the first section is "Results, Act and Causation" (including the function of causation, proof of causation, and specific controversial issues), and the second section is "The Objective Attribution of Consequential Offense".[34] The objective attribution therein is also used in a narrow sense.

In conclusion, "the method of the theory of objective attribution aims to realize the systematization of the attribution basis by classifying the factual danger and the normative danger while judging the prior creation of danger and the subsequent realization of danger on the premise of the existence of the conditional relation of fact."[35] Therefore, in *German Criminal Law* textbooks, whether it adopts the concept of objective attribution in a broad or narrow sense, the factual causation will usually be discussed at the beginning, and then the results attribution will be further tested normatively. Obviously, Liu's article basically uses the concept of objective attribution in a broad sense, while Zhou's article uses the concept of objective attribution in a narrow sense.

To sum up, the following conclusions can be drawn about the relationship between causation and objective attribution. (A) if the concept of causation in a narrow sense and the objective attribution in a narrow sense are used, then the theory of objective attribution is not the theory of causation, but the theory of normative evaluation after the determination of causation. (B) if the concept of causation in a broad sense and the objective attribution in a broad sense are used, then the two are not antagonistic, but both include the factual causation and normative evaluation. (C) if the concept of causation in a narrow sense and the concept of objective attribution in a broad sense are used, then the theory of objective attribution includes the theory of causation. (D) if the concept of causation in a broad sense and the concept of objective attribution in a narrow sense are used, then the theory of causation contains the theory of objective attribution.[36]

(2) The Relationship between the Theory of Objective Attribution and the Theory of Constitutive Elements

Liu's article holds that the theory of objective attribution is not the theory of constitutive element, but the theory of causation. In this article, this view is debatable. Even if the causation is considered to include normative evaluation, the theory of objective attribution cannot be considered as the theory of causation.

From the above introduction about the formation of the theory of objective attribution, it can be seen that the theory of objective attribution actually contains the perpetrating acts and causation, and even partially contains the result elements.

---

[34] U. Kindhäuser, *Strafrecht Allgemeiner Teil*, 5.Aufl., Nomos, 2011,S.76ff.

[35] 日山中敬一:《刑法总论》，成文堂2008年版，第250页。Yamanaka Keiichi.(2008) *General Theory of Criminal Law*, Seibundo Publishing Co, 250.

[36] Of course, since the theory of objective imputation includes the theory of perpetrating acts, in this regard, the theory of causation in a broad sense may not completely include the theory of objective imputation in a narrow sense.

According to the viewpoints of German scholars, the analysis of causation is carried out after the results have happened, and the judgment of risk is analyzed from an ex-post perspective. As long as any factual situation can be identified as the cause after the event, then it must also be an element of risk beforehand. If it is identified that one person threw a cigarette with a spark in a dry forest and caused a forest fire. Then it can be considered that the throwing is an element of risk before a forest fire occurs.[37] Obviously, the risk judgment of act is actually the judgment of the perpetrating acts. For example, Professor C.Roxin stated with respect to the danger of creating unpermitted risk in objective attribution that though the infringement of legal interest has occurred after complying with all traffic regulations, the creation of this infringement is not an act that meets the constitutive elements. This applies to both negligent crimes and intentional crimes equally.[38] The result that "in a storm, one sent another to the forest, and hoped that the person would be struck by lightning cannot be attributed to the man as a killing because he didn't create significant danger".[39] That is to say, the act of sending others to the forest is not a killing. Obviously, the requirement of creating unpermitted dangers means that the acts of constitutive elements shall exist actually.

For another example, when Professor C.Roxin discussed the scope of validity on the constitutive elements,[40] he quoted a case that in a motorcycle competition between A and B who both had criminal responsible liability after drinking, B died due to his own fault. Professor C.Roxin pointed out that "although the existing risks had realized, the results were not within the scope of the protection of the provisions, thus he shall not be attributed... This is because A does not meet the objective constitutive elements of Articles 222 and 212, even if A tolerates the fatal accident of competitor from the beginning, he also cannot be punished. That is to say, when the 'intent' mentioned above is directed to the act which lacks constitutive elements, it cannot be the foundation for *Strafbarkeit*."[41] This passage shows that the theory of objective attribution not only discusses the act of the constitutive elements, but also evaluates the results of the constitutive elements normatively. That is to say, if the results are not within the scope of the constitutive elements, the objective attribution also cannot be carried out.

---

[37] U. Kindhäuser, *Strafrecht Allgemeiner Teil*, 5.Aufl., Nomos, 2011,S.9.1.

[38] C.Roxin,*Strafrecht Allgemeiner Teil, Band I*, 4.Aufl., C.H.Beck,2006,S.383.

[39] C.Roxin,*Das strafrechtliche Unrecht im Spannungsfeld von Rechtsgüterschutz und individueller Freiheit*, ZStW 116(2004),S.935. the ordinary text is: daβ der Veranlasser kein rechtlich relevantes Risiko geschaffen habe und daβ der Erfolg ihm aus diesem Grunde nicht als Ttungshandlung zuzurechnen sei.

[40] The theory of objective imputation in Germany generally takes two rules as the main body, namely creation of risk and realization of risk. "Roxin's system has some characteristics, especially in addition to the two main rules on creation and realization of risks, in addition, the scope of the constitutive elements(Die Reichweite des Tatbestandes)as the third main rule"(林钰雄:"第三人行为介入之因果关系及客观归责(下)"，载《台湾本土法学》2006年第80期Lin Yu Xiong. (2006) "Causation and Objective Imputation in Cases of Intervention by a Third Party (II),"as cited in *Taiwan Law Journal*, No. 80.).

[41] C.Roxin,*Strafrecht Allgemeiner Teil, Band I*, 4.Aufl., C.H.Beck,2006,S. 402f.

It is not difficult to see that according to the Chinese and Japanese scholars' understanding of the constitutive elements, the perpetrating acts, results and causation are the basic elements of the constitutive elements. There are there specific contents of the theory of objective attribution. The first is to discuss the perpetrating acts (the creation of unpermitted danger by the act). The second (the realization of dangers) is the question of objective attribution in the actual or narrow sense or results attribution (which may also contain the content of the perpetrating acts). The third (the scope of validity on constitutive elements) discusses both the perpetrating acts and results. In addition, since constitutive elements are one of illegal types, the theory of objective attribution cannot directly deal with the problem of wrongdoing, that is, whether the act shall be prohibited or not. In a word, the theory of objective attribution is the theory of constitutive elements, or it actually discusses the perpetrating acts, results and causation of the constitutive elements.

Therefore, Professor Frisch pointed out that "the theory of objective attribution treats the problems that limited objective constitutive elements as the result attribution. Many of the questions that are interpreted by the theory of objective attribution as results attribution are not related to it, but related to the question of 'whether there is a bound and prohibited act of constitutive element'".[42] For example, Professor Ida Makoto also points out that the theory of objective attribution in Germany combines "the judgment on the behavioral of perpetrating acts (and the behavioral of accomplice) and causation" in the Japanese theory of criminal law.[43] As for whether the theory of objective attribution should become the theory of constitutive element is another matter, but in reality, the objective attribution which is widely used in Germany is the theory of constitutive elements, or the theory of conformity of elements of crime.

It thus appears that, the denial in Liu's article upon the theory of objective attribution as the theory of constitutive elements lacks foundation. Of course, from the point of view of this article, Liu's article does not deny the theory of objective attribution in fact, but it hopes that the theory of objective attribution can only discuss the causation in a broad sense. In other word, it expects that the theory of objective attribution can be only oriented to the theory of causation in a broad sense. The second part of Liu's article observes that the theory of objective attribution is a theory of *Strafbarkeit*, that is to say, "the objective attribution seems to have developed from the so-called theory of constitutive elements to the superior concept of the tripartite system of the crime which includes the conformity of elements of crime, wrongdoing and accountability. It does not seem to discuss the question of attribution, but more like analyzing the question of whether a crime is established or not. It is also not like a theory of attribution, but like a general theory of the

[42] 德沃尔冈夫·弗里希:"客观的结果归责", 蔡圣伟译, 载陈兴良主编:《刑事法评论》(第30卷), 北京大学出版社2012年版, 第253页。Wolfgang Frisch, trans. Cai Shengwei, (2012) *Objective Result Attribution*, as cited in Chen Xingliang ed. *Criminal Law Review*, No. 30, Peking University Press, 223–224.

[43] 日井田良:《刑法总论の理论构造》, 成文堂2005年版, 第63页。Ida Makoto.(2005) *Theories of General Theory of Criminal Law*, seibundoh, 63.

establishment of crime". (Liu's article, P. 1221). Therefore, Liu's article cannot deny that the theory of objective attribution is the theory of constitutive elements at first because it is impossible to establish a crime without the conformity of elements of crime. It is not difficult to see that Liu's article denied that the theory of objective attribution is the theory of constitutive elements on the one hand, and on the other hand, it holds that the theory of objective attribution develops from the theory of constitutive elements to the general theory of the establishment of crime. The two aspects are contradictory.

In connection with the discussion in the first part, it can be argued that the theory of objective attribution is not only a theory about whether the result can be attributed to act, but also a theory about what act constitutes the acts of constitutive element and what result is the consequence of constitutive elements. Therefore, the theory of objective attribution includes both the factual judgments and the theory of constitutive elements of normative evaluation.

3.3 The Evaluation of the Theory of Objective Attribution

Zhou and Liu's articles respectively evaluated the theory of objective attribution from positive and negative perspectives. For example, Liu's article believes that the theory of objective attribution includes the judgment about wrongdoing and subjective attribution, at the cost of blurring the tripartite system of the crime, it greatly weakens its function of safeguarding human rights. Therefore, it is a combination of different contents. Zhou's article believes that the above feature of the theory of objective attribution can just use multiple rules to ensure that there is no omission during the application process, and it can establish the test standard for positive judgment and reverse test interaction, and highlight the hierarchy and sufficiency of evaluation. The conclusions drawn by the two professors are basically their own value judgments, yet not necessarily inevitable conclusions from the view of logics.

First of all, the evaluation of the theory of objective attribution in Germany should be carried out in the theoretical context of German theory of criminal law. At this point, Liu's article may have obvious defects.

For example, Liu's article pointed out that "the content and judgment of the theory of objective attribution quietly switched to the field of wrongdoing from the field of constitutive elements upon the concept of 'risk unlawfulness'". (Liu's article, P. 1222). In fact, as mentioned below, "the risk prohibited by law" in the theory of objective attribution shall be generally judged independent of specific events, while the judgment of wrongdoing in the field of wrongdoing is the judgment on specific events, they are not the same. It's also questionable about Liu's article's criticism based on specific examples. "For example, a heroic passer-by found that a child was going to be hit by a bus and he pushed the child away, but unfortunately, this child suffered a head injury because of his act" (Liu's article, P. 1223). Liu's article criticized that "according to the tripartite system of the crime, it should be confirmed that the passer-by's act constitutes the conformity of elements of crime at first. However, with the judgment of wrongdoing, it can be identified as justifiable cause (necessity), so this act does not establish a crime. However, according to the theory of objective attribution, this kind of grounds which should be judged by wrongdoing has already been discussed as the question of conformity of elements of crime, and such discussion will be done by means of wrongdoing... This means that the justifications in the theory of wrongdoing, such as necessity and justifiable defense, have been replaced by the theory of objective attribution. The theory of wrongdoing seems to be redundant after the theory of objective attribution". (Liu's article, P. 1223).

However, firstly, Liu's article's criticism is on the basis of his own understanding about necessity, it does not meet the necessity in the theory of objective attribution in Germany. In Germany, simply risk reduction (for example, a brick was originally going to fall on the victim's head and caused his death, but the actor pushed the victim away and caused the brick to fall on the victim's shoulder, finally, the victim got minor wound) cannot be objectively attributed. The necessity refers to replace the original high-risk with a newly low-risk, such as throwing the child on the fire brigade's rescue cloth is to prevent him from being killed in the fire, but causing the child to be injured, which also called the risk replacement.[44] The example cited in Liu's article originally belongs to the necessity, but it is not the state of simply risk reduction in the theory of objective attribution. To develop further, if a child was going to be killed by a bus, the passer-by pushed him, caused the child's leg to be injured by bus, which will be the state of risk reduction. Of course, it is difficult to distinguish them in some cases. Hence, the theory of objective attribution in Germany does not include the necessity, but Liu's article incorporates cases of necessity into objective attribution, thus improperly criticizing the theory of objective attribution. Secondly, the theory of objective attribution does not discuss the justifiable cause which meets the constitutive elements in field of the theory of objective attribution. This is because the theory of objective attribution discusses the state that does not meet the constitutive elements. If the act meets the constitutive elements, it needs to be examined in the case of justifiable cause. It is natural to take the concept of wrongdoing as a guide when carried out the objective attribution and to consider the necessity of general deterrence, because the constitutive elements belong to the type of wrongdoing originally.

For another example, the third part in Liu's article argues that the objective attribution is actually the subjective attribution because the actor's special cognition and subjective prediction possibility will be taken into account when the judgment of objective attribution is being made. However, such criticism is also questionable. On one hand, taking actor's special cognition as judgment information of objective attribution may be related to the intention censorship, but the two are different: special cognition must exist beforehand, and the intention censorship is used after objective attribution. Even if the subject intent is taken into account in the objective

[44] H.Jescheck/T.Weigend,*Lehrbuch des Strafrechts.Allgemeiner Teil*, 5.Aufl.,Duncker & Humblot 1996,S.287f.

attribution, it does not mean that the subjective attribution is not needed. "The reason why 'objective attribution is called objective' is not because subjective elements are not important, but because of the acts upon the constitutive elements which are comprised by attribution, such as killing, injury or damage and so on. Acts mentioned above are objective acts, and intent in the subjective constitutive elements can be added after these acts occurred."[45] In the field of criminal negligence, although there are contradictions, according to Professor C.Roxin, "it is negligence that can be attributed in objective constitutive elements. The concepts on violation of duty of care, prediction possibility, possibility of recognition, and possibility of avoidance that the traditional theory of negligence attempts to understand are superfluous and can be discarded".[46] Therefore, it cannot be considered that the theory of objective attribution is imputing subjectively. Moreover, although the theory of objective attribution uses special cognition and other content as judgment information in some occasions, it does not confuse objective attribution with accountability, as Liu wrote.[47] This is because the dominant ideology of German theory of criminal law incorporates the intent, as the element of wrongdoing, into the constitutive elements. Therefore, even if the theory of objective attribution includes the judgment of intent, it cannot be considered that the theory of objective attribution confuses the relationship of constitutive elements, wrongdoing and accountability. In fact, the theory of objective attribution does not incorporate the elements of responsibility, such as capacity liability, the possibility of cognition of wrongdoing and reasonableness (*Zumutbarkeit*), into the judgment information of objective attribution. Therefore, the theory of objective attribution does not confuse the tripartite system of the crime.

Secondly, the evaluation of the theory of objective attribution is largely compared with the theory of *Adäquanz*. It's helpful to have a better perception of the theory of objective attribution by understanding the theory of *Adäquanz*. However, the evaluation of the theory of *Adäquanz* in Japan should also be understood in the system of Japanese theory of criminal law. From this point, Zhou's criticism of the theory of *Adäquanz* may be debatable.

For example, Zhou's article argues that the theory of *Adäquanz* "lacks specific rules for judging the acts of constitutive elements, i.e. perpetrating acts". (Zhou's article, P. 236). However, in Japan, before the discussion of causation, there is a discussion of the perpetrating acts, and the rule for judging the perpetrating acts is

[45] 德骆克信:"客观归责理论"，许玉秀译，载《政大法学评论》1994年第50期。C.Roxin, trans. Xv Yuxiu, (1994) *The theory of objective imputation*, as cited in *Chengchi Law Review*, No. 50.

[46] 德骆克信:"客观归责理论"，许玉秀译，载《政大法学评论》1994年第50期。C.Roxin, trans. Xv Yuxiu, (1994) *The theory of objective imputation*, as cited in *Chengchi Law Review*, No. 50.

[47] The imputation is the upperseat concept, the subordinate concepts are "the objective imputation"(belonging to the constitutive elements) and "the subjective imputation" (belonging to guilt or responsibility)"(德骆克信等:"问题研讨"，许玉秀、郑铭仁译，载《政大法学评论》1994年第50期C.Roxin, et,al., trans. Xv Yuxiu, (1994) *Symposium on Jurisprudential Questions*, Zheng Mingren, as cited in *Chengchi Law Review*, No. 50.).

not originally in the adequacy.[48] For another example, in Zhou's article, the theory of *Adäquanz* "ignores the effect of 'ranking' on the judgment of conditions for the establishment of crime". Therefore, "the problems which should be resolved in the judgment of the conformity of elements of crime are left in the later judgment process". For example, the theory of *Adäquanz* means "uses the theory of necessity to explain or deny the establishment of aider when acts reduce the risk of legal interest" (Zhou's article, Pp. 236–237). However, this criticism is questionable. Since the theory of objective attribution includes the judgment of the perpetrating acts, the order of examination of the theory of objective attribution is: causation—creation of danger (perpetrating acts)—realization of danger—the scope of validity of the constitutive elements. Since the theory of *Adäquanz* basically does not include the judgment of perpetrating acts, the order of examination of adequacy as a whole is: results—perpetrating acts—causation—the judgment of adequateness. It is difficult to think that the theory of *Adäquanz* lacks the effects of ranking if it is evaluated in the criminal system of Japan. Many states that cannot be objectively attributed in the theory of objective attribution are judged to be lacked of perpetrating acts in the theory of *Adäquanz*. For example, Professor Yamaguchi Atsushi pointed out that "in the case where the duty to prevent the result is fulfilled in response to the reduction of the dangerousness of the act, the result is that the dangerousness is reduced and the act (perpetrating act) that constitutes the criminal negligence is lost, and there is no need to call it a permitted danger in the first place."[49]

In fact, German scholars call "the theory of objective attribution a continuation and complement of the theory of *Adäquanz* or the theory of importance" without hesitation.[50] The difference between the theory of *Adäquanz* and the theory of objective attribution is not in the objective result attribution, but in the content arrangement of the theory of constitutive elements. As Professor C.Roxin says, the theory of *Adäquanz* includes a formula of adequateness, and it is partially consistent with the theory of objective attribution. "If the risk created by the actor is realized in a causation process, this process is adequate. So far, the theory of *Adäquanz* and

---

[48] However, it is also difficult to think that the theory of *Adäquanz* does not consider the perpetrating acts at all. For example, according to Professor Nishida Noriyuki, in the case that A urged other to walk in the woods and expected other to be struck by lightning accidentally, as a result, that man was killed by lightning when he was walking in the woods. "It cannot be said that there is a adequacy in the empirical law. Therefore, the act of A in this case lacks the 'perpetrating acts' of the crime of homicide, and does not establish the crime of attempted homicide. This is also an applicable scenario for the theory of *Adäquanz*"(日西田典之:《刑法总论》，弘文堂2010年版，第101页Nishida Noriyuki.(2010) *General Theory of Criminal Law*, Koubundou Publishers Inc., 101.)This is obviously from the point of view of whether a certain act can usually lead to death, to judge whether the act belongs to the the crime of homiceide that conforms to the constitutive elements.

[49] 日山口厚:《刑法总论》，有斐阁2007年版，第231页。Yamaguchi Atsushi.(2007) *General Rules of Criminal Law*, Yuhikaku Press, 231.

[50] 德沃尔冈夫·弗里希:"客观的结果归责"，蔡圣伟译，载陈兴良主编:《刑事法评论》(第30卷)，北京大学出版社2012年版，第227页。Wolfgang Frisch, trans. Cai Shengwei, (2012) *Objective Result Attribution*, as cited in Chen Xingliang ed. *Criminal Law Review*, No. 30, Peking University Press, 227.

objective attribution are the same. However, the questions about risk reduction, the permitted risk, the protection purpose of attention norms or the scope of validity of the constitutive elements cannot be included in the formula of adequateness".[51] However, the theory of *Adäquanz* discusses the risk reduction and other issues in the elements of constitutive elements, such as results, perpetrating acts, which are prior to the causation. In a word, if the theory of *Adäquanz* is evaluated in the system of criminal law in Japan, it will be found that the defects of the theory are not as much as Zhou said. And there is no significant difference in the conclusion of the case. For example, Zhou's article pointed out that "if B was severely injured by A, and then was infected with bacteria after being sent to the hospital. The theory of *Adäquanz* holds that the bacterial infection in the hospital is not an abnormal phenomenon, so there is adequateness between the injury act of A and the death of B. This is to check whether the intervention factor is abnormal from the reverse side. However, from the positive perspective, bacterial infection is an unavoidable risk that can be tolerated in life, especially in hospital. It has 'social adequateness' and cannot be attributed from the results" (Zhou's article, P. 239). However, Zhou's conclusion is questionable. In fact, the result will be attributed for such state even if the theory of objective attribution is adopted.[52] For another example, Zhou's article pointed out that "A, who knew that B was competitive, urged him to participate in the wrestling competition. As a referee, A changed the order of lottery intently, then B was seriously injured by C because he was arranged to compete with C, who was the strongest opponent. D took this chance to kill B during the hospitalization of him. Is A culpable for the serious injury or death of B, or is it not responsible at all? In this case, it can be concluded that there is a causation between A's act and B's injury according to the theory of *Adäquanz*" (Zhou's article, P. 239). However, firstly, scholars who advocate the theory of *Adäquanz* will first deny that A's act is the act of constitutive element on killing and injury. Secondly, even if they take a step back and reach a positive conclusion, they will not admit that there is adequacy between them. Zhou quoted Professor B.Schünemann's argument that "the victim's close relatives who were died due to stir of knowing the victims were seriously injured in a car accident. And there are other examples of sequel, such as the death of the victim after infecting several years of AIDS. 'All of these adequate results are completely caused by previous infringement'". (Zhou's article, p. 237). However, in author's opinion, this may be the conclusion about the theory of *Adäquanz* in the early stage of Germany, but it cannot be the assertion of Japanese scholars who advocate the theory of *Adäquanz*.

---

[51] 德骆克信等:"问题研讨"，许玉秀、郑铭仁译，载《政大法学评论》1994年第50期。C. Roxin, et,al., trans. Xv Yuxiu, (1994) *Symposium on Jurisprudential Questions*, Zheng Mingren, as cited in *Chengchi Law Review,* No. 50.

[52] C.Roxin,*Strafrecht Allgemeiner Teil, Band I*, 4.Aufl., C.H.Beck,2006,S. 385. If the victim does not go to the hospital for treatment, he will die at home. This situation is quite abnormal, and it is difficult to impute death to previous injury. Therefore, in any case, the result of death cannot be attributed to serious injuries. This argument obviously does not make sense.

Finally, the evaluation of the theory of objective attribution in Germany will also be related to whether China should learn from the theory of objective attribution and what should be learned from it. In other words, when we evaluate the theory of objective attribution from the standpoint of German doctrine and a conclusion can be drawn that the theory is incomparably superior, it does not mean that China's theory of criminal law can adopt the theory directly. The author will discuss the reference problem of the theory of objective attribution in the following. As a foreshadowing, the author will firstly make own value judgment on the merits and demerits of the theory of objective attribution.

In this article, the theory of objective attribution has the following advantages. Firstly, it is difficult to judge the perpetrating acts on crimes of homicide and injury because they lack constancy. The theory of objective attribution can avoid the judgment dilemma of crimes on homicide and injury.[53] Secondly, the theory of objective attribution can both take advantage of the theory of *Conditio-sine-qua-non-Formel* or the theory of *Conditio-sine-qua-non-Formel* with lawfulness to avoid the arbitrary judgment of facts, and it can overcome the defects of the theory of *Conditio-sine-qua-non-Formel* and avoid *Regressus ad infinitum*. Thirdly, "the objective constitutive elements have important status through the modern theory of attribution, and also relatively reduce the value of subjective constitutive elements".[54] In particular, the objectification of the judgment on criminal negligence is conducive to avoid the arbitrariness of judgment. Fourthly, the theory of objective attribution judges from the ontology to the theory of normative judgment, and it is systematized. Despite this, the theory of objective attribution is still unsatisfactory.

As mentioned above, the theory of objective attribution includes the judgment on perpetrating acts of constitutive element and even the whole problem of limitation on conformity of elements of crime, which is not conducive to the independent judgment on elements of constitutive elements, and weakens the function of the doctrine of *nulla poena sine lege* which the concept on conformity of elements of crime had. This is the biggest problem of the theory of objective attribution. In addition, part of the lower rule concerning the hierarchy of the theory of objective attribution is not perfect.

---

[53] For example, in the case that A is completely capable of causing death to B, but B is only harmed to the extent that hospitalization is required. However, B died due to the arson of the hospital during his hospitalization. Whether the theory of objective imputation is adopted or not, people will think that A's act is not killing but injury, and there is no causation between A's act and B's death. However, if one episode is added, that is, A is accidentally aware that C, who does not know him, will harm B when he sets fire to the hospital, and uses the arson of C to cause the death of A, then people will think that A's act is killing. There is a causation between the act of A and the death of B. But why do judgments about the character of the perpetrating acts and its causation come to different conclusions when they are objectively identical? It is difficult to reasonably explain from the perspective of the perpetrating acts and causation, and the theory of objective imputation solves this problem.

[54] 德骆克信:"客观归责理论"，许玉秀译，载《政大法学评论》1994年第50期。C.Roxin, trans. Xv Yuxiu, (1994) *The theory of objective imputation*, as cited in *Chengchi Law Review*, No. 50.

Firstly, the first lower rule concerning the hierarchy of the theory of objective attribution is the unpermitted danger which is created by acts, and there are many issues to be researched.

(A) Professor C.Roxin points out that "the permitted danger means although the act creates a significant danger in law, but such danger is also generally (unrelated to the specific case) permitted. Therefore, unlike the justifications, such act has been considered to prevent the attribution of objective constitutive elements. A typical example of the permitted danger is driving a motor vehicle in compliance with all the traffic rules." "The failure to create/cause dangers within the permitted limitation prevents the sufficiency of objective constitutive elements",[55] which is agreed by Professor Feng Jun.[56] What is not discussed is that whether it can be distinguished successfully about 'the permitted danger of the act' and 'the creation of danger is not occurred'.[57] However, it is not appropriate to judge whether the act creates the unpermitted danger and whether the act conforms to the constitutive elements. The basic logic of the theory of objective attribution is that since certain acts are inevitably with dangers, such acts are prohibited in the social development and the danger of such acts should be permitted, thus it does not meet the objective constitutive definition of crime. Professor C.Roxin further points out that "it is undeniable that road traffic causes a significant danger in life, health and property. Additionally, accident statistics also can support this conclusion to be irrefutable. However, legislators still allow road traffic (within the scope of certain provisions for attention) based on the significant benefits of public welfare."[58] According to statistics, the number of people killed in traffic accidents in China is about 200,000 per year, as Professor Feng Jun pointed out years ago. Despite this, legislators still allow people to engage in driving because more important interests are depended on traffic driving.[59] Professor Lin Yuxiong also points out that "other modern industrial facilities (such as oil refineries, nuclear power plants) or products (drugs, home appliances, etc.) are produced by dangers. If legislators allow a certain degree of danger within the statutory safety standards and accidents are caused, such dangers are permitted by legislators, which should not be the objective constitutive elements, such as injury,

---

[55] C.Roxin,*Strafrecht Allgemeiner Teil, Band I*, 4.Aufl., C.H.Beck, 2006,S. 383f.

[56] 参见冯军:《刑法问题的规范理解》，北京大学出版社2009年版，第137~138页。See Feng Jun. (2009*) Normative Understanding of Criminal Law Issues*, Peking University Press, 137–138.

[57] Professor C.Roxin points out that it is not easy to distinguish the permitted danger and the situations in which important dangers are not created.(C.Roxin, *Strafrecht Allgemeiner Teil, Band I*, 4.Aufl.,C.H.Beck,2006,S.383).

[58] C.Roxin,*Strafrecht Allgemeiner Teil, Band I*, 4.Aufl., C.H.Beck,2006,S.383.

[59] 冯军:《刑法问题的规范理解》，北京大学出版社2009年版，第137页。Feng Jun. (2009*) Normative Understanding of Criminal Law Issues*, Peking University Press, 137.

killing."[60] However, these views may confuse legislative policy and the interpretation of criminal law. When a kind of act has the danger of the infringement of legal interest, it is a matter of legislative policy whether the legislature allows or prohibits. Whether a specific act in real life creates the danger of the infringement of legal interest and whether it meets the objective constitutive elements of a crime, it's a problem about the interpretation of criminal law (or the theory of conformity of elements of crime). It is undeniable that legislators can generally predict in advance that traffic driving will cause many deaths every year. It is an issue of legislative policy about whether it is possible to prohibit all the traffic driving. However, this is completely different from the issue about whether it will lead to the death of many people as permitted items without penalty.[61] Similarly, it is an issue of legislative policy to decide whether to develop the aviation industry, to build high-speed railways or nuclear power plants after weighing their usefulness, necessity and danger. In the interpretation of criminal law, only individual and specific acts can be discussed.[62] These acts can only be judged whether the act meets the constitutive elements based on specific cases. In other words, although the conformity of elements of crime is a judgment of typology, while whether the act conforming to the constitutive elements will inevitably depend on the specific facts of the specific case. However, whether the act claimed by the theory of objective attribution is permitted is not related to specific cases. That is to say, the theory of permitted danger is not discussed in relation to specific dangerous acts, but it takes the general admissibility of dangerous cause as issues.[63] Therefore, it is impossible to judge whether the specific case meets the constitutive elements of a certain crime based on general conclusions.[64]

(B) It is generally not doubtful that the act of risk reduction does not meet the constitutive elements. However, it is not so simple to apply this in specific cases. For example, when a brick is about to fall on the victim's head and the victim shall surely be seriously injured, the actor pushes him, and the brick only fell on the victim's shoulder, causing the victim to be slightly injured. The actor is not considered to create dangers in common circumstances. However, in certain special circumstances, if the victim wishes to have a serious injury on his

---

[60] 林钰雄:《新刑法总则》，中国人民大学出版社2009年版，第127页。Lin Yu Xiong. (2009) *General Provisions of New Criminal Law*, China Renmin University Press, 127.

[61] 参见日平野龙一:《刑法总论I》，有斐阁1972年版，第199页。See Hirano Ryuuichi.(1972) *General Rules of Criminal Law I*, Yuhikaku Press, 199.

[62] 参见日内藤谦:《刑法讲义总论》(中)，有斐阁2001年版，第631页。See Naitou Ken. (2001) *General Lectures on Criminal Law (Medium)*, Yuhikaku Press, 631.

[63] 日篠田公穗:"许された危险の理论についての一考察"，载《刑法杂志》第27卷(1986年)第2号。Shinoda Kimiho.(1986) "A research on the theory of premissible risk", as cited in *Journal of Criminal Law*, Vol. 27, No. 2.

[64] 参见张明楷:"论被允许的危险的法理"，载《中国社会科学》2012年第11期。See Zhang Mingkai. (2012) "On the Jurisprudence of the Allowed Danger Doctrine", as cited in *Social Sciences in China*, No. 11.

head, it is difficult to deny the objective attribution of act (the conformity of elements of crime) without using the presumption of commitment.[65] For another example, if the victim is a child and the actor is the parent, the actor can push the victim twice in order to avoid minor wound. However, the actor does not push the child twice and causes the child slightly injured. Although the act reduces the danger of injuring, it is difficult to deny the wrongdoing and objective attribution of the act (the conformity of elements of crime).[66]

(C) There are some problems difficult to solve when considering that all actions of risk reduction do not meet the constitutive elements. For example, if a doctor removes the tongue of a cancer patient to save his life, the harm caused by the treatment and the benefits of the treatment should be independently evaluated by the criminal law., in addition, this act cannot be considered to be inconsistent with the constitutive elements of injury just based on risk reduction.[67] That is to say, in the situation mentioned above, it is necessary to admit that the treatment meets the constitutive elements of the crime of injury, but the balance of legal interests prevents wrongdoing. If the treatment is considered to be inconsistent with the constitutive elements of injury, then the arbitrary treatment (such as the removal of the patient's tongue without his consent) does not meet the constitutive elements of assault, (because the risk is reduced), therefore, it does not constitute assault. This conclusion is obviously not appropriate.[68]

(D) According to Professor C.Roxin, when an existing danger is not enhanced in a measurable way, it should be identified as a lack of danger creation, and the act does not meet the constitutive elements. Therefore, it cannot be objectively attributed. For example, the act of a man who poured a basin of water into a flooded reservoir is difficult to be identified as crime of breaching dikes.[69] It is true that the behavior of the actor cannot be considered as crime of breaching dikes, which is indeed because it is hardly to prove that whether the breaching of dikes or breaching in advance was caused by a basin of water and causes death in advance. But this is basically an issue of evidence rather than a matter of substance. That's like saying if one cannot be proved that killed someone, he cannot be said that meets the constitutive elements of killing, which doesn't make sense in reality. If this causation can be proved, the conclusion will be

[65] U. Kindhäuser, *Strafrecht Allgemeiner Teil*, 5.Aufl., Nomos, 2011,S.94.

[66] 参见德沃斯·金德霍伊泽尔:"故意犯的客观和主观归责"，樊文译，载《清华法律评论》(第3卷第1辑)，清华大学出版社2009年版，第156页。See Urs Kindhäuser, trans. Fan Wen, (2009) *Objective and Subjective Imputation in Intentional Crimes*, as cited in *Tsinghua Law Review*, (Vol.3, No.1), Tsinghua University Press, 156.

[67] 参见日町野朔:《患者の自己決定权と法》，东京大学出版会1986年版，第171页。See Machino Saku.(1986) *Patients' Right to Self-Determination and the Law*, University of Tokyo Press, 171.

[68] 参见德沃斯·金德霍伊泽尔:"故意犯的客观和主观归责"，樊文译，载《清华法律评》(第3卷第1辑)，清华大学出版社2009年版，第156页。See Urs Kindhäuser, trans. Fan Wen, (2009) *Objective and Subjective Imputation in Intentional Crimes*, as cited in *Tsinghua Law Review*, (Vol.3, No.1), Tsinghua University Press, 156.

[69] C.Roxin,*Strafrecht Allgemeiner Teil, Band I*, 4.Aufl., C.H.Beck,2006,S.377.

totally different. For example, the victim was hung on a cliff with only one rope, and the rope was slowly breaking because it was difficult to bear the weight of the victim. The actor cut the rope one second before the victim fell. The victim's life is absolutely protected even in the last second, and the behavior of the actor still constitutes homicide.

Therefore, what behind the exclusion of unlawfulness due to risk reduction is the evaluation issues based on real facts and general rules, which are answered by means of consent, presumed consent or necessity. A common short description (short formula) of risk reduction is very helpful for the classes, but it is not enough to solve academic problems.[70]

Secondly, the second lower rule concerning the hierarchy of the theory of objective attribution is that it does not allow the realization of danger, and it is the real theory of result attribution.

(A) The attribution cannot be applied before the danger really realized. For example, A shot the victim with intent of killing, and the victim was burned to death because of a fire occurring in a hospital to cure the shot wound. In this case, the danger of shooting is not realized, so it cannot be objectively attributed. In the cases which the cause of death are different (death by gunshot or burning), it is easy to see whether the danger of act is realistic when the specific view of the results is adopted (e.g. death by poison or death by thirst are totally different), thus overcoming the defects of the theory of *Conditio-sine-qua-non-Formel*. However, doubts also haunt when the causes of death are the same. For example, A pushed C who is not good at swimming, into the reservoir and left away, but C was able to grab the plank nearby to keep his life. However, at the same time, B, who had no connection with A, quickly took the plank away and caused C's death. In this case, the theory of objective attribution may not be able to give clear and consistent answers.

(B) The unpermitted danger cannot be attributed before it realized, such as the well-known case "*Ziegenhaar-Fall*". This is expressed as the lack of the possibility of preventing the result in Japan's theory of criminal law. And in the theory of *Adäquanz* in Japan, the lack of the possibility of result avoidance is called the lack of conditional relation.[71] If so, the theory of objective attribution has no advantage over the theory of *Adäquanz* in this issue.

(C) China's theory of criminal law should learn from the viewpoint about protection purpose of attention norms. But it is also worth discussing whether it is a problem of lacking the perpetrating acts or a problem of risk which is not realized. For example, when the act of constitutive elements which is stipulated in

[70] U. Kindhäuser, *Strafrecht Allgemeiner Teil*, 5.Aufl., Nomos, 2011, S.94.

[71] 参见日町野朔:《刑法总论讲义案I》，信山社1995年版，第155页； 日山口厚:"因果关系论"，载日芝原邦尔等编:《刑法理论の现代的展开(总论)I》，日本评论社1988年版，第43页。See Machino Saku.(1995) *Handouts of General Theory of Criminal Law (I)*, Shinzansha Publisher Co., 155; Yamaguchi Atsushi.(2007) "The theory of causal relationship", as cited in Shibahara Kuniji et al., ed.(1998) *The modern development of criminal law theory(General Theory I)*, NIPPON HYORON SHA Co., 43.

the criminal law's specific provisions is premised on violating the attentions, it is necessary to judge whether the act violates the attention norms before judging whether it meets the constitutive elements. And During the judge of whether the act violates the attention norms, it is necessary to consider the protection purpose of attention norms. Therefore, the protection purpose of attention norms can be understood as the content of the perpetrating acts (see the content described later in this article). If it is only considered as a question about whether the danger is realized, it may be inappropriate to identify the cases without perpetrating acts originally as attempted crime.

(D) The theory of objective attribution in Germany has a fierce controversy on the lawful alternative acts and the theory of risk enhancement.[72] Therefore, it is not just the adoption of an the theory of objective attribution that can lead to a completely same theory in specific case.[73]

Thirdly, it is also skeptical of the scope of validity of constitutive elements. Professor C.Roxin denied the objective attribution of participating in self-endangerment because the defendant, who intentionally participates in the victim's intentional suicide or self-injury, shall not be punished in principle according to the provisions of *German Criminal Law*. Thus, the defendant shall not be subject to the punishment when he or she participates in others' self-endangerment, nor can he or she be punished for negligently participating in others' self-endangerment, which is less serious than the former.[74] In other words, since the act of intentional soliciting or aiding

---

[72] C.Roxin,*Strafrecht Allgemeiner Teil, Band I*, 4.Aufl., C.H.Beck,2006,S.392ff.

[73] "The question of what degree of danger is punishable when it is created, or what occasion are meant by the realization of danger, is impossible to unravel without reference to the types of cases suggested by the proponents of the theory of objective imputation"(日山本高子:"客观的归属论否认论——Zieschang《刑法总论第二版》の检讨", 载《比较法杂志》2012年第46卷第1号Yamamoto Takako.(2012) "Denial theory of objective attribution——discussion of Zieschang *General Theory of Criminal Law [2nd Edition]*", as cited in *Journal of Comparative Jurisprudence*, Vol. 46, No. 1). There is not usually an unpermitted risk of going to the slums because there are many people who come and go without risk, says Professor C. Roxin. But if there are special risks for a particular person, for example, if there are already many passengers killed in a particular area, so that the city's administration strongly warns foreigners not to embark on a journey. If passengers who have no idea of this news are asked to this area, it can definitely be considered that there is an unpermitted danger"(德骆克信等:"问题研讨", 许玉秀、郑铭仁译, 载《政大法学评论》1994年第50期C.Roxin, et,al., trans. Xv Yuxiu, (1994) *Symposium on Jurisprudential Questions*, Zheng Mingren, as cited in *Chengchi Law Review*, No. 50.)However, Professor C. Roxin's view does not necessarily extend the scope of homicide. On the other hand, in the case that A provides diabetic patient with syrup and causes death, Professor C.Roxin believes that "the supply of syrup and the result of death cannot be attributed to A's act, because the risk is permitted. Every diabetic patient has to be mentally prepared. The drinks and food he gets may contain too much sugar for him and he should examine and return it by himself"(德骆克信等:"问题研讨", 许玉秀、郑铭仁译, 载《政大法学评论》1994年第50期)However, Professor C. Roxin's view does not necessarily shrink the scope of homicide. From this point of view, when we use the theory of objective imputation to discuss cases in which the proponents of this theory are not discussed, there is still a lot of doubt about what conclusions should be concluded in the theory of objective imputation should draw.

[74] C.Roxin,Strafrecht Allgemeiner Teil, Band I, 4.Aufl., C.H.Beck,2006,S.402.

others to commit suicide is not within the function of constitutive element (out of the protection of norms), it is impossible for the act of negligently soliciting or aiding the victim to endanger himself or herself to be in accordance with the constitutive element. However, this reason is not established, the corollary hereof is also doubtful.[75] On the surface, it is true that the defendant participated in the victim's intentional suicide (self-infringement) is more serious than involving in the victim's potentially lethal act (self-endangerment). However, from the perspective of the victim's own decision, the former victim not only recognizes the damaging results, but also expects and hopes that it will occur. The latter victim only recognizes the danger of the act and opposes the occurrence on the damaging results.[76] The evaluation of the result must be related to the subject's attitude about legal interest. In the case of victim's self-infringement, the victim has given up the legal interest. While on the occasion of participating in the self-endangerment, the legal interest has not been abandoned. In summary, if the commitment about the suicide or self-injury is valid, the act of soliciting or aiding self-infringement will not violate legal interest while the act of soliciting or aiding self-endangerment will violate the legal interest. In that case, it should not be considered that participating in the victim's self-infringement is more serious than participating in the self-endangerment. It is true that in some cases, if judged from the objective dangerous situation, the act of self-infringement (suicide) endangers the life more than the act of self-endangerment. In this sense, since the participation in a more dangerous act (instigating or aiding to commit suicide) is undeserving of punishment, the participation in a less dangerous act should be even more unpunishable. However, it is still difficult to be an argument that the participation in self-endangerment is always unpunishable. In the case of participating in self-endangerment, even if the victim doesn't wish and allow the consequence of death to occur, there is still a high risk of death led by the victim's act. For example, there are a lot of cases of attempted suicide and a large number of self-endangerment. It shows that the level of danger is not the distinction between the self-infringement and self-endangerment. That is to say, it shall not be believed that the act of self-endangerment is certainly less dangerous than that of self-infringement. Therefore, the impunity of participation in self-endangerment cannot be proved by that of participation in suicide (self-infringement).[77] Of course, this article does not argue for the establishment of a crime by participation in

---

[75] 参见德英格博格·普珀:《法学思维小学堂》，蔡圣伟译，元照出版公司2010年版，第135页。See Ingeborg Puppe, trans. Cai Shengwei, (2010) *Kleine schule des juristischen denkens*, Angle Publishing Co., Ltd., 135.

[76] 参见日曾根威彦:《刑事违法论の研究》，成文堂1998年版，第169页。See Sone Takehiko.(1998) *A Study of Criminal Illegality*, Seibundo Publishing Co., 169.

[77] 日岛田聡一郎:"被害者による危险引受"，載日山口厚编著:《クロ-ズアップ刑法总论》，成文堂2003年版，第141页。Shimada Souichirou.(2003) "Result of the victims' assumption of risk", as cited in Yamaguchi Atsushi ed. *Close-up General Theory of Criminal Law*, Seibundo Publishing Co., 141.

self-endangerment, but simply argues that[78] it is doubtful to deny the objective attribution of such act by the scope of the constitutive elements.

The negative comments about the theory of objective attribution mentioned above doesn't mean that the total negation of the theory of objective attribution. What the author wants to say is that the theory of objective attribution should not be regarded as truth, and it is not necessary to regard it as a standard.

3.4 The Reference of the Theory of Objective Attribution

Generally speaking, the author thinks that China's theory of criminal law cannot fully use the theory of objective attribution of Professor C.Roxin, but should learn from its judgment methods of norms and some of specific contents.

Firstly, China's theory of criminal law should emphasize the concept of conformity of elements of crime.[79] The reason is that the constitutive element, which emphasizes the concept of conformity of elements of crime, bears the function of the doctrine of *nulla poena sine lege*, and plays an important role in implementing the rules of this doctrine. Although the theory of objective attribution is also the theory of constitutive elements, it also involves three elements: perpetrating acts, result and causation. However, this theory does not separately discuss each element, whereas it mixes and discusses three elements together. Moreover, the cases which lack constancy in perpetrating acts are discussed, such as killing, injury and destruction of property and it is difficult to be applied in all crimes. However, in the theory of interpretation which is considered as the general provisions of criminal law, it is necessary to abstract out the common problems in subdivision, that is, to discuss not only the conformity of elements of crime, but also all elements of constitutive elements. If the theory of constitutive element is completely replaced by the theory of objective attribution, the value about the concept of conformity of elements of crime will be devalued. It is true that the theory of objective attribution can deny the conformity of elements of crime by denying the objective attribution, and it is consistent with the concept of conformity of criminal elements. However, parts of elements about constitutive elements are took into account, thus it can only take part of crimes into consideration. And the establishment of all crimes must meet the conformity of elements of crime. In China, if this point is not emphasized, it will not be conducive to implement the doctrine of *nulla poena sine lege*.[80]

---

[78] 参见张明楷:"刑法学中危险接受的法理"，载《法学研究》2012年第5期。See Zhang Mingkai. (2012) "The Jurisprudence of Assumption of Risk in Criminal Law", as cited in *Chinese Journal of Law*, No. 5.

[79] The constitutive elements in this article refer to the constitutive elements in the tripartite system of the crime, but does not include intent and negligence.

[80] For example, the behavior object is discussed as constitutive elements in China's criminal law, while judicial practice often convicts a crime in spite of considering the existence of the object.(For example, the act of trafficking flour is convicted the crime of drug dealing, the act of objectively

Secondly, China's theory of criminal law should retain the concept of the acts of constitutive elements or perpetrating acts, and it is not appropriate to discuss the perpetrating acts in the theory of objective attribution.

(A) In connection with the point mentioned above, it is not the crime of killing, injury and destruction of property that have the perpetrating acts, but all the crimes have the perpetrating acts. In other words, "the 'bound act' of constitutive element in a narrow sense is the basic element of every criminal act"[81] Retaining the concept of perpetrating acts is of special significance for preventing subjective attribution and guaranteeing the freedom of movement on citizens.

(B) In China, the division of perpetrating acts and causation (or results attribution) into two different elements bears great significance for the determination of attempted crimes. The identification of attempted crime in *German Criminal Law* does not depend on the concept of perpetrating acts. Article 22 of *German Criminal Law* provides that "according to the actor's conception of an act, it is an attempted crime to directly meet the constitutive elements", according to which, even if the concept of perpetrating acts is not implemented, it will not affect the identification of attempted crime. The Paragraph (1) of Article 23 of China's *Criminal Law* provides that "Attempted crime refers to a state that an offender has already started to commit a crime but is prevented from completing it for the reasons independent of his will". Since the criminal law punishes the attempted crime in principles, the concept of perpetrating acts should be stipulated in China's theory of criminal law.[82] Also, it is entirely possible to affirm the attempted crime even if the causation or result attribution is denied. Meanwhile, when it is necessary to deny the perpetrating act, it is obviously inappropriate to convict an attempted crime if it only denies the causation or the result attribution. For example, as the river surged, it seeped into the basement of B's house on the shore, but B and his family were not at home. Neighbor

delivering property to a liar is considered as bribery, the person who objectively purchased a pile of waste article was identified as the crime of selling counterfeit money, etc). If the elements of behavioral objects are not emphasized, the adoption of subjective imputation in judicial practice may be more.

[81] 德沃尔冈夫·弗里希:"客观的结果归责"，蔡圣伟译，载陈兴良主编:《刑事法评论》(第30卷)，北京大学出版社2012年版，第254页。Wolfgang Frisch, trans. Cai Shengwei, (2012) *Objective Result Attribution*, as cited in Chen Xingliang ed. *Criminal Law Review*, No. 30, Peking University Press, 254.

[82] Zhou's article points out that in the dominant ideology of criminal law in China, the discussion of perpetrating acts is discussed in the theoretical framework of the execution and the attempt (the unfinished form of crime), so that the perpetrating acts, as the beginning of causation, is not adopted in the judgment of the theory about the conformity of criminal constitutive elements, and it is difficult to be perfect in the construction of the criminal theory system (Zhou's article, P. 136). This article fully agrees with the explanation of the defects in Zhou's article. However, this defect cannot be overcome only by adopting the theory of objective imputation in Germany. The general part of our criminal law has a section of "act" or "perpetrating acts", in which the discussion of the normative judgment of perpetrating acts is without hesitation.

A found this situation and blocked the basement window of B by himself. Professor Urs Kindhäuser pointed out that A's act only prevented a larger flood. "Since people can explain the actual damage with causation to B without considering A's act, A's act is not the cause of the specific result".[83] In such cases, however, it is possible to draw the conclusion that A's act is attempted crime if it does not deny that A's act does not meet the constitutive elements at first, but deny the causation or result attribution. This is obviously not appropriate.

(C) The crime stipulated by the criminal law includes the consequential offense and *Tätigkeitsdelikte* (if the action and the result take place simultaneously, the causation or result attribution is not needed to be considered). In *Tätigkeitsdelikte*, the concept of perpetrating acts is of great significance.

(D) Even from the standpoint of *Handlungsunwert*, the content on the violation of norms needs to be clarified. If the concept of perpetrating acts submerged in the theory of objective attribution, it is not conducive to the clarity of acts of constitutive element. It is difficult for the citizen to know from the judgment which act is prohibited in the criminal law.[84] It is easy to say that, according to the theory of *Conditio-sine-qua-non-Formel* or the theory of *Conditio-sine-qua-non-Formel* with lawfulness, as the theory of objective attribution, the act that reduces the risk is regarded as the injury at first, and then denies the objective attribution. It is not conducive to give play to the function of the behavior norms of criminal law. As Professor W.Frisch said that "under correct understanding, those actions that reduce risk are not prohibited at all. Likewise, even if those who deliver the certain daily necessities hurt themselves because of carelessness, their delivering will not be prohibited. In principle, in all the problems involving the so-called creation of danger deserves been blamed, there is a question of 'whether there is a bound act with blame of constitutive element', rather than involving result attribution. What is true is that there is some connection between this requirement and the result attribution. If the actor has not engaged in the bound act of constitutive elements at all, then the result that occurred (of course) cannot be attributed to him, but the reason is the absence of the bound act of constitutive element."[85]

(E) In fact, the whole content of the unpermitted danger created by the act described in the theory of objective attribution in Germany, as well as some contents in the realization of danger and the scope of validity of constitutive elements can be fully included in the judgment of the perpetrating acts. For example, in Professor C.Roxin's case that A provided heroin for others even with the knowledge that others were going to commit suicide will solved by the scope

[83] U. Kindhäuser, *Strafrecht Allgemeiner Teil*, 5.Aufl., Nomos, 2011,S .93.

[84] 日井田良:《刑法总论の理论构造》，成文堂2005年版，第63页。Ida Makoto.(2005) *Theories of General Rules of Criminal Law*, seibundoh, 63.

[85] 德沃尔冈夫·弗里希:"客观的结果归责"，蔡圣伟译，载陈兴良主编:《刑事法评论》(第30卷)，北京大学出版社2012年版，第253页。Wolfgang Frisch, trans. Cai Shengwei, (2012) *Objective Result Attribution*, as cited in Chen Xingliang ed. *Criminal Law Review*, No. 30, Peking University Press, 253.

> of validity of constitutive elements. As a matter of fact, it can be considered that this act does not meet the constitutive elements of killing without this theory. That is to say, "from the light prescribed punishment of required homicide in *German Criminal Law* (Article 216), the object of homicide is limited to people without the intention of death. It follows that it is also entirely possible to argue that the act of assisted suicide does not meet the constitutive elements of homicide. In addition, the act of delivering heroin is merely a dangerous act that is harmful to life, instead of directly posing a danger to other's life. Therefore, it is sufficient to review the composition of homicide only in the range of its constitutive elements, without considering the intentional self-endangerment, and to deny the danger as perpetrating acts".[86]

Thirdly, if the current constitutive elements or the basic framework of the perpetrating acts, objects, results, and causation in the objective constitutive elements are maintained, then, the theory of objective attribution advocated by Professor C.Roxin is applied to the causation as a whole, which will lead to the repetitiveness of the judgment (after judging the perpetrating acts, it is judged again in the causation), thus impairing the economics of judgment. It is true that the theory of objective attribution and the theory of perpetrating act are not mutually exclusive.[87] It is not inappropriate to repeatedly test whether an act constitutes a crime. However, repeatedly testing does not rely on the repetition of the program set by the theory. In the theory of criminal law, if the contents of testing standards A and B are identical, only one of them can be retained. On the contrary, even if there is no repeated content in the tripartite system of the crime, it can be tested repeatedly. When one concludes that the conformity of constitutive elements are met in a case and enters the wrongdoing without finding justifiable causes, but then believes that it should not be treated as a crime, one may still go back and judge the conformity of constitutive elements again. Similarly, when people think that a certain act meets the constitutive elements, when making a causation judgment, they can either think that the result cannot be attributed to the act, or they can go back again to judge whether the act belongs to the act of constitutive elements. This repetition of thinking is not premised on the repetition of content on the theoretical system. Just like a security check before boarding, if someone finds a problem, he can still re-examine it without several identical security devices.

The theory of objective attribution often emphasizes the principle of non-attribution from the opposite side. Zhou's article fully affirms the significance of his methodology. However, it should be noted that the system of the crime should be arranged on the basis of the conditions for establishing the crime, and it is not

[86] 日曾根威彦:"客观的归属论の体系论的考察"，载日冈野光雄等编:《西原春夫先生古稀祝贺论文集》(第1卷)，成文堂1998年版，第71~72页。Sone Takehiko.(1998) "A systematic examination of objective attribution theory", as cited in Okano Mitsuo et al., ed., *A Collection of Congratulatory Essays by Mr. Haruo Nishihara in His Seventies(Vol, 1)*, Seibundo Publishing Co, 71–72.

[87] 参见日山中敬一:《刑法总论》，成文堂2008年版，第279页。See Yamanaka Keiichi. (2008) *General Theory of Criminal Law*, Seibundo Publishing Co, 279.

possible to arrange according to the elements that exclude the establishment of the crime. Therefore, the exclusion of the establishment of the crime in priority is not the reason for arranging the system of criminal theory. Firstly, there are too many issues that do not establish a crime, and it is difficult for the theory of criminal law to give priority to examine the issues which exclude the establishment of crime. Secondly, the theory of criminal law cannot be arranged on the basis of the elements that exclude the establishment of a crime. For example, a child was pushed into the water by A, who did not reach the age of responsibility, while the child's father B who was present did not rescue the child in time, thus causing the child to drown. On such occasions, people do not carefully study whether the death can be objectively attributed to A, but directly exclude the establishment of crime on the ground that A does not reach the age of responsibility. However, this does not mean that age of responsibility must be arranged before the objective constitutive elements. Thirdly, the so-called exclusion of the establishment of the crime in priority only exists in the concept or logic, but has no practical significance. For example, in the tripartite system, the judiciary does not detain or arrest an actor as long as the act meets the constitutive elements, nor is it possible to arrest an actor as long as the act meets the constitutive elements and the act is illegal, but only when all the conditions for conformity of elements of crime, wrongdoing and accountability of the constitutive elements are fully met, the actor can be detained and arrested. Therefore, in order to exclude the establishment of crimes as soon as possible, it is inappropriate to include justifiable causes and causes of preventive culpability in the stage of conformity of elements of crime.

The above three points have determined that the theory of objective attribution in Germany should not be fully incorporated into the 'causation' in our current theory of criminal law.

Fourthly, even under the basic framework of maintaining the perpetrating acts, the object of acts, the result and the causation in the part of constitutive elements, the normative judgment method of the theory of objective attribution and part of concrete content can and should be used for reference.

(A) The part involves 'perpetrating acts' should refer to the specific content of the creation of unpermitted danger in the theory of objective attribution, and the content of judging the perpetrating acts in the realization of danger and the scope of validity of constitutive elements.

The reason is, as mentioned above, the creation of unpermitted danger in the theory of objective attribution is actually a normative judgment of the act of the constitutive elements. At the same time, it is also a problem about how to normative evaluate the perpetrating acts that lacks constancy to a large extent. Therefore, our theory of criminal law must make a substantive interpretation of the constitutive elements of the act, and can only evaluate the acts that infringe the legal interests or the behavior standards that have the urgent dangers on infringement of the legal interests as perpetrating acts. In addition, it is necessary to learn from the specific rules upon the creation of unpermitted danger and to determine the perpetrating acts.

Other rules of the theory of objective attribution that fall within the scope of perpetrating acts that are worthy of consideration can also be incorporated into the perpetrating acts. For example, Professor C.Roxin points out that "the normalization is not merely a permitted danger determined after weighing value, but can be corroborated by the fact that 'the realization of unpermitted dangers is not a purely factual process, but depends on the protective purpose of the attention norms qualified by the permitted dangers.' For example, if a driver of a car who was initially speeding and then slowed down to within the permissible standard range, collides in an objectively unavoidable manner with a child who suddenly jumps out from the side of the road, which is merely an accident and not an act of physical injury. This is because, although the driver exceeded the permitted danger, and assuming that the accident would not have occurred without the exceed of that danger, the reason is that the driver would not have been in the position where the child jumped out if the speed limit had been consistently observed. However, the protection purpose of the speed limit still excludes the result attribution. The speed limit is not intended to prevent the car from driving to the accident site at a safe speed at the time of the accident. It is intended to prevent the limitation of the possibility of avoidance caused by speeding in similar cases and the sharp increase when collision occurs. These dangers do not exist in the cases the author cited, thus the physical injury act which meets the objective constitutive elements should be denied."[88] Therefore, it can be seen that the protection purpose of attention norms is actually the identification of constitutive element of act. In this case, if the independent parts of perpetrating acts are still remained in the general principles of our criminal law, this question should be discussed in perpetrating acts. It should be emphasized that the theory of the protection purpose of the attention norms should be introduced into the theory of criminal law and judicial practice in China. In our judicial practice, especially in the process of determining the crime of causing traffic casualties, basically the amount of traffic rules violated by the actor and the victim to determine who is primarily responsible, without even considering the protection purpose of specific traffic rules, and without considering the results caused by which of the acts in the violation of traffic rules, so it leads to the confusion of the determination of the crime of causing traffic casualties. What is even more absurd is that some actors have criminal culpability for traffic accidents only because they escape afterwards.[89] However, escaping after traffic accidents cannot be the perpetrating acts of the crime of causing traffic casualties, and it is even less likely to be the cause of the previous consequences. The introduction on the theory of protection purposes of attention norms is obviously conducive to the proper identification of negligent crimes, such as the crime of causing traffic casualties.

---

[88] C.Roxin,*Das strafrechtliche Unrecht im Spannungsfeld von Rechtsgüterschutz und individueller Freiheit*, ZStW 116(2004),S.931f.

[89] 参见汤玉婷、范福华:"意外被撞逃跑'跑'来有罪指控"，载《检察日报》2007年2月4日。See Tang Yu Ting & Fan Fu Hua. (2007) "'Run' after Being Hit by Accident 'Runs' into Criminal Charge," as cited in *Procuratorate Daily*, 4 February 2007.

(B) The part involves 'result' should draw on the position of the normative judgment of the theory of objective attribution. Only the result of infringement of the legal interest can become the consequence of constitutive elements. Also, even if it is the result of infringement of the legal interest, it must be further judged that whether the result is prohibited by the specific criminal law norms. For example, when the act is determined to be a crime of intentional injury, the victim's medical expenses, such as property damage, should not be considered as the result of the crime of intentional injury. Because property damage is not the result of a specific rule of the crime of intentional injury, there is no need to discuss the result attribution hereof.

(C) The part involves 'causation' should draw on the basic content of the unpermitted danger in the theory of objective attribution. To put it bluntly, the part involves 'causation' in our theory of criminal law should be divided into two steps: the first step is to discuss the causation of facts, and the second step is to discuss the result attribution after affirming the factual causation.

When the factual causation is discussed, the theory of causation discussed in the theory of objective attribution in a broad sense must be referenced. Since the theory of objective attribution is premised on the factual causation, in this respect, theory of criminal law needs further research. In fact, the difficulty of many cases is not the difficulty of normative evaluation, but the difficulty of determining the factual causation before this. Because of this, some of *German Criminal Law* textbooks cover more discussion of factual causation than the objective attribution in a narrow sense.[90]

Zhou's article criticized not only the theory of *Conditio-sine-qua-non-Formel* (Zhou's article, P.228 below), but also the theory of *Conditio-sine-qua-non-Formel* with lawfulness. (Zhou's article, P. 231 below). However, it is no doubt that "when confirming causation, the supporters of theory of attribution and the courts are either using the unimaginable nonexistence formula of the theory of equivalence, or using the theory of *Conditio-sine-qua-non-Formel* with lawfulness",[91] which results from the fact that the normative evaluation in the theory of objective attribution is based on the factual causation. As Professor C.Roxin says, "in the absence of an objective, natural science proof of causation, judges should not take replacement by subjective confirming by a free evidence evaluation method."[92] If neither the theory of *Conditio-sine-qua-non-Formel* nor the theory of *Conditio-sine-qua-non-Formel* with lawfulness is adopted, the theory of objective attribution cannot be objective simply by conducting normative evaluation. The 'law' of the theory of *Conditio-sine-qua-non-Formel* with lawfulness includes not only the laws of science but also the empirical

---

[90] H.Jescheck/T.Weigend,*Lehrbuch des Strafrechts.Allgemeiner Teil*, 5.Aufl.,Duncker & Humblot 1996,S. 272ff.

[91] 德沃尔冈夫·弗里希:"客观的结果归责"，蔡圣伟译，载陈兴良主编:《刑事法评论》(第30卷)，北京大学出版社2012年版，第229~230页。Wolfgang Frisch, trans. Cai Shengwei, (2012) *Objective Result Attribution*, as cited in Chen Xingliang ed. *Criminal Law Review*, No. 30, Peking University Press, 223–224.

[92] C.Roxin,*Strafrecht Allgemeiner Teil, Band I*, 4.Aufl., C.H.Beck,2006,S.356.

laws which are not contradictory to the laws of science,[93] "and it is a direct and concise method of judgment".[94] The causation of epidemiology is not only considered to be an empirical causation, but also considered to be a causation in the natural sciences, rather than a non-conformity of laws, as Zhou said. It is impossible to draw conclusions that whether a certain additive can cause human casualties in the abstract. However, it is entirely possible to draw conclusions through scientific or empirical rules about whether a specific food additive can cause casualties.

In this article, in terms of the part on the factual causation, China's theory of criminal law needs to conduct intensive research on the theory of *Conditio-sine-qua-non-Formel* and the theory of *Conditio-sine-qua-non-Formel* with lawfulness, which are not an opposite relationship. "In fact, the formula of conditional relation, as the dominant ideology, is the same with the formula of conditional relation with lawfulness in conclusion".[95] This is because the conditional relation between act and result is actually premised on the knowledge of causation rules. As mentioned above, in a case that A got a heart attack and died after taking a drug which was still in the experimental stage given by B, it was difficult to determine the conditional relation because there was no knowledge of causation rules in this respect. If the drug is later found to have side effects that could cause heart disease, or if the person taking the drug gets a heart attack in general, it can affirm the conditional relation and the conditional relation with lawfulness.

However, the theory of *Conditio-sine-qua-non-Formel* and the theory of *Conditio-sine-qua-non-Formel* with lawfulness may also lead to different conclusions in certain special cases. On one hand, if the theory of *Conditio-sine-qua-non-Formel* draws a positive conclusion, the theory of *Conditio-sine-qua-non-Formel* with lawfulness may lead to a negative conclusion. For example, "A accidentally hit a tree while driving, the passenger B in the same car broke the left thigh, and he died in the hospital from the sepsis caused by the doctor's negligence. In this case, German courts convict routinely the actor who caused the first result of the crime of negligent homicide".[96] One reason for this is that the theory of *Conditio-sine-qua-non-Formel* has been adopted. If the theory of *Conditio-sine-qua-non-Formel* with lawfulness is adopted, it is not necessarily considered that there is a causation between the act of A and the death of B. On the other hand, if the theory of *Conditio-sine-qua-non-Formel* draws a negative conclusion, the theory of *Conditio-sine-qua-non-Formel* with lawfulness may also lead to a positive conclusion. For example, the defendant A was driving a car on a straight road which was 6-meter-wide, and the B was riding the bicycle in the same direction on the right. According to the

---

[93] When introducing the causation with lawfulness, the author points out that "if the empirical law is not contradictory to the law of science, this empirical law is also included in the 'legal rule'"(张明楷:《刑法学》，法律出版社2011年版，第177页See Zhang Mingkai, (2011) *Criminal Law*, Law Press China, 177.).

[94] 日井田良:《讲义刑法学·总论》，有斐阁2008年版，第121页。Ida Makoto.(2008) *Handout of Criminal Law·General Rules*, Yuhikaku Press, 121.

[95] 日井田良:《讲义刑法学·总论》，有斐阁2008年版，第121页。Ida Makoto.(2008) *Handout of Criminal Law·General Rules*, Yuhikaku Press, 121.

[96] 德骆克信:"客观归责理论"，许玉秀译，载《政大法学评论》1994年第50期。C.Roxin, trans. Xv Yuxiu, (1994) *The theory of objective imputation*, as cited in *Chengchi Law Review*, No. 50.

rules, cars and pedestrians should maintain a distance of 1.5 m, but A only maintains a distance of 0.75 m. However, B was drunk and fell down, but unfortunately he was run over by the rear wheel. According to the theory of *Conditio-sine-qua-non-Formel*, even if A keeps the car at an appropriate distance from B, the probability of the same accident is still high, and B will die. Therefore, there is no causation between the act of A and the death of B. However, according to the theory of *Conditio-sine-qua-non-Formel* with lawfulness, there is causation. For another example, regarding the double causation, if both A and B deliver a lethal dose of poison to the victim's cup without intention liaison. The theory of *Conditio-sine-qua-non-Formel* denied that the acts of the two men and the death of the victim have causation. The theory of *Conditio-sine-qua-non-Formel* with lawfulness holds the view that if the poisons of A and B all play a role in the death of the victim, thus there is causation between the act of the two men and the death of the victim. If it is proved that the victim died because of the poison of A before B used his poison, it can only be confirmed that there is causation between the act of A and the result. If only a poison is found to be effective, but it cannot be proved who put this useful poison, according to the principle of *in dubio pro reo*, it can only be denied that there is a causation between the acts of A and B and the death of the victim. From the conclusions of the above cases, the theory of *Conditio-sine-qua-non-Formel* with lawfulness is superior to the theory of *Conditio-sine-qua-non-Formel.*

On the contrary, in determining the crime of abuse of authority, the crime due to dereliction of duty and other crimes of malfeasance in China's criminal law context, if only the theory of *Conditio-sine-qua-non-Formel* with lawfulness adopted but no involvement of the theory of *Conditio-sine-qua-non-Formel*, it's possible those accusations will never be confirmed. For example, on November 6, 2008, *Notice of the Supreme People's Procuratorate on Issuing the Guiding Opinions on Strengthening the Work of Investigating and Handling the Crime of Malfeasance Which Endangers Land Resources* points out that implementers and supervisors who know that the decision-makers have made wrong decisions and do not raise objections, or do not correct, stop or investigate, thus causing serious damage to the national land resources, should be held responsible for the crime of malfeasance depending on the circumstances." However, in such an occasion, it may be quite difficult to determine that there is a conditional relation with lawfulness between the act of the implementer and the supervisor and the result, but if the theory of *Conditio-sine-qua-non-Formel* is adopted, the factual causation relationship may be affirmed.

Thus it can be seen that the question about whether the theory of *Conditio-sine-qua-non-Formel* and the theory of *Conditio-sine-qua-non-Formel* with lawfulness can be respectively adopted in different occasions and in what occasions need to be in-depth researched based on foreign doctrines.

When the result attribution is discussed, the theory of objective attribution should be learned. That is, after affirming the factual causation, it is necessary to make further normative judgments. In this respect, the specific rules of the theory of objective attribution that belong to the result attribution in a narrow sense are worth learning. Of course, we cannot take Professor C.Roxin's the theory of objective attribution as the whole content of the theory of objective attribution in Germany. Other German scholars' specific views on the theory of objective attribution are also worth learning. At the same time, it is necessary to learn from the theory of *Adäquanz* of Japan and Anglo-American theory of legal causation for reference.[97] The theory of *Adäquanz* and the theory of legal causation is actually the theory of result attribution, which is the normative evaluation after the factual causation. At the same time, as for the discussion of various intervention factors, the theory of *Adäquanz* of Japan and Anglo-American theory of legal causation are more detailed and practical.

From this point of view, we do not need to particularly emphasize the differences between the theory of objective attribution in Germany, the theory of *Adäquanz* of Japan and Anglo-American theory of legal causation, but shall pay attention to their common points. If our theory of criminal law divides the traditional causation into two parts: the causation and the result attribution, it will inevitably absorb the strengths of the above theory, thus perfecting our theory of criminal law.

Fifthly, as mentioned above, the application of the theory of objective attribution in the affirmation of criminal negligent is of great significance. According to Professor C.Roxin, as long as the unpermitted danger is objectively created and realized, the criminal negligent can be affirmed. There is an important difference between this normative theory of negligence and the psychological theory of negligence which is now prevailing in China. The former makes the affirmation of the criminal negligent objective and standardized, and the latter often falls into the difficulty of affirmation which leads to the arbitrariness of judgment. Therefore, the theory of criminal negligent in China about how to learn from the theory of objective attribution has become an important issue that needs to be researched.

References

Amaguchi Atsushi.(2007) *General Rules of Criminal Law*, Yuhikaku Press, 231.

C.Roxin, *Das strafrechtliche Unrecht im Spannungsfeld von Rechtsgüterschutz und individueller Freiheit*, ZStW 116(2004), S.929f, 931f, 935.

C.Roxin, *Strafrecht Allgemeiner Teil,* Band I, 4.Aufl., C.H.Beck, 2006, S.206,343ff,350,356,372,373,377,383f,385,392ff,402f,403ff.

C.Roxin, trans. Xv Yuxiu, (1994) *The theory of objective imputation*, as in Chengchi Law Review, No. 50.

C.Roxin, et al., trans. Xv Yuxiu, (1994) *Symposium on Jurisprudential Questions,* Zheng Mingren, as in Chengchi Law Review, No. 50.

Feng Jun. (2009) *Normative Understanding of Criminal Law Issues*, Peking University Press, 137,137-138.

[97] The Anglo-American theory of criminal law divides causation into factual causation (factual reason) and legal causation (legal reason). In the factual reason, not only the conditional relation is discussed, but also the compound factual reason (including the reason that promotes the result to occur, the sufficient reason that causes the concurrence, the reason that interrupts) is further discussed. The discussion of proximate reason, direct reason and interventing factors in legal reasons is quite specific.(参见美约书亚·德雷斯勒:《美国刑法精解》，王秀梅等译，北京大学出版社2009年版，第164页以下Joshua Dressler, trans. Wang Xiumei, (2009) *Understanding Criminal Law*, Beijing: Peking University Press, 1–164).

H.Jescheck/T.Weigend, *Lehrbuch des Strafrechts. Allgemeiner Teil*, 5.Aufl., Duncker & Humblot 1996, S. 272ff,287f.
Hirano Ryuuichi.(1972) *General Rules of Criminal Law I,* Yuhikaku Press, 199.
Ida Makoto.(2005) *Theories of General Rules of Criminal Law,* seibundoh, 63.
Ida Makoto.(2008) *Handout of Criminal Law·General Rules,* Yuhikaku Press, 1-113,121.
Ingeborg Puppe, trans. Cai Shengwei, (2010) *Kleine Schule des juristischen Denkens*, Angle Publishing Co., Ltd., 135.
Joshua Dressler, trans. Wang Xiumei, (2009) *Understanding Criminal Law*, Beijing: Peking University Press, 1-164,167.
Lin Yu Xiong. (2006) "Causation and Objective Imputation in Cases of Intervention by a Third Party (II)," as in Taiwan Law Journal, No. 80.
Lin Yu Xiong. (2009) *General Provisions of New Criminal Law*, China Renmin University Press, 127.
Machino Saku.(1986) *Patients' Right to Self-Determination and the Law,* University of Tokyo Press, 171.
Machino Saku.(1995) *Handouts of General Theory of Criminal Law (I)*, Shinzansha Publisher Co., 155; Yamaguchi Atsushi.(2007) "The theory of causal relationship", as in Shibahara Kuniji et al, ed.(1998) The modern development of criminal law theory(General Theory I), NIPPON HYORON SHA Co., 43.
Maeda Masahide.(2011) *Handouts of General Rules of Criminal Law,* University of Tokyo Press, 1-178,1-182.
Naitou Ken.(2001) *General Lectures on Criminal Law (Medium)*, Yuhikaku Press, 631.
Naitou Ken.(2007) *Historical Development of Criminal Theory*, Yuhikaku Press, 596.
Nishida Noriyuki.(2010) *General Theory of Criminal Law*, Koubundou Publishers Inc., 101.
Ohya Minoru.(2009) *Lectures on Criminal Law(New Edition)*, Seibundo Publishing Co, 216.
Saeki Hitoshi.(2004) "Causal relationship (2)", as in Hogaku Kyoshitsu, August (No. 287).
Shimada Souichirou.(2003) "Result of the victims' assumption of risk", as in Yamaguchi Atsushi ed. Close-up General Theory of Criminal Law, Seibundo Publishing Co., 141.
Shinoda Kimiho.(1986) "A research on the theory of permissible risk", as in Journal of Criminal Law, Vol. 27, No. 2.
Sone Takehiko.(1998) "A systematic examination of objective attribution theory", as in Okano Mitsuo et al, ed., *A Collection of Congratulatory Essays by Mr. Haruo Nishihara in His Seventies(Vol, 1)*, Seibundo Publishing Co, 71-72.
Sone Takehiko.(1998) *A Study of Criminal Illegality*, Seibundo Publishing Co., 169.
Tang Yu Ting & Fan Fu Hua. (2007) " 'Run' after Being Hit by Accident 'Runs' into Criminal Charge," as in Procuratorate Daily, 4 February 2007.
U. Kindhäuser, Strafrecht Allgemeiner Teil, 5.Aufl., Nomos, 2011, S.9.1,76ff,79,88f,93,94.
Urs Kindhäuser, trans. Fan Wen, (2009) *Objective and Subjective Imputation in Intentional Crimes*, as in Tsinghua Law Review, (Vol.3, No.1), Tsinghua University Press, 156.
Wolfgang Frisch, trans. Cai Shengwei, (2012) *Objective Result Attribution,* as in Chen Xingliang ed. Criminal Law Review, No. 30, Peking University Press, 223-224,227,253,254.
Yamaguchi Atsushi.(2007) *General Rules of Criminal Law*, Yuhikaku Press, 1-49.
Yamanaka Keiichi.(1997) *The Theory of Objective Attribution in Criminal Law*, Seibundo Publishing Co., 1.
Yamanaka Keiichi.(2008) *General Theory of Criminal Law*, Seibundo Publishing Co, 1-248,1-251,250,279.
Zhang Mingkai. (2011) *Criminal Law*, Law Press China, 177.
Zhang Mingkai. (2012) "On the Jurisprudence of the Allowed Danger Doctrine", as in Social Sciences in China, No. 11.
Zhang Mingkai. (2012) "The Jurisprudence of Assumption of Risk in Criminal Law", as in Chinese Journal of Law, No. 5.

Chapter 4
Theory of Wrongdoing from the Perspective of Behavioral Utilitarianism

Although both behavioral utilitarianism and rule utilitarianism are types of utilitarianism, the views on some specific issues and how to deal with them are not exactly the same. This article attempts to apply behavioral utilitarianism to the field of wrongdoing in criminal law, so as to lay a philosophical foundation for *Erfolgsunwert*.

4.1 The Basic Premise

"Finding out wrongdoing and culpability are different materials to build the system of criminal law... they are major achievements of criminal hermeneutics and once being established, there is no way to ignore."[1] In tripartite system in the countries like Germany or Japan, "although the judgment of conformity of criminal constitutive element at the first stage can be distinguished from that of justifiable causes at the second stage, the two stages are all the judgments of wrongdoing. Therefore, the essential judgments to criminal law can be divided into judgment of wrongdoing and of culpability in general situations. The pillars of theoretical system of crime are are the two categories of wrongdoing and culpability."[2] What is discussed in the

*The original title is "Theory of Wrongdoing from the Perspective of Behavioral Utilitarianism", published in ***China Legal Scienc***e, 2011, Vol. 5.

[1] 德许迺曼:"区分不法与罪责的功能"，载许玉秀、陈志辉编:《不移不惑献身法与正义——许迺曼教授刑事法论文选辑》，台北春风和煦学术基金2006年版，第416页。Bernd Schünemann, (2006) *Distinguishing the Illegality and Culpability*, as cited in Chen Zhihui, ed., *Unbestechlich und unbeirrbar im dienst von recht unechtigkeit: abhandlungen zur gesamten strafrechtswissenschaft von BERND SCHUNEMANN*, Taiwan: taedp.org.tw, 416.

[2] 日井田良:《刑法总论の理论构造》，成文堂2005年版，第1页。Ida Makoto.(2005) *Theories of General Rules of Criminal Law*, seibundoh, 1.

M. Zhang, *The Fundamental Issues upon Criminal Law Theories*, Masterpieces of Contemporary Jurisprudents in China,
https://doi.org/10.1007/978-981-95-1276-8_4

theory of wrongdoing is which kind of act is improper and prohibited by criminal law. While what is discussed in the theory of culpability is that if the premise of the actor's implement of illegal acts has met the constitutive element, what conditions are required for punish the illegal acts.

Currently, for the theory of criminal law in most countries, it is almost certain that the criminal culpability, the possibility of cognition of wrongdoing and reasonableness are the elements of culpability (or as cause of preventive culpability from a negative perspective). There is no doubt that objective elements infringing the legal interests such as acts and results are the elements of wrongdoing. The main issue of the debate is how to understand and determine the wrongdoing? Are intention and negligence the elements of culpability or the elements of wrongdoing? Therefore, whether the act that infringes the legal interests objectively without intention or negligence is an unjustifiable act prohibited by the criminal law, and whether the act violating a certain rule that protects the legal interests objectively with intention or negligence is an illegal act in criminal law, become questions to discuss.

Technically speaking, wrongdoing refers to the implementation of acts prohibited by criminal law, which must be evil acts. The question then arises: what are standard to decide the good and evil of acts? The substantial question is, what kind of act should be prohibited by the criminal law? Why is it prohibited? Ethics discusses the standards of good and evil on acts, and the standard for judging acts justified or not, among which the most influential doctrines are behavioral utilitarianism (action utilitarianism) and rule utilitarianism (standard utilitarianism). Roughly speaking, "the action utilitarianism judges right or wrong acts is based on the good or bad effects produced by the act itself; the standard utilitarianism judges right or wrong action is based on the good or bad effects produced by the action following the rule in the same situation."[3] Rule utilitarianism believes that "the right or wrong of a given act depends on whether it complies with effective moral rules; according to the rule utilitarianism, if (generally) universal adherence to these rules will promote rule utilitarians to achieve their highest goals, which is to brings the greatest cumulative consequences to all relevant persons, then these rules can be effective".[4] According to the behavioral utilitarianism, the problem is not which rule has the greatest utility, but which act has the greatest utility; in contrast, according to the rule utilitarianism, "the problem is not which act has the greatest utility, but rather which standard has the greatest utility".[5]

These two theories have been clearly reflected in the criminal law. As is well known, there is a fundamental disagreement in the area of wrongdoing between

---

[3] 澳斯马特、威廉斯:《功利主义:赞成与反对》，牟文武译，中国社会科学出版社1992年版，第9页。Smart, J J C & Williams, Bernard, trans. Mou Wenwu, (1992) *Utilitarianism:For and against*, China Social Sciences Press, 9.

[4] 美汤姆·雷根:《动物权利研究》，李曦译，北京大学出版社2010年版，第211页。Tom Regan, trans. Li Xi, (2010) *The Case for Animal Rights*, Peking University Press, 211.

[5] 美弗兰克纳:《伦理学》，关键译，三联书店1987年版，第81页。William Frankena, trans. Guan Jian, (1987) *Ethics*, SDX Joint Publishing Company, 81.

Erfolgsunwert (results worthless) and dualism. The basic situation of *Erfolgsunwert* emphasizes that the purpose and mission of criminal law is to protect legal interests, and the essence (or basis) of wrongdoing is the infringement of legal interests and the related danger. The acts without the infringement of legal interests are not illegal act, even if it violates social ethical order, or lacks the grounds of social sufficiency and certain rules. The wrongdoing should be investigated objectively, while the subjective elements are not elements for determining wrongdoing, which means, the intention and negligence are not illegal elements, but culpability elements.The object of the evaluation of wrongdoing is the objective facts identified after the fact. Dualism treats both *Erfolgsunwert* and *Handlungsunwert* (behaviors worthless) as grounds of wrongdoing. It should be noted that the view that *Handlungsunwert* refers to the act violates ethics, or the act lacks the social sufficiency has already been sifted out in today's academia. The reason for that is, there were flaws in those statements *per se*, but not because they were diachronically right, yet fell behind of the development of society. Today, the so-called behavioral utilitarianism stated by the most influential dualists means that the act has a feature of normative violation, in which the "normative" refers to the behavioral norms and rules that are not related to ethics and morality, which must be observed to protect the legal interests. The dualism mentioned in this article is basically limited to this. Professor Ida Makoto, a Japanese scholar who adopted this dualism, pointed out that "even the dualism of wrongdoing that is now in place, it must basically stand on the standpoint of utilitarianism, as *Erfolgsunwert*. If there is any difference between the two, it is that *Erfolgsunwert* is behavioral utilitarianism (action utilitarianism). However, the author will be a supporter for rule utilitarianism. That means, it is impossible to make a sound criminal judgment without considering 'what negative effect on society is produced when a certain act is generally permitted' and 'in order to prevent such negative effects, it is proper to show what kind of action rules are observed' (based on such considerations, when the act negatively [strong or weak] is evaluated, the evaluation can only be an evaluation of the behavioral utilitarianism)."[6] Although it is still not certain that Professor Ida Makoto is in terms of the legitimacy of act, or the legitimacy of punishment, it is almost certain that the argument between *Erfolgsunwert* and dualism reflects action utilitarianism and rule utilitarianism in the field of wrongdoing.

Generally, there is no disagreement between *Erfolgsunwert* and dualism on the judgment of wrongdoing, because the act violating the rule is usually an act infringing the legal interests, vice versa. However, in the tripartite system, "it is confusing that the object of study is how to prevent the wrongdoing in the field of wrongdoing. However, we must realize that the conformity of criminal constitutive element is concerned with wrongdoing, all the characteristics that make an act manifest as a violation of a norm protected by criminal law, which is illegal as long as the admissibility provision does not intervene. Thus, the facts that are decisive for

---

[6] 日井田良:《变革の时代における理论刑法学》，庆应义塾大学出版会2007年版，第119页。Ida Makoto.(2007) *Theoretical Criminal Law in the Age of Change*, Keio University Press Inc., 119.

unlawfulness will be distributed between the two evaluative strata of the constitutive element in the construction of the crime and 'wrongdoing'. To some extent, the wrongdoing itself is just a result of conformity of constitutive element and lack of justifiable causes".[7] In other words, in the tripartite system, the constitutive elements are types of wrongdoing, which means that the acts that conform to the constitutive elements are illegal in principle, and there is not active illegal elements besides the constitutive elements. Therefore, what is discussed in the field of wrongdoing is the acts conforming to the constitutive element under what circumstances can prevent wrongdoing. It is certain that in the tripartite system, the acts conforming to the constitutive element are acts that "damage"[8] the legal interests. For example, the general intentional homicide and the justifiable defense causing death, both of which result in death (damaging the lives of others), there is no difference between them in such regard. However, though an act complying with the constitutive element and "damage" the legal interest shall be illegal, in exceptional circumstances, there can be some act being justified and not illegal. Therefore, it is necessary to discuss what act, conforming to the constitutive element and "damage" the legal interest, is justified and not illegal in criminal law (prevent the wrongdoing). For sure, the consideration that an act that meets the constitutive elements and "damage" the legal interest is not illegal is necessarily the result of individual balancing. So what is the principle behind this consideration? What is the standard of consideration? The specific problem is that the reason why the act conforming to the constitutive element prevents the wrongdoing, is that the act conforms to the rules (or the exception rules), or the act protects the superior or at least equal legal interest. According to the view of the dualism, as long as an act conforming to the constitutive element does not conform to the rule, even if it protects superior or at least equal legal interest objectively, wrongdoing of the act will not be prevented.[9] Obviously, *Erfolgsunwert* adopts the position of balancing the legal interests, belonging to the behavioral utilitarianism; dualism is not directly balancing the legal interests, but judging whether the act violates the rules that need to be observed for the protection of legal interests, thus it shall belong to rule utilitarianism.

This article has no intention to discuss what behavioral utilitarianism and rule utilitarianism are and what problems they are with, it will only apply the most basic viewpoints of behavioral utilitarianism and rule utilitarianism in ethics to the field of wrongdoing of criminal law, and examines whether behavioral utilitarianism (*Erfolgsunwert*) or rule utilitarianism (dualism) should be adopted to the field of wrongdoing. There are two notable questions here: which act is justified in criminal

[7] 德冈特·施特拉腾韦特、洛塔尔·库伦:《刑法总论I——犯罪论》，杨萌译，法律出版社2006年版，第81页。Giinter Stratenwerth & Lothar Kuhlen, trans. Yang Meng, (2006) *Strafrecht Allgemeiner Teil I: Die Straftat*, Law Press, 81.

[8] The author didn't use the term "infringe" here because the term "infringe" in Chinese itself contains a negative evaluation. However, legitimate acts such as justifiable defense have damaged the life and body of the illegal infringer, but they cannot be negatively evaluated.

[9] There is no dispute about that an act which fully complies with the rules of criminal law (including exception rules) cannot confirm a crime.

law?[10] And which punishment is justified in criminal law? In other words, the legitimacy of act in criminal law and the legitimacy of certain punishments are not the same problem, although they are usually linked. If the two are both balanced by utilitarianism, the former question discussed is whether the specific act produces the greatest utilitarianism, and thus whether it is justified; while the latter discussed the question of whether the penalty for certain acts produces the greatest utilitarianism, thus whether the penalty is justified. As discussed later, one of the criticisms of behavioral utilitarianism is that it will also argue for punishing justifiable act when the greatest utilitarianism can be gained by punishing it. But it is clear that justifiable act under criminal law should never be punished by criminal law; the consequences of a state punishing justifiable act under criminal law by criminal law would be unthinkable. Therefore, the State can only select the middle part of the unjustifiable acts to be punished. It is for this reason that we can independently discuss what act is justified[11] and what act is unjustified in the sense of criminal law. In this article, we will only discuss from this perspective the question of why an act that meets the constitutive elements may prevent wrongdoing, which is the basis for the prevention of wrongdoing, and arguably the question of why the justifications are justified, without discussing the justification basis for the penalty. In other words, the question discussed in this article is that under what conditions, the infringement of the "behavioral norms" is justified and not illegal. Therefore, the author do wish the audience will not confuse the topics such as benign violations of the law, the rule of law, the rule of norm, and the principle of legality (*nulla poena sine lege*), and so on with the author's aim. To be clearer, the audience shall not have an impression that behavioral utilitarianism is to advocate benign violations of the law, to provoke the opposite directions of rule of law, rule of norm, and the principle of legality, while rule utilitarianism is surely to advocate obeying the law strictly, rule of law, rule of norm, and the principle of *nulla poena sine lege*.

Also, as the author myself am a supporter of *Erfolgsunwert*, the author is in favor of the idea that, applying the behavioral utilitarianism to the field of wrongdoing may lead to a negative evaluation of *Handlungsunwert* supported by the rule utilitarianism. In addition, since ethics is not my research domain, the citations about ethical materials in this article may not be comprehensive, and interpretation of ethical literature is likely to be one-sided.

---

[10]The purpose of criminal law is different from that of ethics. The legitimate act in criminal law may be coincident with the legitimate act in ethics, but it may not be completely the same. The legitimate act referred to in this article is the legitimate act in criminal law, not that in ethics.

[11]Although criminal law is a law that stipulates crimes and penalties, it seems to have nothing to do with legitimate act, but it is not the truth. In the tripartite system, the theory fo wrongdoing actually discusses the legitimate ground.

4.2 The Basic Theory

In criminal law, it is not necessary to introduce ethical concepts to discuss how acts can meet constitutive element, or under what conditions those acts can prevent wrongdoing. However, in the tripartite system, even if the act conforms to the constitutive element, as long as there is justifiable cause (justifications), it becomes a justifiable act in criminal law. The behavioral utilitarianism and rule utilitarianism about justifiability can indeed serve as a theoretical ground for determining the justifiable causes. Therefore, applying the opposing views of behavioral utilitarianism and rule utilitarianism to the field of wrongdoing is conducive to analyzing the pros and cons of *Erfolgsunwert* and dualism. If the reason why the act conforming to the constitutive element prevents wrongdoing is balancing the legal interests based on the behavioral utilitarianism, it is reasonable for *Erfolgsunwert* to understand the nature of the wrongdoing as the infringement of legal interests; If the reason is just that the act obeys the rules protecting the legal interests, then it is justifiable for the dualism to understand the nature of the wrongdoing as a normative violation.

1. Theoretical Position

The status of rule utilitarianism is very embarrassing for lacking an internal and consistent theoretical system. If rule utilitarians emphasize that experiences can proves the violation of certain rules often brings bad results and person must abide by these rules in any case, they will then become deontologists. If rule utilitarians deny themselves to be deontologists and defense the rule through the result of an act, they will then become behavioral utilitarians. The reason for that is, when rules and utilitarian (final results) conflict, rule utilitarianism either violates the rules to pursue good results, or maintains rules to for sake good results. "As David Lyons proposed, assuming that an act beyond the provisions of the standard R produces the best possible effect can prove that the standard R should be amended so that it can cope with this exceptional event, which leads to a new standard formula. That is, 'acting according to the standard R except in the case C'. With such a revision, the 'reasonable' standard utilitarianism is the same as action utilitarianism. J. J. C. Smart believes that it will become reasonable after changing the norms of standard utilitarianism and taking consideration on the consequences. In Smart's view, reasonable standard utilitarianism is not only the same as the principle of action utilitarianism in practice, but it includes one principle in fact: the 'maximum possible interest' of action utilitarianism."[12] This kind of rule utilitarianism contains only one principle, and bears no difference from behavioral utilitarianism.

As everyone knows, there are exceptions to the saying like no hurting others and do keep the promise. For example, justifiable defense may hurt others, and when you can save others' lives, you can break your promises, and so on. "the person can get utility from the exceptions of the moral rules, like no hurting others and keep

[12] 龚群:"论斯马特的行动功利主义"，载《齐鲁学刊》2003年第2期。Gong Qun. (2003) "On Smart's Act Utilitarianism,"as cited in *Qilu Journal,* No. 2.

one's promises. If this is true, then rule consequentialism is forced to approve the rules with exceptions by their own rule selection standard. Similar reasoning will benefit special exceptions in all situations, and in these situations, compliance with certain rules will not have the best consequences. Once all the exception clauses have been added, the rule consequentialism will have all the same implications of behavioral consequentialism, which is a disaster."[13]

The current theory of *Handlungsunwert* is basically in form with dualism, one position of which is "the entities of wrongdoing are first an infringement on or a threat to the legal interests. It should not leave *Erfolgsunwert* in this sense, and only consider the simple *Handlungsunwert*... On the contrary, *Erfolgsunwert* that determines the content of wrongdoing by it, is too rigidly attached to the concept of wrongdoing, it may distort the straightforward understanding of the situation... Therefore, the wrongdoing can be correctly evaluated only when both considering *Erfolgsunwert* and *Handlungsunwert*."[14] Thus, when determining of wrongdoing, whether the act results in good or bad consequence, and whether the act violates the rules (or ethical norms) shall be taken into consideration. This dualism has no obvious connection with rule utilitarianism, and this article chooses not to discuss such position. Another position is whether the act violates the criminal law depends on whether the act violates the rules designed to protect the legal interests. The result of the infringement of legal interest is only an additional factor limiting the scope of the punishment.[15] Generally speaking, the latter position emphasizes the observance and maintenance of rules, and its status is the same as the rule utilitarianism.

Here is a frequently seen ethical example: "During World War II, a Dutchman hid the Jews in his own attic. How should we feel about it? According to the standard utilitarianism's point of view, when the Gestapo (*Geheime Staats Polizei*) went to their home to search for Jews, should they tell the truth (the basis of the judgment is: in general, lying always causes more misfortune than honesty, so person should not lie). However, the standard utilitarian will deal with this matter in accordance with the general principle: 'Lie is not right, unless that lie can save lives of innocent persons'".[16] However, according to the view of behavioral utilitarianism, the cherish of the results and the restrictions and exceptions to the rules has already shifted to the direction of behavioral utilitarianism (*Erfolgsunwert* in the criminal law); additionally, if rule utilitarian insists that lying is violating the rules without exception,

[13] 美布拉德·胡克:"规则后果主义"，载美休·拉福莱特主编:《伦理学理论》，龚祥主译，中国人民大学出版社2008年版，第223页。Brad Hooker, trans. Gongxiang et al., (2008) *Rule Consequentialism*, as cited in Hugh LaFollette ed., *The Blackwell Guide to Ethical Theory*, China Renmin University Press, 233.

[14] 日大塚仁:《刑法概说(总论)》，有斐阁2008年版，第368页。Otsuka Hitoshi.(2008) *Overview of Criminal Law*, Yuhikaku Press, 368.

[15] 参见日井田良:《刑法总论の理论构造》，成文堂2005年版，第15页。Ida Makoto.(2005) *Theories of General Rules of Criminal Law*, seibundoh, 15.

[16] 美唐纳德·帕尔玛:《西方哲学导论》，杨洋、曹洪洋译，上海社会科学院出版社2009年版，第274~275页。Donald Palmer, trans. Yang Yang, Cao Hongxiang, (2009) *An Introduction to Western Philosophy*, Shanghai Academy of Social Sciences Press, 274–275.

then the rule utilitarian becomes a deontologist. In such case, it means that the Dutchman must tell the truth, and the result can only be bad. Thus, even if the act of telling the truth caused the infringement of legal interest, the act of the Dutchman was justified because the Dutch followed the common rule. Obviously, this conclusion is difficult for us to accept.

Take justifiable defense and defense by accident as other examples. "You shall not kill" is obviously a set rule, but exceptions do exist to this rule. When the actor consciously committed act of defence in the face of serious infringement of legal interest and killed the illegal infringer, the rule utilitarianism will say that "killing is not justified, except for proper justifiable defense." At this time, rule utilitarianism will share the same conclusion as behavioral utilitarianism, or to say, the dualism is the same as *Erfolgsunwert* in such case. However, when the actor objectively suffered the serious infringement of legal interest, but the actor intentionally killed the illegal infringer, the dualist did not propose an exception rule, and still let the accidental defender take the culpability of intentional homicide. Hence, the dualist did not consider the results and utility, having evolved into monist *Handlungsunwert*. From this point of view, "although the standard utilitarianism has an intuitive appeal,[17] it is still a compromise between utilitarianism and common sense".[18] Because of this, dualism is basically the unitary *Handlungsunwert* in the result. Because of this, the dualism is not only criticized by *Erfolgsunwert*, but also by the unitary *Handlungsunwert*.

According to the view of behavioral utilitarianism, it is the result of act to define whether it's justifiable. Therefore, when the Gestapo went to the Dutch to search for Jews, the Dutchman's lie was justified because though this lie violated the rules yet it could avoid bad results and prevent wrongdoing. Similarly, in cases of justifiable defense and defense by accident, behavioral utilitarianism can draw conclusions that crimes are not established[19] because the utility of the two are identical. There is no vacillating phenomenon in behavioral utilitarianism. Applying behavioral

[17] The reason why people think that defense by accident is not justified is that: First, they attach importance to the intent of accidental defenders; second, they do not pay attention to the interests of innocent people; third, they attach importance to their intuition. However, on the one hand, this is ignoring the purpose of the legal protection of criminal law, and the moral concept is about the performance of the criminal law concept; on the other hand, "intuition may be the wrong product of historical stereotypes and prejudice"(美唐纳德·帕尔玛:《为什么做个好人很难?》，黄少婷译，上海社会科学出版社2010年版，第170页Donald Palmer, trans. Huang Shaoting, (2010) *Why It's Hard to Be Good?*, Shanghai Academy of Social Sciences Press, 170.)

[18] 美詹姆斯、雷切斯特著，斯图亚特、雷切斯特第5版修订:《道德的理由》，杨宗元译，中国人民大学出版社2009年版，第112页。James Rachels, trans. Yang Zongyuan, (2009) *The Elements of Moral Philosophy* (revised. Stuart Rachels), China Renmin University Press, 112.

[19] Even if *Erfolgsunwert* believes that the defense by accident is an attempted homicide, nor is it because the defense by accident violates the rules, but because the defense by accident has the danger of violation of law.(参见日西田典之:《刑法总论》，弘文堂2010年版，第171、307页以下Nishida Noriyuki.(2010) *General Theory of Criminal Law*, Koubundou Publishers Inc., 171, 1–307).

utilitarianism to the field of wrongdoing in criminal law will make the identification of wrongdoing clearer and prevent the judiciary from reckless judging.

2. Purpose of Criminal Law

Utilitarianism emphasizes the purpose, without which there can be no utilitarianism. The formulation and implementation of the criminal law also has its purpose. This is confirmed by both behavioral utilitarianism and rule utilitarianism. Moreover, both *Erfolgsunwert* and the dualism believe that protecting legal interests is the purpose and task of criminal law.

The purpose and task of criminal law need 'wrongdoing' to be well defined. When the criminal law prohibits certain act A, it has three effects on the average persons: (1) the average persons may not implement the act A, so as not to cause the infringement of legal interests. (2) the average persons can prevent or stop others from implementing the act A, thereby avoiding the infringement of legal interests. (3) the average persons' legal interests corresponding to the acts are protected by promise (the average persons realizes that the state protects its legal interests from certain act A). Obviously, it is directly relevant to the protection of legal interests. However, the dualism will not examine whether the act itself infringes the legal interests, but to investigate whether it infringes the legal interests because of violating a certain rule, or whether it violates the rules for protecting the legal interests. Conversely, the dualism is not to examine whether the act itself directly protects the legal interests, but to examine whether the act protects the legal interests by obeying certain rules, or whether it complies with the rules laid down to protect the legal interests. "The standard utilitarianism insists should also follow the best general guidelines, even knowing that obeying the rules in exceptional circumstances can have bad consequences."[20] That is, when the act complies with the general rules settled for protecting legal interests, even if it objectively infringed the legal interests, it must be allowed; when the act violates the general rules, objectively protecting the legal interests, it must be banned. "In Smart's view, the standard utilitarianism is the 'standard worship'. He criticized the standard utilitarianism, saying that standard utilitarians often defend their principles and always believe they are working for human happiness. But the question is, when he knows that in current situation, it is not the most beneficial to abide by certain standard, why does he still try to promote such a standard?"[21] R.B.Brandt, a rule utilitarian, does not believe that "rule utilitarianism leads to the person's 'standard worship'. In his view, moral rules are not universally applicable and absolutely unchanging; the choice of rules does not rely solely on past experience, but takes into account the current realities of society; it is also established as a flexible choice to address the realities of different social groups, and such a principle cannot be a blind adherence to the common sense of past experience. When solving the problem of conflicts of moral

[20] 牛京辉:《英国功用主义伦理思想研究》，人民出版社2002年版，第202页。Niu Jing Hui. (2002) A Study on British Utilitarian Ethical Thought, People's Publishing House, 202.

[21] 龚群:"论斯马特的行动功利主义"，载《齐鲁学刊》2003年第2期。Gong Qun. (2003) "On Smart's Act Utilitarianism,"as cited in *Qilu Journal,* No. 2.

obligations, Brandt believes that moral principles will require person to make choices flexibly according to the strength of their obligations, and will not require person to perform principles blindly like deontologist, regardless of the actual interests, thus bringing negative effects to the society."[22]

In this regard, this article summarizes the following points:(1) if Brandt's view is applied, which blindly follows the rules that considering the reality of current society and actual interests, and making a flexible choice in the conflict of obligations, it is then no longer rule utilitarianism; (2) from the logical relationship between means and purpose, since the rules are settled to protect legal interests, why do persons are required to follow the rules at the expense of legal interests being infringed on certain occasions? It may be risking big things for the sake of small ones; (3) the dualism ostensibly establishes a rule intermediary between act and result, but in fact it protects the rules as the purpose itself, in conflict with what they claim to protect legal interests as the purpose of criminal law; and (4) from the actual consequences, dualism is also not conducive to the realization of the purpose of criminal law.

Take the defense by accident as another example: A was aiming at B to pull the trigger, at the same time, C fired a shot at A without knowing that, and objectively stopped A to kill B. If, rule utilitarianism in criminal law is applied, or according to the dualism, there can only be two endings: (1) in the case that C "complying" to the rules without shooting, innocent B is killed, and A is condemned by intentional homicide (may be the death penalty); (2) in the case that C "violating" the rule with shooting, innocent B is not killed, a deliberately murdered A is shot, and C is guilty of intentional homicide (may be the death penalty). Investigating these two endings according to the common sense, the author is afraid no one will think that the former is better than the latter. At this point, the dualism clearly sees the general rules as more important than human life. It would rather defend rules than save innocents' life, which is contrary to the purpose of protecting legal interests of.[23] Moreover, the above-mentioned "complying" to the rules and "violating" the rules only stay in the innermost of the actor, or only the inner obedience and infringement of the rules, rather than the observance and infringement of the rules by objective act. For example, when A was aiming at B to pull the trigger, the uninformed C1 deliberately shot the head of A with intent of killing, and the informed C2 shot the heart of A with a sense of defense. The time was exactly the same. According to the dualism's point of view, C1 violated the rules for protecting legal interests, and C2 did not. However, the *actus reus* of C1 and C2 is exactly the same, the *mens rea* will be different.

---

[22] 吴映平:"黑尔之功利主义观述评"，载《武汉理工大学学报》(社会科学版)2008年第2期。Wu Ying Ping. (2008) "*A Review of Hare's View on Utilitarianism,*" as cited in *Journal of Wuhan University of Technology* (Social Science Edition), No. 2.

[23] As mentioned earlier, rule utilitarianism recognizes the exception of homicide: "the killing is not justified, except for proper justifiable defense". This exceptional rule can be transferred to another rule without exception: "We cannot deliberately kill an innocent, this is a non-violable norm"(美詹姆斯、雷切斯特著，斯图亚特、雷切斯特第5版修订:《道德的理由》，杨宗元译，中国人民大学出版社2009年版，第119页James Rachels, trans. Yang Zongyuan, (2009) *The Elements of Moral Philosophy* (revised. Stuart Rachels), China Renmin University Press, 119.)

Finally, C1 was sentenced to penalties only because of his internal infringement of the rules, which caused his act to be improper. This article cannot agree with that conclusion. If we further examine the question of whether the defense by accident can be defended again, the conclusion of the dualism may be even worse. According to the dualism's point of view, the aforementioned defense by accident act of C is unjustified and is an ongoing infringement of legal interest. Therefore, D can implement a justifiable defense and kill C. However, the result of D's act must be: C protecting B's life is being killed by E, and innocent B is killed by A, and A is alive (of course he will be sanctioned by law). It is difficult to believe that the use of dualism supported by rule utilitarianism in criminal law is conducive to protect legal interests.

Being common, or let's say universality, is one of the characteristics of the law. Only in the context of the universality of statute law, the purpose of criminal law can be realized by considering its special situations to the maximum extent because the specific provisions of the criminal law on the constitutive elements may literally contain acts that vary greatly. Both German and *Japanese Criminal Law* scholars believe that murder and the killing under justifiable defense are in line with the constitutive element of homicide. "Criminal law attempts to make itself more flexible in the most significant areas of this situation to suit individual circumstances: the independent jurisdiction of judges on issues related to the implementation of punishment, the consideration of forgivable circumstances and the possibility of pardon, are all means to achieve this."[24] Thus, to achieve the purpose of protecting legal interests of criminal law, we can only follow a principle of "benefit maximization". To follow this principle, it must be flexible in responding to exceptions.

The ethicist Friedrich Paulsen pointed out: "If the fullest and freest development and use of human physical strength and ability is the supreme interest of human life, then... the legal order may provide a means of serving this supreme interest by serving to harmonize the strength of many individuals with the least expenditure of energy, or by balancing the interests of persons with the least harm to many intersecting spheres of interest. The more fully a statute law fulfills this purpose, the closer it comes to achieving the goal of law, or rather the goal that morality demands and expects the law to achieve. But the legal system can never fully achieve this end. The reason for this is the mechanical nature of a mechanical process, that is to say, it acts only in accordance with general laws and not in accordance with the specific requirements of particular cases. The legal system acts in the same way: individual cases are determined by general rules."[25] It is not difficult to find that if rule utilitarianism is applied to criminal law, the practice of individual circumstances is almost determined by general rules, and the ending can only prevent the realization of the

[24] 德弗里德里希·包尔生:《伦理学体系》，何怀宏、廖申白译，中国社会科学出版社1988年版，第544页。Friedrich Paulsen, trans. He Huaihong, Liao Shenbai, (1988) *System der Ethik*, China Social Sciences Press, 544.

[25] 德弗里德里希·包尔生:《伦理学体系》，何怀宏、廖申白译，中国社会科学出版社1988年版，第542页。Friedrich Paulsen, trans. He Huaihong, Liao Shenbai, (1988) *System der Ethik*, China Social Sciences Press, 542.

purpose of criminal law. More importantly, the judgment of justifiable causes is not a typed judgment, but an individual judgment. The nature of this judgment determines that justifiable cause cannot be judged according to the general rules. In other words, the use of rule utilitarianism in the field of wrongdoing actually leads to the conversion of individual judgments of justifiable cause into typed judgments, thus it does not conform to the nature of the judgment of justifiable cause.

"Behavioral utilitarianism advocates a more flexible attitude, and it could set aside general norms for better results."[26] This is because, if the rules of criminal law are formulated to protect legal interests, the rules must be subject to the purpose of protecting legal interest. Such rules are only general rules, but there are always exceptions. So in exceptional circumstances, priority must be given to the protection of legal interests, not rules maintaining themselves. Take the aforementioned defense by accident as an example. When behavioral utilitarianism is applied to criminal law, it would be found that because the shooting of C prevented the killer A from acting and protected the life of innocent B, the act of C is an act of protecting legal interests, and thus it is justifiable. Similarly, D should not carry out justifiable defense against C. (If D knowing that C is in defense by accident killed C, he established the crime of intentional homicide; if D did not know the truth, just thinking that C was simply killing A and murdered C, it was a defense out of imagination).

3. Behavioral Norm

The application of rule utilitarianism to criminal law aims to inform the citizen in advance what act is permitted and what is prohibited, so that the requirement of general precautionary of the criminal law are saturated into the theory of crime. As the Japanese scholar Professor Ida Makoto said: "The diversity of *Handlungsunwert* and *Erfolgsunwert* is neither whether to adopt a stance of moralism, nor whether it tends to draw conclusions from the general terms of 'social equivalence'. The differences between the two are whether or not to recognize the function of 'informing the citizen permissible act beforehand' as the guiding principle of the wrongdoing, and whether to make the theory of *nulla poena sine lege* and the general prevention under the criminal norms into the theory of crime."[27] Because of this, the dualists adore the rules as much as rule utilitarian. The specific manifestation is that as long as the act violates the general rules that need to be observed in order to protect the legal interests, it should be considered illegal even if it does not infringe the legal interests. However, in criminal law, the use of rule utilitarianism is always counterproductive.

Firstly, the rule utilitarianism is too restrictive for citizen's freedom of action. The logic of dualism is that a rule that is often useful for protecting the legal

[26] 牛京辉:《英国功用主义伦理思想研究》，人民出版社2002年版，第202页。Niu Jing Hui. (2002) A Study on British Utilitarian Ethical Thought, People's Publishing House, 202.

[27] 参见日井田良:《变革の时代における理论刑法学》，庆应义塾大学出版会2007年版，第113页。Ida Makoto.(2007) *Theoretical Criminal Law in the Age of Change*, Keio University Press Inc., 113.

interests must be unconditionally applied to any occasion. Therefore, in order to protect human life, murders without justification must be prohibited and illegal. And it is necessary to inform citizens that only murder with justification is allowed.

Moreover, the dualism pursues the utilitarian nature of penalty, thus it prohibits all killing acts without justification. In other words, because prohibition on defense by accident can produce utilitarian penalty (in case of preventing others from killing), it seems to be a must for prohibiting defense by accident. But as mentioned earlier, criminal law can only prohibit improper act. A kill that is prohibited in the criminal law under normal circumstances may become a legitimate act in special situations, as is the case with justifiable defense; a kill that is unjustified under normal circumstances may become a legitimate murder in special situations, as is the case with occasional defense. Dualism hence has obviously made a perversion about cause and results, which believes that as long as a certain act can prevent certain types of act if it is prohibited, then that act must be prohibited. For example, as long as the prohibition of defense by accident is conducive to protecting ones' lives, even if defense by accident protects the others' lives, it is prohibited by criminal law. Moreover, the dualism actually wants to achieve the effect of protecting the legal interests by partially prohibiting the act protecting the legal interests. However, this practice has led to a fact that certain acts that protect the legal interests are also prohibited by the criminal law, which limits the freedom of action of citizens.

More importantly, there is a large number of criminal negligence in criminal law, while criminal negligence often lack the stereotype of act (such as negligent homicide), thus the dualism adopts the new theory of negligence (the theory of baseline act). "The new theory of negligence is not seeking the entities of negligence for the possibility of foreseeability, but for the infringement of the obligation of result evasion. That means, negligence is the result of slacking off the general requirements of social life."[28] In other words, the new theory of negligence will actually violate the rules of daily life (the general negligence) or the administrative law rules (the business negligence) as the standard for the judgment of negligence. However, the "rule of daily life" that deviates from the possibility of foreseeability must be unclear and cozy, meanwhile the business negligence has become an aggravated offense of administrative regulations.[29] In summary, the "violates the rules protecting the legal interests" as claimed in the dualism is not limited to violate the rules of criminal law, but includes violations of daily life rules. This does not limit, but expands the range of punishment for negligent crime.

Also, rules are always lagging behind. "Today's rules are often solutions to yesterday's problems. Events, crises, and arguments often occur before rules change".[30]

---

[28] 日西田典之:《刑法总论》，弘文堂2010年版，第258页。Nishida Noriyuki.(2010) *General Theory of Criminal Law*, Koubundou Publishers Inc., 258.

[29] 日山口厚:《刑法总论》，有斐阁2007年版，第226页。Yamaguchi Atsushi.(2007) *General Rules of Criminal Law*, Yuhikaku Press, 226.

[30] 美詹姆斯·马奇、马丁·舒尔茨、周雪光:《规则的动态演变》，童根兴译，上海人民出版社2005年版，第45~46页。James G March & Martin Schulz & Xueguang Zhou, trans. Tong Genxing, (2005) *The Dynamics of Rules*, Shanghai People's Publishing House, 45–46.

Some state agencies like to make rules, especially the rules that simply restrict citizen's freedom (citizens cannot benefit from the rules). Moreover, after a rule is formulated, even if there is a problem with the rule, it will not be immediately amended and abolished, which is unreasonable. However, if citizens did not abide by the old rules, their acts would be deemed illegal, which inevitably formed the negative effects of restricting the freedom to move of citizens. Similarly, it is inappropriate to deny that the act does prevent wrongdoing for not obeying the old rules.

For example, the former passage of Article 32, Paragraph 1 of the *Forest Law of the People's Republic of China,* "For the harvest of the trees on woodlands, an application shall be made for a harvest permit, and the harvest shall be gathered as required by the harvest permit." While Paragraph 2 of Article 39 stipulates that: "In the case of deforestation, the forestry department of the people's government shall order trees of 5 times the trees removed in the deforestation within the specified period, and impose a fine of not less than 2 times nor more than 5 times the value of the trees so removed." Article 345 of *Chinese Criminal Law* provides the crime of deforestation According to the *Forest Law* and related regulations, even if one cuts the dead trees, the approval of authorities is needed. *Document No. 15 (2003)* issued by the State Forestry Administration clearly stipulates that the harvesting of forest trees destroyed by natural disasters, such as "burning dead wood", without applying for a harvest permit shall be qualified as the crime of illegally felling trees or the crime of deforestation respectively, in accordance with the law.[31] According to this, even the farmers who contracted the forest land, in order to plant trees, did not apply for permits and cut dead trees, he also established the crime of deforestation. But the author can't agree with that. Although deforestation of the dead trees that contracted the forest land in order to plant live trees, is in violation of relevant rules, but it did not damage forest resources, and conversely protected these trees. Even if it is in line with the constitutive element of the crime of deforestation, it should be considered to be justifiable cause.

Someone may argue that this is an unreasonable example to illustrate the problem. The author admits that even rule utilitarians must have a negative attitude toward rules without the utility (such as rules that simply restrict citizens' freedom). The problem is that humans are impossible to have the ability to develop a system of rules that will maximize every interest. Or, there is no guarantee that all rules will benefit the most. Otherwise, there will be no dispute between behavioral utilitarianism and rule utilitarianism.

Secondly, even utilitarians cannot deny that there always are exceptions to rules. On one hand, it is difficult to enumerate all of its exceptions for any rule. For example, it is difficult to clarify how many exceptions to the rules of prohibiting killing persons. If you want to exhaust all the exceptions, then it only can be an abstract rule: "Do not kill, except for legitimate killing". But how to decide whether it is legitimate or not? Obviously, the abstract induction of exceptions does not really

[31] On March 3, 2003, State Forestry Administration published *Response to the Qualitative Determination of the Behavior of Unexplored Forest Harvesting Permits to Log Fired Dead Wood.*

make any sense. Therefore, let alone the rule utilitarians, even the deontologist, did not "give us a system that sets out the specific norms of no conflict, no exceptions that we should act in reality".[32] On the other hand, if an exception is included in the rule, it will result in too many rules or the rules are too specific to be observed. "The rules being more complex for persons, the higher the cost of learning the rules will be. At some point, learning more rules, more complex rules, will pay more than the benefits. Therefore, the rules that have the best consequences for their education and internalization are limited in their quantity and complexity".[33] In addition, the author would like to repeat that "For any rule, person can at least find an exception wherever they are, and when you include all possible exceptions in the rules, you are actually promoting behavioral utilitarianism".[34]

As is well known, the field of wrongdoing in criminal law is actually dealing with exceptions. Generally, the constitutive element is a types of wrongdoing. Acts that conform to the constitutive element are in principle illegal, but in exceptional cases, when the act that meets the constitutive element is justified, the wrongdoing is prevented. Obviously, the field of wrongdoing actually discussed exceptions. Nevertheless, criminal law cannot stipulate all exceptions. So the theory of criminal law of the world recognizes the supra-law justifiable cause. The existence and recognition of supra-law justifiable cause prevent the use of rule utilitarianism in the field of wrongdoing.

Thirdly, "Smart believes that the basis of the rule utilitarians to establish their moral principles is past experience. Therefore, these rules are only 'rough common sense', which only requires person to blindly follow the customary act, but has no practical meaning."[35] In today's society, special and abnormal situations are becoming more and more common, many rules that person have settled in advance are nothing more than "clumsy rules" or "rough guidance of act".

For example, according to the rules, the minimum speed of the outer road of expressway in the Beijing Capital Airport is 60 km per hour; the minimum speed of the middle road is 80 kilometers; and the minimum speed of the inner road is 100 km. Obviously, it cannot be said that such rules are unreasonable. For example, the outside are indeed conducive to smooth traffic for new drivers, but it is impossible for person to follow this rule completely. The author often finds that the vehicles on the outer side are sometimes much faster than the vehicles on the inner side.

---

[32] 美弗兰克纳:《伦理学》，关键译，三联书店1987年版，第53~53页。William Frankena, trans. Guan Jian, (1987) *Ethics*, SDX Joint Publishing Company, 53–53.

[33] 美布拉德·胡克:"规则后果主义"，载美休·拉福莱特主编:《伦理学理论》，龚祥主译，中国人民大学出版社2008年版，第223页。Brad Hooker, trans. Gongxiang et al., (2008) *Rule Consequentialism*, as cited in Hugh LaFollette ed., *The Blackwell Guide to Ethical Theory*, China Renmin University Press, 233.

[34] 美雅克·蒂洛、基思·克拉斯曼:《伦理学与生活》，程立显、刘建等译，世界图书出版公司2008年版，第42页。Jacques Paul Thiroux & Keith W. Krasemann, trans. Chen Liyu, Liu Jian, (2008) *Ethics: Theory and Practice*, World Publishing Corporation, 42.

[35] 吴映平:"黑尔之功利主义观述评"，载《武汉理工大学学报》(社会科学版)2008年第2期。Wu Ying Ping. (2008) "*A Review of Hare's View on Utilitarianism,*" as cited in *Journal of Wuhan University of Technology* (Social Science Edition), No. 2.

The reason is that this kind of regulation of speed is only a rough and general guide to act.

It is true that once the criminal law is enacted, it becomes behavioral norms of citizens, all persons should generally abide by. However, the question is whether the norms provided by the criminal law to citizens are complete and sufficient. For example, citizens learned from the Articles 232 and 233 of *Chinese Criminal Law* that they are not allowed to kill. However, citizens must also know that killing on certain occasions does not violate the criminal law. On what occasions killing does not violate the criminal law is difficult to learn from the provisions of the criminal law. Therefore, the specific content of the criminal law norms that citizens should abide by is not necessarily clear to citizens.

Since the rules are nothing more than "clumsy rules" and "rough guidance of act", it is not possible to judge whether the act is illegal in criminal law based on whether the act violates the rules. According to Smart, "If you use it (shallow rules—note from the author) as the standard of one's act, it will lead persons to blindly worship the rules in some special situations, and make unreasonable judgments on the reality. Thus rule utilitarianism choosing the optimum cannot solve the moral conflicts that occur in all specific situations. It even allows some acts that do not produce good effects to exist, which brings unnecessary disasters to society."[36] In other words, as long as a certain act protects a superior or equal legal interest, even if it violates the clumsy rules, the wrongdoing is prevented.

Fourthly, the conflicts between rules are common. To prevent crimes by making citizens obey the rules will cause them being confused in many cases.

There can be occasion that persons are supposed to do act A according to one rule when facing two or more conflicting obligations or rules, another rule is leading to act B. Under this condition, he is impossible to guarantee both rules to be adhered to at the same time, which becomes a dilemma. If he chooses to do A, he will fall into anxiety because he have not followed the rules contained in B. Also, he can't choose neither A or B since avoiding to do anything may bring a double rule violation.[37] Such is the case in obligations conflict. Certainly, the rule utilitarians will say that in the event of obligations conflict, it is entirely possible to determine a general rule, that is, to perform a major obligation to slack off the minor obligation. The question then is how to determine major obligations and minor obligations? In fact, on this occasion, person does not need to consider the importance of the obligation itself, which does not matter. He only needs to consider performing what kind of obligations will protect the more important legal interest. Hence, even if the moral obligation is fulfilled and the statutory obligation is violated, it is justified to protect the superior interests. This is the argument of the behavioral utilitarianism.

---

[36] 吴映平:"黑尔之功利主义观述评"，载《武汉理工大学学报》(社会科学版)2008年第2期。Wu Ying Ping. (2008) "*A Review of Hare's View on Utilitarianism,*" as cited in *Journal of Wuhan University of Technology* (Social Science Edition), No. 2.

[37] 参见牛京辉:《英国功用主义伦理思想研究》，人民出版社2002年版，第199页。See Niu Jing Hui. (2002) A Study on British Utilitarian Ethical Thought, People's Publishing House, 202.

For example, A and B are twin brothers who are very similar in appearance. When A was hurting X, B was also on the scene, but A's act was not related to B. After the police arrived at the scene, X and witnesses all identified B as the injurer. Therefore, the police brought B to the public security bureau. Y, at the scene, knew that X and witnesses had misidentified and explained the truth to the police, but the police believed the identification of X and the majority, so B was detained. B found Y after escaping from the detention center. Y harbored B, and explained the truth to the police again. The question is when the police go to Y's house to ask B's whereabouts, how should Y answer? Y has only two choices: one is to hand over B to the police; the other is to continue to harbor B. But at this time there are two conflicting rules: the first is "to conceal the whereabouts of B to the police is not justified" or "to harbor suspects is not justified"; the second is "to help the police to detain innocents is not justified". In this case, asking Y to act according to above two rules will push Y at a loss. Rule utilitarianism is likely to deem that the act of Y is found to be the crime of harboring a criminal, for that the former rule should be observed previously. That is hard to be accepted.

"Behavioral consequentialism argues that if and only if the actual (or predictable) good produced by a particular act is at least as great as the good of other acts that the actor is easy to take, the act is morally justified (permitted and necessary)."[38] According to the view of behavioral utilitarianism, when a violation of a rule can bring a larger and wider range of utility, the act is justified (prevent the wrongdoing).

First of all, *Erfolgsunwert* is not without rules. On one hand, in normal circumstances, obeying the rules means protecting the legal interests, so in this case *Erfolgsunwert* must also advocate obeying the rules. But the reason why *Erfolgsunwert* advocates obeying the rules is that the compliance with rules can protect legal interests, rather than just complying with rules per se. On the other hand, *Erfolgsunwert* has a simple, basic rule (to protect legal interests), and implements the rule in a specific situation. Behavioral utilitarianism opposes the use of predetermined "rules" to correct person's act under exceptional circumstances, and emphasizes the particular situation, where protecting legal interests is the basic rules of act. Therefore, in the special situation, there is no need to artificially set the intermediary of "rules" in advance. General rules are neither necessary nor possible for act choices in specific situations. In everyday life, especially facing conflicts, in the sense of being associated with criminal law, persons only need to consider one question: "Can my acts best protect the interests of the law, even though they meet the constitutive elements?" They don't need to consider "although it meets the constitutive element of a crime, does my act comply with the settled rules and is an exception allowed by the rules?" It is not difficult to find that the theory of *Erfolgsunwert* has its unique charm in the face of conflicts, namely, the theory boasts simplicity and flexibility.

---

[38] 美布拉德·胡克:"规则后果主义", 载美休·拉福莱特主编:《伦理学理论》, 龚祥主译, 中国人民大学出版社2008年版, 第219页。Brad Hooker, trans. Gongxiang et al., (2008) *Rule Consequentialism*, as cited in Hugh LaFollette ed., *The Blackwell Guide to Ethical Theory*, China Renmin University Press, 219.

Moreover, "a widespread criticism of behavioral utilitarianism is because, under its principle, when persons are prepared to do something, they must make a calculation of the happiness and pain that produced by this act, and only when the person expect that happiness are more worthwhile than pain, their act can be moral and therefore should be done. However, on one hand, the person don't have so much time to do this calculation before doing each act. On the other hand, due to the complexity of the matter, the calculation beforehand is difficult to be accurate, sometimes even impossible to calculate".[39] Regardless of whether this criticism of traditional utilitarianism is appropriate, there is no such problem in the field of criminal law. Even if this criticism of traditional utilitarianism is appropriate, it is out of that different persons have different understandings of happiness, which makes it difficult to calculate the amount of happiness and pain.[40] However, when applying behavioral utilitarianism to the field of wrongdoing in criminal law, calculating happiness and pain are the problems of balancing the legal interests. On one hand, from the perspective of behavioral norms, if the actor considers his or her act beforehand, then it is only necessary to balance whether the act infringes the legal interest, if the act has infringed the legal interest and whether it protected superior or at least equal legal interests by necessity. This requirement is not excessive because the person can easily balance it. On the other hand, from the perspective of adjudication norms, judges only need to make objective *ex post* judgments, and do not need to consider the calculation of the gains and losses of the legal interests in the actor's heart: if the legal interests are protected objectively, it is justified in criminal law; if the legal interests are infringed objectively, it is not justified in the criminal law (the rest is the question of whether or not there is culpability).

Finally, we also need to distinguish between the effects of the act itself and the effect of advocating or condemning the act itself. The effect of defense by accident itself is to protect legal interests, which must be affirmed. According to the view of behavioral utilitarianism, it is justified in criminal law. As for criminal justice, it is quite another thing to punish defense by accident whether has utility or not. As mentioned above, justifiable acts in criminal law should not be punished, so criminal justice cannot punish defense by accident. But, what the author wants to point out is that, such criminal judgment, that defense by accident is justified, protects the legal interests of accidental defenders, and does not encourage defense by accident or misdirect the actor when someone is intentionally killing. If someone keeps track of his enemies for a long time because of the legality of defense by accident, and

---

[39] 张传有:《伦理学引论》，人民出版社2007年版，第160页。Zhang Chuan You. (2007) *Introduction to Ethics*, People's Publishing House,160.

[40] Jeremy Bentham has used "seven standards in an attempt to create a way to measure happiness and pain. These seven standard are: strength, duration, certainty, approximation, richness, purity and scope of happiness. Müller holds different view towards this. He evaluates happiness by quantity and quality. But Müller fails to prove how the standard of utilitarianism is put forward if happiness is evaluated in this way." (美弗兰克纳:《伦理学》，关键译，三联书店1987年版，第71页William Frankena, trans. Guan Jian, (1987) *Ethics*, SDX Joint Publishing Company, 71.)。

intends to kill the enemy when the enemy is killing, then his act is already a justifiable defense, which is not illegal.

4. The Nature of Wrongdoing

"Rule consequentialism claims that an act is permitted if, and only if, it is permitted by a rule which can reasonably be expected to produce as much good as any other identifiable rule can reasonably be expected to produce."[41] Dualism also argues that wrongdoing refers to the infringement of the norms that should be observed to protect legal interests. Therefore, dualism will draw the conclusion that, when the act conforming to the rules infringes the legal interests, the act is justified and legal; when the act violating the rules protects the legal interests, the act is also improper and illegal.

However, norms and rules of certain conduct do not correspond exactly to the infringement of the legal interest; not all act rules already exist when any act is committed, and those that do exist may be superfluous and unnecessary, and many of the so-called rules are not known. Dualism confuses the general situation with the special situation, and it requires persons to act in accordance with the rules of the general situation in special situations. Nor, in aggregate, is it consistent with the effects sought by the rule utilitarianism that underpin dualism.

An example of the dualist goes as: when X passed through the intersection of the green light signal, X collided with Y, who ignored the red light signal, causing the death of Y. *Erfolgsunwert* believes that the act of X infringed legal interests. Therefore, X's act is illegal, and then it is only a matter of discussing whether X has responsibility. But such views are against common sense. According to the dualism's point of view, although the act of X caused the infringement of legal interests, X does not violate the rules that need to be observed to protect the legal interests. Therefore, X's act is not illegal.[42] Nevertheless, In this case, the author does not agree with the view that X caused the infringement of legal interest, but that Y caused his own death by violating the law. If X was found to have caused the infringement of legal interest in this case, would we say that the owner of the building or the builder caused Y's death when he accidentally hit the building with his car? Moreover, if Y first broke into the crossing, while X stroke Y and caused Y to die, as long as there is a causality between the act of X and the death of Y, X's act is unjustified in criminal law.[43]

As mentioned earlier, rule utilitarianism also admits that there are exceptions to the rules, but they admit that for gaining greater utility. However, rule utilitarianism

---

[41] 美布拉德·胡克:"规则后果主义"，载美休·拉福莱特主编:《伦理学理论》，龚祥主译，中国人民大学出版社2008年版，第219页。Brad Hooker, trans. Gongxiang et al., (2008) *Rule Consequentialism*, as cited in Hugh LaFollette ed., *The Blackwell Guide to Ethical Theory*, China Renmin University Press, 219.

[42] 日井田良:《刑法总论の理论构造》，成文堂2005年版，第3页。Ida Makoto.(2005) *Theories of General Rules of Criminal Law*, seibundoh, 3.

[43] 参见日西田典之:《刑法总论》，弘文堂2010年版，第131~132页。Nishida Noriyuki. (2010) *General Theory of Criminal Law*, Koubundou Publishers Inc., 131–132.

ignores any subtle differences between various acts, thus making these differences become exceptions. For example, rule utilitarianism recognizes that, if one's life is protected by damaging the property of another worth 990,000 Yuan by necessity, there should be an exception to the rule of "no damage of other person's property". However, if one protects his property worth 1,000,000 Yuan by damaging the property of another person worth 990,000 Yuan by necessity, the rule utilitarianism opposes it. For example, Professor Liu Mingxiang pointed out: "The kind of necessity that causes serious damage to others in order to protect one's own interests can hardly be said to be beneficial to society. For example, causing serious disability to another person in order to save one's own life, or destroying another person's property worth 990,000 Yuan in order to save one's own property worth 1,000,000 Yuan. This kind of transfer of danger to others is not in line with our traditional moral values. Even in terms of the overall interests of the society, although it avoids greater losses, it cannot deny but admit that the damage to the legitimate interests of others is still a disaster, and the view that necessity causing such disasters is socially beneficial is naturally unreasonable."[44]

However, this view needs further discussion. Firstly, this view is questionable in terms of perspective. If one takes an individualistic view, one should not pass on the distress one faces to others; but from the standpoint of society as a whole, when one of the two legitimate interests has to be lost, it is ideal to preserve the higher value interest, regardless of whose interest it is, and it is on the basis of consideration of the interests of society as a whole that necessity is permissible under criminal law.[45] Therefore, it is fully established that necessity is beneficial to society. Secondly, the above-mentioned view that the necessity may be harmful to society and the examples it cites are clearly judged only from a subjective point of view, ignoring the nature and results of the objective act. According to its logic, it is harmful for A to damage B's interest worth 990,000 Yuan for his own interest worth 1,000,000 Yuan and for A to maim B in order to preserve his own life; it is beneficial for A to damage C's interest worth 990,000 Yuan for B's (including the state and the collective) interest worth 1,000,000 Yuan and for A to maim C in order to preserve B's life. However, the necessity of A and C are objectively identical. Except their respective motives and purposes, the former is for themselves, the latter for others. According to the provisions of the criminal law, the necessity for their own or for others are both legal. Why is there a difference between the nature of acts of A and C (harmful and beneficial)? This is hard to be accepted. The reason is nothing more than bringing the moral evaluation into the field of criminal law. Morality pays attention to the inner heart of the person. Therefore, any necessity that damages others' interests for their own interests will be regarded as selfish, which violates social ethical order and is harmful to society. From this point of view, it is questionable to evaluate

---

[44] 刘明祥:"论紧急避险的性质", 载《法学研究》1997年第4期。Liu Ming Xiang. (1997) "On the Nature of the Necessity Defense," as cited in *Chinese Journal of Law*, No. 4.

[45] 参见日平野龙一:《刑法总论II》, 有斐阁1975年版, 第229页。See Hirano Ryuuichi. (1975) *General Theory of Criminal Law II*, Yuhikaku Press, 229.

whether the act is beneficial or harmful based solely on the subjective motivation and purpose of the actor.

Only when there are conflicts, the necessity to determine whether there is justifiable cause is required. Rule utilitarianism always requires person to act in accordance with predetermined rules when facing conflicts. "It is true that legal procedures can be used to seek change in a democratic society; but this is not enough to explain that the use of illegal means is wrong. With legal methods existing, but the prospects of using them to effect change in the foreseeable future are still likely to be bleak. When the person make slow and painful progress through legitimate channels (perhaps without progress), the unreasonable mistakes that are trying to stop themselves may still continue."[46] Therefore, when it is difficult for a citizen to protect a superior legal interest by obeying the rules, even if the protection of superior or equal legal interest violates certain rules, it should be considered as justifiable cause.

For example, a factory built near a village which exhausted smoke made the visibility extremely low extremely polluted the environment. Being unable to see things clearly, passing vehicles could only drive slowly, and the lives of the villagers were obviously threatened. The villagers repeatedly reported to the higher authorities that they requested to close the factory. But the superior did not agree with the request, nor did they require the factory to rectify. As a result, the villagers organized to not allow vehicles to enter the factory through the only necessary road, which caused the factory to halt production. Normally, villagers should continue to use legal procedures to seek solutions to problems, but we cannot believe that the act of the villagers is illegal. Even if the act of the villagers caused the loss of the factory and met the constitutive element of a crime, the act protected the superior legal interests and prevented culpability.

As mentioned above, in the field of wrongdoing in criminal law, what is discussed is the justifiable cause, such as the justifiable defense, necessity, which embodies the behavioral utilitarianism in criminal legislation. The reason why admit that justifiable defense and necessity are justifications is because the act is utility in terms of results. Moreover, this kind of utility should not be abstract, but must be specific.

With regard to the limits of necessity, the general theory of criminal law in China believes that when the damage caused by necessity is less than the damage avoided, it does not exceed the necessary limit; as long as the damage caused by the necessity is equal to the damage avoided, it exceeds the necessary limits. According to this, in order to protect certain interests, the actor, who infringes the same interests of others and exceeds the necessary limits by necessity, should be investigated for criminal culpability. One of the reasons for this is that the necessity is mostly about protecting one's own interests in practice at the expense of others of equal value by necessity, and this subjective selfishness (a violation of ethical norms) becomes the basic justification for holding them criminally responsible. However, from the standpoint

[46]美彼德·辛格:《实践伦理学》，刘莘译，东方出版社2005年版，第294页。Peter Singer, trans. Liu Xin, (2005) *Practical ethics*, People's Oriental Publishing & Media Co., Ltd., 294.

of behavioral utilitarianism: Firstly, nor is it necessarily more than necessary to impair an equivalent interest in a case of last resort. That is, if the only way to protect interest A is to harm interest B, in a situation where interest A is equal to interest B, then at best, the necessity can be considered meaningless. This is because the system of necessity is not designed to protect an ethic of mutual care, but rather "a system that prevents the diminution of the interests of society as a whole from the point of utilitarian".[47] In the above case, however, the legal interest is not harmed in terms of society as a whole. This being the case, it cannot be considered a crime. *Handlungsunwert* usually holds that it is not appropriate to sacrifice other person's property worth 1,000,000 Yuan in order to preserve one's own equal property. But this is only an ethical inappropriateness, not a criminal inappropriateness. When legal interest A conflicts with legal interest B, the only effective way to protect the interest A is to damage the interest B. As a whole, the act of necessity actually does not cause new damage. Even if the actor sacrifices the same interests of others for his own interest, it is only culpability in moral and civil law, and he cannot be held criminally culpable. Secondly, when the damage caused by necessity is less than the damage avoided, it may exceed the necessary limit. For example, in the event of a forest fire, in order to prevent the spread of fire, it is necessary to cut trees to form a separation belt. If a 20-meter-wide isolation belt is enough according to the objective situation at the time, the actor ordered a large number of felled trees to form a 50-meter-wide isolation belt. Although the area of forest protected is much larger than the area of forest that has been felled, it cannot be considered that it does not exceed the necessary limit. It is not difficult to see that only by balancing specific legal interests, will it be beneficial to protect the legal interests.

Next, it is necessary to respond to the criticism from those who oppose in perspective of criminal law.

Germain Grisez once said: "Good faith shall not be used for comparison unless there is a standard that can be applied to all good. Nor can they be commensurate unless all good is called 'good' in exactly the same sense, which can be applied to all good. The author denies that the word 'good' in the choice of ethical judgment can have a single meaning, where it means anything that can be measured by the same common standard."[48] According to this view, human's good is incomparable and incommensurable; correspondingly, human's evil is also incomparable and incommensurable. In the sense of criminal law, this critique is completely appropriate for another dualism that advocates that "only the infringement of legal interests violating social ethical norms are illegal."[49] Because when an act infringes the legal

---

[47] 日西田典之:《刑法总论》，弘文堂2010年版，第142页。Nishida Noriyuki.(2010) *General Theory of Criminal Law*, Koubundou Publishers Inc., 142.

[48] 转引自林庆华:"天主教新自然法学派论结果主义伦理学"，载《宗教学研究》2008年第2期。As cited in Lin Qing Hua. (2008) "The Catholic Neo-Natural Law School on Consequentialist Ethics", as cited in *Religious Studies*, No. 2.

[49] 周光权:"违法性判断的基准与行为无价值论"，载《中国社会科学》2008年第4期。Zhou Guang Quan. (2008) "On the Criterion for Judgment of Wrongfulness and the Act Wrongfulness Doctrine", as cited in *Social Sciences in China*, No. 4.

interests but conforms to the so-called ethics, or the contrary, it is difficult for the dualist to draw conclusions through comparison. On the contrary, according to *Erfolgsunwert*, there is a single standard, that is the infringement of legal interests and the balancing of legal interests.

"In Grisez's view, in the context of conflicts, the 'greater evil' is not necessarily the only substitute for 'lesser evil', so the basic principles of consequencialism are not self-evident. Joseph J.Boyle and William E.May similarly argued that the basic consequentialist principle that 'the greater good should be chosen and the lesser evil should be chosen' is not self-evident... One cannot reasonably assess and measure good and evil because he or she will encounter questions such as those about what the measure is, how to decide on the consequences and how many and to whom, which are difficult to resolve... If a woman is considering having an abortion, then if she follows consequentialism she will list separately the good and bad consequences of the decision to go for an abortion or the decision not to have an abortion. One of the bad consequences is that the woman may deliberately choose to kill her own unborn child. The expected good result may be that she may maintain her physical and mental health, gain peace, harmony and wholeness in her family, and so on. And the human good of life, family, and peace is an incomparable value. The woman is obviously not sure which is the greater or lesser evil: the killing of her unborn child, the loss of her health, etc."[50] The criticism may be ethically appropriate, but as mentioned earlier, this criticism is not right for the view of behavioral utilitarianism in the field of criminal law. This is because only when there is a conflict between legal interests, it is allowed to sacrifice one legal interest to protect another in criminal law settings. In other words, in criminal law, the only way to protect superior legal interest is to sacrifice another minor or equal legal interest, where necessity is permitted. Therefore, it can be considered that the basic principle of behavioral utilitarianism in criminal law is self-evident.

5. The Principle of Culpability

An important feature in Ethics is to consider the actor's subjective content (motivation) to judge whether the act is justified or not. The same is true of rule utilitarianism. Rule utilitarianism or dualism treat intention and negligence as the standard for judging whether the act itself is justified or not. The first reason put forward by *German Criminal Law* scholars is: "The significance of intention is that it contains a decision against a legally protected interest that is lacking in criminal negligence, so that this makes its classification as an element of wrongdoing significant, since, if the actor is aware of the legal interest that is included and deliberately infringes it, it is clearly a more serious infringement of the norms protected by criminal law than an act that negligently harms the legal interest. Intention is therefore one of the elements of the act threatened by the penalty, and these elements determine the degree

[50] 林庆华:"天主教新自然法学派论结果主义伦理学"，载《宗教学研究》2008年第2期。Lin Qing Hua. (2008) "The Catholic Neo-Natural Law School on Consequentialist Ethics", as cited in *Religious Studies*, No. 2.

of wrongdoing, i.e. intent is an integral part of wrongdoing."[51] In fact, there is no serious infringement of the criminal law norms. The homicide and theft are not different from the infringement of the norm. It cannot be said that the homicide violates all the norms (100%) or completely violates the norms, while the theft only violates the specific norm (60%) or partly (60%) violates the norms. Similarly, criminal intent and criminal negligence have the same degree of infringement of the norm. It cannot be said that criminal intent violate the norms completely (100%), and criminal negligence violate the norms partly (60%). Different degree of wrongdoing doesn't refer to the different degree of violating the norm, but the different degree of substantive wrongdoing, that is, different infringement of legal interests, or to say the different degree of the same infringement of legal interest. It is precisely out of that the intent killing one person is the same as negligent killing from the point of legal interests and the degree of infringement, that intention and negligence are not an element of wrongdoing but an element of culpability.

One of the criticisms of behavioral utilitarianism is to use good or evil of the result as the ultimate standard, without considering ethical standards. "The best-effective act is not always the right act, and the right act which is morally commendable may not always be the best-effective act. In many cases, we also need to take into account a number of other elements such as the motive for the act. Let us say that an assassin murders a president who is respected and supported by the persons. But the bullet misses and hits a rocky outcrop, resulting in the discovery of a huge oil field that has since enriched the persons of the area. The assassin's act is effective, but the motive is questionable. We do not think that an assassination becomes the right act because it works well. Another example is a doctor who volunteers to go to Africa to help the persons in a poor village, but inadvertently brings a disease to the local population. His act is ineffective, but we do not consider his act to be immoral because his motives is good"[52] In this article, even if it is believed that in ethics, "from the internal point of view, the most moral act is the act driven by the impartial and unmotivated motives".[53] The failure to consider the content of motivation is an ethical flaw in behavioral utilitarianism, a flaw that is also absent in criminal law.

In the case of the above oil field, the discovery of oil field is a good result; the specific threat to the president's life is a bad result. However, these two results are not based on conflicts. It is not the only way to assassinate the president to discover the oil field, nor is it as long as the oil field is found to inevitably assassinate the president. Therefore, the discovery of oil field cannot be justifiable cause, and the

---

[51] 德冈特·施特拉腾韦特、洛塔尔·库伦:《刑法总论I——犯罪论》，杨萌译，法律出版社2006年版，第108页。Giinter Stratenwerth & Lothar Kuhlen, trans. Yang Meng, (2006) *Strafrecht Allgemeiner Teil I: Die Straftat*, Law Press, 108.

[52] 陈真:《当代西方规范伦理学》，南京师范大学出版社2006年版，第70页。Chen Zheng. (2006) *Contemporary Western Normative Ethics*, Nanjing Normal University Press, 70.

[53] 美R.尼布尔:《道德的人与不道德的社会》，蒋庆等译，贵州人民出版社2009年第2版，第152页。Reinhold Niebuhr, trans. Jiang Qing, (2009) *Moral Men and Immoral Society*, Guizhou People's Publishing House, No.2, 152.

assassin still has to take the culpability of attempted homicide. Hence, the rule utilitarians did not consider the specific threat to the president's life; while it can also be argued that the ethical comparison of good and evil is not standardized, thus it is quite different from balancing the legal interests in criminal law.

As far as the doctor is concerned, it is of course legitimate for the doctor to volunteer to help poor villagers in Africa; however, it is not legitimate for him to bring the diseases to local residents whether he has intent or not. There is no conflict between the two. It is true that if he does not go to Africa, he will not bring the diseases to Africa. However, going to Africa does not mean bringing the diseases to Africa. Therefore, it cannot be justified that the doctor's motivation is good to bring the diseases to African residents. The reason why rule utilitarianism does not think that doctor's act is immoral is that there is no distinction between whether the act itself is justified and whether it should be condemned.

In fact, it is human nature to distinguish whether the act itself is justified (illegal) and whether it should be condemned (culpability). Even children can grasp this. A 3-year-old child broke the bowl on the ground, when his parents asked "What happened", all the children in such situation almost always said "I didn't mean it" or "I was careless". At this time, children will never argue that it is correct and proper to break the bowl on the ground. They are just to justify that they have no responsibility or no intent, and hope that parents will not condemn themselves. A 13-year-old boy used computer after school, when his parents blamed "Why didn't you finish your homework", his answer may be "No homework today", "I have done my homework", "I am checking the information on the computer" or "What's wrong with using the computer?" Obviously, he is justifying his acts. Therefore, the author is in favor (criminal law scholars should agree as well) of the act utilitarian Smart, who distinguished whether the act is correct between whether the act is rational, and whether the act is correct between whether the actor is a good person. He said: "let us use the word 'rational' to praise the act that is not only optional for the actor but also causing the best effect probably; let us use the word 'correct' to praise the act that produces the best results actually. That is to say, rational act is to try to take correct acts and produce the best results... In this way, we can say, for example, that this actor has taken the correct act, but the way of act is irrational... We can also say that the way he acts is rational, but he does something wrong because of bad luck, because there are the most sufficient reasons to explain what he might have done just happened." He also said: "We do need a term that sympathizes with actors and motivations. I suggest using the words 'good' and 'bad' to satisfy this requirement. A good actor is a person who is closer to the general best way of action than the average persons. A bad actor is a person who does not act in the best way as the average persons... In special situations, a good person may do something wrong, a bad person may do the right thing. A correct act may come from a bad motive, and a wrong act may come from a good motive. Many of the special arguments against utilitarianism are due to the confusion of these differences."[54] Similarly, dualism does not actually distinguish between the legitimacy of the act itself and the good of the actor, resulting in a mixture of wrongdoing and culpability.

Friedrich Paulsen pointed out: "under certain circumstances, it may be ethical for a person to do something that is not legally permissible. It is legally wrong for a person to dispose of an object entrusted to him at the expense of the owner of the object, and this is punishable as an act of breach of trust. But it can be morally right; if the only way he can save himself and others from a great misfortune is to misappropriate the thing entrusted to his care, he may be able to do so without being reproached by his conscience. He may be guilty and punishable before the law, but he is innocent before the court of conscience and morality."[55] He also cited provisions of necessity, which is the prevention of culpability in *German Criminal Law*, to show that the law itself would recognize the above situation, and that this is the contradiction of the law in dealing with real life matters, which is intended to avoid conflicts with the ideal of justice. In fact, this is the secret of the criminal law to clearly distinguish between wrongdoing and culpability, and it is also the key to distinguish criminal law from ethics.

6. The Concept of Justice

Rule utilitarianism has a distinct advantage in that it avoids unjust utility by settling rules that are consistent with justice. However, this does not mean that behavioral utilitarianism necessarily leads to injustice.

Mc Cloakey asked us to consider the following case. "Suppose a Utilitarian visits an area where there is racial conflict and during his visit a black man rapes a white woman, the result of this crime is that there will be a race riot and a white mob, with the connivance of the police, beats and kills the black man in anger. The following is even more hypothetical: the utilitarian happens to be present at the time of the crime, so his testimony may declare a particular black person guilty. If he knows that arresting the suspect as soon as possible will stop the riots and stop the lynching of blacks, as a utilitarian he will no doubt conclude that it is his duty to tolerate the bearing of false witness and the punishment of an innocent man." But "it is again wrong to cause an innocent man to be sentenced to death. And again, utilitarianism entails that this is right; therefore, utilitarianism must be incorrect".[56] In summary, behavioral utilitarianism will conflict with the idea of justice. Conversely, rule

54 澳斯马特:"功利主义:赞成与反对"，载万俊人主编:《20世纪西方伦理学经典》(I)，中国人民大学出版社2004年版，第319~320页。*Century Western Ethics (I): Foundations of Ethics—Principles and Theories*, China Renmin University Press, 319–320.

55 德弗里德里希·包尔生:《伦理学体系》，何怀宏、廖申白译，中国社会科学出版社1988年版，第544~545页。Friedrich Paulsen, trans. He Huaihong, Liao Shenbai, (1988) *System der Ethik*, China Social Sciences Press, 544–545.

56 美詹姆斯、雷切斯特著，斯图亚特、雷切斯特第5版修订:《道德的理由》，杨宗元译，中国人民大学出版社2009年版，第104~105页。James Rachels, trans. Yang Zongyuan, (2009) *The Elements of Moral Philosophy* (revised. Stuart Rachels), China Renmin University Press, 104–105.

utilitarianism avoids this defect: it is better for society to observe a norm such as "do not tolerate false testimony against the innocent". "Thus, the norm against imputing guilt to the innocent should be accepted, and by appealing to it we conclude that in Mc Cloakey's case the man should not have given false testimony against the innocent."[57] This can avoid the above phenomenon that does not conform to the concept of justice.

Smart pointed out: "No matter how reluctant are the behavioral utilitarianism to accept the conclusion, they must admit that when they are in this situation, they would draw unjust conclusions." "If the theory of ethic is utility, it sometimes has to accept injustice, and those who are receiving orthodox in fact dislike this possibility."[58] It is believed that Smart came to this conclusion as a necessary logical consequence of his adherence to theory of effectiveness. Based on the view of the utilitarian, as long as an action works better than other alternative actions, whether just or unjust, it is a good act.[59]

However, 1) although in Smart's point of view, ethically unjust conclusions must be drawn, it is impossible to draw such unjust conclusions in criminal law. Because the criminal law adopts the principle of '*Nulla poena sine lege*' and criminal procedures applies the principle of 'presumption of innocence', it is impossible to convict someone by false charge or frame-up, or perjury. Moreover, the principles mentioned above are not denials of behavioral utilitarianism. On the contrary, they are required by behavioral utilitarianism. Criminal law, which is based on the principle of utility, is impossible to express or imply that, in extreme cases, penalties are imposed on innocents to achieve greater utility. This is because if the criminal law makes such an endorsement, then in such extreme cases it is not possible to achieve what it intends to achieve. Take a case filed by the opponent as an example. If the criminal law allows for the punishment of innocent person in extreme circumstances, then the person may suspect that the person who was declared a criminal is a scapegoat (fall guy) for the government. Justice is still not fulfilled. And not only atrocities and riots will not stop (unless the mobs only take the opportunity to revenge the aliens, regardless of the true criminal), but also the authority of the criminal law is bound to be reduced. Not only that, but in other cases it is doubtful whether the criminal law, by declaring an act to be a crime and imposing a penalty, really makes persons feel that justice has been done and that they are no longer threatened by the criminals. There is every reason to suspect that those in power are using criminal law to deceive them, and potential criminals seem to prefer to defy the deterrent effect of criminal law because they too may feel that even if they

[57] 美詹姆斯、雷切斯特著，斯图亚特、雷切斯特第5版修订:《道德的理由》，杨宗元译，中国人民大学出版社2009年版，第112页。James Rachels, trans. Yang Zongyuan, (2009) *The Elements of Moral Philosophy* (revised. Stuart Rachels), China Renmin University Press, 112.

[58] 澳斯马特、威廉斯:《功利主义:赞成与反对》，牟文武译，中国社会科学出版社1992年版，第68~69页。Smart, J J C & Williams, Bernard, trans. Mou Wenwu, (1992) *Utilitarianism:For and against*, China Social Sciences Press, 68–69.

[59] 参见龚群:"论斯马特的行动功利主义"，载《齐鲁学刊》2003年第2期。See Gong Qun. (2003) "On Smart's Act Utilitarianism,"as cited in *Qilu Journal,* No. 2.

commit a crime they may have some unlucky scapegoat to take the blame for them. On the other hand, good persons will worry that they will become scapegoats one day. Obviously, if the criminal law wants to achieve its prescriptive goal of utilitarianism, it must stipulate that it can only punish a person who is proved guilty, which is embodied in the principle of '*Nulla poena sine lege*' or 'a presumption of innocence'. Therefore, in the field of criminal law, the result of behavioral utilitarianism hoped can only be achieved under the premise of these principles. At this point, there is no difference between behavioral utilitarianism and rule utilitarianism.

2) "As in the case of such hypothesis, it is better to observe the rule of non-perjury, given that unobtainable knowledge is usually presupposed, so that the witness cannot be sure whether perjury will result in a conviction or perjury will go undetected. When one takes into account the inevitable uncertainty, the result is that utilitarianism in fact recommends against perjury."[60] So it is difficult to draw the critics' conclusions.

3) It cannot be concluded that the result of penalizing innocent persons by making false testimony is good. "In the case described by Mc Closkey, if the utilitarian tried to convict an innocent person in order to stop the riots, he may not succeed and his lie may be exposed, causing the situation even worse than before. Even if he lies successfully and the real criminal is not arrested, so that the real criminal may commit more crimes. If this criminal group is later arrested (which is always possible), this lie may cause more trouble and person's trust in the criminal justice system will be undermined. The moral here is that while one may think that the best result will come through such act, one cannot be sure of this. In fact, experience tells us the opposite: the utility can not be gained by framing innocent persons."[61] Therefore, the act of perjury for stopping the riots does not lead to greater utility, and thus fails to eliminate wrongdoing. Perhaps the opponents will insist that nobody's leak will hardly give birth to worse results. But how do opponents know such a fact?

4) The case envisaged above is almost impossible to become a reality. Even if such a case occurs in modern society, there are many ways to prevent, stop, and calm the riots. Punishing innocence is not the only way. Therefore, we cannot believe that behavioral utilitarianism will violate the concept of justice. If the act violating a certain concept of justice and basic principles is the only way to protect greater legal interests, we can only doubt this kind of justice concept and basic principles. For example, the prohibition of torture is considered a basic principle without any exceptions. Is it true? On September 27, 2002, the suspect G kidnapped a banker's 11-year-old son and attempted to claim EUR 1,000,000. According to the plan of the German police in Frankfurt, the suspect was arrested when he received

[60] 美丹尼尔·豪斯曼、迈克尔·麦克弗森:《经济分析、道德哲学与公共政策》，纪如曼、高红艳译，上海译文出版社2008年版，第136页。Daniel Hausman & Michael McPherson, trans. Ji Ruman, Gao Hongyan, (2008) *Economic Analysis, Moral Philosophy, and Public Policy*, Shanghai Translation Publishing House,136.

[61] 美詹姆斯、雷切斯特著，斯图亚特、雷切斯特第5版修订:《道德的理由》，杨宗元译，中国人民大学出版社2009年版，第110页。James Rachels, trans. Yang Zongyuan, (2009) *The Elements of Moral Philosophy* (revised. Stuart Rachels), China Renmin University Press, 110.

the ransom before September 30. However, in the next interrogation, the suspect repeatedly refused to disclose the location of the victim's detention. Although the police have taken many measures, they still cannot find the victims. The next day, considering that the victim may be at great risk of life due to lack of necessary water and food, Daschner, a Frankfurt police chief, ordered that information about the victim's hiding place be extracted by intimidating the suspect and even inflicting physical pain on him if necessary, under the supervision of a doctor. Under the intimidation of the police to impose corporal punishment, the suspect finally explained the location of the victim's hiding place and the fact that the victim had been killed by him on the evening of September 27. The German court found that the act of Daschner constituted crime of coercion and did not recognize that the justifiable cause existed. The basic reason for this is that "it is not allowed to use torture even to protect the life and dignity of the victim". However, "this position shows the indifference of life that makes it somewhat untenable".[62] In fact, according to a survey by the German media, 63% German citizens believed that the act of the police in this case should be legal or at least not subject to criminal penalties. It is difficult to believe that 63% German citizens lacked the concept of justice. It may be said that "it is not allowed to use torture even to protect the life and dignity of the victim" is a judgment that violates the sense of justice. According to the view of behavioral utilitarianism, the infliction of pain on the body of the criminal, even by the police, which is necessary to protect the life of the victim, has a justifiable cause because it protects a more superior interest.[63] It is true that persons may worry that, "From the perspective of realistic consequences, it can be argued that once the rescue of torture is legalized exceptionally, it is difficult to divide a defined boundary in practice and avoid the risk of abuse by state agencies. It may make the torture quickly expand to the point where it is 'difficult to be tolerated by the rule of law': 'when torture begins, it will not stop again'".[64] However, since it is only an exception, it is impossible to generalize, and make boundaries unclear. To take a step back, if it is considered that the legalization of the rescue of torture will bring more serious and bad results, it should be banned. This is also the conclusion of behavioral utilitarianism.

One of the biggest criticisms on behavioral utilitarianism is: "It can recognize very unequal distribution of good and evil. Since the goal set in this theory is accumulative and to require our acts to bring the greatest balance of good and evil to all concerned. Therefore, critics believe that in this case: some individuals will be required to bear unequal evil, so that others can collectively get the most good. The

[62] 英朱利安·巴吉尼:《一头想要被吃掉的猪》，张容南、杨志华译，上海三联书店2008年版，第50页。Julian Baggini,trans. Zhang Rongnan, Yang Zhihua, (2008) *The Pig That Wants to Be Eaten*, READWAY, 50.

[63] It is another matter as to whether the act of torture against the actor is a justifiable defense, or a necessity, or other legitimate grounds.

[64] 王钢:"出于营救目的的酷刑与正当防卫"，载《清华法学》2010年第2期。Wang Gang. (2010) "Torture for Lifesaving and Justifiable Defense", as cited in *Tsinghua University Law Journal*, No.2.

hedonism utilitarianism and preference utilitarianism all face the challenge of whether murder is moral, which which can be deemed as a rebuttal. When an individual is killed, the result is the best overall accumulation result. The survivors got the benefit and the victim lost everything. This situation will certainly shock us, which is too unfair; however, if the consequences including the side effect are the best, then the act utilitarian... will certainly admit that this situation will not lead to moral complaints."[65] For example, "Sam is a basically normal, hard-to-describe but 'very good' person. He went to the hospital to visit his aunt in illness who was his only still alive relative. When he went to the hospital, there were just five urgent patients in the hospital, who required transplantation of the liver, spleen, lungs, heart and pineal gland respectively. These five patients are extremely important and well-loved person, and their death will bring great grief and real physical discomfort to many persons. On the other hand, Sam's death will not make anyone feel sad (except for his aunt, who may feel sad for his death when she is conscious). The senior management staffs in hospital are uncompromising utilitarians. They lured Sam into the operating room, removed all the important organs from him, and assigned them to those in need. They greatly comply with the principle of utilitarianism, that is, (thinly) doing things with the greatest happiness of the most people."[66]

However, 1) "These absurd examples are actually irrelevant to the choice of actual principles. For these examples, Utilitarians may say that the principles we accept should be useful in practice, we need to cultivate that kind of intuition, which should be something that can be called 'the most highly acceptable'."[67]

2) As Professor Nishida Noriyuki said: "On such occasions, it does not exist that 99.9% of the cases where killing is the only means (supplementary) can be affirmed."[68] It can be argued that it may be absolutely non-existent for five organs of one person, as described above, to meet the needs of five patients for organ transplantation at the same time.

3) Since it is recognized that the use of life as a means can lead to extremely common and serious consequences, it should in principle be prohibited, or any use of life as a means should be illegal. However, if it is not allowed to protect more life by sacrificing one's life, it means that more persons will rather die than sacrifice one person's life, which is difficult to be accepted by the general concept of the society, and does not necessarily conform to the utilitarian nature of the society. From this point of view, at least the act of protecting the lives of the majority and sacrificing

---

[65] 美汤姆·雷根:《动物权利研究》，李曦译，北京大学出版社2010年版，第192页。Tom Regan, trans. Li Xi, (2010) *The Case for Animal Rights*, Peking University Press, 192.

[66] 美唐纳德·帕尔玛:《西方哲学导论》，杨洋、曹洪洋译，上海社会科学院出版社2009年版，第273页。Donald Palmer, trans. Yang Yang, Cao Hongxiang, (2009) *An Introduction to Western Philosophy*, Shanghai Academy of Social Sciences Press, 273.

[67] 转引自孙伟平:"赫尔的功利主义思想述评"，载《南京社会科学》2001年第8期。As cited in Sun Weiping. (2001) "A Review of Hare's Utilitarian Thought",Nanjing Journal of Social Sciences, No.8.

[68] 日西田典之:《刑法总论》，弘文堂2010年版，第144页。Nishida Noriyuki.(2010) *General Theory of Criminal Law*, Koubundou Publishers Inc., 144.

one's life by necessity should rule out the establishment of the crime.[69] "If there is no other means to save lives, it should also be acknowledged that there is room for the doctor to implement the necessity."[70] However, a person's life can only be sacrificed to protect the lives of others if the person being sacrificed is specific (for example, if the person is in the position of the person being sacrificed, meanwhile, if the person being sacrificed is otherwise about to die, etc.), and the judgement of "by necessity" should be stricter.. Therefore, in the above-mentioned liver transplantation, it is not possible to arbitrarily select a healthy person for liver transplantation.[71] Otherwise, no one will dare to enter a hospital or even pass near one, which will inevitably end in more deaths, which will inevitably lead to more deaths. This is also a violation of behavioral utilitarianism. However, if it is a situation in which a particular person must be killed, it is possible to sacrifice the lives of a few person to save more lives. Take *Trolley Problem* proposed by Philippa Foot as an example. "The tram was out of control, and a crazy philosopher bundled five persons in the front of the track. Fortunately, you can pull an organ that allows the tram to go on another track but there is also a person tied to that track. So, should you pull the organ and exchange one life for five lives? Most philosophers believe it is morally permissible. John Mikhail, a philosopher and legal theorist, did a series of experiments and found that most persons would agree with that."[72]

To be clear, people shall not be seen as tools or means, but shall be the purpose. However, "the distinction between treating a person as a mean and treating a person as their own purpose is never clear. Kant said that we cannot 'just' treat a person 'as a mean'. So what if we 'usually' treat a person 'as a mean'?... The situation in real life often puts us in a dilemma. No matter what we do, our acts can always be understood as using others."[73] For example, an important motivation for me to teach criminal law is to maintain a livelihood. Does it prove that I am using my students as a mean to achieve my goals? In the case of the aforementioned torture for the purpose of rescue, not to torture the kidnapper is to treat the kidnapper as a human being; but not to torture the kidnapper is, I fear, to fail to treat the kidnapped person as a human being, to allow the kidnapper to use the kidnapped person as a tool. In the aforementioned *Trolley Problem*, pulling organ (gate) is considered to use one person as a tool; however, if the organ is not pulled, the mad philosopher is tolerated and

---

[69] For other situations,参见黎宏:"紧急避险法律性质研究"，载《清华法学》2007年第1期。

[70] 参见黎宏:"紧急避险法律性质研究"，载《清华法学》2007年第1期。See Li Hong. (2007) "Research on the Legal Nature of Necessity", as cited in T*singhua University Law Journal*, No.1.

[71] Otherwise, the crime of intentional homicide or the crime of intentional injury is established.

[72] 美劳伦斯·索伦:《法理词汇》，王凌皞译，中国政法大学出版社2010年版，第126页。Lawrence Solum, trans. Wang Linghao, (2010) *Legal Theory Lexicon*, China University of Political Science and Law Press, 126.

[73] 美唐纳德·帕尔玛:《西方哲学导论》，杨洋、曹洪洋译，上海社会科学院出版社2009年版，第285页。Donald Palmer, trans. Yang Yang, Cao Hongxiang, (2009) *An Introduction to Western Philosophy*, Shanghai Academy of Social Sciences Press, 285.

allowed to use the five men as tools. Therefore, it is not appropriate to use life as a mean to criticize the view of behavioral utilitarianism.[74]

7. The Protection of Right

Another criticism of behavioral utilitarianism is based on that, "action consequentialism requires us to make a huge sacrifice in order to maximize the donation of hunger relief supplies. It also requires self-sacrifice even if the interests of others are only slightly more than the costs of the actors."[75] In other words, behavioral utilitarianism requires persons to sacrifice their own small interests in pursuit of the great interests of mankind.

In perspective of criminal law, this issue is mainly related to omission in criminal law, but it has a strict condition for the establishment of omission, and will not expand the range of punishment. Even crimes such as failing to save a person in danger, as in section 323c of *German Criminal Law*, are subject to the condition that it is easy to save another person, or that saving another person does not place an obvious burden on the actor. Establishing strict conditions for omission is also a requirement of behavioral utilitarianism. If anyone must rescue them at all times, our society will be caught in confusion.

Some criticized that consequentialism denies person's freedom to choice. The establishment of consequentialism must satisfy two conditions: one is that person must choose freely, and the other is that the selector must determine that one of the choices can provide greater good or less evil. These two conditions are incompatible because the choice of a possibility or possibilities (including 'doing nothing') can only be morally significant and required if the possibility or possibilities available remain attractive. One can choose something because it is good. However, if a choice is considered to bring greater good or less evil, then other choices that promise to bring less good or greater evil will be less attractive and the person will not choose them. The reason why the person doesn't choose them is that choosing greater good or smaller evils provide every possible reason choosing less good or greater evil.[76]

However, criminal law actually offers two choices: one is to choose legitimate or illegal act, even if choosing illegal act will bring greater evil, some person do

---

[74] "Every afternoon, Kant would take a long time walk, and his servant Lampe would carry an umbrella with him to prevent Kant from getting wet. Kant did not apply the principle that 'a person cannot be used as a means, but must be treated as a purpose' (nothing is more terrible than the will of one person is subject to the will of another)"(英马丁·科恩:《哲学野史》，邱炳译，新华出版社2010年版，第150页Martin Cohen, trans. Qiu Bing, (2010) *Philosophical Tales*, Xinhua Publishing House, 150.)。

[75] 美布拉德·胡克:"规则后果主义"，载美休·拉福莱特主编:《伦理学理论》，龚祥主译，中国人民大学出版社2008年版，第230页。Brad Hooker, trans. Gongxiang et al., (2008) *Rule Consequentialism*, as cited in Hugh LaFollette ed., *The Blackwell Guide to Ethical Theory*, China Renmin University Press, 230.

[76] 参见林庆华:"天主教新自然法学派论结果主义伦理学"，载《宗教学研究》2008年第2期。See Lin Qing Hua. (2008) "The Catholic Neo-Natural Law School on Consequentialist Ethics", as cited in *Religious Studies*, No. 2.

choose; another is that, in the conflict of obligations, the ending of choosing which kind of good is still to choose good or evil. So behavioral utilitarianism does not deny a person's freedom to choice.

4.3 General Conclusion

By contrast, it can be found that when the act conforms to the constitutive element, the basis for preventing wrongdoing is that the act protects superior or at least equal legal interests, rather than the act conforming to certain rules. The tripartite system itself means the validity of the view on the wrongdoing of the behavioral utilitarianism: Acts that violate the rules (such as the killing that meets constitutive element), while protecting the superior or at least equal legal interests (such as justifiable defense), can prevent wrongdoing.

In Ethics, some scholars have integrated or compromised behavioral utilitarianism and rule utilitarianism. Then, can it be compromised in criminal law?

> Given that common sense is not always in line with utilitarianism, it requires the person not to treat these rules as absolute as dogmatic intuitionists, but to acknowledge the imperfections of these rules and to use utilitarianism to continually improve them, especially when the requirements of these rules conflicted. This shows that Sidgwick examines utilitarianism from different levels. He hides this view in his thoughts, 'A civilized person, when reflecting on such common sense, would (a) observe the rules of dogmatic intuitionism when there is no difficulty in them; (b) apply a utilitarian approach when there are doubts and conflicts; and (c) carefully modify the rules of common sense ethics to fit the course of history, when necessary, in the light of changing conditions and with reference to the utilitarian approach hidden beneath the existing rules'.[77]

R. M. Hare believes that moral thinking can be divided into intuitive thinking and critical thinking. For intuitive thinking, moral judgment is based on the generally accepted and highly convincing principle of moral intuition, which is the standard that rule utilitarianism moral judgment is based. However, Hare has repeatedly emphasized that this principle of intuitive moral thinking is simple, general, and insufficient, because it cannot solve the problem of moral conflict. Hare cites an example that intuitionism philosophers have always liked: I first promised the children to take them to the Oxford River for a picnic, and on the same day my old friend suddenly visited me from Australia and could only stay in Oxford for an afternoon, hoping that I can take him and his wife to visit the college. Obviously I was supposed to take my children to the college, and I should abide by my commitment to the children. Hare also cites another example:,if the commander, on a small frigate faces a dilemma, did not drop a deep water bomb, the enemy submarine would slip away and continued to sink more ships and hurt more person; if he

[77] 陈江进、郭琰:"试析西季威克功利主义的性质及其影响", 载《道德与文明》2007年第3期。Chen Jiangjin & Guo Yan. (2007) "An Analysis of the Nature and Influence of Sidgwick's Utilitarianism", as cited in *Morality and Civilization*, No. 3.

dropped a bomb, it would kill the survivors in the water. Situations such as these, where there are conflicting responsibilities, cannot be resolved by principle of intuition alone and must rely on the critical thinking dimension and adopt an approach of behavioral utilitarianism. In Hare's view, intuitive thinking can provide the principle of intuition that is consistent with the rules and practices that persons have formed in historical life, which is rule utilitarianism. But in the case of daily moral rules conflicted, the choice of principles and the resolution of moral conflict must be carried out at the level of critical thinking, which is behavioral utilitarianism.[78]

The above-mentioned compromise theory has one thing in common, that is, taking behavioral utilitarianism in the event of conflicting. In the field of wrongdoing in criminal law, what needs to be solved is a situation of conflict, that between the behavioral norms and the ultimate standard of act. Therefore, even if behavioral utilitarianism has problems in ethics, when it is applied to specialization of dealing with the conflicts in the field of wrongdoing, there is no problem.

There is also a view that proper understanding of behavioral utilitarianism is only a legitimate theory, rather than decision-making process. "The reason of legitimacy is a theory that is stated on the basis of the bestact or result, and a theory about how we act our moral thinking is constructed on the basis of the development of character and making ourselves a particular type of personto construct."[79] And the theory of wrongdoing is a theory for evaluating whether a act is justified. Therefore, it can only be judged whether the act is illegal according to the result of the act or the possible result of the act, which also requires the theory of criminal law to adopt behavioral utilitarianism in the field of wrongdoing.

In summary, the legitimate act in criminal law should never be punished by law. The judgement of whether an act is justified or not should adopt behavioral utilitarianism, and that is *Erfolgsunwert*. In the case of two legal interests conflicting, the judgment whether the act is justified or not should be judged by balancing the legal interests. An act in conformity with the constitutive element, even if it violates certain rules, as long as it protects the superior or equal legal interests, becomes justifications. Whether the act is justified or not is different from whether the actor should be condemned. Therefore, theory of criminal law must strictly distinguish between wrongdoing and culpability. The intent and negligent of the actor does not affect the legitimacy of the act itself, and thus are only elements of culpability, not elements of wrongdoing.

---

[78] 参见吴映平:"黑尔之功利主义观述评"，载《武汉理工大学学报》(社会科学版)2008年第2期。See Wu Ying Ping. (2008) "*A Review of Hare's View on Utilitarianism,*" as cited in *Journal of Wuhan University of Technology* (Social Science Edition), No. 2.

[79] 美弗雷:"行动功利主义"，载美休·拉福莱特主编:《伦理学理论》，龚祥主译，中国人民大学出版社2008年版，第211页。R.G. Frey, trans. Gongxiang et al., (2008) *Act-utilitarianism*, as cited in Hugh LaFollette ed., *The Blackwell Guide to Ethical Theory*, China Renmin University Press, 211.

References

Bernd Schünemann, (2006) *Distinguishing the Illegality and Culpability*, as cited in Chen Zhihui, ed., Unbestechlich und unbeirrbar im dienst von recht unechtigkeit: abhandlungen zur gesamten strafrechtswissenschaft von BERND SCHUNEMANN, Taiwan: taedp.org.tw, 416.

Brad Hooker, trans. Gongxiang et al., (2008) *Rule Consequentialism*, as cited in Hugh LaFollette ed., The Blackwell Guide to Ethical Theory, China Renmin University Press, 219, 230, 233.

Chen Jiangjin & Guo Yan. (2007) "An Analysis of the Nature and Influence of Sidgwick's Utilitarianism", as cited in Morality and Civilization, No. 3.

Chen Zheng. (2006) *Contemporary Western Normative Ethics*, Nanjing Normal University Press, 70.

Daniel Hausman & Michael McPherson, trans. Ji Ruman, Gao Hongyan, (2008) *Economic Analysis, Moral Philosophy, and Public Policy*, Shanghai Translation Publishing House, 136.

Donald Palmer, trans. Huang Shaoting, (2010) *Why It's Hard to Be Good?,* Shanghai Academy of Social Sciences Press, 170.

Donald Palmer, trans. Yang Yang, Cao Hongxiang, (2009) *An Introduction to Western Philosophy,* Shanghai Academy of Social Sciences Press, 273, 274-275, 285.

Friedrich Paulsen, trans. He Huaihong, Liao Shenbai, (1988) *System der Ethik*, China Social Sciences Press, 542, 544, 544-545.

Giunter Stratenwerth & Lothar Kuhlen, trans. Yang Meng, (2006) *Strafrecht Allgemeiner Teil I: Die Straftat*, Law Press, 81, 108.

Gong Qun. (2003) "On Smart's Act Utilitarianism," as cited in Qilu Journal, No. 2.

Hirano Ryuuichi. (1975) *General Theory of Criminal Law II*, Yuhikaku Press, 229.

Ida Makoto. (2005) *Theories of General Rules of Criminal Law*, seibundoh, 1, 3, 15.

Ida Makoto. (2007) *Theoretical Criminal Law in the Age of Change,* Keio University Press Inc., 113, 119.

James G March & Martin Schulz & Xueguang Zhou, trans. Tong Genxing, (2005) *The Dynamics of Rules*, Shanghai People's Publishing House, 45-46.

James Rachels, trans. Yang Zongyuan, (2009) *The Elements of Moral Philosophy* (revised. Stuart Rachels), China Renmin University Press, 104-105, 110, 112, 119.

Jacques Paul Thiroux & Keith W. Krasemann, trans. Chen Liyu, Liu Jian, (2008) *Ethics: Theory and Practice*, World Publishing Corporation, 42.

Julian Baggini, trans. Zhang Rongnan, Yang Zhihua, (2008) *The Pig That Wants to Be Eaten*, READWAY, 50.

Lawrence Solum, trans. Wang Linghao, (2010) *Legal Theory Lexicon*, China University of Political Science and Law Press, 126.

Li Hong. (2007) "Research on the Legal Nature of Necessity", as cited in Tsinghua University Law Journal, No.1.

Lin Qing Hua. (2008) "The Catholic Neo-Natural Law School on Consequentialist Ethics", as cited in Religious Studies, No. 2.

Liu Ming Xiang. (1997) "On the Nature of the Necessity Defense," as cited in Chinese Journal of Law, No. 4.

Martin Cohen, trans. Qiu Bing, (2010) *Philosophical Tales*, Xinhua Publishing House, 150.

Niu Jing Hui. (2002) *A Study on British Utilitarian Ethical Thought*, People's Publishing House, 202.

Nishida Noriyuki. (2010) *General Theory of Criminal Law*, Koubundou Publishers Inc., 1-307, 131-132, 142, 144, 171, 258.

Otsuka Hitoshi. (2008) *Overview of Criminal Law*, Yuhikaku Press, 368.

Peter Singer, trans. Liu Xin, (2005) *Practical Ethics,* People's Oriental Publishing & Media Co., Ltd., 294.

Reinhold Niebuhr, trans. Jiang Qing, (2009) *Moral Men and Immoral Society*, Guizhou People's Publishing House, No.2, 152.

R.G. Frey, trans. Gongxiang et al., (2008) *Act-utilitarianism*, as cited in Hugh LaFollette ed., The Blackwell Guide to Ethical Theory, China Renmin University Press, 211.

Smart, J J C & Williams, Bernard, trans. Mou Wenwu, (1992) *Utilitarianism: For and against*, China Social Sciences Press, 9, 68-69.

Sun Weiping. (2001) "A Review of Hare's Utilitarian Thought", Nanjing Journal of Social Sciences, No.8.

Tom Regan, trans. Li Xi, (2010) *The Case for Animal Right*s, Peking University Press, 192, 211.

Wang Gang. (2010) "Torture for Lifesaving and Justifiable Defense", as cited in Tsinghua University Law Journal, No.2.

William Frankena, trans. Guan Jian, (1987) *Ethics*, SDX Joint Publishing Company, 53-53, 71, 81.

Wu Ying Ping. (2008) "A Review of Hare's View on Utilitarianism," as cited in Journal of Wuhan University of Technology (Social Science Edition), No. 2.

Yamaguchi Atsushi. (2007) General Rules of Criminal Law, Yuhikaku Press, 226.

Zhang Chuan You. (2007) Introduction to Ethics, People's Publishing House, 160.

Chapter 5
Basic Nature of Defense by Accident

The typical case of defense by accident is so rare that the discussion of it does not bear obviously-practical significance. However, in theory, the conclusion of handling defense by accident is the touchstone for judging whether a scholar holds *Handlungsunwert* or *Erfolgsunwert*. For another side, if *Handlungsunwert* does not properly deal with defense by accident, it indicates that *Handlungsunwert* itself has questions, and vice versa.

In general, defense by accident refers to that the actor has objectively defended against the on-going unlawful infringement, but he or she subjectively has no defense consciousness. Defense by accident can be divided into two types: emergency rescue and justifiable defense The example of the former is that B intently (negligently or accidentally) killed C while C was deliberately killing D. The act of B protected D's life, but B knew nothing about the fact that C was killing D. The example of the latter is that B intently (negligently or accidentally) killed C, and B had no idea that at the same time C was deliberately killing himself or herself.[1]

For defense by accident, there are the following opinions in theory of criminal law: Firstly, some *Handlungsunwert* believers hold that the establishment of justifiable defense requires defense consciousness (subjective element of justification) and

*The original title is "On Defense by Accident", published in ***Tsinghua University Law Journal***, 2012, Vol. 1.

[1] As long as the defensive result is caused objectively, and there is no defense consciousness subjectively, it can be described as defense by accident. Therefore, focusing on the subjective content of accidental defenders, defense by accident can be divided into intentional defense by accident (the result of justifiable defense caused by intentional acts of crime), negligent defense by accident (the result of justifiable defense caused by negligence) and unexpected defense by accident (the result of justifiable defense caused by negligence unexpected acts). This article focuses on the intentional defense by accident. Because if intentional defense by accident is acquitted, negligent defense by accident and unexpected defense by accident should be acquitted as well.

M. Zhang, *The Fundamental Issues upon Criminal Law Theories*, Masterpieces of Contemporary Jurisprudents in China,
https://doi.org/10.1007/978-981-95-1276-8_5

defense by accident can be seen as an accomplished crime because of lacking defense consciousness (the theory of accomplishment of *Handlungsunwert*). Secondly, some *Handlungsunwert* believers (also known as dualists) consider that the establishment of justifiable defense requires defense consciousness. Defense by accident caused a legitimate result, thus lacking *Erfolgsunwert* while *Handlungsunwert* existed, therefore, the attempted crime shall establish (the theory of attempt of *Handlungsunwert*). Thirdly, part of *Erfolgsunwert* believers think that although the establishment of justifiable defense does not require defense consciousness, defense by accident shall establish as the attempted crime because of the risk of causing an infringement of legal interests due to accidental reasons that do not result in an infringement of legal interests (the theory of attempt of *Erfolgsunwert*). Fourthly, part of *Erfolgsunwert* believers view the emergency rescue (one type of defense by accident) as justifiable defense, and consider justifiable defense (another type of defense by accident) commit an attempted crime (the dualism of *Erfolgsunwert*). Fifthly, some *Erfolgsunwert* believers think that the establishment of justifiable defense does not require defense consciousness and defense by accident belongs to justifiable defense (the theory of innocence of *Erfolgsunwert*).[2]

Obviously, the differences between different viewpoints are mainly manifested in three aspects: (A) Does the establishment of justifiable defense require defense consciousness? *Handlungsunwert* believers consider the theory of necessity of defense consciousness, yet *Erfolgsunwert* believers hold the theory of unnecessary of defense consciousness. (B) How to judge the danger of act? Namely, does the act of defense by accident have danger of infringing the legal interest? Both the theory of attempt of *Handlungsunwert* and the theory of attempt of *Erfolgsunwert* may lead to affirmative conclusions; however, the theory of innocence of *Erfolgsunwert* leads to a negative conclusion. (C) What is the essence of wrongdoing? In other words, what is the substantive basis for preventing wrongdoing? This is the fundamental difference between *Handlungsunwert* and *Erfolgsunwert*.[3] As a *Erfolgsunwert* believer, the author have repeatedly discussed that the essence of wrongdoing is the infringement of legal interest, and expressed my own views on the judgment of danger.[4] As a result, this article mainly analyzes and discusses critically the above mentioned four opinions and the reasons within the specific scope of defense by accident, thus affirming the rationality of the theory of innocence of *Erfolgsunwert*.

---

[2] 参见　　日关根彻:"偶然防卫について"，载日川端博等编:《立石二六先生古稀祝贺论文集》，成文堂2010年版，第191页。See Sekine Tsuyoshi.(2010) "Of accidental defense", as cited in Kawabata Hiroshi et al., ed., *A Collection of Congratulatory Essays by Mr. Tateishi Niroku in His Seventies,* Seibundo Publishing Co., 191.

[3] In addition, there involves the relationship between the constitutive elements and the justifiable cause (cause of justification) in the three-tier criminal system.

[4] 参见张明楷:《刑法的基本立场》，中国法制出版社2002年版，第152页以下；张明楷:《法益初论》，中国政法大学出版社2003年版，第269页以下；张明楷:"行为无价值论的疑问"，载《中国社会科学》2009年第1期。See Zhang Mingkai. (2002) *Basic Standpoints of Criminal Law*, China Legal Publishing House, 1–152.; Zhang Mingkai. (2003) *Preliminary Study on Legal Interests*, China University of Political Science and Law Press,1–269; Zhang Mingkai. (2009) "Doubts on the Theory of Act Valorization", as cited in *Social Sciences in China*, No. 1.

5.1 The Theory of Accomplishment of *Handlungsunwert*

(1) Doctrine in Germany and Japan

In Germany, only a few scholars advocate defense by accident constitute an accomplished crime. The reason is that to punish the actor of defense by accident as an unlawful infringer who attempts to commit a crime is away from the basis of authenticity. Because as long as "the actor has satisfied the subjective and objective elements of unlawful act" and causing "result fitting with the constitutive elements", the existence of the attempted crime will be excluded.[5]

However, this doctrine has lost its influence in Germany because the constitutive elements are illegal type, and the basis for *Erfolgsunwert* is not the formal result of constitutive elements, but the unlawful result. Although the defense by accident infringes the interests of the unlawful infringer, the lack of a wrongful result due to the fact that the unlawful infringer was in a state of being defended and the act of defense by accident objectively protected the legal interests of an innocent person does not establish an accomplished crime, even according to *Handlungsunwert*.[6]

In Japan, scholars such as Professors Ooya Minoru and Otsuka hitoshi are supporters of the theory of accomplishment of *Handlungsunwert*. The reasons put forward by Professor Ooya Minoru are: "First, the act in the criminal law consists of subjective elements and objective elements. This premise is true of defensive act as well. The subjective elements of the wrongdoing are the conditions for the establishment of the crime, conversely, the subjective element of justification should be recognized. Second, if an attack which is implemented out of a criminal intent and causes the actor's expected result is deemed to be a justifiable defense, the unlawful infringer will be protected and the purpose of justifiable defense by law to ensure social order will be violated. Therefore, on occasions where the result of defence is incidental happened (defense by accident)... should not be considered justifiable defense because of a lack of defense consciousness. Third, it should be considered that the term "for" defense rights used in Article 36 of *Japanese Criminal Law* indicates that defense consciousness is necessary. One opinion of the theory of necessity of defense consciousness is that since the elements of justifiable defense are objectively satisfied, there is no *Erfolgsunwert* and the attempted crime is established because of the lack of defense consciousness and *Handlungsunwert*. However, since the object of preventing wrongdoing is the totality of the facts that satisfy the constitutive elements, it is inappropriate to evaluate the act separately from the

---

[5] 参见张明楷:《刑法的基本立场》，中国法制出版社2002年版，第152页以下；张明楷:《法益初论》，中国政法大学出版社2003年版，第269页以下；张明楷:"行为无价值论的疑问"，载《中国社会科学》2009年第1期。See Zhang Mingkai. (2002) *Basic Standpoints of Criminal Law*, China Legal Publishing House, 1–152.; Zhang Mingkai. (2003) *Preliminary Study on Legal Interests*, China University of Political Science and Law Press,1–269; Zhang Mingkai. (2009) "Doubts on the Theory of Act Valorization", as cited in *Social Sciences in China*, No. 1.

[6] C.Roxin, *Strafrecht Allgenmeiner Teil, Band I*, 4.Aufl, C.H.Beck, 2006,S.645; H.Jeschck/T. Weigend, *Lehrbuch des Strafrechts.Allgemeiner Teil*, 5.Aufl., Duncker & Humblot, 1996,S.330.

result. Therefore, since one stands for the theory of necessity of defense consciousness, one should generally argue for the establishment of an accomplished crime."[7] The reason given by Professor Otsuka hitoshi is exactly the same.[8]

This article raises the following objections to the above points and reasons.

Firstly, the crime is an illegal and culpable act that conforms to the constitutive elements. In the context of traditional Chinese theory of criminal law, the unification of objectivity and subjectivity is required of the criminal act, rather than the non-criminal act. In other words, it cannot be considered that a non-criminal act must be the unification of subjectivity and objectivity. Otherwise, the acts failing to achieve the unification of subjectivity and objectivity are neither criminal acts nor non-criminal acts. This is hard to accept. "Acts in criminal law consists of subjective and objective elements", which works only in relation to criminal acts. Acts in criminal law that prevent the establishment of crime do not necessarily consist of subjective and objective elements. For example, the accident resulted in death without intention or negligence can also be acts in criminal law (Article 16 of *Chinese Criminal Law* stipulates such acts). And those acts are not composed of subjective elements and objective elements. Similarly, the act of justifiable defense is not a crime and certainly does not require the unification of subjectivity and objectivity. It is therefore inappropriate to argue that the subjective element of justification must also be present to establish justifiable defense on the grounds that the establishment of a crime requires a subjective element of justification. Even if the defense consciousness is taken as the element of justifiable defense, it can only be said that the act without defense consciousness is not a justifiable defense, in addition, it cannot be directly concluded that the act is a crime, to say the least.

Secondly, although the actor in defense by accident subjectively defended with a criminal intent and caused the expected result, the result of defense by accident is permitted by criminal law. Because the judgment of whether the result is allowed by the criminal law only depends on objectivity, which is independent from the intent of the actor. For example, when Y's life is in an imminent danger, as long as X objectively protects Y's life with criminal intent, it cannot be assumed that X's act has caused bad results. For another example, if A attacks C with a defense consciousness while C is killing D and protects D's life, this result is allowed by law. Similarly, B attacks C in a defense by accident who is killing D and protects D's life, it cannot be denied that the result is legally permissible because B has a criminal intent. Where the objective result is identical, to evaluate the result differently simply because the intention of the actor was different is in fact motivated by a subjectivism that is difficult to accept. In other words, results which are objective are independent from the will of the actor. An objective analysis leads us to find that in the case of the defense by accident of B, the result of B's act is allowed and even encouraged by law. There are both killing of C expected by B and protection of D's

---

[7] 日大谷实:《刑法讲义总论》，成文堂2009年新版，第288~289页。See Ohya Minoru. (2009) *General Handouts on Criminal Law(New Edition)*, Seibundo Publishing Co, 288–289.

[8] 参见日大塚仁:《刑法概说(总论)》，有斐阁2008年版，第390页。Otsuka Hitoshi.(2008) *Overview of Criminal Law*, Yuhikaku Press, 390.

life which is not expected by B in the results. The latter result cannot be denied because B does not anticipate. However, once the latter result and the fact that C is being illegally infringed are considered, it is inevitable to think that B's act has good result. It is not difficult to find that in the defense by accident of B, to confirm that B's act is justifiable defense and protects the life of innocent D, rather than protecting the unlawful infringer. To hold that B's defense by accident is an attempted crime means that B's act was prohibited by the criminal law. However, the end of the prohibition of B's act will necessarily be to cause the innocent D to be killed by C. Such an end cannot be considered to be the desired outcome of criminal law.

Professor Ooya Minoru believes that the purpose of justifiable defense is to maintain social order through the law, which is consistent with his view on the substance of wrongdoing. Professor Ooya Minoru pointed out that the essence of wrongdoing is "the infringement of legal interests in violation of social ethics".[9] An attack committed by defender by accident with criminal intent is necessarily an unethical act and therefore illegal. However, first, although the ethical norms and the criminal law norms have similarities in principle, the two bear little value within themselves but they are valuable to protect certain values. Because of this, criminal law and ethics are not mutually exclusive in their purpose of protecting certain values, so that a number of ethical norms overlap with criminal law norms. Yet even if the criminal law norms incorporate some ethical norms, it is not intended for promoting a particular person's ethics, only because some of the values protected by ethics have something in common with the values protected by criminal law. Moreover, not all ethical norms are incorporated into the criminal law.[10] The requirement that the infringement of legal interests be predicated on a breach of social ethics is in fact intended to protect social ethics. However, penalty is not an appropriate means to maintain social ethics. Because of the relativity of ethics, maintaining social ethics as a task of criminal law is easy to force others to obey own ethical concepts in the name of criminal law. The task of the criminal law is only a prerequisite for ensuring the common life of people with different values, therefore, it is sufficient that a specific, objectively ascertainable interest or state of affairs (legal interest) of value to the maintenance of the common life of the nation is the object of protection. In principle, criminal law applies only when the will of others are violated and major infringement or danger to the legal interests of others are caused. Second, the criminal law stipulates that justifiable defense prevents wrongdoing, not because justifiable defense conforms to social ethical order. The reason why the justifiable defense prevents wrongdoing is it conforms to the social ethical order, then the time and limits for justifiable defense will be canceled. For example, people may think that to kill a thief who is stealing is socially ethical.[11] Nor can it be said

---

[9] 日大谷实:《刑法讲义总论》，成文堂2009年新版，第236页。Ohya Minoru.(2009) *Lectures on Criminal Law(New Edition)*, Seibundo Publishing Co, 236.

[10] 参见日西田典之:《刑法总论》，弘文堂2010年版，第31页。See Nishida Noriyuki.(2010) *General Theory of Criminal Law*, Koubundou Publishers Inc., 31.

[11] This phenomenon often occurs in real life, and even the phenomenon of killing thieves afterwards occurs. People may think that to kill a thief who is stealing is socially ethical.

in general that the justifiable defense stipulated in criminal law is to maintain social order. This is because social order is a very broad and unclear concept. Based on this ground, it is impossible to raise conditions such as the time and limits for the justifiable defense. It should be considered that the justifiable defense provided for in criminal law is in order to protect the legal interests from on-going unlawful infringement. The reason why justifiable defense prevents wrongdoing is that it protects a superior or at least equal legal interest while damaging another. The act of defense by accident protects legal interests of the innocent while infringing the legal interests of unlawful infringers, therefore, treating it as justifiable defense is fully in line with the purpose hereof.

Thirdly, the expression "for" is used in Article 36 of *Japanese Criminal Law*, Article 32 of *German Criminal Law*, and Article 20 of *Chinese Criminal Law* for the justifiable defense.[12] It is undeniable that the expression "for protecting..." in Article 20 of *Chinese Criminal Law* is easy to be accepted. This seems to indicate that the criminal law in Japan, Germany and China all adopt the theory of the necessity of defense consciousness. However, this statement is not enough to be the legal basis for the theory of the necessity of defense consciousness.

If Article 20 of *Chinese Criminal Law* is interpreted in accordance with the ordinary or general literal meaning, it may be understood that defense consciousness includes defense cognition and defense intention (especially to emphasize the defense purpose). That is to say, on the one hand, the justifiable defense requires the actor to know that the unlawful infringement is on-going and justified, on the other hand, the actor acted for the purpose or intent to protect the State, the public interest, his or her person, property and other rights from an ongoing wrongful infringement.[13] However, if the emphasis is on the need for the actor to have the defense intention, it means that a counter-attack committed purely out of anger at the unlawful infringer (without any thought of what legal interest to protect) does not establish justifiable defense. However, such understanding clearly and unduly narrows the scope of justifiable defense. On the other hand, if the defense consciousness only requires defense cognition, it does not conform to the literal meaning of "for protecting". Because the ordinary literal meaning of "for protecting" obviously means to achieve a certain purpose, not just to aware of the on-going unlawful infringement. From this point of view, even if "for" is interpreted one of subjective element of justification, in fact it is impossible to explain in accordance with its ordinary literal meaning.

Since the ordinary literal meaning of "for protecting" does not work at all, it is only possible to systematically being explained within the meaning that the term may have.[14] The term "ため" in Article 36 of *Japanese Criminal Law* does not nec-

[12] Article 36 of *Japanese Criminal Law* uses "ため", and Article 32 of *German Criminal Law* uses "um-zu". In this regard, the following mainly discusses the provisions of Chinese criminal law.

[13] 参见陈兴良:《规范刑法学》，中国人民大学出版社2008年版，第142~143页。Chen Xingliang. (2008) *Normative Criminal Law*, China Renmin University Press, 142–143.

[14] *Modern Chinese Dictionary* writes that "for indicate the reason, people generally use 'because' rather than for'" (中国社会科学院语言研究所词典编辑室:《现代汉语词典》，商务印书馆

essarily mean the purpose. The Japanese dictionary clearly states that this term has the meaning of "to express causation". Article 32 of *German Criminal Law* uses the expression "*um-abzuwenden*" (for avoiding), but as mentioned later, *German Criminal Law* only adopts the theory of defense cognition.[15] Professor C.Roxin pointed out that although Article 32 of *German Criminal Law* requires the defense 'for avoiding... necessary for the on-going unlawful infringement', however, 'for' refers to 'the nature of objective defense rather than the intention of the actor'."[16] In this article, "for protect the State, the public interest, his or her person, property and other rights from an ongoing wrongful infringement" in Article 20 of *Chinese Criminal Law* can be explained that the unlawful infringement is objectively existing from which the act of defense protect legitimate rights and interests. In other words, "'for' can also express reason, meaning 'because'".[17] Mr. Lv Shuxiang once said that the most commonly used relational terms for reason (generally) are '因为(because)' and '为了(for)' in vernacular Chinese, and '以','为','由' in classical Chinese. These relative terms can introduce reason complements or connect causal clauses. The reason complement is usually between the subject and the verb. Before the reason complement, the vernacularism Chinese uses '为了(for)' more than '因为(because)'. For example, "He was so anxious to sleep for three nights for solving this issue".[18] Chairman Mao (Mao Zedong; the founder of the People's Republic of China) once said:" a peasant association in a district of Xiangtan did not get along well with a township peasant association 'for one thing' ('为了一件事'), the chairman of the township peasant association declared that to oppose the unequal treaty of the district peasant association."[19] Therefore, "for (为了)" therein clearly means "because (因为)". Chairman Mao also said:" In the society of private property, closing the door is a must at sleep time of night. Everyone knows that this is for preventing thieves, not for making troubles."[20] The latter "for" indicates the reason, which is equivalent to "because", and the former "for" shows the purpose. Mr. Feng Zikai once wrote in his *Remembrance of Childhood* that "The taste of crabs is so good that our five sisters and brothers like, but also for our father's preferences." "The ceremony of moon appreciation on the Mid-autumn Festival was originally held for

---

2005年版，第1422页Dictionary Editing Office, Institute of Linguistics, Chinese Academy of Social Sciences.(2005) *Modern Chinese Dictionary*, The Commercial Press, 1422.), Since 'for' is not used for reasons only "generally", it does not preclude the use of 'for' for reasons in special cases.

15 日新村出编:《广辞苑》，岩波书店1983年版，第1514页。Shinmura Izuru ed.(1983) *Kojien*, Iwanami Shoten Publisher, 1514.

16 C.Roxin, *Strafrecht Allgenmeiner Teil, Band I*, 4.Aufl., C.H.Beck 2006,S.642.

17 孟田:《关联词语例释》，黑龙江人民出版社1981年版，第94页。Meng Tian.(1981) *Examples and Explanations of Conjunctions*, Heilongjiang People's Publishing House, 94.

18 吕叔湘:《中国文法要略》，商务印书馆1982年版，第388页。Lü Shuxiang. (1982) *Essentials of Chinese Grammar,* The Commercial Press,388.

19 《毛泽东选集》(第1卷)，人民出版社1991年版，第35页。*Mao Zedong Selected Works (vol 1)* (1991), People's Publishing House,35.

20 《毛泽东选集》(第3卷)，人民出版社1991年版，第904页。*Mao Zedong Selected Works (vol III)* (1991), People's Publishing House, 904.

father's preferences and for eating crabs."[21] All "for" clearly express reason. In fact, the use of "for" indicates the reason can be traced back to the ancient vernacular. The expression of "for" indicates the reason in modern Chinese is the inheritance of ancient vernacular, which is common in literature of the 1930s. Although there are fewer in contemporary literature, it is still used in causal sentences and cause and effect sentences as well as some specific environment.[22] Since "for" can indicate reason, then Article 20 of the Criminal Law is interpreted "because the protection of the State, the public interest, his or her person, property and other rights from being infringed upon by an ongoing wrongful infringement" as an objective condition for justifiable defense, there are no obstacles or problems at all.

Even if this interpretation of Article 20 of *Chinese Criminal Law* is beyond the ordinary people's understanding, the principle of *nulla poena sine lege* is not violated. Because this kind of interpretation only expands the scope of the justifiable defense, not the range of punishment for crimes. Actually, the range of punishment for crimes is narrowed down. Some people think that such interpretation harms the predicted possibility of unlawful infringers. Because unlawful infringers believe that defense can only be carried out when others know that unlawful infringement is on-going; if others can defend unlawful infringers when they do not know that there is an on-going unlawful infringement, unlawful infringers will not commit unlawful infringement. Obviously, criminal law will not protect this predicted possibility of unlawful infringers.

Fourthly, even if one takes *Handlungsunwert*, one should not conclude that the defense by accident shall establish the accomplished intentional crime. This is because the result, as the standard of the accomplished crime, is not only the result expected by the actor, but also the result which violates legal interests and is prohibited by the criminal law. In the case of defense by accident of B, on the one hand, because C is killing D illegally and in a state of being defended, so within the limits of defense, damage to C caused by B cannot be evaluated as prohibited by the criminal law. On the other hand, even if it is believed that the damage to C violates legal interest, B's act of defense by accident cannot be considered to causing the result prohibited by the criminal law for protecting superior legal interests of innocent D after being weighed. The theory of accomplishment of *Handlungsunwert* actually says that the result of the rescue of the innocent person's life is evaluated as an illegal result. So the opposite party or the third party can prevent or obstruct the occurrence of this result. This is obviously not appropriate.

In addition, concerning Professor Ooya Minoru's views on justifiable defense, defense against objects and imaginative defense, we can also find that there is self-contradiction in the theory of accomplishment of *Handlungsunwert*. For example, A thought he was being attacked by a wild animal and fired, when in fact it was not

---

[21] 丰子恺:《丰子恺文集》，人民文学出版社2008年版，第38~39页。Feng Zikai. (2008) *Collected Works of Feng Zikai*, People's Literature Publishing House, 38–39.

[22] 参见邵则遂:"'为了'表示原因刍议"，载《培训与研究》(湖北教育学院学报)1999年第4期。See Shao Zesui. (1999) "On the Use of 'Weile' to Express Cause", as cited in *Training and Research* (Journal of Hubei Institute of Education), No. 4.

a wild animal that attacked A, but a man, but A did not recognize this.. Professor Ooya Minoru pointed out that "on such occasions, although the act is negligent, it can be considered as justifiable defense because it can be found to have the consciousness to exclude the attack."[23] According to this point, the justifiable defense requires the combination of the objective defense against person and the subjective defense consciousness against objects. However, on the one hand, the intentional crime is accomplished when the intentional act causes the defense results, so when the negligent act causes defense results, it should also be regarded as a negligent crime. It is not difficult to see that Professor Ooya Minoru's views are not coordinated. On the other hand, when discussing the defense against objects, Professor Ooya Minoru said that "because the wrongdoing is a problem caused by human act, the infringement of animals' legal interests cannot be the object of justifiable defense but the object of necessity."[24] Since the infringement from animal cannot be the object of justifiable defense, how can the consciousness of excluding the infringement from animal be treated as the consciousness of justifiable defense? Professor Ooya Minoru came to this conclusion simply because when one has the consciousness to exclude the infringement from animal, the actor is not subjectively reprehensible and therefore cannot be considered guilty of negligence, whereas when one excludes infringement with criminal intent of another person, one is subjectively reprehensible and is therefore considered to have accomplished the intentional crime This is obviously a subjectivism position. For another example, Professor Ooya Minoru believes that imaginative defense is a mistake of law. As long as its imagination has no reasonable grounds, it will establish an intentional crime.[25] A link between the Professor Ooya Minoru's treatment of defense by accident and imaginative defense reveals an incongruity. That is, the defense by accident fully satisfies the objective conditions of justifiable defense, but not the subjective defense consciousness. The imaginative defense does not meet the objective conditions of justifiable defense, but is subjective in nature, and is thus the opposite of defense by accident. According to the logic of Professor Ooya Minoru, since imaginative defense is a mistake of law (wrongly thinking that own act is allowed by law), then defense by accident is the inverse mistake of law (wrongly thinking that own act is prohibited by law), which shall belong to offense under illusion and cannot be punished as a crime.

(2) Doctrine in America

The author only read the discussion materials of American scholars about whether the defense by accident shall establish a crime, but did not find the discussion of whether the defense by accident shall establish an accomplished crime or an

[23] 日大谷实:《刑法讲义总论》，成文堂2009年新版，第290页。See Ohya Minoru.(2009) *General Handouts on Criminal Law(New Edition)*, Seibundo Publishing Co, 290.

[24] 日大谷实:《刑法讲义总论》，成文堂2009年新版，第283页。See Ohya Minoru.(2009) *General Handouts on Criminal Law(New Edition)*, Seibundo Publishing Co, 283.

[25] 日大谷实:《刑法讲义总论》，成文堂2009年新版，第297页。See Ohya Minoru.(2009) *General Handouts on Criminal Law(New Edition)*, Seibundo Publishing Co, 297.

attempted one. The general speculation in this article is that since the system of the crime in the United States treats justifiable defense as *justification*, and, acts with criminal act and criminal intent, but without any ground for defense shall belong to crimes. In addition, because the result of the defense by accident occurred, the defense by accident shall establish the accomplishment of a crime as long as it holds the theory of necessity of defense consciousness. Therefore, the author classifies the American doctrine into the theory of accomplishment of *Handlungsunwert*. Admittedly, this speculation is not necessarily true. However, even if some materials show that American scholars advocate that the actor of defense by accident commits an attempted crime, the author's following rebuttal is also tenable.

For example, Doctor Alex intended to kill the patient David and was ready to inject air into David's vein, so Alex got close to David and got out the syringe secretly. At this moment David was mad at Alex because of medical bill, and he slammed Alex's nose with his fist and caused Alex to fall unconsciously. After describing the case, American scholar Fletcher pointed out: "A few years ago, Paul Robinson published an article in the *UCLA Law Review*. In the article, he hold the request for justification is applicable whether or not the defendant knew of the circumstances of justification. His argument is that the norms of justification is purely objective which does not require subjective mental state as the basis for its establishment. At the time, the author wrote an article to response and explain that all legal systems in the world demand a subjective element of justifiable defense and necessity, which seems to be correct. In the example given above, David is responsible for criminal assault and battery And Alex's attack is meaningless objectively. From then on, it is fair to say that we have been trying to change our position, but neither party has been able to make an overwhelming argument."[26]

Fletcher admitted that "there is an intuitive support, at least partial support, for the theory of objectivity in the public sentiment".[27] However, Fletcher's intuition was that David's action constituted assault and battery.[28] So he needed to find reasons for his instincts. After analyzing the relationship between norms and privileges, he pointed out: "The most appropriate description of the relationship between prohibitive norms and privileges is that people are obliged to comply with prohibitive norms and have the privilege to violate this obligation in the case of *iusta causa*." "The knowledge of *iusta causa* is a necessary condition for the violator to exercise privileges. There are three arguments that support this conclusion: First, the violation of norms upon *iusta causa* (the objective factor is enough to prevent conviction), and in its basic terms, does not have to extend to the realm of privilege.

[26] 美乔治·弗莱彻:《刑法的基本概念》，蔡爱惠等译，中国政法大学出版社2004年版，第133页。George P, Fletcher, trans. Cai Aihui, (2004) *Basic Concepts of Criminal Law*, China University of Political Science and Law Press, 133.

[27] 美乔治·弗莱彻:《刑法的基本概念》，蔡爱惠等译，中国政法大学出版社2004年版，第134页。George P, Fletcher, trans. Cai Aihui, (2004) *Basic Concepts of Criminal Law*, China University of Political Science and Law Press, 134.

[28] 美乔治·弗莱彻:《反思刑法》，邓子滨译，华夏出版社2008年版，第408页。George P, Fletcher, trans. Deng Zibin, (2008) *Rethinking Criminal Law*, Huaxia Publishing House, 408.

Second, the conceptual analysis of the 'exercise of privilege' supports a view that 'exercising' or 'acting on privilege' is premised on knowing the existence of *iusta causa*." Third, "the claims of *iusta causa* represent an exception to the prohibitive norms. As an exception, these claims should only apply to those who have special circumstances. The inclusion of this element makes the intention of the actor important, since objective circumstances alone are not sufficient to establish a person's special right to trample on the legal interests of others. A person who has breached norms may also enjoy an exception, and he must at least be aware of the circumstances supporting his claim to the exception."[29] However, Fletcher's argument is questionable.

Firstly, Fletcher believes that all legal systems require subjective elements of justification. The view that "in the United States or other countries, there is no support for Robinson's theory of objectivity" does not capture support.[30] Because he wrote clearly that some cases in Europe also support the view of pure objective justification... Lately, judges in Austria ruled that objective standard is sufficient to support the legitimacy of the act."[31] Moreover, the requirement of subjective elements of justification is basically derived from theoretical doctrine rather than the explicit provisions of criminal law. Therefore, Fletcher's above statement is unfounded, and scholars advocating the theory of the necessity of defense consciousness should not use Fletcher's above statement as an argument.

Secondly, Fletcher's three arguments are not reasons, but conclusions. In other words, Fletcher only uses conclusions to argue the conclusions. For example, why does not the violation of norms of *iusta causa* have to extend to the realm of privilege? He did not answer. For another example, why the precondition for exercising the privilege is to know the existence of *iusta causa*? He also did not explain. And why did the exceptional *iusta causa* make the intention of actor important? He also did not explain at all.

Thirdly, justifications can actually be negative constitutive elements. For example, if there is no general provision of criminal law regarding justifiable defense, then the crime of intentional homicide should be expressed as "intentional homicide other than in justifiable defense is punishable by...". Therefore, on the one hand, intentional homicide requires its establishment condition to be met, on the other hand, there must not be a justifiable defense. Thus, Fletcher's treatment of prohibitive norms and privileges depends on the systemic arrangement of the theoretical system of crime. If other systems are adopted, Fletcher's view does not apply. Moreover, even if the theory of negative constitutive elements is denied, it may be difficult to distinguish in certain contexts (such as consent of the victim) whether a

---

[29] 美乔治·弗莱彻:《反思刑法》，邓子滨译，华夏出版社2008年版，第414页。George P, Fletcher, trans. Deng Zibin, (2008) *Rethinking Criminal Law*, Huaxia Publishing House, 414.

[30] 美乔治·弗莱彻:《刑法的基本概念》，蔡爱惠等译，中国政法大学出版社2004年版，第134页。George P, Fletcher, trans. Cai Aihui, (2004) *Basic Concepts of Criminal Law*, China University of Political Science and Law Press, 134.

[31] 美乔治·弗莱彻:《反思刑法》，邓子滨译，华夏出版社2008年版，第411页。George P, Fletcher, trans. Deng Zibin, (2008) *Rethinking Criminal Law*, Huaxia Publishing House, 411.

certain behavior is the prevention to the conformity of constitutive elements or to wrongdoing. In this case, Fletcher's point of view simply does not work. Therefore, he has to admit that "unfortunately, this method (Fletcher's point of view) is not enough to accurately solve the ambiguity between the constitutive elements and *iusta causa*."[32]

Fourthly, it is difficult to implement the view in other relevant cases that exercising exceptional privileges beyond rules requires the actor has subjective elements of justification. For example, Article 30 of the *Gun Control Law of the People's Republic of China* states: "No unit or individual may transport firearms without permission. Those wishing to transport firearms must give a true report to the public security authority with regard to the type and quantity of the firearms and the route and method of transport, and apply for a transport permit." Obviously, it is impossible to establish the crime of illegal transportation of firearms if unit or individual transports firearm with permission. Even if A, who has obtained a permit, forgets after a period of time that he has obtained a permit and transports a firearm that he was originally permitted to transport during the validity of the permit with the intent to commit the crime of transportation of firearms and ammunitions, it is unlikely that he will be found guilty of a crime.

5.2 The Theory of Attempt of *Handlungsunwert*

(1) A view that defense by accident has *Erfolgsunwert* and lacks *Handlungsunwert*

According to previous prevailing views in Germany, subjective elements of justification were not required. But since Paragraph 3, Article 23 of *German Criminal Law* provides for that impossibility defense is punishable, in order to maintain consistency between the handling of defense by accident in practice and provisions of Paragraph 3, Article 23 of *German Criminal Law*, the dominant ideology consider that the actor of defense by accident commits an attempted crime of impossibility defense. In Germany, where dualism is dominant, an act can only be legal if it has neither *Erfolgsunwert*, nor does it have *Handlungsunwert*. However, defense by accident has *Handlungsunwert*, so it cannot be viewed as an attempted impossibility defense.[33] Most of the dualists in Japan also hold this position. For example, Professor Ida Makoto pointed out that to recognize the effect of preventing wrongdoing from *Handlungsunwert* requires not only the existence of an objective fact that qualifies as justifiable cause (such as justifiable defense), but also that the actor committed the act in awareness of that fact... When an actor commits an act without recognizing the fact that it is justifiable cause, he commits the act in order to realize the fact that he recognizes an infringement of a legal interest or a danger that is not

[32] 美乔治·弗莱彻:《反思刑法》，邓子滨译，华夏出版社2008年版，第416页。George P, Fletcher, trans. Deng Zibin, (2008) *Rethinking Criminal Law*, Huaxia Publishing House, 416.

[33] C.Roxin, *Strafrecht Allgenmeiner Teil, Band I*, 4.Aufl., C.H.Beck 2006,S.641,644.

justified, so that the wrongdoing of the intentional crime can be confirmed. Even if by chance an objective fact consistent with the justifiable cause has arisen, there is still no *Handlungsunwert* and the wrongfulness of the act is affirmed."[34]

The reason why *Handlungsunwert* advocators view defense by accident as an attempted crime is as follows.[35] First, *Handlungsunwert* believes that intention and negligence are subjective elements of wrongdoing. Corresponding to it, the ground for *iusta causa* requires subjective *iusta causa*, so the establishment of justifiable defense requires defenders to have defense consciousness. Because defense without consciousness has *Handlungsunwert*, "however, the unlawfulness is denied because it is clear afterwards that an objectively justified result was produced. Thus, as a situation where, although there is a unlawful act, no result of unlawfulness produces, the wrongdoing is affirmed within the limits of the attempt."[36] Second, *Handlungsunwert* believes that "the function to inform the national of the admissibility of act beforehand" as the guiding principle of the theory of wrongdoing, while at the same time, soaks the principle of the *nulla poena sine lege* and the general precautionary requirements of the criminal law as much as possible in wrongdoing.[37] Thus, an act that may violate legal interests under normal conditions must be punished even if it does not infringe under special conditions. Otherwise, others will follow the act, thus resulting in infringement of legal interest. This is the case with defense by accident. However, above reasons are also questionable.

First, *Handlungsunwert* has adopted the theory of violating norm on the issue of wrongdoing. Since the purpose of criminal law is to protect norms, at the same time, intentional acts "seriously violate the norms protected by criminal law" compared with negligence. Therefore, intention is one of the elements of the conduct threatened by the penalty, and these elements determine the degree of wrongdoing, which means intention is an integral part of unlawfulness."[38] However, it will inevitably lead to a paradoxical situation if (a) to recognizing the subjective element of wrongdoing in the establishment of the crime and including intention and negligence into the element of wrongdoing, and (b) to requiring a subjective element of justification for justifiable cause and incorporating defense consciousness into the subjective element of justification. For example, when C is illegally killing D, B accidentally leads to C's casualties without any intention or negligence, thus avoiding D's death. According to *Handlungsunwert*, since B lacks intention and negli-

---

[34] 日井田良:《讲义刑法学·总论》，成文堂2008年版，第258页。Ida Makoto.(2008) *Handout of Criminal Law·General Rules*, Yuhikaku Press, 258.

[35] As being discussed later, the believers of *Handlungsunwert* in Germany and Japan do not advocate that all defense by accident be treated as attempted crimes.

[36] 日井田良:《讲义刑法学·总论》，成文堂2008年版，第260页。Ida Makoto.(2008) *Handout of Criminal Law·General Rules*, Yuhikaku Press, 260.

[37] 日井田良:《变革时代の理论刑法学》，庆应义塾大学出版会2007年版，第113页。 Ida Makoto.(2007) *Theoretical Criminal Law in the Age of Change*, Keio University Press Inc., 113.

[38] 德冈特·施特拉腾韦特、洛塔尔·库伦:《刑法总论I——犯罪论》，杨萌译，法律出版社2006年版，第108页。Giinter Stratenwerth & Lothar Kuhlen, trans. Yang Meng, (2006) *Strafrecht Allgemeiner Teil I: Die Straftat*, Law Press, 108.

gence, his conduct is not unlawful, however, since B does not have the subjective element of justification, his conduct is unlawful. Perhaps *Handlungsunwert* believers will say that as the conformance of the constitutive elements is judged before, so B has no intention and negligence, of course, not illegal, if C has the intention to kill, he has the wrongdoing of attempted homicide, if C has the defense consciousness, justifiable defense shall be established. However, (a) Although it is possible to conclude at the first stage that there is no wrongdoing, if one goes further to the second stage, it can only conclude that there is wrongdoing. Originally, in the tripartite system, the criminal constitutive elements are the type of wrongdoing, the field of wrongdoing is about the justifiable cause, both the constitutive element and wrongdoing are about wrongdoing, and an act that does not meet the constitutive element cannot be criminally illegal. However, the theory of attempt of *Handlungsunwert* creates a situation in which an act that does not meet the constitutive elements also has a criminal wrongdoing; (b) These contradictory situations may be neglected in the tripartite system, but in other systems it must be quite obvious. However, the tripartite system is not necessarily the only correct system; (c) Even in the tripartite system, the theory of attempt of *Handlungsunwert* is questionable. According to the tripartite system and the theory of attempt of *Handlungsunwert*, in the stage of conformity of the constitutive elements, the first shall be to affirm the constitutive elements of a sufficient attempted crime of defense by accident, only to identify an attempted crime at the stage of wrongdoing. It will then go back to deny the constitutive elements of a sufficient attempted crime of defense by accident[39]; (d) The logic of the theory of attempt of *Handlungsunwert* is that: the intention is the content of the constitutive elements and an important element indicating *Handlungsunwert*; the constitutive elements are types of wrongdoing, and act conforming to the constitutive elements are illegal in principle. Wrongdoing includes *Handlungsunwert* and *Erfolgsunwert*. Therefore, in order to make justifiable causes exist, it is necessary not only to exclude *Erfolgsunwert*, but also to exclude *Handlungsunwert* (exclude the intention). Since the defense by accident was intentional, it cannot be ruled out *Handlungsunwert* and therefore an attempted crime was established. However, the only difference between defense by accident and justifiable defense upon defense consciousness is whether the actor recognizes the premise of justifiable defense. From this, it can be clearly seen that in the case where the objective facts are identical, *Handlungsunwert*, which determines wrongdoing solely on the basis of the subjective content of the actor, falls into a subjectivist position.

Second, *Handlungsunwert* has adopted the position of rule utilitarianism. Accordingly, as long as the act violates the general rules that need to be observed in order to protect the legal interest, it should be considered illegal even if it does not result in the infringement of legal interest. However, the status of rule utilitarianism is very embarrassing for lacking an internal and consistent theoretical system. If rule utilitarians emphasize that experience proves that violations of certain rules

[39] Vgl.,V.Krey, *Deutsches Strafrecht Allgenmeiner Teil, Band I*, W.kohlhammer 2001,S.158.

often infringe legal interest, people must abide by these rules in any case and that's how rule utilitarians become deontologist, however, deontology conflicts with the freedom guarantee function of criminal law. If rule utilitarianism denies that it is deontological and at all times justifies rules of act by the consequences of the act, then it turns to act utilitarianism (*Erfolgsunwert*); if violating a certain rule produces better results, rule utilitarians may defend based on act utilitarianism. The reason for this is that when rules and utilitarian (final results) conflict, rule utilitarianism either violates the rules to pursue good results, or maintains rules to discard good results.[40] In connection with this, rule utilitarianism may not only limit the freedom of actions of nationals, but may also be detrimental to the protection of legal interests and thus be inappropriate. For example, when the infringement of the rules of act does not cause infringement of legal interest and danger, but instead protects the legal interest, *Handlungsunwert* believers also consider the act is illegal, which ignores the limitations and exceptions of the rule. For another example, the conflict between rules is a common occurrence and the notion of preventing crime by making the nations comply with the rules can, on many occasions, render the nation helpless. In summary, it is too indirect and unrealistic to achieve the purpose of protecting legal interest by obeying the rule of act.[41]

Third, according to the viewpoint of *Handlungsunwert*, because the defense by accident is carried out by the actor under the domination of crime intent, if such act is repeated in another time and another place, the infringement of legal interest will occur. In order to prevent crime, the defense by accident must be considered as a crime. However, since the defense by accident occurs at this time and this place, it should not be placed at that time and that place to judge the danger of the infringement of legal interest. Since defense on specific unlawful infringers has conducted at this time and this place and resulted in the protection of legal interest, therefore, its wrongdoing should be denied. To identify an attempt crime in order to prevent others from following suit would clearly be to use the defender of accident as a tool to prevent crime. he most obviously, if the infringement of legal interest cannot be conducted at this time or in this place, as long as the infringement of legal interest occurs at another time and in another place, the wrongdoing of such act must also be declared, then, the national can only commit acts that at no time could lead to the infringement of a legal interest. This unduly restricts the freedom of nationals and is therefore undesirable.

---

[40] 参见美汤姆·雷根:《动物权利研究》，李曦译，北京大学出版社2010年版，第211页；美布拉德·胡克:“规则后果主义”，载美休·拉福莱特主编:《伦理学理论》，龚群主译，中国人民大学出版社2008年版，第223页。See Tom Regan, trans. Li Xi, (2010) *The Case for Animal Rights*, Peking University Press, 211; Brad Hooker, trans. Gongxiang et al., (2008) *Rule Consequentialism*, as cited in Hugh LaFollette ed., *The Blackwell Guide to Ethical Theory*, China Renmin University Press, 223.

[41] 参见张明楷:“行为功利主义违法观”，载《中国法学》2011年第5期。See Zhang Mingkai. (2011) “The Conception of Wrongfulness in Behavioral Utilitarianism”, as cited in *China Legal Science*, No. 5.

According to the logic of *Handlungsunwert*, when the actor thinks that his act violates the criminal law, but in fact it does not, it is also sanctioned by the imposition of a penalty, which otherwise does not prevent the actor from committing future acts when he knows that the criminal law has been violated, nor does it prevent others from committing acts when they know that the criminal law has been violated. Indeed, *Handlungsunwert* advocators will say that the act, on such occasion, should not be criminalized because criminal constitutive elements are not met. However, the logic is the same. Even if the above-mentioned answer to *Handlungsunwert* is acknowledged, its believers will have difficulties in distinguishing the preventing of the conformity of elements of crime and the wrongdoing. For example, Y prepares to give X a gift, and X intentionally takes the gift away with theft without knowing the truth. If the consent of the victim can prevent the conformity of elements of crime, then *Handlungsunwert* advocators will think that X's act does not constitute a crime. If the consent of the victim can prevent the wrongdoing, then *Handlungsunwert* advocators will think X commits an attempted theft. However, no matter what cause the consent of the victim is, according to the logic of *Handlungsunwert*, a change in the time and place of X's act may lead to the infringement of legal interest. As a result, the same handling should be done, but in fact, it does not. It cannot be denied that this is a contradiction.

According to *Handlungsunwert*, the law does not object to the good results of an act with criminal intent, but it still opposes the act itself. In other words, the evaluation of act can or should be independent of the result of the act. As far as defense by accident is concerned, the reason why evaluate its *Handlungsunwert* independently of the result is that if the act is not prohibited, the actor or other person may cause and infringe legal interests under other conditions. Therefore, whether an act is illegal is not determined by whether the act may cause and infringe legal interest, but entirely by whether the act requires being general prevented. However, what determines whether an action requires being general prevented? The answer may only be that the act may cause and infringe legal interest. In this case, it should be judged whether the actions that have caused or may result in the infringement of legal interest, and cannot leave this point to determine whether an action requires being general prevented. In addition, since *Handlungsunwert* does not oppose, even favour the result of defense by accident, such act shall not be prohibited because the prohibition of the act will result in the prohibition of good results.

It is manifested that the view of *Handlungsunwert* is mainly about the future regardless of the reality. For example, B shot C without knowing that C was preparing to rape women D and caused a serious injury to C. B's act objectively stopped the criminal act of C. According to the viewpoint of *Handlungsunwert*, B's act is illegal, that is, the criminal law prohibits B from shooting at C. Thus, there can only be two endings: (1) B obeys the norm and does not shoot, D is raped, and C is convicted of rape, or (2) B violates the norm and shoots, and B was charged with the crime of intentional homicide or the crime of intentional injury, C was shot and D was raped. However, both endings are unsatisfactory. In other words, *Handlungsunwert* considers general prevention on the premise of sacrificing the legal interests of reality. According to the viewpoint of *Handlungsunwert*, since the criminal law prohibits B's defense by accident, it is illegal for B to shoot and should be punished. Therefore, in the normative sense, it means to prevent others from committing crimes by sacrificing D's legal interests. It has to be argued that *Handlungsunwert* prevents crimes through the indulgence of crimes (the act of C).

Fourth, the theory of attempt of *Handlungsunwert* cannot be implemented in *Tätigkeitsdelikte* where act and result occur simultaneously. For example, Professor C. Roxin pointed out: "*Tätigkeitsdelikte* means that the positive act ends, and at the same time, the constitutive elements are met. Thus there will be no result separating from the act." At the same time, he pointed out that "all crimes have results, in the case of *Tätigkeitsdelikte*, the result exists in the act which is sufficient to constitutive elements implemented by the actor."[42] Since the act and result of *Tätigkeitsdelikte* occur at the same time, then it is impossible to believe that the infringement of legal interest result does not occur (lacking *Erfolgsunwert*) and the act is illegal (lacking *Handlungsunwert*) when the actor intentionally commits *Tätigkeitsdelikte* and the criminal constitutive elements are adequately satisfied, and the subjective elements of justifiable cause are met as well. In other words, in this case, *Handlungsunwert* believers either think that the act constitutes an accomplished intentional crime (because the act has been implemented and the result has already occurred), or think that the act does not constitute a crime (denying the occurrence of the act because the result has not occurred). However, in any case, the theory of attempt of *Handlungsunwert* may fall into a dilemma.

Fifth, *Handlungsunwert* thinks that defense by accident is illegal, but it has to be acknowledged that it is impossible to defend and prevent such defenders of accident who are objectively within the scope of justifications because they create a legal state that should not be banned.[43] Obviously, there are many problems herein.

There are four main contradictions in the theory of attempt of *Handlungsunwert*:

1) The defense by accident is illegal, this kind of illegal act cannot be defended at the time of the act, or it means helping the unlawful infringers to invade the innocent. So, what are the reasons for not to defend? There may be many answers. First of all, defense by accident leads to a legal state, which is a good result, so it cannot be defended. But why should an act that objectively causes good results be considered illegal? The only conclusion is that the actor carries out a defense by accident with the criminal intent. This is basically not about *Handlungsunwert*, but about unworthiness of mood. Moreover, the reason why defense by accident cannot be defended against is that the unlawful infringer cannot defend the defender of accident. Therefore, other third parties cannot defend the defender of accident. Yet *Chinese Criminal Law* stipulates defense for the public interest. Even if the unlawful infringer does not have the right to defend, the third party is likely to defend against the ongoing illegal act. More importantly, *iusta causa* are the interest conflict and rival between multiple participants. "If the act of the actor is legal, the infringed counterpart can only

[42] C.Roxin, *Strafrecht Allgenmeiner Teil, Band I*, 4.Aufl., C.H.Beck, 2006,S.330.

[43] C.Roxin, *Strafrecht Allgenmeiner Teil, Band I*, 4.Aufl., C.H.Beck, 2006,S.330.

endure this infringement."[44] Since the unlawful infringer C can only endure the attack of B, it indicates that the act of B is justified. Finally, according to Professor C.Roxin's point of view, "An attempted impossibility defense is not an attack. It is true that in the case of attempted impossibility defense, although there is no lack of interests confirmed by law, the necessity of protection lacks. Therefore, if a person knows that the infringer's pistol has no bullets, he will not be allowed to knock him down".[45] Since defense by accident is an attempt that cannot be committed, the need for defence is lacking. However, this view separates the interests confirmed by law from the interests protected by law and is hardly favourable. Moreover, in the case of defense by accident, as long as the interests of innocent D are considered, it is necessary to affirm the wrongdoing of C's act, as B's act is an act in opposition to C's, the legality of B can only be affirmed. In addition, defense does not mean casualties. If the wrongdoing of defense by accident is affirmed, then defense is only a matter of limitation, not a matter of it cannot be defended.

2) The defense by accident is unlawful, but, at the time of the act, not only may it not be justified, but it may not be prevented or hindered in any way, on the contrary, it may only be allowed and permitted to be carried out. This is also because an informed third party can only allow or even help the defender to carry out his or her actions in the case of defense by accident. Hindering or preventing means to help the unlawful infringers to commit the illegal act. Thus, there is a conclusion in *Handlungsunwert*: some illegal acts can only be allowed and indulged at that time or some acts prohibited by criminal law must be allowed to be implemented at that time. However, it is difficult to accept such a conclusion in this article.
3) The defense by accident is not defensible or preventable at the time of the act and is to be indulged and allowed, but is punishable by criminal penalties afterwards. However, since the act was allowed at the time of the act, why is it necessary to punish such act afterwards? The answer of *Handlungsunwert* must be that legal interests will be infringed when the time and place changed and others will imitate and infringe the legal interest if the punishment was not carried out. However, the criminal judgment that defense by accident is not illegal does not bring negative effects. This is because such criminal judgment protects the legal interests of defenders of accident, and does not lead to the effect of defense by accident in anticipation of one's own actions in the event of an intentional killing. That is, when B's defense by accident caused death but was acquitted by the court, others could not imitate defense by accident. If someone does follow his enemy for a long time with the intention of killing him when he kills him because defense by accident is not illegal, he is already acting in justifiable defense with defense consciousness, which is also not illegal. In summary, a criminal justice

---

[44] 日井田良:《犯罪论の现在と目的的行为论》，成文堂1995年版，第151页。 Ida Makoto. (1995) *The Present of Criminology and the Theory of Purposive Action*, Seibundo Publishing Co., 151.

[45] C.Roxin, *Strafrecht Allgenmeiner Teil, Band I*, 4.Aufl., C.H.Beck, 2006,S.659.

declaration that defense by accident is not illegal is unlikely to have the effect of encouraging people to implement defense by accident.

4) The defense by accident belongs to the attempted impossibility defense. "Even if the attempted impossibility defense is punishable, justifiable defense towards it shall not be allowed, because the attempted impossibility defense does not pose a danger to the individual's legal interests."[46] However, on the one hand, when the unlawful infringer is killing another person, even if the attack by the defense by accident poses a danger to the infringer, it is permitted by law and is not illegal. Since defense by accident does not pose a danger to personal legal interests, it should be considered been prevented wrongdoing. However, the theory of attempt of *Handlungsunwert* advocates the punishment of the defense by accident, which is also self-contradictory. On the other hand, "Although formally speaking, wrongdoing in criminal law refers to the violation of a criminal law norm (the norms of evaluation), since wrongdoing is the property and evaluation, of the state of affairs in which the criminal law norm makes a negative evaluation, its content is determined by the purpose of criminal law. In other words, what acts will be forbidden is determined by the purpose of law. In this sense, the virtual understanding of the concept of the essential wrongdoing and wrongdoing is based on that of the tasks and purpose of criminal law".[47] Since Professor C.Roxin considers that the purpose and task of criminal law is to protect the legal interest,[48] it is only possible to treat as unlawful an act that infringes or poses a danger to the legal interest. Therefore, there is a contradiction in finding the defense by accident that does not pose a danger to a person's legal interests to be unlawful.

Sixth, the subjective position of *Handlungsunwert* on the issue of defense by accident is quite obvious. For example, when C1 and C2 jointly implement the violent robbery of D's property, A and B use violence to C1 and C2 respectively. The difference is that A knows the existence of the robbery, but B does not. According to *Handlungsunwert*, A's act is justifiable defense, yet the act of B is an attempted crime. However, the objectively identical act becomes the boundary of identifying the establishment of crime simply depending on whether the actor knows the truth subjectively. The use of the defender's crime consciousness and lack of defense consciousness as a basis for *Handlungsunwert* of attempted crime is a good indication that *Handlungsunwert* is nothing more than unworthiness of mood, and there is little differ from subjectivism, if at all. For another example, when C was illegally killing D, A and B shot D at the same time without meaning connect, and C's heart

---

[46] C.Roxin, *Strafrecht Allgenmeiner Teil, Band I*, 4.Aufl., C.H.Beck, 2006,S.654.

[47] 日山口厚:《刑法总论》，有斐阁2007年版，第101页。Yamaguchi Atsushi.(2007) *General Rules of Criminal Law*, Yuhikaku Press, 101.

[48] 参见德克劳斯·罗克信:"刑法的任务不是法益保护吗?"，樊文译，载陈兴良主编:《刑事法评论》(第19卷)，北京大学出版社2007年版，第146页以下。Claus Roxin, trans. Fan Wen, (2007) *Rechtsgütern nicht zu den Aufgaben des Strafrechts?*, as cited in Chen Xingliang ed., *Criminal Law Review*, No.19, Peking University Press, 1–146.

was hit by two bullets; but A knew that C was killing D, and B did not know that. *Handlungsunwert* will conclude that B's act is illegal and constitutes a crime of intentional homicide; but A's shooting is not illegal and does not constitute a crime. The implication is that the act of saving D's life is legal on the condition that the actor knows C is killing D; if the actor does not know C is killing D, the saving of D's life is illegal. However, such a conclusion is also a reflection of subjectivism, and it is hard to agree.

Seventh, regarding the content of defense consciousness, the dominant ideology in Germany is that "it is substantially sufficient for justification that the actor committed the act to the extent that it was objectively justified and had subjective knowledge of the state of justification. The actor then has the intention to commit the justified act objectively. The mere awareness of the state of legitimacy precludes the act from *Handlungsunwert*, at the same time, precludes wrongfulness. The actor is not required to further commit the act for the purpose of justification."[49] *Handlungsunwert* believers in Japan consider that "the original meaning of defense consciousness is to actively defend the rights of oneself or others from unlawful infringement (the theory of purpose or intention). However, even an instinctive act of self-defence does not negate the fact that it is based on defense consciousness. Moreover, there is no doubt that the justifiable defense also take into account instinctive counter-attacks. Therefore, in the absence of positive defense intentions and motives, it is not possible to identify the existence of defense consciousness. Therefore, even if there is no positive defense consciousness due to excitement, embarrassment, anger or coexistence of attack and defense intention, defense consciousness should not be denied immediately".[50] However, firstly, *Handlungsunwert* advocators require subjective elements of wrongdoing to correspond to subjective *iusta causa*. Since *Handlungsunwert* advocators view criminal intent as one of subjective element of wrongdoing and considers intent to be the unity of the cognition element and will element,[51] then the subjective element of justification should also be the unity of the cognition element and will element. However, in the case of defense by accident, *Handlungsunwert* requires defense cognition, which is somewhat self-contradictory. Secondly, the paradox is that when A says to the defender of accident B that "C is killing somebody", the act of B should be viewed as justifiable defense because he has realized the infringement of legal interest of C. How weird it is that a stranger can make a sinner become sinless.

Eighth, if the defense by accident is the attempt crime, then B conducts defense by accident against C with murder intent when C is intentionally killing D. B fails to kill C, causing or not causing injury of C, then there are two attempts: (a) there is

---

[49] C.Roxin, *Strafrecht Allgenmeiner Teil, Band I*, 4.Aufl., C.H.Beck, 2006,S.641.

[50] 日大谷实:《刑法讲义总论》，成文堂2009年新版，第289~290页。See Ohya Minoru. (2009) *General Handouts on Criminal Law(New Edition)*, Seibundo Publishing Co, 289–290.

[51] Vgl.,C.Roxin, *Strafrecht Allgenmeiner Teil, Band I*, 4.Aufl., C.H.Beck, 2006.S.437; H.Jeschck/T. Weigend, *Lehrbuch des Strafrechts.Allgemeiner Teil*, 5.Aufl.,Duncker & Humblot, 1996,S.293; 日大谷实:《刑法讲义总论》，成文堂2009年新版，第165页。Ohya Minoru.(2009) *General Handouts on Criminal Law(New Edition)*, Seibundo Publishing Co, 165.

an attempt to cause the expected death result, and (b) due to lack of the attempt of *Erfolgsunwert*, thus forms the "attempted attempt".[52] But it's incredible. The counter-argument of *Handlungsunwert* is that the reason to affirm that the defense by accident constitutes an attempted crime is that its wrongdoing can only be affirmed on condition that the illegal results constitute the attempted crime, rather than acknowledging the "attempted attempt". The criticism of the theory of attempt is only conceptual, not essential.[53] However, since the attempted crime is to be considered, it is impossible to disregard the concept of attempted crime. The attempted crime is not only a matter of the stage of wrongdoing, but also of the stage of conformity of the constitutive elements, and an attempt can only be one that has been undertaken without having reached the stage of accomplishment, and not one that has not reached the stage of attempt. It does not accord with the guiding principles of the stability of the criminal law to determine substantively attempted crime or to apply (or quasi-apply) the provisions of attempted crime.

Ninth, *Handlungsunwert* in Germany is to punish defense by accident as attempted impossibility defense. Professor C.Roxin pointed out that "when the actor lacks an understanding of the objective situation of justifiable defense, his act is evaluated as an impossibility defense."[54] Article 23 of *German Criminal Law*, which deals with attempted crime, provides in its Paragraph 3: "If the actor, out of great ignorance, did not realize that the type of object of attempt or the method used could not have achieved the attempt at all, the court may waive the penalty or reduce it at its discretion." According to this stipulation, the attempted impossibility defense cannot be committed when the actor mistakes a wild animal for an enemy to kill, and when he mistakes sugar for arsenic. This is in fact the conclusion of the pure subjectivism or the theory of abstract danger. Obviously, in China, as long as we do not adopt the pure subjectivism or the theory of abstract danger, we cannot accept the conclusions of German scholars. However, there are many flaws in the pure subjectivism and the theory of abstract danger that cannot be used as a basis for determining the attempted crime.[55] In the case of defense by accident, Japanese Professor Ida Makoto pointed out that "to affirm the wrongdoing of act is limited to the fact that the actor does not realize that the justifiable cause exists, and the average people do not have the opportunity to recognize the fact."[56] Obviously this is the point of view of the theory of specific danger. However, the theory of specific dan-

---

[52] 参见日西村克彦:"いわゆる'偶然防卫'について", 载《判例时报》第824号(1976年)。Nishimura Katsuhiko.(1976) "So-called 'accidential defense' ", as cited in *Case Law Times*, No. 824.

[53] 日井田良:《犯罪论の现在と目的的行为论》，成文堂1995年版，第134页。Ida Makoto. (1995) *The Present of Criminology and the Theory of Purposive Action*, Seibundo Publishing Co., 134.

[54] C.Roxin, *Strafrecht Allgenmeiner Teil, Band I*, 4.Aufl., C.H.Beck, 2006,S.719.

[55] 参见张明楷:《刑法的基本立场》，中国法制出版社2002年版，第236页以下。See Zhang Mingkai. (2002) *Basic Standpoints of Criminal Law*, China Legal Publishing House, 1–236.

[56] 日井田良:《讲义刑法学·总论》，成文堂2008年版，第260页。Ida Makoto.(2008) *Handout of Criminal Law·General Rules*, Yuhikaku Press, 260.

ger is not satisfactory.[57] It is not difficult to see that it is impossible to accept the conclusion of Japanese scholars as long as the theory of objective danger or the corrected theory of objective danger is to be reasonable adopted. It should also be noted that in Germany and Japan, the penalties for attempted crimes are subject to certain restrictions. Therefore, even *Handlungsunwert* believers do not advocate that the defense by accident shall be established as the attempted crime.

(2) A view that defense by accident has *Handlungsunwert* and lacks *Erfolgsunwert*

Several *Handlungsunwert* believers have argued that justifiable defense is premised on defense consciousness. The defense by accident is not only *Handlungsunwert*, but also *Erfolgsunwert*.

For example, Professor Takahashi Norio in Japan pointed out that "there is a view that defense by accident lacks *Erfolgsunwert*, and it only has *Handlungsunwert*, so the attempted crime shall be established. However, the attempted crime shall have *Handlungsunwert* and *Erfolgsunwert* (in the sense of specific danger of legal interests), the mere fact that *Handlungsunwert* does not provide a basis for an attempted crime. In the case of defense by accident, the absence of defense consciousness means that it cannot be considered to be in the nature of a counter-attack, but, as the end is justified, there is both a breach of the norms of act and the result of a constitutive element has occurred. However, such result cannot be considered as 'illegal' results, and sanctions can only be imposed at an attempted limit. Therefore, provisions of attempted crime can be quasi-applied. That is to say, the crime is not purely attempted because the result of the constitutive elements has occurred, but *Erfolgsunwert* because the result of defence has been produced and the result is reduced, so the penalty is quasi-attempted."[58]

The above viewpoints consider the specific danger to legal interest as a punishment basis of attempted crime. The author fully agrees on that. However, there is no room for discussion about the point of view that the punishment of defense by accident should be quasi-apply with the standard of attempted crime.

First, for distinguishing attempt crimes and impossibility defense, Professor Takahashi Norio believes that the corrected theory of objective danger is basically appropriate. He also believes that "the presence or absence of the specific danger is a problem of danger results and is a requirement for launching sanctions". "The dangerousness of the perpetrating act is established by a prior judgment at the time of the act, if there is an abstract danger to the legal interest. However, the establishment of an attempted crime is an *ex post facto* judgment as to whether or not the sanctioning norm was activated, and therefore an *ex post facto* judgment should be made as to what degree of danger existed to that object at the time of the act."[59]

[57] 参见张明楷:《刑法的基本立场》，中国法制出版社2002年版，第239页以下。See Zhang Mingkai. (2002) *Basic Standpoints of Criminal Law*, China Legal Publishing House, 1–239.

[58] 日高桥则夫:《刑法总论》，成文堂2010年版，第268页。Takahashi Norio.(2010) *General Theory of Criminal Law,* Seibundo Publishing Co., 268.

[59] 日高桥则夫:《刑法总论》，成文堂2010年版，第375~376页。Takahashi Norio.(2010) *General Theory of Criminal Law,* Seibundo Publishing Co., 375–376.

However, as the discussion later, since the specific danger is used as the punishment basis of the attempted crime, and the corrected objective theory of danger is taken, it is quite difficult to affirm the specific danger of defense by accident.

Second, there are two kinds of provisions for the quasi-application of attempted crime: (a) neither the attempted crimes nor accomplished crime is established originally, but the rule of the former is quasi-applied, and (b) accomplished crimes are established, but the rules of attempted crimes are used for some reason. The quasi-application of the former occasion clearly violates the principle of *nulla poena sine lege*. The latter type of quasi-application is unreasonable and contradictory. This is because, since the act has already constituted an accomplished crime, it is not allowed to quasi-apply the rules of the attempted crime.

5.3 The Theory of Attempt of *Erfolgsunwert*

(1) Reasons of the Theory of Unnecessary of Defense Consciousness

Erfolgsunwert denies subjective elements of justification, so the theory of unnecessary of defense consciousness is taken. In summary, there are the following reasons for the theory of unnecessary of defense consciousness:

First, the expression "for" defense rights used in Article 36 of *Japanese Criminal Law* can be understood as an act committed objectively for the purpose of defending the right, and does not have to be understood as a subjective purpose of defending the right.[60] As stated before, "for avoiding" used in Article 32 of *German Criminal Law* expresses the objective nature of justifiable defense. Article 20 of *Chinese Criminal Law* also uses "for". But as mentioned before, the expression of "for" not only express the purpose, but also indicate the reason. Therefore, it is absolutely feasible to understand justifiable defense objectively without the need to take defense consciousness as a subjective element of justifiable defense.

Second, according to the viewpoints of *Erfolgsunwert*, intention and negligence are the elements of culpability rather than subjective elements of wrongdoing. The subjective element of justification is not required, since justifiable defense is justifiable cause. For example, Professor Yamaguchi Atsushi said that "according to *Erfolgsunwert*, it is not required to take the defense consciousness as the element of justifiable defense (the theory of unnecessary of defense consciousness). When the defense consciousness is understood as the intent and motivation of defense, a simple element of mood may become an element of culpability. In understanding the defense consciousness as the knowledge of facts belonging to a justifiable defence such as a situation of justifiable defence, it is simply the 'intent' of justifiable defence as an element of culpability (cautiously, this is a metaphor; correctly, as described later, the existence of intent is denied when there is knowledge of facts

[60] 参见日浅田和茂:《刑法总论》，成文堂2007年补正版，第227页。Asada Kazushige. (2007) *General Theory of Criminal Law (Supplementary Edition)*, Seibundo Publishing Co, 227.

belonging to a justifiable defence such as a situation of justifiable defence). As long as the general criminal intents are not taken as subjective elements of wrongdoing, namely, as *Handlungsunwert*, the nature of defense by accident as an element of wrongdoing is denied (simple awareness of facts, infringement of legal interests or dangers, and advocacy of legal interest as a hindrance element will not affect the wrongdoing of the act). Therefore, defense by accident may constitute a justifiable defense."[61]

Third, even if the act is committed with a criminal intent, if justifiable defense is achieved as its result, there is no *Erfolgsunwert*. According to *Erfolgsunwert*, it is appropriate to assume that they are *iusta causa*. For example, when C is killing D, defender of the accident B just kills C in advance. Because D and C are the relationship between "justifiable and unjustifiable", even if B does not have the defense consciousness, B and C are in a "justifiable and unjustifiable", relationship, which is in line with the characteristics of justifiable defense. Therefore, the justifiable defense does not require the defense consciousness as a subjective element of justification.[62]

Fourth, justifiable defence is a sudden act of counter-attack, even an instinctive one, and to require a defense consciousness would narrow the scope of justifiable defence significantly and would therefore be inappropriate.[63] Professor Fukuda taira, who holds the theory of necessity of defense consciousness, pointed out that the defense based on the instinct, even if it is basically unconscious reflections, can generally be considered to have the defense consciousness.[64] However, if the instinctive and reflective actions are not necessarily evaluated as acts, then it is far-fetched to identify it as an act with defense consciousness.

Fifth, if the theory of necessity of defense consciousness is taken, then, when negligent act stops the on-going unlawful infringement, it cannot be considered as justifiable defense because there is no defense consciousness. This is obviously inappropriate.[65] Professor Fukuda taira, who holds the theory of necessity of defense consciousness, pointed out that since the counterattack based on the instinct can also be recognized as the existence of defense consciousness, the negligent counterattack can also be justifiable defense.[66] However, "When C was shooting D, B shot C accidentally. Regardless of whether his actions were unconscious, he obviously

[61] 日山口厚:《刑法总论》，有斐阁2007年版，第124页。Yamaguchi Atsushi.(2007) *General Rules of Criminal Law*, Yuhikaku Press, 124.

[62] 参见日曾根威彦:《刑法总论》，成文堂2008年版，第104页。See Sone Takehiko.(2008) *General Theory of Criminal Law*, Seibundo Publishing Co., 104.

[63] 日山中敬一:《刑法总论》，成文堂2008年版，第463页。Yamanaka Keiichi.(2008) *General Theory of Criminal Law*, Seibundo Publishing Co, 463.

[64] 参见日福田平:《全订刑法总论》，有斐阁2004年版，第158页。See Fukuda Taira.(2004) *General Theory of Criminal Law (Full Edition)*, Yuhikaku Press, 158.

[65] 日平野龙一:《刑法总论II》，有斐阁1975年版，第243页。See Hirano Ryuuichi.(1975) *General Theory of Criminal Law II*, Yuhikaku Press, 243.

[66] 参见日福田平:《全订刑法总论》，有斐阁2004年版，第158页。See Fukuda Taira.(2004) *General Theory of Criminal Law (Full Edition)*, Yuhikaku Press, 158.

did not recognize the situation of justifiable defense. To assume the defense consciousness on such occasions is either a strong argument or self-defeating".[67]

Why do some *Erfolgsunwert* believers advocate that defense by accident shall be established as the attempted crime while standing for the theory of unnecessary of defense consciousness? Are these reasons valid?

(2) A View that *Erfolgsunwert* regarding the Attempted Crime Exist in Defense by Accident.

Unlike *Handlungsunwert*, which holds that there is *Handlungsunwert* in defense by accident, *Erfolgsunwert* believes that the defense by accident has attempted *Erfolgsunwert*.

Professor Nishida Noriyuki pointed out that defense by accident "lacks *Erfolgsunwert* indeed, but it may also be considered that there is a danger that the result may happens. This question can be considered in parallel with the following questions. For example, when a person did not know that the other party was a corpse, and he thought that the other party was still alive and fired. Afterwards, the forensic identification showed that the other party had died. Is the act an attempted homicide? Obviously, how to deal with this problem ultimately comes to what kind of insights can be made about the impossibility defense, which will be discussed later. Although this article applies the theory of unnecessary of defense consciousness, it believes that defense by accident should have the attempted *Strafbarkeit*".[68] Professor Nishida Noriyuki takes hypothetical probability on impossibility defense: "If a strict *ex post facto*, scientific judgment is made, all attempts are apt to become impossibility defense. Therefore, in determining the happening of results, it is important to explore both the reasons and circumstances under which the result did not occur, and also what change in circumstances could have caused the result, and to what extent such a change in circumstances would have probability. The end of this inquiry is that when there is no probability, or very low probability, then danger should be denied and the impossibility defense should be identified. Such an insight can be called the theory of hypothetical probability."[69] Apparently, the reason why Professor Nishida Noriyuki believes that the defense by accident shall be established as the attempted crime is because of the probability that C did not kill D at the time of the act. In other words, if the probability of C not killing D was high at the time of the act, then the risk of infringement of legal interest of B's defense by accident would have been high, and therefore the attempted crime should have been deemed to have been committed. Professor Yamaguchi Atsushi also pointed out that "where it can be found that there is a possibility of achieving the constitutive elements without being based on justifiable defense, there is also scope for interpreting

[67] 日山中敬一:《刑法总论》，成文堂2008年版，第463页。Yamanaka Keiichi.(2008) *General Theory of Criminal Law*, Seibundo Publishing Co, 463.

[68] 日西田典之:《刑法总论》，弘文堂2010年版，第171页。Nishida Noriyuki.(2010) *General Theory of Criminal Law*, Koubundou Publishers Inc., 171.

[69] 日西田典之:《刑法总论》，弘文堂2010年版，第310~311页。Nishida Noriyuki.(2010) *General Theory of Criminal Law*, Koubundou Publishers Inc., 310–311.

this as establishing an attempted crime, based on the understanding of an attempted crime."[70] However, this article is skeptical of the above views.

First, since defense consciousness is not required to establish justifiable defense, it follows that defense by accident satisfies the conditions for justifiable defense and is therefore a justifiable cause. At this point, it is possible to deny the establishment of the crime, and on this premise it is inappropriate to say that defense by accident shall be established as an attempted crime.

Second, if there is a danger of infringement of legal interest caused by defense by accident, it is because C may not have committed the act of killing D, then, the defense by accident of B may infringe on the life of C who did not kill D. The above judgment is questionable. In this case, the above viewpoints only depend on using the facts recognized by the accidental defenders without using the objective facts that the accidental defenders do not recognize. Since the B's act is affirmed as defense by accident afterwards, it means that C was carrying out the illegal act of killing D. Under this circumstance, no matter what kind of situation is envisaged, the probability of C not killing D is none or very law. On the other hand, the probability of B's infringement of legal interest are none or extremely low.

Third, even if one considers that C may not have committed the unlawful infringement and may be an innocent person, and that B's defense by accident may infringe the legal interests of an innocent person, one cannot directly affirm that B's act constitutes an attempted crime. This is because the other side of the fact is that B's act objectively protected the life of D, or that B's act prevented the legal interest from being infringed. The result of weighing the infringement of legal interest and the danger of infringement of legal interest must be that B's act is not unlawful. In detail, according to *Erfolgsunwert*, in the case of conscious justifiable defense for the interest of a third party, since the unlawful infringer is in a state of defense, the infringed person is not obliged to endure the unlawful infringement, and the balance between the legal interests of the unlawful infringer and the legal interests of the infringed person leads to the conclusion that the legal interests of the infringed person are absolutely superior, and the measure of legal interests becomes the rationale for preventing wrongdoing.[71] Since it is so, in the case of defense by accident, the legal interests of the infringed person must also be included in the scope of measuring legal interest. Once the legal interests of the infringed Are included, even if the defense by accident of B is considered to have the danger (may not conduct infringement) to C's life, but it objectively protects D's life whose legal interest is in superior position, so the wrongdoing of B's act should be denied.

Fourth, to extend the question a little further, it will be even more inappropriate to say that B's act is considered as an attempted crime because of the danger to the life and body of D. In the context of a defense by accident, the danger of shooting an innocent person as opposed to the objective protection of an innocent person's

[70] 日山口厚:《刑法总论》，有斐阁2007年版，第124页。Yamaguchi Atsushi.(2007) *General Rules of Criminal Law*, Yuhikaku Press, 124.

[71] 参见日山口厚:《刑法总论》，有斐阁2007年版，第113~114页。Yamaguchi Atsushi. (2007) *General Rules of Criminal Law*, Yuhikaku Press, 113–114.

life (the innocent person's life cannot be protected if there is no danger of shooting the innocent) will have to be allowed (this is the result of measuring legal interest, not the conclusion from *Handlungsunwert*). Moreover, even if it is not defense by accident but the justifiable defense with defense consciousness (shooting the unlawful infringer), the life of the innocent is equally in danger of which the defender is fully aware. But B's act cannot be considered as an attempted crime. For example, to rescue hostages been kidnapped, it is often to shoot criminals. Under such circumstances, even if the criminal was hit, and shooting posed a certain danger to the hostage's life, it is still allowed.

It can be seen from the above that there is still a difference between the judgment of whether the defense by accident has the risk of infringement of the legal interest, and whether the intentional act in the general occasion has the risk of infringement of the legal interest. Because in the latter case (such as shooting to the bed for killing someone, and the victim was not hit because he gone to bathroom at night), there is no fact of protecting legal interest in killing, so there is no need to measure the legal interest. However, in the case of defense by accident, because there is objective fact of protecting legal interests, therefore, when making a judgment of danger and weighing the legal interests, it is necessarily different from an ordinary judgment.. However, the above-mentioned theory of attempt of *Erfolgsunwert* ignores this point and is therefore not taken in this article.

(3) A View that Unworthiness of Danger Exist in Defense by Accident

Professor Yamanaka Keiichi, who holds the theory of unnecessary of defense consciousness,[72] believes that the unworthiness of danger exist in defense by accident. For example, when C was killing D intentionally, the defender of accident B fired at C which happened to result in justifiable defense. Whether B's act is slightly earlier, or slightly later, B commits a crime of intentional homicide. This is true in all cases of defense by accident Therefore, even if we do not take the theory of specific danger judged in advance but take the after-the-fact observation, we can also say that B's act has caused a dangerous state that brings illegal results. For example, C conducted infringement in the last moment after the shooting of B, and the act of B has already posed a specific danger. In this case, although there is a result of justifiable defense without *Erfolgsunwert*, the dangerous state of the wrongdoing that has occurred cannot be justified. In summary, without *Erfolgsunwert*, there is still unworthiness of danger.[73] However, this view is questionable.

First, "since the unworthiness of danger implies the risk of a result occurring, there is no unworthiness of danger on the occasion of making an *ex post facto* observation that there is no *Erfolgsunwert* (fully lawfulness)".[74] In other words, the dan-

[72] 日山中敬一:《刑法总论》，成文堂2008年版，第435页。Yamanaka Keiichi.(2008) *General Theory of Criminal Law*, Seibundo Publishing Co, 435.

[73] 日山中敬一:《刑法总论》，成文堂2008年版，第465页。Yamanaka Keiichi.(2008) *General Theory of Criminal Law*, Seibundo Publishing Co, 465.

[74] 日浅田和茂:《刑法总论》，成文堂2007年补正版，第230页。Asada Kazushige.(2007) *General Theory of Criminal Law (Supplementary Edition)*, Seibundo Publishing Co, 230.

gerous state itself is the result. Since it is considered that defense by accident lacks *Erfolgsunwert*, it should not be considered that defense by accident has the unworthiness of danger.

Second, it cannot be argued that there is an unworthiness of danger in defense by accident on the grounds that a slight advance or postponement of defense by accident would have established the crime of intentional homicide. Since one takes an *ex post facto* observation, one cannot change the facts itself to determine what might have happened a little earlier or a little later. In fact, even in the case of a justifiable defense with defense consciousness, there are many occasions when a slight advance or postponement may be an untimely defense and the intentional crime. However, it cannot be considered that justifiable defense with defense consciousness has the unworthiness of danger.

Third, when legal interests are in urgent danger, justifiable defense can be carried out. For example, when C is aiming at D with a gun, it can be properly defended even if the trigger has not been pulled. Therefore, the so-called situation that "C conducted infringement in the last moment after the shooting of B, and the act of B has already posed a specific danger" is hardly tenable.

5.4 The Dualism of *Erfolgsunwert*

The dualism of *Erfolgsunwert* holds that the emergency rescue (one type of defense by accident) is justifiable. This article is in favor of this. Why the justifiable defense (another type of defense by accident) is shall be established as an attempted crime?

Professor Sone Takehiko, who advocates this view, pointed out that on the occasion of B killed C with intent to homicide and in fact C was committing an intentional act of killing against B, "there is a conflict between their legal interests, and the law could not take either of them in a superior position". "They are not in a 'justifiable and unjustifiable' relationship, it is difficult to determine that B's act is justified without the premise of lacking justifiable defense. In this respect, the ending in this case is that the defense consciousness plays a role as a subjective element of justification, but it must be noted that this is because the legal interest of B, who does not have a defense intent, is evaluated as an unjustified interest, and not because the mental state of B, who does not have a defense intent, itself lays the basis for the wrongdoing of the act, as *Handlungsunwert* suggests. However, although it cannot be assumed that B's act constitutes a justifiable defense, it should be considered that the degree of its wrongdoing is only within the limits of criminal attempt. It is true that C has died, and B's act is in line with the constitutive elements of accomplished homicide (this is also true in the case of normal justifiable defense). But since the legal interest of C is also an interest that is not worthy of protecting by law, thus a legal evaluation which is different from homicide should be made. However, due to the actual results, provisions of attempted crime should be applied, rather than quasi-applying the attempted crime."[75] This view is somehow reasonable, and may also conform to the ordinary people's feelings of law. However, this article has different views on this.

First, when judging the danger, Professor Sone Takehiko takes the theory of objective danger, namely, All the facts identified afterwards and existing at the time of the act are used as information to judge the presence or absence of danger by general human standards of science.[76] However, "in order to bring defense by accident, people can also say that they are in a 'justifiable and unjustifiable' relationship from the observation after the defense",[77] thus it conforms to the characteristics of justifiable defense. In other words, as long as it is found afterwards that C was carrying out the act of killing B, it can be concluded that B's life was in an imminent danger. Even if B killed C a little earlier, it cannot be denied that B's act meets the conditions of justifiable defense. People may ask whether C's act is justifiable defense if B kills C a little earlier before C kills B. This article also holds a positive attitude towards this. "To determine whether there is the justifiable defense, the first essential point is to judge from its result."[78] The objective judgment after the defense always find that the party who is "striking preemptively" constitutes a justifiable defense. People may say that this is exactly a 'justifiable and justifiable' or 'unjustifiable and unjustifiable' relationship. In fact, there are two 'justifiable and unjustifiable' relationships: when C is conducting the defense by accident and kill B, C is justifiable and B is unjustifiable; when B is conducting the defense by accident and kill C, then B is justifiable and C is unjustifiable.

Second, on the one hand, Professor Sone Takehiko argued that B's act did not establish justifiable defense was not based on a lack of defense consciousness as a basis for wrongdoing, as *Handlungsunwert*, while on the other hand, he argued that B's lack of defense consciousness led to his legal interest being evaluated as an unjustified interest. In the view of this article, this is simply a different formulation, which in effect treats the defense consciousness as a subjective element of justification and conflicts with Professor Sone Takehiko's position of *Erfolgsunwert*.

Third, professor Sone Takehiko uses the premise that "justifiable defense (one type of defense by accident) belongs to the relationship of 'unjustifiable and unjustifiable'" to argue that defense by accident is illegal. This is actually a mutual argumentation of premise and conclusion.[79] It is true that Professor Sone Takehiko puts

---

[75] 日曾根威彦:《刑法の重要问题(总论)》，成文堂2005年版，第94~95页。Sone Takehiko. (2005) *Important Issues of Criminal Law General Theory(General Theory)*, Seibundo Publishing Co., 94–95.

[76] 日曾根威彦:《刑法总论》，弘文堂2008年版，第230页。Sone Takehiko.(2008) *General Theory of Criminal Law*, Seibundo Publishing Co., 230.

[77] 日浅田和茂:《刑法总论》，成文堂2007年补正版，第230页。Asada Kazushige.(2007) *General Theory of Criminal Law (Supplementary Edition)*, Seibundo Publishing Co, 230.

[78] 日山中敬一:《刑法总论》，成文堂2008年版，第463页。Yamanaka Keiichi.(2008) *General Theory of Criminal Law*, Seibundo Publishing Co, 463.

[79] 参见日前田雅英:《现代社会と实质的犯罪论》，东京大学出版会1992年版，第149页。See Maeda Masahide.(1992) *Contemporary Society and Substantive Crime Theory*,

forward a basic reason. The reason why the defender of accident is unjustifiable is that the lack of defense consciousness. Therefore, legal interests of the defender of accident are not worth to be protected by criminal law. However, an objectively existing legal interest will certainly lose the protection of criminal law just because the subject of the legal interest has criminal intent or lacks defense consciousness; only when the subject of the legal interest is implementing unlawful infringement, he can be placed in a position of defense. Since justifiable defense (one type of defense by accident) objectively protects one's own life, and the other party's act belongs to the unlawful infringement, then it cannot be considered that the defender of accident loses the protection of the criminal law because of lack of defense consciousness.

Fourth, the conclusions of the dualism are also uncoordinated, that is, the defense by accident that protects the third party's legal interests, is not a crime. But defense by accident which protects own legal interests is an attempted crime. This more or less brings ethical judgment into the realm of criminal law.

5.5 The Theory of Innocence of *Erfolgsunwert*

The critique of the above-mentioned various theories generally means that the theory of innocence of *Erfolgsunwert* is reasonable. The following is a brief summary of the two basic views of that.

(1) A View that the Theory of the Necessity of Defense Consciousness

Professor Li Hong points out: "From the legislative history of China's criminal law concerning justifiable defense, with the exception of *Criminal Law of the People's Republic of China (1995 Draft)* concerning the elements of the establishment of justifiable defense, which used the phrase 'for defending...', a phrase that purely emphasizes objective facts, after which successive drafts of the criminal law as well as the current criminal law have used the highly subjective term 'for... protect oneself from an ongoing unlawful infringement'. In this context, as long as the principle of *nulla poena sine lege* is upheld, the standpoint that no matter whether the actor has the defense consciousness, justifiable defense always constitutes is hard to be tenable."[80] In view of this, Professor Li Hong takes the theory of the necessity of defense consciousness, according to which, defense by accident does not constitute justifiable defense. However, Professor Li Hong also pointed out: "the view that defense by accident does not constitute justifiable defense does not mean that defense by accident constitutes a crime. According to the current criminal law, defense by accident does not constitute a crime. In the light of the provisions of

University of Tokyo Press, 149.

[80] 黎宏:《刑法总论问题思考》，中国人民大学出版社2007年版，第324~325页。Li Hong. (2007) *Reflections on Issues in the General Theories of Criminal Law*, China Renmin University Press, 324–325.

Article 13 of *Chinese Criminal Law* concerning the concept of crime, a crime is an act which is socially dangerous in substance to the extent that it merits a penalty and which violates the provisions of criminal law in form. Specifically speaking, whether an act is a crime or not, objectively, the act of the actor need to be socially harmful, infringing or threatening the legal interests protected by the specific provisions of criminal law, subjectively, the actor need to be aware of the result which infringes or threats legal interests caused by his act. These two aspects are indispensable elements for the establishment of the crime, without which the crime cannot be established. In the occasion of defense by accident, although the actor carried out killing under the control of subjective criminal purpose (the intention of homicide), but since, in retrospect, the act not only did not have the serious consequence of depriving an innocent person's life, but instead gave rise to the legally permissible effect of saving one's own life or the life of another in justifiable defense. Therefore, the act objectively does not have the effect of infringing or threatening the legal interest, that is, it is not socially harmful. This being the case, it is clear that, from the point of view of crime being the unity of objective harm and subjective offense, both of which are indispensable, the act of defense by accident does not meet the requirements for the establishment of a crime and can hardly constitute a specific offense under criminal law.."[81] This article agrees with Professor Li Hong's conclusion, but it is difficult to agree with his reasons.

First of all, as mentioned above, "for" is a term with a strong subjective color and a term to express objective reasons. Therefore, since *Erfolgsunwert* is adopted, people need to choose the latter meaning of "for" and give up the theory of the necessity of defense consciousness. In other words, the adoption of *Erfolgsunwert* means to take the theory of the unnecessary of defense consciousness, which will not violate the principle of *nulla poena sine lege*.

Moreover, Professor Li Hong only substantially discusses that defense by accident does not constitute a crime. However, under the bipartite system or the tripartite system, when the constitutive elements are met, a purely substantive argument that the act is not illegal, leading to a conclusion of innocence, is not only unconvincing but also tends to undermine the security of the criminal law and denies the principle that the constitutive elements are types of wrongdoing. In China, under the quadripartite system of crime, when the four elements of the crime are met, arguing purely on substance that the act lacks social harm and thus concluding that it is not guilty can also lead to arbitrariness in judgment and undermine the stability of criminal law. In summary, no matter what kind of system of the crime is adopted, when objective "damage" is caused, the actor is acquitted on the grounds either that the act does not conform to the constitutive elements, or that there is a justifiable cause or impediment on responsibility. And the actor should not be acquitted directly on the grounds that the act has no criminal nature.

[81] 黎宏:《刑法总论问题思考》，中国人民大学出版社2007年版，第344页。Li Hong. (2007) *Reflections on Issues in the General Theories of Criminal Law*, China Renmin University Press, 344.

Finally, according to Professor Li Hong's point of view, defense by accident is a supra-law justifiable cause. However, it is always easy to dispute whether the supra-law justifiable cause can be recognized. As a result, as long as the judicial personnel do not recognize the supra-law justifiable cause, the defense by accident will be considered as a crime. Therefore, when people are controversial about whether a sinless act is a statutory justifiable cause or a supra-law justifiable cause, it should be classified in the former. That is to say, when a sinless act prevents the wrongdoing, the priority should be given to the application of the criminal law on the justifiable cause. In fact, as long as the theory of unnecessary of defense consciousness is taken, defense by accident can be the statutory justifiable cause, thus the arbitrariness of identification is avoided.

(2) A View that the Theory of Unnecessary of Defense Consciousness

This article takes *Erfolgsunwert* and the theory of unnecessary of defense consciousness.

The essence of wrongdoing is the infringement of legal interests, not the violation of norms, much less a lack of ethical violation and social equivalence. Accordingly, an act prevents wrongdoing either because it protects a more superior or at least equivalent legal interest (such as justifiable defense, necessity, etc.) or because the victim waives the protection of legal interests (such as consent of the victim). Just like normal justifiable defense, as long as defense by accident does not exceed the limits of necessary limits, it means to protect a superior or at least equivalent legal interest, thus preventing wrongdoing.

Whether the act infringes the legal interest is an objective fact. Therefore, intention and negligence are the elements of responsibility, not the elements of wrongdoing. Correspondingly, the so-called defense consciousness is not an element that affects wrongdoing. As a result, the establishment of justifiable defense does not base on the premise that the defender has defense consciousness subjectively (the theory of unnecessary of defense consciousness). And it cannot be considered illegal because the defender of accident lacks defense consciousness.

Because the defense consciousness does not affect the wrongdoing and the justifiable defense is justifiable cause, when the defense by accident meets the various objective elements of justifiable defense, it is considered that the wrongdoing is prevented. With this premise, it is self-contradictory to say that defense by accident shall be established as an attempted crime. The intent to kill or injury other person of the defender of accident is simply *mens rea*. However, the pure *mens rea* is impossible to establish a crime.

In defense by accident, "the objective existence of an imminent and unjustified fact of infringement, as well as the act of defense and the effect of defense, are objectively in a 'justifiable and unjustifiable' relationship, so that there is an objective interest that is confirmed by law".[82] In accordance with the path from objective

[82] 日内藤谦:《刑法讲义总论(中)》，有斐阁1986年版，第344页。See Naitou Ken.(1986) *General Lectures on Criminal Law (Medium)*, Yuhikaku Press, 344.

to subjective determination of crime, the establishment of crime should be excluded. "Whether observed *ex ante* or *ex post*, the defense by accident objectively prevents the basis for the wrongful content of the crime as an attempt and should be acquitted."[83]

The defense by accident is not limited to the so-called intentional defense by accident, but also includes the so-called negligent (or accidental) defense by accident. The latter is divided into two types: (a) when C is illegally killing D, B is cleaning his gun nearby and B's gun discharges and hits C because of negligence (or accident), thus protecting D's life, and (b) A mistaken thought to be attacked by a beast because of negligence (or accident), in fact, it was a human being not a beast. According to the theory of innocence of *Erfolgsunwert*, the act of A and B is a justifiable defense and does not constitute a crime.

In short, the defense by accident shall be established as a justifiable defense, and shall be acquitted. As *Handlungsunwert* believers say: "An objective examination of the wrongdoing is consistent in its resolution of this issue."[84] "The doctrine of impunity, which implements the principle of the *ex post facto* of the judgment of wrongdoing, is indeed consistent with the adoption of the theory of objective danger of punishment for attempted crime. As long as *ex post facto* judgment is adopted, on occasions where the object is not available, there is objectively no object worth protecting and the danger of violation of law cannot be affirmed. Likewise, in the case of defense by accident, if the standard of *ex post facto* judgment is adopted, the wrongdoing cannot be affirmed in any sense."[85]

It should be noted that the above discussion about defense by accident is limited to the act and intent of defenders of accident which are towards to objective unlawful infringers. If the act and intent of accidental defenders are towards to the innocent and casualties to the unlawful infringer are caused accidentally, then it is an issue that needs to be discussed separately. For example, the fugitives A and B both fired at the police officer C, but A's bullet hit B. Under this circumstance, although the act of A to B is defense by accident and does not constitute a crime, because A is aimed at the police C, his act has the danger of killing C, and A commits an attempted intentional homicide against C.[86] Moreover, the defense by accident is not illegal just in terms of the act of defense by accident. Therefore, it does not exclude the act of defense by accident is a preparation for a crime. For example, in order to kill B, A prepares a weapon beforehand and investigates the whereabouts of B. Later, when he is killing B, B is killing C at the same time. The statement that defense by accident is sinless refers to the 'perpetrating act' that A killed B is not a crime. As

---

[83] 日林幹人:《刑法总论》，东京大学出版会2008年版，第197页。Hayashi Mikito.(2008) *General Theory of Criminal Law*, University of Tokyo Press, 197.

[84] C.Roxin, *Strafrecht Allgenmeiner Teil, Band I*, 4.Aufl., C.H.Beck, 2006,S.640.

[85] 日井田良:《犯罪论の现在と目的的行为论》，成文堂1995年版，第135页。Ida Makoto. (1995) *The Present of Criminology and the Theory of Purposive Action*, Seibundo Publishing Co., 135.

[86] 参见日松原芳博:《刑法总论》，日本评论社2013年版，第152页。See Matsubara Yoshihiro.(2013) *General Theory of Criminal Law*, NIPPON HYORON SHA Co., 152.

for the preparatory act previously carried out by A, it is indeed possible to constitute a murder preparation. Obviously, there is no contradiction to reach the above conclusions.

References

Asada Kazushige. (2007) *General Theory of Criminal Law (Supplementary Edition)*, Seibundo Publishing Co., 227, 230.

Chen Xingliang. (2008) *Normative Criminal Law*, China Renmin University Press, 142-143.

C.Roxin, Strafrecht Allgenmeiner Teil, Band I, 4.Aufl., C.H.Beck, 2006, S.330, 437, 640, 641, 642, 644, 645, 654, 659, 719.

Claus Roxin, trans. Fan Wen. (2007) Rechtsgütern nicht zu den Aufgaben des Strafrechts?, as cited in Chen Xingliang ed., Criminal Law Review, No. 19, Peking University Press, 1-146.

Dictionary Editing Office, Institute of Linguistics, Chinese Academy of Social Sciences. (2005) Modern Chinese Dictionary, The Commercial Press, 1422.

Feng Zikai. (2008) *Collected Works of Feng Zikai*, People's Literature Publishing House, 38-39.

Fukuda Taira. (2004) *General Theory of Criminal Law* (Full Edition), Yuhikaku Press, 158.

George P. Fletcher, trans. Cai Aihui. (2004) B*asic Concepts of Criminal Law*, China University of Political Science and Law Press, 133, 134.

George P. Fletcher, trans. Deng Zibin. (2008) *Rethinking Criminal Law*, Huaxia Publishing House, 408, 411, 414, 416.

Giunter Stratenwerth & Lothar Kuhlen, trans. Yang Meng. (2006) *Strafrecht Allgemeiner Teil I*: Die Straftat, Law Press, 108.

Hayashi Mikito. (2008) *General Theory of Criminal Law,* University of Tokyo Press, 197.

Hirano Ryuuichi. (1975) *General Theory of Criminal Law II,* Yuhikaku Press, 243.

H.Jeschck/T.Weigend, Lehrbuch des Strafrechts. *Allgemeiner Teil*, 5.Aufl., Duncker & Humblot, 1996, S.293, 330.

Ida Makoto. (1995) *The Present of Criminology and the Theory of Purposive Action*, Seibundo Publishing Co., 134, 135, 151.

Ida Makoto. (2007) *Theoretical Criminal Law in the Age of Change*, Keio University Press Inc., 113.

Ida Makoto. (2008) *Handout of Criminal Law·General Rules,* Yuhikaku Press, 258, 260.

Li Hong. (2007) *Reflections on Issues in the General Theories of Criminal Law,* China Renmin University Press, 324-325, 344.

Lü Shuxiang. (1982) *Essentials of Chinese Grammar*, The Commercial Press, 388.

Maeda Masahide. (1992) *Contemporary Society and Substantive Crime Theory*, University of Tokyo Press, 149.

Mao Zedong. *Mao Zedong Selected Works* (vol 1, vol III) (1991), People's Publishing House, 35, 904.

Matsubara Yoshihiro. (2013) *General Theory of Criminal Law,* NIPPON HYORON SHA Co., 152.

Meng Tian. (1981) *Examples and Explanations of Conjunctions*, Heilongjiang People's Publishing House, 94.

Naitou Ken. (1986) *General Lectures on Criminal Law (Medium)*, Yuhikaku Press, 344.

Nishida Noriyuki.(2010) *General Theory of Criminal Law*, Koubundou Publishers Inc., 31, 171, 310-311.

Nishimura Katsuhiko. (1976) "So-called 'accidential defense' ", as cited in Case Law Times, No. 824.

Ohya Minoru.(2009) *General Handouts on Criminal Law (New Edition)*, Seibundo Publishing Co, 165, 283, 288-289, 289-290, 290, 297.

Ohya Minoru.(2009) Lectures on Criminal Law (New Edition), Seibundo Publishing Co, 236.
Sekine Tsuyoshi.(2010) "Of accidental defense", as cited in Kawabata Hiroshi et al, ed., A Collection of Congratulatory Essays by Mr. Tateishi Niroku in His Seventies, Seibundo Publishing Co., 191.
Shinmura Izuru ed. (1983) *Kojien*, Iwanami Shoten Publisher, 1514.
Shao Zesui. (1999) "On the Use of 'Weile' to Express Cause", as cited in Training and Research (Journal of Hubei Institute of Education), No. 4.
Sone Takehiko. (2005) *Important Issues of Criminal Law General Theory (General Theory),* Seibundo Publishing Co., 94-95.
Sone Takehiko. (2008) *General Theory of Criminal Law*, Seibundo Publishing Co., 104, 230.
Takahashi Norio. (2010) *General Theory of Criminal Law,* Seibundo Publishing Co., 268, 375-376.
Tom Regan, trans. Li Xi. (2010) *The Case for Animal Rights*, Peking University Press, 211
Brad Hooker, trans. Gongxiang et al. (2008) Rule Consequentialism, as cited in Hugh LaFollette ed., The Blackwell Guide to Ethical Theory, China Renmin University Press, 223.
Vgl., V. Krey, Deutsches Strafrecht Allgenmeiner Teil, Band I, W. Kohlhammer, 2001, S.158.
Yamaguchi Atsushi. (2007) *General Rules of Criminal Law,* Yuhikaku Press, 101, 113-114, 124, 435, 463, 465.
Zhang Mingkai. (2002) *Basic Standpoints of Criminal Law,* China Legal Publishing House, 1-239, 1-152, 1-236
Zhang Mingkai. (2003) *Preliminary Study on Legal Interests*, China University of Political Science and Law Press, 1-269.
Zhang Mingkai. (2009) "Doubts on the Theory of Act Valorization", as cited in Social Sciences in China, No. 1.
Zhang Mingkai. (2011) "The Conception of Wrongfulness in Behavioral Utilitarianism", as cited in China Legal Science, No. 5.

Chapter 6
Basic Legal Principles of Risk Assumption

Cases of risk assumption occur a lot in daily life. However, as no specific research for that has been conducted in China, there is no theoretical guidance on dealing with those cases in judicial practice, which make some cases very hard to understand: in the same case, the defendants found guilty for criminal culpability while also found no civil responsibility in civil judgments. This article aims to throw some light on this field by bringing up some immature suggestions about the basic legal principle of risk assumption.

6.1 General Theory of Risk Assumption

6.1.1 Types of Risk Assumption

Broadly speaking, risk assumption can be divided into three types in general[1]:

The first type is the victim's spontaneous self-endangerment in a narrow sense: the victim has continued to act and further endangered himself or herself, even though the victim has already realized the act will endanger his or her own legal interests. In this case, only the victim has conducted the act that has a causality with the infringement of legal interest. For example, the victim has realized the danger of

*The original title is "Jurisprudence Principles of Risk Assumption in Criminal Studies", published in ***Chinese Journal of Law*** in 2012, Vol 5.

[1] 参见日吉川敏雄:"'合意のある他者危殆化'について"，载日冈野光雄等编:《西原春夫先生古稀祝贺论文集》(第1卷)，成文堂1998年版，第407页以下。See Yoshikawa Toshio. (1998) "On 'Endangerment of others with consent'", as cited in Okano Mitsuo et al., ed., *A Collection of Congratulatory Essays by Mr. Haruo Nishihara in His Seventies(Vol, 1)*, Seibundo Publishing Co., 1–407.

M. Zhang, *The Fundamental Issues upon Criminal Law Theories*, Masterpieces of Contemporary Jurisprudents in China,
https://doi.org/10.1007/978-981-95-1276-8_6

falling down but still climbs the tree to pick up fruits, and he or she is badly injured as a result. Obviously, such case has no significance regarding criminal law,[2] this article thus will not discuss it.

The second type is the involvement in self-endangerment: the victim has realized and conducted the dangerous acts that lead to the damaging results, which also has a physical or psychological causality with the defendant's involvement. To be brief, the defendant has participated in the victim's spontaneous self-endangerment. For example, there is such a case in Germany: The victim held and injected heroin by asking to use the defendant's syringe, and died thereafter. The German court used to determine this act as crime of negligent homicide, but denied the establishment of such crime in case above (*case of heroin*).[3]

The third type is the endangerment by the third party based on consensus (*Einverständnis*): although the damaging results has been caused by others, the victim has realized and approved the danger brought to him or her (or to say, the victim only agreed with the danger but doesn't agree with the result). In *case of Memel River* in German: two passengers ignored the warning of "danger" from the ferryman and required him to take them across the river when the furious storm was coming. The ferry wrecked and passengers died. The German court held that the ferryman shall not been convicted of crime of negligent homicide for he had no special duty for protecting the passengers and didn't violate the duty.[4]

The description above gives the impression that all cases related to risk assumption will prevent the establishment of crime. But it is not the fact. For example, the victim still sat in the car drove by the defendant even though he or she knew the defendant was drunk. The car collided with an oncoming car when crossing the central reservation due to the defendant's erroneousness, leading to a serious injury to the victim in the same car (both of the drivers were badly injured). The court in Germany held that the defendant's act accorded with the Article 315a and 316 of *German Criminal Law*, even if the victim taking the same car had realized the danger, the wrongdoing of defendant's act would still not be prevented. That is because the two provisions above are aimed to protect not only the bodies and lives of traffic participants, but also the traffic and public safety, and therefore the defendant's act shall be convicted of crime of negligent homicide.[5] However, Professor C. Roxin believes that attributing the consequence of death and injury to the defendant's act is not satisfying.[6] In fact, lots of scholars agree to find the ferryman in *case of Memel*

---

[2] It is certainly necessary to distinguish whether the victim's self-endangerment is caused by themselves, or caused by the actions of others. Generally speaking, if the defendant's act imposes physical or psychological pressure on the victim, leading to the victim's self-endangerment, it then cannot be regarded as spontaneous self-endangerment but shall affirm that there is a causal relationship between the actual result of the injury and the actors' act (See Zhang Mingkai, "*Criminal Law*", Law Press,2007:185 and below).

[3] BGHSt 32(Urt.v.124.2.1984),S.262ff.

[4] RGSt 57(Urt.v.3.1.1923),S.172ff.

[5] BGHSt 6(Urt.v.24.6.1954),S.232.

[6] C.Roxin,Strafrecht Allgemeiner Teil,Band I,4.Aufl.C.H.Beck, 2006,S.411.

Rivert that guilty of crime of negligent homicide.[7] Therefore, it is worthwhile to do the research no matter which kind of risk assumption in what condition and on what ground has prevented the constitution of crime.

6.1.2 The Relationship Between Involvement in Self-Endangerment and Endangerment by the Third Party Based on Consensus

There are three common features of involvement in self-endangerment and endangerment by the third party based on consensus: firstly, the damaging results from the interaction between defendant's and victims' attitudes of ignorance. Secondly, neither the defendant nor the victim wishes or allows the damaging result to occur; instead, they hope and expect it will not happen. Thirdly, the victims "negligently" participate in resulting the result, and the issue faced by both of them is whether the defendant shall eventually take the criminal culpability of negligence.[8]

Owing to the features shared in common, the theory of criminal law has concluded the two types above as risk assumption. It will be meaningful only when the two types have been treated differently or it will be meaningless. As it is known, according to the tripartite system, the conditions for determining a crime are conformity with constitutive element, wrongdoing and culpability. Correspondingly, if the situation does not accord with the constitutive element, or is short of justifiable cause or culpability, there will be no crime. It shall be assured that the risk assumption is a question of conformity with constitutive element and wrongdoing (the two are collectively known as 'illegal'), rather than a question of culpability.[9] Therefore, in essence, whether it is the involvement in self-endangerment or endangerment by the third party based on consensus, the question shall only be solved from the perspective of wrongdoing.[10] In this regard, there is no difference in dealing with both situations. However, it cannot

---

[7]Vgl.,D.Dölling,Fahrlässige Tötung bei Selbstgefhrdung des Opfers,GA 1984,S.93; 日曾根威彦:"过失犯における危险の引受", 载《早稲田法学》第73卷(1997年)第2号; 日深町晋也:"危险引受け论について", 载《本乡法政纪要》2000年第9号。Sone Takehiko.(1997) "Assumption of risk in the case of negligent criminals", as cited in *Waseda Law Journal*, Vol. 73, No. 2; Fukamachi Hhinya.(2000) "Of the theory of assumption of risk", as cited in *A Summary of the Local Legal and Political Affairs*, No. 9.

[8]参见日盐谷毅:《被害者の承诺と自己答责性》, 法律文化社2004年版, 第178页。See Shiotani Takeshi.(2004) *Victim's Consent and Self-assumed Liability*, Houritsu Bunka Sha, 178.

[9]There are also a few scholars who deny that the defendant's act constituting a crime on the grounds of responsibility prevention.参见日神山敏雄:"危险引き受けの法理とスポ-ツ事故", 载日大谷实等编:《宫泽浩一先生古稀祝贺论文集》(第3卷), 成文堂2000年版, 第36页以下。See Kamiyama Toshio.(2000) "The Legal Doctrine of Assumption of Risk and Sports Accidents", as cited in Ohya Minoru, et al., ed., *A Collection of Congratulatory Essays by Mr. Miyazawa Kouichi in His Seventies(Vol, 3)*, Seibundo Publishing Co., 1–36.

[10]Moreover, all participants in risk assumption are with faults, so even if the theory of anti-value act were adopted, the problem can only be solved from the objective level (such as the conformity of objective constitutive elements, *Lehre vonder objektive zurechnung*, etc.).

directly identify the endangerment by the third party based on consensus as not in accordance with the constitutive element only because the involvement in self-endangerment doesn't meet the constitutive element. Or to say, although the "inconformity with constitutive element and justifiable cause exclude the acts from being crimes" can be applied to all cases, act B shall not be denied as crime only for the act sharing the same characteristics with act A, which doesn't constitute a crime. In sum, the major premises of elimination of crime are the same, but the specific facts differ from each other. As a result, it is necessary to distinguish the situations of involvement in self-endangerment from those of endangerment by the third party based on consensus,[11] due to the significant factual differences that affect value judgments.

Professor Schünemann, a German scholar, pointed out that for one thing, the standard for distinguishing the two lies in the chronological sequences of acts of the defendant and the victim: if the victim's act comes later, it is the involvement in self-endangerment; otherwise, it is the endangerment by the third party based on consensus. For another thing, to handle the two types of endangerment shall be exactly the same: both of the involvement in self-endangerment and endangerment by the third party based on consensus will prevent the establishment of such crime from the perspective of the victim's risk assumption.[12] But the author doesn't agree with such view. First of all, according to this theory, if a victim died after eating the globefish whose liver wasn't handled properly by the chief, as the victim's act came later than the chief's cooking, the case therefore should be an involvement in self-endangerment. Obviously, this over-formalized view is not conductive to make a reasonable judgment that whose act the damaging result shall be attributed to. Moreover, just as instigating and helping suicide is not the same as promised killing, negligently helping others to commit suicide is not the same as death caused by negligence, different legal assessment shall be made on lending the drug syringes to victims and injecting drugs directly into victims.

Japanese Professor Yamanaka Keiiti believes that after the danger has been firstly created, in case the victim realized it but still participated in the act, it is the involvement in self-endangerment; if the victim's dangerous act functions at the same time with the danger firstly created, it is the endangerment by the third party based on consensus.[13] However, such distinction is too formalized and it is not conductive to determine whose act has essentially caused the damaging result. That is because the

[11] M.C. Meli, a Spanish scholar, argues that it is problematic to classify risk assumption into involvement in self-endangerment and hazardization caused by others based on consensus. This classification "tends to have only symbolic significance. It also fails to provide adequate problem-solving mechanisms. Besides, the classification cannot prejudge the solutions. [M.C.Meliá,Victims and Self-Liability in Criminal Law: Beyond Contributive Negligence and Foreseeabikity (Without Blaming the Victim),Pace Law Review,Vol.28(2007–2008)] In fact, this is based on his indiscriminate view that cases of risk assumption all prevent the establishment of a crime. As mentioned later, a clear distinction between the two is of great significance for the proper handling of risk assumption cases.

[12] B.Schünemann, Moderne Tendenzen in der Dogmatik der Fahrlässigkeits-und Gefährdungsdelikte, JA 1975, S,715ff.

[13] 日山中敬一:《刑法における客观的归属の理论》，成文堂1997年版，第731页。See Yamanaka Keiichi.(1997) *The Theory of Objective Attribution in Criminal Law*, Seibundo Publishing Co., 731.

timing of involvement is not the only element to decide the damaging result. According to Professor Yamanaka Keiiti, if the female victim is surely aware of the fact that the male defendant is suffering from AIDS, but still has sex with him without protection and further infected with AIDS (*AIDS case*), it will be a endangerment by the third party based on consensus.[14] It explicitly expands the scope of endangerment by the third party based on consensus.[15]

This article holds that the two shall be distinguished from the perspective of perpetrator, and the standard is the subject of conducting the self-endangerment or endangerment by the third party. That is to say, when the victim himself or herself dominates the damaging result, the defendant's act is the involvement in self-endangerment; when the defendant's act plays the dominant role in creating the damaging result, it is the realization of dangers caused by others based on consensus. In other words, in the case of involvement in self-endangerment, the defendant is the accomplice and the victim is the perpetrator, while the defendant is the perpetrator and the victim is the accomplice in the situation of endangerment by the third party based on consensus.[16] Such distinguishing standard is both definite and practical.

The controversial issue lies in the situation in which it is hard to distinguish the principal offender and the accomplice, which means, there can be a problem upon how to distinguish the actual danger results from the interaction or joint action of the victim and the defendant. This article believes that three conclusions may be drawn concerning the said problem: firstly, even though the victim can freely determine whether to endanger himself or not, if the act creating the damaging result has been dominated by the defendant, it is endangerment by the third party based on consensus. For example, the victim clearly knew that the defendant was drunk, and sat on the car drove by the defendant, and the defendant's negligence resulted in the casualties of the victim. The victim could not choose not to take the defendant's ride, the act that led to the casualties should be deemed as being dominated by the defendant; secondly, if the act that creates the damaging result is determined by the victim, or to say, the victim has dominated the act that leads to the damaging result, it shall be identified as involvement in self-endangerment. In the aforementioned case of AIDS, the defendant's act shall be identified as involvement in self-endangerment. In such occasion, it is the functions of both of them that essentially result in the victim's infection of AIDS. However, the defendant neither forced the victim nor hid the fact of being infected. Whether to have sex and further be infected

---

[14] 日山中敬一:《刑法における客观的归属の理论》，成文堂1997年版，第741页以下。See Yamanaka Keiichi.(1997) *The Theory of Objective Attribution in Criminal Law*, Seibundo Publishing Co., 1–741.

[15] The Bavarian State Court of Germany held that in the case of AIDS, the defendant's behavior was his own involvement in self-endangerment and would take the responsibility by himself at his will. It doesn't constitute the crime of dangerous injury provided in Article 223 of the Criminal Law (OLG Bayern, NJW 1990, S.131).

[16] 参见日岛田聡一郎:"被害者による危险引受"，载日山口厚编者:《クロ-ズアップ刑法总论》，成文堂2003年版，第140~141页。Shimada Souichirou.(2003) "Result of the victims' assumpution of risk", as cited in Yamaguchi Atsushi ed. *Close-up General Theory of Criminal Law*, Seibundo Publishing Co., 141.

with AIDS is totally dominated by the victim, and therefore the defendant cannot be deemed as the one who dominates the damaging result; thirdly, if the result is jointly dominated by the victim and defendant in essence, the case shall be classified as involvement in self-endangerment. For example, A and B rode a bicycle together. A hold the handlebars and B pushed on the pedals and A got seriously injured when the bike jerked down. In such case, both of their acts have played essential roles in leading to the result. However, in the case of risk assumption, even though the principle of joint crime may have been applied, it is still impossible to adopt the principle that parts of the accomplices taking full culpability for the victim is not the defendant. Once the principle above has not been adopted, the result shall not be attributed to the act of the defendant B, that is, the defendant B cannot be identified as dominating the occurrence of the result. Therefore, it can only be affirmed as involvement in self -endangerment.[17]

6.1.3 The Relationship Between Risk Assumption and Consent of the Victim

There are two distinct differences between the risk assumption and the consent of the victim (agreement): one is that risk assumption is basically concerned with the negligent crime; meanwhile, although consent of the victim can be seen in negligent crime, it is mainly related to intentional crimes. The other is that, when it is the risk assumption, the victim only realizes the dangerousness of the act but he or she neither promises the damaging result nor gives up his or her legal interest; when it is the consent of the victim, the victim has abandoned the legal interest while giving consent to the damaging result.[18]

Since the beginning of the twentieth century, German has been discussing the subject of consent in negligent crime, or to say, does the mere act of consent prevent the law violation, or only the agreed result will prevent the violation of law? For example, B, C and D all sat on the car drove by A even though they realized that A was drunk. Three of them all got seriously injured due to A's negligence. If the object of consent is the act, then A is not subject to criminal culpability for serious injuries of B, C and D since all of the victims have agreed with the act of drunk driving. Therefore, A's act shall not be held as crime of traffic accident (or crime of serious injury out of negligence), but the crime of dangerous driving. However, if the result has been regarded as the necessary contents of consent, A shall bear the criminal culpability of crime of traffic accident (or crime of serious injury out of

[17] The second case mentioned above may be difficult to distinguish from the third one, or to say, the second case may be incorporated into the third case. However, since both of them belong to involvement in self-endangerment, whether they can be distinguished or not does not affect the conclusion.

[18] Of course, there will no difference on this issue if the content of the consent of the victim is only deemed to be the dangerous act.

negligence) for B, C and D have only agreed with the act of drunk driving, rather than the result of serious injuries.[19]

H.Welzel believes that, the logic of wrongdoing for negligent crime is the necessary act of care in social life, which means, the breach of the duty of care (*Handlungsunwert*). The occurrence of result (*Erfolgsunwert*) only has the function of restricting rather than constituting the unlawful acts. It is the violation of duty of care as well as the absence of justifiable cause that lay the foundation for the wrongdoing of negligent crime. Therefore, it is enough as long as the acts violating duty of care has been approved by the victim. In other words, the approval to the dangerous acts have prevented *Handlungsunwert* of negligent crime, and prevented the wrongdoing therefore.[20] Professor Ida Makoto holds the similar idea: "the contents of rights of self-determination include the freedom of permitting one's interests not only to be violated, but also to be endangered, or to say, the freedom of taking the risk to enjoy certain interest that surpasses the risk typical cases are combating sports such as judo, boxing and the dangerous surgery conducted by doctors, etc. 'In such occasion, the protection of criminal law to the victim's legal interest may be negated to the extent that the victim has realized the danger of the act but still gives his or her consent to such act the perpetrating act refers to the dangerous act that beyond the permitted scope'. It is the consent of the victim that makes the danger permitted by the law."[21]

However, the author found these views are not convincing. First, as the underlying logic is the theory of *Handlungsunwert*, namely, the wrongdoing of the negligent crime lies in the violation of duty of care, therefore, as long as the victim gives approval to the dangerous act, there is no *Handlungsunwert* and hence the act is not illegal. However, without taking issues concerning theory of *Handlungsunwert* into consideration, even if the wrongdoing of negligent crime has been considered as violation of duty to act, the mere approval of the victim will still not be deemed as preventing wrongdoing of negligent crime. That is because, the theory of consent of the victim may be entirely illustrated by that "the victim gives up his or her legal interests after knowing the actual consequence of damaging result, and therefore has no duty of care to the abandoned legal interest"; "instead of deducting the theory of object of consent sorely by the theory of *Handlungsunwert*. Or to say, the theory of object of consent could only be analyzed within the theory itself".[22] Second, "what the law ultimately denies is not the act itself that caused the accident, but the

[19] 参见日岛田聡一郎:"被害者による危険引受"，載日山口厚编著:《クロ-ズアップ刑法总论》，成文堂2003年版，第126页。See Shimada Souichirou.(2003) "Result of the victims' assumpution of risk", as cited in Yamaguchi Atsushi ed. *Close-up General Theory of Criminal Law*, Seibundo Publishing Co., 126.

[20] H.Welzel,Das Deutsche Strafrecht,11Aufl.,Walter de Gruyter & Co.1969,S.136.

[21] 日井田良:"被害者の同意"，载《现代刑事法》第14号(2008年)。Ida Makoto.(2008) "Consent of Victims", as cited in *Modern Criminal Law*, No. 14.

[22] 日深町晋也:"危险引受け论について"，载《本乡法政纪要》2000年第9号。Fukamachi Hhinya.(2000) "Of the theory of assumption of risk", as cited in *A Summary of the Local Legal and Political Affairs*, No. 9.

state of legal interest damage. The reason why an act has been determined as illegal is that there is a possibility (danger) for the legal interest to be damaged by such act, which, in law, is only a way of causing the consequence. It is not the aim of the law to ban the act itself. Moreover, to the victim, the concern is whether the legal interest has been protected or violated, rather than the issue of whether the perpetrator has violated the duty of care or not. Therefore, the consent of the victim is to the final damaging result, not the act being the premise of such result."[23] Third, since the consent of the victim has been treated as the realization of right of self-determination, the factor of will is indispensable. That is, it is not the realization of self-determination right if the victim is only aware of the danger of the act; only when the victim has the will to realize the danger, will it be called the realization of right of determination. Fourth, the victim, in fact, has only agreed with the danger he knows, but not the realization of danger. In other words, even though the danger has been approved, it only means that the danger, rather than the danger to the victim is justified by law. Fifth, it is doubtful that the above view has equated the due professional conduct with the consent of the victim, or that taking the due professional conduct as an example to illustrate that the victim shall only be committed to the conduct. The reason why that the due professional conduct has prevented the wrongdoing is not only because the victim accepts the danger, but for the conduct itself is legitimate and is able to protect superior legal interest.

Professor Maeda Masahide believes that the consent of the victim has prevented the wrongdoing in both crime of intentional and negligent crime. However, in the latter situation, it is most likely that the consequence is out of the party's expectation and therefore there are fewer cases in which the victims give explicit consents to the consequence. In the case of negligent crime, for this reason, the wrongdoing shall be prevented even though the content of consent is more abstract. Or to say, the victim shall be considered as giving consent to the predictable dangerous consequence if he or she has actively put himself or herself in a high risk, even if the victim doesn't agree with the consequence in a strict sense.[24] Professor Mikito Hayashi also holds that, what makes the consent of the victim and the risk assumption different is that there is a low possibility for the victim, who doesn't want the consequence to occur, to realize the consequence or there is only an abstract knowledge about the consequence in the latter occasion. But such distinction has no

---

[23] 日曾根威彦:"过失犯における危险の引受"，载《早稻田法学》第73卷(1997年)第2号。Sone Takehiko.(1997) "Assumption of risk in the case of negligent criminals", as cited in *Waseda Law Journal*, Vol. 73, No. 2.

[24] 日前田雅英:《刑法总论讲义》，东京大学出版会2011年版，第409页；日前田雅英:"许された危险"，载日中山研一等编:《现代刑法讲座》(第3卷)，成文堂1979年版，第46页。Maeda Masahide.(2011) *Handouts of General Rules of Criminal Law*, University of Tokyo Press, 409; Maeda Masahide.(1979) "Premissible risk", as cited in Nakayama Kenichi et al., ed., *Issues in Contemporary Criminal Law(Vol. 3)*, Seibundo Publishing Co, 46.

influence on applying the theory of consent of the victim to the case of risk assumption (theory of quasi consent).[25]

Both the professors' views are questionable, however. First, the views above actually show that in the case of intentional crime, the victim is required to be aware of the consequence of damaging result; as to the negligent crime, however, the victim who makes the commitment is only required to know the possibility of the consequence. Obviously, the elements constituting intention and negligence have been confused with the consent of the victim in the crime of intention and negligence. Second, the above viewpoints have actually fictionalized the victim's realization of danger as the victim's consent to the damaging result.[26] However, even if the danger has been aware, it doesn't mean that the subject of legal interest hopes or tolerates such result. If the realization of danger is held as tolerating the consequence of damaging result, it actually denies the phenomenon of risk assumption. In fact, in the situation of risk assumption, the victim doesn't tolerate the consequence. On the contrary, he or she expects or hopes that the damaging results will not happen. For example, when an acrobat throws a flying knife at a beautiful lady, the lady only accepts the danger but will not allow the knife stabbing at her body. Third, the reason why the consent of the victim can prevent the wrongdoing is that the victim has decided to abandon the legal interest. Therefore, the consent of the victim requires the victim not only to realize the consequence of damaging result but also to agree with it. The victim in the case of risk assumption, however, only gives consent to the dangerous act of the victim rather than the occurrence of the consequence. Therefore, the victim cannot be held as abandoning his or her own legal interest.

Latterly, W. Beulke, the German scholar has pointed out that the question of risk assumption shall be unitarily solved by the consent of the victim. That is because it is unnatural and unrealistic for the victim to bring forward that the damaging result has not been taken into consideration afterwards, as he or she has already known the danger but still gives consent to it. In other words, in the case of risk assumption, it shall be affirmed that the victim has made the commitment to the result. The criminal law only punished the intentional act of homicide that gets committed, thus it shall not be held that the committed act of negligent homicide should get punished and convicted of a crime. Otherwise, the doctrine of a legally prescribed punishment for a specified crime will be contradicted.[27]

However, there are three problems with this view. First, as discussed above, it is not the fact that the victim has committed to the damaging result in the case of risk assumption. The "adventurous" person, in the real life, is not always the one who

---

[25] 日林幹人:《刑法总论》，东京大学出版会2008年版，第173页以下。Hayashi Mikito. (2008) *General Theory of Criminal Law*, University of Tokyo Press, 173.

[26] 参见日林慎一郎:"被害者による危険の引受けについて"，载《立命馆法政论集》2004年第2号。See Hayashi Shinichiro.(2004) "On the assumption of risk by victims", as cited in *Ritsumeikan Law and Politics Review*, No. 2.

[27] 参见日北川敦子:"Werner Beulke'刑法における被害者の自律性'"，载《早稲田法学》第85卷(2009年)第1号。See Kiragawa Atsuko.(2009) "Werner Beulke'Victim Autonomy in Criminal Law'", as cited in *Waseda Law Journal*, Vol. 85 No. 1.

is willing to accept the damage. If the expression of negligent crime will be borrowed, the victim only has "the negligence of over-confidence" in the case of risk assumption, or to say, the victim has foreseen the danger but mistakenly believes that the danger will occur. Second, it is not proper to come to the conclusion that the consent of the victim is invalid to the act of intentional homicide but is valid to the negligent homicide based on the fact that the criminal law only punishes the intentional homicide act being committed. That is because the invalid commitment to intentional homicide means that the commitment to death is invalid. In other words, the criminal law's absolute protection to life has negated the commitment to death. Third, since the defendant may be convicted of crime of homicide when he or she has committed to the victim's death, the defendant's behavior is more punishable when the victim does not commit to death, but only realizes the danger of death.

Therefore, the risk assumption shall not be solved with the theory of consent of the victim. Or to say, cases of risk assumption are different from those of consent of the victim. Therefore, if the case can be evaluated as the type of consent of the victim, it will be not proper to deal with it with the legal principle of risk assumption.

6.1.4 The Theoretical Premises of Risk Assumption

To discuss the risk assumption, the following premises shall be clarified[28]:

First, the cases of risk assumption shall be premised on the consequence of damaging result. If the defendants have conducted the dangerous act that permitted by the victim, but lead to no damaging result, then there is no significance in criminal law.

Second, the victim shall have the ability of acknowledgement and control. For example, the defendant hands over large quantities of drugs to the victim when the latter is kicking a drug addiction and out of control and died after taking drugs, it shall not be regarded as the case of risk assumption and the defendant shall be convicted of the corresponding crime.

Third, the victim shall have a clear understanding of the dangerous facts. If the victim is lack of the acknowledgement for the defendant conceals the truth, the case shall not be solved as risk assumption. For example, the defendant conceals the fact that he or she is suffering from serious STD but still has intercourse with others and uses no condoms, which, as a result, causes others to be infected. In such case, the defendant shall be convicted of crime of intentional injury.

Fourth, when the defendant acts when the victim has not been aware of the danger and had to be subject to the danger, it is not the case of risk assumption. For

[28] 参见日岛田聪一郎:"被害者による危险引受"，载日山口厚编著:《クロ-ズアップ刑法总论》，成文堂2003年版，第130页以下。Shimada Souichirou.(2003) "Result of the victims' assumpution of risk", as cited in Yamaguchi Atsushi ed. *Close-up General Theory of Criminal Law*, Seibundo Publishing Co., 1–130.

example, the defendant A set B's house on fire. B rushed into the burning house to save the family members but he blacked out and died due to carbon monoxide poisoning. A shall bear criminal culpability for B's death.

Fifth, for the crime violating public legal interest, there is no problem of risk assumption. For example, B knew that A, a prostitute, had serious STD but still had sex with her without any protection, and he later got infected with serious STD. Whether A was guilty of inflicting serious injury to B out of negligence is the question of risk assumption. However, even if A had not been declared guilty of inflicting serious injury out of negligence, it was still undeniable that her act had constituted the crime of propagating sexually transmitted disease that violated the public legal interest.

Sixth, after conducting the self-endangerment or endangerment by the third party based on consensus, the defendant doesn't rescue the victim even though he or she is able to do, whether the defendant shall be convicted of omission crime is not the question of risk assumption itself. On the one hand, the self-endangerment or endangerment by the third party based on consensus shall not be directly identified as a crime only because the actor has failed to perform the duty to act. The former may be the crime of intentional omission, while the latter is the negligent crime. On the other hand, the self-endangerment or endangerment by the third party based on consensus based on consensus shall not be directly negated as a crime only because the actor has no duty to act or be lack of possibility of act. For example, the victim asked the taxi driver to speed up for the victim was in a hurry. The right side of the car, due to the speeding, had crashed into a telegraph pole and the victim was badly injured and then died because the rescue was not in time. The serious injury of the victim is the concern of risk assumption. Whether the driver had the duty to rescue and whether he or she could rescue the victim on time is a matter of omission. The endangerment by the third party based on consensus based on consensus can not be directly identified as a crime only because the omission has been affirmed; and vice versa.

6.2 Involvement in Self-Endangerment

One of the dominant characteristics of involvement in self-endangerment is that the victim's act is the direct reason that leads to the damaging result, or to say, the victim himself or herself has dominated the damaging result while the defendant has only participated in such process. The basic point of this article is that, in the case of involvement in self-endangerment, as long as the aforesaid premise of the risk assumption has been met, the damaging result cannot be attributed to the defendant's act (the defendant's act is not a crime). The problem was how to explain it.[29]

6.2.1 View of Outside the Protection of Norms

After the 1970s, the general theory of Germany denied that the involvement in self-endangerment was a crime according to the functional scope of constitutive elements of *Lehre vonder objektive zurechnung*. The basic reason is that, according to *German Criminal Law*, the defendant, who intentionally involves in the victim's intentional suicide or self-injury, shall not be punished in principle; in this case, the defendant shall not be subject to the punishment when he or she involves in others' intentional acts that endanger themselves; nor can he or she be punished for negligently involving in others' self-endangermentt, which is less serious than the former.[30] In other words, since the act of intentional instigating or helping others to commit suicide is not within the functioning scope of constitutive elements (outside the protection of norms), it is impossible for the act of negligently instigating or helping the victim to endanger himself or herself to be in accordance with the constitutive elements.

Chinese Criminal Law doesn't specify the punishment for instigating and helping others to commit suicide, and the theory of criminal law also disputes on dealing with such problem.[31] However, the judicial practice usually punishes such acts in most circumstances. Such situation seems to make it harder to discuss the issue of risk assumption. Or to say, the following conclusion may be reached according to the German theory of criminal law: if Chinese criminal law punishes the act of instigating and helping others to commit suicide, the act of involving in self-endangerment shall not be directly affirmed as innocent. Other reasons shall be found if the act will be identified as innocent; if Chinese criminal law doesn't punish the act above, the involvement in self-endangerment cannot be convicted of crime according to the principle of natural interpretation.

However, as the dominant ideology of German is not established, the corollary is also doubtful.[32] On the surface, it is true that the defendant's involvement in the

[29] Most of German and Japanese scholars try to solve the involvement in self-endangerment and-hazardization caused by others based on consensus by one principle. Therefore, the later theory on involvement in self-endangerment also becomes the reason for the involvement in self-endangerment to prevent the establishment of crime.

[30] Vgl.,C.Roxin,Strafrecht Allgemeiner Teil,Band I,4.Aufl.C.H.Beck, 2006,S.402.

[31] 参见陈兴良:《判例刑法学》(下卷)，中国人民大学出版社2009年，第154页以下。See Chen Xingliang. (2009) *Case Studies in Criminal Law* (vol. 2),China Renmin University of Press, 1–154.

[32] 参见德 Ingeborg Puppe:《法学思维小学堂》，蔡圣伟译，元照出版有限公司2010年版，第135页。Ingeborg Puppe, trans. Cai Shengwei, (2010) *Kleine schule des juristischen denkens*, Angle Publishing Co., Ltd., 135.

victim's intentional suicide (self-infringement) is more serious than involving in the victim's potentially lethal act (self-endangerment). However, in the former case, the victim not only realizes the damaging result, but also hopes or wishes the occurrence of such result from the perspective of the victim's self-determination; but in the latter case, the victim has only realized the danger of the act and is against the occurrence of such damaging result.[33] The result shall be evaluated by considering the attitude of the legal interest body to the legal interest. In the case of victim's self-infringement, the victim has given up the legal interest; while on the occasion of involving in self-endangerment, the legal interest has not been abandoned. In summary, if the commitment to the suicide or self-injury is valid, the act of instigating or helping self-infringement will not violates legal interest while instigating or helping others to realize the dangers will violate the legal interest. In that case, it should not be considered that involving in the victim's self-infringement is more serious than involving in self-endangerment.

It is true that in some cases, if judged from the state of objective danger, the act of self-infringement (suicide) endangers the life more than the act of self-endangerment. In this sense, since the involvement in a more dangerous act (instigating or helping to commit suicide) is undeserving of punishment, the involvement in a less dangerous act should be even more unpunishable. However, it is still difficult to be an argument that the involvement in self-endangerment is not always unpunishable. In the case of involvement in self-endangerment, even if the victim doesn't wish or allow the consequence of death to occur, there is still a high risk of death led by the victim's act. For example, there are a lot of cases of attempted suicide and a large number of self-endangerment cases. It shows that the level of danger is not the distinction between the self-infringement and self-endangerment. Namely, it shall not be believed that the act of self-endangerment is certainly less dangerous than that of self-infringement. Therefore, the impunity of involvement in self-endangerment cannot be proved by that of involvement in suicide (self-infringement).[34]

6.2.2 Comparison with Negligent Abettor and Aider

If the criminal law only punish the negligent perpetrator, but not the negligent abettor and aider, there is no reason to punish the involvement in self-endangerment. That is because when the third party's legal interest has been violated by the negligent or even intentional perpetrator, the negligent act of abetting and aiding has

[33] 参见日曾根威彦:《刑事违法论の研究》，成文堂1998年版，第169页。See Sone Takehiko.(1998) *A Study of Criminal Illegality*, Seibundo Publishing Co., 169.

[34] 参见日岛田聡一郎:"被害者による危险引受"，载日山口厚编者:《クロ-ズアップ刑法总论》，成文堂2003年版，第141页。Shimada Souichirou.(2003) "Result of the victims' assumption of risk", as cited in Yamaguchi Atsushi ed. *Close-up General Theory of Criminal Law*, Seibundo Publishing Co., 141.

not been punished, therefore, when the victim's legal interest has been violated by himself or herself, the negligent act of abetting and aiding (involvement in self-endangerment) should even less be punished.

Obviously, such reason is premised on narrowing down the concept of negligent crime. If the concept of unified perpetrator has been taken, the conclusion above will not be drawn since the negligent abettor and aider will be included as perpetrator.

"H.Welzel, who advocates *finale Handlungslehre*, argued that it is inherently wrong to adopt the same standard of perpetrator in intentional and negligent crimes, or more correctly, in *Begehungsdelikte* and other crimes.

There is no distinction between perpetrator and accomplice in the case of negligent crime without purposive act (and the criminal omission), and thus advocates the dualism or dualistic concept of perpetrator in which all acts that provoke the results of constitutive elements."[35] Professor C. Roxin pointed out that in the case of intentional crime, "the 'restricted concept of perpetrator' is the correct insight, whereby the perpetrator is in principle limited to the acts of constitutive elements described in the specific provisions of criminal law. Abetting and Aiding, on the other hand, is based on penal expansion, and its *Strafbarkeit* goes beyond the core of *Strafbarkeit* known as the perpetrator. In this way, one also finds the boundary between the perpetrator and the accomplice: this boundary exists in the realization of the constitutive elements, not in the causality."[36] However, "in the current German criminal law, the unified concept of perpetrator is indeed generally used in the field of negligent crime. Since the criminal law expressly presupposes the existence of intent for the establishment of an abettor or an aider (Article 26 and 27), there can be no abettor or aider in the field of negligent crime. Thus, any actor who negligently causes the results of constitutive elements is always a perpetrator of a negligent crime. Of course, the possibility of a negligent joint perpetrator is not excluded."[37]

According to such view, the one who intentionally helps others to commit suicide is not the perpetrator; but the one who negligently helps others to commit suicide will be the perpetrator of negligent homicide. Applying this dual concept of perpetrator to the case of participating in self-endangerment will affirm the *Strafbarkeit* of involvement in self-endangerment. That is because the one who negligently helps others to commit suicide and leads to others' death is not a negligent aider but a negligent perpetrator, and his or her *Strafbarkeit* cannot be denied.

However, it is hard to accept the view that the criminal law not only punishes the negligent abettor and aider but also punishes them as the negligent perpetrator,

---

[35] 日松宫孝明:《过失犯论の现代的课题》，成文堂2004年版，第251~252页。Matsumiya Takaaki.(2004) *Contemporary Issues of the Theory of Negligent Crime*, Seibundo Publishing Co., 251–252.

[36] C.Roxin,Strafrecht Allgemeiner Teil,Band II,C.H.Beck,2003,S.7.

[37] C.Roxin,Strafrecht Allgemeiner Teil,Band II,C.H.Beck,2003,S.8.

hence it is hard to apply it in China. First, criminal law adheres to the principle of punishing intentional crimes and takes the punishment to negligent crimes as exceptions. If the negligent acts of abetting and aiding have been regarded as negligent perpetrator, the range of punishment will be infinitely enlarged, which doesn't accord with the exception. Second, Paragraph 2 of Article 15 of *Chinese Criminal Law* expressly provides that: "the criminal culpability shall be borne for negligent crimes only when the law so provides." There is no single provision that provides punishment to the negligent act of abetting and aiding in the specific provisions of criminal law. Article 25 of the general provisions has narrowed down the joint crime to intentional crimes. Therefore, punishing the negligent abetting or aiding as perpetrator possibly violates the doctrine of *nulla poena sine lege*. Third, the punishment to negligent abetting and aiding will inevitably lead to the atrophy of citizens' acts. Briefly speaking, punishing the act of abetting out of negligence may prevent citizens to communicate with others in language or writing; punishing the negligent act of aiding may frighten the citizens out of providing properties to others. Such an outcome is obviously not consistent with the criminal law's purpose of protecting the freedom of the people. Fourth, it should be pointed out that the deduction of German scholars that "any actor who negligently leads to the consequence of constitutive elements is always the perpetrator of negligent crime", "from no abettor or aider can exist in negligent crime" is only a logic one. In fact, the opposite conclusion can be drawn: since punishing abettors and aiders is premised on the actor's intent, negligent abettor and aider without intent will not be punished.

It can be seen from the above that as long as the concept of restricted perpetrator is applied in the negligent crime and the negligent abetting and aiding are hold to be unpunishable, the involvement in self-endangerment will not be punished due to lack of intention. However, such argument is still unsatisfactory. First, it has not been decided whether the criminal law in China has adopted the concept of restricted perpetrator or unified perpetrator. That is because the provisions of Article 25 of the *Criminal Law* do not explicitly oppose to the use of uniform concept of perpetrator for the negligent offense.[38] Second, if the involvement in self-endangerment is unpunishableit is only because the defendant has no intention, which means that the involvement itself, which accords with the establishment condition of act of abetting and aiding, is still illegal but lacks the culpability for the intention according to the theory of *Erfolgsunwert*. However, it is not appropriate.

In a word, although it is possible to draw the conclusion that the involvement in self-endangerment is not a crime compared with the negligent abetting and aiding, it is not the ideal way.

---

[38] 参见张明楷:《刑法学》，法律出版社2011年版，第365页。See Zhang Mingkai, (2011) *Criminal Law*, Law Press China, 365.

6.2.3 Application of the Principle of Derivativeness of Accomplice

This article will draw the conclusion that the involvement in self-endangerment is not a crime by denying the conformity of criminal constitutive element and applying the principle of derivativeness of accomplice.

Although it is not the joint crime in the essence, the involvement in self-endangerment is the same as the joint crime in the sense that the damaging result are created by the acts of more than two people. The joint crime is an illegal pattern. In terms of wrongdoing, the problem solved by the legislation and theory of joint crime is to attribute the unlawful facts to participants. The judicial organ's determination of whether the acts of two or more people have constituted the joint crime in specific cases is aimed to solve the issue of *Lehre vonder objektive zurechnung* of more than two persons' acts. In the case of involvement in self-endangerment, it can be said that more than two persons' acts have jointly resulted in the damaging result and therefore having similarities with the joint crime. That is to say, both of them have to solve the problems that whose act has directly lead to the damaging result (perpetrator) and whose act results in the damaging result through others' act (accomplice). Hence, the distinction between the perpetrator and accomplice in joint crime can be totally applied in the circumstances of involvement in self-endangerment (as discussed later, it can also be applied in the case of endangerment by the third party based on consensus). That is, on the occasion of involvement in self-endangerment, the victim is the perpetrator and his or her act neither accords with the constitutive element nor violates the law if the victim is going to take the risk. For example, seriously injuring others due to negligence refers to "negligently injuring another person and causing severe injury"(Article 235 of *Criminal Law*); negligently causing others to die refers to causing the death of "another person", which doesn't include the actor himself or herself.[39] When the victim is seriously injured or died due to his or her own negligence, the act does not accord with the constitutive element of crime of serious injury caused by negligence or crime of negligent homicide. Since the act of the perpetrator doesn't satisfy the constitutive element, then according to the theory of derivativeness of accomplice, it is impossible for the acts of abetting and aiding to be crimes no matter which theory (any theory of derivativeness will require the perpetrator's act to accord with the constitutive element) has been taken as to the level of derivativeness.

For example, Zhou Qiang, Liu Qing and Liu Min were college students who made a date to go swimming in a river. Liu Min proposed to go to the deepest part

[39] People can say that "intentional killing" case can be a homicide or a suicide, but you cannot say that people can kill himself in a manslaughter case. And since conscientious act shall not be prevented, while suicide can be prevented, then suicide is seemingly illegal , then, theone who is killed in "intentional killing" can be oneself. However, if people try to prevent others based on the possibility of danger, it will inevitably infringe the freedom of others, which is obvious not proper. For example, when someone climbs a mountain, no one can prevent him from climbing a mountain on the grounds that he or she may fall to death by mistake.

to see how deep the river was. Zhou Qiang and Liu Qing agreed. For fear of danger, the three decided to go into the water hand by hand but fell into the river because their hands were slipped. When others heard the call for help, Liu Min was rushed to the beach and climbed ashore. Liu Qing was rescued but Zhou Qiang sank into the water and was not found until the next afternoon. In this case, the act of holding hands was a dangerous act to all of them. However, Zhou Qiang's act didn't meet the constitutive element of crime of negligent homicide. Since it is so, Liu Min and Liu Qing, who participated in it, could not be the negligent abettor and aider. It is absolutely right to not handle it as criminal case.[40]

However, in the judicial practice of China, identifying the involvements in self-endangerment as crimes has always been seen.

For example, on the morning of January 29, 2010, Gu X(male, 42 years old) and Ni X, the victim, and others were on a boat in Beixin Town, Qidong City. Gu X felt bored and tried to have some fun. Gu X had reminded of a game he used to play with Ni X in the summer. The game is that he threw 50 Yuan into the river and asked Ni X to get the money, which would belong to Ni X if the money had been got. Gu X once again proposed to play the game but Ni X refused to do so for the water was so cold in the winter. Therefore, Gu X had raised it to 100 Yuan and Ni X agreed. Gu X soon threw 100 Yuan of cash into the river. Ni X jumped into the cold river but drowned to death since the river was too cold. The court sentenced Gu X to one year's imprisonment for the crime of negligent homicide.[41]

The point of this case is that the defendant instigated the victim to carry out his dangerous act of fishing for money in the river. Although the victim did not wish or allow himself to die, he did so. Therefore, the act of the defendant is a typical involvement in self-endangerment. It is certain that the cause of death is the victim's act of jumping into the river (the victim himself negligently caused his own death). However, such act doesn't accord with the constitutive element of crime of negligent homicide. As mentioned above, the "person" whose death has led by negligence shall only be another person, rather than the victim himself or herself. Therefore, the defendant doesn't participate in the act that meets the constitutive element. On the other hand, there is no difference between the defendant's and the victim's knowledge on the issue of risk; nor can it be considered that the behavior of the defendant objectively imposes psychological or physical coercion on the victim. In a word, the defendant's behavior does not conform to the establishment

[40] In the civil lawsuit, Zhou Qiang's parents brought a lawsuit that demanding Liu Qing and Liu Min to share the liability for compensation. The court's final judgment held that "the three men's appointment of testing the depth of the water is self-willed and risky. They should bear their own responsibilities for the consequences and then the court rejected Zhou Qiang's parents' lawsuit request" (程成:"相约游泳试水身亡，甘愿冒险责任自负"，载《检察日报》2008年11月1日 Cheng Cheng.(2008) "Drowning during trial swim by mutual agreement: willing assumption of risk and self-responsibility", as cited in *Procuratorial Daily*,November 1)).

[41] 徐德高、张晋中:"为取乐，诱人下水去取钱贪小财，溺水身亡真可悲"，载《检察日报》2010年5月15日。Xu Degao & Zhang Jinzhong. (2010) "Lured into Water for Fun, Drowned for Petty Cash: A Tragic Case", as cited in *Procuratorate Daily*, May 15.

condition of indirect perpetrator. Therefore, the defendant's act doesn't constitute the crime of negligent homicide from every standpoint.

Another example: at about 8 a.m. on March 8, 2011, Xiao Fengqin, suspected of defiance and array, was summoned by the police to the police station for interrogation. Before going to the police station, Xiao Fengqin told her sister Xiao Fengxia about it and asked Xiao Fengxia to buy pesticides and send them to the police station so as to frighten the police by drinking pesticides. Xiao Fengxia and Wong went to the store and bought two bottles of imidacloprid and gave them to Xiao Fengqin at the police station. Xiao Fengqin received the pesticides and went to the bathroom. When she came out, the police, who found her flushed and was foaming at the mouth, immediately called emergency service and sent her to the hospital, but the attempts had failed. The court held that the defendant Xiao Fengxia, who was fully aware that the pesticides would lead to death but still brought them to others, causing serious consequence of other's death, should be convicted of crime of negligent homicide and sentenced to a fixed-term imprisonment of three years, and under probation of five years.[42]

The point of this case is that the defendant aided others to conduct the endanger themselves. However, the defendant didn't intentionally lead to the death of the victim, who had the dangerous act of drinking pesticides but did not wish or allow herself to die. Therefore, the act of the defendant is a typical involvement in self-endangerment. Since the victim's act doesn't accord with the constitutive element of negligent crime, the defendant who negligently offered help should also not be convicted of crime of negligent homicide.[43]

In a word, as to the involvement in self-endangerment, the victim, as the perpetrator, will not be convicted of any crime since he or she's act doesn't accord with the constitutive element of any crime. According to the aforesaid viewpoint, if the defendant and the victim jointly lead to the damaging result, the defendant's act should not be regarded as a crime but shall be identified as involvement in self-endangerment. For example, on the evening of July 28, 2006, when Zhang Dongyue, the defendant, had sex with the victim Yu on Zhang Dongyue's Santana, Zhang was asked to help the victim to jointly throttle her neck with bare hands. Zhang Dongyue had immediately sent Yu to the hospital with others as soon as he found Yu passed out. However, the efforts to revive Yu were futile and Yu was died of mechanical asphyxia caused by external force after conducting the forensic authentication. The court held that the defendant's throttling the victim's neck had caused the mechanical asphyxia of the victim. Subjectively speaking, the defendant was negligent in the victim's death and his act had constituted the crime of negligent homicide. And he

[42] (2011)Xi Yi County Xing Chu Zi No.194, published on http://vip.chinalawinfo.com/case/Display.asp?Gid=117856890&KeyWord=Xiao Fengxia, visited on February 11th,2012.

[43] It is true that the purchase of pesticides is "intentional", but this intent is not intentional to the death of the victim, therefore it is not the intent in the sense of criminal law.

should be sentenced to a fixed-term imprisonment of 6 years.[44] According to the author, if the defendant has throttled the victim's neck by his own hands, it is the endangerment by the third party based on consensus. However, in this case, the defendant and the victim had jointly throttled the victim's neck, thus the result of death shall not attribute to the defendant's act. As it is known, the so-called principle of "full culpability for partial involvement" refers to that when it is joint perpetrator, even if the defendant only performs part of the acts, it should be affirmed that the defendant's act is the reason of the damaging result. That is because the acts of making use of others and completing others' acts have unified each defendant's act with others', leading to the result in the case of joint perpetrator. If considered separately, it will be difficult to determine whose behavior has caused the result. Besides, in the joint perpetrator, all perpetrators are "the defendants". However, in the above case, even if it can be determined that the joint acts of the victim and the defendant have caused the damaging result, the victim is still not the defendant. The causality between victim's act and the damaging result cannot be the reason for affirming the causality between other's behavior and the result. Therefore, the so-called principle of "full culpability for partial involvement" may not be applied. Obviously, if the victim's act has not been taken into consideration, it means that only the defendant's act will be examined. Once the defendant's act is solely examined, it will be impossible to conclude that there is a causality between the defendant's act and the victim's death, or to say, the defendant's act cannot be regarded as dominating the occurrence of the death. In this case, it can only be denied that the defendant's act accords with the constitutive element.

6.3 Endangerment by the Third Party Based on Consensus

As discussed before, there are differences between the endangerment by the third party based on consensus and involvement in self-endangerment. But most of the theories of criminal law in German and Japan have tried to illustrate that both of them are unpunishable with only one principle but multiple reasons.[45] This article here can only comment on some representative views and then expresses its own opinions.

---

[44] "The Verdict of the Case that a Policeman of Hejian 'throttled' a Karaoke Girl for Sexual Pleasure" Has Been Issued"(Original one is unsigned), published on http://www.hbktv.com/portal.php?mod=view&aid=825, visited on February 9th, 2012.

[45] Such as consent of the victim Theory, Causal Process Manipulation Theory, Dangerous Community Theory, Victim's Jurisdiction Theory, Self-bearing Danger Theory, Social Equivalence Theory, Partial Sociology Theory, Responsibility prevention Theory, Permissible Danger Theory, Trust Principle Theory, Prohibition of Retroactivity Theory, et al.(参见日盐谷毅:《被害者の承诺と自己答责性》，法律文化社2004年版，第263页以下 See Shiotani Takeshi.(2004) *Victim's Consent and Self-assumed Liability*, Houritsu Bunka Sha, 1–263)。

6.3.1 View of Outside the Protection of Norms

As mentioned above, Professor C. Roxin holds that when it is the involvement in self-endangerment, the consequence shall not attribute to the act of involving in self-endangerment because the result is not under the protection of norms. C. Roxin further points out that when the act of endangerment by the third party based on consensus can be equated with the act of involving in self-endangerment in all important aspects, the objective attribution shall be denied. In other words, only when the endangerment by the third party based on consensus also outside the protection of norms, *Lehre vonder objektive zurechnung* shall be denied. C. Roxin, on one side, points out that it is impossible to equate them because those who delegate their own endangerment to others (i.e., on the occasion of endangerment by the third party based on consensus) are more at the mercy of events than those who try to control the danger with their own strength and then make themselves endangered (i.e., on the occasion of self-endangerment). On the other hand, it is pointed out that when the following conditions are met, the two can be regarded as the same: first of all, the damaging result is the realization of the danger faced by the defendant, rather than being created by other faults; second, the victim being endangered and the defendant conducting the dangerous act shall be equally responsible for their joint act. Moreover, as long as the victim and the defendant had equally foreseen the endangerment, they shall bear the same level of culpability and *Lehre vonder objektive zurechnung*, thereby, shall be negated.[46]

However, the above views of Professor C. Roxin can be further discussed.

First of all, in the situation of involvement in self-endangerment, the victim has dominated the result, while in the case of endangerment by the third party based on consensus, the defendant dominated the damaging result, therefore it is impossible to hold that the two can be equated with each other if certain conditions have been met. It is true that from the perspective of the theoretical foundation that the freedom shall be determined by oneself, there seems to be no essential difference between the two. But in the case of involvement in self-endangerment, the involvement of the defendant is only subsidiary and should be placed outside the regulation of criminal law. In the occasion of endangerment by the third party based on consensus, the defendant's dangerous act is the object that examined by the criminal law, and the consent of the victim is only the attached condition that indirectly affects the degree of criminality.[47]

Then, the two conditions proposed by Professor C. Roxin not only lack practical significance, but also lead to the strict equivalency of the two. The first condition is of no value because even in the case of involvement in self-endangerment, the damaging result is the realizations of the danger. If it is not, it is not the case of risk

[46] C.Roxin, Strafrecht Allgemeiner Teil,Band I,4.Aufl.C.H.Beck, 2006, S.411.

[47] 参见日曽根威彦:"过失犯における危险の引受"，载《早稻田法学》第73卷(1997年)第2号。Sone Takehiko.(1997) "Assumption of risk in the case of negligent criminals", as cited in *Waseda Law Journal*, Vol. 73, No. 2.

assumption.[48] The second condition is also incapable of providing basis of negating *Lehre vonder objektive zurechnung* for danger created by others based on consensus. That is because in the occasion of involvement in self-endangerment, the victim and the defendant have the same degree of predictions. For example, there is no distinction in the prediction of the danger of death led by the drugs, whether it is to lend drug syringes (involvement in self-endangerment) or directly injects drugs to addicts (endangerment by the third party based on consensus). Therefore, the way of dealing the cases of endangerment by the third party based on consensus is almost the same with that of involvement in self-endangerment and both of them deny the *Lehre vonder objektive zurechnung*. It is clearly not appropriate. Moreover, C. Roxin doesn't provide any convincing reason why the second condition will equate the endangerment by the third party based on consensus with involvement in self-endangerment (why the same predictions shall be objectively attributed equally). The endangerment by the third party based on consensus refers to that the injury is not directly led by the victim's act, but by the defendant's dangerous act. Therefore, the same predictions of the defendant and the victim shall not be considered as negating the fact that the damaging result should attribute to the defendant's act. Or to say, in the case of endangerment by the third party based on consensus, higher conditions must be put forward to deny the attribution of the result.

Last, it can be further found that Professor C.Roxin's views are self-contradictory: on the one hand, he clearly distinguishes the involvement in self-endangerment from endangerment by the third party based on consensus and holds that the latter can not generally equate with the former; on the other hand, he sets very low condition for objective attribution that denies the endangerment by the third party based on consensus which leads almost the same decision on handling both of them.

6.3.2 Theory of Victim's Self-Accountability

Theory of victim's self-accountability is one of the contents of the theory of *Lehre vonder objektive zurechnung*. When it comes to the risk assumption, however, this theory will not discuss the normative protection, but the allocation of the victim's and the defendant's accountability. However, the viewpoints that deny dangers created by others based on consensus as reason of crime by applying the theory of victim's self-accountability are distinguished, thus the conditions for excluding the establishment of the crime are more inconsistent. Following are some representative viewpoints.

---

[48] 参见日岛田聡一郎:"被害者による危险引受"，载日山口厚编者:《クロ-ズアップ刑法总论》，成文堂2003年版，第142页。Shimada Souichirou.(2003) "Result of the victims' assumpution of risk", as cited in Yamaguchi Atsushi ed. *Close-up General Theory of Criminal Law*, Seibundo Publishing Co., 142.

6.3.2.1 View of Professor R.Zaczyk

Professor R. Zaczyk puts forward that the self-accountability is an issue of wrongdoing. The wrongdoing in criminal law refers to the attack on the personality of each individual, that is, the reduction of the freedom of each individual. Normally, cases related to the wrongdoing are manifested in the opposition between the positive part of one party and the negative part of the other party, so self-infringement does not mean the wrongdoing. That is because the self-infringement act lacks connection with specific personalities. Based on it, Professor R. Zaczyk points out that, "self-infringement with conscious" refers to the victim who knows the result but commits the act of infringing his or her own legal interests, and the victim intends the result to occur. Here, it is the victim who creates the "unity of intention, act and result". The victim is the center and also the goal of the act. In such occasion, the defendant shall be exempted from accountability while the victim shall bear all the accountability. However, in the occasion of risk assumption, the victim supposes the result will not occur, thus this will not create the "unity of intention, act and result" as the self-infringement with conscious. Therefore, the victim shall not take full accountability. In other words, the reason why the defendant has been punished as negligent perpetrator in the case of risk assumption is that the result is accidentally caused by the defendant, not by the victim. Then how to determine who should be accountable? Professor R. Zaczyk brings forward two stage examinations. The first stage is that "in the form determined by law, can the victim trust others to dominate the process leading to the infringement based on other's attitude that suitable for performing the obligation?" If the answer is YES, the victim shall not take the accountability while others shall be accountable; the victim shall be self-accountable and others will not if negative answer will be given. However, even if the victim's self-accountability has been confirmed, the examination of the second stage will be conducted taht "in the form determined by law, can the victim believe that he or she has no any possibility of promoting the danger to him or her?" If it the answer is positive, the victim's self-accountability shall be denied and others shall bear the accountability. However, this affirmation of the accountability of others is only limited to exceptional circumstances because generally speaking, the defendant has no duty to supervise the victim. The result is that, as long as the defendant doesn't violate the duty of care, there will be no possibility for attribution. Therefore, in *Memel River case*, the victim shall bear the accountability since the boatman has no special duty to supervise. Conversely, in the drug case, (where the defendant delivers drugs or injections to the victim, and the victim dies from excessive injection of drugs), the defendant's act violates the law on drugs and the duty of care, so it is not the victim's accountability, but that of defendant.[49]

In the authors opinion, Professor R.Zaczyk's view is flawed. Firstly, Professor R. Zaczyk makes the judgment to the possibility of trust in two stages. The

[49] R.Zaczyk,Strafrechtliches Unrecht und die Selbstverantwortung des Verletzten, C.F.Mller Verlag 1993, S.25ff.

defendant's obligation of dominating the causation process of the danger is the first stage of the judgment and the defendant's duty to supervise to the victim is the second stage of the judgment. Professor R. Zaczyk also takes the victim's self-endangerment with conscious as one of the facts of determining whether the defendant has violated the duty of care. Clearly, it only explains whether the defendant violates the duty of care but no further explanation.[50] Secondly, although the theory seems to be well constructed, there is no specific standard to determine who makes the unity of intention, act and result. Thirdly, according to the basic opinion of Professor R. Zaczyk, in the occasion of risk assumption, the victim always bear the self-accountability even though the victim should not do so. Fourthly, although Professor R. Zaczyk has divided the self-endangerment with conscious and risk assumption, he doesn't distinguish the involvement in self-endangerment and the endangerment by the third party based on consensus, which may lead to the fact that the latter may not be crimes while the former may constitute a crime. This conclusion is hard to be accepted.

6.3.2.2 View of Professor Shioyaki

Although the Japanese scholar Shioyaki has distinguished the involvement in self-endangerment from endangerment by the third party based on consensus, he holds that when the following three conditions have been met, the crime will be prevented: firstly, the victim fully recognizes the danger of the act and the possibility of the occurrence of specific result of constitutive elements; secondly, victim's ability to recognize and evaluate (ability of self-accountability) the dangers above and the freedom to decide by will; thirdly, objectively, the victim does not simply entrust the development of the situation to the defendant, but shows at least the same degree of positive attitude (attitude of self-accountability) as the defendant does when the result occurs. Although involvement in self-endangerment can usually satisfy the third condition, the endangerment by the third party based on consensus doesn't necessarily meet the third requirement. Only when the victim seizes the overall "initiative" of the situation and the damaging result attributes to the victim's are of accountability, can the third condition be met.[51]

It is hard to accept the view of Professor Shioyaki. Firstly, Professor Shioyaki has regarded risk assumption as an issue of *Lehre vonder objektive zurechnung*. The conditions that require the victim to take the self-accountability, however, are basically subjective conditions. Secondly, the so-called victim's overall "initiative" of the situation does not mean that the victim dominates the result, but that the victim

[50] 参见日深町晋也:"危险引受け论について"，载《本乡法政纪要》2000年第9号。Fukamachi Hhinya.(2000) "Of the theory of assumption of risk", as cited in *A Summary of the Local Legal and Political Affairs*, No. 9.

[51] 日盐谷毅:《被害者の承诺と自己答责性》，法律文化社2004年版，第371页以下。Shiotani Takeshi.(2004) *Victim's Consent and Self-assumed Liability*, Houritsu Bunka Sha, 371.

can decide whether to participate in dangerous acts. In the occasion of endangerment by the third party based on consensus, however, if the result has directly caused by the defendant objectively, the victim should not be considered as taking the "initiative" of the whole situation. For example, in the *Memel River case*, the victim should not be assumed as having the "initiative" over the whole situation because the victim had asked to cross the river. Thirdly, on the one hand, Professor Shioyaki believes that in the situation of endangerment by the third party based on consensus, as the defendant's act has directly led to the result, "in principle, the defendant can be presumed as the perpetrator, and there must be certain special situations to identify the victim as self-accountable". On the other hand, he hold that the defendant in the *Memel River case* had already pointed out the danger and persuaded the victim not to cross the river, but the latter still asked to cross the river. Therefore, "the victim's initiative to the result can be determined". The victim has the characteristic of indirect perpetrator while the act of the defendant shall be evaluated as act of helping.[52] Although Professor Shioyaki seemingly believes that the principle of endangerment by the third party based on consensus does not accord with the third condition for the victim's self-accountability, the analysis of specific cases is basically based on the victim's self-accountability. This is obviously contradictory.

6.3.2.3 View of Professor Feng Jun

Professor Feng Jun holds that the defendants act may not be crimes by applying the theory of victim's self-accountability. There are four conditions for the victim's self-accountability: first, the victim's ability of recognizing the danger of causing the result and preventing the danger from realizing (into the result); second, the victim has caused the danger that leads to the damage; third, the victim strengthens the danger even though he or she can manage the danger; and fourth, the law doesn't provide special duty for others to prevent dangers from realizing. The victim shall be culpable for the consequence of damage result both for his or her involvement in self-endangerment ("carry out dangerous act by intention") and for the endangerment by the third party based on consensus ("permit others to conduct the dangerous act").[53] It is obviously that Professor Feng Jun has dealt with involvement in self-endangerment and endangerment by the third party based on consensus in the same way.

First of all, it shall be clarified that the intention of Professor Feng Jun's intentionally carrying out dangerous acts does not mean that the victim wishes or allows

[52] 日盐谷毅:《被害者の承诺と自己答责性》，法律文化社2004年版，第373~374页。See Shiotani Takeshi.(2004) *Victim's Consent and Self-assumed Liability*, Houritsu Bunka Sha, 373–374.

[53] 冯军:"刑法中的自我答责"，载《中国法学》2006年第3期。Feng Jun. (2006) "Self-Responsibility in Criminal Law", as cited in *China Legal Science*, No. 3.

the damaging result; otherwise, it will totally become a case of the consent of the victim without necessarily adopting the theory of victim's self-accountability.

Also, it should be admitted that four conditions of the victim's self-accountability hold by Professor Feng Jun are the most complete. The problem is whether the endangerment by the third party based on consensus has met the second and third condition, or to say, whether it can be believed that it is the victim that causes or intensifies the dangers that leading to the damage? This article is doubtful about that. For example, in June 2005, the defendant Tian Yufu and his wife Kang Tengqing were brought to the Family Planning Technical Guidance Station of Banlishu Town by the staff to have a ligation surgery due to the illegal birth of the third child. At about 11 a.m. on June 25, the defendant, Tian Yufu, lied to the staff that his wife wanted to take a bath in the in-patient department's bathroom on the third floor in order to make his wife escape from the surgery. After getting trust from the staff, the defendant first broke the wooden window of the bathroom with bare hands, then tied a prepared nylon rope to his wife's chest and tried to lower his wife down to escape. However, the rope severed halfway and his wife fell down from the third floor and died right on the spot (the court convicted the defendant's act of crime of negligent homicide).[54] It is a typical case of endangerment by the third party based on consensus. The victim was undoubtedly aware of the danger, which is completely controlled by the defendant, however. The defendant's negligent act had dominated the damaging result. Thereby, it is difficult to regard the victim as the one caused and strengthened the danger. It is definite that the victim may not give consent to the defendant's act. However, it cannot be held that the victim caused and strengthened the danger of death only because she had the right to determine. More importantly, in the current society, it is the act causing the damaging result of infringement of legal interest that shall deserve more attention compared with the act causing the danger. Therefore, to take a step back, even if the victim is considered to have caused the danger, the importance of the defendant's infringement act of realizing the danger can not be denied. Therefore, the endangerment by the third party based on consensus done not accord with the conditions set by Professor Feng Jun and the victim should not bear the accountability by himself or herself.

6.3.2.4 Common Problems

There are some common problems about the theory of victim's self-accountability:

Firstly, in general, the theory of victim's self-accountability is quite confusing: (a) although scholars holding this theory all believe that the victim's self-accountability is a problem of *Lehre vonder objektive zurechnung*, the theory is neither clear nor unified about whether the victim's self-accountability refers to that the defendant's behavior does not increase the risk or that the risk is not realistic, or

[54] People's Court of Mayang Miao Autonomous County of Hunan Province(2005)Ma Xing Chu Zi(No.111), published on http://www.pkulaw.cn/fulltext_form.aspx?Db=pfnl&Gid=117613765&keyword=&EncodingName=&Search_Mode=accurate, visited on February 11th, 2012.

the risk outside the protection of the constitutive element; (b) scholars who advocate this theory have set different conditions for the victim's self-accountability; in fact, each scholar has his or her own conclusion on various cases in advance, and then sets the conditions according to such a conclusion; (c) correspondingly, scholars who advocate this theory have not reached the same conclusion in dealing with the same cases.

Secondly, the victim's self-accountability and the consent of the victim are based on the same theoretical foundation, that is the victim's right of self-determination. Since the endangerment by the third party based on consensus cannot be excluded by the consent of the victim, why does the principle of self-accountability, which bases on the same theory (right of self-determination), can be applied to exclude the wrongdoing?[55] It is hard to be answered by the theory of victim's self-accountability. This is because, since the consent of the victim to life is invalid, or to say, even if the consent of the victim is obtained, the infringement of his or her life is still illegal. Then it is even more impossible to deny the wrongdoing of the actor's infringement of life when the victim does not make a commitment but only gives consent to the act endangering his or her life. Alternatively speaking, when the victim has made a commitment to life, the wrongdoing of the killer's act cannot be denied only because of the victim's culpability. In this case, when the victim doesn't make a commitment to life but only consents to act endangering life, the wrongdoing of the actor's infringement on life cannot be denied due to the victim's culpability.

Thirdly, the principle of victim's self-accountability has something in common with the principle of *Viktimodogmatik* for both of them holding that the subject of legal interest has the duty to protect his or her own legal interests.[56] However, this view is untenable. First, this view conflicts with the legal principle of the consent of the victim. If the subject of legal interest has the duty to protect his or her legal inter-

---

[55] 参见日曾根威彦:"过失犯における危险の引受", 载《早稲田法学》第73卷(1997年)第2号。Sone Takehiko.(1997) "Assumption of risk in the case of negligent criminals", as cited in *Waseda Law Journal*, Vol. 73, No. 2.

[56] For example, Professor Shioyaki who holding this theory points out that: "Criminal law is a social mechanism that aiming at protecting the legal interest at the first place. The protection of the legal interest is not only reflects in that 'others shall not intervene or violate the legal interest", but also in the inherent responsibility for protecting the legal interest. It is exactly what the law expects that the subject of legal interest should undertake his or her duty and not make the legal interest endangered. When the danger to legal interest has caused by the cofunction of subject of legal interest (the victim) and others (the defendant), it is necessary to clarify the role of the subject of legal interest who should be the first to bear the responsibility for the protection of legal interest in its situation (and the occurrence of results). In this regard, the identification of the victim's "self-accountability" is of significance. That is to say, on the premise that the victim satisfies certain subjective elements (self-accountability, etc.) and shows his or her own attitude (self-responsible attitude) of taking the initiative in an event, the danger of the defendant and the consequences shall belong to the field where the victim shall bear the accountability as the "principal offender". The defendant can at best be regarded as an accomplice or a helpful participant in the situation."参见日盐谷毅:"自己危殆化への関与と合意による他者危殆化について(四)", 载《立命馆法学》1997年第1号。See Shiotani Takeshi.(1997) "On participation in self-endangerment and consensual endangerment of others (IV)", as cited in *Ritsumeikan Law Review*, No. 1.

est, then it will be a infringement of legal duty when he or she agrees that others infringe upon his or her own legal interests. The value of self-determination has been denied then and the consent of the victim will not be the justifiable cause. Moreover, there will be no intrinsic difference between self-infringement and other's infringement. It is even possible to punish the self-infringement act by criminal law. It not only conflicts with the existing law, but also doesn't accord with the objective facts, however.[57] Second, the assertion that the victim has the duty to protect his or her own legal interests "is likely to permit the excessive involvement of the state in the lives of citizens".[58] For example, in the areas where theft occurs frequently, the state can force its citizens, who otherwise will violate duty to protect their legal interests, to lock their doors and windows. However, this practice of forcing subjects of legal interests to protect their own legal interests in a specific way is "impossible to reconcile with the current legal order based on 'personal freedom'".[59]

Fourthly, if there is only the victim in a case, the criminal law, whose purpose is to protect legal interest, will not get involved at all. As long as the defendant has acted and infringed on the legal interests of others, it must be judged whether the act has the constitutive elements like conformity, wrongdoing and culpability. The victim's self-accountability theory, however, is like the principle of contributory negligence in the tort law of British and America: "in the scope… that the loss is allocated by fault, the individual shall act 'reasonably' to avoid injuring others or himself (herself), or he or she shall subject to all the losses; it is the same if the individual has been injured by others who act equally unreasonably. It means that if I was the victim of the accident and my act is unreasonable, I shall take all the culpability even if the inflictor's act is also improper. That is the rule of contributory negligence. It has been abandoned by many states since it is so foolish." "A classic criticism to contributory negligence is that 'it imposes on one party the full burden of losses assumed to be caused by both parties'… In other words, although both of the defendant and the victim are at fault, the principle of contributory negligence is still patchy."[60] The theory of victim's self-accountability is the same. Even if the perpetrator has caused damaging result to the legal interests of the victim, as long as the victim recognizes the danger and still agrees the defendant to carry out such a dangerous act, he or she must be imposed on all the burdens. It is the typical case of favoring one (the defendant) more than the other (the victim).

[57] 参见日东雪见:"法益主体の危险引受け(一)"，载《上智法学论集》第47卷(2003年)第2号。See Higashi Yukimi.(2003) "Assumption of Risk by the Legal Interest Holder (I)", as cited in *Sophia Law Review*, Vol. 47, No. 2.

[58] 日曽根威彦:"过失犯における危险の引受"，载《早稲田法学》第73卷(1997年)第2号。Sone Takehiko.(1997) "Assumption of risk in the case of negligent criminals", as cited in *Waseda Law Journal*, Vol. 73, No. 2.

[59] 日小林宪太郎:"被害者の关与と结果の归责"，载《千叶大学法学论集》第15卷(2000年)第1号。Kobayashi Kentarou.(2000) "Victims' involvement and the attribution of result", as cited in *Chiba University Law Review*, Vol. 15, No. 1.

[60] Guido Calabresi, "Ideals, Beliefs, Attitudes and the Law", trans. Hu Xiaoqian,Peking University Press 2012:22,128.

6.3.3 *Principle of* Viktimodogmatik

If the theory of victim's self-accountability considers the accountability relationship between the victim and the defendant, the jurisdictional relationship between the victim and the state is what the principle of *Viktimodogmatik* considers.

The basic idea of the principle of *Viktimodogmatik* is that "in the legal order composed not of paternalism but of liberalism, the first jurisdiction to maintain and not to endanger legal interests is directed at the victim himself or herself, who is the subject of legal interests."[61] As Professor K. Amelumg pointed out, the criminal law is the last way of protecting the legal interests of the state. If the victim himself or herself can use appropriate means to protect the legal interests without using them at will, there is no room for criminal law to intervene.[62] Professor Schünemann points out that, the traditional theoretical system of criminal law, which determines the conformity, wrongdoing and culpability based on the defendant's act, cannot fully explain the criminal acts intervened by the victim's act; the victim's act has its independent status for the establishment of a crime; the necessity of the criminal punishment on the defendant and the necessity for the protection of victims are relative because as the state's last resort of preventing the social harmfulness, the criminal punishment shall not be applied when the victims are able to but do not protect themselves due to negligence. Or to say, when the victim is not worthy of protecting and does not need to be protected by the state, there is no room and also not necessary to punish the defendant.[63] Therefore, "In contrast with the potential victims who may or could successfully protect themselves, criminal law shall be a subsidiary way of protection or stands third in protecting those victims".[64]

According to this point of view, the attitude of the victim to his or her own legal interests is of great importance. Where the victim can be expected to protect his or her own legal interests and avoid the damaging result, even if the defendant has participated in this occasion, he or she should not bear the culpability. In the case of endangerment by the third party based on consensus, therefore, the defendant shall not be held responsible by criminal law since the victim doesn't protect his or her

[61] U.Neumann, Die Strafbarkeit der Suizidbeteiligung als Problem der Eigenverantwortlichkeit des Opfers, JA 1987,S.248.

[62] 参见申柳华:《德国被害人信条学研究》，中国人民公安大学出版社2011年版，第96页。See Shen Liuhua. (2011) *Research on German Victim Dogmatics*, Press of People's Public Security University of China, 96.

[63] 参见德伯恩特·许乃曼:"刑事制度中之被害人角色研究"，王秀梅、杜澎译，载《中国刑事法杂志》2001年第2期；王梅英、林钰雄:"从被害者学谈刑法诈欺罪"，载《月旦法学杂志》1998年第4期。Bernd Schunemann, trans. Wang Xiumei, Du Peng, (2001) *The Role of the Victim within the Criminal Justice System--A Concept with Three Columns*, as cited in *Criminal Science*, No.2; (1998) *On the Crime of Fraud in Criminal Law from the Perspective of Victimology*, as cited in *The Taiwan Law Review,* No.4.

[64] 转引自申柳华:《德国被害人信条学研究》，中国人民公安大学出版社2011年版，第97页。As cited in Shen Liuhua. (2011) *Research on German Victim Dogmatics*, Press of People's Public Security University of China, 97.

legal interests properly. Some scholars even believe that as long as the victim has a relatively moderate and abstract understanding of the danger, or the possibility of understanding, the criminal culpability of the defendant should not be pursued. For example, if the victim has realized that the defendant is a prostitute, he or she shall have an abstract understanding of the danger. The act of the prostitute shall not be affirmed as negligent crime even if the prostitute conceals the truth that she has AIDS and the victim is finally infected with AIDS without realizing the specific possibility of AIDS infection.[65]

It is doubtful that the victim is the first responsible to protect his or her legal interests regardless of the circumstances and occasions. Admittedly, if the victim buys over-the-counter drugs from the pharmacy and does not use them according to the instructions, resulting in death or injury, it is impossible for others to bear criminal culpability. However, this view cannot be thoroughly applied, or to say, cannot be carried out in all the cases. First, it will violate the spirit of criminal law if the principle of *Viktimodogmatik* has been regarded as a general rule of criminal law so that the necessity of punishment depends on the necessity of protecting the victim. For example, the defendant's act should not be denied as the crime of theft even if the victim is negligent of protecting his or her own properties and results in the theft of those properties. In the occasion of endangerment by the third party based on consensus, if the victim has been excluded from the protection of the criminal law for the victim trusts the actor easily, it also does not accord with the spirit of criminal law. Second, the principle of *Viktimodogmatik* cannot be deduced from the criminal law's complementary, the basic content of which is that if the social harmfulness can be prevented by the state by using a slight method, there will be no room for the application of criminal law. Apparently, this principle is aimed at the acts of state rather than the common citizens. It doesn't mean that "there is no room for the application of criminal law if the citizens can be protected by themselves". In other words, the principle of complementary is that when the state has multiple ways for protection, the way with the least degree of interference to the fundamental rights of citizens shall be chosen. However, the so-called principle of *Viktimodogmatik* has shifted the responsibility of protecting the legal interests to the citizens themselves. Protecting citizens' legal interests, however, is originally the important purpose and significance as well as the basis of the legitimacy of the existence of the country. Thereby, the victim cannot be regarded as the first responsible for protecting his or her legal interests. Third, the principle of *Viktimodogmatik* expands the principle of complementary of criminal law to the principle of "requiring citizens to protect themselves", which also does not accord with the history. Seen from the historical development, the prohibition of using lynching and entrusted the only power of punishment to the state is to relieve the citizen's burden of protecting themselves. Fourth, the principle of *Viktimodogmatik* is against the criminal policies. If the individual will not get the protection from the country only for trusting others easily,

---

[65] M.C.Meli, Opfer Verhalten und objective Zurechnung,ZStW 111,S.378.

he or she will always be filled with anxiety in public life and the freedom of act will thereafter being limited.[66]

In addition, scholars who hold the theory of *Viktimodogmatik* also think that the theory of victim's self-accountability is too rigid and the principle of *Viktimodogmatik* is flexible in three aspects: first, it is of hierarchical diversity because it can be not only applied to *Lehre vonder objektive zurechnung*, but also used as justifiable cause as well as an important principle of interpretation for the specific provisions of criminal law. Second, it is non-exclusive and will balance the legal interests combined with other principles so that the last resort principle of criminal law can be carried out. Third, it provides the direction of thinking that can be followed and avoids the rigid judgment of either or the other.[67] Therefore, it can be seen that the principle of *Viktimodogmatik* doesn't provide a clear standard for the case of risk assumption. The case held as innocent by the principle of victim's self-accountability may be convicted of crime according to the principle of *Viktimodogmatik*.[68] Moreover, since the principle of *Viktimodogmatik* is flexible, scholars who adopt the same principle may also come to different conclusions; even if the same conclusion of not guilty has been drawn, some may give the reason of lack of wrongdoing while some may believe that it is lack of wrongdoing.

6.3.4 Theory of Negating the Danger of Act

Professor Yamaguti Atushi used to point out that, in the case of "accepting the danger of death", although the subject of legal interest doesn't agree with the result of death, he or she gives consent to the danger of death (the danger of act). The danger of act is an important element for determining the adequate causation or objective attribution. Therefore, within the limit of identifying the degree of danger of the victim's consent, the "danger of the act" can be normatively denied and the adequate causation or objective attribution relationship can be further denied. As a result, the conformity of elements of crime will not be affirmed and the negligent crime will thereby not be established.[69] Later, Professor Yamaguti Atushi pointed out that the subject of legal interest has the freedom of preventing his or her legal interest from being endangered, which can be reflected in involvement in self-

[66] Vgl.,C.Roxin,Strafrecht Allgemeiner Teil,Band I,4.Aufl.C.H.Beck 2006,S.607ff.

[67] 参见申柳华:《德国被害人信条学研究》，中国人民公安大学出版社2011年版，第293页以下。See Shen Liuhua. (2011) *Research on German Victim Dogmatics*, Press of People's Public Security University of China, 1–293.

[68] 参见申柳华:《德国被害人信条学研究》，中国人民公安大学出版社2011年版，第292页。See Shen Liuhua. (2011) *Research on German Victim Dogmatics*, Press of People's Public Security University of China, 292.

[69] 日山口厚:"被害者による危险の引受と过失犯处罚"，载《研修》第599号(1998年)。Yamaguchi Atsushi.(1998) "Assumption of risk by victims and punishment of negligence offenses", as cited in *Kenshuu*, No. 599.

endangerment or endangerment by the third party based on consensus. Since the subject of legal interest realizes and agrees to carry out dangerous acts, the criminal culpability for resulting in the consequence that could not be objectively and subjectively avoided should not be taken by the actor. If the criminal culpability has been pursued, it will be contradictory to the permission of dangerous act. Conversely, if there is the objective and subjective possibility of avoiding the result, there is no reason to deny the actor's act as a crime.[70]

However, this view is still questionable. First, as it is known, Professor Yamaguti Atushi is a total supporter of *Erfolgsunwert*, but his attitude of denying the conformity of criminal constitutive element by denying the danger of act on this issue seems to conflict with theory of *Erfolgsunwert*. Second, if someone has abandoned the legal interests for he or she realizes that others' acts will cause damaging result to the legal interests, it is totally possible to deny the danger of the act by normative evaluation. That is because, as long as the victim has abandoned the legal interests that had been infringed, the infringement will not be illegal any more. However, if the subject of legal interest has only realized the danger rather than the damaging result, it will be groundless to deny the danger of the act only on the basis that the subject has already realized the danger.[71] In other words, in the case of endangerment by the third party based on consensus, the normative evaluation that denies the dangers of act is groundless. Third, if the danger of the defendant's act has been denied only for the victim has given consent to the act that endangers his or her life, when the victim agrees to be killed by others, the defendant's dangerous act shall be more denied. However, it is not the case (it can be illustrated by the fact that the promised killing is punished by all the countries).[72] Fourth, in fact, Professor Yamaguti Atushi has equally dealt with the victim's consent to danger and to the result of damaging result. Or to say, he has fictionalized the consent to danger as the consent to the result of damaging result. However, if the commitment to life is invalid, why does the act endangering life cannot be pursued criminal culpability only for the subject of legal interests has given consent to such act? Those are the questions not answer by Professor Yamaguti Atushi.[73] Besides, in the case of endangerment by the third party based on consensus, the defendant shall not be regarded as being unable to objectively and subjectively prevent the result only for the victim gives permission to the dangerous act.

---

[70] 日山口厚:《刑法总论》，有斐阁2007年版，第170~171页。Yamaguchi Atsushi.(2007) *General Rules of Criminal Law*, Yuhikaku Press, 170–171.

[71] 参见日深町晋也:"危险引受け论について"，载《本乡法政纪要》2000年第9号。See Fukamachi Hhinya.(2000) "Of the theory of assumption of risk", as cited in *A Summary of the Local Legal and Political Affairs*, No. 9.

[72] 参见日须之内克彦:《刑法における被害者の同意》，成文堂2004年版，第252页。 See Sunouchi Katsuhiko.(2004) *Victims' consent in criminal law,* Seibundo Publishing Co., 252.

[73] 参见日佐伯仁志:"被害者の同意とその周边(2)"，载《法学教室》第296号(2005年)。See Saeki Hitoshi.(2005) "Victims' consent and its surroundings (II)", as cited in *Hogaku Kyoshitsu*, No. 296.

6.3.5 View of this Article

To sum up, various theories that attempt to exclude the endangerment by the third party based on consensus from crimes are unsuccessful. This article holds the view that the endangerment by the third party based on consensus could only be analyzed from the perspective of the conformity with criminal constitutive elements, wrongdoing as well as culpability. The endangerment by the third party based on consensus is not an issue of culpability, but a problem of conformity with constitutive element and wrongdoing. As to the conformity with constitutive element, however, since the act has resulted in others' injuries or death, it does accord with the constitutive elements of crime of negligent homicide or crime of serious injury out of negligence. Even if the theory of *Lehre vonder objektive zurechnung* has been taken, it still can not be held that the endangerment by the third party based on consensus doesn't create unacceptable danger, let alone denying the realization of danger as well as holding it outside the protection of constitutive elements. In the aspect of wrongdoing, since the endangerment by the third party based on consensus doesn't provide protection for the more advantageous interests, there is no justifiable cause for it.[74] In view of this, there is no reason for endangerment by the third party based on consensus to exclude the establishment of a crime.

For example, at about 12:00 on December 26, 1999, the defendant Zhong Ping and Long Lijuan drove a XiaLi to the south side of Guanting Reservoir in Yanqing County. In order to watch wild ducks at close range, Zhong Ping inspected the thick ice layer that is about 30 centimeters, and walked seven or eighty meters forward on the ice surface. He thought that the ice layer could carry his car and suggested driving across the ice surface. Long Lijuan agreed with that and Zhong Ping drove Long Lijuan to the North Bank of the reservoir. When the car reached the north of the anabranch, the ice broke down and the car fell into the ice water, causing Long Lijuan drown to death. Zhong Ping went ashore without taking rescue measures or reporting the case. He quietly returned to Beijing and was arrested on June 11, 2004. The procuratorial organ suggested the defendant Zhong Ping convicted the crime of negligent homicide. Both the defense counsel in the first and second trial believed that Zhong Ping is of no negligence and the case was an accident. But all the judgments held that Zhong Ping's act was convicted of crime of negligent homicide.[75] This case didn't hold the defendant's act as negligent crime, or to say, it was a typical case of endangerment by the third party based on consensus. It is for sure that the victim may not be in the car. However, it cannot be held that the victim caused and even created the danger of death by herself only because she had the right to determine. In any case, it should be considered that the defendant's acts caused the

[74] If the more advantageous interests has been protected as the therapeutic act, it will be another matter(it is not necessary to handle the case as risk assumption.)

[75] The First Intermediate People's Court of Beijing(2006)Yi Zhong Xing Zhong Zi(No.1871),published on http://www.pkulaw.cn/fulltext_form.aspx?Db=pfnl&Gid=117670800&keyword=&EncodingName=&Search_Mode=accurate,visited on February 11th,2012.

danger of death and made the danger realistic. Alternatively speaking, although the victim has realized the danger, the danger is completely controlled by the defendant, and the latter's negligent act has dominated the consequence of death. Since the defendant's act completely accord with the constitutive elements of the crime of negligent homicide, and there is no justifiable cause and cause of preventive culpability. The judgment that identifies the defendant's act as crime of negligent homicide is correct.

If the *Memel River case* occurs in China, it should also be punished as negligent crime. That is because the boatman had more knowledge about ferrying and also had the duty for making a safe crossing of the river.[76] The passengers certainly trusted the boatman to cross the river safely even though the boatman drove the boat upon the passenger's request. In such circumstance, the boatman's act cannot be denied as constituting the crime of negligent homicide.[77] Based on the same reason, when the passenger requires the taxi driver to overspeed in order to catch a plane and a car accident thereby occurs, resulting in the passenger's death, the crime of traffic accident (or crime of negligent homicide) has also been established.

If the victim, who takes a ride in the drunken defendant's car, dies due to the defendant's negligence, the defendant shall also bear the criminal culpability of the result. That is because the consequence is created by the defendant's act without any excuse for preventing the culpability. Most of the aforesaid theories of victim's self-accountability hold that the defendant shall only be responsible for the crime of dangerous driving rather than the crime of negligent homicide or traffic accident in such occasion. It is hard to be accepted by this article. Since the dangerous driving act that results in the consequence of death has been forbidden by the criminal law, and the victim doesn't commit to such consequence and the equally or more advantageous legal interests haven't been protected by the act, there will be no reason to deny the defendant's culpability to the crime of negligent homicide or crime of traffic accidents (see Paragraph 1, Article 133 of *Chinese Criminal Law*).

Obviously, the view of this article that endangerment by the third party based on consensus doesn't prevent the constitution of crime is premised on the defendant's act of perpetrator that meets the constitutive element. Therefore, if the victim is the indirect perpetrator and it is the defendant's act that leads to the consequence of legal interest infringement on the surface, the conformity of elements of crime will not be identified and the defendant shall not be hold responsible for the result. Or to say, although on the surface, the defendant is the one who leads to the result, he or she is in fact under the overwhelming domination of the victim's intention and the circumstance can be essentially evaluated as a judgment that it is the victim that

[76] If the defendant was only an ordinary fisherman rather than the boatman who was responsible for ferrying, or the victim handled the boat after getting abroad, the conclusion will be different.

[77] 参见日恩田祐将:"刑法における危険引受けと过失犯の成否"，載《创价大学大学院纪要》2008年号。See Onda Yusuke.(2008) "Assumption of risk in criminal law and the establishment of negligence offenses", as cited in *Soka University Graduate School Bulletin*, 2008 issue.

leads to the result and the defendant shall not be responsible for it.[78] That is because when the victim himself or herself has become the indirect perpetrator that violated his or her own legal interest, such an act doesn't satisfy any constitutive element. Therefore, based on the principle of derivativeness of accomplice, the defendant's involvement will also be impossible to accord with the constitutive element. There are:

Firstly, the victim dominates the development of causal process by coercing the defendant.

For example, on the afternoon of October 16, 2002, Yu Li, the police of Shanghuang Police Station of Public Security Bureau of Wuxi County, led Chen Hao and other policemen to set up a road card from Shanghuang Town to Gulu Town for traffic inspection. Deng Guangzhong, the defendant, drove an unlicensed motorcycle by this road without driver license, was detained by Yu Li and others. Yu Li ordered Deng Guangzhong, the defendant, to drive Yu Li to Shanghuang Police Station for disposal. When Deng Guangzhong drove the car to the right turning of 1 km + 200 m Shangshuo-Gulu Road, the vehicle collided with the rocks along the road due to the excessive speeding and improper operation, resulting in serious injury to Yu Li (Grade I disability). The liability certificate made by the Traffic police detachment of public security bureau of Wuxi County confirmed that the defendant born full responsibility for the accident. The People's Court of Wuxi found that the defendant's act convicted of crime of traffic accident and shall be sentenced to a fixed-term imprisonment of 1 year. After hearing, the Second Intermediate People's Court of Chongqing held that the appellant Deng Guangzhong, who caused serious injuries to the victim due to improper operation, drove the motorcycle without a license under the temporary permission and direction of the law enforcer. In such case, Deng Guangzhong had no possibility of choosing other legitimate acts sand, thus he should not bear the culpability of traffic violation. In sum, his act didn't meet the constitutive elements of crime of traffic accident. However, Deng Guangzhong, the appellant, had the obligation to foresee the consequences that his driving might cause injury to others based on his knowledge and ability of understanding. The appellant should have fulfilled his duty of care for driving safely. However, without improper driving and effective measures to avoid roadside obstacles, the appellant has subjective negligence and objectively resulting in one person's serious injury. His act fully conforms to the constitutive elements of the crime of serious injury caused by negligence and should be punished as such crime. The Second Intermedia People's Court of Chongqing exempted the appellant from criminal punishment in view of the minor circumstances.[79]

---

[78] 日曽根威彦:"过失犯における危险の引受"，載《早稻田法学》第73卷(1997年)第2号。Sone Takehiko.(1997) "Assumption of risk in the case of negligent criminals", as cited in *Waseda Law Journal*, Vol. 73, No. 2.

[79] The Second Intermediate People's Court of Chongqing, (2003) Yu Er Zhong Xing Yi Zhong Zi (No.91), published on http://www.pkulaw.cn/fulltext_form.aspx?Db=pfnl&Gid=117560922&keyword=&EncodingName=&Search_Mode=accurate, visited on February 11th, 2012.

The defendant's is not a crime in the view of this article. When the defendant was investigated and punished for driving without a license, the victim, as a police officer who was exercising the power of traffic inspection and investigating traffic violations, required the defendant to continue driving and carry him even though he clearly knew that the defendant is not qualified to drive. Therefore, this should be evaluated as coercing the defendant. In other words, under that circumstance, it is impossible for the defendant to resist the victim's act. Hence, the victim's act shall be regarded as dominating the occurrence. The appellate court gave a judgment only by considering whether the defendant had the negligence and it formally decided that serious injury was caused by the defendant's negligence without substantively determining who should be attributed to the victim's serious injury. Therefore, it is not proper. As it can be conformed that the victim has dominated the occurrence of the consequence, and such self injured behavior doesn't accord with the constitutive element of negligently injured "others" that provided in Article 235, the defendant's act, according to the principle of derivativeness of accomplice, is also not a crime. In contrary, if the defendant is badly injured, the victim shall bear the criminal culpability.

Secondly, the victim has more advantageous knowledge about the serious act and dominates the development of causal process.

Chiba racing case in Japan is a case in point: the victim had seven years of racing experience and found that the defendant who first learnt racing was poor in technology. When the defendant was practicing, the victim asked to sit on the car and gave technical guidance to the defendant. With the victim's instructions, the defendant improperly handled the car during the practice of racing, causing it to lose control and crash into the protective fence and overturned. The pillar of the protective fence pierced window on the victim's side and resulted in the death of the victim. The court found that the defendant's act was not a crime.[80]

In this case, the victim not only realized the danger of the car racing sport, but also dominated the danger to a large extent by suggesting and instructing the defendant based on his advantageous knowledge. Although the defendant was the one who created the damaging result, it was the victim who stands in the position of indirect perpetrator. Or to say, substantially, the victim's act of infringement had caused his own death. Since the act didn't satisfy any constitutive elements and therefore, based on the principle of derivativeness of accomplice, the defendant's act also does not accord with the constitutive elements.

In addition, it shall be illustrated that the endangerment by the third party based on consensus may well be solved by others means. For example, when the death is caused by the rule-breaking boxing, it can be solved by the due professional conduct even though it can be regarded as the endangerment by the third party based on consensus. So is the act of treatment. What's more, if the actor's act accords with the constitutive element and is also illegal, the establishment of the crime shall be excluded when the actor has no negligence to the damaging result. But this is no longer a matter of risk assumption.

---

[80] 日西田典之等编:《刑法判例百选I(总论)》，有斐阁2008年版，第314页。Nishida Noriyuki et al., ed., (2008) *Selected criminal law cases I (General theory)*, Yuhikaku Press, 314.

References

B.Schünemann, *Moderne Tendenzen in der Dogmatik der Fahrlässigkeits-und Gefährdungsdelikte,* JA 1975, S,715ff.

Bernd Schünemann, trans. Wang Xiumei, Du Peng, (2001) *The Role of the Victim within the Criminal Justice System--A Concept with Three Columns,* as cited in Criminal Science, No.2; (1998) On the Crime of Fraud in Criminal Law from the Perspective of Victimology, as cited in The Taiwan Law Review, No.4.

C.Roxin, *Strafrecht Allgemeiner Teil, Band I, 4.* Aufl. C.H. Beck, 2006, S.402, 411, 607ff.

C.Roxin, *Strafrecht Allgemeiner Teil, Band II,* C.H. Beck, 2003, S.7, 8.

Chen Xingliang. (2009) *Case Studies in Criminal Law (vol. 2),* China Renmin University of Press, 1-154.

Cheng Cheng.(2008) "Drowning during trial swim by mutual agreement: willing assumption of risk and self-responsibility", as cited in Procuratorial Daily, November 1.

Feng Jun. (2006) "Self-Responsibility in Criminal Law", as cited in China Legal Science, No. 3.

Fukamachi Hhinya.(2000) "Of the theory of assumption of risk', as cited in A Summary of the Local Legal and Political Affairs, No. 9.

Guido Calabresi.(2012) "Ideals, Beliefs, Attitudes and the Law", trans. Hu Xiaoqian, Peking University Press, 22,128.

H.Welzel, *Das Deutsche Strafrecht,* 11 Aufl., Walter de Gruyter & Co. 1969, S.136.

Hayashi Mikito.(2008) *General Theory of Criminal Law,* University of Tokyo Press, 173.

Hayashi Shinichiro.(2004) "On the assumption of risk by victims", as cited in Ritsumeikan Law and Politics Review, No. 2.

Higashi Yukimi.(2003) "Assumption of Risk by the Legal Interest Holder (I)', as cited in Sophia Law Review, Vol. 47, No. 2.

Ida Makoto.(2008) "Consent of Victims", as cited in Modern Criminal Law, No. 14.

Ingeborg Puppe, trans. Cai Shengwei, (2010) *Kleine schule des juristischen denkens,* Angle Publishing Co., Ltd., 135.

Kamiyama Toshio.(2000) "The Legal Doctrine of Assumption of Risk and Sports Accidents", as cited in Ohya Minoru, et al, ed., A Collection of Congratulatory Essays by Mr. Miyazawa Kouichi in His Seventies (Vol. 3), Seibundo Publishing Co., 1-36.

Kiragawa Atsuko.(2009) "Werner Beulke 'Victim Autonomy in Criminal Law'", as cited in Waseda Law Journal, Vol. 85 No. 1.

Kobayashi Kentarou.(2000) "Victims' involvement and the attribution of result", as cited in Chiba University Law Review, Vol. 15, No. 1.

Maeda Masahide.(1979) "Premissible risk", as cited in Nakayama Kenichi et al, ed., Issues in Contemporary Criminal Law (Vol. 3), Seibundo Publishing Co, 46.

Maeda Masahide.(2011) *Handouts of General Rules of Criminal Law,* University of Tokyo Press, 409.

Matsumiya Takaaki.(2004) *Contemporary Issues of the Theory of Negligent Crime,* Seibundo Publishing Co., 251-252.

M.C.Meli, *Opfer Verhalten und objective Zurechnung,* ZStW 111, S.378.

Nishida Noriyuki et al, ed., (2008) *Selected criminal law cases I (General theory),* Yuhikaku Press, 314.

Onda Yusuke.(2008) "Assumption of risk in criminal law and the establishment of negligence offenses", as cited in Soka University Graduate School Bulletin, 2008 issue.

R.Zaczyk.(1993) *Strafrechtliches Unrecht und die Selbstverantwortung des Verletzten,* C.F.Mller Verlag, S.25ff.

Saeki Hitoshi.(2005) "Victims' consent and its surroundings (II)", as cited in Hogaku Kyoshitsu, No. 296.

Shen Liuhua. (2011) *Research on German Victim Dogmatics,* Press of People's Public Security University of China, 1-293, esp. 96, 97, 292.

Shiotani Takeshi.(1997) "On participation in self-endangerment and consensual endangerment of others (IV)", as cited in Ritsumeikan Law Review, No. 1.
Shiotani Takeshi.(2004) *Victim's Consent and Self-assumed Liability,* Houritsu Bunka Sha, 1-263, 178, 371, 373-374.
Shimada Souichirou.(2003) "Result of the victims' assumption of risk", as cited in Yamaguchi Atsushi ed. Close-up General Theory of Criminal Law, Seibundo Publishing Co., 1-130, 126, 141, 142.
Sone Takehiko.(1997) "Assumption of risk in the case of negligent criminals", as cited in Waseda Law Journal, Vol. 73, No. 2.
Sone Takehiko.(1998) *A Study of Criminal Illegality,* Seibundo Publishing Co., 169.
Sunouchi Katsuhiko.(2004) *Victims' consent in criminal law,* Seibundo Publishing Co., 252.
Xu Degao & Zhang Jinzhong. (2010) "Lured into Water for Fun, Drowned for Petty Cash: A Tragic Case", as cited in Procuratorate Daily, May 15.
Yamaguchi Atsushi.(1998) "Assumption of risk by victims and punishment of negligence offenses", as cited in Kenshuu, No. 599.
Yamaguchi Atsushi.(2007) *General Rules of Criminal Law,* Yuhikaku Press, 170-171.
Yamanaka Keiichi.(1997) *The Theory of Objective Attribution in Criminal Law,* Seibundo Publishing Co., 1-741, esp. 731.
Yoshikawa Toshio.(1998) "On 'Endangerment of others with consent'", as cited in Okano Mitsuo et al, ed., A Collection of Congratulatory Essays by Mr. Haruo Nishihara in His Seventies (Vol. 1), Seibundo Publishing Co., 1-407.

Chapter 7
How to Dealing with Specific Method Mistake

Cognition mistakes of facts can be divided into concrete (specific) cognition mistakes of facts and abstract cognition mistakes of facts. Concrete cognition mistakes of facts refer to the situation that the facts recognized by the actor are inconsistent with the facts that actually occur, but they are within the situations that constitute same crime (also referred to the mistake within the composition of the same crime). The theory of criminal law generally believes that concrete cognition mistakes of facts include object mistake, method mistake, and causality mistake.[1] Concerning the concrete cognition mistakes of facts, there is mainly a dispute between the doctrines of concrete accord and the doctrines of legally prescribed.[2] The former believes that when the facts recognized by the actor are specifically consistent with the actual facts, then the intentional accomplished crime can be established; the latter argues that as long as the facts recognized by the actor and actual facts are consistent within constitution of a crime, then the intentional accomplished crime can be established.[3]

*The original title is "On Specific Method Mistake", published in ***Peking University Law Journal*** in 2008, Vol.2.

[1] 参见日前田雅英:《刑法总论讲义》，东京大学出版会2006年版，第243页。See Maeda Masahide. (2006) *Handouts of General Rules of Criminal Law*, University of Tokyo Press, 243.

[2] Because the doctrines of concrete accord and the doctrines of legally prescribed both require the consistency and conformity of subjective cognition and objective elements within the same constitutive elements. Therefore, the Japanese scholar, Professor Hirano, believes that the doctrines of concrete accord and the doctrines of legally prescribed can also be called specific statutory conformity theory, and abstract statutory conformity theory respectively. (参见日平野龙一:《刑法总论I》，有斐阁1972年版，第175页). Obviously, the abstract doctrines of legally prescribed is different from the abstract conformity theory. In this article, I prefer to call them the doctrines of concrete accord and the doctrines of legally prescribed.

[3] To be mentioned, there is a theory called abstract conformity in criminal law which is a theory adopted for abstract fact errors. The basic viewpoint of that theory is, when the subjective cognition of the perpetrator and the objective elements belong to constitutive elements of different

M. Zhang, *The Fundamental Issues upon Criminal Law Theories*, Masterpieces of Contemporary Jurisprudents in China,
https://doi.org/10.1007/978-981-95-1276-8_7

The object mistake of the specific fact mistakes means that, the actor mistakenly infringes object A as object B under certain situation where A and B are in the same criminal composition, and the actor's cognition content and objective facts are consistent with the same crime. For example, A intents to harm his enemy X, but A mistakenly kills his father Y due to bad sight in the night. According to the doctrines of legally prescribed, the crime of murder in criminal law is designed to protect human life, not just to protect X or Y particularly. Therefore, as long as the actor has the meas rea and commits murder, the requirements of murder would be satisfied, and the murder thus is accomplished. The doctrines of concrete accord also believes that this kind of object mistake is not important, thus it does not affect the establishment of the intentional crime. Because when the actor wanted to kill Y, and actually he committed a killing, that shall satisfied the requirements of concrete accord. Therefore, the accomplished intentional homicide should be established.[4] In other words, when object mistake happens, the so-called "actor A intents to kill the enemy X" means that initially, A wants to kill X; and when committing killing, A believed the "person" (Y) was the right target to kill. This situation is in line with the concrete accord.[5] Therefore, in terms of such object mistakes, the doctrines of concrete accord and the doctrines of legally prescribed have the same conclusion. However, there are fierce debates in the theory of criminal law in terms of how to deal with method mistakes.

7.1 The Scope of Method Mistakes

Method mistakes (diverted criminal act, *aberratio ictus*) mean that, influenced by the mistake of the behavior, the actor attacks the actual victim who is not his previous target, but such mistake still does not exceed the situation of the constitution of the crime. For example, A mistakenly shoots Y who is next to the real target X, leading to the death of Y (Case 1). This is a typical example of a method mistake recognized by theory of criminal law in civil law countries such as Germany and Japan.

Method mistakes do not occur only in crimes targeting humans, but they may also occur in crimes regarding objects. For example, as desire for killing a dog raised by X pushed him to shoot the dog, but he shoots the dog raised by Y by mistake (Case 2). A's cognition (killing the dog raised by X, namely, intentional destruction of X's property) is inconsistent with objective facts (killing the dog raised by Y, namely, destroying Y's property). But both dogs can be the object of the crime of intentionally destroying property as stipulated in Article 275 of *Chinese Criminal*

crimes, the perpetrator shall at least be convicted of a accomplished crime within the limits of the lighter crime. However, this view has basically been forsaken.

[4] 参见日山口厚:《刑法总论》，有斐阁2007年版，第205~206页; Yamaguchi Atsushi, (2007) *General Rules of Criminal Law*, Yuhikaku Press, 205–206. C.Roxin,Strafrecht Allgemeiner Teil,Band I,3.Aufl.,C.H.Beck, 1997,S.448f.

[5] Obviously, while conducting acts of perpetrating, as to the subjective cognition of the perpetrator and objective elements, there is no object error.

Law. Therefore, A's cognition mistake does not exceed the same constitution of crime and it is a specific method mistakes.

Some scholars in China believe that method mistake "has nothing to do with the subjective cognition mistake of the actor. It is purely a mistake or an objective diverted criminal act of objective behavior. Therefore, it is not within the range of mistake of the criminal law."[6] This view attributes the method mistake to the objective mistake of the behavior, thus it is concluded that the actor does not know the cognition mistake subjectively. In fact, the problem to be solved by the theory of cognition mistake is whether the actor can bear the intentional culpability for the actual result. In Case 1, there is a question that whether A should bear the culpability of intentional homicide for the death of Y. This is exactly the problem to be solved by the theory of cognition mistake. Therefore, the cognition mistake of facts in criminal law is not limited to the subjective mistake of the actor, but rather about the situation in which the subjective cognition of the actor does not conform to the objective fact.[7] In cases regarding cognition mistakes, the subjective cognition of the actor (shooting X) and the objective facts (causing Y's death) are inconsistent and should be studied in the cognition mistake. It is also true for Case 2, if the method mistake is not considered to be a cognition mistake, another theory must be established to deal with the method mistake. But in fact, the handling of method mistake is also applicable to other theories regarding cognition mistakes (hereinafter called the theory for handling the cognition mistakes as "the theory of mistake").

Of course, not all general situations in which subjective cognition is inconsistent with objective facts can be called method mistakes. The subjective cognition in method mistakes refers to the crime intent; the objective fact refers to the fact (result) that meets the objective constitutive elements. Therefore, first, if the actor has no intention of committing a crime subjectively, even if the result meets the constitutive elements of the crime, it is not a method mistake. For example, the actor wanted to shoot and kill a mad dog, but because he failed to aim correctly, he shot others instead. Since he has no intention of committing a crime subjectively, it is not a method mistake but a distinction between negligence and an accident.[8] Second, if

---

[6] 何秉松主编:《刑法教科书》(上卷)，中国法制出版社2000年版，第336页。笔者也曾发表过类似观点(参见张明楷:《犯罪论原理》，武汉大学出版社1991年版，第306页)。

He Bingsong ed. (2000) *Treatise on Criminal Law (Vol. 1)*, China Legal System Publishing House, 336. The author has also expressed similar views. (See Zhang Mingkai. (1991) *Fundamentals of the Theory of Crime*, Wuhan University Press, 306.)

[7] Of course, it does not refer to all situations in which objective elements are inconsistent with subjective cognition. For example, A wants to steal X's mobile phone, but he steals X's handheld computer instead. This kind of error has no significance in conviction.

[8] For the same reason, if the perpetrator wants to shoot and kill a mad dog, but mistakenly takes other person as mad dog in the dark and causes the death of that person, it is not an object error, but a distinction between a negligent manslaughter and an accident. Errors in the Anglo-American common law can cover such instance. "For example, suppose D had sexual intercourse with V without V's consent, and he mistakenly believed that V agreed to do so. D is accused of rape... Because rape is a general intentional crime, the court uses the punishable method to analyze the factual error of D; if he believes that the factual error that V has agreed is reasonable, then he will

the actor has the criminal intent subjectively, but he objectively does not cause a crime, it is still not a method mistake. For example, the actor wanted to shoot and kill others, however, he failed to aim correctly and shot a mad dog. Since there is not result meets the constitutive elements of the crime, it is not a method mistake but a attempted crime (if there is no danger of killing others, it is an incapable crime which is unpunishable).[9]

Obviously, the method mistake is different from the mean mistake or tool mistake included in theory of criminal law in China (in the past). For example, earlier textbooks pointed out that "the cognition mistake of the criminal means, which usually refers to the actor's incorrect understanding of whether the means or method used can cause damaging results. It may manifest that the means used are not sufficient to cause a damaging result, and the actor mistakenly believes that it can cause a damaging result. For example, in order to kill his girlfriend he hates, A purchased 40 tablets of chlordiazepine for her to take down. In fact, 40 tablets of chlordiazepine could not kill human. His girlfriend wakes up later… It may also show that the means taken can cause a damaging result, which the actor mistakenly believes that it will not cause. For another example, Li X mistakenly used dichlorvos as medicinal liquor, and told the guests who complained of back pain, causing the death of the guests by poisoning."[10] In the context of this article, the former situation, that is, the behavior of A, is not the cognition mistake but the difference between the attempted crime and unpunishable incapable crime which should be discussed in the attempted crime. This is because the incapable crime "is in an intangible relation with the perpetrating act, that is, the situation adjacent to the content of the perpetrating act". The incapable crime "lacks the danger required by the crime meeting constitutive elements of the crime, thus it does not conform to the characteristics of the perpetrating act".[11] In other words, as for the former case, the question to be solved is whether A has begun to implement the murderous conduct. Therefore it is a question of whether an attempted crime is established, and there is no question about whether A should bear the intentional culpability of the death he envisions. The latter case, Li X's behavior is not a cognition mistake, but a difference between a negligent crime and an accident. Because in such case, the problem to be solved is whether Li X is at fault for the victim's death, not whether he is willing to take culpability for the victim's death. In the recent textbooks, the former

not be convicted (美约书亚·德雷斯勒:《美国刑法精解》，王秀梅等译，北京大学出版社2009年版，第143页). Obviously, this factual error identification in the Anglo-American common law is not the factual errors in theory of criminal law of the civil law countries, and it's not the same as mentioned in this article.

[9] For the same reason, if the perpetrator wants to shoot other person, but mistakenly shoots the mad dog and causes the death of the mad dog, it is not an object error, but a distinction between the incapable crime undeserving punishment and an attempt.

[10] 高铭暄主编:《中国刑法学》，中国人民大学出版社1989年版，第142页。Gao Mingxuan ed. (1989) *Chinese Criminal Law*, China Renmin University Press, 142.

[11] 日西原春夫:《犯罪实行行为论》，戴波、江溯译，北京大学出版社2006年版，第5~6页。Nishihara Haruo, trans. Dai Bo & Jiang Su. (2006), *Theory of Criminal Conduct*, Peking University Press, 5–6.

case is still treated as a cognition mistake.[12] However, the method mistakes discussed in this article do not include such so-called mean mistake and tool mistake.

7.2 The Relation Between the Theory of Mistake and the Theory of Intention

Regarding the content of criminal intent, criminal laws overseas generally stipulate no clear provisions, and there are many different doctrines in theory of criminal law.[13] However, it is certain that the establishment of intent at least requires that the actor has an understanding of the facts meeting the objective constitutive elements. If it is possible for the actor to know the facts of the objective constitutive elements, and lacking realistic understanding, he can only be charged a negligent crime. Therefore, the criminal intent will be affected by the cognition mistake of facts in line with criminal constitutive elements. Some of them will affect the establishment of specific intentions, while some will affect whether the actor is guilty of the criminal result (influencing the form of crime).

As mentioned above, the cognition mistake means that the subjective cognition of the actor is inconsistent with the objective fact, which does not necessarily mean that the actor has subjectively formed a wrong understanding (in this article, the cognition mistake refers only to the cognition mistake of facts). The theory of criminal law always discusses cognition mistakes in relation to intentional crimes rather than negligent crimes.[14] Therefore, the relation between the theory of mistake and the theory of intention has become an important issue.

One view is that the theory of mistake is about evaluating the intentional perpetrating acts as a whole (the result included), which plays an independent role and hence is different from the theory of intention, thus it has a unique principle.[15] The point of this view is that, when it is not possible to affirm the intent of the actor about the result based on the theory of intention, the theory of mistake may be helpful. Therefore, the theory of mistake has become another way to affirm intents. But this article doesn't agree with that. Article 14 of *Chinese Criminal Law* clearly pro-

---

[12] 参见高铭暄、马克昌主编:《刑法学》，北京大学出版社、高等教育出版社2007年版，第136页。See Gao Mingxuan & Ma Kechang eds. (2007) *Criminal Law*, Peking University Press & Higher Education Press, 136.

[13] 参见张明楷:《外国刑法纲要》，清华大学出版社2007年版，第215~217页。 See Zhang Mingkai. (2007) *Essentials of Foreign Criminal Law*, Tsinghua University Press, 215–217.

[14] For example, the perpetrator mistakenly takes the property of another as his and destroys it. This is not a problem which the error theory solves.

[15] 日佐久间修:"错误论における结果归属の理论"，载日福田平/大塚仁博士古稀祝贺论文集:《刑法法学の综合的检讨》(上卷)，有斐阁1993年版，第146页。See Sakuma Osamu. (1993) "Theory of result attribution in error theory", as cited in Hirata Taira. *A Collection of Congratulatory Essays by Dr. Otsuka Hitoshi in His Seventies: Comprehensive Studies on Criminal Law (Vol. 1)*, Yuhikaku Press, 146.

vides the general definition of intent. In addition, the objective constitutive elements of specific crimes regulate the cognition content and will the mistake theory of intents. Obviously, when the subjective content of the actor does not meet the requirements stipulated in Article 14 of *Chinese Criminal Law*, and where there is a lack of cognition of the facts, it is impossible to establish criminal intents. In this context, of course, the theory of mistake cannot be regarded as another way to affirm intent.

Another view is that the theory of mistake is the opposite of the theory of intention. This article is in favor of this view. Because "mistakes discussed in criminal law are not all cases of inconsistency between the subjective and objective aspects, but are limited to the situation in which there is the criminal intent or not. When some major matters happen objectively (such as a death of some person) and the subjective recognition of offender of the outcome shall be deemed as a standard to test whether it is consistent with the objective outcome, therefore it shall be an mistake in sense of theory of criminal law".[16] Obviously, there is an exterior-interior relation between the cognition mistake and intent, and to deal with cognition mistake is to resolve whether the actor bears intentional culpability for the result. Therefore, it is a must to maintain the proposition that the theory of mistake is opposite to the the theory of intention must be kept (*Kehrseite*). Hence, when intent becomes a problem, there is no case which is 'not applicable to the theory of mistake'; when there is no intent according to the the theory of intention, it cannot be determined according to the theory of mistake".[17]

However, it will be extreme to take the idea that the theory of mistake and the theory of intention are completely equivalent. Some scholars deny the intent-regulating function of the subjective element, but believe that the establishment of intent does not require cognition of the facts that meet the objective constitutive elements, as long as the actor recognizes the meaning of the facts; in other words, those scholars believe that as long as the actor is aware of wrongdoing and content of culpability that belong to the constitutive elements, the criminal intent would be demonstrated. Otherwise, when the actor's subjective cognition and objective facts do not fall neatly in the same constitutive elements due to some cognition mistake, as long as the wrongdoing and content of culpability of the two crimes are the same, the actor should also bear the culpability for not foreseeing the objective facts and take the culpability for intentionally committing the crime.[18] Therefore, the theory of mistake is somehow another the theory of intention. However, on the one hand, it will make the constitutive elements lose the function of principle of *nulla poena*

---

[16] 日井田良、丸山雅夫:《ケ-ススタディ刑法》，日本评论社2004年版，第112页。Ida Makoto & Maruyama Masao. (2004*) Case Study Criminal Law*, NIPPON HYORON SHA Co., 112.

[17] 日平野龙一:《刑事法研究最终卷》，有斐阁2005年版，第3页。Hirano Ryuuichi. (2005) *Final Volume of Criminal Law Research*, Yuhikaku Press, 3.

[18] 参见日町野朔:《刑法总论讲义案I》，信山社1995年版，第229~230页。

See Machino Saku. (1995) *Handouts of General Theory of Criminal Law (I)*, Shinzansha Publisher Co., 229–230.

sine lege that not conducive to the identification of intent, and denying intent-regulating function of the objective constitutive elements. Moreover, scholars who hold the above viewpoints also believe that "the establishment of an intentional crime requires the actor... have an understanding of all the facts corresponding to the constitutive elements."[19] As it is, the objective constitutive elements have the intent-regulating function. Additionally, if there is no cognition mistake of the actor, it is then unnecessary to apply the theory of mistake, to apply the theory of intention will meet the needs. On the contrary, it is necessary to apply both the theory of mistake and the the theory of intention where the actor does have cognition mistake. Therefore, the theory of mistake and the theory of intention though have an exterior-interior relation, they are not the same thing and shall not be equalized.

It is just because the theory of mistake and the the theory of intention though have an exterior-interior relation that the consistency of the subjective cognition and the objective elements of the actor will not only be a matter of content of intent cognition but also a matter of the theory of mistake. What is certain is that only when the facts recognized by the actor and the actual facts happen are "consistent within the scope of the constitutive elements", can he be affirmed an offender who completes an intentional crime. In other words, the constitutive elements should be a benchmark to decide whether a certain fact is an important fact as a cognition object (or content) of intent; if there is a cognition mistake to an important fact, it will prevent the accomplishment of an intentional crime; otherwise, an intentional crime completes. But the question is, what on earth are the meanings of the terms such as "constitutive elements" and "inconsistent"? One view is that the constitutive elements should be taken as the standards, and the facts meeting the constitutive elements should be given an abstract grasp, without considering the individuality and specificity of those facts. If the facts meet certain constitutive element, its specificity should not be the cognition content of intent. For example, the victim in the constitutive elements of intentional homicide is an important part, however, the specific status and identity of the victim does not matter. So, the establishment of the crime of intentional homicide requires the actor to know that he is killing a person, not necessarily who the person is.[20] This is the statement of the doctrines of legally prescribed. Other view exists too, that the constitutive elements should be taken as the standards, and the facts that meet the constitutive elements should be given an

---

[19] 日町野朔:《刑法总论讲义案I》，信山社1995年版，第220页。

See Machino Saku. (1995) *Handouts of General Theory of Criminal Law (I)*, Shinzansha Publisher Co., 220.

[20] 参见日团藤重光:《刑法纲要总论》，创文社1990年版，第298页See Dandou Shigemitsu. (1990) General Outline of Criminal Law, Kodansha Publishing Co, 298；日大塚仁:《刑法概说(总论)》，有斐阁1997年版，第205页Otsuka Hitoshi.(1997) *Overview of Criminal Law*, Yuhikaku Press, 205.；日大谷实:《刑法讲义总论》，成文堂2007年新版，第184~187页 Ohya Minoru.(2010) *General Handouts on Criminal Law(New Edition)*, Seibundo Publishing Co, 184–187；日前田雅英:《刑法总论讲义》，东京大学出版会2006年版，第246~247页 Maeda Masahide.(2006) *Handouts of General Rules of Criminal Law*, University of Tokyo Press,246–247.；Puppe, Zur Revision der Lehre vom "konkreten" Vorsatz und der Beachtlichkeit der aberratio ictus,GA 1981,S.1；等等。法定符合说(即德国的等价说)在德国并非主流观点。

abstract grasp, but the individuality and specificity of the subject of legal interests should not be abandoned (or even the individuality and specificity of the object of the criminal act itself cannot be abandoned, such as property in theft). And for cases concerning cognition mistakes in the subjects of legal interest, the conformity of elements of crime should be judged according to the subject of legal interests. For example, in Case 1, A wants to kill X, but when Y is killed because of a method mistake, the conformity of the constitutive elements of X and Y should be judged respectively. Obviously, A constitutes an attempted intentional homicide against X and constitutes a negligent homicide against Y.[21] This is exactly what the doctrines of concrete accord claims. In addition, there is the theory of behavior planning between the theory of mistake and the theory of intention.

7.3 The Doctrines of Concrete Accord

According to the doctrines of concrete accord, in Case 1 concerning method mistakes, when the objective facts are not consistent with the specific subjective cognition of the actor, A bears the culpability of attempted killing for X, and culpability of negligent homicide for Y; since there is only one act, Case 1 is the ideal concurrence and A would be convicted of a more serious crime. Obviously, the doctrine of concrete accord emphasizes the difference in the subjects of legal interests, and considers that the cognition content of intent includes the understanding of the specific legal subject. However, this article is going to discuss some flaws in the doctrines of concrete accord.

(1) According to the doctrines of concrete accord, there is only one act in Case 1, so the actor only can be charged with a more serious crime, which is attempted intentional homicide. However, the actor cause death to another person with meas rea, the conviction of attempted intentional homicide is against the general social concepts. The theory of criminal law should not cause such confusion to the general social concepts. One of the important reasons why the establishment of a crime requires the actor to have *vorwerfbarkeit* is that it derives from views accepted by the general social concepts.[22] In other words, to investigate and to affix the criminal culpability of the actor only based on his objective act and the criminal result but the

---

21 参见日平野龙一:《刑法总论I》，有斐阁1972年版，第175页See Hirano Ryuuichi. (1972) *General Theory of Criminal Law I,* Yuhikaku Press, 175；日铃木茂嗣:《刑法总论(犯罪论)》，成文堂2001年版，第103~104页Suzuki Shigetsugu.(2001) *General part of criminal law (theory of crime)*, Seibundo Publishing Co., 103–104.；日山口厚:《刑法总论》，有斐阁2007年版，第206页See Yamaguchi Atsushi.(2007) G*eneral Part of Criminal Law.*Yuhikaku Press,206；等等。The doctrines of concrete accord is both a powerful statement from Japan and a mainstream doctrine in German theory of criminal law(Vgl.,C.Roxin, Strafrecht Allgemeiner Teil, Band I,3. Aufl.,C.H.Beck, 1997,S.437f).

22 参见日前田雅英:《刑法总论讲义》，东京大学出版会2006年版，第54、200页。See Maeda Masahide. (2006) *Handouts of General Rules of Criminal Law (4th Edition)*, University of Tokyo Press, 54、200.

criminal intent (meas rea), negligence and other factors indicating the *vorwerfbarkeit* lose, it will confuse the general social concepts or cause the national normative consciousness. On the contrary, when discussing method mistakes, it is against the general social concepts that A bears no culpability while being charged with attempted intentional homicide in Case 1.

Of course, grounds based on "the general social concepts" may be modest to be convincing. Scholars holding the doctrines of concrete accord can find supportive cases in which the convictions are consistent with the general social concepts. For example, A wants to kill X but (Case 3) shoots the daughter Y instead. In terms of doctrines of concrete accord, the assumption that A constitutes an attempted intentional homicide against X and constitutes a negligent homicide against Y is consistent with the general social concepts, since A cannot be assumed to have an intention of murder against his own daughter Y in common sense. However, Case 3 can hardly be a powerful proof for the doctrines of concrete accord. As mentioned above, for object mistakes, the doctrines of concrete accord and the doctrines of legally prescribed have exactly the same conclusion. If we make some slight change to Case 3, the conclusion drawn from the doctrines of concrete accord will be then questionable: finding enemy X with a gun, A killed his daughter Y in the dark for taken her mistakenly as X (Case 4). According to the doctrines of concrete accord, it should be convicted that A bears the culpability of intentional homicide for the death of Y. Because A wants to kill "that person" (Y) in front of him, and successfully kills "that person" (Y), this is a concrete match. Therefore, scholars holding the doctrines of concrete accord would consider A has a intention of homicide against Y according to the general social concepts. This seems to be self-contradictory. Obviously, only considering A has criminal intent to the death of Y in Case 1, Case 3, and Case 4 can avoid contradictions.

(2) According to the doctrines of concrete accord, when the actor A shoots X, as long as it does not cause the death of X, regardless of whether it causes the death of Y or others, A only bears the culpability of attempted homicide, it will lead to an imbalance between crime and punishment. For example, A shoots X, but causing many people such as C, D, Y, Z to die because of a method mistake (Case 5). According to the doctrines of concrete accord, A in Case 5 can only be punished with an attempted intentional homicide. This is obviously not an appropriate punishment for such crime. China's scholars advocating this theory have realized and explained: "According to the provisions of Article 23, Paragraph 2 of *Chinese Criminal Law*, an offender who attempts to commit a crime may, in comparison with one who completes the crime, is given a lighter or mitigated punishment (not shall) which means that judges may be impose the same penalties on the attempted crime and the accomplished crime according to the specific circumstances of the case. In this way, there will be no irrational phenomenon that criminals are too lightly sentenced."[23] By implication, the behavior of A in Case 5 shall be convicted

[23] 刘明祥:《刑法中错误论》，中国检察出版社2004年版，第181页。Liu Mingxiang. (2004) *Treatise on the Doctrine of Mistake in Criminal Law,* China Procuratorial Publishing House, 181.

as an attempted crime, but when it comes to the sentence phase for punishment, A shall be punished as an accomplished criminal. Or to say, A shall be convicted as intentional homicide, but be found as an intentional actor when sentenced. This is a contradictory. In Germany and Japan, in order to make A only bear the culpability of the attempted crime and thus get a mitigated punishment, it is advocated that A will be charged with the attempted intentional homicide and be punished. If A was not given a mitigated punishment, the doctrines of concrete accord will lose its meaning. Meanwhile, the claim of advocator of the doctrines of legally prescribed that A should be charged with the accomplished homicide avoids mitigating punishment for A. Therefore, the above viewpoints of Chinese scholars have apparently adopted the doctrines of concrete accord, and the actual adoption is still the doctrines of legally prescribed. Moreover, according to the above viewpoints of Chinese scholars, A who wants to kill X objectively kills Y shall not be given a lighter or mitigated punishment, which completely loses the meaning to adopt the doctrines of concrete accord.

(3) According to the doctrines of concrete accord, the actor A originally plans to steal the wallet of X wearing the suits, but actually steals the wallet of the Y wearing the jacket because of the method mistake. As a result, A constituted the unaccomplished theft against X and negligent theft against Y (Case 6). Because German and Japanese criminal law expressly stipulates the attempted theft, the behavior of A can at least be treated as a crime. In this regard, defects of the doctrines of concrete accord are not obvious. However, in China, there is usually no penalty for attempted theft. Negligent theft cannot constitute a crime, therefore, in China, A will not be guilty, which certainly seems unreasonable. Those who adopt the doctrines of concrete accord may propose two points for arguing this: the one is, China's criminal law does not prohibit punishing the attempted theft. On the contrary, according to the general provisions of China's criminal law, the attempted theft is punishable in principle. Therefore, A in Case 6 can still be charged with attempted theft. The other point is, in judicial practice, if the attempted theft is serious, it should be treated as accomplished theft. The behavior of A in Case 6 can be considered serious, so he may be charged with the accomplished theft. However, first, although China's criminal law does not prohibit punishing the attempted theft, according to the nature of the crime and judicial practice, in fact, only the serious theft has been criminalized. Therefore, the first point of the said counter-argument cannot be found. Being not so, it will inevitably lead to the arbitrary punishment of the attempted theft. Second, considering the fact that A has stolen the wallet of Y, the accomplished theft of A by stealing Y's wallet in Case 6 is obviously more serious. However, according to the viewpoint of the doctrines of concrete accord, A stole the wallet of Y negligently; however, the China's criminal law does not prohibit negligent theft, so negligent theft cannot be the evaluation object of the criminal law. If the court takes both the attempt and the negligence of theft in to account, and determines that the consequence of attempted theft is serious, it means that the criminal fact is proved by the facts not prohibited in China's criminal law. This

obviously forms an indirect punishment and violates the principle of legality of the crime.[24]

For another example, actor A wanted to cut off X's pinkie finger, however, A cut off Y's pinkie finger because of the method mistakes (Case 7). According to the doctrines of concrete accord, A can be convicted an attempted intentional minor injury against X and a negligent minor injury against Y. In Germany and Japan, A can be charged with the crime of harming the body of others (Article 223 of the *German Criminal Law*) or the crime of violence (Article 208 of the *Japanese Criminal Law*) at least. In this regard, the flaws of the doctrines of concrete accord are not obvious. However, in China, the attempted intentional injury, especially that of minor injury, is not punishable, and the offender who negligent injuries cannot be punished. And there is no provision in criminal law of the crime of harming the body of others, or any provision of the crime of violence; if the doctrines of concrete accord is adopted in China, it means that there will be no crime for A's conduct, which is also difficult to agree with. If the offender is charged with the attempted injury, it will also cause an arbitrary and indirect punishment for the attempted punishment.

Upon these comparisons, its evident that there may be obvious flaws of the doctrines of concrete accord in China while the case is not the same with that in Germany and Japan.

(4) The doctrines of concrete accord advocates that the intentional culpability shall be borne only when the actor's subjective cognition and the objective facts (result) are in specific consistency. But, what degree the "specific" shall be as in those consistency? This is an unsolved problem.

For example, A wanted to smash the computer in the left hand of X who is carrying one computer in his each hand. However, what A really smashed is the computer on X's right hand because of a method mistake (Case 8). According to one of the viewpoints in the doctrines of concrete accord, it is believed that at this time, because the objects do not have the same identity, it should be denied that A has an intention to destroy the computer on X's right hand (the doctrine based on the identity of the object). Thus, in Case 8, A can be convicted of the attempted intentional damage of properties against the computer on left hand, and the crime of negligent damage of properties against the computer on right hand. If it is so, A will not be charged with any crime.[25] However, with the same subject of the legal interests, it seems to go too far to consider that A is not guilty of anything. That is not conducive

---

[24] 参见张明楷:"结果与量刑——结果责任、双重评价、间接处罚之禁止"，载《清华大学学报》(哲学社会科学版)2004年第6期。See Zhang Mingkai. (2004) "Consequences and Sentencing: Consequential Liability, Double Evaluation, and Prohibition of Indirect Punishment", as cited in *Journal of Tsinghua University* (Philosophy and Social Sciences), No. 6.

[25] 参见日町野朔:《刑法总论讲义案I》，信山社1995年版，第242~244页See Machino Saku. (1995) *Handouts of General Theory of Criminal Law (I)*, Shinzansha Publisher Co., 242–244；日佐伯仁志:"故意·错误论"，载日山口厚、井田良、佐伯仁志:《理论刑法学の最前线》，岩波书店2001年版，第113~116页。Saeki Hitoshi.(2001) "Intent and error theory", as cited in Yamaguchi Atsushi, Ida Makoto & Saeki Hitoshi. *The Forefront of Theoretical Criminal Law*, Iwanami Shoten Publisher, 113–116.

to the protection of legal interests. Therefore, another argument of the doctrines of concrete accord is that, because the subject of legal interest are the same, A has intention to destroy the computer of X right hand, and then A completes the crime of intentional destruction of property (the doctrine based on the identity of the subject of legal interests).[26]

However, lets slightly change the case then well see there will be some doubts about the doctrines of concrete accord. For example, X carries his own computer on his left hand with Y's computer on his right hand (assuming that X is only the assistant possessor of Y's computer, not the real possessor). A planed to smash the computer on left hand, but smashed the computer on the right hand because of a method mistake (Case 9). According to the doctrines of concrete accord, A's behavior is unpunishable. Because the subject of legal interests is different, A constitutes the attempted intentional damage of properties against the computer on left hand (unpunishable), and he may be convicted of the crime of negligent damage of properties against the computer on right hand (unpunishable). However, in Case 9 and Case 8, there is no difference in wrongdoing and the intention content of the actor. Yet, with different conclusion reached, the author finds impossible to agree with the doctrines of concrete accord.

Moreover, the actor carries out a spate of bombings to kill a number of government officials, but causing the death of innocent civilians due to method mistakes. The doctrines of concrete accord is either to insist that the actor has no intention to the death of innocent civilians for the consistency of the theory or to abstract the "concrete accord" to some extent in order to draw a reasonable conclusion. However, the former conclusion is obviously unreasonable, and the latter no longer is from the angle of the doctrines of concrete accord.

(5) As mentioned above, according to the doctrines of concrete accord, when A takes Y as X mistakenly and kills Y (object mistake), the intentional homicide against Y is still established; if A plans to kill X but causes the death of Y due to the method mistake, A constitutes the attempted homicide against X and the crime of negligent homicide against Y. However, when the object mistake and the method mistake are indistinguishable, the doctrines of concrete accord will cause confusion.

For example, A gave poisoned wine to X for killing X, but X did not drink. A few months later, X's wife who doesn't know the wine is poisoned, gave it to Y who died after drinking it. A did not expect the death of Y (Case 10). For another example, A installed the ammunition on the X's car to kill X. But when Y, X's wife, was accidentally driving the car and was killed (Case 11). A further example, in order to extort property, A made a threatening phone call to X's office, and the call was answered by X's secretary Y. Y was terrified, and delivered the property to A (Case 12). In these three Cases, the actor A target a specific person, be that person X or Y? The conclusions drawn from the doctrines of concrete accord are not the same.

[26] 参见日西田典之:《刑法总论》，弘文堂2006年版，第209页；See Nishida Noriyuki.(2006) *General Theory of Criminal Law*, Koubundou Publishers Inc., 209.日山中敬一:《刑法总论I》，成文堂1999年版，页317~318。Yamanaka Keiichi.(1999) *General Theory of Criminal Law (I)*, Seibundo Publishing Co., 317–318.

Some people think that there is an object mistake in the above three cases, while others think that it is a method mistake. In fact, in the above three cases, whether Y is "the specified one", in another word, whether A constitutes the accomplished intentional homicide against Y or the accomplished crime of extortion by blackmail against Y are met torrent of differences among those who hold the doctrines of concrete accord.[27] This is because the doctrines of concrete accord does not have the specific standard for the legal entity.

China's criminal law with meticulous specific provisions has led to more questions in which it is difficult to distinguish between object mistakes and method mistakes. For example, actor A found a forged credit card, and he used it as a valid one (Case 13). Objectively speaking, A conducted the act of "using a forged credit card" though A did not realize that. Subjectively speaking, A intended to implement the act of using other peoples credit cards, but he did not objectively use other people's real and effective credit cards. It is obviously inappropriate to consider that the conduct of A is not a crime. Because if A picks up a real and valid credit card and uses it, it will undoubtedly constitute a credit card fraud. Suppose A picks up a forged credit card but he thinks it is real and valid and uses it, after which there would be no consequences, it is clearly against the fairness and justice spirit of the criminal law. China's theory of criminal law does not treat similar problems as cognition mistakes, but only discusses whether credit cards, financial instruments and so on used falsely by actors must be true and effective.[28] And it seems impossible to solve the problems. In fact, the above problems should be solved as cognition mistakes of facts. As for whether it is an object mistake or a method mistake, it is difficult to define, but as long as the doctrines of legally prescribed is adopted, it can be considered as accomplished crime of credit card fraud. If the doctrine of concrete accord is adopted, it must first distinguish whether it is an object mistake or a method mistake, and the conclusion must be different from person to person, which is not conducive to the proper handling of the Case.

---

[27] 参见日浅田和茂:《刑法总论》，成文堂2007年补正版，第313~314页；Asada Kazushige. (2007) *General Theory of Criminal Law* (Supplementary Edition), Seibundo Publishing Co, 313~314.日井田良、丸山雅夫:《ケ-ススタディ刑法》，日本评论社2004年版，第122~123页；Ida Makoto & Maruyama Masao.(2004) *Case study criminal law,* NIPPON HYORON SHA Co., 122~12.日松宫孝明:《刑法总论讲义》，成文堂2004年版，第188~189页。Matsumiya Takaaki.(2004) *Handouts of General Theory of Criminal Law*, Seibundo Publishing Co., 188–189.

[28] 刘华:《票据犯罪研究》，中国检察出版社2001年版，第177页；Liu Hua. (2001) *Research on Crimes Related to Bills*, China Procuratorial Press, 177.王明、康瑛、杨克:"票据诈骗若干问题研究"，载赵秉志、张军主编:《中国刑法学年会文集(2003年度)——第二卷:刑法实务问题研究》(上册)，中国人民公安大学出版社2003年版，第259页；Wang Ming, Kang Ying. & Yang Ke. (2003) "Research on Several Issues of Instrument Fraud", as cited in Zhao Bingzhi & Zhang Jun. eds, *Annual Conference Proceedings of Chinese Criminal Law Society (2003) – Volume 2: Research on Practical Issues in Criminal Law (Part 1)*, Press of People's Public Security University of China, 259.李文燕主编:《金融诈骗犯罪研究》，中国人民公安大学出版社2002年版，第144页。Li Wenyan ed. (2002) *Research on Financial Fraud Crimes*, Press of People's Public Security University of China, 144.

(6) Even if the doctrines of concrete accord can propose reasonable standard for distinguishing between object mistakes and method mistakes, there are still some cases in judicial practice which concern method mistake for the abettor and an object mistake for the actor. In such case, the doctrine of concrete accord necessarily leads to different conclusions and is therefore not desirable.

In this article, the above views are trying to make some conclusions of the perspective of the doctrines of concrete accord. Although the views bear theoretical consistency, yet the conclusions are obviously unacceptable. There are obvious defects in Viewpoint b: since X is not present, it is obviously inappropriate to assume that B has begun to kill X; moreover, even if X is present, the act of killing Y conducted by B is difficult to be recognized as a attempted homicide against X at the same time. Viewpoint c finds the shortcomings of Viewpoint a and reaches a reasonable conclusion, but its theory lacks consistency. Because in Case 14, it is considered that there is an object mistake in A, that is, Y is mistaken for X by A, and there is no basis. Viewpoint d and Viewpoint e both attempt to avoid inappropriate conclusions and try to maintain the consistency of the theory. The end result is that when A is determined to be a method mistake, the conclusions drawn is not appropriate; when A is identified as an object mistake, it is lacking the consistency of theory. Moreover, Viewpoint e has deviated from the misconception.

(7) The doctrine of concrete accord is not helpful to solve the problems of misunderstanding of the selective constitutive elements in specific provisions in China's criminal law. For example, the criminal object of the crime of women and children trafficking can be either a woman or a child. If the actor thinks that the person of his trafficking is a woman who has reached the age of fourteen is actually a 13-year-old boy, according to the doctrines of concrete accord, the actor establishes the attempted trafficking of women (or may be an incapable crime) and the negligent trafficking of children, but the latter is not penalized. Such a conclusion is certainly not convincing for the public. Also, the object of the crime theft of firearms and ammunition can be either a firearm or an ammunition. When the actor thinks that he is stealing a gun, but the real thing he stole is ammunition, according to the doctrines of concrete accord, the actor accomplishes the attempted crime of gun-stealing (maybe a incapable crime) and the negligent theft of ammunition (unpunishable), and then this is hardly for the article to accept such views. Some people may think that the above two cases are object mistakes and should be considered as accomplished crimes. However, the theory of mistake is the opposite of the theory of intention. The claim of the doctrines of concrete accord means that the actor must recognize the specific facts of the criminal constitutive elements. However, in the last two cases, the actors do not realize that the specific behavior objects are 13-year-old children and ammunition. According to the point of view of the doctrines of concrete accord, it should not be considered as crimes.

(8) The doctrines of concrete accord actually leads to the fact that the theory of mistake is completely equivalent to the the theory of intention, and it is not in harmony to deal with cases regarding abstract fact mistakes. The basic idea of the doctrines of concrete accord is to determine what the specific result of the reality is firstly, and then determine whether the actor has the cognition of the specific result.

If the actor has the cognition, then an intentional crime constitutes; if not, no intentional crime constitutes. Thus, the theory of mistake is completely integrated with the theory of intention, and it is not conducive to dealing with abstract fact mistakes.

For example, actor A throws stones to destroy the camera of X, however, the stone hits the video camera of X due to a method mistake (Case 15). According to the true and thorough doctrines of concrete accord, the result happening in reality needs to be determined firstly, that is, to determine the result of the destruction of the camera, and then to examine and decide whether A recognizes that he wants to destroy the video camera of X, which of course is not his intent. Therefore, A constitutes the attempted crime of intentional destruction of property against the camera and constitutes the negligent destruction of property against the video camera, neither of which can be punished.[29] Obviously, if it is true with such thinking, in terms of the accomplishment of intentional crimes, it is only necessary to examine and judge whether the actor has any knowledge of the specific results of the reality, and the theory of mistake completely loses its meaning. More importantly, this kind of thinking plays no role in making types of the criminal constitutive elements. It is true that the crime should be determined from the objective to the subjective, namely, to find out the objective facts, and then to examine the subjective content. However, when objective facts are being identified, it is inevitable to use the constitutive elements as a guide to analyze objective facts in the sense of constitutive elements, rather than to examine the subjective content of the actor after determining the natural facts. In Case 15, the behavior of A causes the destruction of X's camera. The reason why it is taken as a criminal case is because the camera is the property protected under Article 275 of *Chinese Criminal Law*. Thus, it is enough that the actor has the intention to destroy property when throwing stones.

Take the abstract fact mistake (object mistake) as an example. The actor A takes a forgotten object of Y which is actually a possession of X (Case 16). According to the thinking of the doctrines of concrete accord, the specific result happening in reality needs to be determined firstly, that is, the possession of X being stolen, and then to decide whether A recognizes that the property is possessed by X. If the actor has the cognition, then crime of theft constitutes; if not, no crime constitutes. In Case 16, because A does not realize that it was the possession of X, so no theft is accomplished. However, scholars who hold doctrines of concrete accord do not believe that A in Case 17 constitute no crime, but they advocates the establishment of a crime within the limits of the overlapping. That is to say, the scholars who hold the specific conformity almost agree that A's subjective cognition and objective facts are coincident in the scope of the crime of encroachment (forgotten property), so they claim to convict the actor of the accomplished the crime of embezzlement. It is because there is a "common constitutive element" on the forgotten property of the crime of encroachment and theft.[30] Obviously, the way regarding the doctrines

[29] 参见日町野朔:"故意论と错误论", 载《刑法杂志》1984年第26卷第2号。See Machino Saku. (1984) "Theory of intent and error", as cited in *Journal of Criminal Law*, Vol. 26, No. 2.

[30] 日西田典之:《刑法总论》，弘文堂2006年版，第219页；See Nishida Noriyuki.(2006) *General Theory of Criminal Law*, Koubundou Publishers Inc., 219. 日山口厚:《刑法总论》，有

of concrete accord deals with specific fact mistakes is inconsistent to the handling of abstract fact mistakes because in the case of a specific method mistake, there is not only the "common constitutive elements" but the "same constitutive elements". However, in case of a specific method with the "same constitutive elements", the scholar for the doctrines of concrete accord does not recognize the accomplished intentional crime; on the occasion of the abstract fact mistakes with "common constitutive elements", they admit the establishment of the accomplished intentional crime.

(9) The specific fact mistakes are various. When it comes to whether the crime is established or not, any constitutive elements shall be equivalent, but the special handling of the method mistakes by the doctrines of concrete accord lacks theoretical basis.[31]

7.4 Theory of Behavior Planning

With regard to specific method mistakes, the doctrine of concrete accord takes dominant role in German theory of criminal law. However, some scholars have proposed intermediate doctrines because of the doubts and shortcomings from the doctrines of concrete accord, among which, theory of behavior planning proposed by Professor C.Roxin is representative.

Professor C.Roxin took the theory of objective will to analyze the difference between the intention and negligence. He believes that whether a certain psychological state is intentional or negligent should be decided objectively, which means, to decide whether the result is consistent with the actor's plan in order to see whether he is intentional or he is negligent. For example, if the actor intentionally causes an accident, knowing that a third party may be infringed in the accident, even if the actor doesn't want that infringement, it should be considered that the actor has intention in the infringement on the third party. On the other hand, when a person smokes on a hotel bed and causes a fire, even if he realizes that risk, it cannot be considered that he has the intention to set fire.[32] In terms of specific method mistakes, the theory of behavior planning proposed by Professor C.Roxin believes that if the method mistake leads to the failure of the behavior planning, the intentional crime will not be accomplished; on the contrary, the intentional crime accomplished. For example, in the aforementioned Case 3, A with intention to kill X shoots his daughter mistakenly, which should not be considered as intentional homicide. Because A has an mistake in aiming, his behavior plan (to kill X) failed. For another example, A throws snowballs to passers-by for prank, but the snowball does not hit

斐阁2007年版，第222页。Yamaguchi Atsushi. (2007) *General Theory of Criminal Law* Yuhikaku Press, 222.

31 参见日林幹人:《刑法总论》，东京大学出版会2008年版，第253~254页。Hayashi Mikito. (2008) *General Theory of Criminal Law*, University of Tokyo Press, 197.

32 Vgl.,C.Roxin,Strafrecht Allgemeiner Teil,Band I,3.Aufl.,C.H.Beck,1997,S.365f.

the X who is aimed at, but hits the face of Y walking behind (Case 17). A's act should be considered as accomplished intentional injury.[33]

However, this article believes that the theory of behavior planning is flawed and should not be adopted in China's theory of criminal law.

Firstly, there is no clear standard to evaluate whether a behavior plan is achieved or not. The result in Case 3 is the death of the actor's daughter, which is obviously not the behavior plan of the actor. Even if it were not his own daughter but a stranger Y when A takes the shot in this case, the theory of behavior planning also believes that the results does not conform to the behavior plan (to kill X). On the other hand, for Case 17, the theory of behavior planning believes that the behavior plan does not fail because the realization of the behavior plan does not depend on the identity of the victim.[34] Obviously, the relation between the deceased and the actor and the way in which it behaves affect the distinction between the accomplishment and attempt of crime. Suppose terrorist A's wife and children he loves deeply die in an explosion conducted by terrorist A due to wrong methods (Case 18). According to the theory of behavior planning, because the death of his wife and children is not in his plan, terrorist A only bears the negligent culpability. It cannot be denied that this is a manifestation of incorporating ethical concepts into the concept of criminal law, and it is also a replacement of intention in normative meaning by its natural meaning. In addition, when A wants to kill his enemy X but mistakenly shoots his own daughter Y (object mistake), it does not conform to A's behavior plan. In this Case, A's act should also be considered as the concurrence of attempted intentional homicide and negligent death. However, according to Professor C.Roxin's view of object mistakes, this is not the case. Obviously, it is hard for the theory of behavior planning to implement.

Secondly, when solving the problem of method mistake, Professor C.Roxin proposed to distinguish whether the behavior plan was realized according to the actor's answer to a landmark question: "will the actor do this when he foresees that there will be a method mistake?" Obviously, if the actor's plan is based on a specific object, then he will not do so when he foresees that there will be a method mistake. Therefore, it is necessary to adopt the doctrines of concrete accord. Conversely, if the actor's plan is not specific, even if he foresees that there will be a method mistake, this will be done, and then the doctrines of legally prescribed should be adopted.[35] That's to say, when the actor has a general intent, the doctrines of legally prescribed determines that the actor is culpable for the result of an intentional crime; while when the actor has additional intent, the doctrines of concrete accord determines the actor does not bear the culpability of the result of intentional crime. However, there is no substantial difference among the general intent, the determined intent and the indeterminate intent which includes alternative intent and eventual

[33] Vgl.,C.Roxin,Strafrecht Allgemeiner Teil,Band I,3.Aufl.,C.H.Beck,1997,S.439.

[34] Vgl.,C.Roxin,Strafrecht Allgemeiner Teil,Band I,3.Aufl.,C.H.Beck,1997,S.439f.

[35] Vgl.,C.Roxin,Strafrecht Allgemeiner Teil,Band I,3.Aufl.,C.H.Beck,1997,S.439f.

intent. The theory of behavior planning has made a substantial difference among the above, and thus it lacks rationality.

Thirdly, under the theory of behavior planning, to decide whether the actor is intentional will be on the basis of extremely specific object identity. For example, the actor A wanted to use a toxic substance to deprive X of fertility, but the toxic substance used blinded X instead of causing X to lose fertility (Case 19). According to Professor C.Roxin's point of view, because As behavior plan has failed, A has no intent to cause the blindness of X, negligence at best (when there was no foreseeable possibility, it was an accident); A just constitutes an attempt crime regarding X's loss of fertility.[36] Given the stipulations of Article 226 of the *German Criminal Law*, Professor C.Roxin's views may be justified. However, if this view is adopted in China, the conclusions will probably not be accepted. The severe injuries stipulated in Article 234 of the *Chinese Criminal Law* include not only the situation whoever negligently injures another person and causes severe injury (aggregated consequential offense included) but also the situation whoever intentionally inflicts injury upon another person and causes severe injury. For example, the actor A wanted to poisoned the witness X to make him deaf and blind, but the poison only caused X to be blind and X still can testify (Case 20). According to the theory of behavior planning, A constitutes an attempted crime of making X deaf and mute, and established a negligent crime towards his blindness. This has created difficulties in law application. First, it is difficult for people to accept to determine A constitute an attempted intentional injure because A's behavior has already caused severe injuries. Second, if A is convicted the crime of negligent injury, it is even less acceptable because A has the intent of causing severe injury. Third, if it is determined that A has the intent of causing light injury, but serious injury is caused by negligence (aggregated consequential offense), A is still culpable for the serious injury (binocular blindness), which obviously does not meet the facts of the case, because A planned to cause severe injury. Fourth, if it is determined that A has a severe injury intent (making X deaf and mute), and is culpable for the severe injury (binocular blindness), it is still uncertain how to apply the law. Fifth, it is reasonable to assume that A has the intention of causing severe injuries (making X deaf and mute) and bear the culpability for severe injuries (binocular blindness). But this is not the viewpoint of the theory of behavior planning, but the conclusion of the doctrines of legally prescribed.

Fourthly, Professor C.Roxin admits that theory of behavior planning is a doctrine between the doctrines of legally prescribed and the doctrines of concrete accord, and conclusion drawn from is closer to the latter.[37] Being so, the above-mentioned criticism of the doctrines of concrete accord in this article also applies to the same and similar aspects in the theory of behavior planning.

---

[36] Vgl.,C.Roxin,Strafrecht Allgemeiner Teil,Band I,3.Aufl.,C.H.Beck,1997,S.435f.

[37] Vgl.,C.Roxin,Strafrecht Allgemeiner Teil,Band I,3.Aufl.,C.H.Beck,1997,S.439.

7.5 The Doctrines of Legally Prescribed

This article is in favor of the doctrines of legally prescribed, in Case 1, the actor A has murder intent (to X), and his act of killing also causes the death of other person (Y) objectively. Although Y and X are with different legal interests, they are the "person" in the intentional homicide as provided in Article 232 of *Chinese Criminal Law*. Therefore, the subjective intention and the objective behavior of A are completely consistent in the criminal constitution of intentional homicide, and thus the intentional homicide shall be accomplished. Obviously, the doctrines of legally prescribed pays attention to the nature of legal benefits, but does not pay attention to the difference between legal subjects. In other words, the doctrines of legally prescribed not only pays attention to whether A has an intention of killing "person", but also whether A objectively kills "person", while which one is objectively killed is not important. The doctrines of legally prescribed is only supported by a minority group in Germany, but it occupied dominant position in Japan. In addition, the principle of transferred malice or transferred intention in the Anglo-American common law countries is also a doctrine of legally prescribed.[38]

It's no doubt that, adopting the doctrines of legally prescribed can avoid defects of the doctrines of concrete accord. For example, in Case 1, Case 3 and Case 5, the accomplishment of intentional homicide is in line with social general concept and is conducive to the principle of suiting punishment to crime. For another example, the accomplishment of theft in Case 6, the accomplished crime of intentional injury, accomplished intentional injury, accomplished intentional injury in Case 7, 19, 20 respectively and the accomplished intentional destruction of property crime in Case 8, 9 and Case 15 are appropriate. Another example is that for Case 10 to Case 13, the doctrines of legally prescribed can also not strictly distinguish between object mistakes and method mistakes, and treats the actors with intentional crimes. For instance, if the facts of joint crimes are misunderstood (Case 14) and the indiscriminate killings, abductions, etc. (Case 18) for terrorists, the legally prescribed can also lead to proper conclusions (in Case 14, A constitutes the abettor of intentional homicide, and in Case 18 A assumes the intentional culpability for the death of his wife and children). Besides that, the doctrines of legally prescribed has many other advantages.

Firstly, the doctrines of legally prescribed is conducive to equal protection of legal interests. If A wants to kill X, even if he causes the death of Y, or causes the death of X and Y at the same time, it should be considered as accomplished intentional homicide, so that X's life and Y's life are equally protected. And the degree of protection of the victim's life by the criminal law is not influenced by cognition mistakes of the actor. It is true that human life is exclusive legal benefits, so the "person" in the crime of intentional homicide is specific, not abstract. X and Y are both specific persons and protected by criminal law. No matter whether the act of A

[38] J. Dressler. Understanding Criminal Law(second edition)[M].Mathew Bender & Company,Inc.,1995:107.

causes the death of X or the death of Y, as long as he has an intention of homicide, he has the same wrongdoing (infringement of legal benefits). If the behavior of A causes the death of X and Y at the same time, his wrongdoing increases, and it is reasonable to give a heavier sentence. Obviously, taking the doctrines of legally prescribed is more conducive to the equal protection of human life and other legal interests.

Secondly, the adoption of the doctrines of legally prescribed conforms to the nature of culpability and is conducive to the purpose of penalties. The nature of culpability is that illegal acts meet criminal constitutive elements and actors can be blamed based on that culpability. To punish acts that lack culpability is impossible to prevent the same "criminal" behavior from occurring in the same situation in the future (no effect of preventing the crime). In other words, the criminal law makes citizens produce the motive for not committing crimes through passing the notices and sanctions on the infringement of legal interests. Only when citizens can generate the motive for not committing a crime, and only when the national can choose other legal acts rather than committing illegal acts, is the prevention of crime effective. The intention and negligence are two forms of culpability, while *vorwerfbarkeit* of intent is heavier than negligence. The necessity of preventing intentional crime is also greater than that of negligent crime. Because when the actor realizes the legal interests being infringed on, an objection motive can be generated. If the actor still implements the act, it indicates active infringement of the legal interests; and when the actor has an understanding of the possibility of violation of law but no realistic understanding, there is only the possibility of generating an objection to the motive at that time, and if the actor still carries out the act, it only shows his negative unprotected attitude towards the legal interests. For example, actor A intentionally shot at X, and actor B intentionally shot at X but hit Y. The degree of culpability between those two should not be different. Because A and B know not only the same facts, but also the possibility of opposing the formation of motives. Additionally, the expectation of conducting legal behavior is exactly the same. In this sense, whether the actor has intention to the result is determined by the content of his or her behavior and the content of the will, and it cannot be determined afterwards. Also, taking the doctrines of legally prescribed is conducive to prohibiting intentional crimes, namely, the prevention necessity of the actor who intends to kill X but shoots someone else decreases, even if it causes the death of Y due to a method mistake. If the doctrine of concrete accord is adopted, it is inconsistent with the necessity of prevention to charge B with intentional homicide; the adoption of doctrines of legally prescribed and charging B with intentional homicide is just in line with the necessity of prevention.

Thirdly, the adoption of the doctrines of legally prescribed makes possible to reasonably distinguish the perpetrator and the accomplice in narrow sense. For example, A prepares to kill the X who is passing by in the dark, B has known A's behavior plan, and B makes his enemy Y pass the place where A waited. A mistakes Y as X and kills Y (Case 21). According to the doctrines of concrete accord, whether the victim is X or Y has important differences in the constitutive elements, so it is inevitable to conclude that B is the perpetrator of killing Y rather than the accomplice.[39] However, according to the doctrines of legally prescribed adopted in this article, since A dominates the fact of murder, he is the perpetrator who killed Y. Although B makes A to kill Y rather than X, but Y's life is equivalent to that of X. They both are the object of intentional homicide. The behavior of B has no dominant role in killing, thus B should be convicted as a secondary offender (accomplice). It is true that since A has an intention of homicide, B is not an abettor of homicide. A kills Y due to the object mistake. And at that time, A just killed the "that person" (Y), and B lured Y to the place where A was waiting, which helps A kill Y. Moreover, what is certain is that in China's judicial practice, it is almost impossible to conclude that B is the principal offender but it can only be considered that B is an accomplice.

It is undeniable that the doctrines of legally prescribed also faces difficulties and criticisms. Therefore, the criticism and questions from the doctrines of concrete accord shall be answered during adopting the doctrines of legally prescribed.

The first question is about how to deal with excessive results and concurrent results.

For example, A wants to kill X, but A causes the death of X and Y because of method mistakes (Case 22, this is so-called excessive result), how to handle the case? According to the doctrines of concrete accord, it is easy to understand and accept conclusion that A establishes an intentional homicide to X and the crime of negligent homicide to Y. But for the doctrines of legally prescribed, it becomes a problem.

There are two solutions to the problem: First, it is considered that there is no cognition mistake in Case 22, thus the theory of mistake is not applicable. A wants to kill X, and objectively kills X. Of course, the intentional homicide is accomplished. Meanwhile, Y dies due to As negligence. However, since A only conducted one act, he would be identified as the imaginative joinder of offense and be convicted of intentional homicide, and there is no need to apply the theory of mistake.[40] But this article does not agree with it. Because A causes the death of X and Y at the same time with the intention of homicide of X, it is completely inconsistent with subjective cognition and objective elements. Of course, it is a cognition mistake in Cases where the theory of mistake should be applied to solve problems. Second, the application of the theory of mistake can solve the problem of excessive results and concurrent results. The theory of multi-intention in the doctrines of legally prescribed thinks that A's act constitutes the accomplished intentional homicide against X and against Y respectively; the theory of one-intention considers that A's act con-

[39] Some think that B is a (one-sided) coprincipal(参见日山口厚:"实行行为と责任非难"，载日三井诚等编:《铃木茂嗣先生古稀祝贺论文集》上卷，成文堂2007年版，第211页See Yamaguchi Atsushi.(2007) "Conduct of execution and blameworthiness", as cited in Mitsui Makoto et al., ed., *A Collection of Congratulatory Essays by Mr.* Suzuki Shigetsugu*in His Seventies* (Vol. 1), Seibundo Publishing Co., 211.); some believe that B is an indirect principal offender (C. Roxin, Strafrecht Allgemeiner Teil, Band II, CHBeck, 2003, S. 45).

[40] 参见日福田平:《刑法解释学の诸问题》，有斐阁2007年版，第43页。See Fukuda Taira. (2007) *Various Issues in Criminal Law Interpretation*, Yuhikaku Press, 43.

stitutes the accomplished intentional homicide against X and the negligent homicide to Y when he contains the one intention of killing X but causing the death of X and Y. Because he has achieved the purpose of killing X and the death of Y is an excessive result which cannot be explained by criminal intention but negligence. However, the theory of one-intention bears defects both in practice and theory. From a practical viewpoint, there exist irrational solutions to problems. For example, A intends to kill X, but a bullet causes both X and Y to die (Case 23, this is the so-called "concurrent results" or "concurrent facts"). According to the theory of one-intention, A first establishes the accomplished intentional homicide against Y. Since A only has one intention, it is obviously inappropriate to constitute a crime of negligent injury against X. Theoretically, the theoretical basis of the theory of one-intention is that in Case 23, the intention of homicide of A against X can be transferred to Y within the scope of the doctrines of legally prescribed. Therefore, whether A establishes intentional homicide against Y is not a problem of intention itself, but a problem whether the intention of homicide against X can be transferred to intention of homicide against Y through the theory of mistake.[41] In other words, in the viewpoint of the theory of one-intention, the theory of mistake is an exception to the theory of intention, not the opposite. This is hard to agree with in this article. Therefore, this article takes the theory of multi-intention. As far as Case 22 is concerned, A has constituted intentional homicide both against X and Y. A is convicted as an imaginative joinder of offense due to one act conducted and is charged with one crime. As to Case 23, A has established an attempted intentional homicide against X, and an accomplished intentional homicide against Y. And A would be convicted of the crime of accomplished intentional homicide because he only conducted one act.

Professor Nishida Noriyuki made the following criticism regarding the theory of multi-intention that "the theory of multi-intention believes that when A wants to kill B, the actor contains intention towards all the death results or death risks that have (considerable) causality with the killing behavior since such a treatment was criticized as a infringement of the principle of culpability. To respond this criticism, the theory of multi-intention claimed that as the cognitive concurrence, it does not violate the principle of culpability to deal with several intentions as a crime. However, in judicial practice, the actor in Case 3 is sentenced to the death penalty in principle. If A kills 3 people separately, as a combined crime, of course, the death penalty will be imposed. Furthermore, when a actor kills three persons at the same time by throwing a bomb, he would be given a death penalty since there is only one act that belongs to the cognitive concurrence. However, if A causes the death of C and D rather than B who he intends to kill, A cannot be sentenced to death penalty as a cognitive concurrence. Suppose A bears the culpability for killing three persons but only has one intention, and then it is a infringement of the principle of culpability. Therefore, although it is a matter of expediency to views regarding to the theory of

---

[41] 参见日福田平:《刑法解释学の主要问题》，有斐阁1989年版，第90页。See Fukuda Taira. (1989) *Main Issues in Criminal Law Interpretation*, Yuhikaku Press, 90.

multi-intention as the cognitive concurrence, it is also a infringement of the principle of culpability."[42] However, in China, taking the theory of multi-intention does not mean that A in Case 22 has established several intentional homicides rather than being convicted of the intentional homicide as an imaginative joinder, hence it does not violate the principle of culpability. Moreover, during the sentencing, the sentence of intentional homicide does not solely depend on the number of victims. The severity of culpability has a major impact on sentencing. In fact, even if the several crimes between the killing of several people under the imaginative joinder of offense in Case 22 and the intentional killing several people are same, there is significant difference in culpability. Therefore, the sentence should be different accordingly. For example, in Chinese judicial practice, if anyone who kills two or more persons intentionally is sentenced to death executed immediately, then the imaginative joinder of offense caused more than two deaths based on the method mistake should not be sentenced to immediate execution.

The second question is about the theoretical consistency of the doctrines of legally prescribed.

Professor Nishida Noriyuki also points out that "the doctrines of legally prescribed holds a critical attitude: if the abstraction of objects is not recognized, then, when A throws a stone at X's car, but hits and destroys Y's car (Case 24), it is not appropriate to convict A of attempted intentional destruction of property and negligent destruction of property, because those two crimes are punishable. However, if A throws a stone at X's car, but hits Y next to X and causes the death of Y (Case 25). Those who in favor of doctrines of legally prescribed also reckon the destruction of property is imaginative concurrence of unpunishable attempted crime and the homicide is negligent. If Y's car is next to X's car, it is admitted that A is intentional; if it is Y rather than Y's car, A shall be considered as not intentional. This situation is theoretically inconsistent."[43]

The above criticism is not sufficient to explain the inconsistency of the doctrines of legally prescribed in this article. First, to decide the conformity of elements of crime will be a problem. In Case 24, in the view of the doctrines of legally prescribed from objective wrongdoing to subjective culpability, the behavior of destroying the car (property) of Y and the intention of destroying X's car lead us to attribute the objective behavior and results to A, so A should be convicted of intentional destruction of property crime. However, in Case 25, although the objective elements are in line with the objective constitutive elements of intentional homicide, since A does not have the intention of killing, the intention of destroying property cannot be the subjective attribution of the crime of intentional homicide. Thus A's behavior constitutes negligent homicide. Second, lets look Case 24 and Case 25 from the other way: in both cases, A only has the intention to destroy the car of X. According to the doctrines of legally prescribed, as long as the car is destroyed, intentional

---

[42] 日西田典之:《刑法总论》，弘文堂2006年版，第207页。See Nishida Noriyuki. (2006) *General Theory of Criminal Law*, Koubundou Publishers Inc., 207.

[43] 日西田典之:《刑法总论》，弘文堂2006年版，第208页。See Nishida Noriyuki.(2006) *General Theory of Criminal Law*, Koubundou Publishers Inc., 208.

destruction of property crime shall be established without asking whose car is ruined. However, if the car is not destroyed, the criminal law does not punish the attempted destroy the property. Then, of course, intentional destruction of property crime is not established. A in Case 24 actually destroys Y's car, so A's act constitutes intentional destruction of property crime; in Case 25 A does not destroy Y's car, and of course A's act does not constitute intentional destruction of property crime. In other words, when A implements the behavior of destroying X's car, if Y's car next to X's is destroyed, A indeed constitutes the accomplished crime of intentional destruction of property; if Y is next to X's car, even if it causes the death of Y, nor does it establish a crime of intentional destruction of property, it can be seen that there is no inconsistency in the doctrines of legally prescribed. Supporters of the doctrines of concrete accord seem to believe that only when A's act in Case 25 being convicted of the accomplished crime of intentional destruction of property or the accomplished crime of intentional homicide that the theoretical consistency of the doctrines of legally prescribed can be concluded. However, the conclusion that A's act in Case 25 constitutes the accomplished crime of intentional destruction of property or the accomplished crime of intentional homicide is the viewpoint of the theory of abstract conformity.[44] The doctrines of legally prescribed requires consistency of the subjective cognition and the objective elements within the same constitutive elements, which is different from the theory of abstract conformity. In Case 24, subjective cognition and objective elements are consistent within the same constitutive elements. In Case 25, subjective cognition and objective facts are not consistent within the same constitutive elements, and of course different conclusions should be drawn. Third, Case 24 is a specific fact mistake, while Case 25 is an abstract fact mistake. The doctrines of legally prescribed does not just require the consistency of the subjective cognition and the objective elements. More specifically, this consistency needs to be within the same constitutive elements. Therefore, since Case 24 satisfies the above condition, the actor in Case 24 is convicted of the accomplished crime of intentional destruction of property; there exists no consistency within the same constitutive elements in Case 25, so the actor is neither convicted of the accomplished crime of intentional destruction of property, nor the accomplished crime of intentional homicide. In this regard, the doctrines of legally prescribed is theoretically consistent.

The reversed conditions can make further demonstration. For example, A intends to kill X and throws the stone to X, but the car of Y next to X is broken due to a method mistake (Case 26). According to the doctrines of concrete accord and the doctrines of legally prescribed, A's act constitutes the attempted intentional homicide against X, and constitutes the negligent destruction of property crime against Y's car, so A cannot be punished. The advocators of the doctrines of concrete accord also criticize the doctrines of legally prescribed lacks consistency. However, as far as Case 26 is concerned, conclusions drawn from the doctrines of legally prescribed

[44] Even if it is an abstract conformity, it will be considered that A in Case 25 constitutes the accomplishment of intentional destruction of property crime rather than intentional homicide.

are consistent with its main idea. Because Y's car is destroyed and could not be evaluated as a human death, A's act does not constitute the intentional homicide (not in conformity with the constitutive elements of intentional homicide). On the other hand, the intention of homicide that A holds against X cannot be evaluated as the intention of destroying property, thus A's act cannot be identified as intentional destruction of property (it is inconsistent with the constitutive elements of intentional destruction of property crime).

Then, in the doctrines of legally prescribed, since A's act constitutes the accomplished crime of intentional destruction of property crime when A wants to destroy X's car but destroys Y's car, why does A constitute negligent homicide rather than the crime of intentional destruction of property when A wants to destroy X's car but kills Y? This is because, the same with the doctrines of concrete accord, the doctrines of legally prescribed also requires subjective cognition and objective elements to be consistent within the same constitutive elements. Therefore, the legal interests recognized by the actor A must be the same as that of objective infringement. The difference between the doctrines of legally prescribed and the doctrines of concrete accord is that the latter requires the legal interests subject recognized by the actor A to be the same as the legal interests subject that is objectively infringed, while the former does not require the same. As a result, when A destroys Y's car rather than the car of X which he intends to (such as Case 24), because the doctrines of legally prescribed and the doctrines of concrete accord have the same legal interests, but the different legal interests objects, the doctrines of legally prescribed claims to constitute the accomplished crime of intentional destruction of property, and the doctrines of concrete accord claims to constitute the attempted crime of intentional destruction of property and crime of negligent destruction of property (unpunishable). However, when A wants to destroy X's car but crushes Y to death (as Case 25) or the reverse happens (as Case 26), because the legal interests recognized by A subjectively is different from that of objective behavior and there exists no consistency in the same constitutive elements, the conclusion consistent with the doctrines of concrete accord is drawn.

In addition, Professor Hirano Ryuichi points out in his response to the criticism of the doctrines of concrete accord: "For specific doctrines of legally prescribed, some people criticize on the grounds that unreasonable conclusions will arise in the destruction of property. For example, A wants to damage X's car and throws stones, but smashes Y's car next to X's. According to the specific doctrines of legally prescribed, A's act constitutes the attempted crime of intentional destruction of X's car and negligent destruction of property against the car of Y, but A shall not be given penalty since both of them are not punishable according to the current law. This is not appropriate. Whether it is improper or not is a matter of punishment. However, since the current law neither penalizes the attempted crime of intentional destruction of property nor punishes negligent destruction of property, it can be said that the conclusion drawn from the specific doctrines of legally prescribed is in line with the purpose of criminal law. At least it cannot be said that there is irrationality to some degree that must exclude the specific doctrines of legally prescribed. Moreover, cases undeserving punishment in similar situations still exist. For example, A shoots one object taking it as a person mistakenly, except for the most exceptional occasions, there is no attempt to kill, so the actor cannot be punished. Compared to the above-mentioned car-crushing, this case is obviously more unreasonable. However, in spite of this, those who adopt the (abstract) doctrines of legally prescribed have to say that this is a legislative incompleteness. However, if the conclusion is unreasonable and the actor should be identified to have the destruction intention against the car of Y in the above car-crushing case, then in this case, it is inconsistent to claim that the actor contains the intention to destroy the property.' '[45] However, this is the object mistake when A intends to throw stones to X to death but destroys the car of Y due to the object mistake (Case 27). According to the doctrines of concrete accord and the doctrines of legally prescribed, if there is no person at the side of Y's car, A's behavior is the incapable crime and negligent destruction of property (both unpunishable), and A is not guilty. This is not a theoretical contradiction in the doctrines of legally prescribed. The above conclusions are reached because there is no perpetrating acts of killing in Case 27, and A's subjective cognition and objective elements are not consistent within the same constitutive elements.

Obviously, there are similarities in the doctrines of legally prescribed and the doctrines of concrete accord, that is, both of them require the consistency of subjective cognition and objective elements within the same constitutive elements. In this case, the two may reach the same conclusion in some cases. As a result, it is not possible to conclude that there is a contradiction in the doctrines of legally prescribed because the conclusions reached in some Cases are the same as the conclusions drawn from the doctrines of legally prescribed.

The third question is the basic position of the doctrines of legally prescribed.

Supporters for doctrines of concrete accord have put forward another criticism of the doctrines of legally prescribed: under the general social ethical norms, the ordinary people are not targeted to be killed but the 'specific one' and 'that one', which means, the norms of intentional homicide are not to kill specific person. "The norms of intentional homicide will be applied when the actor is about to conduct acts of perpetrating. The norms at this time are not expressed in the general form of 'not killing ordinary people', but are working in the form of 'not killing that one' recognized by the actor. As to the understanding of the norms, the abstract doctrines of legally prescribed confuses social ethics norms and criminal law norms."[46]

But this article does not reckon such criticism tenable. First, the so-called "under the general social ethical norms, the ordinary people are not targeted to be killed" does not mean that social ethics norms prohibit the killing of abstract people, but also refers to social ethics norms prohibiting the killing of any specific person. The criminal laws provision on intentional homicide also prohibits the killing of any

[45] 日平野龙一:《刑事法研究最终卷》，有斐阁2005年版，第5~6页。Hirano Ryuuichi. (2005) *Final Volume of Criminal Law Research,* Yuhikaku Press, 5–6.

[46] 日佐伯仁志:"故意·错误论"，载日山口厚、井田良、佐伯仁志:《理论刑法学の最前线》，岩波书店2001年版，第107~108页Saeki Hitoshi.(2001) "Intent and error theory", as cited in Yamaguchi Atsushi, Ida Makoto & Saeki Hitoshi. *The forefront of theoretical criminal law*, Iwanami Shoten Publisher, 107–108.

specific person, not just the person whom the actor is targeted. At this point, social ethics norms are no different from criminal law norms. It is true that the purpose of criminal law is not to protect ethics, but to protect legal interests. However, ethical norms and criminal law norms have the same structure in principle as long as they are derived from the needs of society. That is to say, the ethical norms and the criminal law norms have no value, and the reason for their existence is that the objects they protect have certain value. Therefore, criminal law and ethics are not mutually exclusive in terms of protecting certain interests."[47] This works for the prohibition on murder. Second, "the constitutive elements are abstract and typed. It is enough to determine the conformity within the scope of the statutory acts of perpetrating. It is at the risk of denying the necessity of constitutive elements to require the specific conformity besides."[48] Therefore, it is the consistency of the doctrines of legally prescribed and the constitutive elements stipulated in the criminal law, rather than method mistakes according to social ethics.

7.6 Conclusion

The theory of mistake is the opposite of the theory of intention. Therefore, the dispute between the doctrines of concrete accord and the doctrines of legally prescribed is over the content of intention and the degree of "conformity" between subjective cognition and objective elements. The objective constitutive elements are characterized of types. Therefore, the objective elements of cases must be summarized with the objective constitutive elements, which also have the intention regulatory function. Thus, the establishment of intention only requires recognizing the facts that meet the objective constitutive elements, and does not require the facts that are of no significance in criminal law to be recognized. In other words, as long as the facts recognized by the actor and the facts happening in reality are in conformity with the same constitutive elements, it is necessary to assume intentional culpability for the facts that occur in reality. This is the conclusion drawn from the doctrines of legally prescribed.

To some degree, the doctrines of concrete accord and doctrines of legally prescribed are manifested as the following conflicts: Should the theory of culpability be consequence valueless as much as possible, or should elements of culpability such as intent be of behavior valuelessness? Standing in the position of consequence valuelessness, the wrongdoing is objective. However, this does not mean that the intentional responsibility can only be judged afterwards. Since the actor has realized or may recognize the fact that the legal interests have been infringed during the perpetrating act, and the actor has the possibility of forming an anti-motivation.

---

[47] 日西田典之:《刑法总论》，弘文堂2006年版，第30页。Nishida Noriyuki (2006) *General Theory of Criminal Law,* Koubundou Publishers Inc., 30.

[48] 日大谷实:《刑法讲义总论》，成文堂2007年新版，第184页。Ohya Minoru.(2007) *Handouts of General Theory of Criminal Law (New Edition)*, Seibundo Publishing Co.,184.

Therefore, elements of culpability can be inspected from the perspective of the actor. In other words, in terms of culpabilitybility blame, the difference between the consequence recognized subjectively by the actor and the consequence in the reality does not affect the culpability of the actor, so this difference is not important.[49] This is also the conclusion of the doctrines of legally prescribed.

References

Asada Kazushige. (2007) *General Theory of Criminal Law (Supplementary Edition)*, Seibundo Publishing Co, 313-314.

Dressler. (1995) *Understanding Criminal Law* (second edition). Mathew Bender & Company,Inc., 107.

Gao Mingxuan ed. (1989) *Chinese Criminal Law*, China Renmin University Press, 142.

He Bingsong ed. (2000) *Treatise on Criminal Law (Vol. 1)*, China Legal System Publishing House, 336. The author has also expressed similar views. (See Zhang Mingkai. (1991) *Fundamentals of the Theory of Crime*, Wuhan University Press, 306.)

Hirano Ryuuichi. (2005) *Final Volume of Criminal Law Research*, Yuhikaku Press, 3,5,6.

Horiuchi Shouzou. (2000) *General Theory of Criminal Law*, Yuhikaku Press, 288.

Hayashi Mikito. (2008) *General Theory of Criminal Law*, University of Tokyo Press, 197.

Ida Makoto & Maruyama Masao. (2004a) *Case Study Criminal Law*, NIPPON HYORON SHA Co., 112.

Ida Makoto & Maruyama Masao. (2004b) *Case study criminal law,* NIPPON HYORON SHA Co., 122-12.

Li Wenyan ed. (2002) *Research on Financial Fraud Crimes*, Press of People's Public Security University of China, 144.

Liu Hua. (2001) *Research on Crimes Related to Bills*, China Procuratorial Press, 177.

Liu Mingxiang. (2004) *Treatise on the Doctrine of Mistake in Criminal Law,* China Procuratorial Publishing House, 181.

Maeda Masahide. (2006) *Handouts of General Rules of Criminal Law*, University of Tokyo Press, 246-247. Puppe,Zur Revision der Lehre vom "konkreten" Vorsatz und der Beachtlichkeit der aberratio ictus,GA 1981,S.1;

Matsumiya Takaaki. (2004) *Handouts of General Theory of Criminal Law*, Seibundo Publishing Co., 188-189.

Nishihara Haruo, trans. Dai Bo & Jiang Su. (2006), *Theory of Criminal Conduct*, Peking University Press, 5–6.

Nishida Noriyuki (2006a) *General Theory of Criminal Law,* Koubundou Publishers Inc, 30.

Ohya Minoru. (2007) *Handouts of General Theory of Criminal Law (New Edition)*, Seibundo Publishing Co., 184

Ohya Minoru. (2010) *General Handouts on Criminal Law(New Edition)*, Seibundo Publishing Co, 184–187

Otsuka Hitoshi. (1997) *Overview of Criminal Law*, Yuhikaku Press, 205.

Saeki Hitoshi. (2001a) "Intent and error theory", as cited in Yamaguchi Atsushi, Ida Makoto & Saeki Hitoshi. *The forefront of theoretical criminal law*, Iwanami Shoten Publisher, 113-116.

Saeki Hitoshi. (2001b) "Intent and error theory", as cited in Yamaguchi Atsushi, Ida Makoto & Saeki Hitoshi. *The forefront of theoretical criminal law*, Iwanami Shoten Publisher, 107-108.

[49] 参见日前田雅英:《刑法总论讲义》，东京大学出版会2006年版，第247~248页。See Maeda Masahide. (2006) *Handouts of General Rules of Criminal Law (4th Edition)*, University of Tokyo Press, 247–248.

See Dandou Shigemitsu. (1990) General Outline of Criminal Law, Kodansha Publishing Co, 298.
See Fukuda Taira. (1989) *Main issues in criminal law interpretation*, Yuhikaku Press, 90.
See Gao Mingxuan & Ma Kechang eds. (2007) *Criminal Law*, Peking University Press & Higher Education Press, 136.
See Machino Saku. (1995a) *Handouts of General Theory of Criminal Law (I)*, Shinzansha Publisher Co., 220, 229-230.
See Hirano Ryuuichi. (1972) General Theory of Criminal Law I, Yuhikaku Press, 175, 337.
See Machino Saku. (1984) "Theory of intent and error", as cited in *Journal of Criminal Law*, Vol. 26, No. 2.
See Machino Saku. (1995b) Handouts of General Theory of Criminal Law (I), Shinzansha Publisher Co., 242-244
See Maeda Masahide. (2006a) Handouts of General Rules of Criminal Law, University of Tokyo Press, 243.
See Maeda Masahide. (2006b) *Handouts of General Rules of Criminal Law(4th Edition)*, University of Tokyo Press, 54, 200
See Maeda Masahide. (2006c) *Handouts of General Rules of Criminal Law(4th Edition)*, University of Tokyo Press, 247-248.
See Nishida Noriyuki. (2006b) *General Theory of Criminal Law*, Koubundou Publishers Inc., 207-209, 219.
See Sakuma Osamu. (1993) "Theory of result attribution in error theory", as cited in Hirata Taira. *A Collection of Congratulatory Essays by Dr. Otsuka Hitoshi in His Seventies: Comprehensive Studies on Criminal Law (Vol. 1)*, Yuhikaku Press, 146.
See Sone Takehiko. (2008) *General Theory of Criminal Law*, Seibundo Publishing Co., 287.
See Yamaguchi Atsushi. (2007a) "Conduct of execution and blameworthiness", as cited in Mitsui Makoto et al, ed., *A Collection of Congratulatory Essays by Mr.* Suzuki Shigetsugu*in His Seventies* (Vol. 1), Seibundo Publishing Co., 211.); some believe that B is an indirect principal offender (C. Roxin, Strafrecht Allgemeiner Teil, Band II, CHBeck, 2003, S. 45).
See Yamaguchi Atsushi. (2007b) *General Part of Criminal Law*. Yuhikaku Press, 206.
See Yamanaka Keiichi. (1999) General Theory of Criminal Law, Seibundo Publishing Co, 316.
See Zhang Mingkai. (2004) "Consequences and Sentencing: Consequential Liability, Double Evaluation, and Prohibition of Indirect Punishment", as cited in *Journal of Tsinghua University* (Philosophy and Social Sciences), No. 6.
See Zhang Mingkai. (2007) *Essentials of Foreign Criminal Law*, Tsinghua University Press, 215-217.
Suzuki Shigetsugu. (2001) *General part of criminal law (theory of crime)*, Seibundo Publishing Co., 103-104.
Vgl.,C. Roxin, Strafrecht Allgemeiner Teil, Band I,3.Aufl.,C.H. Beck, 1997,S.365f.
Vgl.,H. Jescheck & T. Weigend, Lehrbuch des Strafrechts allgemeiner Teil,5.Aufl., Duncker &Humblot, 1996, S.690ff.
Wang Ming, Kang Ying. & Yang Ke. (2003) "Research on Several Issues of Instrument Fraud", as cited in Zhao Bingzhi & Zhang Jun. eds, *Annual Conference Proceedings of Chinese Criminal Law Society (2003)—Volume 2: Research on Practical Issues in Criminal Law (Part 1)*, Press of People's Public Security University of China, 259.
Yamaguchi Atsushi, (2007) *General Rules of Criminal Law*, Yuhikaku Press, 205-206, 222. C.Roxin, Strafrecht Allgemeiner Teil, Band I,3.Aufl.,C.H. Beck, 1997,S.448f.
Yamanaka Keiichi. (1999) *General Theory of Criminal Law (I)*, Seibundo Publishing Co., 317-318.

Chapter 8
Jurisprudence of Reasonableness

The reasonableness, also the Probability of Anticipation, AKA expectability (*Zumutbarkeit*) has various meanings, and the sorting out of the theory is conducive to applying the reasonable contents to the criminal justice practice in China.

8.1 Basic Issues of Reasonableness

The principle of "alternate possibilities" (or to say, alternative possibilities) plays a governing role in the philosophical discussion of free will. "This principle holds that a person can be morally responsible for an act he has done only if he could be able to perform others."[1] In other words, "In order to be morally responsible for own actions, a person must have (at some relevant point in reaching that action) a certain type of alternate possibilities, which should be a basic and broad assumption. This basic idea has encapsulated in the 'principle of alternate possibilities', various versions of which require that moral responsibility should be accompanied by the emergence of alternate possibilities."[2] Accordingly, the moral responsibility of the

*The original title is "Theoretical Compendium of Reasonableness", published in *Chinese Journal of Law*, 2009, Vol.1.

[1] 美哈里·法兰克福:"可供取舍的可能性与道德责任"，载徐向东编:《自由意志与道德责任》，江苏人民出版社2006年版，第359页。Harry Frankfurt, (2006) *Alternate Possibilities and Moral Responsibility*, as cited in Xv Xiangdong ed. *Free Will and Moral Responsibility*, Nanjing: Jiangsu People's Publishing House, 359.

[2] 美约翰·马丁·费尔希:"法兰克福式例子与半相容论"，载徐向东编:《自由意志与道德责任》，江苏人民出版社2006年版，第392页。John Martin Fischer, (2006) *Frankfurt-Style Examples and Semi-Compatibilism*, as cited in Xv Xiangdong ed. *Free Will and Moral Responsibility*, Nanjing: Jiangsu People's Publishing House, 392.

M. Zhang, *The Fundamental Issues upon Criminal Law Theories*, Masterpieces of Contemporary Jurisprudents in China,
https://doi.org/10.1007/978-981-95-1276-8_8

Act A and its consequences[3] presupposes that the actor would have been able to implement Act B, Act C or others at the time of implementing Act A. This alternate possibilities is "possibility of other acts" in theory of criminal law.

Whether to recognize alternate possibilities and to what extent this possibility recognized are long debated issues among philosophers and jurists. The determinism does not recognize free will of man and alternate possibilities: Some scholars reject "a person can be morally responsible for an act he has done only if he could be able to perform other actions" but affirm that "a person can be morally responsible for failing to perform a given action only if he could be able to perform that action".[4] This article will not launch the discussion now, but rather to analyze alternate possibilities from the indeterminism.

The reason for taking the indeterminism is that the concept of culpability in criminal law was originally formed on the premise of free will. As is known, "the one who defined the concept of culpability in a systemic sense and made a significant contribution to the development of the culpability in criminal law was the Enlightenment thinker, Samuel Pufendorf (1632–1694). He holds that a man is a rational being who acts by free will, that is, a being who can decide to perform good or bad acts by free will. Thus, he argued that only when such a free act can be subjectively attributed to the actor is there a culpability. Understanding the act as a product of free will and making free will as the center of *Zurechnung* by Samuel Pufendorf greatly influenced subsequent doctrines."[5] In criminal law, Samuel Pufendorf "proceeded from the premise of free will to conclude that culpability will be established only when there is the capacity for attribution and identification, thus creating a new doctrine of culpability in criminal law. The establishment of morality for the purpose of the state limits education and deterrence as the purpose of criminal law, and prevention replaces revenge. Samuel Pufendorf's idea of moral coercion by penal deterrence preceded Samuel Feuerbach's doctrine of psychological coercion".[6] It can be argued that the present concept of culpability in criminal law would be difficult to exist without the premise that the actor has free will.

---

[3] Moral responsibility is a concept that is contrary to causal responsibility. Moral responsibility does not necessarily reflect the right and wrong in morality, but it is about the reactive attitude. It can be argued that in criminal law, causal responsibility is objective imputation, and moral responsibility is about subjective imputation. However, this does not mean that the responsibility in criminal law is an ethical responsibility or a moral responsibility.

[4] 美约翰·马丁·费尔希:"法兰克福式例子与半相容论"，载徐向东编:《自由意志与道德责任》，江苏人民出版社2006年版，第394页以下。John Martin Fischer, (2006) *Frankfurt-Style Examples and Semi-Compatibilism*, as cited in Xv Xiangdong ed. *Free Will and Moral Responsibility*, Nanjing: Jiangsu People's Publishing House, 394.

[5] 日堀内捷三:"责任论の课题"，载日芝原邦尔等编:《刑法理论の现代的展开—总论I》，日本评论社1988年版，第172~173页。Horiuchi Shouzou.(1988) "Issues in the theory of responsibility", as cited in Shibahara Kuniji et al., ed., *The modern development of criminal law theory — General part I,* NIPPON HYORON SHA Co., 172–173.

[6] 日堀内捷三:"责任论の课题"，载日芝原邦尔等编:《刑法理论の现代的展开—总论I》，日本评论社1988年版，第172~173页。Horiuchi Shouzou.(1988) "Issues in the theory of responsibility", as cited in Shibahara Kuniji et al., ed., *The modern development of criminal law theory — General part I,* NIPPON HYORON SHA Co., 172–173.

Taking the indeterminism is also based on several reasons: First, although free will is difficult to prove, it is worth aspiring to and protecting. Prohibition of some crimes in criminal law (e.g., rape, coercion in foreign criminal law, etc.) protect not only a person's freedom of action, but also his or her freedom of conscious activity. If a person has no free will and every action is completely determined, then there is no need for the law to protect his or her freedom of conscious activity. Second, the denial of free will ends either in advocating a penal code without culpability and punishment, as Ferri, one of the representatives of The New School, did,[7] or in arguing that legal culpability is not predicated on free will. However, the former does not work, and the latter cannot account for culpability in criminal law. Third, recognizing the free will can solve many problems in criminal law. For example, it is because a person have free will that criminal law norms can influence him or her to make appropriate volitional decisions, so that the prevention of crime is possible and becomes the purpose of punishment. Fourth, an important function of criminal law is to guarantee the freedom of the accused, and it is more beneficial to the accused to recognize free will. The result of denying free will is either to deny culpability, then the penalty cannot be limited by culpability, thus resulting in an excessive penalty, or to determine the severity of the penalty solely by the necessity of general prevention, thus making the defendant an instrument to prevent others from committing crimes. Fifth, even if free will is considered to be an assumption, this assumption is as positive as the social contract theory. Indeed, even criminal law scholars who do not (fully) recognize free will or do not use the concept of free will often presuppose that people have free will.[8] In short, it is better to recognize that people have free will than to deny it.

To recognize people have free will means to recognize possibility of other acts. The possibility of other acts, in general, means the possibility of lawful acts (in special cases, it may means the possibility of less harmful acts). Conversely, the possibility of other acts implies the avoidability of criminal acts. As described later, this possibility of other acts is indistinguishable from reasonableness of other acts (lawful acts) in criminal law.

Germany is the birthplace of the doctrine of reasonableness, however, it is "difficult to believe" for *Chinese Criminal Law* scholars that this doctrine has been

[7] 参见意恩里科·菲利:《实证派犯罪学》，郭建安译，中国人民公安大学出版社2004年版，第185页以下。Enrico Ferri, trans. Guo Jianan, (2004) *Positive school of criminology: three lectures*, Press of People's Public Security University of China, 1–185.

[8] For example, the German scholar C. Roxin advocates the normative theory of possibility of answering. When the actor is acting, his spirit and psychology are in a state of being able to respond to the call of the norms, and has the possibility of making a norm-oriented behavioral decision psychologically. There is a psychological controlling possibility of the healthy adult in a specific case, the responsibility of actor can be affirmed. This kind of responsibility does not involve hypotheses that cannot be proved, but involves the intelligence of empirical science. Responsibility is the mixing of empirical materials with normative materials; the ability of controlling and the normative possibility of answering are empirically determined; the possibility of legitimate acts is the requirement of the norms. In criminal law, the freedom of the possibility of other acts is a normative assumption that is neither verifiable nor rebuttable (C.Roxin, *Strafrecht Allgemeiner Teil, Band I*, C.H.Beck 4.Aufl.,2006,S.851ff).

neglected and has become insignificant precisely in Germany.[9] Other scholars argue that the fate of reasonableness has declined with the objectification of *Verschulden*.[10] So, what is the reason for the neglect of reasonableness in Germany? In what sense is reasonableness that has been neglected? The answers to these questions will help our theory of criminal law and judicial practice to treat the doctrine of reasonableness correctly. This is the question of the overall fate of the doctrine of reasonableness.

In addition, there are significant controversies in the domestic and international theories of reasonableness regarding the following specific issues:

(1) The Status of Reasonableness

That is, is the reasonableness a positive or negative element of culpability? If reasonableness is considered to be a positive element, is it a constitutive element of intention or negligence, or is it an element of culpability alongside criminal capacity, intention and negligence? If reasonableness is considered to be a negative element, it means that the lack of reasonableness is a cause of preventive culpability, then for what reasons should criminal law set up criminal capacity, intention and negligence as elements of culpability? In China, the specific problems encountered in theory of criminal law and judicial practice is whether reasonableness be discussed within or beyond the theory of intention and negligence, and whether the public prosecutor need to prove that the accused has reasonableness Related to this is that the relationship between the criminal capacity and reasonableness is also controversial in our theory of criminal law. One view is the reason why a person under the age of 14 is not criminally culpable is he or she lacks the ability to recognize and control and cannot be expected to perform a lawful act.[11] Others point out that the lack of reasonableness is the basis for a mental patient not to be criminally culpable.[12] Another view states that "an incapacitated person will not bear criminal culpability is not connected with and the doctrine of reasonableness."[13]

---

[9] 参见陈兴良:"期待可能性问题研究"，载《法律科学》2006年第2期。See Chen Xingliang. (2006) "Research on Issues of Doctrinal Possibility of Expectation", as cited in *Legal Science*, No. 2.

[10] 参见劳东燕:"罪责的客观化与期待可能性理论的命运"，载《现代法学》2008年第5期。See Lao Dongyan. (2008) "Objectification of Criminal Culpability and the Fate of Doctrinal Possibility of Expectation", as cited in *Modern Law Science*, No. 5.

[11] 苗玉红:"期待可能性理论"，载《黑龙江政法干部管理学院学报》2001年第3期。Miao Yuhong. (2001) "Doctrinal Possibility of Expectation", as cited in *Journal of Heilongjiang College of Political Science and Law*, No. 3.

[12] 欧锦雄:"期待可能性理论的继承与批判"，载《法律科学》2000年第5期。Ou Jinxiong. (2000) "Inheritance and Critique of Doctrinal Possibility of Expectation", as cited in *Legal Science*, No. 5.

[13] 李立众:"期待可能性研究诸失误之匡正"，载《现代法学》2004年第3期。Li Lizhong. (2004) "Rectification of Fallacies in Research on Doctrinal Possibility of Expectation", as cited in *Modern Law Science*, No. 3, 102–107.

(2) The Legal Nature of Reasonableness

Is the lack of reasonableness a general supra-law cause of preventive culpability, or is it a cause of preventive culpability only when it is provided for in the criminal law? In China, the problem faced by theory of criminal law and judicial practice is that, although the *Specific Provisions of Criminal Law* does not expressly state close kinship as a cause of preventive culpability for the crime of harboring and shielding, can the lack of reasonableness of harboring and shielding between close relatives be denied as a crime?

(3) The Standard of Reasonableness

Although each has its own rationale, the well-known "actor standard theory", "average man standard theory" and "legal norms standard theory" have been criticized, which is also the problem faced by our theory of criminal law and judicial practice. For example, can Xu Ting be acquitted because of the lack of reasonableness? If a married woman who fled to another country because of a disaster or was trafficked to another country and married another person, can she not be guilty of bigamy due to lack of reasonableness?

(4) The Cognition Mistake of Reasonableness

The cognition mistakes of reasonableness include positive mistakes and negative mistakes. The former situation refers to the actor mistakenly believed the matter that there was no such thing that lack of reasonableness existed. The latter situation refers to the actor mistakenly thought the matter that there was such thing that lack of reasonableness did not exist. For example, what should be done if the actor mistakenly destroys the evidence of another person's crime as own, or vice versa? This is also a problem that needs to be solved in our theory of criminal law and judicial practice.

In this article, it seems that an important reason for the above controversy is that the concept of reasonableness used by scholars is not specific. In other words, the controversy may imply that reasonableness has multiple meanings.

8.2 Multiple Meanings of Reasonableness

After a careful study, it is possible to find at least four not completely same senses in which the concept of reasonableness is used in theory of criminal law.

(1) Reasonableness: As Psychological Coercion Possibility, Basis of Culpability

The theory of reasonableness is the logical conclusion of the theory of normative culpability. The theory of normative culpability is characterized by understanding culpability in relation to legal norms. After all, legal norms are expressed in terms of orders and prohibitions to individuals. As far as the actor is concerned, such orders and prohibitions are only appropriate if they can be complied with, that is, in case of the acts other than criminal acts can be performed. Therefore, *Vorwerfbarkeit* under culpabilities is based on the expectation that the actor had the possibility of performing lawful acts. In other words, there is no *Vorwerfbarkeit* without reasonableness. Reasonableness in this sense is not just an element of culpability alongside criminal capacity, intention and negligence, but is the basis of culpability.

The inclusion of accountability as an essential definition of crime is a fundamental requirement of substantial justice. The concept of justice requires a substantial fit relationship between the essential definition of crime and legal effects. Penalty is a punishment for the actor's criminal act, and such punishment is rightly predicated on *Vorwerfbarkeit*. It is also a fundamental requirement of the purpose of penalty to make accountability a condition for the establishment of a crime. That's because, if the penalty is imposed for an act committed in a state of mind in which the penalty cannot have an effect, the effect hereof will not be achieved, and the punishment for an act without accountability cannot prevent the same "criminal act" from occurring in the future in the same condition (that is, without prevention effect). In short, the penalty can only be imposed if there is *Vorwerfbarkeit*.

"What provides the basis for *Vorwerfbarkei* can be called 'possibility of other acts' (it means the ability to evade the unlawful act that meets the constitutive elements and to perform other acts). Although there is a dichotomy between determinism (it means the decision of a person's intention and acts hereof belong to a result of some reasons, which should be determined in this sense) and indeterminism (it means a person is free to determine own intention and choose acts) with regard to human behavior, it is not possible to impose on a person who has done unlawful acts that meets constitutive elements in the absence of 'possibility of other acts'. Only when there is 'possibility of other acts' and the person's unlawful act meets constitutive elements, is it possible to bring the objects that 'the act should not be committed' and the punishment. The 'possibility of other acts' mentioned above means that the unlawful act that meets the constitutive elements will not be committed by further unleashing the normative consciousness (or under the existence of a stronger normative consciousness). Nonetheless, the punishment will be imposed if an unlawful act that meets the constitutive elements still is committed."[14] In summary, according to the theory of normative culpability, 'possibility of other acts' is the basis of culpability.

Hence, what is the relationship between 'possibility of other acts' and 'reasonableness of other acts'? If the general or objective standard is adopted for the possibility of other acts, and the personal or subjective standard is adopted for reasonableness of other acts, there may be a difference between them. In fact, the two are not only closely related, but also almost impossible to distinguish. Therefore, many scholars use 'possibility of other acts' and 'reasonableness of other acts' in an equivalent sense. For example, Professor Noriyuki Nishida points out that "The third element of the establishment of a crime is accountability or culpability:

[14] 日山口厚:《刑法总论》，有斐阁2007年版，第181~182页。See Yamaguchi Atsushi. (2007) *General Part of Criminal Law*. Yuhikaku Press, 366.

Accountability means to blame the actor for the unlawful acts that meets the constitutive elements. This element derives from the purpose of the penalty. In other words, the criminal law prohibits certain acts for protecting legal interests and imposes penal sanctions to the unlawful acts by foreseeing, thus refraining nationals from committing crimes. Therefore, the premise is that it is possible to perform a motive not to commit a crime, that is, the actor has the possibility to perform another lawful act at the time of committing the crime. This is the 'possibility of other acts', which also can be called "reasonableness' in the sense of being able to expect to commit a lawful act, instead of committing an offense. In a nutshell, 'Accountability' refers to the blame under the law for the unlawful acts even if the performance of lawful acts ('possibility of other acts' and 'reasonableness') can exist."[15] For another example, when discussing 'doctrine of culpability' and 'reasonableness', Professor Noriyuki Nishida respectively states that "the principle that 'there is no penalty without culpability (*Vorwerfbarkei*)' is called 'doctrine of culpability'. Generally speaking, *Vorwerfbarke* can be considered only when 'the actor committed the crime despite the possibility that he or she could have committed other acts". At the same time, "To blame the actor, it is necessary to require the possibility that, in the specific circumstances at the time of acting, the actor can be expected not to commit the illegal act, but to be able to perform other lawful acts. This possibility is called 'reasonableness'".[16] Accordingly, it can be said both that the basis of blame is 'possibility of other acts' and 'reasonableness of other acts'. Other scholars point out that "the doctrine of culpability is about the evaluation of the cause of the actor for the wrongful act… If the intention of the actor to perform the unlawful act is due to some special circumstances, the actor cannot be responsible for own unlawful act… From the concept of culpability in general terms, the so-called culpability refers to the possibility (ability) of the actor to control what he does. Or from another point of view, it also refers to reasonableness for the actor to act lawfully. And because the actor can be expected to act lawfully, but he or she fails, therefore, the law can impose punish the liable and blamable actor."[17] So reasonableness is the basis of culpability.

On the one hand, if the actor does not have possibility of other acts, there is necessarily no reasonableness of other acts. On the other hand, if the actor has possibility of other acts, the legal order will expect him to perform it. In other words, 'possibility of other acts' is both the premise of reasonableness of other acts and the basis of it. Thus, the judgment of the possibility of other acts and reasonableness of other acts are the same. Because of this, the theorist of normative culpability will use the concept of 'reasonableness' in the basis of culpability.

---

[15] 日西田典之:《刑法总论》，弘文堂2006年版，第191页。See Nishida Noriyuki. (2006) *General Theory of Criminal Law,* Koubundou Publishers Inc., 191.

[16] 日前田雅英:《刑法总论讲义》，东京大学出版会2007年版，第53、370页。See Maeda Masahide. (2007) *Handouts of General Rules of Criminal Law(4th Edition)*, University of Tokyo Press, 53–370.

[17] 黄荣坚:《基础刑法学(下)》，元照出版有限公司2006年版，第635~636页。Huang Rongjian. (2006) *Fundamental Criminal Law (Vol. 2)*, Angle Publishing Co., Ltd., 635–636.

(2) Reasonableness: As Element of Culpability, in a Narrow Sense

Just as the infringement of legal interest as the basis of wrongdoing must be concretized as a constitutive element, the above-mentioned 'reasonableness' as the basis of culpability also must be concretized as an element of culpability. Criminal capacity, intent, negligence and the possibility of cognition of wrongdoing are essentially the concretization of 'possibility of other acts' and 'reasonableness' as the basis of culpability.[18] In other words, when a person with criminal capacity has cognition of the objective constitutive element (intentional) or the possibility of foreseeability them (negligence), and has the possibility of cognition of wrongdoing, it is possible to expect that the motivation to refrain from committing an illegal act that meets the constitutive elements will arise, thus avoiding committing this act, then, if the actor commits it, he or she shall be deemed culpable.

However, the above elements of culpability are set up on the premise that the actor can be expected to perform other lawful acts. In other words, the situation that 'the existence of criminal capacity, intent, negligence and the possibility of cognition of wrongdoing are worth to be blamed' is set for the usual condition, or is predicated on the normalcy of the circumstances accompanying the act. In social life, it is not excluded that in rare cases, due to the abnormal circumstances accompanying the act, a person with criminal capacity cannot be expected to commit other lawful acts, even if he or she is aware of or may be aware of the fact that the constitutive elements are met, and even if he or she has the possibility of knowledge of unlawfulness. Therefore, reasonableness in a special situation must be considered as an element of culpability, and reasonableness in this sense can be called 'reasonableness in a narrow sense'.[19] reasonableness discussed in our theory of criminal law is, by and large, this 'reasonableness in a narrow sense'.

(3) Reasonableness: As Compulsory Coercion Possibility, in Criminal Omission

An act that violates prohibitions is an 'action' and an act that violates orders is an 'omission'.[20] In other words, 'action' refers to the performance of a prohibited act and 'omission' refers to the failure to perform an expected act. Three conditions are necessary for the realization of orders: First, commandee has the intention and action. The order shall fail to perform without the intention and action. Second, the possibility of an act as an association between the commandant and the commandee, that is, commandant can influence the commandee. Third, commandee has the

[18] For example, when the actor does not foresee and can not foresee that his act would result in the infringement of legal interest, he would not have the motivation to give up this act, thus cannot take other acts, so there is not the possibility of other acts (without reasonableness) Therefore, the establishment of the crime is necessary for the actor to be intent or negligence.

[19] 参见日平野龙一:《刑法总论II》，有斐阁1975年版，第154页。See Hirano Ryuuichi. (1975) General Theory of Criminal Law II, Yuhikaku Press, 154.

[20] Other standards for differentiating act and omission is mostly to the specification for distinguish the violation of forbidding norm and the violation of mandatory norm.

possibility to control the intention and is able to perform the act required by the orders.[21]

In the case of criminal omission, it is not certain that the constitutive elements are met as long as there is a causality between the omission and the infringement of the legal interest. For example, in the case of a drowning child who dies without being rescued, if the omission of who might rescue the drowning child is considered to meet the constitutive elements of intentional homicide, it would be an obvious expansion of the punishment. Thus, theory of criminal law considers the duty to act based on the status of a guarantor as an element of the criminal omission, which means, the person who has a special duty to prevent the result occurs is the "guarantor" and the said special duty is "the duty to act". Therefore, the theory of criminal law must firstly determine which persons are under special duty to prevent the occurrence of the result, that is to say, where the special duty originates (the basis for the occurrence of the obligation). It is obvious that the performance of the obligation presupposes that the guarantor has the possibility of act.

"The possibility of act" means that the guarantor has the possibility to perform the duty (to take positive measures). Legal norms and the legal orders only require those who are able to perform their duty to do so and will not force those who cannot.[22] The question is whether the possibility of act is a precondition for the duty to act or an element alongside the duty to act? One view is that if the actor does not have the possibility of act, he or she will lose the precondition for the duty to act (i.e., there is no duty to act without the possibility of act).[23] Another view is that the possibility of act and the duty to act are different problems.[24] Obviously, if the possibility of act and the duty to act are both considered to be issues at the stage of wrongdoing, the above controversies are not particularly relevant. However, once it is considered that the duty to act is a matter of the stage of wrongdoing and the possibility of act is a matter of the stage of culpability, the above controversies are of significance. These questions, in turn, depend on the answer to the question about what are the standard for judging the possibility of act and what is the relationship between the possibility of act and reasonableness?

The first argument is "the establishment of an omission requires the possibility of act in addition to the duty to act… For example, on the occasion of mother A's failure to rescue her drowning child on the bank of a river, an omission shall not be

[21] 参见日青井秀夫:《法理学讲义》，有斐阁2007年版，第44页。See Aoi Hideo. (2007) *Lectures on jurisprudence,* Yuhikaku Press, 44.

[22] Some specific provisions of China's *Criminal Law* clearly provide that the possibility of acting can be the establishment condition of criminal omission (see Articles 429 and 445 of the *Criminal Law*).

[23] 日西田典之:"不作为犯论"，载日芝原邦尔等编:《刑法理论の现代的展开——总论I》，日本评论社1988年版，第80页。Nishida Noriyuki. (1988) "Theory of omission offenses", as cited in Shibahara Kuniji et al., ed., *The modern development of criminal law theory — General part I,* NIPPON HYORON SHA Co., 80.

[24] 日山口厚:《刑法总论》，有斐阁2007年版，第93页。See Yamaguchi Atsushi. (2007) *General Part of Criminal Law.* Yuhikaku Press, 93.

established when A does not know how to swim and it is in fact impossible to rescue someone. That is, for an omission to be established, there must be a possibility of preventing the results by acting. This is different from the mental possibility in the so-called reasonableness, which is a factual possibility."[25] Now therefore, when there is a lack of the possibility of act and the conformity of the constitutive elements of an omission, the possibility of act is not related to reasonableness. However, the conformity of the constitutive element is a type of judgment whose standard cannot be different from one person to another. Therefore, the said view is doubtful because it sets the specific possibility of act of the guarantor as the constitutive element. On the other hand, since the constitutive element is the type of wrongdoing, the said view inevitably leads to the judgment of wrongdoing being influenced by personal ability of the guarantor, thus moving toward a subjective theory of wrongdoing. In addition, it remains doubtful whether a clear distinction can be made between the possibility of fact and psychology when judging whether the guarantor has the possibility of act. For example, if a mother A can swim, but is afraid to go into the water to help her drowning son because of high waves and fears that she will also die, it is difficult to conclude whether the said occasion is a factual or a psychological impossibility.

The second view holds that the possibility of act as a matter of conformity of the constitutive elements, and also recognizes that "the omission is also bound by the instruments at the specific situation and by the criminal capacity of the specific actor" (e.g., "the result can be attributed to the omission only if the person who failed to act was in fact capable of performing the act that theoretically could have prevented the result. Therefore, there is no 'omission' of those who do not use the boats to rescue those who fall overboard if there are no boats available, and those who cannot swim and fails to rescue people from drowning are also not have 'omission'"). It is also argued that "in the criminal omission, 'unanticipated' is a general principle limiting the obligation to act, but also contains some special justifiable cause and exemptions applicable to *Begehungsdelikte*",[26] without indicating the relationship between the possibility of act and reasonableness. This is largely true of German theory of criminal law.[27] However, as discussed later, the fact that German theory of criminal law generally recognizes the role of reasonableness in the criminal omission at least suggests that the possibility of act and reasonableness are closely related.

The third view points out that the possibility of act lays the foundation for the duty to act as a constitutive element and should be judged against the general

---

[25] 日平野龙一:《刑法总论I》，有斐阁1972年版，第154页。Hirano Ryuuichi. (1972) *General Rules of Criminal Law I*, Yuhikaku Press, 154.

[26] 德冈特·施特拉腾韦特、洛塔尔·库伦:《刑法总论I——犯罪论》，杨萌译，法律出版社2006年版，第377~378、386页Giinter Stratenwerth & Lothar Kuhlen, trans. Yang Meng, (2006) *Strafrecht Allgemeiner Teil I: Die Straftat*, Law Press, 377~378、386.。显然，这种观点将作为可能性视为作为义务的前提。

[27] Vgl.,H.Jescheck/T.Weigend,Lehrbuch des Strafrechts Allgemeiner Teil, Duncker & Humblot,5. Aufl.,1996, S.634; Schnke-Schrder, Strafgesetzbuch, Kommentar, C.H.Beck,26.Aufl.,2001,S.596.

perception of the average person or society. The possibility of act of a specific actor is a matter of culpability. For example, if the waves are too high and dangerous and it is basically impossible to carry out rescue, the parents have no duty to act when their child drowns and there is no omission.. In contrast, if it is in fact impossible to rescue the child because the parents cannot swim, there is a duty to act and it is only the question about culpability.[28] In view of the above, when there is a possibility of act according to the general concept of society, and the actor does not have the possibility of act, it is a question of the theory of culpability. What, then, is the problem in the theory of culpability? Obviously, this occasion lack of factual possibility of act is neither a question of intention or negligence, nor a question of the criminal capacity and cognition of wrongdoing, Thus, it can only be a question of reasonableness.

The fourth viewpoint is that, since the standard for judging as possibility is only personal ability, it is questionable to include it as a constitutive element and appropriate to include it as an element of culpability. However, since it is easier to discuss 'possibility of act' in the context of causation, in addition, 'possibility of act' is the element of culpability that limits unlawful acts, it is possible to exceptionally include it as a constitutive element. "However, even with the said interpretation, reasonableness of performing the duty to act must be left at the level of culpability."[29] It thus appears that the said view recognizes the possibility of act is about reasonableness.

In any case, the judgment of the possibility of act shall take into account both the normality of the attached circumstances and the personal capacity of the guarantor. Even if it is considered that possibility of act is a judgment of conformity to the constitutive elements and therefore can only be judged by the general concept of society, it cannot be denied that it is also necessary to make a judgment based on the personal capacity of the guarantor. The latter is actually a matter of reasonableness as well. Since the establishment of an omission is predicated on the possibility of act, moreover, the absence of reasonableness of performing the duty to act means that there is no possibility of act, thus preventing the conformity of the constitutive elements and the wrongdoing. In this case, although German theory of criminal law denies the establishment of an omission on the grounds of lack of possibility of act or the duty to act, it has actually placed reasonableness in the consideration of the conformity of the constitutive elements of the omission. Of course, it does not mean that the German theory of criminal law confuses the possibility of act with reasonableness, but because the judgment of these two possibilities are based on the same condition in the case of an omission. For example, in the case of a child drowning, on the one hand, in the absence of a boat (accompanying situation), the legal order cannot expect the actor to use the boat, on the other hand, in the case where the actor does not know how to swim (personal ability), the legal order cannot expect the

[28] 日大谷实:《刑法讲义总论》，成文堂2007年新版，第152页。Ohya Minoru.(2007) *Handouts of General Theory of Criminal Law* (New Edition), Seibundo Publishing Co., 152.

[29] 日山口厚:《问题探究刑法总论》，有斐阁1998年版，第44页。Yamaguchi Atsushi. (1998) *Problematic Criminal Law Overview*, Yuhikaku Press, 44.

actor to swim. Obviously, when the accompanying situation of the act and the personal ability lead to the fact that the guarantor cannot be expected to perform the duty to act and the result is inevitable, it can be considered that the guarantor lacks the possibility of act and reasonableness.

(4) Reasonableness: As Establishment Condition of the Negligent Crime, Establishment Requirement of Negligent Crime

In the past, the theory of psychological culpability was adopted in judging the entity of culpability, it holds that the entity of culpability is the psychological relationship of the actor, and based on the different psychological relationship, the culpability can be divided into intention and negligence, moreover, the actor is held responsible when he or she has intention and negligence in addition to the criminal capacity. This doctrine dominated in the late 19th and early 20th centuries. Even if the normative theory of culpability is adopted, it does not mean that the mental element of negligence will be completely abandoned. For example, the possibility of foreseeability in negligence with carelessness does not lose its significance because of the normative theory of culpability.

According to the old theory of negligence centered on the possibility of foreseeability the result, the negligent crime shall not be established when the actor cannot foresee that the infringement of legal interest will occur by own actions. The question is about what is the relationship between the lack of the possibility of foreseeability without results and reasonableness. Obviously, when the actor cannot foresee the result of own acts, he or she cannot be expected to foresee it, nor can be expected to choose other lawful acts. Therefore, even if the actor does not choose other lawful acts, *Vorwerfbarkeit* will not stand. In this occasion, it can be said either that the actor is not guilty of negligence because lacking the possibility of foreseeability, or that because lacking reasonableness of other acts and foreseeing the results.

According to the new theory of negligence, even if there is a possibility of foreseeability the result, the negligence shall not be established if the duty to prevent the result is fulfilled. In this way, the center of the duty of care in negligent crime is shifted from the duty to foresee the result to the duty to prevent the result. Moreover, as an objective behavioral baseline, the duty to prevent the result is set as an objective duty of care, thus treating it an element of wrongdoing. The new theory of negligence treats negligence not only as a matter of culpability but also as matters of conformity of the constitutive element and wrongdoing, so it focuses not only on negligence in a mental state but also on the side of acts. Since the new theory of negligence regard the breach of duty of care as a unlawful issue of the negligent crime, "the next disagreement centers on what requirements should be set for such a breach of duty that together constitute unlawful reasons, whether a breach of a general (objective) duty of care is sufficient or whether the actor is required to exercise the necessary care that he or she could have exercised according to personal criminal capacity".[30]

The first view (the dominant view in Germany) adopts a "two-tier theory". When the objective duty of care is violated, there is conformity of the constitutive elements of the negligent crime and wrongdoing.. This objective duty of care varies according to the division of labor, the field of life and the specific situation, instead of the onerous individual. Whether the actor has the ability to perform the objective duty of care is then a matter of accountability.[31]

The second view (the minority view in Germany) is that the constitutive elements of negligent crime include not only a breach of an objective duty of care, but also a breach of a duty determined according to the personal capacity of the actor.[32]

The third view (the compromise theory in Germany) holds that the criminal capacity in below-average does not preclude the conformity of the constitutive elements of negligent crime and wrongdoing, but only with culpability. This is because the realization of the constitutive elements cannot depend on individualized standard, otherwise the distinction between wrongdoing and culpability is confused.[33]

According to the first and third views above, incapacity (lack of ability to perform the duty of care) impedes the accountability of the negligence. According to the second view, incapacity impedes the conformity of the constitutive elements and the wrongdoing. However, what is the relationship between incapacity and lack of reasonableness is a question worth discussing. Although some scholars clearly distinguish between incapacity and lack of reasonableness, the judicial decisions in Germany sometimes do not distinguish them.[34] In this article, it is quite difficult or even impossible to distinguish between incapacity and lack of reasonableness in the case of negligent crime. This is because no one who lacks the criminal capacity to perform the duty of care can be expected by the legal order to perform the duty of care. Because of this, some German scholars have pointed out that reasonableness has a double function in a negligent crime: first, it determines the objective duty of care to be performed or not in the field of wrongdoing, second, it determines the subjective duty to foresee in the field of culpability.[35]

Our criminal law distinguishes negligence into negligence with carelessness and negligence with undue assumption. In the case of negligence with carelessness, when the actor lacks the possibility of foreseeability (cannot foresee), the criminal

---

[30] 德冈特·施特拉腾韦特、洛塔尔·库伦:《刑法总论I——犯罪论》，杨萌译，法律出版社2006年版，第402页。Giinter Stratenwerth & Lothar Kuhlen, trans. Yang Meng, (2006) *Strafrecht Allgemeiner Teil I: Die Straftat*, Law Press, 402.

[31] Vgl.,H.Jescheck/T.Weigend,*Lehrbuch des Strafrechts Allgemeiner Teil*, Duncker & Humblot 5.Aufl.,1996, S.563ff.

[32] 参见德冈特·施特拉腾韦特、洛塔尔·库伦:《刑法总论I——犯罪论》，杨萌译，法律出版社2006年版，第404页。Giinter Stratenwerth & Lothar Kuhlen, trans. Yang Meng, (2006) *Strafrecht Allgemeiner Teil I: Die Straftat*, Law Press, 404.

[33] Vgl.,C.Roxin, *Strafrecht Allgemeiner Teil, Band I*, C.H.Beck 4.Aufl.,2006,S.1083f.

[34] Vgl.,C.Roxin, *Strafrecht Allgemeiner Teil, Band I*, C.H.Beck 4.Aufl.,2006,S.1108f.

[35] Vgl.,Wessels/Beulke, *Strafrecht Allgemeiner Teil*, C.F.Müller 30. Aufl.,2000,S.139.

law cannot expect him or her to foresee (should not foresee), then, the negligent crime cannot be established In the case of negligence with undue assumption, when the actor has foreseen the infringement of legal interest and cannot prevent the result, he or she cannot be expected to prevent the result (there is a crossover and overlap with the omission). Only when the actor foresees the infringement of legal interest and can abandon the act or take effective measures to prevent the result, the criminal law can expect him or she to abandon the act or take effective measures, thus affirming the establishment of negligent crime.

Thus, regardless of whether negligence is a matter of culpability or a matter of constitutive elements and wrongdoing, when the actor cannot foresee and prevent the infringement of legal interest, in other words, when the actor cannot perform the duty to foresee the result to the duty to prevent the result, the negligent crime cannot be established. If the actor cannot foresee or prevent the result, the theory of criminal law can be considered that the actor lacks reasonableness of other acts. The said reasonableness is actually the condition for the establishment of the negligent crime.

8.3 The Overall Fate of Reasonableness

Once the multiple meanings of reasonableness are clarified, the following questions can be answered: What is the reason for the neglect of reasonableness in Germany? In what sense is reasonableness that has been neglected? How should reasonableness be treated in China?

Firstly, the theory of reasonableness, as the basis of culpability, is the natural conclusion of the normative theory of culpability. One of the important reasons why this theory has neglected in Germany is that some scholars have adopted the theory of functional culpability (or theory of preventive culpability) instead of (fully) adopting the normative theory of culpability.

For example, Professor G. Jakobs argues that only 'purpose' can give substance to the concept of culpability, and that the content of the concept of culpability is determined solely by the purpose of general prevention, and that the presence or absence of the need for general prevention determines the culpability of the actor. In other words, the culpability is premised not on *Verschulden*, but on the real or possible need for prevention. The question of whether the actor could have committed other lawful acts without committing the unlawful acts that meet the constitutive elements is replaced by the question of whether it is necessary or superfluous to make the actor culpable.[36] This theory of functional culpability leaves no room for the concepts of *Verschulden*, the possibility of other acts and reasonableness.

It is not difficult to find that if the theory of functional culpability, which is the general theory, is adopted, the theory of reasonableness still has an important position. In fact, in Germany, scholars who are negative to the theory of functional

[36] G.Jakobs, *Strafrecht Allgemeiner Teil*, 2.Aufl.,Walter de Gruyter 1993,S.480ff.

culpability affirm the important status and role of reasonableness.[37] On the other hand, the theory of functional culpability is not universally accepted in Japan, so reasonableness is not as cold in Japan as it is in Germany. So, the key here is how to evaluate the theory of functional culpability.

The greatest flaw in the theory of functional culpability is the confusion between criminal law and criminal policy. First, if the state does not regard the notion of "the end justifies the means" as the supreme guiding principle of state act, then the imposition of the most severe penalties must be justified on special grounds of rationality. In other words, it is not enough to point out the instrumental usefulness of punishment; it must be presented as a measure that the nation can accept as reasonable and just.[38] However, "the theory of functional culpability replaces the concept of culpability with prevention, thus rendering the limiting function of the doctrine of culpability in its relation to general prevention. It is inappropriate to confirm culpability for the critical mentally ill patients or to determine heavy culpability for the recidivist who has difficulty complying with the law on a general prevention view. The same is true when the concept of culpability is affected by the purpose of prevention. The traditional doctrine of culpability is a norm for the protection of constitutionally ordered actors, and therefore must not be infringed upon by skillful theories. Second, in the case of the theory of functional culpability, there is also no clear standard that can stabilize the order trust. This ultimately leaves the concept of culpability in the hands of the legislator or the judge and confuses the establishment of the crime unclear".[39] Because the conditions under which the criminal law can play a general preventive role is a question that has not been answered so far. Once again, the doctrine of culpability prevents the state from punishing an illegal act without culpability in pursuit of the general preventive effect. In other words, the doctrine of culpability is not only treated as a rationalization principle, but also necessarily becomes a principle that exerts a limiting influence on penalties. Thus, culpability, as complete independent of the concept of prevention, has the detailed connotation of a state governed by the rule of law.[40] "Moreover, theoretically, from the perspec-

---

[37] 参见德冈特·施特拉腾韦特、洛塔尔·库伦:《刑法总论I——犯罪论》，杨萌译，法律出版社2006年版，第236页以下。Giinter Stratenwerth & Lothar Kuhlen, trans. Yang Meng, (2006) *Strafrecht Allgemeiner Teil I: Die Straftat,* Law Press, 1–236.

[38] 参见德许迺曼:"罪责原则在预防刑法中的功能"，载许玉秀、陈志辉编:《不移不惑献身法与正义——许迺曼教授刑事法论文选辑》，公益信托春风煦日学术基金2006年版，第608页。Bernd Schünemann, (2006) Functions of Culpability in Preventing Crimes, as cited in Chen Zhihui, ed., Unbestechlich und unbeirrbar im dienst von recht unechtigkeit: abhandlungen zur gesamten strafrechtswissenschaft von BERND SCHUNEMANN, Taiwan: taedp.org.tw, 608.

[39] 韩李在祥:《韩国刑法总论》，韩相敦译，中国人民大学出版社2005年版，第262~263页。Lee, Jae-sang. (2005*) General Theory of Korean Criminal Law*, trans. Han Xiangdun, Renmin University of China Press, 262–263.

[40] 参见德许迺曼:"罪责原则在预防刑法中的功能"，载许玉秀、陈志辉编:《不移不惑献身法与正义——许迺曼教授刑事法论文选辑》，公益信托春风煦日学术基金2006年版，第609、611页。Bernd Schünemann, (2006) *Functions of Culpability in Preventing Crimes,* as cited in Chen Zhihui, ed., *Unbestechlich und unbeirrbar im dienst von recht unechtigkeit: abhandlungen zur gesamten strafrechtswissenschaft von BERND SCHUNEMANN*, Taiwan: taedp.org.tw, 606.

tive of the (positive) theory of general prevention, the standard of criminal attribution cannot be different from those of the traditional concept of guilty. In this regard, the functional meaning of the guilty is merely conceptually confusing."[41] Finally, the functional concept of guilty inevitably leads to the objectification of culpability, then inevitably leads to the instrumentalization of the actor in the imposition of punishment, as well as the security measures, thus creating a situation where there is only a security measure but no punishment. In short, the theory of functional culpability lacks appropriateness and feasibility.[42]

The theory of criminal law previously in China has always equated intention and negligence with guilt and adopted the theory of psychological culpability. However, However, this article argues that we should adopt the general theory of normative culpability that is the norm in the world today. First, as mentioned earlier, in specific cases, even if the psychological fact of having intention or negligence is found, there are situations in which blames cannot be given. This is because criminal law imposes statutory penalties for crimes with the intention of create an opposing motive for the crime. Although, in general, in the case of the existence of intent, negligence, criminal capacity and the possibility of the cognition of wrongdoing, an opposing motive should or can be generated, "However, on certain occasions… especially when the inner root impulse of the actor is much stronger than the horror of the suffering foreseen by the law, the setting of an opposing motive is meaningless. For example, in a bounded state such as necessity for protecting life, human vulnerability and the instinct for self-preservation are significant".[43] On such occasions, the actor is not culpable. Second, Article 16 of *Criminal Law of the People's Republic of China* contain the idea of the opposing of normative culpability this article provides that "although an act objectively creates harmful consequences, if it does not result from intention or negligence but rather stems from irresistible or unforeseeable causes, it is not a crime.." The so-called irresistible, means that although the actor recognizes that own actions will occur damaging results, but due to the constraints of the subjective and objective conditions at the time, it is impossible to exclude or prevent the results. Obviously, the actor of an irresistible event lacks reasonableness. Third, the theory of normative culpability presupposes the possibility of other acts, and as mentioned earlier, it is reasonable to start the discussion of the theory of culpability with the possibility of other acts. Fourth, the theory of normative culpability does not imply the denial of the mental element, on the

[41] 德冈特·施特拉腾韦特、洛塔尔·库伦:《刑法总论I——犯罪论》，杨萌译，法律出版社2006年版，第205~206页。Günter Stratenwerth & Lothar Kuhlen, trans. Yang Meng, (2006) *Strafrecht Allgemeiner Teil I: Die Straftat*, Law Press, 205–206.

[42] Many scholars in Germany have strongly criticized the theory of the theory of functional responsibility(参加李文健:《罪责概念之研究》，作者发行1998年版，第237页以下).

[43] 日青井秀夫:《法理学讲义》，有斐阁2007年版，第59页。See Aoi Hideo. (2007) *Lectures on jurisprudence*, Yuhikaku Press, 59.

contrary, intention and negligence are still elements of culpability. In other words, "although it is a theory of psychological culpability, it is not an unregulated consideration of culpability. Although it is a theory of normative culpability, it is not a denial of the existence of the psychological element... only that the theory of normative culpability holds that even in cases where a person with criminal capacity to act is aware of the facts of the crime and commits the act, there are cases where the person cannot be accused but rather examining the process of forming the 'psychological' motive at first."[44] Therefore, reasonableness also should also be discussed in addition to intention and negligence. Fifth, the theory of normative culpability does not imply that culpability is irrelevant to crime prevention. "Culpability, as *Vorwerfbarkeit* for the actor who has committed unlawful acts that meet the constitutive elements, is required as an element that justifies the imposition of penalties that have the nature of blameness... penalties are imposed under the conditions or constraints of such blames in pursuit of the purpose of crime prevention."[45] As mentioned earlier, imposing punishment for acts without the possibility of other acts is unlikely to have the effect of preventing crimes. The premise of reasonableness is precisely to achieve the purpose of preventing crimes.

Secondly, whereas reasonableness has multiple meanings, "it may be an aggregate concept encompassing different situations,"[46] and its underlying rationale has played out differently in different contexts with other concepts.

"The doctrine of reasonableness is originally developed according to the basic principle of cause of preventive culpability. However, according to the explanation of scholars, the complementary function of reasonableness is not only applicable to the cause of preventive culpability, but also can be used to explain the propriety or even unlawfulness of the constitutive elements for omission and negligent crime. There are several opinions on propriety or even unlawfulness of the constitutive elements against unreasonableness: First, the unreasonableness determines the scope of the duty to act in the case of pure criminal omission, so the appropriateness of the constitutive elements is prevented.[47] Second, not only in the case of pure criminal omission, but also in the case of impure criminal omission, the propriety of the constitutive elements is prevented. Third, in the case of negligence other than omission, reasonableness determines the performance of the objective duty of care in the

[44] 日平野龙一:《刑法总论II》，有斐阁1975年版，第271页。See Hirano Ryuuichi. (1975) *General Theory of Criminal Law II*, Yuhikaku Press, 271.

[45] 日山口厚:《刑法总论》，有斐阁2007年版，第181~182页。See Yamaguchi Atsushi. (2007) *General Part of Criminal Law*. Yuhikaku Press, 181–182.

[46] 德冈特·施特拉腾韦特、洛塔尔·库伦:《刑法总论I——犯罪论》，杨萌译，法律出版社2006年版，第236页。Giinter Stratenwerth & Lothar Kuhlen, trans. Yang Meng, (2006) *Strafrecht Allgemeiner Teil I: Die Straftat*, Law Press, 236.

[47] In this view, the possibility of acting is a prerequisite for the duty to act. So the absence of reasonableness (without the possibility of acting) means the absence of the duty to act.

realm of wrongdoing, and has the dual significance of determining the subjective duty of anticipation with respect to culpability."[48]

In this article, one of the important reasons[49] why theory of criminal law in Germany generally recognizes the significance of reasonableness in omission and the duty to foresee the result to the duty to prevent the result in negligent crime need to be solved according to the principle of reasonableness. In other words, in Germany, the concept of reasonableness, which originally belongs to the field of culpability, actually plays a role in the stage of conformity to the constitutive elements in the case of omission, and in the stage of conformity of the constitutive elements and wrongdoing in the case of negligent crime (new theory of negligence) or in the conditions for the establishment of negligence (old theory of negligence).

As far as the intentional *Begehungsdelikte* is concerned, the lack of reasonableness is relatively rare in today's society. Objectively speaking, *Begehungsdelikte* is manifested by committing an act prohibited by law with a positive physical action, and the requirement that the actor not commit the *Begehungsdelikte* with a positive physical action is not excessive under normal circumstances. This is because, "in terms of reasonableness, what can be more easily expected from the same person is a negative failure to do unlawfulness. What can be more hardly expected is that the actor will actively do lawfulness. Not only is there a gap between the two, but there is often a huge gap".[50] That is to say, in the case of intentional *Begehungsdelikte*, what the legal order expects is only negative non-action of unlawfulness, and thus usually has reasonableness. Subjectively speaking, 'intentional' means that the actor has recognized the infringement of the legal interest, and thus producing the motive of opposition, and it is not too much to require that he or she does not produce the motive of crime. Therefore, there is little room for the doctrine of reasonableness to be applied to the intentional *Begehungsdelikte*. On the other hand, the theoretical system of crime in Germany is built around the intentional *Begehungsdelikte*, it means, the intentional *Begehungsdelikte* should be discussed first and foremost, and then the negligent crime and omission are discussed. The lack of reasonableness is indeed rare in the doctrine of intentional *Begehungsdelikte*, so that the doctrine of reasonableness is "left out". In other words, the theory of criminal law in Germany only considers reasonableness to be insignificant in the doctrine of intentional *Begehungsdelikte*.

Unlike the theoretical system of crime in Germany, China discusses the intentional *Begehungsdelikte* with the criminal omission and negligence together. Obviously, in crime system in China, it is impossible to say in general that reasonableness is insignificant.

[48] 韩李在祥:《韩国刑法总论》，韩相敦译，中国人民大学出版社2005年版，第303页。Lee, Jae-sang. (2005) *General Theory of Korean Criminal Law*, trans. Han Xiangdun, China Renmin University Press, 303.

[49] Vgl.,C.Roxin, *Strafrecht Allgemeiner Teil, Band I*, C.H.Beck 4.Aufl., 2006,S.857.

[50] 黄荣坚:《基础刑法学(下)》，元照出版有限公司2006年版，第733页。Huang Rongjian. (2006) *Fundamental Criminal Law (Vol. 2)*, Angle Publishing Co., Ltd., 733.

Thirdly, in Germany, the lack of reasonableness has basically been explicitly provided for in the criminal law as a ground for elimination of crimes, so the lack of reasonableness beyond the statute is not common anymore.

Article 33 of General Part of *German Penal Code* exempts from punishment those who defend themselves improperly due to panic, fear or fright, and Article 35 provides for exemption from culpability for necessity. These two articles are based on the doctrine of reasonableness. Specific Provisions of *German Penal Code* also provides for circumstances in which the lack of reasonableness is not punishable. For example, Article 138 of *German Penal Code* provides for the crime of failing to prosecute a planned criminal act, and Article 139(3) provides that even failure to prosecute a crime is not punishable if efforts are made to prevent the crime by a relative. As another example, Article 258 of *German Criminal Law* provides that prevention of criminal justice committed for oneself or for one's relatives is not punishable. Another example is that the reason why *German Criminal Law* does not punish simple escape (i.e., escape without the use of violence, coercion, destruction of custodial facilities, etc.) is based on the actor lacks reasonableness.[51]

Obviously, if the criminal law already provides for all acts lacking reasonableness in the criminal law, the lack of reasonableness cannot be a supra-law cause of preventive culpability, but only a theoretical basis for statutory cause of preventive culpability. However, in China, many situations that clearly lack reasonableness have not been legalized. That being the case, we cannot deny that the lack of reasonableness can be a supra-law cause of preventive culpability, as theory of criminal law in Germany does.

Fourthly, in today's Germany, due to the full development of the society and the perfection of the law, the nationals enjoy full freedom within the law and the lack of reasonableness at the time of the act is indeed rare. For example, the well-known case *Leinenfaenger*. Today, under German labor law, the actor in case *Leinenfaenger* is no longer under compulsion, in other words, if the case *Leinenfaenger* had occurred in Germany today, the actor would be criminally liable for negligent injury.[52]

In conclusion, in Germany, reasonableness is still important in the case of omission and negligence. If the theory of normative culpability is adopted instead of the theory of functional culpability, reasonableness as the basis of culpability is still important. It is only in the case of intentional action that there is no room for the narrowly defined reasonableness to play an important role.

[51] *Japanese Criminal Law* is also based on the principle of reasonableness, which stipulates more impediment on responsibility. Because of this, the state of the crime does not establish because of the absence of reasonableness is rare in Japan.(参见黎宏:《日本刑法精义》，法律出版社2008年版，第227页See Li Hong. (2008) Essentials of Japanese Criminal Law, Law Press China, 227.).

[52] Vgl.,C.Roxin, *Strafrecht Allgemeiner Teil, Band I*, C.H.Beck 4.Aufl.,2006,S.1107.

8.4 Specific Issues of Reasonableness

The following discussion focuses on the specific issues of reasonableness in a narrow sense, while also addressing reasonableness as a basis for culpability.

(1) Is Reasonableness a Positive or Negative Element of Culpability?

Reasonableness, which is a basis for culpability, is neither a positive nor a negative element of culpability. What is in dispute is whether reasonableness in the narrow sense is a positive or a negative element of culpability? How does it relate to intent, negligence and criminal capacity?

The composite concept of culpability asserts that intent, negligence, criminal capacity and reasonableness are positive elements of culpability, in other words, reasonableness is the third element of culpability alongside with criminal capacity, intention or negligence. The pure concept of culpability asserts that intention or negligence is a matter of wrongdoing, and only criminal capacity, the possibility of the cognition of wrongdoing and reasonableness are elements of culpability, but what is discussed on the title of accountability is actually a cause of preventive culpability, so the lack of reasonableness is a cause of preventive culpability. Or it asserts that the criminal capacity, intention or negligence are the principle elements of culpability and reasonableness is the exceptional element of culpability, so the lack of reasonableness is a cause of preventive culpability.[53]

In fact, the two views mentioned above are not substantially opposed to each other, at best, they are only differences in judgment methods, because the cause of preventive culpability and the elements of culpability are two sides of the same coin. On the one hand, in order to blame a person for commit an illegal act that meets the constitutive elements, it is required that the actor has reasonableness to commit other acts. In this sense, reasonableness is an element of culpability. On the other hand, since people in general usually have reasonableness of performing lawful acts, it is not necessary for the public prosecution to prove that the actor has reasonableness when determining the crime. However, if in a special case, the actor does not have reasonableness, the culpability is prevented. Therefore, from the former side, reasonableness is a positive element, from the latter side, the lack of reasonableness is a cause of preventive culpability. In other words, from the perspective that *Vorwerfbarkeit* is conditional on reasonableness, the conclusion that 'reasonableness is positive element' is established, from the perspective that the lack of reasonableness prevents the granting of *Vorwerfbarkeit*, the conclusion that 'the lack of reasonableness is a cause of preventive culpability' is also established. The specific issues of the two arguments are not difficult to resolve. For one thing, advocates of the pure concept of culpability point out that if reasonableness is considered as a positive element of reasonableness, then it is unreasonable and in fact not true

[53] 参见韩李在祥:《韩国刑法总论》，韩相敦译，中国人民大学出版社2005年版，第263页。Lee, Jae-sang. (2005) *General Theory of Korean Criminal Law*, trans. Han Xiangdun, China Renmin University of Press, 263.

that the public prosecution must positively prove the existence of reasonableness for every case. In fact, since people in general usually have reasonableness to perform lawful acts, it is not necessary for the public prosecution to actively prove it in each case. For another, advocates of the composite concept of culpability point out that if reasonableness is not a positive element of culpability, it cannot explain the role of reasonableness in mitigating culpability. In fact, this view may not distinguish between reasonableness as the basis of culpability and as an element of culpability. As a cause of preventive culpability, there is no question of the magnitude of culpability. As long as reasonableness is lacking, there is no culpability. Conversely, in the case of reasonableness, the magnitude of reasonableness only affects the sentencing. Even from a narrow perspective of reasonableness, since lack of reasonableness is a cause of culpability, it is an element of culpability to have reasonableness. Therefore, the magnitude of reasonableness certainly plays a role in determining the severity of culpability.

The above conclusion can also be drawn by comparing it with the criminal capacity. In the sense that the establishment of a crime must require that the actor has the criminal capacity which is a positive element of culpability. However, people who have reached a certain age usually have the criminal capacity, so it is not necessary for the public prosecution to prove it. Because of this, the criminal law of each country provides for criminal capacity from a negative perspective, that is, the act of a person without the criminal capacity is not a crime. Accordingly, incapacity is an element to prevent the culpability, and therefore a negative element of culpability. However, this does not mean that there is no degree of criminal capacity for culpability, on the contrary, the diminution of criminal capacity for culpability reduces the degree of culpability of the actor, provided that there is criminal capacity.

In a nutshell, reasonableness, as the basis of culpability, of course, has a degree, so it also materializes as a cause of mitigating culpability (for example, one of the important reasons why excessive defense and excessive necessity are applied to mitigate or exempt from punishment is the small reasonableness. On the contrary, the reason why criminal law provides for lenient punishment for surrender is that it is rational for the offender to flee after committing a crime, and the offender cannot be expected to stay in place or surrender to the judicial authorities after committing the crime). However, since a person with the criminal capacity is generally capable of generating an objectionable motive when he or she foresees or may foresee the infringement of legal interest, it may be more appropriate to consider the lack of reasonableness in the narrow sense as a cause of preventive culpability (negative element of culpability) in the theoretical system of crime.

In addition, as mentioned earlier, some scholars in China argue that the reason why an incapable person is not culpable for his or her acts and results is because of the lack of reasonableness. Some scholars have countered that "criminal capacity is the first element of accountability, and if the actor does not have the criminal capacity, he or she is naturally not accountable and does not constitute a crime... In criminal law in Germany and Japan, even if an incapable person commits an illegal act that meets the elements of composition, it does not apply the theory of reasonableness to explain their non-criminal, the incapacity itself is sufficient reason for decriminalization."[54] In this article, the opposition between the two views arises from the use of the concept of reasonableness in different senses. The former uses the concept of reasonableness in the sense of the basis of culpability, the latter uses the concept of reasonableness in a narrow sense. If one further asks "why is an incapable person not culpable? Why does the act committed by an incapable person not constitute a crime?" The answer should be that an incapable person neither has the possibility of recognizing wrongdoing nor can he or she be expected to commit other lawful acts (of course, there are also criminal policy reasons for not punishing people who have not reached the legal age). In this sense, the element of criminal capacity is, in fact, a concretization of reasonableness as a basis for culpability.

(2) Is the Lack of Reasonableness a General Supra-Law Cause of Preventive Culpability, or Only When the Criminal Law Provides for It?

Reasonableness, which is the basis of culpability, will necessarily also become the theoretical basis of the cause of preventive culpability, and can become the basis of not only the statutory cause of preventive culpability, but also the supra-law cause of preventive culpability. It is impossible for the criminal law to fully specify reasonableness as the basis of culpability, so there are situations where the positive elements of culpability, such as intention and negligence, are met, and there are no other illegal cause of preventive culpability and statutory cause of preventive culpability, and they can only be saved from penal sanctions by the lack of reasonableness in a narrow sense.

On this issue, the positions of Germany and Japan are not the same. The general view in Germany is that the lack of reasonableness is only the theoretical basis for the cause of preventive culpability under criminal law, or rather, the lack of reasonableness is limited to the cause of preventive culpability under law, not the general supra-law cause of preventive culpability. For example, the criminal law in Germany provides for the non-punishment of the excessive defense due to panic, fear or fright and the necessity for prevent the culpability, based on the theory of reasonableness. In the absence of an express provision in the law, the lack of reasonableness cannot be used as a reason to exclude culpability. The main reason for this view of theory of criminal law in Germany is that "the supra-law cause of preventive culpability for lack of reasonableness, whether understood subjectively or objectively, weakens the general preventive effect of criminal law and leads to inequality in the application of the law. This is because the so-called 'lack of reasonableness' is not a standard for possible application. Moreover, under the clear system of law, the exemptions are placed in exceptions that cannot be extended in application. Even for people facing difficult life situations, the community may require them to endure great sacrifices in order to comply with the law".[55] The general opinion in Japan, on the

[54] 李立众:"期待可能性研究诸失误之匡正"，载《现代法学》2004年第3期。Li Lizhong. (2004) "Rectification of Fallacies in Research on Doctrinal Possibility of Expectation", as cited in *Modern Law Science,* No. 3, 102–107.

[55] H.Jescheck/T.Weigend,*Lehrbuch des Strafrechts Allgemeiner Teil,* Duncker & Humblot 5. Aufl.,1996, S.504.

other hand, is that the lack of reasonableness can be the supra-law cause of preventive culpability. The reason is that since the idea of reasonableness exists behind the actual law, it should be interpreted as the prevention of culpability in the absence of reasonableness. If the doctrine of reasonableness is only used as the explanatory principle for cause of preventive culpability under criminal law, the doctrine cannot be fully utilized.[56] However, in the jurisprudence of the Supreme Court of Japan, there is no case in which acquittal was based on the lack of reasonableness. This shows that there is no significant difference in the ending between the two views mentioned above after the basic situation of lack of reasonableness has been stipulated in the criminal law.

This article argues that in China, it is still necessary to use the lack of narrowly defined reasonableness as a supra-law cause of preventive culpability.

Reasonableness, which is the basis of culpability, is necessarily reflected in the specific provisions. In other words, when the specific provisions stipulate the constitutive elements, it will generally exclude the situations lacking reasonableness from the crime. For example, if the actor makes a false confession, destroys or falsifies evidence, or covers up or conceals any proceeds of crime and gains accrued by such proceeds, although criminal justice was prevented, the criminal law does not provide for punishment of the actor (such as 'the subject of the perjury does not include the perpetrator', 'assist parties concerned in destroying, falsifying evidence shall belong to crime', 'only those who are not guilty of this crime are guilty of covering up or concealing any proceeds of crime and gains accrued by such proceeds'), simply because the actor cannot be expected not to commit said act after committing the crime.

As mentioned earlier, in Germany and Japan, acquittals based directly on the lack of reasonableness are indeed rare. This is because the lack of reasonableness is basically typified in the criminal law, which makes the lack of reasonableness basically no longer exist outside of the express provisions of the criminal law. Therefore, the theory of criminal law in Germany and some Japanese scholars deny the lack of reasonableness as a supra-law cause of preventive culpability. However, this does not mean that China must also hold a denial attitude, because criminal law in China obviously does not fully typify the lack of reasonableness in the criminal law. The lack of reasonableness, which has been legalized in ancient China and old China, as well as the lack of reasonableness, which has been legalized in the criminal law of Germany and Japan today, are not provided in criminal law in China as a statutory cause of preventive culpability. Since this is the case, we must recognize the lack of reasonableness as a supra-law cause of preventive culpability, and not as a crime. The following are a few examples:

Firstly, crime of impairing testifying. If criminal suspects, defendants in a criminal case commit this crime, is he or she guilty of this crime? One view is that a criminal suspect or defendant who himself or herself adopts illegal means to

---

[56] 参见日大谷实:《刑法讲义总论》，成文堂2007年新版，第356页。See Ohya Minoru. (2009) *General Handouts on Criminal Law(New Edition)*, Seibundo Publishing Co, 356.

impairing testimony also constitutes this crime.[57] However, there are doubts about this view. According to the basic viewpoint of the theory of normative culpability, if the suspect or defendant adopts general methods such as entrusting, requesting, or persuading to prevent others from testifying or instructing others to commit perjury, the crime of impairing testifying should not be punished because of the lack of reasonableness. Only when the suspect or defendant uses violence, threat or bribery to prevent others from testifying or instructs others to commit perjury, it can be considered that there is no lack of reasonableness and thus be considered as the crime of impairing testifying.

Secondly, the crime of assisting the parties concerned in destroying or falsifying evidences. If the actor helps the spouse or close relative (the party) to destroy or falsify evidence, is this crime established? Although such behavior is usually treated as a crime in judicial practice, this approach is contrary to the doctrine of culpability and should be acquitted as a situation lacking reasonableness.

Thirdly, the crime of harboring and shielding. If the person who committed the crime harbors or shields himself, this crime is not established because of the lack of reasonableness. The question is how to deal with the harboring or shielding committed by the spouse or close relatives of the actor. Although such acts are generally treated as crimes in judicial practice as well, it is appropriate to acquit the actor for lack of reasonableness.

Fourthly, simple escape. The acting subjects of crime of escaping is the criminals (convicted criminals), defendants and suspects who are imprisoned in accordance with the law. The question is whether a person who is in fact innocent can be the subject of the act of this crime? The affirmative and negative arguments essentially involve the question of whether to give priority to the protection of national interests or personal interests. In terms of law, the affirmative and negative arguments involve the question of reasonableness, in addition to how to understand and judge "in accordance with the law". In the opinion of this article, as long as the judicial authorities meet the legal procedural and substantive conditions at the time of detention, it should be considered as a legal detention, and the criminal, defendant, or suspect in detention can become the subject of the act. However, it cannot be ignored that in the case where the actor is originally innocent and is detained solely due to the mistake of the judicial authorities, the actor simply escapes and should be considered as lacking reasonableness and not be treated as a crime.

Fifthly, necessity for life. If life is equivalent and quantifiable, then it is possible to protect equivalent life by sacrificing life, and especially it is possible to protect the life of the majority by sacrificing the life of one person. However, life is an essential element of personality, the nature of which cannot be compared by any measure, and the legal order does not allow the use of human life as a means to achieve any end. For example, a person's liver cannot be arbitrarily removed for transplantation when it could be used by five liver patients for liver transplantation

[57] 参见周道鸾、张军主编:《刑法罪名精释》，人民法院出版社2007年版，第601页。See Zhou Daoluan. & Zhang Jun. eds. (2007) *Exact Explanatuin for Accusations of Criminal Law*, People's Court Press, 601.

and thus save the lives of five people.[58] In this sense, any act that uses life as a means to an end is illegal. However, if it is not allowed to protect the lives of more people by sacrificing one person's life, it means that it is better to cause the death of more people than to sacrifice one person's life, which is difficult to be accepted by the general concept of society and is not necessarily in line with the socially utilitarian nature of necessity. Thus, it seems that at least for the protection of the lives of the majority of people who have no choice but to sacrifice the life of one person, the crime should be excluded.[59] However, first of all, one person's life can be sacrificed to protect the lives of others only when the person being sacrificed is specific (e.g., the person promises to sacrifice himself, the person is the only one in the position of the person being sacrificed, etc.), and the judgment of "necessary" should be stricter. Therefore, in the above-mentioned example of liver transplantation, a healthy person cannot be arbitrarily selected for liver transplantation. Moreover, since the legal order does not allow the use of human life as a means, the above act may still be illegal. However, it should be considered that the actor of necessity lacks reasonableness and thus is not culpable, i.e., it is treated as a supra-law necessity. For the same reason, the act of sacrificing the lives of specific others as a last resort in order to protect own life or the lives of friends and relatives can also be regarded as supra-law necessity.

It is clear from the above that the doctrine of reasonableness still has a lot of room for application in China. In other words, in China, there are still many supra-law cause of preventive culpability (some of which are already statutory cause of preventive culpability abroad), and the basis for preventing the culpability is the lack of reasonableness.

(3) What Standard Should Be Used to Determine Reasonableness?

The standard for judging reasonableness refers to the standard for judging whether the actor has reasonableness of lawful conduct when committing the illegal act that meets the constitutive elements.

"Actor standard theory" asserts that the standard is the actor's own criminal capacity in the specific situation at the time of the act. If the actor cannot be expected to perform the lawful act in the specific situation at the time, the lack of reasonableness is indicated. However, if the actor himself or herself cannot perform the lawful act without expecting to do so, then there is no lawful order. Moreover, this doctrine does not account for the culpability of the religion criminal, because most of the religion criminal believes that own actions are justified, and if the actor is the standard, these people lack reasonableness and thus cannot be held culpable, which is

---

[58] Some scholars believe that if the truth is true, the doctor's removal of a person's liver for transplantation is also a necessity. However, in the case of 99.9%, there is not such "forced" situation in most cases.(参见日西田典之:《刑法总论》，弘文堂2006年版，第134页以下See Nishida Noriyuki.(2006) *General Theory of Criminal Law*, Koubundou Publishers Inc., 1–134).

[59] For other situations,参见黎宏:"紧急避险法律性质研究"，载《清华法学》2007年第1期。See Li Hong. (2007) "Research on the Legal Nature of Necessity", as cited in T*singhua University Law Journal*, No.1.

not the case. "Average man standard theory" says that if an average man in the actor's state can be expected to perform a lawful act, then the actor also has reasonableness. If the average man in the actor's state cannot be expected to perform a lawful act, then the actor also does not have reasonableness. However, this theory does not take into account the situation that the average man can be expected but the actor cannot be expected, which is not in line with the intention of the theory of reasonableness. "Legal norms standard theory" or "national standard theory" advocates that the specific requirements of the legal order of the state is the standard to determine whether there is reasonableness. Because the so-called "expected" refers to the expectation of the legal order to the actor, not the actor's own expectation, so whether there is reasonableness can only be based on the requirements of the legal order as the standard, not the expected actor or the average man. However, the doctrine of reasonableness is supposed to give the remedy of law against the human weakness of the actor, so those who cannot adapt to the expectation of the legal order should be considered, which is not considered by the legal norms standard theory. Moreover, it is an unclear question in what occasion the legal order expects the actor to perform the lawful act, therefore, the legal norms standard theory actually does not propose any standard.

In fact, the above three doctrines only grasp part of the sides of the standard for judging reasonableness, and their oppositions are not significant. In other words, "actor standard theory" focuses on the judgment information, "average man standard theory" focuses on the judgment benchmark and "legal norms standard theory" focuses on the subject of anticipation. However, the three can be applied without contradiction.

In terms of the physical and psychological condition of the actor, it is necessary to take the specific actor as the basis, rather than general person, but this does not mean that culpability is prevented on the grounds that "it is not possible because it is this actor". The "average person" does not mean the average person in the statistical sense, but the majority of other people with the characteristics of the actor. "This concept of 'average' is a technical concept that is indispensable for judging the likelihood of the actor's legal behavior, because it is impossible to judge the likelihood of a particular person's behavior without comparing it with others. Thus, there is no difference in the practical meaning of the so-called "actor, average man or type of person."[60]

"Legal norms standard theory" is not opposed to "personal standard theory" either. Because the judgment of reasonableness is not a reasonable conclusion that can be drawn simply from the observation of the possibility of other acts on the side of the actor, but the need of the legal order must be considered. In other words, the judgment of reasonableness is a judgment of the tension between the individual and the legal order.

[60] 黄荣坚:《基础刑法学》(下)，元照出版有限公司2006年版，第664页。Huang Rongjian. (2006) *Fundamental Criminal Law (Vol. 2)*, Angle Publishing Co., Ltd., 664.

The result can only be that, from the standpoint of protecting the legal interest, based on the physical and mental conditions of the actor at the time and the accompanying circumstances, and by comparing with most other people with the characteristics of the actor, it can be judged whether the actor at the time can be expected to refrain from committing the illegal act by performing his or her criminal capacity.[61] For example, in the case of Xu Ting, based on his criminal capacity, it was fully expected that he would not withdraw money at that time, therefore, there was no lack of reasonableness. If a married woman formed a *de facto* marriage with another person because of suffered from natural disasters to exile to earn a living, or because she has serious difficulties in family life on the ground of the spouse's long-term whereabouts, or because of forced or arranged marriages or fleeing due to abuse after marriage, or because of being trafficked, all of the above situations are compelled by objective conditions, therefore, there is an absence of reasonableness, thus deterring culpability and making it inappropriate to punish them as bigamy. However, there is reasonableness for the said woman who then goes to the marriage registration office to register with another person.

(4) What Is the Nature of Cognition Mistakes of Reasonableness?

Generally speaking, the cognition mistake of reasonableness in the narrow sense, which belongs to cognition mistake of the objective elements of culpability, exists in two main cases.

Firstly, a positive mistake, it means something without reasonableness that did not exist originally, but which the actor mistakenly thought existed. The first view is that a positive mistake prevents intent.[62] This view is reasonable if one considers that the cognition content (the object) of intent includes the fact of blameness. However, intent is the knowledge and recognition of the fact of wrongdoing that meets the objective constitutive elements, and reasonableness is not the cognition content of intent, but the element of culpability other than intent. The second view is that positive mistakes of reasonableness should be treated like a prohibited mistake. If the mistake is unavoidable, the culpability shall be prevented.[63] Although this view proposes a principle of treatment, it lacks foundation. The third view is that a negligent crime is established if the actor is negligent for falling into the cognition mistakes.[64] This view also holds that the lack of reasonableness is a cause of preventive culpability, however, since reasonableness exists in principle when the actor has intent, negligence and the criminal capacity, it is obviously improper to affect the establishment of intention and negligence by the mistakes of

[61] 参见日山口厚:《刑法总论》，有斐阁2007年版，第251~252页。See Yamaguchi Atsushi. (2007) *General Part of Criminal Law*.Yuhikaku Press, 251–252.

[62] 参见日团藤重光:《刑法纲要总论》，创文社1990年版，第331页。See Dandou Shigemitsu. (1990) *General Outline of Criminal Law*, Kodansha Publishing Co, 331.

[63] 参见日福田平:《全订刑法总论》，有斐阁2004年版，第222页。See Fukuda Taira. (2004) *General Theory of Criminal Law (Full Edition)*, Yuhikaku Press, 222.

[64] 参见日中山研一:《刑法总论》，成文堂1982年版，第397页。See Nakayama Kenichi. (1982) *General Theory of Criminal Law*, Seibundo Publishing Co., 397.

reasonableness after the actor had intention or negligence. The fourth view is that "in the case of a positive mistake regarding reasonableness which should be judged directly by the mental state of the actor himself or herself. In other words, it is not based on whether there is negligence in the error or whether the mistake could have been prevented, but rather on whether there is a mental state sufficient to negate reasonableness. Therefore, in the case of a positive mistake concerning reasonableness, it should be considered that culpability has been prevented or diminished at the level of normative culpability."[65] However, to entirely recognize a positive mistake of reasonableness as preventing or diminishing culpability would lead to an undue expansion of the scope of preventing the culpability and undermine the stability of criminal law. The fifth view is that although a positive mistake of reasonableness makes the actor lack reasonableness, should be considered to exist if the actor, by exercising his subjective ability, can recognize the existence of reasonableness. Therefore, it is appropriate to resolve the positive mistakes of reasonableness within the judgment of reasonableness.[66]

This article believes that this should be distinguished into two situations for consideration: 1) when the criminal law cannot impose punishment because of the lack of reasonableness, and in the occasion that what is stipulated in the constitutive elements is not lack of reasonableness, the positive mistake is actually the mistake of the constitutive elements, thus preventing the establishment of intent. For example, what should be done if the doe A destroys the evidence of another person's crime by mistake as his own evidence of crime? It is undeniable that the act of destroying evidence of own crime cannot be established as a crime because of the lack of reasonableness. In this sense, the criminal law includes the element of "assist parties concerned in destroying" from the perspective of culpability. However, once it is included, it should be considered as constitutive elements and not an element of culpability. If this is not the case and the "parties" is treated as an element of culpability, then, since the element of culpability does not need to be recognized for the establishment of intent, the destruction of evidence of another crime as evidence of own crime cannot be regard punishable because the reduction of culpability is not certain. This is a clear violation of Paragraph 2 of Article 307 of *Criminal Law of the People's Republic of China*. Since Article 307 expresses the constitutive element as "assist parties concerned in destroying" evidence, it requires the actor to recognize that what he or she destroyed was evidence of another person's crime. In the case where A did not realize that he was destroying evidence of parties involved and thought he was destroying evidence of his own crime, he lacked the intent and certainly did not commit the crime.[67] Of course, strictly speaking, this cognition

[65] 日浅田和茂:《刑法总论》，成文堂2007年补正版，第361页。Asada Kazushige.(2007) *General Theory of Criminal Law (Supplementary Edition),* Seibundo Publishing Co, 361.

[66] 参见日前田雅英:《刑法总论讲义》，东京大学出版会2007年版，第372页See Maeda Masahide.(2007) *Handouts of General Rules of Criminal Law(4th Edition)*, University of Tokyo Press, 372.

[67] 参见日山口厚:《刑法总论》，有斐阁2007年版，第33页。See Yamaguchi Atsushi.(2007) *General Part of Criminal Law*. Yuhikaku Press, 33.

mistake is no longer a cognition mistake of reasonableness, but a factual cognition mistake of the constitutive element; 2) when the positive mistake of reasonableness is not related to intent, it is appropriate to take the fifth view above and resolve it within the judgment of reasonableness. For example, B mistakenly believes that his life is in imminent danger and mistakenly holds that the only way is to perform necessity against the lives of others, and thus kills others. If the actor can be expected not to make such a mistake at that time, then culpability cannot be prevented and the guilty of intentional homicide shall be found. Conversely, if the actor could not be expected not to make such a mistake at that time, then culpability is prevented.

Secondly, a negative mistake, it means something without reasonableness existed originally, but which the actor mistakenly thought it not existed. Since there is actually something that lacks reasonableness, there is an absence of special prevention for the actor. And since such negative mistakes are extremely rare, there is no need for general prevention, so blameness shall not stand.[68]

8.5 Conclusion

To sum up, even in Germany, reasonableness is neglected in intentional *Begehungsdelikte*, and in China, it is still necessary to reasonably apply the doctrine of reasonableness.

A distinction should be made, if necessary, between the concept of reasonableness, which was previously used in a different sense in theory of criminal law. In the opinion of this article, problems that can be solved at the stage of wrongdoing should not be considered as reasonableness in the field of culpability. In other words, since the theory of criminal law recognizes reasonableness as a matter of accountability, it is not appropriate to treat the objective constitutive elements and the wrongdoing aspect as reasonableness. Therefore, the possibility of act in an omission is not a matter of culpability and should not be discussed as an reasonableness. In other words, what can exclude the establishment of a crime in the objective constitutive element stage and the wrongdoing stage should not remain in the theory of culpability. Therefore, the issue of conflicting duty is appropriate to be judged in the stage of wrongdoing, but not in the stage of accountability. On the other hand, when reasonableness, which is the basis of culpability, has been specified as relevant, it is inappropriate to discuss it as the issue of reasonableness. For example, the criminal capacity and the possibility of foreseeability the negligence, although these are questions of culpability, should not be treated as a question of reasonableness. Otherwise, it will lead to confusion of concepts and tedious judgment.

It is necessary to distinguish between reasonableness as a basis of culpability and reasonableness as an element of culpability (lack of reasonableness as cause of

[68] 参见日浅田和茂:《刑法总论》，成文堂2007年补正版，第361页。Asada Kazushige. (2007) *General Theory of Criminal Law (Supplementary Edition)*, Seibundo Publishing Co, 361.

preventive culpability). On the one hand, for some provisions of criminal law concerning the cause of preventive and reduced culpability, the theory of criminal law can be explained from reasonableness as the basis of culpability; on the other hand, if there is really no reasonableness and there is no other express basis for acquittal, acquittal should be made as a supra-law justifiable cause.

However, it is true that the narrow theory of reasonableness cannot be abused, i.e., acquittal cannot be readily based on the lack of reasonableness of the perpetrator (supra-law justifiable cause). The criminal law doctrine should typify the justifiable cause that should be typified in criminal law but have not yet been typified (causes of lack of reasonableness). Outside of typification, the conclusion of acquittal for lack of reasonableness is possible only in very exceptional cases.

References

Asada Kazushige. (2007) *General Theory of Criminal Law (Supplementary Edition)*, Seibundo Publishing Co, 361

Bernd Schünemann, (2006) Functions of Culpability in Preventing Crimes, as cited in Chen Zhihui, ed., Unbestechlich und unbeirrbar im dienst von recht unechtigkeit: abhandlungen zur gesamten strafrechtswissenschaft von BERND SCHUNEMANN, Taiwan: taedp.org.tw, 608， 606

Daoluan. & Zhang Jun. eds. (2007) *Exact Explanatuin for Accusations of Criminal Law*, People's Court Press, 601.

Enrico Ferri, trans. Guo Jianan, (2004) *Positive school of criminology: three lectures*, Press of People's Public Security University of China, 1-185.

Giinter Stratenwerth & Lothar Kuhlen, trans. Yang Meng, (2006) Strafrecht Allgemeiner Teil I: Die Straftat, Law Press, 1-236, 377-378, 386, 402.

Harry Frankfurt, (2006) *Alternate Possibilities and Moral Responsibility*, as cited in Xv Xiangdong ed. *Free Will and Moral Responsibility*, Nanjing: Jiangsu People's Publishing House, 359.

Hirano Ryuuichi. (1972) *General Rules of Criminal Law I*, Yuhikaku Press, 154.

Horiuchi Shouzou. (1988a) "Issues in the theory of responsibility", as cited in Shibahara Kuniji et al, ed., *The modern development of criminal law theory — General part I,* NIPPON HYORON SHA Co., 172-173.

Horiuchi Shouzou. (1988b) "Issues in the theory of responsibility", as cited in Shibahara Kuniji et al, ed., *The modern development of criminal law theory — General part I,* NIPPON HYORON SHA Co., 172-173.

Huang Rongjian. (2006) *Fundamental Criminal Law (Vol. 2)*, Angle Publishing Co., Ltd., 635-636, 664, 733.

G.Jakobs, *Strafrecht Allgemeiner Teil*, 2.Aufl., Walter de Gruyter 1993,S.480ff.

H.Jescheck/T.Weigend, *Lehrbuch des Strafrechts Allgemeiner Teil,* Duncker & Humblot 5.Aufl.,1996, S.504.

John Martin Fischer, (2006) *Frankfurt-Style Examples and Semi-Compatibilism*, as cited in Xv Xiangdong ed. *Free Will and Moral Responsibility*, Nanjing: Jiangsu People's Publishing House, 392, 394.

Li Lizhong. (2004) "Rectification of Fallacies in Research on Doctrinal Possibility of Expectation", as cited in Modern Law Science, No. 3, 102-107.

Lee, Jae-sang. (2005) *General Theory of Korean Criminal Law*, trans. Han Xiangdun, China Renmin University Press, 262-263, 303.

Miao Yuhong. (2001) "Doctrinal Possibility of Expectation", as cited in Journal of Heilongjiang College of Political Science and Law, No. 3

Nishida Noriyuki. (1988) "Theory of omission offenses", as cited in Shibahara Kuniji et al, ed., *The modern development of criminal law theory — General part I,* NIPPON HYORON SHA Co., 80.
Ohya Minoru. (2007) Handouts of General Theory of Criminal Law (New Edition), Seibundo Publishing Co., 152.
Ou Jinxiong. (2000) "Inheritance and Critique of Doctrinal Possibility of Expectation", as cited in Legal Science, No. 5,
See Aoi Hideo. (2007) *Lectures on jurisprudence,* Yuhikaku Press, 44, 59.
See Chen Xingliang. (2006) "Research on Issues of Doctrinal Possibility of Expectation", as cited in *Legal Science*, No. 2.
See Dandou Shigemitsu. (1990) *General Outline of Criminal Law*, Kodansha Publishing Co, 331.
See Fukuda Taira. (2004) *General Theory of Criminal Law (Full Edition)*, Yuhikaku Press, 222.
See Hirano Ryuuichi. (1975) *General Theory of Criminal Law II*, Yuhikaku Press, 154,271.
See Nishida Noriyuki. (2006) *General Theory of Criminal Law,* Koubundou Publishers Inc., 191.
See Lao Dongyan. (2008) "Objectification of Criminal Culpability and the Fate of Doctrinal Possibility of Expectation", as cited in *Modern Law Science*, No. 5.
See Li Hong. (2007) "Research on the Legal Nature of Necessity", as cited in T*singhua University Law Journal*, No.1.
See Li Hong. (2008) *Essentials of Japanese Criminal Law,* Law Press China, 227.)
See Maeda Masahide. (2006) *Handouts of General Rules of Criminal Law(4th Edition)*, University of Tokyo Press, 53, 37, 372.
See Nishida Noriyuki. (2006) *General Theory of Criminal Law*, Koubundou Publishers Inc., 1-134, 397.
See Ohya Minoru. (2009) *General Handouts on Criminal Law(New Edition)*, Seibundo Publishing Co, 356
See Yamaguchi Atsushi. (2007) *General Part of Criminal Law*. Yuhikaku Press, 33,93,181-182,251-252,366.
Vgl.,C. Roxin, Strafrecht Allgemeiner Teil, Band I, C.H.Beck 4.Aufl.,2006,S.857,1107, 1108f,1083f.
Vgl.,C. Roxin, Strafrecht Allgemeiner Teil, Band I, C.H.Beck 4.Aufl.,2006,S.1107.
Vgl.,H.Jescheck/T.Weigend,Lehrbuch des Strafrechts Allgemeiner Teil, Duncker & Humblot,5. Aufl.,1996, S.634; Schnke-Schrder, Strafgesetzbuch, Kommentar, C.H.Beck,26. Aufl.,2001,S.596.
Vgl.,H.Jescheck/T.Weigend,Lehrbuch des Strafrechts Allgemeiner Teil, Duncker & Humblot 5.Aufl.,1996, S.563ff.
Vgl.,Wessels/Beulke, *Strafrecht Allgemeiner Teil*, C.F.Müller 30. Aufl.,2000,S.139.
Yamaguchi Atsushi. (1998) *Problematic Criminal Law Overview,* Yuhikaku Press, 44.

Chapter 9
The Legal Nature of Abandonment of Crime

To discuss the legal nature of the abandonment of crime is to discuss the basis of a mitigated punishment or an exempted punishment for an offender who abandon the crime with. Only by clarifying the legal nature of the abandonment of crime, can the relevant issues in legal practice be handled well.

9.1 Statement of Problems

The basis for an offender who abandon the crime be exempted from punishment or be given a mitigated punishment are not directly provided in different criminal laws all over the world; yet there are provisions concerning the establishment condition for the abandonment of crime. However, the interpretations of criminal law provisions may vary due to the language expression itself. Whether abandonment of crime can be admitted shall be in accordance with provisions in the criminal law, its crucial to understand and apply the legal basis of mitigating or exempting punishment of the abandonment of crime. For example, although Article 24 of the *Criminal Law* in China expressly provided that "the abandonment of crime refers to a case where, in the course of committing a crime, the offender voluntarily and effectively prevents the consequences of the crime from occurring." However, whether it is required that no criminal result occurred or only required that the perpetrator voluntarily takes effective measures to prevent the consequences of the crime from occurring depends on the understanding of the basis for an offender who abandon the crime be given a mitigated punishment or be exempted from punishment. If it is considered that the basis (or one of them) for an offender who abandon the crime be

*The original title is "The Basis of Mitigating or Exempting Punishment of the Abandonment of Crime", published in ***Peking University Law Journal***, 2015, Vol. 5.

M. Zhang, *The Fundamental Issues upon Criminal Law Theories*, Masterpieces of Contemporary Jurisprudents in China,
https://doi.org/10.1007/978-981-95-1276-8_9

given a mitigated punishment or be exempted from punishment is the reduction of wrongdoing (the reduction of the infringement of legal interest), then the former understanding established; otherwise, the latter understanding established. As another example, how to understand "the voluntarily" and whether or not a perpetrator is required to abandonment of crime because of repentance also depend on the understanding of the basis for an offender who abandon the crime be given a mitigated punishment or be exempted from punishment.

Of course, the interpreter may also take reference in accordance with the provisions of establishment condition for an offender who abandon the crime be given a mitigated punishment or be exempted from punishment in *Chinese Criminal Law*. For example, if the view that voluntarily and effectively prevent the consequences of the crime from occurring in Article 24 of the *Criminal Law* means crime consequences are prevented, there should be no criminal result occurred, then, it is possible (not necessarily) to consider the reduction of wrongdoing as a basis (or one of the bases) for an offender who abandon the crime be given a mitigated punishment or be exempted from punishment.

So far, the theory of criminal law in China has basically adopted the Japanese theory of criminal law to discuss the issue of an offender who abandon the crime shall be given a mitigated punishment or be exempted from punishment. The mainstream is the combination or synthesis of the law theory (reduction of wrongdoing, reduction of culpability) and policy theory.[1] In the old era of criminal law before 1997 in China, it was understandable to adopt such a route because the punishment provision of abandonment of crime in the old criminal law in China are the same as that in *Japanese Criminal Law* which is shall be given a mitigated punishment or be exempted from punishment.[2] Keeping walking down such route, the theory of criminal law in China seems to be able to take a whole reference from Japanese theory of criminal law.

The reason why the past theory of criminal law in China did not take the reference from German criminal theory regarding the basis for the offender who abandon the crime be exempted is because the previous provisions of the *Criminal Law* in China on the mitigated or exempted penalty are different from the provisions of *German Criminal Law*. As known, *German Criminal Law* provides that, the offender who abandon the crime will not be punished, nor be punished. If the abandonment of crime includes another accomplished misdemeanor, the offender who abandon the crime will not be punished, but the act which constitutes an accomplished misdemeanor is still punishable. For example, when the actor abandon a burglary, the abandonment of burglary is not punishable, but the actor shall still be punished for

---

[1] 参见陈兴良:《口授刑法学》，中国人民大学出版社2007年版，第304页； 张明楷:《刑法学》，法律出版社2011年版，第338页;黎宏:《刑法学》，法律出版社2012年版，第253页;周光权:《刑法总论》，中国人民大学出版社2011年版，第196页。See Chen Xingliang. (2007) *Lectures on Criminal Law*, Renmin University of China Press, 304; Zhang Mingkai. (2011) Criminal Law, Law Press China, 338. See Li Hong. (2012) *Criminal Law*, Law Press China, 253; Zhou Guangquan. (2011) *General Part of Criminal Law*, China Renmin University of Press, 196.

[2] Article 21, paragraph 2, of the old criminal law of China provides that "An offender who discontinues a crime shall be exempted from punishment or be given a lighter punishment". Article 43 of Japanese *Criminal Law* provides that "An offender who abandons a crime on his own will shall be exempted from punishment or be given a lighter punishment".

the accomplished illegal trespassing; when the actor abandon a murder, he shall be punished for the accomplished crime of intentional injury if any harm is caused.[3] Such regulations are obviously different from the provisions of the old criminal law in China. Therefore, it is difficult for China's past theory of criminal law to take reference from the theory of penalty purpose which in *German Criminal Law*.

However, in general, the offender who abandon the crime shall still be given a mitigated punishment or be exempted from punishment according to China's current criminal law, which is significantly different from the provisions of the old version. That is to say, the current criminal law does not adopt flexible provisions, instead, it specifically provides that "an offender who abandon the crime shall, if no damage is caused, be exempted from punishment or, if any damage is caused, be given a mitigated punishment." So, is this regulation more similar to the provisions of *Japanese Criminal Law*, or is it more similar to the provisions of *German Criminal Law*? Is it appropriate to transplant the theory formed by provisions regarding mitigated punishment and exemption from punishment based on the flexibility of *Japanese Criminal Law* to the Chinese legislation where criminal law clearly distinguishes between exemption conditions and mitigating conditions? In a word, whether the discussion on penalty mitigating and exemption basis for abandonment of crimes in China's criminal theory should be changed (based on the current criminal law in China and the German doctrine) is a question worthy of further study.

9.2 Path of Japanese Doctrines

Japanese Criminal Law is flexible regarding the provisions for the offender who abandon the crime shall be given a mitigated punishment or be exempted from punishment. In some cases, the offender may be exempted from punishment when some damages are caused (for instance, the abandonment of the murder with minor injuries), even the criminal result is prevented. While in other cases, a crime is abandoned and no damage is caused (murder without any harm), the offender may only be given a mitigated punishment. Such provision has brought a lot of trouble as a result of its flexibility to the discussion on the basis for the mitigated punishment and exemption from punishment of abandonment of crime.[4]

Let's assume, if the content of the law theory is recognized, and the basis for the mitigated punishment and exemption from punishment of abandonment of crime has eliminated the wrongdoing and the culpability, then the opponent will ask: since the wrongdoing and culpability have been eliminated, why the punishment is still mitigated? Moreover, how can the existed wrongdoing and culpability be

---

[3] Vgl.,H.Jescheck/T.Weigend,Lehrbuch des Strafrechts.Allgemeiner Teil, 5.Aufl., Duncker & Humblot, 1996, S.549.

[4] Scholars do not have to discuss or hardly discuss what kind of abandonment of crime should be exempted from punishment, or what kind of abandonment of crime can only be given a mitigated punishment.

eliminated? Similarly, if the basis for the mitigated punishment and exemption from punishment of abandonment of crime is considered to be a reduction in wrongdoing and culpability, then the dissident will further ask: since the wrongdoing and culpability are only mitigated and not eliminated, why is the punishment exempted? As a result, the theory regarding to mitigated wrongdoing, eliminated wrongdoing, mitigated culpability and eliminated culpability in China's theory of criminal law have emerged. In this way, it seems that when the wrongdoing and culpability are reduced, the punishment for the offender who abandon the crime should be mitigated; if the wrongdoing and culpability are eliminated, the offender should be exempted from punishment.[5] Can the wrongdoing and culpability of the abandonment of crime be eliminated or reduced?[6] This can be broken down into three questions for discussion.

The first question: can the wrongdoing and culpability of the abandonment of crime be eliminated? This article holds a negative answer. In terms of wrongdoing, before the act is abandoned, it has already threatened the legal interests and even caused some damages to the legal interests of the victim. This already formed threat and damage which cannot be eliminated by the actor's abandonment or prevention of the final result. For example, An illegally invaded the house and wanted to rape a woman named B by violence, and caused a slight injury to B, but A abandoned the adultery because of B's pleading. Although the rape was suspended, the wrongdoing of the illegal invasion of the house could not be eliminated, the wrongdoing of minor wound caused by violent acts also could not be eliminated. For the same reason, the culpability of abandonment of crime cannot be eliminated. Culpability is the criminal responsibility of wrongdoing, not the mere subjective malice or personal danger.[7] As mentioned above, in the case of abandonment of crime, the perpetrator has already initiated the crime,[8] and may even be considered that the wrongful act has been implemented in accordance with the constituent requirements, and the perpetrator is culpable for the wrongdoing already caused. In this case, the culpability of the perpetrator cannot be eliminated. Because of this, the Japanese theory of criminal law now does not believe that the wrongdoing and culpability of abandonment of crimes may be eliminated.[9]

---

[5] 参见张明楷:《未遂犯》，中国法律出版社、日本国成文堂1997年联合出版，第332以下。See Zhang Mingkai. (1997) *Inchoate Offenses: A Comparative Study,* China Law Press & Seibundo Publishing Co., 1–332.

[6] Without special explanation, the reduction of culpability(responsibility) in the elimination theory refers to the culpability (responsibility) as a condition for establishing a crime.

[7] 参见张明楷:《责任刑与预防刑》，北京大学出版社2015年版，第275以下。See Zhang Mingkai. (2015) *Responsibility and Prevention in Sentencing*, Peking University Press, 1–275.

[8] In China, although there may be an abandonment in the preparatory stage of a crime, but, it is basically impossible to be acquitted in judicial practice. Therefore, the abandonment of crimes handled in practice are all after the commencement. In addition, for the convenience of expression, this article only discusses the criminal abandonment after the commencement of a crime.

[9] Contemporary Japanese Criminal Law textbooks generally adopt the expression of reduction of wrongdoing and responsibility reduction, but there is no expression of wrongdoing elimination and responsibility elimination (参见日前田雅英:《刑法总论讲义》，东京大学出版会2011年版，第167页; 日山口厚:《刑法总论》，有斐阁2007年版，第278页; 日井田良:《讲义刑法学·总

The second question: can the wrongdoing of the abandonment of crime be reduced? It is true that, compared with the accomplished crime, the wrongdoing of the abandonment of crime has indeed decreased. Because Article 24 of *Chinese Criminal Law* provides that one of establishment conditions for a abandonment of crime is no criminal result. The abandonment of crime will not be established if the perpetrator fails to prevent the criminal consequence from happening after sincere efforts.[10] Therefore, from the views of wrongdoing, it is only practical to compare the abandonment of crime with the accomplished crime: if the result of the crime has already been caused, the abandonment of crime will not be established. At the same time, compared with the accomplished crime, we can explain why the abandonment of crime is established based on the fact that no criminal result has been caused. Despite this, the reduction of wrongdoing can only provide a partial basis for the penalty mitigation of the abandonment of crime, and it is not possible to provide any punishment basis for the exemption of the abandonment of crime.

Compared with the attempted crime, the wrongdoing of the abandonment of crime has not decreased because both of them may threaten or have caused damaged to certain legal interests. The penalty of the attempted crime can be lightened or mitigated because there is no criminal result, but the offender who abandon the crime should be given a mitigated punishment or be exempted from punishment. In this regard, considering the reduction of wrongdoing as the basis for the punishment reduction of the abandonment of crime is obviously lack of persuasiveness. Besides that, the reduction in wrongdoing (compared to the attempted crime) cannot explain the abandonment in a joint crime.[11] For example, in the joint crime, if the perpetrator abandon the crime, but the abettor and the aider shall still establish attempted crime and are not likely to be treated as offenders who abandon the crime. If the wrongdoing of the abandonment of crime is reduced, because the wrongdoing is conjoint and the accomplice in the narrow sense is subordinate to the perpetrator it is necessary to recognize that the wrongdoing of the aider and abettor is also reduced, and the punishment imposed on them should be reduced accordingly. However, from the aspect of law and fact, this is not the case.

Dr. Wang Zhaowu points out that the criminal acts happened before the abandonment and the abandonment *per se* should be considered as a whole which uniformly constitutes a dynamic evaluation object in wrongdoing. Since the offender "abandon the crime voluntarily'" and the attempted crime is "been forced to abandon",

论》，有斐阁2008年版，第422页;日松原芳博:《刑法总论》，日本评论社2013年版，第316页; 等等)。See Maeda Masahide.(2006) Handouts of General Rules of Criminal Law(4th Edition), University of Tokyo Press, 167; Yamaguchi Atsushi.(2007) General Rules of Criminal Law, Yuhikaku Press, 278; Ida Makoto.(2008) Handout of Criminal Law General Rules, Yuhikaku Press, 422 See Matsubara Yoshihiro.(2013) General Theory of Criminal Law, NIPPON HYORON SHA Co., 316.

[10]参见高铭暄、马克昌主编:《刑法学》，北京大学出版社、高等教育出版社2011年版，第158~159页。. Gao Mingxuan & Ma Kechang eds. (2011) Criminal Law, Peking University Press & Higher Education Press, 158~159.

[11]Vgl.,C.Roxin, StrafrechtAllgemeinerTeil, Band II, C.H.Beck, 2003,S.481f.

"although there exists the danger of the accomplishment of the crime in both the mentioned situations, there is a fundamental difference between the abandonment of crime and the attempted criminal in the risk of accomplishment crime. In contrast to the attempted ones who have accidentally prevented the crime from completing for reasons independent of his will, the wrongdoing of the offender who attempts to commit is reduced.[12] This article will not deny certain rationality in such view, while still be suspicious about it.

Firstly, the overall reviewing method (take it as a whole) believes that the act that already started to commit a crime and abandonment are two independent acts, which are as constitutive elements from the perspective of value.[13] However, the overall reviewing method is difficult to justify itself. Theoretically, the act that already started to commit a crime with wrongdoing (prohibited by the criminal law) and the abandonment with wrongdoing (encouraged by the criminal law) of a crime are fundamentally different.[14] The act that already started to commit a crime conforms to the constitutive elements of crime, and the abandonment of crime does not; the former is an act of violation of law, and the latter is to prevent or avoid the infringement of legal interests; additionally, the former is deliberately implemented and indicates that the perpetrator is punishable, and the latter act shows that the perpetrator obeys the legal normative. In this case, the act of abandonment and the previous act that already started to commit a crime should be separate and different. The criminal law regulates people's behavior and tells the citizens what behaviors are prohibited by criminal law, and what acts are not prohibited or even encouraged by criminal law. The overall reviewing method of the abandonment is not conducive to the function of the criminal law as a code of conduct. Taking a divided reviewing method can make the citizens know what behavior (the act that already started to commit a crime before the abandonment) is prohibited by the criminal law, and what behavior (which avoids or prevents the infringement of the legal interests) is encouraged by the criminal law.[15] From a practical point of view, the overall reviewing method is difficult to solve specific cases. For example, A intentionally used violence against B in order to rape B. And to avoid being raped, B offered to give A 5000 Yuan in cash, A took 5000 Yuan the money and gave up raping. If the overall reviewing method is adopted, it may be considered that the abandonment of rape conducted by A caused property damage of the victim, namely, "the damage is caused" in the abandonment of rape. However, this conclusion is not appropriate. This is because, in this case, as long as the offender simply abandons the rape

[12] 王昭武:"论中止犯的性质及其对成立要件的制约"，载《清华法学》2013年第5期。Wang Zhaowu. (2013) "On the Nature of Withdrawal from Attempted Crime and Its Restricting Effect on Constitutive Requirements", *Tsinghua University Law Journal,* No. 5.

[13] Vgl.,Lang-Hinrichsen, Bemerkungen zum Begriff der "Tat" im Strafrecht,in:Festschrift für Engisch, Frankfurt am Main, 1969, S.370ff.

[14] It is true that certain abandoning acts may also violate other crimes at the same time, or may coincide with other criminal acts, but the abandonment per se should not be identified as illegal.

[15] 参见日町田行男:《中止未遂の理论》，现代人文社2005年版，第47页以下。See Machida Yukio.(2005) *Theory of voluntary abandonment,* Gendaijinbun-sha, 1–47.

without taking active measures to prevent the result from happening, he will be convicted as an abandonment of crime of rape. However, the act of simple abandonment of rape cannot cause damage to the property of others. For another example, A put poison in the food of victim B. Seeing the pain was unbearable for B, A was regretful and drove B to the hospital immediately, but he drove the car into a lamppole negligently on the way to hospital, resulting in the death of B. Taking the behavior of A as a whole, it seems that A has caused the death of B, thus completing the crime of intentional homicide. However, this conclusion actually attributes the result caused by A's negligence to A's previous intentional behavior, which is difficult for people to understand and accept.

Secondly, the above views incorporate the culpability or the necessity of special prevention into the evaluation of wrongdoing. The so-called abandonment of crime is "to abandon the crime voluntarily", and the attempted crime "accidentally" prevents the crime from completing for "reasons independent of own will". The focus of latter situation expression is whether the offender stops conducting the criminal behavior voluntarily, which obliviously fall out of the scope of wrongdoing.

Thirdly, the above views are not entirely in line with the facts. Criminal acts is a process affected by different criminal means and objects. The attempt or abandonment of crime may happen after the beginning of perpetrating acts and before the completion of the crime. If A attempts to commit in the earliest stage of criminal process (he can be given a lightened or mitigated punishment only), and B abandon the crime in the final stage of criminal process (he should be exempted from punishment or be given a mitigated punishment), it is difficult to think that the wrongdoing of B is less than A after comparison. For example, when the criminal act is completed, the risk of occurrence of the criminal result is no less than that of the attempted ones. Some disagreement may arise from this kind of comparison, people may argue that only the abandonment of crime and the attempted criminal in the same criminal process can be compared. That is, only the abandonment of crime and the attempted criminal who are both in the earliest criminal stage can be compared, and the abandonment of crime and the attempted criminal who are both in the final criminal stage can be compared, that's how the conclusion is draw. In fact, even if the said comparison is made, it may not be possible to conclude that the wrongdoing of the abandonment of crime is less than that of the attempted ones. This is because, in many cases, whether the criminal consequence is prevented easily or not does not depend on whether the act stops voluntarily or not, but on many other factors. For example, after the poison is placed in a remote mountainous area for others to consume, the abandonment of the perpetrator is almost useless. Conversely, when the perpetrator is stopped by a third party while killing others, it is easy to prevent the death result. Perhaps for this reason, Dr. Wang Zhaowu used the expression "'the wrongdoing of this type reduces", through which what he wants to demonstrate is that, the wrongdoing of any abandonment of crime is not lighter than the attempted criminal. However, even if it is considered that the wrongdoing of certain situation reduces, there is still a problem in explaining the base of mitigated punishment for the abandonment of crime when the abandonment does not actually reduce the wrongdoing of the offender. It is generally certain that when the crime is completed, even the offender abandoned the crime, the risk of infringement of legal interests that has already occurred cannot be less than that of the attempted ones. In such a case, it is difficult to explain why the abandonment of crime should be exempted from punishment.

The third question: can the culpability of the abandonment of crime be reduced? It is undeniable that "it is easier to explain that the subjective viciousness of the abandonment of crime is less than the attempted ones. The usual explanation in China criminal law community is that the attempted criminal 'cannot complete the crime for reasons beyond his will', and the abandonment of crime abandon the crime 'voluntarily', or he 'voluntarily' and effectively prevents the criminal result from happening, that's why the subjective viciousness of the abandonment of crime is lighter than attempted ones. There should be no objection to this."[16] The question is what is the specific content of "subjective viciousness" here? If subjective viciousness refers to the possibility of re-committing a crime, it is impossible to simply summarize the above viewpoints into the theory of reduction of culpability. Meanwhile, if the subjective viciousness refers to the culpability as one of the criminal establishment conditions, then does the established culpability of perpetrator reduces? Compared it with the subjective viciousness of the accomplished crime, the conclusion is positive. It is because the culpability points at illegal acts. Under the premise of having culpability, the culpability is first determined by the degree of wrongdoing. Since the wrongdoing of the abandonment of crime is less than that of the offender who completes the crime, the culpability for the former is also less than that of the latter. Some scholars in Germany also believe that the abandonment of crime reduces the wrongdoing because of the lack of criminal results, and it also greatly reduces the culpability, so that the offender can be exempted from punishment.[17] However, the affirmative conclusion drawn from the comparison with the criminals still cannot explain why the offender who abandon the crime should be exempted from punishment or be given a mitigated punishment. That is to say, when the wrongdoing and culpability are eliminated, the punishment can be exempted; at the time of simple reduction, it can only lead to the reduction of the punishment, and it may not lead to the exemption of the punishment.

Compared with the attempted crime, it is actually difficult to conclude that the culpability of the offender who abandoned the crime is less than that of the offender who completes the crime. Since culpability decides the *vorwerfbarkei*t towards illegal acts, then when the perpetrator is responsible for implementing the illegal act that meets the constitutive elements, the culpability has already existed objectively. This existing culpability cannot be reduced by the abandonment after the completion of the crime. In other words, the culpability is determined when the crime is accomplished or the criminal act is completed, and the act afterwards cannot reduce

[16]李立众:"中止犯减免处罚根据及其意义"，载《法学研究》2008年第4期。Li Lizhong. (2008) "Grounds for Mitigation or Exemption of Punishment for Withdrawal from Crime and Its Significance", as cited in *Chinese Journal of Law*, No. 4.

[17]Vgl.,K.Ulsenheimer, Grundfragen des RücktrittsvomVersuch in Theorie und Praxis,DeGruyter1976,S.94ff.

the established culpability. Some scholars in Japan observed that "facts determining history does not allow for subsequent changes, but the post-evaluation of the perpetrator's intentions may be changed afterwards."[18] However, how can unchanged facts lead to evaluation changes? What is the basis for the change of evaluation? For such questions, Professor Sone Takehiko accordingly points out that "the voluntariness of the abandonment of crime that differs from the attempted criminal is the intentional abandonment of committing a crime. The basis for the reduction of culpabilities is not the intentional abandonment itself, but the choice to conduct the legal act (the abandonment of crime) with reasonableness of the legal act in the difficult situation (the act of abandonment is carried out voluntarily by the perpetrator who started the crime), *vorwerfbarkeit* thus can reduce. It should be considered that in case of the abandonment of crime, the reason why the crime is not completed is that the offender who abandoned the crime voluntarily, so the culpability is less than that of the attempted criminal (the crime is not completed because of outside obstacles)."[19] This explanation is not unquestionable. Why is reasonableness to behave lawfully for the perpetrator less after he begins to perpetrate? This is because once the perpetrator has a criminal intention, generally he is prone to insist on realizing it. It is true that if the perpetrator is forced to commit a criminal act, reasonableness to conduct legal behavior will be reduced due to the coercion of others. However, in case of abandonment of crime, the criminal intent comes into being by the actor's own. If it is considered that reasonableness of conducting legal act is reduced because of the existence criminal intent, which means the criminal intent is beneficial to the perpetrator. However, the risk intentionally caused by the perpetrator must be borne by him, and the culpability cannot be relieved for previous criminal intent. Therefore, this article agrees with Professor Sone Takehiko.

Dr. Wang Zhaowu also observes that, the past theory of criminal law does not agree with the post-event reduction of wrongdoing, meanwhile he admits that culpability can be reduced afterwards. It is a kind of practice that makes fish of one and flesh of another. However, wrongdoing and culpability are both legal evaluations, which can be reduced afterwards.[20] It is true that the past theory of criminal law has its defects, but in the context of this article, this kind of defect lies in the reduction of culpability afterwards. To overcome this defect, it must be affirmed that it is impossible to reduce wrongdoing or culpability afterwards. In other words, the wrongful act and its culpability before the abandonment cannot be reduced because of the abandonment after the completion of crime. For example, A drives the vehicle to the desert for 10 kilometers and then returns voluntarily because he worries there will be some danger, and B also drives the vehicle to the desert for 10 kilometers but

---

[18] 日香川达夫:《中止未遂の法的性格》，有斐阁1963年版，第97页。Kagawa Tatsuo.(1963) *The legal nature of voluntary abandonment,* Yuhikaku Press, 97.

[19] 日曾根威彦:《刑法总论》，弘文堂2008年版，第227~228页。See Sone Takehiko.(2008) *General Theory of Criminal Law*, Seibundo Publishing Co., 227~228.

[20] 王昭武:"论中止犯的性质及其对成立要件的制约"，载《清华法学》2013年第5期。Wang Zhaowu. (2013) "On the Nature of Withdrawal from Attempted Crime and Its Restricting Effect on Constitutive Requirements", as cited in *Tsinghua University Law Journal*, No. 5.

B's vehicle is stuck in the desert. There is no difference in the fact that both A and B objectively drive to the desert for 10 kilometers, and subjectively have the intention to do that. The only difference is that the situation afterwards.

It is precisely because there are flaws in various theories (namely, to explain why the offender who abandoned the crime should be exempted from punishment), so the general theory of Japanese theory of criminal law combines those theories. Japanese criminal law adopts law theory and policy approach to explain why the offender who abandoned the crime is exempted from penalty. Some scholars advocate the combination of the reduction of wrongdoing theory and the criminal policy theory,[21] while some claims the reduction of culpability theory and the criminal policy theory should be combined,[22] and others advocates the combination of the reduction theory of wrongdoing and culpability and criminal policy theory.[23] The so-called criminal policy theory generally refers to the golden bridge theory proposed by Liszt[24]: "At the moment when the boundaries between the unpunishable preparatory act and the punishable perpetrating act are crossed, the punishment prescribed for the attempted criminal becomes specific. This fact cannot be changed, nor is it allowed to be discarded or obliterated. However, if the law is made based on criminal policies, it could be the excuse for perpetrators being given mitigated punishment or being exempted from punishment. In fact, the legislation recognizes the exemption from punishment for offenders who abandon the crime voluntarily."[25] In other words, provisions of exempting for abandonment of crime from punishment aim to protect the legal interests through the expectation and rewards of

---

[21] 参见日平野龙一:《刑法总论II》，有斐阁1975年版，第333页;日福田平:《全订刑法总论》，有斐阁2001年增补版，第228页;日西原春夫:《刑法总论》，成文堂1987年版，第287页;日大谷实:《刑法讲义总论》，成文堂2012年新版，第384页。See Hirano Ryuuichi. (1975) General Theory of Criminal Law II, Yuhikaku Press, 333; Fukuda Taira.(2001) *General Theory of Criminal Law (Full Edition)*, Yuhikaku Press, 228; Nishihara Haruo.(1987) *General Theory of Criminal Law*, Seibundo Publishing Co., 287; Ohya Minoru.(2012) *Handouts of General Theory of Criminal Law(New Edition)*, Seibundo Publishing Co., 384.

[22] 参见日青柳文雄:《刑法通论I》，泉文堂1978年版，第337页;日前田雅英:《刑法总论讲义》，东京大学出版会2011年版，第168页。See Aoyagi Fumio. (1978) *General theory of criminal law I,* Senbundo Publishing Co., 337. Maeda Masahide. (2011) Handouts of General Rules of Criminal Law, University of Tokyo Press, 168.

[23] 参见日大塚仁:《刑法概说(总论)》，有斐阁2008年版，第257~258页;日藤木英雄:《刑法讲义总论》，弘文堂1987年版，第262页。Otsuka Hitoshi.(2008) Overview of Criminal Law, Yuhikaku Press, 257~258. Fujiki Hideo.(1987) Handouts of G*eneral Theory of* Criminal Law, Koubundou Publishers Inc., 262.

[24] Vgl., C.Roxin, StrafrechtAllgemeinerTeil, Band II, CHBeck, 2003, S.482 (Professor C.Roxin also advocates that the golden bridge theory should be avoided as a criminal policy, because the theory of penalty purpose in Germany today is also based on the consideration of criminal policy); 日山口厚:《刑法总论》，有斐阁2007年版，第278页; 王昭武:"论中止犯的性质及其对成立要件的制约"，载《清华法学》2013年第5期See Yamaguchi Atsushi.(2007) *General Part of Criminal Law*.Yuhikaku Press,278。Wang Zhaowu. (2013) "On the Nature of Withdrawal from Attempted Crime and Its Restricting Effect on Constitutive Requirements", Tsinghua University Law Journal, No. 5.

[25] 转引自日香川达夫:《中止未遂の法的性格》，有斐阁1963年版，第40~41页As cited in Kagawa Tatsuo.(1963) *The legal nature of voluntary abandonment,* Yuhikaku Press, 40~41 。

abandonment at the last moment of the perpetrators criminal act.[26] Therefore, *golden bridge theory* has similarities with the reward theory.[27]

However, the criminal policy theory itself is somehow questionable. First, the criminal policy theory is only a description of the provisions of the criminal law, it does not explain why the legislators set up such golden bridge to stop the crime. Second, the criminal policy theory cannot explain the motive of the perpetrator to abandon the crime, because most of the perpetrators do not know that the criminal law provides for the exemption from punishment for offenders who abandon the crime. "If you want to give the grace to people who don't know the policy, it is necessary to provide the corresponding theoretical basis."[28] which has not been provided in criminal policy theory. Even if a few perpetrators know the exemption from punishment, it does not explain why they begin to commit murder and then abandon the crime at the thought of provisions on exemption from punishment. Moreover, in fact, in most cases, the perpetrators would never consider the consequences in criminal law after they begin to commit.[29] Third, the criminal policy theory cannot provide guidance for the establishment conditions of the abandonment of crime. For example, the criminal policy theory cannot provide any guidance for the voluntariness of abandonment, nor limit the establishment of a abandoned crime to a situation where the crime is not accomplished. According to the criminal policy theory, even if the criminal act before the abandonment violated certain legal interests, in fact, there is still a golden bridge, and no penalty is imposed. However, this does not comply with the provisions of German criminal law and does not comply with the provisions of Chinese criminal law. Fourth, in Japan, the criminal policy theory cannot explain the circumstances under which punishment should be mitigated or the offender should be exempted from punishment. Professor Sone Takehiko points out: "According to the criminal policy theory, the evaluation of criminal theory can be separated from the criminal punishment. Therefore, there is still doubt for the difference between the reasons for the reduction and exemption of punishment."[30] In other words, "with regard to the criminal consequences for offenders who abandon the crime, the policy theory provides no indication at all whether the penalty should be mitigated or the punishment should be exempted.'"[31] This is mainly because

---

[26] 参见日野村稔:《未遂犯の研究》，成文堂1979年版，第119页。See Nomura Minoru. (1979) *Study on Attempted Crimes,* Seibundo Publishing Co., 119.

[27] Vgl.,C.Roxin, Strafrecht Allgemeiner Teil, Band II,C.H.Beck, 2003,S.482.

[28] 日西田典之:《刑法总论》，弘文堂2010年版，第314~315页。Nishida Noriyuki.(2010) General Theory of Criminal Law, Koubundou Publishers Inc., 314~315.

[29] 参见日吉田敏雄:《未遂犯と中止犯》，成文堂2014年版，第136页。See Yoshida Toshio. (2014) *Attempted Crimes and Voluntary Abandonment,* Seibundo Publishing Co., 136.

[30] 日曽根威彦:《刑法の重要问题(总论)》，成文堂2005年版，第276页。Sone Takehiko. (2005) *Important Issues of Criminal Law General Theory (General Theory)*, Seibundo Publishing Co., 276.

[31] 日西田典之:《刑法总论》，弘文堂2010年版，第315页。Nishida Noriyuki.(2010) *General Theory of Criminal Law,* Koubundou Publishers Inc., 315.

"considerations upon theory can only be ex ante, and the discretion of which penalty is inflicted can only be made afterwards."[32]

Professor Xie Wangyuan observes that "with the nature of pursuing fairness and justice, the criminal policy shall be the basis for China's criminal law to give the offender who abandon the crime a mitigated punishment or an exemption from punishment". "When handling the abandonment of crimes, China's criminal policy chooses a broad-minded stand in the first place (exemption from punishment will be the first option), which means, when the perpetrator abandoned the crime without causing *de facto* damages, he can be exempted from criminal punishment; even if the perpetrators criminal act has already caused certain *de facto* damage, but he voluntarily abandon the crime, he shall also be given a mitigated punishment. It can be affirmed that China's criminal law adopts such a position on the criminal abandonment is entirely based on the consideration of the fairness and justice value of the criminal policy which not only encourages criminals to abandon the crime before the occurrence of criminal consequences or effectively prevents them from happening; but reserves appropriate margins for those who cause certain damage, so as to avoid injustice resulted from indulgence of crime."[33]

It is true that fairness and justice can be somehow demonstrated by exempting the offender from punishment if he abandon the crime without causing any damage, or by providing mitigated punishment for abandon the crime with damage. Though this kind of criminal policy theory differing from the golden bridge theory, people can still be confused: first of all, the above viewpoints can only explain that the provisions regarding punishment inflicted on abandonment of crimes in China's Criminal Law can produce the effect of fairness and justice, or help to achieve fairness and justice, but it does not mean that the criminal policy for fairness and justice is the basis for exempting from punishment or a mitigated punishment. Moerover, the criminal policy for fairness and justice is so abstract that it is difficult for people to understand and determine the conditions for the establishment of the abandonment of crime. For example, how to understand voluntariness that is in line with the concept of fairness and justice? Is it different in voluntariness conditions for the abandonment of crime since some exempted from punishment and some are given mitigated punishment? The above example questions are just demonstration for the confusion. Additionally, the above viewpoint actually only covers the concept of retribution and just pays attention to the difference between mitigated punishment and exemption, the status and role of the "'voluntariness'" in abandonment of crime are actually lacking.

It is notable that the provisions of the current China's Criminal Law are quite different from the Japanese one. The criminal policy theory, can it be powerful enough to provide convincing reasons for exempting from punishment and

[32] 日团藤重光:《刑法纲要总论》，创文社1990年版，第361页。Dandou Shigemitsu.(1990) *General Outline of Criminal Law*, Kodansha Publishing Co, 361.

[33] 谢望原:"论中止犯减免处罚之根据"，载《华东政法大学学报》2012年第2期。Xie Wangyuan. (2012) "On the Grounds for Mitigation or Exemption of Punishment for Withdrawal from Crime", as cited in *Journal of the East China University of Political Science and Law*, No. 2.

mitigated punishment? Why don't laws reward the offender who causes damage? Since the offender who abandon the crime at the eleventh hour of the criminal act could be exempted from punishment, then, why can't the offender who abandon the crime before the completion be exempted? This is an important issue before the criminal policy. Dr. Li Lizhong points out that "the purpose to give the abandonment of crime a mitigated punishment or an exemption from punishment is aimed to rescue and protect the legal interests. Therefore, whether to use a mitigated punishment or an exemption depends on how much remedies of the legal interests can be made by the behavior of the perpetrator. When there is only a false alarm and no damaging result to the legal interests, and the perpetrator has the highest degree of protection for the legal interests should be given the greatest reward exemption from punishment; although the perpetrator has eliminated the danger, when a certain degree of damage is caused (for instance the perpetrator abandon a murder but causes severe injury to the victim), it is more appropriate to reward him a mitigated punishment… The punishment is directly proportional to the damage to the legal interests. The greater the damage is, the less mitigated penalty will be, so the perpetrator should try to avoid causing damage to the legal interests when discontinuing a crime; if the crime is accomplished, he will no longer enjoy the preferential treatment of penalty."[34] In the context of this article, the above viewpoint seems to be a statement of the criminal policy, it is actually a description of the degree of reduction in wrongdoing. The so-called damage caused and no damage caused is nothing more than the degree of wrongdoing of the criminal act before the abandonment. However, as mentioned earlier, the reduction of wrongdoing does not explain why the abandonment of crime should be exempted from punishment.

More importantly, how to combine the policy theory and the law theory together? In fact, the previous combination failed to clearly define the relationship between law theory and policy theory, but simply integrated the two. Generally speaking, since people think that the abandonment of crime has less wrongdoing and culpability, it is still impossible to provide a basis for exemption from punishment. Therefore, with criminal policy together, it is possible to explain why the punishment should be exempted. However, the Japanese criminal theory still can't answer why after the reduction of wrongdoing and the culpability, plus the criminal policy considerations, some abandonment of crime still only are given mitigated punishment, and there is no exemption from punishment. Now, some scholars in China are aware of this issue and have raised the question that which theory should be the main one, but the problem of how to merge is still pending solution.

Dr. Li Lizhong points out that "it is often difficult to expect the perpetrator to abandon the crime after the crime has already started. Only by inducing a certain interest to the perpetrator can expect them to abandon the completion of the criminal act. Therefore, legislators make a final effort to prevent the result of the infringement of the legal interests by providing that if the result is prevented, the perpetrator

[34] 李立众:"中止犯减免处罚根据及其意义"，载《法学研究》2008年第4期。Li Lizhong. (2008) "Grounds for Mitigation or Exemption of Punishment for Withdrawal from Crime and Its Significance", as cited in *Chinese Journal of Law*, No. 4.

will be given a mitigated punishment or be exempted from punishment. The mitigated punishment imposed on the offender who abandon the crime aims to induce him to promptly deny himself at that moment and prevent the crime from completing at a critical moment so as to protect legal interests, that is the very purpose of the criminal policy. Of course, the reason why the legislators adopt this criminal policy is based on the fact that the perpetrator objectively eliminates both the risk (reduction of wrongdoing) and the subjective desire (reduction of culpability)."[35]

Dr. Li Lizhong's view is the theory of combination which is largely based on the law theory. However, first, the above viewpoint is still only a description of the provisions of the criminal law, even if it can reflect the legislative reasons for the abandonment of crime, it cannot explain how the criminal policy is applied in specific cases. Second, the adoption of the criminal policy theory is based on the premise of reduction of wrongdoing and/or culpability. The reduction of the two and the encouragement of the policy can eliminate the punishment. However, as mentioned before, this view does not explain why some abandonment of crime cannot be excused from punishment but only get the mitigated punishment. It makes people wonder, with damage caused, why is the punishment only mitigated because of the reduction of wrongdoing and culpability, but not any policy rewards in China? Third, the reduction of wrongdoing is used as the basis for the mitigated punishment or exemption from punishment imposed on the abandonment of crime, while the degree of reduction of wrongdoing is considered again as the content of the criminal policy. As a result, there exists the suspicion of repeated evaluation.

Dr. Wang Zhaowu points out that the policy theory "emphasizes the preventive function of the provisions regarding the abandonment of crime and considers that giving the offender who has already started to commit a crime a mitigated punishment or an exemption from punishment, namely, laying a 'Golden Bridge' can prevent the crime from completing at most. Therefore, the criminal policy theory is also called reward theory." At the same time, he also observes that "the essence of the abandonment of crimes lies in policy-orientated considerations. Policy theory is not a supplement to the law theory but the basis of the law theory and the law theory is the concrete manifestation and reinforcement of the policy theory."[36] He calls his own point of view "new comprehension theory".

However, first, if the policy theory is the basis of the law theory, then, when the perpetrator has made sincere efforts to prevent the consequences from happening after the criminal conduct is completed, yet the consequences are still there, if the punishment is reduced, a return to the Golden Bridge for the perpetrator can also prevent the completion of the crime to the utmost extent, and encourage the

---

[35] 李立众:"中止犯减免处罚根据及其意义"，载《法学研究》2008年第4期。Li Lizhong. (2008) "Grounds for Mitigation or Exemption of Punishment for Withdrawal from Crime and Its Significance", as cited in *Chinese Journal of Law*, No. 4.

[36] 王昭武:"论中止犯的性质及其对成立要件的制约"，载《清华法学》2013年第5期。Wang Zhaowu. (2013) "On the Nature of Withdrawal from Attempted Crime and Its Restricting Effect on Constitutive Requirements", as cited in *Tsinghua University Law Journal*, No. 5.

perpetrator to take active measures to effectively prevent the occurrence of the consequence. Because of this, some German scholars have argued that it is at least necessary to apply analogically the provisions of Article 24 of *German Criminal Law* to the abandonment which is accomplished in form, while in reality it is not accomplished.[37] But China's criminal law provides that criminal abandonment can only be established if the consequence of crime is effectively prevented. Obviously, the policy-based view is difficult to explain the provisions in criminal law regarding penalties imposed on the offenders who abandon crimes. Second, since the law theory is based on policy theory, but when the perpetrator abandon the crime, why can he only be given a mitigated punishment rather than be exempted from punishment? In other words, it is difficult for the "new comprehension theory" to explain the provisions in criminal law regarding penalties imposed on the offenders who abandon crimes. Third, if the law theory is the concrete manifestation of the policy theory, then those two are not in the same class and there is no "comprehensive" issue.

To sum up, there are many doubts and obstacles to adopt the path of Japanese criminal theory which uses the combination of the law theory and the policy theory or the comprehension theory to demonstrate the basis for Chinese criminal law to give the offender who abandon the crime a mitigated punishment or an exemption from punishment.

9.3 Path of German Doctrines

In Germany, the law theory is a doctrine of the nineteenth century and has faded from the historical arena. The golden bridge theory was once dominant in the adjudicature of the German Imperial Court and is now marginalized.[38]

Currently, the dominant theory in Germany is the theory of penalty purpose, which contains two main points of view: the first view is, in the case of abandonment of crime, there is no need for positive general prevention because there is no criminal consequence; and because the perpetrator returned to the position of being faithful to legal norms at a critical moment, there is no necessary need for special precaution. Thus, the abandonment of crime should be exempted from punishment.[39] "From the perspective of positive prevention, it means that the perpetrator has showed that he wants to recognize the norm through the suspension. Therefore, he does not fail the public's confidence in the effectiveness of the norm and does not

[37] 参见德冈特·施特拉腾韦特、洛塔尔·库伦:《刑法总论I——犯罪论》，杨萌译，法律出版社2006年版，第283页。Giinter Stratenwerth & Lothar Kuhlen, trans. Yang Meng, (2006) *Strafrecht Allgemeiner Teil I: Die Straftat*, Law Press, 283.

[38] Vgl.,C.Roxin,StrafrechtAllgemeinerTeil, Band II,C.H.Beck,2003,S.481ff.

[39] Vgl.,C.Roxin,StrafrechtAllgemeinerTeil, Band II,C.H.Beck,2003,S.478.

need to be punished."[40] The second view thinks that the reason for exempting the abandonment of crime from punishment is because there is no need for general prevention because the perpetrator proves the validity of the law by returning to the legal position with the specific actions at a critical moment. Without punishment, the general purpose of punishment will not be impaired.[41] According to the first point of view, the simultaneous loss of general precautionary necessity and the necessity of special precaution become the basis for criminal law to give the offender who abandon the crime an exemption from punishment. According to the second point of view, even if there is a need for special prevention, as long as there is no need for general prevention, it can be the basis for exempting.

Obviously, the above viewpoints correspond to the understanding of the basis for the justification of punishment. If the basis for justification of punishment is considered to be positive general prevention and special prevention, then the first point of view will be taken. For example, the comprehensive prevention theory advocated by Professor C.Roxin is the integration of general positive prevention and special prevention in the sense of re-socialization (to return to society).[42] Professor C.Roxin points out that a rule-of-law society has two opposing goals, namely, society protection and freedom guarantee, which must be in a good balance. In order to protect the whole society, active general prevention must be carried out. At the same time, the human rights of the perpetrator must be guaranteed, and people with a criminal experience cannot be excluded from society, and they must be given the opportunity to re-integrate into society. Therefore, the purposes of punishment are general prevention and special prevention in the sense of re-socialization.[43] According to this, Professor C.Roxin believes that the basis for exemption from punishment is no need of general prevention and special prevention. Conversely, if the basis for justification is considered to be only positive general prevention, then the second view will be adopted.

Since German criminal law provides that the offender who abandon the crime is exempted from punishment, and the wrongdoing and culpability formed before the abandonment of crime are objective and cannot be eliminated, the basis for exempting abandonment of crimes can only be discussed from the perspective of lack of purpose of prevention. Therefore, the theory of penalty purpose becomes dominant in Germany.[44]

---

[40] 德乌尔斯·金德霍伊泽尔:《刑法总论教科书》，蔡桂生译，北京大学出版社2015年版，第302页。Urs Kindhäuser, trans. Cai Guisheng, (2015) *Strafrecht Allgemeiner Teil*, Peking University Press, 302.

[41] Vgl.,E.Schmidhuser,StrafrechtAllgemeinerTeil(Lehrbuch), 2.Aufl.,J.C.B.Mohr, 1975,S.623f.

[42] Vgl.,C.Roxin, Strafrecht Allgenmeiner Teil, Band I, 4.Aufl., C.H.Beck 2006,S.85f.

[43] C.Roxin:"第二次世界大战のドイツにおける刑事政策と刑法学の发展について"，日川口浩一、葛原力三译，载《关西法学论集》第50卷(2000年)第1号。"On the development of criminal policy and criminal law studies in Germany during World War II", Kawaguchi Hirozaku & Kuzuhara Rikizo. (2000) trans., as cited in *Kansai Law Review*, Vol. 50, No. 1.

[44] For the historical development of the German theory of discontinuation of crimes,参见日野译充:《中止犯の理论构造》，成文堂2012年版，第187页以下。See Nozawa Mitsuru.(2012)

As it will be mentioned later, the path of German theory of criminal law is worthy learning for Chinese theory of criminal law. However, regarding the German theory of the justification for punishment, the specific content still seems questionable, thus it is impossible for Chinese criminal law to copy the complete theory.

Firstly, this article acknowledges that criminal punishment has a function of general positive prevention. As a matter of fact, the application of criminal punishment is conducive to enhancing the national awareness of social norms, raising the national legal awareness, promoting the concept of law-abiding and strengthening the national legal identity. Nevertheless, it is quite difficult or even impossible to decide whether the abandonment of crime has the necessity of general prevention. In other words, the argument about the need for positive general prevention is uncertain and cannot be proved empirically.[45] Even scholars who support positive general precautions believe that this theory has no empirical science base.[46] In fact, people only advocate positive general precautions on a symbolic or ideological level, and they try to avoid the empirical provability of that.[47] "A slight exaggeration is that, positive general prevention is so attractive because its effects are not proven by experience, in other precise words, it is because its effects are impossible to prove empirically. Since the positive general prevention is empirically immune, which is basically 'irrevocable' (cannot be prove wrong)."[48] In order to avoid empirical provability, judges cannot make a sentence based on positive general prevention theory, which suggests, criminal punishment is just meaningful symbolically or ideologically, lacking realistic meaning according to positive general prevention theory. In a specific case, because it is impossible to decide whether there is a positive need for general prevention, it is impossible to decide whether or not the punishment should be exempted. For example, when the perpetrator shoots at the victim with murder intent, and how can the law officers judge that there is no need for active general prevention when he can continue to fire but does not fire at all? Does this behavior "not fail the public's trust in the effectiveness of social norms"? It is difficult or even impossible to draw a proper conclusion. In this case, it is difficult to describe the establishment conditions for the abandonment of crime based on the loss of general prevention necessity.

Secondly, from the perspective of strengthening the awareness of norm, people will think that the more severe the penalty is, the more effective it may be in

---

Theoretical Structure of Voluntary Abandonment, Seibundo Publishing Co., 1–187.

[45] W.Hassemer:Generalpr vention und Strafzumessung, in:von W. Hassemer;K.Lüderssen; W.Naucke:Hauptprobleme der Generalprävention, Frankfurt am Main: Metzner 1979, S. 35f.

[46] 参见日城下裕二:《量刑基准の研究》，成文堂1995年版，第132页。

[47] G.Jakobs, Das Strafrecht Zwischen Funktioalismus und Alteuropaischem Prinzipiendenken, ZStW107(1995), S.845.

[48] 美马库斯·德克·达博:"积极的一般预防与法益理论"，杨萌译，载陈兴良主编:《刑事法评论》(第21卷)，北京大学出版社2007年版，第448页。Markus Dirk Dubber, (2007) *Positive Generalpravention und Rechtsgutsheorie: Zwei zentrale Errungenschaften der deutschen Strafrechtswissenschaft aus amerikanischer Sicht*, as cited in Chen Xingliang ed. *Criminal Law Review*, No. 21, *Peking University Press*, 448.

impressing people and strengthening the national normative consciousness. If this is the case, it will not only lead to cruel and unnecessary punishment, but also eliminate the exemption from punishment for the offender who abandon the crime. In fact, there is always a positive need for general prevention, no matter when and where it is, or whether crimes occur. Therefore, the positive general prevention theory does not provide a basis for the exemption from punishment. In other words, although positive general prevention can be one of the effects from sentencing, it is not the doctrine for sentencing,[49] thus it cannot be the basis for the exempting the offender who abandon the crime from punishment.

Thirdly, according to Professor C.Roxin's viewpoint, positive general prevention is preferred to special prevention when sentencing. Therefore, when the perpetrator has no need for special prevention, but has a positive general precautionary necessity, he should be punished and cannot be exempted from punishment. Like the negative general precaution theory, this still deems the perpetrator as a tool to achieve other benefits or purposes. In his defense of the positive general precautionary theory, Professor C.Roxin points out that "the perpetrator himself has the obligation to endure the punishment for the community within the limits of his actions... The perpetrator is a member of the community, to maintain the order of the community, he is culpable for his own actions, it is hence justified. Based on this, the perpetrator is not deemed as a means of the purpose of others, as confirmed in the status of a citizen with equal rights and equal obligations, he is culpable for sharing the fate of all people."[50] However, this argument is not that convincing because the positive general precautionary theory is largely for the sake of argumentation. Even if the offender has no need for special precautions, as long as the necessity for general prevention exists, he should be punished, which suggests that the perpetrator is deemed as a tool for general prevention. Moreover, as mentioned above, positive general prevention may always be necessary because for any crime sentencing, people are expecting to achieve the punishment's effect of learning, trust, satisfaction and confirmation. Therefore, it is necessary to impose a penalty in each crime, which makes it difficult to provide a basis for exempting the abandonment of crime from punishment.

Fourthly, if it is considered that as long as there is no need for general prevention, it is not allowed to impose penalties, even with the necessity of special precaution, it may be in conflict with the purpose of exempting the abandonment of crime.

In balance, although the theory of penalty purpose is worthy studying, there is still a doubt that the loss of necessity of the positive general precaution is the basis for exempting the abandonment of crime.

In addition, it must be noted that the law theory currently no longer prevails in the German criminal theory. This is because, compared with the attempted criminal,

---

[49] 参见日城下裕二:《量刑基准の研究》，成文堂1995年版，第129、136页See Shiroshita Yuuji.(1995) *Study on Sentencing Standards*, Seibundo Publishing Co., 129, 136.。

[50] Roxin:《刑法における责任と预防》，日宫泽浩一监译，成文堂1984年版，第35页。Roxin, trans. Miyazawa Kouichi. (1984) *Responsibility and Prevention in Criminal Law*, Seibundo Publishing Co., 35.

the wrongdoing and culpability of the abandonment of crime has not decreased; moreover, the law theory does not conform to the provisions of Article 24, Paragraph 2 of *German Criminal Law.*[51] However, as will be discussed later, in China's context, the basis for the mitigated punishment or exemption imposed on the abandonment of crimes should be compared with the offenders who complete crimes, so it is necessary to affirm the reduction of wrongdoing and culpability.

9.4 The Basic Position of this Article

As mentioned above, the Chinese criminal theory took the reference of the basis for giving the offender who abandon the crime a mitigated crime or an exemption from punishment mostly similar with the path of the Japanese doctrines (the theory of combination), yet due to obvious defects of the theory, the punishment prescribed in the current Chinese criminal law is significantly different from that of Japanese criminal law, so China needs to stop adopting the theory of Japanese criminal law.

Although the provisions on the punishment imposed on the abandonment of crime in the China's criminal law are quite different from those of Germany, the provisions on exemption from punishment for those who have not caused damage are exactly the same with the German provisions. Therefore, we can take reference from the German theory of criminal law to discuss the basis for giving the offender who abandon the crime a mitigated punishment or an exemption from punishment. However, we cannot discuss the basis in general terms, but should first focus on the basis for exempting the abandonment of crime from punishment. Additionally, Article 24 of China's criminal law on the two legal consequences of the abandonment of crime cannot be completely separated when determining the establishment conditions for two kinds of abandonment. And it is impossible to conclude that the basis for the exemption from punishment is completely different from the basis for the mitigated punishment. For example, it's not proper to consider that the voluntariness for abandonment of crime who is exempted from punishment is higher than the abandonment which was given a mitigated punishment, or to think that the requirements for abandonment of a criminal behavior of the two are different. Therefore, this article believes that the proper sequence shall be: to explain the basis for exempting the abandonment of crime from punishment firstly, then explore the reasons why the criminal who caused the damage should be given a mitigated punishment rather than exemption.

In my opinion, the purposes of criminal punishment include both general prevention and special prevention. The general prevention includes positive general prevention and negative general prevention, and the two are not antagonistic the purpose of those two is to prevent crime, while the difference lies in the emphasis on the function of the penalty, or the demonstration of different views on the

[51] Vgl.,C.Roxin,Strafrecht Allgemeiner Teil, Band II,C.H.Beck,2003,S.481f.

punishments role to prevent crime. However, for enforcing the statutory criminal punishments, the determining, sentencing, and the execution are with different focuses of negative general prevention and positive general prevention. In a specific case, to decide whether to exempt punishment is a sentencing activity. Therefore, the basis should be discussed around the purpose of sentencing.

Firstly, it is notable that the general precaution advocated by Chinese criminal theory mostly refers to negative general prevention, that is, "deterring and shackling potential criminals, preventing criminals from committing crimes by applying criminal penalties to them",[52] but the loss of the necessity of negative general prevention cannot be the basis for exempting offenders who abandon the crime from punishment. Because according to the principle of negative general prevention, in order to deterring general people, it is necessary to apply the penalty instead of exempting the penalty. The loss of the need for negative general prevention means that there are no potential criminals in society, but no one would agree with this conclusion. In this case, the loss of the necessity of negative general prevention cannot be used as a basis for exemption. Moreover, negative general prevention is mainly a statutory sentence theory with certain defects, which cannot be considered as the purpose of sentencing.[53] If the negative general prevention become the focus while sentencing, namely, punishing perpetrator severely in order to deter ordinary people, it will make the perpetrator become a tool for crime prevention, so it is not appropriate. As mentioned above, it is also impossible to view the loss of positive general precautions as a basis for exemption. In summary, the purpose of general prevention is difficult or impossible to consider while sentencing. Therefore, the loss of the necessity of general prevention cannot be used as a basis for exemption.

Secondly, since attention should be given to special prevention while sentencing and general prevention should not take priority before special prevention.[54] The lack of special prevention necessity is the basis for exemption. The relevant provisions of criminal laws in various countries require judges to consider the purpose of special prevention while sentencing. For example, Article 46 of *German Criminal Law* provides that the court should consider the criminal's background, personal and financial situation and post-crime attitudes, especially the efforts made to remedy the damage. Article 32 of the *Austrian Criminal Code* provides that the court should consider the impact of the penalties and other consequences on the future life of the perpetrator in social life. Article 248 of the *Japanese Criminal Procedure Law* provides that when deciding whether to suspend prosecution, "personality, age and circumstances of the offender, the severity and circumstances of the crime, and the

---

[52] 高铭暄、马克昌主编:《刑法学》，北京大学出版社、高等教育出版社2011年版，第224页。Gao Mingxuan & Ma Kechang eds. (2011) *Criminal Law*, Peking University Press & Higher Education Press, 224.

[53] 参见日饭岛畅:"カントト刑罚における预防の意义と应报の限界"，载《香川法学》第28卷(2008年)第2号。See Iijima Mitsuru. (2008) "The significance of prevention and the limits of retribution in Kant's theory of punishment", as cited in *Kagawa Law Review*, Vol. 28, No. 2.

[54] 参见张明楷:《责任刑与预防刑》，北京大学出版社2015年版，第328页以下。See Zhang Mingkai. (2015) *Responsibility and Prevention in Sentencing*, Peking University Press, 1–328.

attitude after the crime" should be considered. Article 48, Paragraph 1 of the revised *Japanese Criminal Law* provides that when applying the punishment, the age, character and experience of the offender, the attitude of the offender after committing the crime and other circumstances shall be taken into account, and the penalty imposed should be conducive to suppressing crime and improving criminals themselves. "The degree of punishment shall be commensurate with the crime committed and the criminal culpability to be borne by the offender" as provided in Article 5 of the *Chinese Criminal Law*, which actually requires the punishment be commensurate with the criminals' recidivism.[55] Special prevention is the future goal by the criminal law. If the perpetrator does not have the risk of recommitting, there is no need for penalty. Since the wrongdoing and culpability of the offender before the abandonment of crime are only reduced but not eliminated, the loss of the need for special prevention can only be used as a basis for exemption.

Thirdly, the basis for justification of punishment is based on the legitimacy of retribution (refers to the culpability retribution) and the rationality of the purpose of crime prevention. Therefore, the retribution punishment is culpability punishment. There may be conflicts between the punishment of culpability and the prevention of punishment. The relation between retribution and prevention is not just a matter of who's first and who's next, but how to use the advantages and overcome the defects of retribution and prevention at the same time. Therefore, the sentencing should adhere to the principle of culpability, but also to prevent crimes for the purpose. To be mentioned, the sentence cannot be used for the purpose of general prevention to make the penalty exceed the degree of culpability. Meanwhile, the purpose of special prevention should be considered within the limits of the culpable penalty. According to the theory, the courts can only consider the need for crime prevention under the culpability; if the necessity of special prevention is small, the penalty should be lightened or mitigated under the punishment of duty, such is the case with juvenile offenders[56]; if there is no necessity of special prevention, the penalty should be exempted, as in the case of the abandonment of crime.

Fourthly, we need to clarify, is the abandonment of crime is a circumstance of the culpable penalty or a circumstance of the special prevention? If it is a circumstance of the special prevention, it can be considered that the offender who attempts to commit and the offender who abandon the crime have the same wrongdoing and culpability. However, there exists the necessity of special prevention for the attempted crime, the punishment cannot be exempted, and the voluntary abandonment of crime indicates the lack of necessity of special prevention, thus punishment needs to be exempted. If it is a circumstance of the culpable penalty, it can be considered that the culpability for the abandonment of crime is lighter than the attempted crime. But it is important to note that, in this case, the

---

[55] 参见张明楷:《刑法学》，法律出版社2011年版，第492页。Zhang Mingkai. (2011) *Criminal Law*, Law Press China, 491.

[56] 参见张明楷:"责任主义与量刑原理——以点的理论为中心"，载《法学研究》2010年第5期。See Zhang Mingkai. (2010) "Doctrine of Culpability and Sentencing Theory: Centered on the Point Theory", as cited in *Chinese Journal of Law,* No. 5.

culpability is not the condition as a criminal culpability, but the culpability of sentencing.[57] The culpability of sentencing and the special prevention necessity of the offender are not in an opposite relationship, but a corresponding relationship.[58] That is to say, the heavier sentencing culpability indicates larger necessity of special prevention, and the lighter sentencing culpability means lighter special prevention. If the sentencing culpability is eliminated, there is no need for special prevention, thus punishment is exempted. From this point of view, no matter which kind of answer is adopted, that is, whether the abandonment of crime is regarded as affecting the circumstances of the culpability of sentencing or as a circumstance affecting the prevention penalty, it should be considered that the fact of the abandonment of crime means that there is no circumstance which needs special prevention for the perpetrator and a statutory sentencing cause of exemption.[59] Because the outcome of sentencing is exemption from punishment, the punishment is blocked.[60]

Anyhow, the voluntary abandonment of crime indicates that the perpetrator voluntary ally returns to the track of legitimacy without the help of others or authorities, in which special prevention thus is no longer needed, and the punishment is thus exempted. It is true that no need for special prevention may be an extremely optimistic forecast,[61] because it cannot be applied in several cases. However, since the criminal law provides for exemption from punishment, it should be considered that the criminal law presumes that there is no necessity of special prevention for offenders, and this legislative presumption does not allow for counter-evidence.[62] Because of the existence of wrongdoing and culpability of abandonment of crime, there is only a lack of special prevention, thus abandonment of crimes is not a reason to hinder the wrongdoing and culpability.

[57] For the concept of sentencing responsibility,见日川崎一夫:《体系的量刑论》，成文堂1991年版，第106页以下。See Kawasaki Kazuo.(1991) *Systematic Theory of Sentencing, Seibundo Publishing Co.*, 1–106.

[58] The responsibility for criminal establishment condition is not the opposite of the necessity of special prevention, but a corresponding relationship. For example, responsibility for intentional crime is heavier than that of negligent crime, and accordingly it can be considered that the special prevention of deliberate crime is greater than that of negligent one. Another example is that the special prevention necessity of an actor who has more reasonableness is greater than that of an actor with less reasonableness.

[59] 参见日西田典之:《刑法总论》，弘文堂2010年版，第316页。Nishida Noriyuki.(2010) *General Theory of Criminal Law*, Koubundou Publishers Inc., 316.

[60] This is also the general theory of German theory of criminal law and jurisprudence. Vgl.,C.Roxin,StrafrechtAllgemeinerTeil, Band II,C.H.Beck,2003, S.488.

[61] 参见日山中敬一:《中止未遂の研究》，成文堂2001年版，第10页。See Yamanaka, Keiichi. (2001) *Study on Discontinuation of Attempt*, Seibundō, 10.

[62] 参见日伊东研祐:"积极的特殊预防と责任非难"，载日内滕谦等编:《刑事法学の课题と展望》，成文堂1996年版，第275页。See Itou Kensuke.(1996) "Positive special prevention and blameworthiness", as cited in Naitou Ken et al., ed., *Issues and Prospects in Criminal Law Studies,* Seibundo Publishing Co., 275.

In addition, it should be noted that if only the loss of special prevention necessity is used as the basis for exemption, then the perpetrator makes a sincere effort to prevent the result from happening after completing a crime based on repentance but fails to prevent the result, under which penalty should also be exempted. However, according to the provisions of Article 24 of the *Chinese Criminal Law,* the perpetrator in this situation is still deemed as an accomplished crime instead of a abandonment of crime. Therefore, the basis for the exemption from punishment must include the reduction of wrongdoing and culpability, that is, objectively, there must be no result of the constitutive elements (no ambiguity), and subjectively, there is no *vorwerfbarkeit.* As mentioned earlier, the reduction of wrongdoing and accountability is only relative to the accomplished crime not to the attempted one.

In Japanese theory of criminal law, the reduction of the wrongdoing and the culpability is relative to the attempted crime. This is because in a broad sense, the abandonment of crime is a special case of the attempted crime, and the punishment principles are different between abandoned crime and the attempted crime because of obstacles in a narrow sense, those two criminal situations should be compared together. However, in China, the abandonment of crime is not a special case of attempted crime, so there is no need to compare those two together. Dr. Li Lizhong points out that "in China, we should discuss the basis of the punishment reduction of abandonment of crime on the basis of comparison between the attempted crime and the preparation for crime, because the sentence rationalization cannot be realized through punishment reduction directly prescribed in specific provisions of criminal law; to reasonably determine the criminal culpability of the abandonment, it must also be compared with the attempted and preparatory cases of the same type the offenders who abandoned, attempted, and prepared the crime have not produced the same result, and all three should be given lenient punishments. What degree of punishment reduction should be given so that the rationality of sentence is achieved? At this time, only a comparison with the attempted crime or preparation for crime can lead to a reasonable conclusion."[63] It is true that the offender who abandoned the crime can be compared with both accomplished one and attempted one. However, the rationality of the comparison with the accomplished one cannot be the reason for not compared with the attempted crime. First, in China, the abandonment and the attempt of crimes are two separate forms, which are criminal uncompleted forms in relation to the completion of crimes, and as mentioned above, there is no difference between the wrongdoing and the accountability of the first two forms. Therefore, when comparing the abandonment of crime with the attempted crime, it is not really comparing the wrongdoing and the culpability of the two, but only comparing the reason for the uncompleted crimes. Second, comparing the abandonment of crime with the accomplished crime means that the wrongdoing and culpability of the abandonment of crime are less than that of the accomplished crime, so it can be explicitly required that the abandonment of crime is based on the premise

[63] 李立众:"中止犯减免处罚根据及其意义"，载《法学研究》2008年第4期。Li Lizhong. (2008) "Grounds for Mitigation or Exemption of Punishment for Withdrawal from Crime and Its Significance", as cited in *Chinese Journal of Law*, No. 4.

that there is no accomplished crime. Third, in connection with above points, if only comparing the abandonment of crime with the attempted crime, the former may be taken as attempted crime, that's why the abandonment of crime is required to be based on the uncompleted crimes. The German and Japanese criminal theories are expressed in this way. For example, Professor Matsubara Yambo points out: "The grace given to abandonment of crime is limited to the punishment of the attempted crime who is the subject of abandonment. It can be said that this indicates that any abandonment of the act reduces the wrongdoing of the attempted crime."[64] Again, Professor Yoshida Minhatsu points out when criticizing the law: "even the offender abandon the crime after the establishment of the attempted crime, the attempted crime is still an attempt."[65] Professor C.Roxin observes such by criticizing the law: "Even if the offender abandon the crime later, an attempted crime is still an attempt."[66] Even if the perpetrator stops the crime after proceeding, the previous attempt still exists. But in China, such a statement is bound to cause ambiguity. Moreover, in China, even if the abandonment of crime is exempted from penalty, he is not exempted from the penalty of the attempted crime, but the penalty imposed by the specific provisions of criminal law as a model of the accomplished crime.[67]

In short, compared with the accomplished criminals, the wrongdoing and culpability of the abandonment of crimes are reduced, and only this can be the reason for reducing the punishment. Since the abandonment of crime returns to the position of legality voluntarily and it leads to the loss of the necessity of special prevention, thus he should be exempted from punishment. In this sense, this article also adopts a theory of combination, only a combination of reduction of wrongdoing, reduction of culpability and lack of special prevention (the theory of sentencing purpose).[68]

Then, why does the punishment of the abandonment of crime causing damage be reduced instead of being exempted? In my view, the reason is that the behavior before the abandonment constitutes another accomplishment of misdemeanor, for which the punishment is made. In case of the accomplishment of misdemeanor, there is no basis for exemption.

The author once pointed out that the "damage caused" in the abandonment of crime bears the following characteristics: First, "damage" is limited to the damaging result caused by the act excluding the danger caused by the act; second, "damage" must be the result of the violation prohibited by the criminal law provisions; third, "damage" is not limited to material results, but also includes non-material

---

[64] 日松原芳博:《刑法总论》，日本评论社2013年版，第319页。See Matsubara Yoshihiro. (2013) *General Theory of Criminal Law*, NIPPON HYORON SHA Co., 319.

[65] 日吉田敏雄:《未遂犯と中止犯》，成文堂2014年版，第133页。See Yoshida Toshio. (2014) *Attempted Crimes and Voluntary Abandonment,* Seibundo Publishing Co., 133.

[66] C.Roxin,StrafrechtAllgemeinerTeil, Band II,C.H.Beck,2003,S.481.

[67] Of course, this article does not object to comparing discontinued offenders with attempted crimes, but only that such comparisons lacks practical significance.

[68] If it is considered that the discontinued offender must not complete the crime as the attempted crime only after comparing it with the attempted crime, then it is regarded that this article only adopts the sentencing purpose theory.

results; fourth, "damage" is limited to damage caused to others, and does not include damage to oneself; fifth, "damage" must be a result of subjective attribution, excluding the results of accidents. Based on the above, it can be concluded that only when the behavior meets the conditions for the establishment of the abandonment of a certain felony, and at the same time it constitutes an accomplishment of a misdemeanor, can it be considered as "damage caused" in the abandonment of crime. For example, the abandonment of rape has constituted the accomplishment of the crime of compulsory defamation of women, the abandonment of intentional homicide has already constituted the accomplishment of intentional assault, the abandonment of burglary has already constituted the accomplishment of the crime of illegal trespassing, the abandonment of crime of extortion has constituted the accomplishment of the crime of fabricating false terrorism; and so on.[69]

Article 24, Paragraph 2 of *Chinese Criminal Law* indicates that the offender who is given a mitigated punishment or be exempted is abandonment of crime. According to this, "damage caused" should be the act of the abandonment of crime. However, the act of abandonment is not a criminal act, and the act before the abandonment is a criminal act that constitutes conformity of elements of crime, wrongdoing and culpability. Therefore, "damage caused" should exclude the behavior of abandonment. In this case, it can be argued that the abandonment of crime who caused damage is given a mitigated punishment instead of being exempted because the previous act has formed a criminal offense.

As mentioned earlier, *German Criminal Law* only provides for a legal consequence of the abandonment of crime, which is exemption from punishment. If the abandonment of crime of intentional homicide is also exempted from punishment, it will inevitably lead to an imbalance in the sentence. Therefore, the general theory of Germany criminal law and the practice of trial practice is that when the abandonment of the felony constitutes the accomplishment of the misdemeanor, it is the concurrence of the abandonment of the felony and the accomplishment of the misdemeanor. It may be imagined concurrence or the concurrence of law articles, but they are all convicted and sentenced as accomplished misdemeanors.[70]

Similar to *German Criminal Law*, Article 16 of the *1960 Soviet Criminal Code* provides: "A person who voluntarily abandon the crime is criminally culpable only if the act he has committed actually contains other criminal constitutions." That is, if the person who voluntarily abandon the crime without committing other crimes, he or she will be exempted from punishment. "So, preparatory acts and attempted acts only have culpability when they manifest as acts that infringe upon other objects and constitute an independent, defamatory crime. For example, in most cases, people who voluntarily abandon the rape of underage women are culpable for defamation, that is, they are culpable for the actual implementation of socially harmful acts (special provisions are made by law, by Article 120 of the *Criminal Code)* instead

[69] 参见张明楷:"中止犯中的'造成损害'"，载《中国法学》2013年第5期。See Zhang Mingkai. (2013) "'Infliction of Harm' in Withdrawal from Crime", as cited in *China Legal Science*, No. 5.

[70] Vgl.,H.Jescheck/T.Weigend,Lehrbuch des Strafrechts.Allgemeiner Teil, 5.Aufl., Duncker & Humblot,1996, S.549.

of being culpable for the attempted rape. The Soviet Supreme Court and the Soviet Supreme Court have repeatedly pointed this out."[71] It is obvious that the Soviet theory of criminal law actually affirmed the concurrence between the abandonment of the felony and the accomplishment of the misdemeanor, and then the offender would be convicted as the accomplishment of misdemeanor. The reason for this is also because the offenders who abandon the crime have not committed a misdemeanor are exempted from punishment. The provisions of Article 56 of the *Italian Criminal Law* on voluntary abandonment of crimes are the same as those of the Soviet-Russian criminal law. Therefore, Italian scholars also points out: "abandonment of crime voluntarily eliminates the *Strafbarkeit* of unfinished crimes, but if the acts that have been committed can constitute other crimes alone, the actor shall bear the corresponding criminal culpability (for example, renunciation of the theft after entering the residence of another person, and the actor shall still be punished according to the infringement of the residence as provided in Article 641, Paragraph 1 of the *Criminal Code*)."[72]

However, Chinese theory of criminal law and judicial practice have not adopted the practices similar to that of Germany, the Soviet Union and Italy, because the Paragraph 2 of Article 24 of *Chinese Criminal Law* clearly provides the punishment for the abandonment of crime which caused damage. If practices in German, Soviet Union and Italy are adopted, and the conviction of a minor offence is convicted and sentenced when the act before the suspension constitutes a misdemeanor, the provisions of Paragraph 2 of Article 24 of *Chinese Criminal Law* will become meaningless. And this is not in line with the basic requirements of the liberal arts explanation. In other words, the purpose provided in the Paragraph 2 of Article 24 of *Chinese Criminal Law* denies the practice that a abandoned felony with damages is convicted and sentenced as an accomplished misdemeanor.

However, this is only a difference in form. The truth of those two practices is bearing criminal culpability for the misdemeanor caused by the criminal act before the abandonment. In Germany, the Soviet Union and Italy, this case is directly convicted and sentenced according to the accomplishment of misdemeanor, but in China, the same case would be convicted a abandoned felony, and the mitigating punishment imposed is generally equivalent to the sentencing of the accomplishment of the misdemeanor. For example, if an offender abandon the homicide act after a serious injury caused, he shall be changed to not less than 3 years but not more than 10 years, which is the statutory penalty of intentional serious injury. For another example, if the victimized woman is threatened by a trespasser violently after his trespassing, and then the rape is abandoned, he shall be given a mitigated punishment which is equivalent to the punishment for the crime of trespass.

[71] 苏联别利亚耶夫、科瓦廖夫主编:《苏维埃刑法总论》，马改秀、张广贤译，群众出版社1987年版，第215页。Н.А. Беляев & М.И. Ковалёв eds., trans. Ma Gaixiu, Zhang Guangxian, (1987) *Общая часть советского уголовного права*, Qunzhong Publishing House, 215.

[72] 意杜里奥·帕多瓦尼:《刑法利刑法原理》(注评版)，陈忠林译评，中国人民大学出版社2004年版，第277页。See Yamanaka, Keiichi. (2001) *Study on Discontinuation of Attempt*, Seibundō, 227.

Of course, due to the complexity of the statutory penalty, the circumstances of mitigating punishments provided in Article 24 of *Chinese Criminal Law* may not completely correspond to the punishment of the accomplice. However, since the "damage caused" in the abandonment of crime actually refers to the another accomplished misdemeanor, the sentence imposed on the offender who abandon the crime must be restricted by the provisions of Article 63 of *Chinese Criminal Law* and coordinate with the statutory punishment and sentencing practice of misdemeanor, that is, it should not exceed the statutory penalty of misdemeanor. For example, if a minor injury is caused by the abandoned intentional homicide, the offender shall be given a statutory punishment for minor injuries (a fixed-term imprisonment of not more than 3 years, criminal detention or public surveillance). However, due to the restrictions imposed by Article 63 of *Chinese Criminal Law* on the mitigation of penalties, the criminal shall be sentenced to a punishment less than the prescribed punishment (the fixed-term imprisonment of not less than 3 years but not more than 10 years). Therefore, the fixed-term imprisonment of 3 years or probation shall be appropriate; if a heavier sentence is imposed, it is obviously difficult to achieve balance between crime and punishment. This should also be the case if the offender who abandon burglary or gun robbery after causing minor injuries, or the offender voluntarily abandon a public rape of a woman in a public place after causing minor injuries.[73]

To sum up, the reason why abandonment of crimes who caused no damage from punishment are exempted is the reduction of wrongdoing and culpability and the non-necessity of special prevention; the reason of mitigating the punishment of the offender who abandoned the crime caused no damages lies in the accomplished misdemeanor constituted by the act before abandonment, thus it cannot be exempted from punishment. As is well known, "voluntariness" is the key to distinguish between abandonment of crime and attempted crime. According to the viewpoint of this article, the substantive basis of "there is no need for special prevention" can be used as a guide to judge whether the perpetrator meets the conditions of "voluntariness".

References

Dandou Shigemitsu. (1990) *General Outline of Criminal Law*, Kodansha Publishing Co, 361.

Fukuda Taira. (2001) *General Theory of Criminal Law (Full Edition)*, Yuhikaku Press, 228;

G. Jakobs, Das Strafrecht Zwischen Funktioalismus und Alteuropaischem Prinzipiendenken,

Gao Mingxuan & Ma Kechang eds. (2011) Criminal Law, Peking University Press & Higher Education Press, 158-159, 224.

Giinter Stratenwerth & Lothar Kuhlen, trans. Yang Meng, (2006) *Strafrecht Allgemeiner Teil I: Die Straftat*, Law Press, 283.

[73] 参见张明楷:"中止犯中的'造成损害'"，载《中国法学》2013年第5期。See Zhang Mingkai. (2013) "'Infliction of Harm' in Withdrawal from Crime", as cited in *China Legal Science*, No. 5.

Н.А. Беляев & М.И. Ковалёв eds., trans. Ma Gaixiu, Zhang Guangxian, (1987) *Общая часть советского уголовного права*, Qunzhong Publishing House, 215.
Ida Makoto. (2008) Handout of Criminal Law·General Rules, Yuhikaku Press, 422
Kagawa Tatsuo. (1963) *The legal nature of voluntary abandonment,* Yuhikaku Press, 40-41, 97.
Kawaguchi Hirozaku & Kuzuhara Rikizo. (2000) trans., as cited in *Kansai Law Review*, Vol. 50, No. 1.
Li Lizhong. (2008) "Grounds for Mitigation or Exemption of Punishment for Withdrawal from Crime and Its Significance", as cited in *Chinese Journal of Law*, No. 4.
Maeda Masahide. (2011) *Handouts of General Rules of Criminal Law,* University of Tokyo Press, 168.
Markus Dirk Dubber, (2007) *Positive Generalpravention und Rechtsgutsheorie: Zwei zentrale Errungenschaften der deutschen Strafrechtswissenschaft aus amerikanischer Sicht*, as cited in Chen Xingliang ed. *Criminal Law Review*, No. 21, *Peking University Press*, 448.
Nishida Noriyuki. (2010) *General Theory of Criminal Law*, Koubundou Publishers Inc., 314-316.
Nishihara Haruo. (1987) *General Theory of Criminal Law*, Seibundo Publishing Co., 287;
Ohya Minoru. (2012) *Handouts of General Theory of Criminal Law(New Edition)*, Seibundo Publishing Co., 384.
Roxin, trans. Miyazawa Kouichi. (1984) *Responsibility and Prevention in Criminal Law*, Seibundo Publishing Co., 35.
Roxin, Strafrecht Allgemeiner Teil, Band II, C.H. Beck, 2003, S.481.
See Aoyagi Fumio. (1978) *General theory of criminal law I,* Senbundo Publishing Co., 337.
See Chen Xingliang. (2007) *Lectures on Criminal Law*, Renmin University of China Press, 304
See Hirano Ryuuichi. (1975) General Theory of Criminal Law II, Yuhikaku Press, 333;
See Iijima Mitsuru. (2008) "The significance of prevention and the limits of retribution in Kant's theory of punishment", as cited in *Kagawa Law Review*, Vol. 28, No. 2.
See Itou Kensuke. (1996) "Positive special prevention and blameworthiness", as cited in Naitou Ken et al, ed., *Issues and Prospects in Criminal Law Studies,* Seibundo Publishing Co., 275.
See Kawasaki Kazuo. (1991) *Systematic Theory of Sentencing,* Seibundo Publishing Co., 1-106.
See Li Hong. (2012) *Criminal Law*, Law Press China, 253;
See Machida Yukio. (2005) *Theory of voluntary abandonment,* Gendaijinbun-sha, 1-47.
See Maeda Masahide. (2006) Handouts of General Rules of Criminal Law (4th Edition), University of Tokyo Press, 167;
See Matsubara Yoshihiro. (2013a) General Theory of Criminal Law, NIPPON HYORON SHA Co., 316.
See Matsubara Yoshihiro. (2013b) *General Theory of Criminal Law*, NIPPON HYORON SHA Co., 319
See Nomura Minoru. (1979) *Study on Attempted Crimes,* Seibundo Publishing Co., 119.
See Nozawa Mitsuru. (2012) *Theoretical Structure of Voluntary Abandonment*, Seibundo Publishing Co., 1-187.
See Shiroshita Yuuji. (1995) Study on Sentencing Standards, Seibundo Publishing Co., 129–136.
See Yamanaka, Keiichi. (2001) *Study on Discontinuation of Attempt*, Seibundō,10,227.
See Sone Takehiko. (2008) *General Theory of Criminal Law*, Seibundo Publishing Co., 227-228.
See Yoshida Toshio. (2014) *Attempted Crimes and Voluntary Abandonment,* Seibundo Publishing Co., 133, 136.
See Zhang Mingkai. (1997) *Inchoate Offenses: A Comparative Study,* China Law Press & Seibundo Publishing Co., 1-332.
See Zhang Mingkai. (2010) "Doctrine of Culpability and Sentencing Theory: Centered on the Point Theory", as cited in *Chinese Journal of Law*, No. 5.
See Zhang Mingkai. (2013) "'Infliction of Harm' in Withdrawal from Crime", as cited in *China Legal Science*, No. 5.
See Zhang Mingkai. (2015a) *Responsibility and Prevention in Sentencing*, Peking University Press, 1-275
See Zhang Mingkai. (2015b) *Responsibility and Prevention in Sentencing*, Peking University Press

Sone Takehiko. (2005) Important Issues of Criminal Law General Theory (General Theory), Seibundo Publishing Co., 276

Urs Kindhäuser, trans. Cai Guisheng, (2015) *Strafrecht Allgemeiner Teil*, Peking University Press, 302.

Vgl.,C. Roxin, *Strafrecht Allgenmeiner Teil,* Band I, 4.Aufl., C.H.Beck 2006, S.85f,481f,481ff,482,478,488.

Vgl.,E.Schmidhuser,StrafrechtAllgemeinerTeil(Lehrbuch), 2.Aufl.,J.C.B.Mohr, 1975,S.623f.

Vgl.,H.Jescheck/T.Weigend, Lehrbuch des Strafrechts.Allgemeiner Teil, 5.Aufl., Duncker & Humblot, 1996, S.549.

Vgl.,K.Ulsenheimer, Grundfragen des RücktrittsvomVersuch in Theorie und Praxis, DeGruyter 1976,S.94ff.

Vgl.,Lang-Hinrichsen, Bemerkungen zum Begriff der “Tat” im Strafrecht,in:Festschrift für Engisch, Frankfurt am Main, 1969, S.370ff.

W.Hassemer: Generalpr vention und Strafzumessung, in:von W. Hassemer;K.Lüderssen;

W.Naucke: Hauptprobleme der Generalprävention, Frankfurt am Main: Metzner 1979, S. 35f.

Wang Zhaowu. (2013) “On the Nature of Withdrawal from Attempted Crime and Its Restricting Effect on Constitutive Requirements”, as cited in *Tsinghua* University Law Journal, No. 5.

Xie Wangyuan. (2012) “On the Grounds for Mitigation or Exemption of Punishment for Withdrawal from Crime”, as cited in *Journal of the East China University of Political Science and Law*, No. 2.

Yamaguchi Atsushi. (2007) General Rules of Criminal Law, Yuhikaku Press, 278;

Zhang Mingkai. (2011) *Criminal Law*, Law Press China, 338, 491.

Zhou Guangquan. (2011) *General Part of Criminal Law*, China Renmin University of Press, 196.

ZStW107, S.845.

Chapter 10
The Identification of Joint Crime

In theory of criminal law, joint crime is arguably the most complex issue. And because joint crime is a frequent phenomenon, how to identify joint crime is an important topic in both theoretical and practical aspects.

10.1 Defects of Traditional Methods

According to China's traditional theory of criminal law, three conditions must be met to establish a joint crime. First, "the subject of a joint crime must be two or more persons who have reached the age and criminal capacity for culpability, or units". Second, "to constitute a joint crime, more than two persons must have a common criminal act" and "the act committed by each actor must be a criminal act, otherwise it cannot constitute a joint crime". Third, "more than two persons must have a common criminal intent to constitute a joint crime".[1] Obviously, the traditional method for identifying joint crime is to determine the conditions for the establishment of joint crime uniformly without distinguishing between different forms of joint crime. If the conditions for the establishment of joint crime are met, it is

*The original title is "The Identification of Joint Crime", published in ***Chinese Journal of Law***, 2014, Vol. 3.

[1] 高铭暄、马克昌主编:《刑法学》，北京大学出版社、高等教育出版社2011年版，第163~165页。Gao Mingxuan & Ma Kechang eds. (2011) Criminal Law, Peking University Press & Higher Education Press, 163–165.

M. Zhang, *The Fundamental Issues upon Criminal Law Theories*, Masterpieces of Contemporary Jurisprudents in China,
https://doi.org/10.1007/978-981-95-1276-8_10

recognized as a joint crime, and a participant in a joint crime is an accomplice.[2] This method has three basic features: (a) it does not distinguish between wrongdoing and culpability, and it is mixed to identify whether joint crime is established. Of the three conditions mentioned above, the first is basically a condition of culpability, the second is a condition of wrongdoing and the third is again a condition of culpability[3]; (b) it does not distinguish between perpetrator and accomplice in a narrow sense, and the identification of whether joint crime is established on the whole. The three conditions discussed above are whether two or more persons can establish a joint crime, rather than discussing whose acts are established as accomplice in a narrow sense (abettor and aider) after the perpetrator determined; c) it only identifies whether the accomplice committed a common criminal act, without separately examining whether there is causality between the acts of accomplice and the following results,[4] it abstractly identifies whether the joint crime is established.

10.1.1 Defects of Mixed Identification of Joint Crime

The mixed identification of joint crime is manifested in the simultaneous identification of joint crime at the levels of wrongdoing and culpability, and the culpability is judged first, followed by the wrongdoing. This method has obvious defects.

10.1.1.1 A. It Is Not Conducive to Dealing with Cases wWhere the Persons Who Are Not Culpable Involved in Joint Crime

Example 1 When 15-year-old A burglarized a home and asked 17-year-old B to look out. With the help of B, A successfully stole 20,000 Yuan in cash from C. According to the general theory, because A has not reached the age for criminal culpability, so A and B do not form a joint crime, and B cannot be punished in the accomplice. However, this conclusion cannot be accepted. If B lookout for the

[2]As is well known, the term "complicity" has different meanings, sometimes it's used in a broad sense, while sometimes in a narrow sense; occasionally, it may place emphasis on either on the act or on the actor. I reckon the audience can also find and understand different connotations in this article, Since this paper here tries to address some long-existed ideas, it's inevitable to use the term or concept such as "complicity" or "joint crime", though which at times I advocate should be paid less emphasis to.

[3]According to the view of the *Handlungsunwert*, the third condition is subjective element of the wrongdoing.

[4]It is true that the general theory holds that there is causality between the joint criminal acts and harmful consequence. However, it emphasizes that there is a causality between the joint criminal acts as the organic whole and harmful consequence.(参见高铭暄、马克昌主编:《刑法学》，北京大学出版社、高等教育出版社2011年版，第164页Gao Mingxuan & Ma Kechang eds. (2011) Criminal Law, Peking University Press & Higher Education Press, 164)Moreover, the general theory states the causality in the sense of determining the ending, that is, as long as two or more persons have joint act and joint intent, the acts of all participants have a causality with the harmful consequence.

18-year-old larcenist, the accomplice of the theft shall be established certainly. Since this is the case, the lookout for 15-year-old larcenist more should be considered a crime. Perhaps some people think that B can be directly treated as an individual commits theft. However, for one thing, it is impossible to punish B as a direct perpetrator because B did not directly commit the act of transferring the property in C's possession to himself or to a third party, and the act of lookout simply does not meet the conditions of a direct perpetrator of theft. For another thing, it is also impossible to punish B as an indirect perpetrator, because only a person who controls or dominates the realization of the constitutive elements as a wire-puller is an indirect perpetrator.[5] B's act that being invited to lookout cannot be established as an indirect perpetrator. This shows that the traditional method is not conducive to the identification of accomplice. Exactly the same problem exists when the person who directly commits the act meets the constitutive elements lacks the elements of culpability such as the criminal capacity, the possibility of cognition of wrongdoing, reasonableness and so on.

10.1.1.2 B. It Is Not Conducive to Dealing with the Cases Where Others Participate in the Unpunishable Afterwards Act of the Offense in Essence

Example 2 The actor of the offense in essence A needs special tools to separate the booty in order to conceal after stolen massive booty, B knew the truth but provided special tools to A, and A divided and concealed booty by these special tools. Whether the act of B belong to the booty crime? According to the traditional view, the actor of the offense in essence cannot become the subject of the booty crime, therefore, B and A does not constitute a joint crime. B's act is also not the perpetrating act of the booty crime which shall not establish the booty crime. However, this conclusion is difficult to be accepted (see the second part of this article).

It is easy to see that an important reason why the traditional method of identifying joint crime is difficult to deal with the above cases is that it fails to distinguish the entity of crime into wrongdoing and culpability, and fails to recognize joint crime as a form of wrongdoing, thus leading to the identification of culpability in the foreground. However, culpability is *Vorwerfbarkeit* of wrongdoing, not a mere mental state, nor a mere will to act or an action plan. Only after the wrongdoing is established can the presence or absence of culpability be judged, and not the other way around.

[5]Vgl.,C.Roxin, *Strafrecht Allgenmeiner Teil, Band II,* C.H.Beck 2003,S.22f; 日西田典之:《刑法总论》，弘文堂2010年版，第328页。Nishida Noriyuki.(2010) *General Theory of Criminal Law*, Koubundou Publishers Inc., 328.

10.1.2 Defects of Integrated Identification of Joint Crime

The integrated identification of joint crime is to determine whether the acts of two or more persons as a whole constitute joint crime, and to determine the nature of joint crime. After concluding that joint crime is established, each accomplice shall be convicted according to the crime, and then the accomplice's role in the joint crime is considered for sentencing. There are many problems with this method.

10.1.2.1 A. Difficult to Identify the "Joint" Criminal Act

In some cases of joint perpetrators (e.g., where all participants are armed with a murder weapon to injury a victim), it is generally easy to determine the existence of a joint criminal act by the participants. However, when the accomplices participate in the crime by abetting or aiding, it is difficult to determine whether there is a joint criminal act. Because "joint" contains the same meaning, the identification of the crime is always from the factual identification to the normative evaluation. If a joint act is denied at the factual stage, the accomplice cannot be recognized in any case. The act of perpetrator is the act that meets the basic elements of the specific provisions, while the abetting and the aiding are not. Especially the aiding, which is obviously different from the act of perpetrator because of the lack of stereotype, at the same time, seemingly every day acts of life may also be established as aiding. Therefore, it is difficult to determine that the aiding is the same as the act of perpetrators.

Example 3 After getting into a cab driven by B, A found that the woman C was carrying a bag in front and asked B to drive close to C. B knew A's intent and still drove close to C. A seized C's bag and asked B to speed up, B immediately speed up and send A to the destination. In this case, it is difficult to consider that B and A have a "joint criminal act". The reason is that when the act of A is judged in isolation, it is impossible to conclude that B has committed a "criminal act", and may even think that B performed a legitimate business practice. In fact, the traditional method of identifying is a circular argument. In other words, it is only after affirming that B is accomplice that B's act is said to be criminal. However, on what grounds is it certain that B is in accomplice? It has to be said that B had committed a criminal act. Obviously, such a circular argument is deficient in persuasiveness.

10.1.2.2 B. Difficult to Identify the "Joint" Intent

Example 4 A proposed to B to "teach" C, B agreed and cooperated with A to commit violence against C jointly, then causing the death of C. Afterwards, it was found that A had the murder intent and B only had injury intent.. The general theory states that "if the content of intent is different, it deviates from the 'joint' intent of the joint crime, and therefore the joint crime cannot establish. For example, if one person's intent is based on injury and the other person's intent is based on murder, even if the same object is committed successively or at the same time, it cannot be regarded as a joint crime and can only be treated separately according to respective crimes and acts."[6] However, if the case is not considered as a joint crime, and it is not possible to identify whose acts directly caused the death of the victim, it can only be identified that the attempted intentional homicide and attempted intentional injury are constituted separately. But this conclusion is inappropriate and not in line with the legislative intent of joint crime (see the second part of this article). If the joint crime is denied and forcibly let A and B be culpable for the death, the principle of *"in dubio, pro reo"* will be violated. Conversely, only when A and B are recognized as joint perpetrators, can the case be properly handled, and the general theory obviously does not provide the basis for handling similar cases. In fact, the person who participates in a specific crime may have the same intent or different intents. Requiring the same intentional content will inevitably make it difficult for many cases to be handled properly.

Besides that, the general theory is paradoxical. For example, the general theory indicates that "the cognition content of the joint crime includes… joint criminals recognize that they and others cooperate with each other to jointly commit the crime" At the same time, in the case of unilateral aiding, "Since they help others to commit crimes, they should be treated as secondary offender in comparison."[7] However, in the case of unilateral aiding, the aider proactively cooperates with the perpetrator while the perpetrator does not cooperate with the aider, therefore, it does not meet the constitutive elements of "cooperate with each other".

10.1.2.3 C. Difficult to Identify the Accomplice in the Status Crime

Example 5 Ordinary citizen B instigates cashier A in state-owned companies to expropriate cash in a safety box. Late one night, A and B arrived at the scene and B opened the iron gate of the accounting office. A opened the safety box with the key owned by himself and took away 100,000 Yuan in cash. Joint intent and joint acts of more than two persons are needed in traditional methods, therefore, when two persons are involved in the status crime and only one of them has a status, the character of the acts of the person with the criminal status will be different from the person without the criminal status, which will cause difficulties of identification. Because of this, the issue that was discussed in theory of criminal law and judicial practice is that how to identify the character of joint crime in the case like Example 5. The judicial interpretation is that the character in the joint crime should be identified in

---

6 王作富主编:《刑法》，中国人民大学出版社2009年版，第138页。Wang Zuofu. ed. (2009) *Criminal Law*, China Renmin University of Press, 138.

7 高铭暄、马克昌主编:《刑法学》，北京大学出版社、高等教育出版社2011年版，第165~166页。Gao Mingxuan & Ma Kechang eds. (2011) *Criminal Law*, Peking University Press & Higher Education Press, 165~166.

accordance with the basic characteristics of the crime of the principal offender.[8] But there are obvious flaws in this view. First of all, in China, the size of the role played by the actor in the joint crime is only the basis for sentencing, not for conviction. The judicial interpretation leads to the identification of the sentencing circumstances first and then the nature of the crime. Moreover, if both the person without the criminal status and the person with the criminal status play the same major role in the joint crime, it is impossible to determine the crime. In Example 5, it is difficult to consider that there is a clear difference between the roles of the two. Although the theory of criminal law holds that the nature of the joint crime should be determined by the nature of the perpetrator's act, this integrated method implies that the person without the criminal status must be guilty of the same crime as the person with the criminal status, and its conclusion is clearly improper (see the second and the third part of this article).

10.1.2.4 D. Difficult to Implement the Theory of Derivativeness of Accomplice

"It is widely accepted that the basis of punishment for the accomplice, like that of the perpetrator, lies in the danger of causing the infringement of legal interest. If the basis of punishment for the accomplice is the same as that of the perpetrator, then the answer to the question of at what stage the accomplice can be punished as the criminal attempt should be essentially the same as the answer to the perpetrator."[9] As discussed later, the reason for punishing the accomplice is that the accomplice participates in causing the infringement of the legal interests by prompting or aiding the perpetrator to commit the perpetrating act. Therefore, it is only logical to treat the perpetrating act committed by the perpetrator as the condition for punishing the accomplice.[10] In other words, the abettor or aider can only be punished if the perpetrator proceeds to commit a crime that places the legal interest in imminent danger. This is precisely the conclusion of the theory of the derivativeness of accomplice. The theory of the derivativeness of accomplice is to uphold the doctrine of *nulla poena sine lege*, to maintain the function of the constitutive elements, and to clarify the boundaries of the punishment of the accomplice, so as to "avoid

---

[8] 参见最高人民法院、最高人民检察院1985年7月8日《关于当前办理经济犯罪案件中具体应用法律的若干问题的解答(试行)》;最高人民法院2000年6月30日《关于审理贪污、职务侵占案件如何认定共同犯罪几个问题的解释》。See Supreme People's Court and Supreme People's Procuratorate, Answers to *Several Questions Concerning the Specific Application of Law in Handling Current Economic Crime Cases (for Trial Implementation)* (Jul. 8, 1985); Supreme People's Court, *Interpretation on Issues Concerning the Determination of Joint Crimes in Adjudicating Embezzlement and Misappropriation of Office Cases* (Jun. 30, 2000).

[9] 日佐伯仁志:"教唆の未遂",载日阿部纯二等编:《刑法基本讲座》(第4卷),法学书院1992年版,第209页。Saeki Hitoshi.(1992) "Attempted instigation", as cited in Abe Junji et al.,ed., *Basic Lectures on Criminal Law (Vol. 4)*, Hogaku Shoin, 209.

[10] 参见日平野龙一:《刑法总论II》,有斐阁1975年版,第347页以下。See Hirano Ryuuichi. (1975) General Theory of Criminal Law II, Yuhikaku Press, 1–347.

the criminal law from considering all acts with causality as the accomplice in a narrow sense, thus causing the excessive proliferation of the boundaries of criminal law and seriously undermining the stability of the law".[11] Adhering to the theory of the derivativeness of accomplice is conducive to preventing improper punishment. In fact, when the instigator merely says "kill someone", even if the other party fully acquiesces, there is no need to punish the instigator.[12] This is because when the instigated person does not commit an act that threatens the interests of the law, even if the instigator is not punished, the smooth life of the nation can be ensured. Similarly, when B provides a knife to A, but A does not use the knife to commit a crime, B should not be punished for the crime. Otherwise, many legitimate acts would be suspected by the judicial authorities, thus infringing the freedom of the nationals. The theory of the derivativeness of accomplice also finds its legal basis in the provisions of the specific provisions of *Chinese Criminal Law* concerning treat the accomplice as perpetrator.[13] However, the integrated identification of joint crime means that it is not a matter of judging who is the perpetrator first, but rather who is jointly criminal with whom as a whole, which makes it impossible to implement the principle of the derivativeness of accomplice. The judicial authorities in China often try joint criminal cases in separate cases and try the aider first, and then use the establishment of the aider as the basis for determining the perpetrator. This approach, which puts the cart before the horse, is not premised on the derivativeness of accomplice and is prone to result in wrongful convictions.

It is easy to see that the traditional method of identification is flawed because it does not identify joint crime in terms of the perpetrator.[14] The idea of integrated identifying joint crime leads to people thinking about, asking and answering questions that do not make sense, which in turn affects the identification of the act of the participants. For example, when someone says that A and B constitute a joint crime, the other party may generally ask, "What kind of joint crime does A and B constitute?" or, "What is the nature of the joint crime of A and B?" In fact, not only are these types of questions meaningless, but they can lead to difficulties in obtaining a conviction.

---

[11] 何庆仁:"我国刑法中教唆犯的两种涵义"，载《法学研究》2004年第4期。He Qingren. (2004) "The Two Implications of Instigator in China's Criminal Law," as cited in *Chinese Journal of Law*, No. 4.

[12] 参见日前田雅英:《刑法总论讲义》，东京大学出版会2011年版，第464页。Maeda Masahide.(2011) *Handouts of General Rules of Criminal Law*, University of Tokyo Press, 464.

[13] 参见周光权:"'被教唆的人没有犯被教唆的罪'之理解"，载《法学研究》2013年第4期。See Zhou Guangquan. (2013) Understanding of 'The Instigated Person Did Not Commit the Crime Instigated', as cited in *Chinese Journal of Law*, No. 4.

[14] As described in the dominant ideology, "The so-called joint criminal acts means that the acts of all actors point to the same crime, connect with each other, and cooperate with each other to form a unified criminal activity as a whole."(高铭暄、马克昌主编:《刑法学》，北京大学出版社、高等教育出版社2011年版，第163页Gao Mingxuan & Ma Kechang eds. (2011) Criminal Law, Peking University Press & Higher Education Press, 163.).

Example 6 A, B and C (female) conspire to extort property, by C pretending to prostitute seduce the victim, A, B immediately to the scene, C quickly left, A and B to extort property from the victim. After the victim realized the truth, A and B used violence to rob the victim's property. The answer of the question "A, B, C constitute what joint crime?" is that neither the answer constitutes the joint crime of robbery nor the answer constitutes the joint crime of extortion.

10.1.3 Defects of Abstract Identification of Joint Crime

The traditional method of abstract identifying whether a participant committed the so-called criminal act, without specifically examining whether there is causality between the act and the result, either improperly expands the scope of the accomplice or improperly expands the scope of accomplished crime.

10.1.3.1 A. Improperly Expanding the Range of Punishment for the Accomplice

Example 7 A sneaked into C's house to steal, just when B found. B knew that A would burglarize, so he took the initiative to look out for A's theft, but A did not know about it, and B's lookout did not objectively play a role in A's theft. According to the traditional method of identification, B implemented the act of aiding with the criminal intent, so the accomplice of theft shall be established for him. However, in Example 7, there is a lack of physical causality and psychological causality between B's act and A's theft of other's property, and in fact there is no promotion of A's theft. There is no basis for treating A in the accomplice of the theft.

10.1.3.2 B. Improperly Expanding the Range of Punishment for Accomplished Crime

The improper extension of punishment for accomplished crime is manifested in two situations: first the failure to adequately consider whether there is causality between the act of the accomplice and the result of the perpetrator, and second, the failure to adequately consider the circumstances that withdrawing from the accomplice.

Example 8 A intended to steal another person's car and B provided the keys used to steal the car, but A was unable to open the door when using the keys. A then stole the car by other means. According to the traditional method, B and A have joint intent and joint act of theft, so the accomplice of theft shall be established, and B bears criminal culpability for the results of the theft.[15] However, although B aided A in the theft, there is neither physical nor psychological causality between his act of aiding and the result of A's accomplished theft. Therefore, it is obviously improper for B to bear the criminal culpability for the accomplished theft.

Example 9 "A, B conspired to kill C, agreed to go to C's house the next day to jointly kill C. A went to C's house as scheduled, and B did not go, A killed C by himself." The general theory points out that "The conspiracy… is a joint criminal preparation, conspirator without carrying out the perpetrating act undoubtedly also have the objective and subjective elements required to establish a joint crime… The killing by A and the participation of B in the conspiracy to kill is inseparable, B should also be culpable for accomplished homicide."[16] Obviously, the general theory is that conspiracy is a preparatory act, therefore, the argument that B should be liable for accomplished homicide is based on the fact that it is a criminal act.. However, a preparatory act of homicide cannot result in death. So, in Example 9, it must be discussed whether B is withdrawing from the accomplice, which means, it must be examined whether there is physical or psychological causality between B's prior conspiracy with A and the result of C's death, but the general doctrine does not do so.

It is easy to see that the reason why the traditional method of identifying joint crime fails to reach the correct conclusion in Examples 7 and 8, and also makes it difficult to draw proper conclusions and give proper reasons for the different situations in Example 9,[17] is because it only abstractly identifies the range of the establishment of joint crime without specifically examining the causality between the acts of each accomplice and the results.

In response to the above-mentioned defects of the traditional method, and according to the characteristics of joint crime, this article proposes the basic method of identifying joint crime with wrongdoing as the focus, perpetrator as the center, and oriented by causality.

---

[15] For example, the dominant ideology pointed out that the entire crime is completed and the crime is accomplished as long as any act of the perpetrators committed by the entire organism that commits crimes directly commits the crime, and all the criminals must be responsible for the accomplished crime."[高铭暄主编:《刑法专论》(上编)，高等教育出版社2002年版，第330页Gao Mingxuan ed. (2002) *Monographs on Criminal Law* (Vol1), Higher Education Press, 330].

[16] 高铭暄主编:《刑法专论》(上编)，高等教育出版社2002年版，第362~363页。Gao Mingxuan ed. (2002) *Monographs on Criminal Law (Vol1)*, Higher Education Press, 362–363.

[17] In China, the term "collusion" actually contains different situations. Since the case of Example 9 is too simple, it is necessary to make a specific judgment on whether B should be responsible for the death of C, the single conclusion can not be drawn.

10.2 Focus on Wrongdoing

Joint crime is a form of wrongdoing.[18] When dealing with joint crimes, one should first identify whether joint crime is established from the level of wrongdoing,[19] and then identify individually whether and what kind of culpability each participant has from the level of culpability. In other words, the special nature of joint crime is only manifested at the level of wrongdoing, and the legislation and theory of joint crime only address at the level of wrongdoing. From the level of culpability, there is no difference between joint crime and individual crime. Therefore, joint crime must be identified with the focus on wrongdoing.

When examined from the viewpoint of substance, a crime can be recognized only if the following two conditions are present: the fact of malfeasance happens (wrongdoing), and, to blame the fact of malfeasance (accountability). Accordingly, the entities of crime are wrongdoing and accountability.[20] However, since criminal law applies the principle of *nulla poena sine lege*, only unlawful acts that meet the constitutive elements become one of the entities of crime. Culpability is a kind of responsibility for wrongdoing,[21] which is *Vorwerfbarkeit* for the fact of malfeasance that the constitutive elements are met, so wrongdoing is a prerequisite for culpability In real life, there is "wrongdoing without culpability" (the act meets the constitutive elements and is illegal, but there is no culpability), but there is absolutely no "culpability without wrongdoing" (the act does not meet the constitutive elements or is not illegal, but the actor is culpable). For the same reason, the identification of crime must be made from wrongdoing to culpability, and not the other way around.[22] The question addressed by the legislation on joint crime in the General Principles of Criminal Law is which participant's act should be attributed to the fact of malfeasance. In the case of a specific case, the identification of whether the acts of more than two persons constitute a joint crime only addresses the objective attribution to more than two persons, or whether the acts of more than two persons are the

[18] This article is discussed under the tripartite system. The so-called "wrongdoing" means that the act meets the constitutive element and is illegal.

[19] The term "crime" is sometimes only at the level of wrongdoing, sometimes in the sense of wrongdoing and responsibility.(参见张明楷:《犯罪构成体系与构成要件要素》，北京大学出版社2010年版，第70页以下See Zhang Mingkai. (2010) *The System of Criminal Constitution and the Elements of Constitutive Requirements*, Peking University Press, 1–70.)Correspondingly, "joint crime" may refer only to joint crimes at the level of wrongdoing, or to joint crimes in the sense of wrongdoing and responsibility.

[20] 参见德乌尔斯·金德霍伊泽尔:"论犯罪构造的逻辑"，徐凌波、蔡桂生译，载《中外法学》2014年第1期; 日前田雅英:《刑法总论讲义》，东京大学出版会2011年版，第29页。Urs Kindhäuser, trans. Xv Lingbo, Cai Guisheng, (2014) *Zur Logik des Verbrechensaufbaus*, as cited in *Chinese Journal of Comparative Law,* No.1. Maeda Masahide. (2006) *Handouts of General Rules of Criminal Law*, University of Tokyo Press, 29.

[21] Vgl.,C.Roxin, *Strafrecht Allgenmeiner Teil, Band I*, 4.Aufl., C.H.Beck 2006,S.226.

[22] 参见张明楷:《犯罪构成体系与构成要件要素》，北京大学出版社2010年版，第49页以下。See Zhang Mingkai. (2010) *The System of Criminal Constitution and the Elements of Constitutive Requirements*, Peking University Press, 1–49.

infringement of legal interest (including the danger). As long as the establishment of a joint crime is determined, the infringement of legal interest must be objectively attributed to the participants (regardless of whether the participants have subjective culpability). As to whether each participant is subjectively culpable for the result attributed to him, it requires to be identified individually, but whether and what kind of culpability the participant has is not special in the joint crime.

Example 10 A and B jointly shot C in conscious liaison. A shot C in the chest and killed C, and B shot C in the thigh and caused C's minor injuries. Even without examining B's actions, it can be concluded that A's actions caused C's death. If A has the elements of culpability such as intent to homicide, it will be established accomplished intentional homicide. However, if the act of B is considered alone, the death of C cannot be attributed to the act of B. Even if B has the elements of culpability such as the intent to homicide, only the attempted intentional homicide is established. If B only has the intent of injury, only the crime of intentional injury (minor injury) is established. However, this conclusion is clearly inappropriate. The legislation and theory of joint crime are designed to objectively impute the results of C's death to B's act. That is, as long as it is found that there is causality between B's act and the result of C's death, then the result of C's death is also unpunishable to B's act. If B has the elements of culpability such as intent to kill, it will be established accomplished intentional homicide. However, in case of B only has the intent of injury, even if there is causality between B's act and the results of C's death, B cannot be found guilty of intentional homicide because A had the intent to kill, but can only be found guilty of causing death by intentional injury in accordance with the content of B's culpability. It can be seen that the joint crime, in fact, only solve the problem of wrongdoing, that is, which participant's act and the results have causality, according to which the results should be attributed to its act. As for the culpability of each participant, it is not a question to be solved by the legislation and theory of joint crime. Since this is the case, judicial practice must determine joint crime with a focus on wrongdoing.

The proposition that "the wrongdoing is (in principle) joint and several and the culpability is individual"[23] also indicates that joint crime is a form of wrongdoing. As is well known, culpability is not joint and several. "The identification of 'culpability' is linked in legal policy to the identification of the propriety of imposing a penalty as a legal consequence of the crime on the person who has committed the unlawful act that meets the constitutive elements."[24] According to the principle of culpability, even if the act meets the constitutive elements and is illegal, if the actor is not culpable, it cannot be treated as a crime and no penalty can be imposed. What is clear is that in determining whether a participant is worthy of being punished, it can only be based on whether each participant is culpable, and that participant B

[23] 参见日山口厚:《刑法总论》，有斐阁2007年版，第300页。See Yamaguchi Atsushi.(2007) *General Rules of Criminal Law*, Yuhikaku Press, 300.

[24] 日内藤谦:《刑法讲义总论(下)I》，有斐阁1991年版，第737页。See Naitou Ken. (2001) *General Lectures on Criminal Law (Medium)*, Yuhikaku Press, 737.

cannot be punished just because participant A is culpable. In fact, the elements of culpability, such as the criminal capacity for culpability, the age of culpability, the content of intent, and the possibility of the cognition of wrongdoing and reasonableness, can only be identified individually. The fact that participant A has the criminal capacity for culpability does not mean that participant B also has the criminal capacity for culpability; the fact that participant A has reasonableness does not mean that participant B has reasonableness.[25] In Example 10, it should be found that the acts of A and B jointly caused the death of C (because of the psychological causality between B's act and C's death), and the result of C's death must be attributed to the acts of both of them, both of which are unlawful (the joint and several nature of the wrongdoing). However, as mentioned above, this does not make both of them culpable for intentional homicide, but rather the elements of culpability of A and B must be identified separately. If A has all the elements of culpability for intentional homicide and B is a mentally ill person who is incapable of culpability, then A is guilty of intentional homicide and B is not guilty (culpability is individual).

Example 11. A, aged 16, and B, aged 13, jointly raped a young girl C in turn. Since they jointly practiced it, the result of C suffering gang rape must be attributed not only to A's act but also to B's act, according to which they established gang rape. Even if B does not reach the age of culpability, the punishment for A is still in accordance with gang rape.[26] It is easy to see that whether the participants have the elements of culpability does not affect whether the results can be attributed to their act. This also shows that joint crime is a form of wrongdoing.

The basis of punishment for the perpetrator is the same as that for an individual. The defects of the theory of culpable accomplice and the advantages of the theory of causal accomplice coincide with the fact that joint crime is a form of wrongdoing.

The theory of culpable accomplice holds that because the accomplice lures the perpetrator into culpability and punishment, the accomplice is also punishable. The classical formulation is that "the perpetrator commits the murder and the abettor creates the murderer". According to the theory of culpable accomplice, the establishment of accomplice presupposes that the perpetrator has the conformity of constitutive elements, wrongdoing, and accountability (the theory of extreme derivativeness). It can be seen that the theory of culpable accomplice actually considers joint crime to be a form of wrongdoing and accountability. However, according to the theory of culpable accomplice, if A abets B to seriously injure A's body,

[25] Because of this, Article 29 of *German Criminal Law* stipulates: "The punishment of each participant shall not consider the responsibility of other persons and may only be punished according to the responsibility of the participants themselves".

[26] The traditional view is that A can not be punished as the crime of gang rape(参见王作富主编:《刑法分则实务研究(中)》，中国方正出版社2010年版，第855页*Research on the Specific Provisions of Criminal Law (Vol2)*, China Fangzheng Press, 2010, 855.)However, there are many flaws in this conclusion.(参见钱叶六:"'轮奸'情节认定中的争议问题研讨"，载《江淮论坛》2010年第5期See Qian Yeliu. (2010) Discussion on Controversial Issues in the Determination of 'Gang Rape' Circumstances, as cited in *Jianghuai Tribune*, No. 5.).

B is established as the crime of intentional injury, and A is established as the abettor of the crime of intentional injury. But this view cannot be accepted. Moreover, according to the theory of culpable accomplice, the harm of an accomplice, especially an abettor, lies mainly in degrading the abetted person. In other words, regardless of the crime committed by the abetted person, the abettor infringes on the comprehensive interests of the abetted person such as freedom, reputation, and social status. However, if the abettor is a "crime of depravity", then the criminal law should provide for an independent statutory penalty for it. However, on the one hand, the legal interests infringed by the abettor are the same as those infringed by the perpetrator, for example, the legal interests infringed by the abettor and the perpetrator of the crime of intentional injury are the same as those infringed by the perpetrator, which are the physical health of the victim. On the other hand, national criminal laws do not provide independent statutory penalties for abettors.[27] Because of this, the theory of culpable accomplice has only doctrinal-historical significance.[28] The decline of the theory of culpable accomplice is due to the fact that it does not consider joint crime as a form of wrongdoing, but rather combines wrongdoing and culpability in a hybrid manner to identify joint crime. The defects of the theory of culpable accomplice and its decline just confirm that joint crime is a form of wrongdoing.

The prevailing view today is the theory of causal accomplice.[29] "The view of the theory of causal accomplice is that 'accomplice is punished because of the causality between it and the infringement of legal interests caused by others', also known as the theory of provocation. In other words, the so-called accomplice is the act of indirectly infringing the legal interest by using other participants as the medium. Therefore, the legal interest infringed must also be protectable vis-à-vis the accomplice himself."[30] For example, A requests the perpetrator B to kill himself (A), and B attempts to kill A. Although A's promise is invalid and B's act establishes the crime of intentional homicide, A does not cause the legal interest to be infringed and

[27] 参见日松原芳博:《刑法总论》，日本评论社2013年版，第368页See Matsubara Yoshihiro. (2013) *General Theory of Criminal Law*, NIPPON HYORON SHA Co., 368。Of course, the Anglo-American criminal law is slightly different. That is, "whether or not the degree of being abetted, the 'abetted crime' is a misdemeanor in common law". Moreover, in the common law, the abetted crime is limited to abetting others to "act to constitute any serious crime, or to be a light crime linked to preventing justice and undermining peace". The provisions of *US Model Penal Code* apply to the incitement of others to commit all crimes.(参见美约书亚·德雷斯勒:《美国刑法精解》，王秀梅等译，北京大学出版社2009年版，第383页以下Joshua Dressler, trans. Wang Xiumei, (2009) *Understanding Criminal Law*, Beijing: Peking University Press, 1–383).

[28] Vgl.,C.Roxin, *Strafrecht Allgenmeiner Teil, Band II*, C.H.Beck 2003,S.133.

[29] In addition to the theory of responsible complicity and the theory of causal complicity, there are also the theory of illegal complicity, which also believes that the establishment of the complicity only requires that the act of the principal offender has the conformity of criminal constitutive elements and wrongdoing. Accordingly, the theory of illegal complicity also recognizes the joint crime is a demonstration of wrongdoing.

[30] 日西田典之:《刑法总论》，弘文堂2010年版，第336~337页。Nishida Noriyuki. (2010) *General Theory of Criminal Law*, Koubundou Publishers Inc., 336~337.

is therefore unpunishable because the criminal law does not require A to protect his own life.[31] Within the theory of causal accomplice., there are the theory of pure provocation, the theory of mixed provocation and the theory of modified provocation,[32] but none of them incorporate the element of culpability into the joint crime.

This article argues that, like the nature of individual crimes, the nature of joint crime is also the infringement of legal interests. The individual perpetrator is the type of crime that directly causes the infringement of legal interests, the joint perpetrator is the type of crime that jointly causes the infringement of legal interests, the indirect perpetrator is the type of crime that causes the infringement of legal interests by dominating the act of others, and the abettor and aider are the type of crime that indirectly causes the infringement of legal interests through the perpetrator. In other words, the punishment of the accomplice is based on the fact that the accomplice indirectly infringes on the legal interest through the perpetrator, i.e., the accomplice is punished because he or she induces and contributes to the direct infringement of the legal interest caused by the perpetrator. The wrongdoing of the accomplice comes from the wrongdoing of the accomplice's act and the wrongdoing of the perpetrator's act. The wrongdoing of the accomplice's act does not mean that the accomplice's act itself has *Handlungsunwert*, but that the accomplice does not have a justifiable cause (recognizing the relativity of the law). First, "the perpetrator" must have committed an illegal act that meets the constitutive elements, otherwise, the abettor and the aider cannot be punished. Therefore, attempted abetment (failure to abet) is not punishable, but attempted abetment (the abetted person proceeds to commit the crime and fails) is punishable. Second, in the case of a perpetrator who commits an illegal act that meets the constitutive elements, as long as the accomplice does not have a justifiable cause, it is necessary to affirm that the accomplice's act is also illegal. In other words, if the legal interest infringed by the perpetrator is not the legal interest that must be protected by the abettor or the aider (the accomplice has a justifiable cause), only the act of the perpetrator is criminalized. In short, only if the accomplice does not have a justifiable cause, then the nature of joint and several of the wrongdoing can be recognized. Conversely, the relativity of the wrongdoing should be recognized under exceptional circumstances. The theory of causal accomplice, which is endorsed in this article, shows precisely that joint crime is a form of wrongdoing.

Since joint crime is a form of wrongdoing, and wrongdoing means that the act meets the constitutive elements and is illegal. Therefore, in identifying joint crime, the first step is to determine whose act among the participants meets the constitutive elements of what crime, and whose act caused the infringement of the legal interest

---

[31] The theory of illegal complicity. denies the relativity of the wrongdoing and believes that A made the principal offender B committed the attempted homicide, he shall be the abettor of the crime of intentional homicide shall be established. But this conclusion is unreasonable.

[32] 参见日曾根威彦:《刑法学基础》，黎宏译，法律出版社2005年版，第137页以下。

See Sone Yoshihiko. (2005) *Fundamentals of Criminal Law*, trans. Li Hong, Law Press China, 1–137.

(or, rather, whose act contributed to the occurrence of the result). This aspect of the identification can be called the identification of the conformity of the constitutive element, which is basically expressed as the identification of the causality of the accomplice (see the fourth part of this article).

In the aforementioned Example 1, 15-year-old A burglarized a home and caused the property damage to others (committing an act that meets the constitutive elements of the crime of theft), and there is a psychological causality between the lookout act of 17-year-old B and the result. Therefore, the result should be attributed to B's act. At the level of wrongdoing, A is a perpetrator and B is an aider or a secondary offender. Under this premise, the respective culpabilities are identified separately. Since A has not reached the age of culpability, his act eventually does not constitute a crime. B has all the elements of culpability and is ultimately guilty of theft, and should be treated as a secondary offender. Based on the same reasoning and identification method, if A in Example 1 is a person who lacks other elements of culpability, B is also a secondary offender to the crime of theft.

In Example 2, whether a third party's act of aiding the actor of the offense in essence to harbor stolen goods constitutes the accomplice depends on the basis for not punishing the actor of the offense in essence. If the reason for not punishing the actor of the offense in essence is that the his act of harboring stolen goods does not have the constitutive elements or is not illegal, then the third party's act of aiding is also not illegal and thus cannot constitute accomplice. On the contrary, if the act of the actor of the offense in essence has the constitutive elements and is illegal, but only lacks culpability, (a) the third party's act of aiding also has wrongdoing and thus is established with the actor of the offense in essence at the level of wrongdoing, (b) the actor of the offense in essence is only non-punishable due to lack of accountability, and (c) a third party is still guilty of accomplice if he has culpability. As is known, the criminal laws in Germany, Japan and other countries provide for the booty crime in the property crime, the larcenist (the actor of the offense in essence) stole other's property and then harbor the stolen goods, the reason why the booty crime is not established, because there is no infringement of the new legal interest (property), the act of harboring committed by the actor of the offense in essence shall belong to the unpunishable afterwards act.[33] In this case, for the third party to aid the actor of the offense in essence to harbor the stolen goods, it is difficult to be recognized as a crime. However, in China, the booty crime is a crime of prevention of justice, and the stolen of other people's property by the larcenist (the actor of the offense in essence), followed by the harboring, also prevents the administration of justice, and has the conformity of constitutive elements and wrongdoing. The reason why the actor of the offense in essence does not establish the booty crime is not because there is no new infringement of legal interest, but because of the lack of reasonableness (i.e., lack of culpability). According to the theory of restricted derivativeness, as long as the perpetrator (the actor of the offense in

[33]参见日山口厚:《刑法各论》，有斐阁2010年版，第349页以下。See Yamaguchi Atsushi. (2010) *Special Part of Criminal Law*. Yuhikaku Press, 1–349

essence A in Example 2) acts with the conformity of constitutive element and wrongdoing, the accomplice can be established. Therefore, if it is recognized that the joint crime is a form of wrongdoing, then it can be concluded that a third party who aids the actor of the offense in essence to harbor stolen goods also establishes joint crime with the actor of the offense in essence for the booty crime, and the actor of the offense in essence is still the perpetrator and the third party is the accomplice. However, because the actor of the offense in essence does not have reasonableness and is unpunishable, and the third party does not lack reasonableness, so it is still established as a secondary offender to the booty crime, such as B in Example 2.

Under normal circumstances, it is presumed that an act has wrongdoing if it meets the constitutive elements. However, since it is impossible for a subject of legal interest to have wrongdoing for the damage caused by his own legal interest (e.g., it is not illegal to harm his own body or destroy his own property), and it is entirely possible for a subject of legal interest to jointly cause damage to his own legal interest with others, therefore, the wrongdoing of the acts of each participant in a joint crime may be relative, thus requiring further to be identified at the level of wrongdoing.

Example 12 Three fugitives, A, B, and C, jointly plan to shoot if they are pursued. In the course of their nighttime escape, fugitive A mistakes accomplice B as a pursuer and shoots him with intent to kill, but no death. The decision of the German Supreme Court held that the victim B was also punishable for attempted homicide.[34] Some scholars in Germany also support this conclusion of the decision.[35] Admittedly, all three fugitives would have been criminally culpable if A had shot the pursuer or someone else. This is because the life of any other person, as opposed to the three fugitives, is a legal interest that they may not infringe. However, B's life and body, although it is a legal interest that A and C may not infringe, is not an interest that B may not harm. Since this is the case, it must be recognized that although there is a psychological causality between B's conspiracy with A and C and the danger to B's life, however, because B's danger to his own life prevents wrongdoing, therefore, at the level of wrongdoing, only A and C are established as joint criminals, and B's danger to his own life prevents the wrongdoing. It is easy to see that the nature of joint and several of wrongdoing is not absolute.

To sum up, joint crime is a form of wrongdoing, and its particularity exists only at the level of wrongdoing. Of course, this does not mean that joint crime in the ultimate sense does not require culpability, but rather that the identification of culpability for each participant in a joint crime is no different from the identification of culpability for an individual crime (of course, the content of each accomplice's intentional cognition content will vary). Therefore, it is not necessary and should not make the content of culpability an important issue when determining joint

---

[34] BGHSt 11,268.

[35] Vgl.,H.Jeschck/T.Weigend, *Lehrbuch des Strafrechts.Allgemeiner Teil*, 5.Aufl., Duncker & Humblot,1996, S.675.

crime. Neither the element of culpability as a condition to identify the establishment of joint crime, let alone identify the culpability before the wrongdoing. “Joint crime” does not mean that each participant is ultimately guilty of a crime. First, although joint crime is established at the level of wrongdoing, some of the participants may not commit the crime ultimately because the lack of the element of culpability, and only some of the participants or even one participant may commit the crime ultimately. This is the case in Example 1. Second, even if all the participants have the so-called joint act and joint intent, some of them may have a justifiable cause and may not establish the joint crime, such as Example 11. Third, because joint crime is only a form of wrongdoing, and the ultimate crime of the participants’ act depends on the content of culpability, so that in the case of the ultimate establishment of joint crime, although all participants are established, but it is entirely possible to establish a different crime. In Example 4, A is guilty of intentional homicide, and B is guilty of intentional injury (causing death), in Example 6, A and B are guilty of robbery, and C is guilty of extortion.

It may be argued that the viewpoint of this article violates Paragraph 1, Article 25 of *Chinese Criminal Law*. This paragraph provides that “The joint crime refers to an intentional crime committed by two or more persons jointly”. Our traditional theory and judicial practice is based on one interpretation conclusion of this paragraph (emphasizing joint intent and joint act, and providing for joint crime at both the level of wrongdoing and culpability). However, more than two interpretations of any one law may be made, and the interpreter should not take one of the interpretative conclusions as the truth, nor should he or she take his or her former understanding as doctrine. In fact, there are multiple interpretations that can be made of Paragraph 1, Article 25. In the opinion of this article, this paragraph only limits joint crime to intentional crimes, rather than requiring more than two persons to have the same intention. If the word “take” is to be added to the above provision, which should be “A joint crime refers to taken an intentional crime committed by two or more persons jointly”, instead of “joint crime means that two or more persons jointly and intentionally commit a crime”.[36] Therefore, this paragraph does not deny that joint crime is a form of wrongdoing. Paragraph 2, Article 25 of *Chinese Criminal Law* provides that “A negligent crime committed by two or more persons jointly shall not be punished as a joint crime; those who should bear criminal culpability shall be individually punished according to the crimes they have committed.” This provision clearly recognizes the fact of joint negligent crime, only that joint negligent crimes are not punished as joint crimes, and does not deny that joint crime is a form of wrongdoing.

[36] 参见张明楷:《刑法学》，法律出版社2011年版，第348页以下Zhang Mingkai. (2011) *Criminal Law*, Law Press China, 1–348; In addition, the paragraph may also be interpreted as a provision for the joint perpetrator.

10.3 Center on the Perpetrator

The joint crime is divided into simple joint crime and complex joint crime. Simple joint crime refers to joint perpetrator.[37] "Complex joint crime refers to joint crime in which there is a certain division of labor among the accomplices. This division of labor is manifested by the fact that some abet others to cause others to commit the crime intentionally, some aid others to commit the crime so that the crime of others can be easily committed, and some directly commit the crime, which means commit the act that constitutes an objective element of that crime."[38] At the level of wrongdoing, any complex joint crime has perpetrator, and there cannot be a joint crime without perpetrator.[39] In determining a complex joint crime, it should not identify which persons are established as joint criminals as a whole, but should first identify the perpetrator, and then identify whether the other participants are established the accomplice with the perpetrator as the center.

"The perpetrator is the central or core figure in the process of achieving the perpetrating act that meets the constitutive elements."[40] Because the essence of crime is to infringe or threaten the legal interest, specifically by causing the result of infringement or dangerous result to the legal interest, and the person who governs the occurrence of such result is the perpetrator. Therefore, when dealing with joint crime, it becomes relatively easy to first confirm the perpetrator and determine whether there is an abettor or an aider under the premise that the act of the perpetrator meets the constitutive elements and is illegal. This is the best path to identify the joint crime, there is no need to abstractly discuss the conditions for the establishment of joint crime.

The causality (including the result attribution) between the act of the perpetrator and the result is easy to determine. When A shoots the victim in the heart with a gun and causes his death, we can easily impute the result of that death to A's shooting. In Example 1, we do not doubt that C's loss was caused by A, and we can affirm that A's act meets the elements of the crime of theft and is unlawful. After affirming that A's act establishes the crime of theft at the level of wrongdoing, and then judging whether B's act contributes to the infringement of A's legal interests, we can conclude whether B is a secondary offender to the crime of theft at the level of wrongdoing. In Example 3, it is easy to identify that the loss of C was caused by A, and

[37] Due to limitation of length in this article, the identification of the joint perpetrator is not argued here, but the method of identification proposed in this article also can be applied to the joint perpetrator. The special feature of the joint perpetrator is to decide whether the participant is a joint perpetrator or an complicity in a narrow sense. This is the internal distinction after the establishment of the complicity in a broad sense.

[38] 高铭暄、马克昌主编:《刑法学》，北京大学出版社、高等教育出版社2011年版，第169页。Gao Mingxuan & Ma Kechang eds. (2011) Criminal Law, Peking University Press & Higher Education Press, 169.

[39] Of course, when the principal offender at the level of wrongdoing lacks the elements of responsibility, there may be only complicity at the level of responsibility without the principal offenders.

[40] C.Roxin, *Strafrecht Allgenmeiner Teil, Band II*, C.H.Beck 2003,S. 9.

thus it can be directly concluded that A shall establish the crime of forcible seizure. Similarly, after affirming the act of A, and then judging whether B's act contributed to the infringement of A's legal interests and whether the justifiable cause exists, it can conclude whether B was established as a secondary offender to the crime of robbery at the level of wrongdoing. Therefore, center on the perpetrator can make the identification of joint crime easier.

According to the restricted concept of perpetrator, which is a general rule in Japan and abroad, "the perpetrator is in principle limited to the acts specified in the constitutive elements of the specific provisions."[41] Since this is the case, it is entirely possible to identify the perpetrator alone. In other words, regardless of whether the abettor or aider is the accomplice, the judiciary can identify a perpetrator without relying on others. Moreover, there is no difference between the identification of a perpetrator and that of an individual crime (individual perpetrator). The center on the perpetrator means that after the perpetrator is identified, it is only necessary to further determine which of the participants' acts constitute the accomplice in a narrow sense. If, instead of centering on the perpetrator, the otherwise clearly identifiable perpetrator is included in the overall identification of all participants, it is not conducive to the proper handling of the case.

Example 13 In 2000, A and B were punished for joint robbery. In the afternoon of the Double-Seventh Festival in 2011, A and B contacted with mobile phone text message that "cheat a girl and do something". At that night, A and B coked C on the car and drive to a park. A dragged C off to the wood and C did not want to, B went to C and yelled "Do you know who I am!" C feared and then went to the woods. A slapped C to the ground and forced C to take off the clothes. C did not want to do as what she was told. So A told B who stood next to "take the knife". B knew that they didn't bring a knife, and A was trying to frighten C, so he stood still. Then, A raped C. During the rape, A asked B to turn over the package of C. B robbed a mobile phone from the package at a distance of one or two meters nearby, and 400 Yuan in cash. Afterwards, about the premeditation said "do", A said it refers to rape, B said it refers to robbery of money. Obviously, A is a perpetrator of the rape, it can be successfully found that A's act is established accomplished rape without considering the act of B. The question is, is B the accomplice of the crime of rape? On this occasion, it would be inappropriate to identify whether the two had a joint intent and joint act of rape, because the initial "conspiracy" did not form a joint criminal intention. The correct approach is to first affirm that A's act is consistent with the elements of the crime of rape and illegal act, established accomplished rape. The next step is to determine whether there is causality between B's act and A's accomplished rape. First of all, from the point of view of act, although B had committed acts of violence and coercion against C before A raped C and objectively promoted to A's accomplished rape, B did not have the intent to rape at this time. In this sense, although B is also the accomplice at the level of wrongdoing, but because of the lack of intent, ultimately cannot be identified as the accomplice of the crime of rape.

[41] C.Roxin, *Strafrecht Allgenmeiner Teil, Band II*, C.H.Beck 2003,S. 7.

Moreover, from the perspective of omission, B's previous acts (including taking C to the park and threatening C) objectively put C in an isolated situation, and under the circumstances put C's sexual autonomy in a state that needed to be protected, so there was a duty to protect C's sexual autonomy, but B did not fulfill this duty. Therefore, there is a causal link with the result of rape and B has the intent to aid, so he is guilty of accomplice by omission in the rape.[42]

According to the theory of the derivativeness of accomplice, the identification of abetting and aiding depends on the perpetrator, and only when the perpetrator's act has the conformity of constitutive elements and is illegal, the act of abetting and aiding may be established as a crime. "The reason for such an identification lies in the understanding of the basis of punishment for the accomplice (abetting and aiding). That is, it is because, since the basis of punishment for the accomplice, like that of an individual perpetrator, lies in the causing of the infringement of legal interests (the result of the constitutive element) (the theory of causal accomplice, i.e., the theory of provocation), then, if there is no infringement and danger of legal interests, which is the basis of punishment, there is no state of affairs that justifies the intervention and prohibition of criminal law (the punishment of the accomplice)."[43] The theory of restricted derivativeness identifies that the perpetrator must be identified first in the process of determining joint crime. As long as the act of the perpetrator has the conformity of constitutive elements and wrongdoing, the accomplice can be established even without culpability. Therefore, the derivativeness of accomplice also requires that the perpetrator be identified as the center of accomplice.

After the perpetrator is identified at the level of wrongdoing, then the accomplice in a narrow sense is identified, which not only overcomes the difficulty of identifying the "joint criminal intent" and "joint criminal act", but also implements the theory of the derivativeness of accomplice, thus it is easy to identify the accomplice in the common crimes, and also easy to solve the problem of the accomplice in the status crime. In fact, there are three aspects of the accomplice in the status crime that are worthy of further discussion.

10.3.1 The Joint Crime Committed by Persons with and without Criminal Status

In cases where a person with criminal status commits a joint crime with a person without criminal status, the perpetrator shall first be determined. The establishment of the perpetrator in the status crime requires, on the one hand, that the actor has a

[42] 参见姚诗:"先前行为与实行过限下知情共犯人的刑事责任"，载《法学研究》2013年第5期。See Yao Shi. (2013) Criminal Liability of the Knowing Joint Offender in Cases of Prior Act and Excessive Execution, as cited in *Chinese Journal of Law*, No. 5.

[43] 日山口厚:《刑法总论》，有斐阁2007年版，第309页。See Yamaguchi Atsushi. (2007) *General Part of Criminal Law*. Yuhikaku Press, 309.

special status and, on the other hand, that the actor commits an unlawful act that meets the constitutive elements.

(a) It is impossible for a person without criminal status to be a perpetrator in the status crime. This is because, in the status crime, the criminal status is the essential constitutive elements for perpetrator, and the "use own status" that is associated with criminal status is also a necessary requirement of the constitutive elements for perpetrator. The acts of the perpetrator must have all the requirements of the constitutive elements. It can be affirmed that in Example 5, ordinary citizen B cannot be the perpetrator of the crime of corruption, but only national staff A can be the perpetrator of the crime of corruption. In the event that A becomes the perpetrator of the crime of corruption, B is the accomplice of the crime of corruption.

(b) The identification of the accomplice in the status crime presupposes that the perpetrator commits an unlawful act that meets the constitutive elements. The question is, what should be done when the act of a person without criminal status meets the constitutive elements in the non-status crime? As mentioned earlier, previous judicial interpretations advocate the identification of the nature of the case by the perpetrator, but the general theory of criminal law advocates the identification of the nature of the case by the nature of the criminal perpetrator.[44] In fact, in the case of joint crime of the status crime, it is entirely possible that such a situation exists: the act of a person with criminal status meets the constitutive elements of the status crime, and is therefore the perpetrator of the status crime, and the act of a person without criminal status meets the constitutive elements of the non-status crime, and is therefore the perpetrator of the non-status crime. In this regard, it is difficult to resolve the current general view.

In this article, the relativity of the perpetrator should be affirmed, while applying the principle of ideal concurrence. First, when a person with criminal status is the perpetrator of the status crime, and the person without criminal status has abetted or aided the perpetrator, and has not committed other crimes, he can only be convicted and sentenced according to the crime committed by the person with criminal status. For example, if a general citizen abets a national staff to accept a bribe, the general citizen can only be found guilty of the crime of bribery (abettor). Second, in the case of a joint crime between a person with criminal status and a person without criminal status, and the person with criminal status is the perpetrator (also the perpetrator and secondary offender of the theft) of the status crime (crime of corruption), and the person without criminal status is the perpetrator (also the secondary offender of the status crime, that is crime of corruption) of the non-status crime (crime of theft), that is, the joint criminal acts of the person with criminal status and the person without criminal status at the same time committed more than two crimes, should be in accordance with the principle of ideal concurrence: if one of the parties is found to be a secondary offender to a more serious crime, which is lesser than the perpetrator

[44] 参见马克昌主编:《犯罪通论》，武汉大学出版社1999年版，第584页；林维:"真正身份犯之共犯问题展开"，载《法学家》2013年第6期。See Ma Kechang ed. (1999) *General Theory of Crime*, Wuhan University Press, 584; Lin Wei. (2013) Unfolding Issues of Complicity in Truly Status-based Offenses, as cited in *Jurists' Review*, No. 6.

of the lesser crime (when the punishment of the perpetrator of a lesser crime is more consistent with principle of suiting punishment to crime), he or she shall be found to be the perpetrator of the lesser crime. Thus, the crime of a person with criminal status may be different from that of a person without criminal status.

It follows that the center on the perpetrator does not mean a blanket center on the status crime. Article 382 of *Chinese Criminal Law* expressly provides that the conduct of internal and external collusion is identified as the accomplice of corruption, which seems to indicate that the status crime is the center.. This is not the case. Article 382, on the one hand, affirms that a person without criminal status can be the accomplice of the status crime, and on the other hand, because the statutory penalty for corruption is heavier than that for theft, it provides that a non-status criminal shall be punished as the accomplice of the crime of corruption. Therefore, if the opposite situation exists, i.e., if the statutory penalty for non-status criminals is heavier, it will expose obvious defects to identify the accomplice with the status crime as the center.

10.3.2 The Joint Crime Committed by Persons with Different Criminal Status

Judicial practice often faces the problem of how to convict persons with different criminal status when they commit crimes together. According to this article, it is very easy to solve the problem as long as the perpetrator is the center, and the relativity of perpetrator is recognized, and the principle of ideal concurrence and legal concurrence is applied.

For example, in the case of a staff A in a non-state-owned company and national staff B who was appointed to this non-state-owned company from state-owned company jointly occupied the property of the non-state-owned company, it should not be determined as a whole what kind of joint crime the two constitute, but first identify the perpetrator. If the two of them jointly corrupted the property only by using the duty convenience of the national staff B, then B is a perpetrator of the crime of corruption, and A is a secondary offender. If the two of them jointly corrupted the property only by using the duty convenience of A's status, then A is a perpetrator of crime of duty encroachment, and B's status is meaningless, and only a secondary offender of crime of duty encroachment. If each of them utilized their respective duty convenience, then A is both a perpetrator of the crime of duty encroachment and a secondary offender of the crime of corruption. B is both a perpetrator of the crime of corruption and a secondary offender of the crime of duty encroachment. At this point, each person has committed two crimes, but because there is only one act, therefore, it should be punished as a felony according to the principle of ideal concurrence. If A is found to be a secondary offender of the crime of corruption, resulting in a lighter punishment than that for the perpetrator of the crime of duty encroachment, A should be identified as the perpetrator of the crime of duty encroachment (at this point, although A and B are established as joint crimes, the accusations are different).[45]

For another example, the deputy secretary of CPC A who in charge of politics and law used the duty convenience to instruct the Judge B to acquit the guilty person, A implemented the act of perpetrator of the crime of abuse of authority, also implemented the act of accomplice (abetting) of crime of bending the law. Since the crime of bending the law is the special provision of the crime of abuse of authority, the act of perpetrator of the crime of bending the law committed by B can also be considered the act of perpetrator of the crime of abuse of authority. Thus, A and B both committed the crime of bending the law and the crime of abuse of authority at the same time. According to the principle of legal concurrence, B can only be punished for the crime of bending the law, then, A can be punished as the perpetrator of the crime of abuse of authority, but also as the accomplice (abettor) of the crime of bending the law. At this point it is necessary to compare the severity of the statutory penalties, and A should be punished as a felony.[46]

10.3.3 The Joint Crime Committed by Persons with Different Criminal Status

Example 14 A, a common civil and B, a company cashier, are close. A lied to buy a car and abetted B to transfer the funds of company for himself, and "promised" that he would return the money when the fixed deposit expired after two weeks. B trusted A and set aside 300,000 Yuan which is the company capital and handed over to A. A used the funds to gamble and made profit, then returned 300,000 Yuan to the company of B within two weeks.

According to Article 272 of *Chinese Criminal Law*, if B knew that A was using the funds for gambling, he would be the perpetrator of the crime of embezzling funds, and A could be the accomplice.[47] However, B was unaware of the fact that A

[45] On June 30, 2000, *The Interpretation of the Supreme People's Court Regarding Several Issues Concerning the Judgment of Corruption and Professional Embezzlement* pointed that "In a company, enterprise or other unit, a person who does not have the status of a national staff collaborates with a national staff member, and uses their respective positions to facilitate the illegal possession of their own property, and is convicted according to the criminal nature of the principal." This interpretation is obviously inappropriate. Since ordinary citizens and national staffs can collude with embezzlers, which thus can constitute the complicity of the crime of corruption, then the person in the companies and enterprises can also constitute the complicity of the crime of corruption.

[46] 另参见张明楷:《刑法学》，法律出版社2011年版，第398页。Zhang Mingkai. (2011) *Criminal Law*, Law Press China, 398.

[47] 参见最高人民法院1998年4月29日《关于审理挪用公款案件具体应用法律若干问题的解释》第8条。See Supreme People's Court. (1998) *Interpretation on Several Issues Concerning the Specific Application of Law in Adjudicating Cases of Misappropriation of Public Funds* (Apr. 29, 1998), Art. 8.

was using 300,000 Yuan for gambling, and did not recognize that A was using the funds for illegal activities, but mistakenly thought that A was using the funds to purchase a car. Therefore, B lacked the intent to commit the crime of embezzling funds. That is, A's act objectively caused B to commit the act of embezzling funds, but did not cause the intent of B.[48] According to the traditional view of theory of criminal law, "the so-called abetted" is to instigate a person with criminal culpability who has no criminal intent to commit a crime."[49] Thus, A's act did not establish the abettor of the crime of embezzling funds. In short, according to the traditional view of China, A and B cannot establish the joint crime of the crime of embezzling funds, and they are not subject to criminal punishment. Perhaps some people believe that A is an indirect perpetrator. However, this view is not valid. The crime of embezzling funds is a typical status crime, in the occasion of it, only the person with the criminal status may become the perpetrator. The indirect perpetrator is a kind of perpetrator, and only the person with the criminal status can become the indirect perpetrator. German theory of criminal law and jurisprudence almost hold without controversy that, in case of the status crime, indirect perpetrator must have criminal status, otherwise they can only be abettors and aiders, and cannot be indirect perpetrators, because indirect perpetrators are perpetrators and not the accomplice, and the identity provided by criminal law is for perpetrators.[50] For example, German scholars point out that "in the absence of special qualifications as a precondition for the constitutive elements of the crime (the typical status crime), indirect perpetrator shall be excluded."[51] German Federal Supreme Court decisions have also held that a person without criminal status cannot be an indirect perpetrator of the status crime.[52] To hold that an indirect perpetrator can be committed without criminal status necessarily deprives the definiteness of constitutive elements and thus violates the principle of *nulla poena sine lege*.[53] For example, if national staff A is away and ask his wife B, who is not a national staff, accept a bribe, A is a perpetrator of the crime of bribery and his wife is aider, rather than his wife is perpetrator and A is

---

48 Under the premise that A returned the funds to the company of B within three months, B's misappropriation of funds to A's "intentional" purchase of cars is not the intent of the crime of embezeeling funds in criminal law.

49 高铭暄、马克昌主编:《刑法学》，北京大学出版社、高等教育出版社2011年版，第176页。; Gao Mingxuan & Ma Kechang eds. (2011) *Criminal Law,* Peking University Press & Higher Education Press, 176.

50 Vgl.,C.Roxin, Strafrecht Allgenmeiner Teil, Band II, C.H.Beck 2003,S.109,138; 德冈特·施特拉腾韦特、洛塔尔·库伦:《刑法总论I——犯罪论》，杨萌译，法律出版社2006年版，第292、309页。Giinter Stratenwerth & Lothar Kuhlen, trans. Yang Meng, (2006) *Strafrecht Allgemeiner Teil I: Die Straftat, Law Press, 292、309.*

51 H.Jeschck/T.Weigend,Lehrbuch des Strafrechts.Allgemeiner Teil, 5.Aufl.,Duncker & Humblot,1996,S.664.

52 BGHSt 9.370，参见日松宫孝明:《刑事立法と犯罪体系》，成文堂2003年版，第259页。See Matsumiya Takaaki.(2003) *Criminal Legislation and Criminal System,* Seibundo Publishing Co., 259.

53 参见日团藤重光:《刑法纲要总论》，创文社1990年版，第155页。Dandou Shigemitsu. (1990) *General Outline of Criminal Law*, Kodansha Publishing Co, 155.

aider.[54] Conversely, even if B coerces A to solicit a bribe and B accepts the property herself, B cannot be an indirect perpetrator for the crime of bribery.

However, in Example 14, it is not appropriate to conclude that both A and B are not guilty of the crime of embezzling funds. In fact, as long as the focus is on the wrongdoing and the center is on the perpetrator, and the theory of the derivativeness of accomplice is used as a guide, the above case is solved: B, who has the status of a company officer, objectively commits the unlawful act that meets the constitutive elements of the crime of embezzling funds (embezzling funds for illegal activities) and is a perpetrator at the level of wrongdoing, but is unpunishable due to the lack of intent, or to say, lack of culpability. However, according to the theory of restricted derivativeness, the abettor and the aider can be established as long as the act of the perpetrator has the conformity of constitutive elements and wrongdoing. In this case, the abetment of A caused the unlawful act that perpetrator conforms the constitutive element and the element of culpability such as intent, so A was established as an abettor of the crime of embezzling funds.[55] This is also true when the person who committed the acts that meet the constitutive elements has the criminal status but does not have other elements of culpability.

It is easy to see that, with the perpetrator as the center, under the premise that the perpetrator's act meets the constitutive elements and is illegal, and then identify the establishment of the accomplice or not, it can make the identification of the joint crime quite smooth, and can reach a proper conclusion. For the same reason, in judicial practice, the cases of joint crime should not be divided into cases. Moreover, it is even more impermissible to try the abettor and the aider first and then the perpetrator, because it is impossible to identify the abettor and the aider in the absence of the perpetrator.

It is true that our criminal law does not use the concept of "perpetrator", but the specific provisions of the criminal law on separate crimes are actually provisions on perpetrator. The general provisions of the criminal law on abetting and aiding also affirm the perpetrator from the opposite side.[56] Therefore, China's criminal law essentially provides for the perpetrator. Just as the criminal law does not have the term "constitutive element", it actually provides for it. Some scholars deny the necessity of the concept of perpetrator based on relatively simple cases of joint crime, and believe that the concept of perpetrator does not play a fundamental role

---

[54] 参见日团藤重光:《刑法纲要总论》，创文社1990年版，第159页; 日大塚仁:《刑法概说(总论)》，有斐阁2008年版，第162页; 日山口厚:《刑法总论》，有斐阁2007年版，第72页。Dandou Shigemitsu.(1990) *General Outline of Criminal Law*, Kodansha Publishing Co, 159; Otsuka Hitoshi.(2008) *Overview of Criminal Law*, Yuhikaku Press, 162. Yamaguchi Atsushi.(2007) *General Rules of Criminal Law*, Yuhikaku Press, 72.

[55] 参见张明楷:"共犯对正犯故意的从属性之否认"，载《政法论坛》2010年第5期。See Zhang Mingkai. (2010) Denial of the Dependence of the Accomplice's Liability on the Principal Offender's Intent, as cited in *Tribune of Political Science and Law*, No. 5.

[56] 参见钱叶六:"双层区分制下正犯与共犯的区分"，载《法学研究》2012年第1期。See Qian Yeliu. (2012) Distinction between Principal Offenders and Accomplices under the Two-tiered Distinction System,as cited in *Chinese Journal of Law*, No. 1.

in resolving whether the actors constitute joint crime.[57] Some scholars also believe that China's criminal law adopts a single system of perpetrator, that is, all participants in the crime are perpetrators, and "there is no need to strictly distinguish between criminal perpetrators, abettors and aiders. There is no need to strictly distinguish between… perpetrators, abettors and aiders, whose acts are all interrelated and mutually exploited, and cannot be singled out for independent evaluation."[58] In fact, such a view is obviously aimed at upholding China's traditional theory of joint crime and identification method, without discovering the essence of the problem and the substance of the joint crime. In fact, as mentioned above, if not centered on the perpetrator, we are helpless to do anything about many crimes, as the above Example 14 fully illustrates.

10.4 Oriented by Causality

Since there is a distinction between attempted and accomplished crimes, whether a participant is the accomplice and whether a participant should be culpable for the infringement of legal interest are two different issues in the joint crime. The question of causality of accomplice is related to both the establishment of accomplice and the extent to which the accomplice should be culpable.

Example 15 Both A and B fired at the same time, but only one bullet hit C. We can set two situations: (1) A hits C, or 2) we cannot find out who hits C. According to the legislation of joint crimes, if A and B establish a joint crime, then in situation 1, B is also culpable for the death of C. In situation 2, both A and B are culpable for the death of C. If A and B do not establish a joint crime, then in situation 1, B shall be punished as attempted homicide, and in situation 2, A and B both punished as attempted homicide. The question is, why must both A and B bear criminal culpability for the death of C once a joint crime is established? Perhaps people will say that this is because of the provision of the criminal law. However, why is the criminal law so stipulated? The answer can only be that because the result of death can be attributed to the acts of A and B, or that there is causality between the acts of both A and B and the result of C's death. Therefore, the causality of accomplice becomes a particularly important element in the theory of accomplice. As Japanese scholars say, "the core of the theory of accomplice is the question of whether the causality of accomplice in the act of accomplice (jointly or indirectly) that causes the infringement of legal interest and danger can be determined, and the question of the

[57] 参见杨兴培:"共同犯罪中的正犯、帮助犯理论的反思与批评"，载《法治研究》2012年第8期。See Yang Xingpei. (2012) Re-examination and Criticism of the Theory of Principal Offenders and Aidors in Joint Crimes, as cited in *Research on Rule of Law*, No. 8.

[58] 刘明祥:"'被教唆的人没有犯被教唆的罪'之解释"，载《法学研究》2011年第1期。Liu Mingxiang. (2011) Interpretation of 'The Instigated Person Did Not Commit the Crime Instigated', as citd in *Chinese Journal of Law*, No. 1.

limitation of the scope of accomplice in which the elements of accomplice are limited under the premise that the causality exists."[59]

As mentioned earlier, the identification of joint crime must be centered on the perpetrator. In the case of the act of the perpetrator is illegal, the identification of whether accomplice is established means determining whether the act of accomplice is causally related to the wrongdoing of the perpetrator. If there is causality, then accomplice is established at the level of wrongdoing, and then whether the participants are intentional. The question is whether the act of accomplice must be causally related to the act of the perpetrator or to the result caused by the perpetrator (the result of the perpetrator). Generally speaking, it is easy to determine the psychological causality between the act of the abettor and the result of the perpetrator,[60] and what needs to be discussed is the causality of the act of aiding.

It is obvious that since the act of the perpetrator is the cause of the result of the perpetrator, there can be no causality between the aiding and the result of the perpetrator if the aiding is not causal to the act of the perpetrator. The question is, when the aiding only promotes to the act of the perpetrator but not to the result of the perpetrator. Or when there is no causality between the aiding and the result of the perpetrator, can the behavioral result of the perpetrator be attributed to the aiding?

The theory of abstract danger holds that, in general, an act which makes the perpetrating of the perpetrator easier at the time when it is perpetrated, indirectly creates a danger to the legal interest, which is the reason for punishment as a secondary offender. Therefore, it is not only not required that there be causality between the aiding and the result of the perpetrator, but also not required that there be causality between the aiding and the act of the perpetrator. For example, as long as, in general, the act strengthens and contributes to the criminal intent of others, it is established as an aider.[61] In our traditional theory, when discussing the conditions for the establishment of joint crime, only two or more persons are required to have a joint criminal act, neither causality between the act of accomplice and the result, nor causality between the act of accomplice and the act of the perpetrator. Basically, this theory of abstract danger is adopted.

However, this theory of abstract danger does not distinguish between punishable and unpunishable aiding and cannot be applied in China.

Example 16 After B and C quarreled, A thought that B would kill C, and then A handed a long knife to B, but B did not kill C at all. According to the theory of abstract danger, A's act also "generally" contributed to B's intent to commit the crime. However, China's criminal law provisions of criminal attempt is for the

---

[59] 日佐伯仁志:《刑法总论の考え方、楽しみ方》，有斐阁2013年版，第370页。Saeki Hitoshi.(2013) *How to Think and Enjoy the General Theory of Criminal Law,* Yuhikaku Press, 370.

[60] Of course, in special circumstances, it is not excluded that the abetting is only causally related to the act of the principal offender.

[61] 参见日野村稔:《刑法总论》，成文堂1998年补订版，第421页以下。See Nomura Minoru. (1979) *General Theory of Criminal Law*, Seibundo Publishing Co., 1–421.

perpetrator, Article 27 of *Chinese Criminal Law* provides that the aider exists only in the joint crime, so A's act is not punishable.

This shows that the theory of abstract danger is not in line with the provisions of our criminal law. On the other hand, if it is held that as long as the actor commits an act of aiding, even if the act of aiding has no effect on the act of the perpetrator, the aider shall be established. It will be impossible to distinguish between aiding to an accomplished crime and aiding to an attempted crime, still less between aiding to an attempted crime and the attempted aiding.[62]

Example 17 A wanted to burglary the property of C and asked B to put the key in the mailbox below the house of A, then B promised and misplaced the key of the C in the mailbox below the house of others. A did not find the key and implemented other methods to burglary the property of the C. B shall be culpable for the crime of accomplished theft if the theory of abstract danger is adopted. However, there is no causality between B's so-called aiding and A's theft and the result of theft. B's aiding is attempted, rather than the aid of the attempted crime, much less the aid of the accomplished crime. Therefore, the result of A's theft should not be attributed to B's act.

The theory of specific danger holds that the causality of the aiding, especially the psychological causality, is difficult to be limited and should be abandoned, and that it is necessary to adopt the formula of "promotion", which is the "the theory of increased danger" that adopts the theory of objective attribution. From the point of view of a person with specialized knowledge at the time of the act, if the aiding is considered to "increased the success of the act of the perpetrator", the accomplished aiding shall be established.[63] Accordingly, a person who provides an entry key should be deemed to have accomplished aiding, even if the perpetrator did not use the key, as long as it can be determined beforehand that the key may be necessary.[64]

Obviously, the theory of specific danger likewise cannot distinguish between aiding to an attempted crime and aiding to an accomplished crime, nor can it distinguish between aiding to an attempted crime and the attempted aiding.

Example 18 The perpetrator A determined to burglary and B knew and provided the key. However, A forgot to bring the key provided by B and turned over the window and burglarized after arriving at the scene. Although it is necessary to confirm that the burglary requires the key beforehand, it is obviously inappropriate to identify the act of B as the accomplished aiding.

---

[62] 参见日山口厚:《问题探究刑法总论》，有斐阁1998年版，第252页。Yamaguchi Atsushi. (1998) *Problematic Criminal Law Overview*, Yuhikaku Press, 252.

[63] Vgl.F.Schaffstein, *Die Risikoerhohung als onjektives Zurechnungsprinzip im Strafrecht,insbesondere bei der Beihilfe, in:Festschrift fur Richard M.Honig*, Otto Schwartz & Co.Göttingen,1970,S.175ff.

[64] R.D.Herzberg,*Anstiftung und Beihilfe als Straftatbeständs*,GA 1971, S.7.

The theory of the act of perpetrator holds that it is sufficient that the aiding is causal to the act of the perpetrator, or that "as long as the aiding makes the act of the perpetrator possible, easy, or promotes or strengthens the act of the perpetrator, the causality of the aiding shall be identified."[65] "German jurisprudence has historically taken the position that it does not require causality between the aiding and the result of the perpetrator; it is sufficient that the aiding promotes (*frdern*) the 'act' of the perpetrator. Accordingly, B handed over the key to A, but A thought that the key did not work and used another method to invade the warehouse and steal property finally. Or B handed iron pliers to A as a tool to invade the warehouse, but A did not use it and invaded the warehouse by using other methods to steal property. Then, the act of B was considered as the aiding of the crime of accomplished theft."[66] There are two reasons for the theory of the act of perpetrator: (a) the criminal aider is one who aids the perpetrator,[67] so that "it is sufficient that the aiding helps the perpetrator by making the act of the perpetrator easier. The causality of the aider should be understood as making it physically or psychologically easier to commit the act of the perpetrator"[68]; and (b) the aiding can only make the act of the perpetrator easier, but cannot be the direct cause of the result. Therefore, it is inherently reluctant to treat the causality between the aiding and the result caused by the perpetrator as an issue and directly prove the causality of aiding. From the theory of the derivativeness of accomplice, the causality between the act of the perpetrator and the result should be considered as the criminal act of the perpetrator, and the infringement of legal interest of the aiding presupposes the causality between the act of the perpetrator and the result, as long as there is a promotion relationship between the aiding and the act of the perpetrator.[69]

However, First, literally speaking, those who aid the perpetrator under criminal law do not mean that they only promote to the act of the perpetrator. Second, it is true that there cannot be a direct causality between the aiding and the result of the perpetrator, but the characteristic of the aider is originally to cause the infringement of legal interest indirectly through others. Therefore, it is possible to determine whether the aiding has indirect causality with the result of the perpetrator, that is, whether the aiding has promoted to the result through the act the perpetrator. Third, the standard for determining the so-called promotion to the result through the act the perpetrator is quite vague. In the case where the perpetrator did not use the tools provided by the aider to break into the warehouse, it is difficult to determine whether

---

[65] H. Jeschck /T.Weigend, *Lehrbuch des Strafrechts.Allgemeiner Teil*, 5.Aufl., Duncker & Humblot,1996,S.694.

[66] 日西田典之:《共犯理论の展开》，成文堂2010年版，第193页。See Nishida Noriyuki. (2010) *Development of Complicity Theory*, Seibundo Publishing Co, 193.

[67] For example, Article 62 of *Japanese Criminal Law* stipulates: "Aiding the principal offender is an accessory."

[68] 日川端博:《刑法总论讲义》，成文堂2006年版，第575页。Kawabata Hiroshi.(2006) *General Lectures on Criminal Law*, Seibundo Publishing Co., 575.

[69] 参见日植松正等编:《现代刑法论争I》，劲草书房1997年版，第341页。See Uematsu Tadashi.(1997) et al., ed., *Modern Debates in Criminal Law I*,Keisoshobo Co., 341.

the aiding promotes the act of the perpetrator. Fourth, if it is considered sufficient that the aiding has causality with the act of the perpetrator, it is impossible to distinguish between the attempted aiding of the perpetrator and the accomplished aiding of the perpetrator. Thus, the act that merely provides the basis for the *Strafbarkeit* of the attempted crime becomes at the same time the basis for culpability for the perpetrator of the accomplished crime. This is clearly inappropriate.[70] Fifth, the theory of the act of the perpetrator is actually the position of the theory of illegal accomplice, but the theory of illegal accomplice has major flaws.[71]

The theory of the result of the perpetrator holds that the aider can be made culpable for accomplished crime only if there is causality between the aiding and the result of the perpetrator.[72] This article advocates this view.

(a) Since the theory of causality of accomplice is adopted, the theory of the result of the perpetrator shall be adopted as well. According to the theory of causality of accomplice, the basis of punishment for the accomplice lies in causing the infringement of legal interest that meets the constitutive element through the perpetrator. Therefore, only if the aiding physically or psychologically promotes or strengthens the result of perpetrator, can the punishment for the aider be justified. If the aiding has no effect on the appearance of the result of constitutive element, it is impossible to attribute the result of perpetrator to the aiding, and the aider cannot be culpable for the accomplished crime. And for the accomplice to be identified to have caused the result of constitutive element through the perpetrator, it is required that the aiding promotes to the result of the perpetrator. Otherwise, it should be impossible to say that the aiding caused the infringement of legal interest result by intervening in the act of perpetrator. In Example 7, although B took the initiative to lookout, but objectively did not have any impact on the result of A's theft, so there is no physical causality. And because A did not know that B was looking out for the theft, B's lookout did not psychologically strengthen and promote A's intent, so there is no psychological causality with the result of A's theft. Not only that, B's lookout and A's theft itself also has no causality. Therefore, B could not be held criminally culpable for A's theft.

(b) As long as a distinction is made between the attempted aiding and the accomplished aiding, it is necessary to adopt the theory of the result of perpetrator. If an act that does not promote to the result is punished as the aider of the accomplished crime, the line between aiding to an attempted crime and aiding to the criminal accomplish is lost. In Example 8, when A committed the theft, he used the key

---

[70] Vgl., C.Roxin, *Strafrecht Allgenmeiner Teil, Band II*, C.H.Beck 2003,S.192ff; 日曾根威彦:《刑法总论》，弘文堂2008年版，第263页。See Sone Takehiko. (2008) *General Theory of Criminal Law*, Seibundo Publishing Co., 263.

[71] 参见杨金彪:《共犯的处罚根据》，中国人民公安大学出版社2008年版，第44页以下。See Yang Jinbiao. (2008) *Grounds for Punishment of Complicity*, Press of Chinese People's Public Security University, 1–44.

[72] 参见日小岛阳介:"精神的帮助における因果关系について"，载《法学论丛(京都大学)》第161卷(2007年)第4号。See Kojima Yousuke.(2007) "On causation in mental assistance", as cited in *Kyoto University Law Review*, Vol. 161, No. 4.

provided by B. In this regard, the aiding of B was still only for the attempted crime. However, the key provided by B did not promote to the result of A's theft of the car. Therefore, B is only criminally culpable for the attempted theft. If B is made criminally culpable for accomplished theft, it shall mean that B would be criminally culpable for results that are not causally related to B's act, which is obviously improper.

(c) The causation is a necessary element for attribution, and it is no exception for the aider. In the case of an individual perpetrator and the perpetrator in a joint crime, the causation is a necessary element for the objective attribution of the result to the perpetrator. If there is no causality between the occurrence of the result and the act of the perpetrator, it is impossible to make the perpetrator culpable for the result. The aider is a kind of ground of the penalty expansion, since the attribution of results to the perpetrator presupposes a causality, it is necessary to make such a requirement for the aider. Otherwise, it would be clearly incompatible with such a ground of the penalty expansion for the aider. It can also be said that the conclusion that the aider is criminally culpable for an accomplished crime even for results that are not causally related to his own acts is the conclusion of subjectivism in theory of criminal law, which is not taken by today's theory of criminal law.

In summary, the aider is culpable for the result of the perpetrator only when there is physical causality or psychological causality between the aiding and the result of the perpetrator. The physical causality between the aiding and the result of the perpetrator is mainly manifested as follows: First, the result of the perpetrator cannot occur without the aiding. For example, the aider provides the key to the perpetrator, and the perpetrator stole the cash in the safe. Second, the aiding extends the range of results of the perpetrator. For example, when a perpetrator borrows a gun from a aider to kill someone, the aider provides a grenade, resulting in multiple deaths. Third, the aiding aggravates the degree of result. For example, the perpetrator asked the aider for narcotics for robbery, and the aider provided the chemicals that caused death, resulting in the death when the perpetrator robed. Fourth, the aidering makes the result of perpetrator in advance. For example, the aider provides the victim's whereabouts, so that the perpetrator quickly kills the victim. Fifth, the aiding makes the risk of the result of the perpetrator increased (so that the result occurs more easily). For example, the perpetrator is ready to break the window to burglarize the house, the aider provides the key to burglarize the house, making it easier for the perpetrator to burglarize. The psychological causality between the aiding and the result of the perpetrator is mainly manifested in strengthening the decision of the perpetrator to cause the result, or to make the perpetrator feel comfortable to carry out the infringement of legal interest and cause the result of infringement.

Example 19 Woman A, who had an inappropriate relationship with man B and said to B when she knew that B wanted to kill his wife C, "If you kill C, I will marry you." A strengthens B's motive to kill and reduced the likelihood that B would give up his intent to commit the crime, finally, B killed C. In this regard, it should be affirmed that there is psychological causality between the act of A and the result of the perpetrator.[73]

Of course, in specific cases, there may be both physical and psychological causality between the aiding and the result of the perpetrator. This is the case, for example, when the act of lookout not only reassures the perpetrator of the theft, but also objectively prevents the victim from immediately discovering the act of perpetrator, thus enabling the perpetrator to accomplish the theft.

There are several other issues that need to be discussed when adopting the theory of the result of perpetrator.

(a) Regarding the relationship between the theory of the act of the perpetrator and the theory of the result of the perpetrator, some scholars in Germany point out that "as long as there is an effect on the way the act of perpetrator, there is actually a causality with the result."[74] Some scholars in Japan also argue that "if the act of the perpetrator is promoted, it can naturally be evaluated as promoting the result of the perpetrator."[75] In fact, the act of promoting the perpetrator should be distinguished from the result of promoting the perpetrator. In Example 8, although B's act of aiding promoted the theft of the perpetrator, it did not promote the result of the perpetrator.

Example 20 The aider provided the key to the perpetrator, and the perpetrator used it too hard that it broke in the lock, so the perpetrator used other methods to open the vault and stole the cash. It can be argued that when the perpetrator used the key provided by the aider, he already started to commit theft, and the aider's act did promote the act of perpetrator. However, since the perpetrator opened the vault by other means, the act of the aider cannot be considered to have promoted the result of the perpetrator. Thus, there is a distinction between the causality of the act of the perpetrator and the causality of the result of the perpetrator.[76]

(b) While adopting the theory of the result of the perpetrator, whether causality is also required between the aiding and the act of perpetrator. Some Japanese scholars have pointed out that "given that the basis of punishment for the accomplice is that the result caused by intervening the act of the perpetrator, as the objective aspect of the constitutive elements of the accomplice (in a broad sense), it requires not only a causality with the final result, but also causality that makes the act of the

---

[73] 参见日松原芳博:《刑法总论》，日本评论社2013年版，第379页。See Matsubara Yoshihiro.(2013) *General Theory of Criminal Law*, NIPPON HYORON SHA Co., 379.

[74] C.Roxin, *Was ist Beihilfe?, in Festschrift für Koichi Miyazawa*, nomos,1995,S.502 f.

[75] 日大塚仁等编:《大コンメンタ-ル刑法》(第五卷)，青林书院1999年版，第576页。See Otsuka Hitoshi et al., ed.,(1999) *The Grand Commentary on Criminal Law* (Vol. 5). Seirin Shoin, 576.

[76] 参见日小岛阳介:"精神的帮助における因果关系について"，载《法学论丛(京都大学)》第161卷(2007年)第4号。See Kojima Yousuke.(2007) "On causation in mental assistance", as cited in *Kyoto University Law Review*, Vol. 161, No. 4.

perpetrator easier."[77] Logically, only the aiding that has causality with the act of the perpetrator may further have causality with the result of the perpetrator. In fact, however, if it is possible to affirm causality between the aiding and the result of the perpetrator, it is necessarily possible to affirm causality between the aiding and the act of perpetrator. On the other hand, if the causality between the aiding and the result of the perpetrator is denied and the causality between the aiding and the act of perpetrator can be affirmed, then it can be recognized as the aider of the attempted crime. This is the case in Example 8 above.

(c) When adopting the theory of the result of the perpetrator, does it require a conditional relation between the aiding and the result of the perpetrator that "there is no latter without the former"? This is controversial in Germany and Japan.[78] In this article, it depends on whether the conditional relation shall be agreed to be modified and how to understand the result of the perpetrator (whether the view of the specific result shall be adopted).

Example 21 A determined to kill D, B and C who knew A's intent did not contact previously but they provided the guns with the same performance to A, and A used the gun provided by B to kill D. According to the theory of the necessity of the conditional relation, B and C are not aiders because A would use the gun provided by C to kill D even without the gun provided by B, and vice versa. However, first, if the conditional relation is amended,[79] then there is a conditional relation between both B's and C's acts and D's death. Second, if the result of death is not the death of D in the abstract sense, but rather that D died at what time and by what gun, then a conditional relation between B's aiding and D's death can be affirmed.. In other words, the causality of the aiding can be affirmed as long as there is a result of the perpetrator that would not have occurred at this time and in this form without the aiding.[80] In this article, it is entirely possible to take the theory of *Conditio-sine-qua-non-Formel* with lawfulness at the same time as the theory of *Conditio-sine-qua-non-Formel*.[81] In Example 21, the gun provided by B legally caused the result

---

[77] 日岛田聡一郎:"他人の行为の介入と正犯成立の限界(二)", 载《法学协会杂志》第117卷(2000年)第3号。Shimada Souichirou.(2000) "Intervention of others' actions and limits of principal offender liability (II)", as cited in *Journal of the Law Association*, Vol. 117, No. 3.

[78] 参见德约翰内斯·韦塞尔斯:《德国刑法总论》, 李昌珂译, 法律出版社2008年版, 第330~331页; 日西田典之:《共犯理论の展开》, 成文堂2010年版, 第189页以下。Johannes Wessels, trans. Li Changke, (2008) *Strafrecht Allgemeiner Teil*, Law Press, 330–331; See Nishida Noriyuki.(2010) *Development of Complicity Theory*, Seibundo Publishing Co, 1–189.

[79] That is, in the case where several acts cause one result, if the result also occur with certain act being removed, while will not occur when all the acts being removed, then all the acts should be the causes of that result. (Vgl.,H.Welzel,*Das Deutsche Strafrecht,* 11.Aufl.,Walter de Gruyter & Co.1969, S.41).

[80] 参见日内田文昭:"帮助の因果性", 载《判例タイムズ》第717号(1990年)。Uchida Fumiaki. (1990) "Causation in aiding", as cited in *Case Law Times,* No. 717.

[81] 参见张明楷:"也谈客观归责理论", 载《中外法学》2013年第2期。See Zhang Mingkai. (2013) "Also on the Theory of Objective Imputation", as cited in *Chinese Journal of Comparative Law,* No. 2.

of D's death, and the physical causality between B's act and D's death shall be affirmed.

(d) The lack of physical causality between the aiding and the result of the perpetrator does not necessarily mean that there is also a lack of psychological causality. In the absence of physical causality, it is necessary to determine whether there is psychological causality, and vice versa. Of course, since physical causality is easier to identify, it should be identified first.[82]

In Example 21, although there is no physical causality between C's act in fact and the result of D's death, C's act also strengthen and promote A's crime intent, and thus have a psychological causality with the result of D's death.[83]

Example 22 A intended to burglary and B provided the tool for breaking in the door after B knew the crime intention of A. A went toward C's house with the tool and the master key he prepared. With a master key, A opened the door of the C's house and stole a large amount of property. In this case, although there is no physical causality between the act of providing the tool of B and the theft of A, but the act strengthens and promotes the theft, thus there is a psychological causality with the result.

It follows that physical aiding and psychological aiding are not equivalent to physical causality and psychological causality. In Example 22, B commits a physical aiding, but has only psychological causality with the result of the perpetrator. For example, if the aider merely dictates to perpetrator of the theft how to open the door and how to start the car, and the perpetrator of the theft steals the car according to the method described by the aider, there is physical causality between the aider's act and the result of the perpetrator. For another example, if the aider provides the perpetrator of the theft with the keys needed to steal the car, and if the aider does not provide the keys, the perpetrator will not decide to commit the crime, the physical aiding of aider actually has a psychological causality with the result.

The question is, under what circumstances does the physical aiding create psychological causality? One view is that the act of providing the key may have psychological causality with the result of the perpetrator even if the perpetrator has had the intent of theft and did not even use the key provided by the aider in the process of implementation.[84] Accordingly, any physical aiding has psychological causality with the result of the perpetrator, and this absolute view would make the identification of causality meaningless. This article argues that, for this type of case, three situations can be distinguished. First, B knew that A would burglarize the house and

[82] Of course, in the case that physical causality does exsit, the identification of psychological causality can be performed. However, this identification only has a certain meaning for sentencing and has no substantial effect on conviction.

[83] 参见日西田典之:《共犯理论の展开》，成文堂2010年版，第199页。See Nishida Noriyuki. (2010) Development of Complicity Theory, Seibundo Publishing Co, 199.

[84] 参见日佐伯仁志:《刑法总论の考え方、楽しみ方》，有斐阁2013年版，第372~373页。Saeki Hitoshi.(2013) How to Think and Enjoy the General Theory of Criminal Law, Yuhikaku Press, 372~373.

provided the key to A, but A arrived at the scene and first used the tools he carried to burglarize the house and stole other's property. In this case, it is still possible to affirm that there is a psychological causality between B's aiding and the result of A's theft. Because A clearly knew during the theft that even if his own key could not open the door, there was still a key provided by B. Therefore, B's aiding strengthened A's criminal intent. Second, after arriving at the scene, A first used the key provided by B, but found that B's key did not work at all, so he used his own key and stole the property. In this case, B's aiding is only physical causality with the act of committing theft, but there is neither physical nor psychological causality with the result of the principal crime. Since A knew that B's key did not play any role, it could not be considered that B's aiding was still strengthening A's criminal intent. Therefore, B is only established as an adier to the attempted crime. Third, if A first used the key provided by B after arriving at the scene, and opened the door and stole the property, it can be considered that the act of providing the key by B and the result of A's theft has both physical causality and psychological causality.

(e) Whether there is causality (especially psychological causality) between the act of accomplice and the result of the perpetrator and whether the aider has intentionality are two different issues. But the conclusion that psychological causality presupposes that there is joint intent is not true. For example, B simply described the fact that the warehouse door and windows were broken, unguarded, and vulnerable to theft, but caused B's criminal intent to steal, then B committed the theft. There is a psychological causality between B's act and the results of A's acts, but A did not abet the intent. This once again shows that it is perfectly feasible to understand and identify joint crime at the level of wrongdoing.

(f) The so-called "withdrawing from the accomplice" is actually also a question of the causality of the accomplice. In other words, when the accomplice abandons or is forced to stop the act of the accomplice and the result is caused by others, under what circumstances is the causality between *Ingerenz* of the accomplice and the result of the perpetrator denied (i.e., affirmed withdrawing from the accomplice), so that only the accomplice is held criminally culpable for the discontinued or attempted crime? In other words, in some cases, although the actor commits an act of accomplice (abetting or aiding), then later eliminates the effect of promotion, thus resulting in no causality between *Ingerenz* of accomplice and the result, it is the so-called "withdrawing from the accomplice". Therefore, it actually means the simultaneous elimination of physical causality and psychological causality between the already committed act of the perpetrator and the result.

Example 23 A invited B lookout for the theft, B agreed. However, after A entered the house, B quietly slipped away and A did not know. In this regard, if it is certain that there is no causality between B's act of leaving and A's accomplished theft, then it is "withdrawing from the accomplice", and B only bears the criminal culpability of the discontinued or attempted crime. Conversely, B still bear criminal culpability for the results of the perpetrator.

Obviously, the identification of "withdrawing from the accomplice" is not substantially different from the aforementioned identification of causality. In the case of Example 23, because A thought that B lookout for the theft, so even if B left, his act still made A feel safe, and therefore there is a psychological causality with the results of A's theft. On the contrary, if, before the accomplished theft, B explicitly told A he wanted to leave and no longer lookout for A, but A still stole alone, the causality between B's previous lookout act and A's accomplished theft. Therefore, "withdrawing from the accomplice" shall establish. In the aforementioned Example 9, B did not arrive at the scene as promised and actually informed A that he would not to participate in the killing, so whether B is culpable for the death caused by A depends on the content of the conspiracy. For example, if B and A conspired the place and method of killing and A killed C according to the content of the conspiracy, or if the content of the conspiracy is that B promoted A to kill C, both situations are certain that there is a causality between B's conspiracy and the result of A's homicide. However, if A proposed to kill C, but only invited B to went to C's house the next day to kill C together or let B lookout, then, B did not arrive at the scene the next day, it cannot be considered that there is a causality between B's conspiracy and the result of A's homicide. At this point, B is withdrawing from the accomplice, at best, only a preparatory to intentional homicide.

Similarly, "withdrawing from the joint perpetrator" is also a matter of identification of causality.

Example 24 A couple who wanted to kill their daughter's illegitimate child, and after they thought that they had killed the child, the husband left. However, the wife later found out that the child was still alive and killed the child alone.[85] The previous killing committed jointly by the husband and wife was causally linked to the child's life being in danger, and therefore the two are joint perpetrator of attempted intentional homicide. However, after the husband left, the result of the wife killed the child alone could not be attributed to the husband's previous act, and therefore, the wife shall bear the criminal culpability of accomplished homicide alone.

Conversely, even if some perpetrators abandon his or her act, he or she shall be culpable for that result as long as there is causality between the act he or she has committed and the result of the other perpetrators.

Example 25 A and B committed violence against woman C with the intent to commit gang rape. After A raped C, B abandoned the rape out of pity. Some scholars have argued that B's act shall establish discontinued crime of rape on the grounds that rape is a personally committing crime and that the act of rape has no substitutability.[86] In fact, the rape is not a personally committing crime.[87] More importantly,

---

[85] Vgl.,C.Roxin, Strafrecht Allgenmeiner Teil, Band II, C.H.Beck 2003,S.79f.

[86] 陈兴良:《共同犯罪论》，中国社会科学出版社2006年版，第372~373页。Chen Xingliang. (2006) *On Joint Crimes*, China Social Sciences Press, 372–373.

[87] The basic sign of 'personally committing crime' is the absence of the possibility of establishing an indirect principal offender. However, The usage of the man without the criminal culpability by the woman that rape other women undoubtedly constitutes an indirect principal offender of crime of the rape.另参见日山口厚:《刑法各论》，有斐阁2010年版，第109页。See Yamaguchi Atsushi.(2010) *Special Part of Criminal Law*. Yuhikaku Press, 109.

although B discontinued the rape there is a causality between the previous violence and the result of the rape. In this case, it is necessary to impute the result of the rape to the act of B. And because B had the intent of committing rape, so B also establishes the accomplished crime of rape.

10.5 Brief Conclusion

To sum up, the identification of joint crime should focus on wrongdoing (from wrongdoing to culpability), center on perpetrator (from perpetrator to accomplice), and be oriented by causality (from physical causality to psychological causality). Therefore, wrongdoing and culpability should not be mixed together to identify joint crime, nor should the establishment or non-establishment of joint crime be discussed as a whole, the identification of causality should not be ignored as well.

The entity of crime is wrongdoing and culpability, and the identification of "what crime" depends not only on wrongdoing but also on culpability, while joint crime solves the problem of wrongdoing, so there is no need to ask and answer the question of "what crime is committed by joint crime". For example, in Example 4, as long as it is identified that A and B jointly committed violence against C, resulting in the death of C, it should be found that they shall establish a joint crime, therefore, the death shall be objectively attributed to their act and they are culpable for the death at the level of wrongdoing (objective attribution). As for the subjective culpability of A and B (the content of their respective intent) and constitutes what crime shall be identified separately. The crime of accomplished intentional homicide is established because of A's intent to kill. While the crime of intentional injury (causing death) is established because of B's intent to injure and negligence in the death. Therefore, the two persons may not be found guilty of the same crime even the joint crime is identified. This being the case, there is absolutely no need to ask the question of what crime is jointly committed by two or more persons.

According to the viewpoint of this article, the concept of "joint crime" can be completely diluted in theory of criminal law and judicial practice. In other words, as long as the focus is on the wrongdoing, the center is on the perpetrator and keep the causality-oriented to identify the case of several persons participating in the crime, then, (1) the perpetrator (including joint perpetrator) should be identified at the level of wrongdoing, and after the perpetrator is identified, the result or danger must be objectively attributed to the act of the perpetrator; (2) the causality between the act of which participants and the result of the perpetrator should be identified, and as long as there is causality, it can be affirmed as the accomplice at the level of wrongdoing; (3) to identify the culpability of each participant separately (such as the age of culpability, the content of intent, etc.), and then to determine the crimes committed by the participants; (4) to sentence each participant separately according to the principle of punishment of the principal, secondary offender, coerced accomplice, and abettor in our criminal law. It is easy to see that at none of these steps is it necessary to ask and answer questions such as "who is guilty of a joint crime with whom" and "what crime is committed jointly".. Therefore, even if the concept of "joint crime" is not used, it is perfectly possible to identify the phenomenon of several persons participating in a crime together. It is true that our criminal law uses the concept of "joint crime", but the provisions of our criminal law on joint crime do have a variety of possibilities of interpreting.

References

Chen Xingliang. (2006) *On Joint Crimes*, China Social Sciences Press, 372–373.

Dandou Shigemitsu. (1990) *General Outline of Criminal Law*, Kodansha Publishing Co, 155, 159;

Gao Mingxuan & Ma Kechang eds. (2011) *Criminal Law*, Peking University Press & Higher Education Press, 163-166, 169, 176.

Gao Mingxuan ed. (2002) *Monographs on Criminal Law* (Vol 1), Higher Education Press, 330, 362–363.

Giinter Stratenwerth & Lothar Kuhlen, trans. Yang Meng, (2006) Strafrecht Allgemeiner Teil I: Die Straftat, Law Press, 292, 309.

H. Jeschck/T. Weigend, *Lehrbuch des Strafrechts. Allgemeiner Teil*, 5.Aufl., Duncker & Humblot, 1996,S.664, 694.

He Qingren. (2004) "The Two Implications of Instigator in China's Criminal Law," as cited in *Chinese Journal of Law*, No. 4.

Humblot, 1996, S.675.

Johannes Wessels, trans. Li Changke, (2008) *Strafrecht Allgemeiner Teil*, Law Press, 330-331; See Nishida Noriyuki. (2010) *Development of Complicity Theory*, Seibundo Publishing Co, 1-189

Joshua Dressler, trans. Wang Xiumei, (2009) *Understanding Criminal Law*, Beijing: Peking University Press, 1-383

Kawabata Hiroshi. (2006) *General Lectures on Criminal Law*, Seibundo Publishing Co., 575.

Liu Mingxiang. (2011) Interpretation of 'The Instigated Person Did Not Commit the Crime Instigated', as citd in *Chinese Journal of Law*, No. 1.

Maeda Masahide. (2011) *Handouts of General Rules of Criminal Law*, University of Tokyo Press, 464

Nishida Noriyuki. (2010) *General Theory of Criminal Law*, Koubundou Publishers Inc., 328, 336-337.

Otsuka Hitoshi. (2008) *Overview of Criminal Law*, Yuhikaku Press, 162.

Press, 370

Principal Offender's Intent, as cited in Tribune of Political Science and Law, No. 5.

R.D. Herzberg, *Anstiftung und Beihilfe als Straftatbeständs*,GA 1971, S.7.

Research on the Specific Provisions of Criminal Law (Vol 2), China Fangzheng Press, 2010, 855.

Roxin, *Strafrecht Allgenmeiner Teil, Band II*, C.H. Beck 2003,S. 7.S.9.

Roxin, *Was ist Beihilfe?, in Festschrift für Koichi Miyazawa*, nomos, 1995,S.502 f.

Saeki Hitoshi. (1992) "Attempted instigation", as cited in Abe Junji et al, ed., *Basic Lectures on Criminal Law* (Vol. 4), Hogaku Shoin, 209.

Saeki Hitoshi. (2013) How to Think and Enjoy the General Theory of Criminal Law, Yuhikaku Press, 372-373

See Hirano Ryuuichi. (1975) General Theory of Criminal Law II, Yuhikaku Press, 1-347

See Kojima Yousuke. (2007) "On causation in mental assistance", as cited in *Kyoto University Law Review*, Vol. 161, No. 4.

See Ma Kechang ed. (1999) *General Theory of Crime*, Wuhan University Press, 584; Lin Wei. (2013) Unfolding Issues of Complicity in Truly Status-based Offenses, as cited in *Jurists' Review*, No. 6.

See Matsubara Yoshihiro. (2013) *General Theory of Criminal Law*, NIPPON HYORON SHA Co., 368, 379.
See Matsumiya Takaaki. (2003) *Criminal Legislation and Criminal System*, Seibundo Publishing Co., 259.
See Nishida Noriyuki. (2010) *Development of Complicity Theory*, Seibundo Publishing Co, 193, 199.
See Naitou Ken. (2001) *General Lectures on Criminal Law (Medium)*, Yuhikaku Press, 737.
See Sone Yoshihiko. (2005) *Fundamentals of Criminal Law*, trans. Li Hong, Law Press China, 1-137.
See Nomura Minoru. (1979) *General Theory of Criminal Law,* Seibundo Publishing Co., 1-421.
See Otsuka Hitoshi et al, ed., (1999) *The Grand Commentary on Criminal Law* (Vol. 5). Seirin Shoin, 576.
See Qian Yeliu. (2010) Discussion on Controversial Issues in the Determination of 'Gang Rape' Circumstances, as cited in *Jianghuai Tribune*, No. 5.
See Qian Yeliu. (2012) Distinction between Principal Offenders and Accomplices under the Two-tiered Distinction System, as cited in *Chinese Journal of Law*, No. 1.
See Sone Takehiko. (2008) *General Theory of Criminal Law*, Seibundo Publishing Co., 263.
See Supreme People's Court. (1998) *Interpretation on Several Issues Concerning the Specific Application of Law in Adjudicating Cases of Misappropriation of Public Funds* (Apr. 29, 1998), Art. 8.
See Uematsu Tadashi. (1997) et al, ed., *Modern Debates in Criminal Law I*, Keisoshobo Co., 341.
See Yamaguchi Atsushi. (2010) *Special Part of Criminal Law*. Yuhikaku Press, 1-349
See Yang Jinbiao. (2008) *Grounds for Punishment of Complicity*, Press of Chinese People's Public Security University, 1-44.
See Yang Xingpei. (2012) Re-examination and Criticism of the Theory of Principal Offenders and Aidors in Joint Crimes, as cited in *Research on Rule of Law*, No. 8;
See Yao Shi. (2013) Criminal Liability of the Knowing Joint Offender in Cases of Prior Act and Excessive Execution, as cited in *Chinese Journal of Law*, No. 5.
See Zhang Mingkai. (2010a) *The System of Criminal Constitution and the Elements of Constitutive Requirements*, Peking University Press, 1-70.
See Zhang Mingkai. (2010b) *The System of Criminal Constitution and the Elements of Constitutive Requirements*, Peking University Press, 1-49.
See Zhang Mingkai. (2013) "Also on the Theory of Objective Imputation", as cited in *Chinese Journal of Comparative Law,* No. 2.
See Zhou Guangquan. (2013) Understanding of 'The Instigated Person Did Not Commit the Crime Instigated', as cited in *Chinese Journal of Law*, No. 4.
Shimada Souichirou. (2000) "Intervention of others' actions and limits of principal offender liability (II)", as cited in *Journal of the Law Association*, Vol. 117, No. 3.
Uchida Fumiaki. (1990) "Causation in aiding", as cited in *Case Law Times*, No. 717.
Urs Kindhäuser, trans. Xv Lingbo, Cai Guisheng, (2014) *Zur Logik des Verbrechensaufbaus*, as cited in *Chinese Journal of Comparative Law,* No.1. Maeda Masahide. (2006) *Handouts of General Rules of Criminal Law*, University of Tokyo Press, 29
Vgl.,C.Roxin, *Strafrecht Allgenmeiner Teil,* Band II, C.H. Beck 2003,S.79f,109, 133, 138, 226;
Vgl.,H.Jeschck/T.Weigend, *Lehrbuch des Strafrechts.Allgemeiner Teil*, 5.Aufl., Duncker & Vgl.,H. Welzel, *Das Deutsche Strafrecht,* 11.Aufl.,Walter de Gruyter & Co. 1969, S.41
Vgl.F. Schaffstein, *Die Risikoerhohung als onjektives Zurechnungsprinzip im Strafrecht, insbesondere bei der Beihilfe, in: Festschrift fur Richard M.Honig*, Otto Schwartz & Co.Göttingen, 1970,S.175ff.
Wang Zuofu. ed. (2009) *Criminal Law*, China Renmin University of Press, 138.
Yamaguchi Atsushi. (1998) *Problematic Criminal Law Overview*, Yuhikaku Press, 252
Yamaguchi Atsushi. (2007) *General Rules of Criminal Law*, Yuhikaku Press, 72, 300.
Zhang Mingkai. (2011) Criminal Law, Law Press China, 1-348, 398;

Chapter 11
Legal Concurrence and Ideal Concurrence

The question about how to distinguish between the legal concurrence and ideal concurrence involves not only multiple theoretical issues of the theory of quantity of crime, but also the principle of punishment for related crimes (for example, whether the special relationship of the legal concurrence could apply the principle of law of serious punishment is prior to law of light punishment as an exception). However, the theory of criminal law in China has not correctly distinguished the legal concurrence and the ideal concurrence, thus resulting in many disputes deviating from the focus, and the related issues have not been properly resolved.

11.1 Necessity of Distinction

There are two differences between the legal consequences of the legal concurrence and the ideal concurrence: (1) In the special relationship of the legal concurrence, when the articles of mitigating punishment belong to the special articles, according to the principle that special law is prior to general law, it cannot be inflicted punishment with one heavier crime and the articles of mitigating punishment must be applied.[1] In contrast, the ideal concurrence will always adopt the principle of

*The original title is "The Difference between Legal Concurrence and Ideal Concurrence", published in ***Chinese Journal of Law***, 2016, No.1.

[1] The regulatory concurrence is not limit to the overlap between one and other articles; it is possible to happen between different paragraphs and sections within one article. For example, there are regulatory concurrence between Paragraph 1, Paragraph 2 and Paragraph 3 of Article 236 of *Criminal Law in China*. For another example, the Article 263 has only one paragraph, among which the eight circumstances of aggravated robbery provided in the latter part is an overlap with the general robbery in the former part (special relationship).

M. Zhang, *The Fundamental Issues upon Criminal Law Theories*, Masterpieces of Contemporary Jurisprudents in China,
https://doi.org/10.1007/978-981-95-1276-8_11

inflicting punishment with one heavier crime. (2) Even if the articles of serious punishment are applied in dealing with other relationships (such as supplement relationships) of the legal concurrence, there is only one article applicable when it is the legal concurrence and other article shall be excluded from application. On the contrary, several articles violated by the act rather than one article shall be applied together in the ideal concurrence. All the crimes committed by the Accused shall be expressed explicitly in the judgment (the function express of the ideal concurrence in the third part of this article)[2] and only the described punishment of the heavier crime will be sentenced. Therefore, the legal concurrence is basically a single crime (the original one crime) while the ideal concurrence are several crimes but only be sentenced as a single.[3] Obviously, "if the legal consequences of ideal concurrence are compared with that of the legal concurrence, there will be an assertion that there is little difference in their legal consequences, except that the lighter punishment may also prevail in legal concurrence". But, "it should not be considered that it should not be concluded from this that, apart from special relationships, all other cases of legal concurrence can be treated as the ideal concurrence."[4] So the legal concurrence and ideal concurrence have been distinguished in theories of criminal law and judicial practices in various countries, and the adoption of a theory of broader concurrence that does not distinguish between the two[5] is not desirable.

As is well known, the criminal law in China has set up a number of "special articles" without any bases,[6] and it will lead to the phenomenon of 'unfitting punishment with crime' if strictly adopting the principle of special law is prior to general law strictly.

The most typical one is that the described punishment in "special articles" is lighter than the described punishment in general articles, and it does not have a mitigating basis, but rather an aggravating reason (Seemingly, it is the concurrence of the basic types and mitigating types. Substantially, it is the concurrence of basic types and aggravating types). For example, according to the accepted theory of criminal law, the crime of fraud only infringes on property, and the crime of insurance fraud infringes

---

[2]参见日只木诚:《罪数论の研究》，成文堂2009年补订版，第187页以下。See Tadaki Makoto.(2009) *Study on the theory of multiple crimes* (revised edition), Seibundo Publishing Co., 1–187.

[3]参见日前田雅英:《刑法总论讲义》，东京大学出版会2015年版，第392、399页; 日山口厚:《刑法总论》，有斐阁2007年版，第365、379页; 日井田良:《讲义刑法学·总论》，有斐阁2008年版，第523、532页。Maeda Masahide.(2015) *Handouts of General Rules of Criminal Law*, University of Tokyo Press, 392、399页. Yamaguchi Atsushi.(2007) *General Rules of Criminal Law*, Yuhikaku Press, 365、379; Ida Makoto. (2008) *Handout of Criminal Law·General Rules*, Yuhikaku Press, 523、532.

[4]德冈特·施特拉腾韦特、洛塔尔·库伦:《刑法总论I——犯罪论》，杨萌译，法律出版社2006年版，第445~446页。Giinter Stratenwerth & Lothar Kuhlen, trans. Yang Meng, (2006) *Strafrecht Allgemeiner Teil I: Die Straftat*, Law Press, 445~446.

[5]参见陈洪兵:"不必严格区分法条竞合与想象竞合——大竞合论之提倡"，载《清华法学》2012年第1期。Chen Hongbing. (2012) "On the Unnecessity of Strictly Distinguishing Legal Concurrence and Ideal Concurrence": An Advocacy of the Grand Concurrence Theory, as cited in *Tsinghua University Law Journal*, No. 1.

[6]The reason why quotation marks are used is that the general theory of criminal law considers these articles as special articles, but I disagree.

not only on property, but also on the financial control order. In this case, the described punishment should be heavier than (at least the same as) that of the crime of fraud when special provisions of the crime of insurance fraud is established.[7] However, on the contrary, the described punishment for the crime of insurance fraud is lighter than the crime of general fraud according to Article 198 of *Chinese Criminal Law*.[8] The principle of fitting punishment with crime is the basic principle of criminal law and shall be implemented. The principle of fitting punishment with crime can be implemented if adopting the principle of the law of serious punishment is prior to law of light punishment, but it may violates the provision of Article 266 of *Chinese Criminal Law* that "except as otherwise specifically provided in this Law". In terms of the relationship between the crime of insurance fraud and the crime of contractual fraud, the crime of insurance fraud shall sill be regarded as special article, and the ending of adopting such article will result in unfitting punishment with crime. If the crime of insurance fraud and the crime of general fraud (or crime of contractual fraud[9]) are not legal concurrence but ideal concurrence, it shall inflict punishment with one heavier crime for implementing the principle of fitting punishment with crime. However, one may have doubts about the conclusion that the two are ideal concurrence.

For quite some time, the theory of criminal law in China has adopted a single and formal standard to distinguish the legal concurrence and ideal concurrence, even by

[7] Actually, people may think that the crime of insurance fraud has the basis of mitigating punishment (参见蔡道通:"特别法条优于普通法条适用"，载《法学家》2015年第5期Cai Daotong. (2015) "On the Application of the Principle That the Special Provision Prevails over the General Provision", as cited in *Jurist*, No. 5.). However, from the perspective of the content of wrongdoing, because the system and order of insurance are becoming more and more important to people, and because the property of insurance companies should also be protected, the insurance fraud shall not be lighter than that of general fraud or contract fraud. There is no reason for the criminal law to adopt the attitude of providing less protection to the victim in insurance fraud cases. The criminal law of Japan doesn't provide special crime of fraud, and the insurance fraud has always been dealt with as the general crime of fraud (as is the case in the criminal laws of the most nations). Article 265 of *German Criminal Law* provides for the punishment of accomplished preparatory crime of insurance fraud and punishes the criminal attempt hereof (equivalent to the punishment of the unfinished preparatory act). It also provides that if the act conforms to the constitutive elements of the general crime of fraud, it shall be punished as the general crime of fraud. All these can prove that, the punishment for crime of insurance fraud shall not be lighter than that of general fraud.

[8] Besides, some of the statutory punishments set by special article and general article are identical in *Criminal Law* in China (the concurrence of basic types and the identical types). For example, the statutory punishment for the crime of forge, alter, buy or sell, steal or rob documents, certificates and seals of armed units in Paragraph 1 of Article 375 of *Criminal Law* is exactly the same as the statutory punishment for the crime of forges, alters, trades in, steals, forcibly seizes or destroys any official document, certificate or seal of a state authority in Paragraph 1 of Article 280 (and the act of destroy is omitted in the Article 375). Also, the statutory punishment of the crime of using methods of violence or threat to prevent military personnel from carrying out their duties stipulated in Article 368 is exactly the same as that of the crime of disrupting public service in Article 277. In this regard, the application of special article will not lead to the unfitting punishment with crime. However, from the legislative point of view, Paragraph 1 of Article 375 and Article 368 are completely unnecessary special articles.

[9] For the purpose here, the following discussion will just take the angle of the crime of insurance fraud and the crime of general fraud.

intervening the fact of case to decide whether there is an inclusive (subsumed) and crossed, or any other relationship between the two articles. As a result, a lot of ideal concurrences have been included in the legal concurrence (In particular, the special relationship hereof), which further leading to the phenomenon that the principle of fitting punishment with crime cannot be followed in handling cases. In other words, although lots of China's scholars have strictly followed to the principle of Germany and Japan that deals with the special relationship of legal concurrence (that is, the special article is prior to the general article), the special relationship itself has not been established in accordance with the German and Japanese theory of criminal law, and therefore leading to the fact that both the absorbing relationship and ideal concurrence in Germany and Japan have all been included in the special relationship. Hence, how to distinguish the legal concurrence and ideal concurrence has become a problem that needs to be re-examined by China's theory of criminal law.

In the view of this article, the formal standard is necessary, but it is only a prerequisite standard rather than the only standard. In addition to the formal standard, there should be a substantive standard: the identity of the legal interests and the inclusiveness of wrongdoing. Or to say, it cannot be affirmed as ideal concurrence or even substantial several crimes, but rather legal concurrence when the formal standard has been met while the substantive standard has not.

11.2 Formal Standard

The legal concurrence is different from the concept of the concepts' relations. However, it is only by rationalizing the relations between the articles that it is possible to clarify which of these situations may or may not establish a legal concurrence.

In general, there are several kinds of relations among the specific provisions of criminal law: (1) The opposite relation (heterogenous relationship or exclusive relationship), which assumes in that matters belong to the concept A cannot belong to concept B, and vice versa. Therefore, an act can only violate one article, not two articles. The typical situations are crimes of embezzlement (of entrusted objects) and theft.[10] The object of the former is the property possessed by the actor, and the object of the latter is the property possessed by others. Therefore, it is impossible for an act to violate the crime of embezzlement (of entrusted objects) and the crime of theft (except, of course, in joint possession). (2) The inclusive relation (subsumed relationship), which assumes in that all matters belong to concept A also belong to concept B, but it is not the case contrarily. For example, any act of killing must go through the process of injuring, and it is impossible that a man dies without being injured (for example, a man who has been poisoned to death must have experienced intestines and stomach injury, and there must be a minor injury that "neck injury and

[10] The full expressions seem a little bit lengthy here, of and for the convenience of discussion, this article will use the names of crime instead.

signs of suffocation" when someone has been strangled to death). Therefore, all the crimes of intentional homicide will violate the crime of intentional injury, or to say, the crime of intentional homicide includes the crime of intentional injury, but it cannot be said the crime of intentional injury violates the crime of intentional homicide at the same time. (3) The crossed relation, which assumes in that parts of matters belong to concept A belong to concept B, and some of the matters included in concept B belong to concept A at the same time. Or to say, when constitutive elements of article A and article B have partly overlapped, it is the crossed relationship (see the contents below). (4) The neutral relation. It refers to that there are no such relations discussed above between two articles judged from their words and contents, but it is still possible for an act to violate two articles at the same time. For example, the crime of intentional homicide is totally different from the crime of intentional destruction of property, but there is a high possibility that the former will violate the latter in the meantime (for example, the act of assassination will destroy the victim's expensive suits).[11]

Obviously, in the context of the opposite relation, not only is it impossible to constitute legal concurrence, but it is essentially impossible to establish the ideal concurrence. The theory of criminal law of China generally holds that where there is an inclusive or crossed relation between articles, it is the legal concurrence.[12] The inclusive or crossed relation between articles will easily be identified by interpreting the constitutive elements without relying on the facts of specific cases. In other words, the relation of legal concurrence is logic rather than a factual relation.[13] The ideal concurrence is that a realistic act has violated several articles, and it is the fact of specific case that violates the law articles, which may not have the inclusive or crossed relationship with each other. Such formal standard for distinction is generally confirmed by this article.

For example, Article 266, which provides for the crime of fraud, and Article 194, which provides for the crime of note fraud; both use the word "fraud" and the object of the fraud is "property". What's more, all the acts of note fraud meet the constitutive elements of the crime of fraud while the latter doesn't necessarily belong to the

---

[11] 以上参见日山火正则:"法条竞合の诸问题(1)"，载《神奈川法学》第7卷(1971)第1号。See Yamabi Masanori.(1971) "Various issues of legal provision competition (1)", as cited in *Kanagawa Law Review*, Vol. 7, No. 1.

[12] 参见陈兴良、龚培华、李奇路:《法条竞合论》，复旦大学出版社1993年版，第22页以下; 吴振兴:《罪数形态论》，中国检察出版社1996年版，第173页; 高铭暄、马克昌主编:《刑法学》，北京大学出版社、高等教育出版社2011年版，第186页; 王作富主编:《刑法》，中国人民大学出版社2009年版，第171页。Chen Xingliang, Gong Peihua & Li Qilu. (1993) *On Concurrence of Legal Provisions*, Fudan University Press, 1–22; Wu Zhenxing. (1996) *On Forms of Imputation*, China Procuratorate Press, 173; Gao Mingxuan & Ma Kechang eds. (2011) *Criminal Law*, Peking University Press & Higher Education Press, 186; Wang Zuofu ed. (2009) *Criminal Law*, China Renmin University of Press, 171.This article regards this crossed relationship as the formal standard of regulatory concurrence only for taking this general theory into account. But as later discussed, all of the crossed relationships belong to ideal concurrence.

[13] 参见陈兴良:《口授刑法学》，中国人民大学出版社2007年版，第372页以下。See Chen Xingliang. (2007) *Lectures on Criminal Law*, China Renmin University of Press, 372;

crime of note fraud. The relation between them has thereby been affirmed as inclusive, and therefore meets the formal standard of legal concurrence. For another example, one of the paragraphs of Article 260 describes the subjects of abuse are the minor, the old, the sick and the disabled, and in Article 261, the subjects are the family members. When the actor has abused the minor, the old, the sick or the disabled family members, there is a crossed relationship, which accords with the formal standard of legal concurrence. Article 263 of *Chinese Criminal Law* provides for eight types aggravated circumstances of robbery, in which there are many crossed relations, such as intruding into others' houses to rob and armed robbery (intruding into others' houses to rob using a gun), armed robbery and bank robbery (bank robbery using a gun), armed robbery and robbery on public transport (armed robbery on public transport), and all of them have the crossed relationships and meet the formal standard of legal concurrence.

It is for sure that when two articles have used the same verbs, it does not mean that the relation between them is legal concurrence. As long as the constitutive element of acts regulated by the two articles could be explained as having inclusive or crossed relationship, the formal standard of the legal concurrence has been met. For example, Article 397, which establishes the crime of abuse of authority, does not use the same verb as Article 400, which establishes the crime of the release of detainee, but the interpretation of the constitutive elements shows that the release of detainee is a specific type of abuse of authority, and that whatever the form of the release of detainee shows, it does not affect the inclusive relationship between the two articles. If other standards are not been taken into consideration, the latter would be the special article of the former. For another example, although Article 131, which stipulates the crime of causing a flight accident, doesn't use the same verb with Article 133 that stipulates the crime of causing traffic casualties, the explanations of their constitutive elements are that the latter can include the former, or to say, the act causing a flight accident is in accordance with the constitutive elements of crime of causing traffic casualties, but the act constitutes latter may not meet the constitutive elements of the former. Therefore, the formal standard of legal concurrence has been met.

However, if the relation between two articles can only be determined by relying on the certain fact of the case (even the inclusive relation), it should not be identified as the legal concurrence since the relationship turns into neutral or even opposed after the fact of case has changed. For example, Article 232 describes the crime of intentional homicide and Article 275 is about the crime of intentional destruction of property, and there is no legal concurrence between them. It is also possible to argue that there is a special relationship between the two if one relies on the facts of the case and the reasonable conclusion that the destruction of another person's clothes (presumably of a large value) in the killing is only the crime of intentional homicide. That is to say, the act of destroying the clothes which belongs to the property, constitutes the crime of intentional destruction of property, while the destruction of clothes caused by intentional homicide will only be convicted of crime of intentional homicide. Therefore, the crime of intentional destruction of property is included in the crime of intentional homicide. Then it is the inclusive relationship between the crime of intentional destruction of property and the crime of intentional homicide, and the former is the special article of the latter. But, that is not the case if the fact has changed. For example, A's act of destroying B's car constitutes the crime of intentional destruction of property and the act of killing B by A afterwards constitutes the crime of intentional homicide. Anyhow, it cannot be seen that there is an inclusive or crossed relationship between the two articles.

For another example, there is no legal concurrence between the Article 118, which stipulates the crime of sabotaging of electrical power equipment, and the Article 264 that regulates the crime of theft. On one hand, the verb used by the former is "sabotage", as long as the utility of the electrical power equipment is reduced or lost, it is "sabotage" and the transfer of the electrical power equipment is not required. The latter uses the verb "theft", which requires the property to be transferred, rather than reducing or eliminating the utility of properties. Thereby, whether an act will violate Article 118 and Article 264 at the same time depends on specific facts of the case. That is, if the actor has only sabotaged the electrical power equipment, it is impossible for Article 264 to be violated. Only when the actor has transferred the electrical power equipment to himself or herself, or the third party, thus reducing or eliminating the utility of it and further endangered the public safety, the two articles above will be violated at the same time. This circumstance, thereby, could not be the legal concurrence, but rather the ideal concurrence.

One of the important reasons for the theory of criminal law of China to include a large number of ideal concurrence into legal concurrence is that it always makes the determination that two articles have inclusive or crossed relationship by discussing specific facts of cases. For example, some textbooks pointed out that, "the crime of perjury stipulated in Article 305 and the crime of harboring and shielding stipulated in Article 310 may haves crossed legal concurrence under the circumstance that the actors are all willing to harbor the criminals."[14] The conclusion, obviously, is drawn by relying on the fact that "the actors are all willing to harbor the criminals". However, from the perspective of the constitutive elements, the crime of harboring and shielding and the crime of perjury have evident distinctions in the behavior subject, behavior state and behavior content, therefore, it is difficult to identify the relation between them as legal concurrence.[15]

With the introduction of German theory of criminal law, some scholars advocated turning the modern theory of quantity of crime in China to the theory of concurrence in Germany.[16] Therefore, it is necessary to discuss that whether articles

---

[14] 王作富主编:《刑法》，中国人民大学出版社2009年版，第170页。Wang Zuofu. ed. (2009) *Criminal Law*, China Renmin University of Press, 170.

[15] Whether an overlap is made between articles shall be firstly decided on the contents of constitutive element, rather than the similar substantive purposes or motivations of two crimes. For example, the crime of theft and the crime of fraud are both bearing premises of illegal possession, but it cannot be considered that there is an overlap between them.

[16] 参见陈兴良:"刑法竞合论"，载《法商研究》2006年第2期;陈兴良:"从罪数论到竞合论——一个学术史的考察"，载《现代法学》2011年第3期。Chen Xingliang. (2006) "*On Concurrence of Criminal Law*", as cited in *Studies in Law and Business,* No. 2; Chen Xingliang.

with neutral relationships could be the legal concurrence. Beling holds that, when two articles are in the neutral relationship, both the legal concurrence and ideal concurrence may exist.[17] It is the dominant ideology in Germany. When it is the neutral relationship, the frequency of the act violating the two articles has determined the distinction between the legal concurrence and ideal concurrence. More specifically, if an act has commonly violated crime A and crime B at the same time, it is the legal concurrence. Otherwise, it is the ideal concurrence or even constitutes several crimes (substantive concurrence). For example, it is the neutral relationship between the crime of intentional injury and the crime of intentional destruction of property. As the act of intentional injury has always destroyed the victim's clothes, it is the legal concurrence (absorbing relationship). However, on other occasions where this is not usual, there is considered to be no legal concurrence between the two articles. For another example, the crime of intruding into others' houses to theft and the crime of intentional destruction of property (breaking the door and window, etc.) have the relationship of legal concurrence (absorptive relationship). But in other contexts where it is not usual, it is not the legal concurrence and an act shall establish the ideal concurrence when it violates two articles.[18] However, it may be hard for scholars in China to accept this view.

The basic framework of the theory of concurrence in Germany is to deal with the circumstance applying only one article as the legal concurrence, which, therefore, equals to the circumstance applying one article. Although several articles should apply, there is an ideal concurrence when there is only one act or one act done. Therefore, ideal concurrence is a single act or a single act done. Otherwise, it is the substantive concurrence (or real concurrence). In other words, in Germany, when the content of wrongdoing (the content of wrongdoing with culpability, hereinafter) of a punishable act can be adequately evaluated by one article, that article shall be applied and the application of other articles shall be excluded, and this is legal concurrence. Obviously, the legal concurrence in Germany does not require a logical inclusive or crossed relationship between the articles, but only that the application of one article adequately evaluates the content of wrongdoing of the act. Hence, the concept of legal concurrence in Germany doesn't deserve its name. For this reason, some scholars in Germany suggest that it is more appropriate to replace the

(2011) "From the Theory of Quantity of Offenses to the Theory of Concurrence: An Academic Historical Investigation", as cited in *Modern Law Journal*, No. 3.

[17] 参见日山火正则:"法条竞合の诸问题(1)"，载《神奈川法学》第7卷(1971)第1号，第8页以下。See Yamabi Masanori. (1971) "Various issues of legal provision competition (1)", as cited in *Kanagawa Law Review*, Vol. 7, No. 1–8.

[18] Vgl.,C.Roxin,*Strafrecht Allgemeiner Teil, Band II*, C.H.Beck,2003,S.858f; 德冈特·施特拉腾韦特、洛塔尔·库伦:《刑法总论I——犯罪论》，杨萌译，法律出版社2006年版，第436页。Giinter Stratenwerth & Lothar Kuhlen, trans. Yang Meng, (2006) *Strafrecht Allgemeiner Teil I: Die Straftat*, Law Press, 436.

traditional and controversial concept of legal concurrence with the concept of single article.[19]

From the perspective of the theory of concurrence, there is no evident defect to include the cases that apply one article into legal concurrence. In Germany, all of the issues concerning quantity of crimes and concurrence shall be categorized into legal concurrence, ideal concurrence as well as substantive concurrence, which leads to a relatively wide range of legal concurrence, especially of the absorbing relationships.[20] This theory of legal concurrence, however, has not been accepted in China in the first place. Moreover, the theory of criminal law in China has already limited the legal concurrence to the circumstances that articles are inclusive or crossed with each other. It is customary and it's not proper to change this formal standard. The criminal jurisprudence is not a subject of natural science. It is quite unrealistic to overturn this notion when one has become completely accustomed to limiting legal concurrence to situations where there is an inclusive or crossed relationship between articles. For example, while it is an advantage to have fewer concepts for the theory of concurrence, the provisions of our specific provisions of criminal law suggest that too few concepts do not summarize the full range of circumstances. What's more, it's impossible in China to abandon multiple concepts originating in the theory of criminal law of Japan. A scholar may give up using certain concepts, while an academic field could not stop concepts from increasing. In fact, it is also impossible for Chinese theory of criminal law to adequately accept German theory of criminal law on the definition of legal concurrence. For example, in China, no one will agree that the crime of intentional injury and the crime of intentional destruction of property has legal concurrence, no matter from the usual meaning of "concurrence" or from the academic tradition. For another example, A embezzles B's property that is kept by A, and tells a lie that the property has been stolen (so called fraud of protecting stolen good), resulting in B's abandonment of the right to claim the return of property. German theory of criminal law puts an emphasis on the relationship between the co-punishable subsequent act and the principle crime, and further improves it to the legal concurrence. That is to say, if the subsequent act of fraud of protecting stolen good belongs to the act of guaranteeing the benefits obtained by the act of embezzlement, it should retreat after the principal crime (crime of embezzlement). Therefore, it is hold that the relationship between co-punishable subsequent act and the crime of embezzlement is the absorbing relationship of legal concurrence.[21] In China, the theory of criminal law focuses on whether the act of protecting stolen goods is a crime of fraud or shall be punished together

---

[19] H. Jescheck /T.Weigend, *Lehrbuch des Strafrechts.Allgemeiner Teil*, 5.Aufl., Duncker & Humblot,1996, S.732.

[20] It should be noted that the scope of the special relationship and supplement relationship of regulatory concurrence in Germany is not broad.

[21] 参见德Ingeborg Puppe:"基于构成要件结果同一性所形成不同构成要件实现之想象竞合"，陈志辉译，载《东吴法律学报》第17卷第3期。Ingeborg Puppe, trans. Chen Zhihui,

with the crime of embezzlement, rather than identifying the relationship as the legal concurrence.[22] Hereby, it is not necessary to confirm the legal concurrence between articles of neutral relationships in China.

Besides, both the theory of criminal law and the judicial practice in China have over-broadly identified the legal concurrence, especially mistakes multiple ideal concurrence as the special relationship of legal concurrence.[23] Under such background, confirming the existence of legal concurrence between articles of neutral relationships will undoubtedly worsen the situation and make the handling of case more inconsistent with the principle of fitting punishment with crime.

In conclusion, the existence of inclusive or crossed relationship between two articles is the formal standard of legal concurrence. If such standard has not been met, it shall be excluded from the legal concurrence. However, even though the formal standard has been met, it may not be legal concurrence, which needed to be judged with the substantive standard.

11.3 Identity of Legal Interests

As discussed above, the determination of inclusive and crossed relations is made by interpreting the constitutive elements of articles, which will inevitably lead to the result that the articles may crossed with each other even though legal interests under protections of the two articles may be totally different. For example, crime of provocative and disturbing acts, which is stipulated in Article 293 of *Chinese Criminal*

Idealkonkurrenz verschiedener Tatbestandsverwirklichungen kraft Identitat der tatbestandsmasigen Erfolge, as cited in *Soochow Law Review*, Vol.17, No.3.

[22] 参见陈兴良主编:《刑法总论精释》，人民法院出版社2011年版，第703页以下; 张明楷:《刑法学》，法律出版社2011年版，第432、906页; 周光权:《刑法总论》，中国人民大学出版社2011年版，第260页。Chen Xingliang ed. (2011) *General Interpretation of Criminal Law*, People's Court Press, 1–703. Zhang Mingkai. (2011) Criminal Law, Law Press China, 432、906; Zhou Guangquan. (2011) *General Part of Criminal Law*, China Renmin University of Press, 296.

[23] According to the theory of criminal law in China, Article 140 is considered as a general article while Article 141–148 special articles. However, Article 149 provides the exceptional principle that article of serious punishment is prior to article of light punishment. Currently, I think we need think twice about this. For example, the maximum penalty for the crime of producing and selling fake and inferior products in Article 140 is life imprisonment, while Article 148 provides that: "Whoever produces cosmetics which do not meet hygiene standards, or knowingly sells such cosmetics, thereby causing serious consequences, shall be sentenced to fixed-term imprisonment of not more than 3 years or short-term custody, with a fine of not less than half but not more than twice the amount of the sales revenue, or shall be sentenced to a fine on the said scale only." If the Article 148 IS a special article, combined with the Article 149, an unanswerable question then come out in front of us: for the purpose of punishing the crime of producting or selling cosmetics that fails to meet hygienic standards, what on earth is the legislator's attitude? A lighter penalty or a heavier one? The idea that Article 148 is a special article actually means that the legislator intends to impose a lighter penalty on such crime. However, for the fear that the penalty would be too light, the Article 149 was set up thereafter. The relationship may be clarified by denying the special relationship while recognizing it as supplementary relationship or ideal concurrence.

Law, provides "assaulting any other person at will, with execrable circumstances". The crime of disrupting the order of the courtroom stipulated in Article 309 has provided "assaulting any judicial staff member". Both of the two articles have used the term "assaulting" and the latter requires the target shall be the judicial staff member. Therefore, the two articles are inclusive. But if the relationship has been regarded as legal concurrence, the crime of disrupting the order of the courtroom will be the special article and the principle that special article is prior to general article will be applied. The result will be the described punishment of "imprisonment of not more than 5 years, limited incarceration or surveillance" shall be applied for "assaulting any other person at will, with execrable circumstances", and the described punishment of "imprisonment of not more than 3 years, limited incarceration or surveillance in addition to a fine" shall be applied for "assaulting any judicial staff member", which is obviously inappropriate. For another example, Article 275 provides that the maximum punishment for the crime of intentional destruction of property is the fixed-term imprisonment of seven years, and the crime of disrupting the order of the courtroom stipulated in Article 309 includes the act of "destroying any of the facilities of the courtroom... with serious circumstances". Purely judged from the logic, the place and the subject of the latter are so special that people may regard the latter as the special article. However, if such conclusion is drawn, the result of applying the principle of "special article is prior to general article" will be that the maximum imprisonment of crime of destruction of general property will be 7 years while the maximum imprisonment for destroying any of the facilities of the courtroom will only be three years, which is clearly not appropriate.[24]

Because of this, theories of criminal law in other countries have always attached importance to distinguish the legal concurrence and ideal concurrence substantively. For example, Professor Ono Seiichiro, who advocates that the nature of crime is the violation of morality and points out that "crime is not a mere violation of norms, but a violation and infringement of morality as well as a punishable act prescribed in the criminal law of the state, whose purpose is to realize its own morality... We must discuss the quantity of crimes under this basic concept... The constitutive elements themselves are the stereotypes of the anti-moral acts, and the adequacy of the constitutive elements reflects the anti-moral nature of the acts... The distinction between ideal concurrence and legal concurrence shall be based on the quantity, whether it's singular or plural, in the meanings of the morality. If the meanings of the morality are the same, it is the legal concurrence, or it is the ideal concurrence."[25] However, for one thing, the idea that crime is a violation or infringement of morality has fallen behind our times and is no longer supported. For another, whether the meanings of the morality are the same or not cannot be judged specifically. In his textbook,

[24] It is sure that some people may argue that "this is a problem of legislation and can only be solved by amending the law, rather than by setting a standard for distinguishing between regulatory concurrence and ideal concurrence". This article, however, holds that it is an issue of the theory of interpretation, not a problem of legislation.

[25] 日小野清一郎:《犯罪构成要件の理论》，有斐阁1953年版，第402页。Ono Seiichirou. (1953) *Theory of Criminal Composition Requirements*, Yuhikaku Press, 402.

Professor Ono Seiichiro argues that there may also be a legal concurrence between the crime of homicide and the crime of destruction of property.[26] However, "on such occasion, in what sense does the identity of morality of the constitutive elements exists"?[27]

The identity of legal interests is the distinctive standard emphasized by the German scholar Maurach. "In the case of legal concurrence, although it can be said that an act conforms to several constitutive elements, only one of them can adequately evaluate the factual contents of wrongdoing." When several constitutive elements "adequately protect the same legal interest, it shall be recognized as legal concurrence, while it is ideal concurrence when different legal interests have been infringed".[28] As long as the nature of crime has been recognized as the infringement of legal interests, and that in the case of a legal concurrence, the application of one article can adequately evaluate the content of wrongdoing of the act, whereas in the case of an ideal concurrence, the application of only one article cannot adequately evaluate the content of wrongdoing of the act. Then, first of all, it is necessary to recognize the identity of legal interests as a substantive standard for distinguishing between legal concurrence and ideal concurrence. Or to say, there is only one fact of infringement of legal interest in the case of legal concurrence while there are several facts of infringement of legal interest in the case of legal concurrence. More specifically, in the case of the legal concurrence, although the act has violated several criminal norms at the same time with the legal interest protected by only one of them infringed, since there is an inclusive or crossed relationship between the norms, it is not necessary and should not be identified that the act is guilty of several crimes, otherwise it would be a repetitive evaluation. Or to say, "from the perspective of protection of legal interest, it is the improper dual punishments if plural legal articles have applied in punishing the same infringement or infringement of legal

[26] 日小野清一郎:《犯罪讲义》，有斐阁1948年版，第266页。Ono Seiichirou.(1948) *Handouts of Crime*, Yuhikaku Press, 266.

[27] 日山火正则:"法条竞合の诸问题(1)"，载《神奈川法学》第7卷(1971)第1号。See Yamabi Masanori.(1971) "Various issues of legal provision competition (1)", as cited in Kanagawa Law Review, Vol. 7, No. 1.

[28] R.Maurach,*Drutsches Strafrecht,Allgemeiner Teil*, 3.Aufl., Karlsruhe, 1965, S.636f. This point of view has been supported by Professor Yamabi Masanori, Suzuki Shigetsugu, Machino Hajime, Maeda Masahide, Yamaguchi Atsushi. 参见日山火正则:"法条竞合の本质"，载《法学》1971年第4号;日铃木茂嗣:《刑法总论》，成文堂2011年版，第275页以下;日町野朔:"法条竞合论"，载日内藤谦等编:《平野龙一古稀祝贺论文集》(上卷)，有斐阁1991年版，第410页以下;日前田雅英:《刑法总论讲义》，东京大学出版会2011年版，第555页;日山口厚:《刑法总论》，有斐阁2007年版，第365、379页。See Yamabi Masanori.(1971) "The nature of legal provision competition", as cited in Hogaku, No. 4; Suzuki Shigetsugu. (2011) *General Theory of Criminal Law*, Seibundo Publishing Co., 275; Machino Saku.(1991) "Theory of legal provision competition", as cited in Naitou Ken et al.,ed., *A Collection of Congratulatory Essays by Mr. Hirano Ryuuichi in His Seventies (Vol. 1)*, Yuhikaku Press, 1–410. Maeda Masahide. (2006) *Handouts of General Rules of Criminal Law*, University of Tokyo Press, 555. Yamaguchi, Atsushi. (2007) *Sōron: Keihō* (General Theory of Criminal Law), Yūhikaku, 365, 379.

interest".[29] In the case of an ideal concurrence, the act that infringes several legal interests protected by criminal norms and therefore violates the criminal norms shall be identified as having committed several crimes..

It shall be pointed out that as some crimes stipulated by the criminal law aims to protect double legal interests (complex objects), the so-called "only one fact of infringement of legal interest" refers to the fact that the legal interest protected by one crime has been infringed; and the so-called "several fact of infringement of legal interest" is the fact that legal interests protected by more than two crimes have been infringed. For example, the act of robbery infringes not only the personal rights but also the property, although the crime of theft has also been infringed at the same time, the legal interests been infringed do not exceed the protection of crime of robbery and therefore it is the legal concurrence (special relationship).[30] On the contrary, it shall be regarded as ideal concurrence that one man steals other's first-aid drug (assuming a large amount) when he or she is under heart attack, resulting in the victim's death. That is because the legal interest protected by the crime of intentional homicide is life rather than the property, while the crime of theft aims to protect the property rather than life. The above act, however, infringes the legal interests protected by two crimes, therefore it is not legal concurrence but ideal concurrence.

So, why does the described punishment of intentional homicide has been imposed in the aforesaid case, instead of recognizing they are legal concurrence by applying the crime of intentional homicide individually? Or to say, why it is a must to identify the act as ideal concurrence and declare it as convicting the crime of intentional homicide and theft simultaneously in the judgment even though it has been sentenced with the punishment of crime of intentional homicide?

(1) The function of criminal law is to protect the legal interest and the national freedom. Only by adequately evaluating the contents of wrongdoing of any case without repeating the evaluation, can we protect both the legal interests and the national freedom. If the judge evaluates a person's act that violates both others' lives and properties as the crime of intentional homicide, the property will be under no protection and it is not conducive to realize the purpose of criminal law to protect legal interests. Conversely, if the act of killing has been announced as crime of intentional homicide as well as the crime of intentional injury, it is the repetitive evaluation and is against the principle of protecting national freedom.

(2) The criminal norms are norms of adjudication. The judge shall accord with those articles, the nature of crimes as well as the specific facts to determine the quantity of crimes. The determination of crime quantity and the determination of whether crimes shall be combined punished are two distinct problems. First of all,

---

[29] 日町野朔:"法条竞合论"，载日内藤谦等编:《平野龙一古稀祝贺论文集》(上卷)，有斐阁1991年版，第420页。Machino Saku.(1991) "Theory of legal provision competition", as cited in Naitou Ken et al.,ed., A Collection of Congratulatory Essays by Mr. Hirano Ryuuichi in His Seventies (Vol. 1), Yuhikaku Press, 1–410.

[30] 参见日山口厚:《刑法总论》，有斐阁2007年版，第367页。See Yamaguchi Atsushi.(2007) *General Part of Criminal Law*. Yuhikaku Press, 367.

although the constitutive elements may be the standard for distinguishing single crime or several crimes, since the constitutive elements of a crime contains all the elements required to establish a crime, it is entirely possible for a case to meet only one relevant element of the constitutive elements of a crime in one respect and adequately comply with two relevant elements of the constitutive elements of a crime in another respect, so that substantive standards are required to determine the quantity of the conformity of constitutive elements of a crime. The result is that the essence of the crime can only be used as a standard to determine how many constitutive elements the act qualifies as. In essence, since the purpose of criminal law is to protect the legal interests, and the nature of the crime is to infringement the legal interests, therefore, it should be evaluated whether the act qualifies as several crimes or several constitutive elements, depending on the amount of legal interest been infringed. Or to say, there will be one crime established if the legal interest protected by only one crime has been infringed; there will be several crimes if legal interests protected by more than two crimes have been infringed; and when an act infringes on the legal interest protected by one crimes for several times, there will be several crimes. In summary, when the Accused's act has infringed on different legal interests protected by several articles, the judgment must affirm that the Accused's act has convicted of several crimes.

(3) Although the criminal law may play the role of behavior norms, "from the perspective that there is no prejudice to truth, it cannot be said that the law is published to the citizens and if it is, the law shall be shaped in a totally different way, which should be more specific and folkloric and expressed in the daily used words, rather than being stipulated in a very limited way. Moreover, it shall be illustrated and taught".[31] In fact, general people is not directly read the articles, but get to know the contents of criminal law through indictments or judgment (including the criminal written orders). On the other hand, "the law is not expressed by explicit provisions, but is clearly shown in the judgments of cases".[32] Although this is a rule of common law, it also applies to statute law. The Japanese scholar points out that "law is the inherent existence in perception. The judgment that interprets it in a correct way is the materialization of the law."[33] Scholars of German also hold that "most laws are materialized and obtain the final clear image through a process of continuous judicial adjudicating, and then can be applied to individual cases. Many articles, in fact, come into being parts of existing laws through adjudication".[34] Criminal law is meaningful only when applied in the daily life. The judgment is a vivid interpreta-

[31] 德亚图·考夫曼:《法律哲学》，刘幸义等译，台北五南图书出版公司2000年版，第119页。Arthur Kaufmann, trans. Liu Xingyi, (2000) *Rechtsphilosophie*, Wu-Nan Book Inc.119.

[32] 美安东尼·刘易斯:《言论的边界》，徐爽译，法律出版社2010年版，第3页。Anthony Lewis, trans. Xv Shuang, (2010) *Freedom for the Thought That We Hate: A Biography of the First Amendment*, China Law Press & Seibundo Publishing Co., 3.

[33] 日平野龙一:"刑法解释中的判例与学说"，黎宏译，载《国家检察官学院学报》2015年第1期。Hirano Ryuuichi.(2015) "Case law and legal doctrines in the interpretation of criminal law", trans., Li Hong, as cited in *Journal of the National Prosecutors College*, No. 1.

[34] 德卡尔·拉伦茨:《法学方法论》，陈爱娥译，商务印书馆2003年版，第20页。Karl Larenz, trans. Chen Aie, (2003) *Methoden lehreder Rechtswissenschaft*, The Commercial Press, 20.

tion of criminal law. The clearer the interpretation is, the easier the content of criminal law will be understood by general people, and the more the criminal law can play the role of behavior norms, so as to achieve the goal of special prevention and general prevention.[35] As to the issue discussed in this article, if the criminal law's role as behavior norms will be played, the express function of ideal concurrence shall be emphasized.

The express function of ideal concurrence refers to that when the Accused's acts have several culpable contents of wrongdoing, if the judgment is pronounced, the contents must be listed one by one and adequately evaluated, so that the Accused and the general people can understand how many crimes that the Accused's act has violated and what kind of acts will constitute crimes through the judgment.[36] In the above-mentioned case of death caused by theft of first-aid drug, if the judgment only declares that the Accused's act constitutes the crime of intentional homicide, it may lead to the misunderstanding to the Accused and the public that the act of stealing drugs will not be identified as crime of theft, which is not conductive to the special prevention and general prevention for the crime of theft. For another example, the Accused A, B, C and others beat the victims A, B, C with no reason after drinking, causing minor injury to victim A, slight injury to victim B and break victim C's cellphone (in relatively large amount). If the judgment only declares the Accused A, B, C and other's acts constitutes the crime of provocative and disturbing acts, the Accused and the public may mistake the act of causing minor injury to others as not constituting crime of intentional injury and the act of destroying others' property after drinking as not constituting crime of intentional destruction of property, which is not conductive for the law to perform its role as behavior norms. Only by specifying the acts of A, B, C and others shall establish the crime of provocative and disturbing acts, the crime of intentional injury and the crime of intentional destruction of property, will it promote the special prevention and general prevention to the acts, such as willful assault and battery, injuring others after drinking and intentionally destroying others' property after drinking.

(4) The criminal judgment is not only about comforting the victims, but also concerned with the compensation and other issues. In the case of legal concurrence, it is not necessary to list all the articles violated by the Accused to solve the problem. For example, Article 263 of *Chinese Criminal Law* is applicable to the case of robbery and is enough to pacify the victims as well as to settle the problems, such as the compensation. Therefore, it is not necessary to apply Article 264. But in the aforementioned case of provocative and disturbing acts by A, B, C and others, if their acts have only been identified as the crime of provocative and disturbing acts, the victim A will not be comforted and it will also not be conductive for the victim

[35] 参见张明楷:"明确性原则在刑事司法中的贯彻"，载《吉林大学社会科学学报》2015年第4期。See Zhang Mingkai. (2015) "On the Implementation of the Principle of Definiteness in Criminal Justice", as cited in *Jilin University Journal Social Sciences Edition*, No. 4.

[36] Vgl.,C. Roxin,*Strafrecht Allgemeiner Teil, Band II*, C.H.Beck, 2003, S.831;H.Jescheck/T. Weigend,*Lehrbuch des Strafrechts.Allgemeiner Teil*, 5.Aufl.,Duncker & Humblot, 1996,S.718.

C to get compensation by filing an incidental civil action since the crime is against the public order.

In a word, it has both theoretical basis and practical significance to regard the identity of legal interests as the standard to distinguish the legal concurrence and ideal concurrence. Generally speaking, according such substantial standard, it is impossible for the relationships among crimes stipulated in different sections of the specific provisions of criminal law to be legal concurrence (there may be exceptions). For example, the legal interests protected by the crime of producing and selling fake and inferior products and the crime of fraud are economic order (the right of consumers to enjoy qualified products) and property respectively. The legal interests of the crime of using counterfeit currency and the crime of fraud are public credit of money and property respectively,[37] and the legal interests under the protections of articles providing by the crime of negligent homicide and the crime of causing traffic casualties are human life and public safety. The crime of fraud and crime of cheating and bluffing respectively protect property and credits of state organ personnel, and legal interests under protection by the case of retaliation and frame-ups and crime of abuse of authority are democratic rights of citizens and the legitimacy, impartiality, effective enforcement as well as citizens' trust. All of the relationships among those articles above cannot be regarded as legal concurrence but ideal concurrence.[38] For another example, the legal interest protected by the crime of negligent homicide is the individual's life, while the crime of medical accident aims to protect the safety of the public's lives and bodies as well as the health management order of the nation. Although protecting the individual's legal interest is the final purpose of protecting the social legal interest, it cannot be said that the individual's legal interest equals or includes the legal interest of society or the nation. Therefore, the relation between those crimes is not legal concurrence but ideal concurrence.[39] Similarly, it is impossible for the relationship between the

[37] 日本刑法理论的通说也不承认二者之间为法条竞合，而是认定为包括的一罪(参见日西田典之:《刑法各论》，弘文堂2012年版，第331页)。例如，山口厚教授认为，法条竞合中并不存在吸收关系，同时认为吸收一罪属于包括的一罪(参见日山口厚:《刑法总论》，有斐阁2007年版，第366页);使用假币罪与诈骗罪属于包括的一罪(参见日山口厚:《刑法各论》，有斐阁2010年版，第423页)。The prevailing view in Japanese criminal law theory does not recognize a relationship of competition of legal provisions between the two offenses, but rather regards it as a case of a compound offense (See Nishida Noriyuki.(2012) *Essays on Criminal Law*, Koubundou Publishers Inc., 331.).For example, Professor Yamaguchi Atsushi argues that there is no absorptive relationship in cases of *lex specialis*, and holds that absorptive offenses fall under compound offenses (See Yamaguchi Atsushi.(2007) *General Part of Criminal Law*. Yuhikaku Press,366.); He also considers the use of counterfeit currency and fraud to be a compound offense. (See Yamaguchi Atsushi.(2010) *Special Part of Criminal Law*. Yuhikaku Press, 423.).

[38] 参见丁慧敏:《论刑法中的法条竞合》，清华大学法学博士学位论文(2013年)，第107页以下。See Ding Huimin. (2013) *On Legal Concurrence of Provisions in Criminal Law*, Doctoral Dissertation, Tsinghua University, 1–107.

[39] 参见吕英杰:"刑法法条竞合理论的比较研究"，载陈兴良主编:《刑事法评论》(第23卷)，北京大学出版社2008年版，第483页。See Lü Yingjie. (2008) "A Comparative Study on the Theory of Legal Concurrence of Provisions in Criminal Law", as cited in Chen Xingliang ed. *Criminal Law Review* (Vol. 23), Peking University Press, 483.

aforesaid crime of provocative and disturbing acts and the crime of disrupting the order of the courtroom to be legal concurrence, but only to be ideal concurrence.

The identity of legal interests also means the identity of the subjects of legal interests. That is, if the act has infringed on the same legal interests of different legal interest subjects, it could not be the legal concurrence. For example, the particular relationship between the crime of intentional homicide and the crime of intentional injury only exists in the case where there is only one legal interest subject; if an act causes A's death and B's injury at the same time, it cannot be identified as legal concurrence but ideal concurrence.[40] For another example, A, the staff of a company, falsely claims that he or she owned the laptop possessed by the company and sold it to B. Although A's act has only infringed on the property, the different legal interest subjects (the company and B relatively) make it impossible to form the relationship of legal concurrence. If it is hold that only one act has been carried out by A, it must be considered as ideal concurrence.[41]

If the substantive standard of the identity of legal interest is strictly adopted, the distinction between the legal concurrence and ideal concurrence will be made clearly. As the Japanese scholar Machino Hajime said, "The identity of legal interest under the protection of criminal law is quite enough to be the standard for judging whether there is the legal concurrence or not, and such standard is decisive."[42] Nevertheless, under the current theoretical background of China, it may be necessary to be forced to admit that if the crimes stipulated in one chapter (section) aims to protect dual legal interests, and crime of the other chapter (section) only protects one of those legal interests, the possibility of legal concurrence cannot be ruled out. For example, crime of fraud and crime of financial fraud are stipulated in the fifth chapter and the third chapter. Since the legal interest protected by the former is only the property while the legal interests protected by the latter are property and financial order, it is totally possible for the public to hold that there is the relationship of legal concurrence. In addition, it is an issue of the theory of interpretation that whether one article aims to protect single legal interest or dual legal interests. In turn, when interpreting the articles, one takes into account the severity of the described punishment and therefore comes to different conclusions. For example, people may believe that the crime of theft only protect the property while the crime of illegally felling trees which protects both the property and the timber resource. Therefore, the former is the general article and the latter is the special article. For another example, before the *Amendment IX* deleted the crime of prostituting girls under the age of 14, it may be hold by the people that such article protects both the

---

[40] It is ideal concurrence if the act fires one shot but leads to the death of two people. Because life is the exclusive legal interest of individuals, the death of two means there are two infringements of legal interests.

[41] Vgl.,C.Roxin, *Strafrecht Allgemeiner Teil, Band II*, C.H.Beck, 2003,S.822.

[42] 日町野朔:"法条竞合论"，载日内藤谦等编:《平野龙一古稀祝贺论文集》(上卷)，有斐阁1991年版，第420页。Machino Saku.(1991) "Theory of legal provision competition", as cited in *Naitou Ken et al,ed., A Collection of Congratulatory Essays by Mr. Hirano Ryuuichi in His Seventies (Vol. 1)*, Yuhikaku Press, 1–420.

sexual autonomy of young girls (or so called physical and mental health) and the social management order. While the legal interest protected by the article regulating the crime of adultery with girls under the age of 14 is only the right of sexual autonomy, so there is a special relationship between those two crimes.[43]

However, a blanket recognition that the above-mentioned situations are belong to the special relationships and that only special articles can be applied will inevitably lead to the unfitting punishment with crime.[44] In other words, if the aforementioned formal standard and the substantive standard of identity of legal interest have been taken, the principle of fitting punishment with crime. Will be violated. For example, if it is considered that there is a special relationship between crime of prostituting girls under the age of 14 and the crime of adultery with girls under the age of 14, according to the principle that "special article is prior to general article", the act of prostituting girls under 14 and resulting in the girls' serious injuries or death will only be applied by the described punishment of the former rather than the punishment to the crime of adultery with girls under the age of 14. Obviously, this conclusion which has violated the principle of fitting punishment with crime is hard to be accepted. It may be one of the important reasons to abolish the crime of prostituting girls under the age of 14 (except that such decision was based on the wrong judgment of the relationship between articles). All the problems will be solved under the ideal concurrence if the act of prostituting girls under the age of 14 and leading to the girls' serious injuries or death is regarded as the ideal concurrence of act of adultery with girls under the age of 14 and act of prostituting girls under the age of 14. Because the contents of crime of prostituting girls under the age of 14 cannot include the result of serious injuries or death. Therefore, the inclusiveness of the wrongdoing, as a substantive standard, shall be also taken.

11.4 The Inclusiveness of Wrongdoing

As mentioned earlier, the legal concurrence is possible only when there is an inclusive or crossed relationship between two articles. The inclusive relationship is an external manifestation of the special relationship. As is well known, the essential feature of the special relationship is that article A (the penal article) records (contains) all the features (or elements) of article B, but also contains at least one further special feature (element) that distinguishes it from article B.[45] In such context, article A is the special article and article B is the general article. For example, the

[43] 参见陈兴良:"法条竞合的学术演进——一个学术史的考察"，载《法律科学》2011年第4期。See Chen Xingliang. (2011) "Academic Evolution of the Concurrence of Legal Provisions: An Academic Historical Investigation", as cited in *Legal Science*, No. 4.

[44] 参见陈兴良:"法条竞合的学术演进——一个学术史的考察"，载《法律科学》2011年第4期。See Chen Xingliang. (2011) "Academic Evolution of the Concurrence of Legal Provisions: An Academic Historical Investigation", as cited in *Legal Science*, No. 4.

[45] Vgl.,C.Roxin, *Strafrecht Allgemeiner Teil, Band II*, C.H.Beck, 2003, S.848.

reason why the crime of intentional homicide is said to be a special article of the crime of intentional injury is that the conditions for the establishment of the crime of intentional homicide contain not only all the elements of intentional injury, but also more (or heavier) elements than those of the crime of intentional injury (homicidal act and homicidal intent). The reason why the crime of robbery is a special article of the crime of theft is that theft refers to the transfer of property in the possession of another person to his or her own possession or to the possession of a third person against the will of the other person, and the act of forcible seizing in robbery also refers to the transfer of property in the possession of another person to his or her own possession or to the possession of a third person against the will of the other person; the crime of robbery contains not only all the features of the crime of theft, but also a further special feature (the use of violence, coercion or other methods).[46] In China, the most problematic and controversial is mainly the special relationship in the legal concurrence. Because when dealing with other relationships in legal concurrence, the result is basically the application of the article of serious punishment, despite the different formulations, while the handling principle of the special relationship is that the special article is prior to the general article. So when faced with a "special article" with a heavy illegal content and a light described punishment, the argument of how to deal with it inevitably arises. In other words, is it necessary to strictly adhere to the principle of the special article is prior to the general article in dealing with special relationships? If strict compliance with this principle leads to unfitting punishment with crime, how should it be handled? The author now sees and thinks of three approaches.

(1) The first approach is to tolerate a situation of unfitting punishment with crime and leave it to the legislator to resolve it, or not to recognize that there is a situation of unfitting punishment with crime (since the legislator so provides, it is the situation of fitting punishment with crime, and the interpreter cannot consider it unfitting).[47]

However, it is not the proper attitude of the interpreter to leave any question to the legislator. It is the task not only of the legislator but also of the interpreter to harmonize the provisions of criminal law. Since Article 5 of *Chinese Criminal Law* establishes the principle of fitting punishment with crime, it must be followed so

---

[46] It is certain that unlike Germany and Japan, Chinese criminal law has a element of "a relatively large amount" for the crime of general theft, so it is difficult to identify crime of robbery as a special article of crime of theft under any circumstances. However, it can be affirmed that robbery with weapons is a special article of armed theft and intruding into dwellings to rob is the special article of theft when compared with theft that doesn't require "a relatively large amount". Also, when premised on "a relatively large amount", crime of robbery is no doubt the special article of crime of theft.

[47] 参见周光权:"法条竞合的特别关系研究"，载《中国法学》2010年第3期;车浩:"强奸罪与嫖宿幼女罪的关系"，载《法学研究》2010年第2期。Zhou Guangquan. (2010) "A Study on the Special Relationship in Concurrence of Legal Provisions", as cited in *China Legal Science*, No. 3; Che Hao. (2010) "On the Relationship between the Crime of Rape and the Crime of Whoring with an Underage Girl", a cited in *Chinese Journal of Law*, No. 2.

that the various crimes are punished accordingly in terms of the theory of interpretation.

It is also not pragmatic to insist that the application of so-called "special articles" cannot lead to fitting punishment with crime. For example, the described maximum punishment for the crime of general theft under Article 264 of *Chinese Criminal Law* is life imprisonment, but the maximum punishment for the crime of illegally felling trees under Article 345 of *Chinese Criminal Law* is the imprisonment of 15 years. If the crime of illegally felling trees is considered to be a special article, is it less illegal than the crime of theft? Obviously not. For example, Article 15 of *Interpretation of Supreme People's Court on Several Issues Concerning the Specific Application of Law in Criminal Cases of Destruction of Forest Resources* enacted on November 22, 2000 stipulates that "Illegal practices of seed collecting, resin tapping, bamboo shoots digging, roots digging and bark peeling for a relatively large amount of economic benefits shall be convicted of crime of theft and punished in accordance with the provisions of Article 264 of *Chinese Criminal Law*." Apparently, if the actor of peeling barks of 100 trees is sentenced to life imprisonment when the amount reaches 1,000,000 Yuan. Then when the actor unlawful felled the same 100 trees, the value of which far exceeds 1,000,000 Yuan, it cannot be considered (or claimed that the legislator considered) that the degree of wrongdoing is less than that of theft just because his act meets the constitutive elements of the crime of illegally felling trees, at the same time, it cannot be considered appropriate to impose the imprisonment of less than 15 years.

Here, the author is compelled to quote Rudolf von Jhering's famous motto in *Ist Die Jurisprudenz Eine Wissenschaft*, "In my eyes, the judge who, in total disregard of the consequences of his decisions, and who places the culpability entirely on the legislator, and who merely applies the provisions of the code mechanically, cannot really be called a judge; he is merely an emotionless, rigid cog in the judicial machine. A judge is not supposed to be like that. The ideal of justice, in my eyes, is not for the judge to extinguish the sense of law in his heart, nor is it for him to forgo all opportunity to pass judgment on law-making under that false notion of loyalty. There was a time when the extinction of independent thought and feeling in the mind of the judge, the total absence of subjectivity, and the total entrustment of his own subjectivity to the law-making, were regarded as the triumph of the idea of justice. That time, gentlemen, has been left behind us. For we find that in all the relations of life rigid rules do not replace human beings; the world is not ruled by abstract rules, but by personalities."[48] In short, the author, who has always advocated the doctrine of substantive interpretation and the resolution of legislative defects by interpreting, will not take the first approach.

(2) The second approach is to conditionally adopt the principle that article of serious punishment shall be prior to article of lighter punishment, in order to achieve the fitting punishment with crime.

---

[48] 德鲁道夫·冯·耶林:《法学是一门科学吗?》，李君韬译，法律出版社2010年版，第81页。Rudolf von Jhering, trans. Li Juntao, (2010) *Ist Die Jurisprudenz Eine Wissenschaft?*, Law Press & Seibundo Publishing Co., 81.

As is known, three decades ago, in a case where the crime of selling counterfeit medicines was punishable only by "fixed-term imprisonment of not more than two years, criminal detention or public surveillance", while the crime of fraud was punishable by "fixed-term imprisonment of not less than 10 years or life imprisonment", Professor Feng Yadong proposed the principle of article of serious punishment is prior to article of light punishment.[49] The author has also been advocating that, when there is a special relationship of legal concurrence, the handling principle is 'special article is prior to general article', but in exceptional cases, the applied principle is 'article of serious punishment is prior to article of light punishment'. "The application of the principle of article of serious punishment is prior to article of light punishment must meet three conditions: (1) the act is committed against the general and the special article of the same law; (2) the described punishment under the special article is clearly lighter than the described punishment under the general article of the same law and lacks a basis for mitigating the described punishment. Moreover, in the circumstances of the case, the application of the special article is clearly contrary to the principle of fitting punishment with crime; (3) the criminal law does not prohibit the application of general articles, or does not indicate that special articles must be applied. Otherwise, the special article must be applied."[50] The above proposition of the author is, on the one hand, to take into account the phenomenon that our theory of criminal law identifies many ideal concurrence as legal concurrence, and on the other hand, to take into account the fact that the expression that the article of serious punishment is prior to the article of light punishment has appeared in our theory of criminal law.

Although the expression that the article of serious punishment is prior to the article of light punishment has been strongly criticized,[51] there is no doubt about the substantive soundness of its conclusion (in conformity with the principle of fitting

---

[49] 冯亚东:"论法条竞合后的从重选择"，载《法学》1984年第4期。Feng Yadong. (1984) "On the Selection of Heavier Punishment after Concurrence of Legal Provisions", as cited in *Journal of Law*, No. 4. However, Professor Feng doesn't strictly distinguish the regulatory concurrence from the ideal concurrence. In this article, the relationship between the crime of selling counterfeit medicines and crime of fraud is ideal concurrence rather than regulatory concurrence.

[50] 张明楷:《刑法学》，法律出版社2011年版，第424页。Zhang Mingkai. (2011) Criminal Law, Law Press China, 424.

[51] 参见肖开权:"法条竞合不能从重选择——与冯亚东同志商榷"，载《法学》1984年第8期;陈兴良:"法条竞合的学术演进——一个学术史的考察"，载《法律科学》2011年第4期;刘明祥:"嫖宿幼女行为适用法条新论"，载《法学》2012年第12期;周光权:"法条竞合的特别关系研究"，载《中国法学》2010年第3期;车浩:"强奸罪与嫖宿幼女罪的关系"，载《法学研究》2010年第2期;王强:"法条竞合特别关系及其处理"，载《法学研究》2012年第1期。Xiao Kaiquan. (1984) "Heavier Punishment Cannot Be Selected after Concurrence of Legal Provisions: A Rejoinder to Comrade Feng Yadong", as cited in *Journal of Law*, No. 8; Chen Xingliang. (2011) "Academic Evolution of the Concurrence of Legal Provisions: An Academic Historical Investigation", as cited in *Legal Science*, No. 4; Liu Mingxiang. (2012) "A New Argument on the Application of Legal Provisions to the Act of Whoring with an Underage Girl", as cited in *Journal of Law*, No. 12; Zhou Guangquan. (2010) "A Study on the Special Relationship in Concurrence of Legal Provisions", as cited in *China Legal Science*, No. 3; Che Hao. (2010) "On the Relationship between the Crime of Rape and the Crime of Whoring with an Underage Girl", as

punishment with crime). On the one hand, "the legal concurrence is not a matter of judging the conformity of the constitutive elements, but of the application of the penal statutory (article) after the establishment of the crime".[52] Thus, there is no doubt that the choice of articles of serious punishment violates the principle of *nulla poena sine lege*. On the other hand, under the restrictions proposed by the author, the choice of articles of serious punishment is consistent with the principle of fitting punishment with crime, and not with the so-called doctrine of severe punishment.

In fact, even in Germany, even when there is a special relation between two articles, the special article is not applied absolutely, but there is a rebirth of the excluded law or a resurrection of the inferior law. For example, the crime of rape is a special article for the crime of forced obscenity, yet once the actor has been deemed as discontinued or attempted rape, German jurisprudence and criminal law doctrine will convict and sentence the actor for accomplished crime of forced obscenity. When the discontinued crime of homicide is established, although crime of homicide is not punished (because the discontinued crime is exempt from punishment), it is considered an accomplished crime of intentional injury if it causes injury.[53] This rebirth of an excluded law or a resurrection of the inferior law is also, in effect, refer to the article of serious punishment is prior to article of light punishment, except that German criminal law doctrine uses a different express.

Nevertheless, this article does not intend to defend and further argue for the article of serious punishment is prior to article of light punishment, but merely proposes the third approach below, drawing on the German and Japanese standard for distinguishing between the special relationship of legal concurrence and the substance standard of ideal concurrence.

(3) The third approach is to exclude the situation where the content of wrongdoing is heavy and the described punishment is light from the legal concurrence, and to consider it as an ideal concurrence. In other words, when an act violates two articles at the same time, only when the application of one of the articles can include the content of wrongdoing of the other article, or when the application of only one of the articles can adequately evaluate all content of wrongdoing of the act, the two articles are belong to the legal concurrence, provided that the two aforementioned standard are met. If the application of either article cannot adequately evaluate all content of wrongdoing of the act, even if the aforementioned two standard are met, it can only be considered as ideal concurrence.[54] In other words, if scholars insist

cited in *Chinese Journal of Law*, No. 2; Wang Qiang. (2012) "The Special Relationship in Concurrence of Legal Provisions and Its Handling", as cited in *Chinese Journal of Law*, No. 1.

[52] 日井田良:《讲义刑法学·总论》，有斐阁2008年版，第524页。Ida Makoto.(2008) Handout of Criminal Law·General Rules, Yuhikaku Press, 524.

[53] Vgl., H.Jescheck/T.Weigend,*Lehrbuch des Strafrechts.Allgemeiner Teil*, 5.Aufl.,Duncker & Humblot, 1996, S.549;日山火正则:"法条竞合の诸问题(2)"，载《神奈川法学》第7卷(1971年)第2号。See Yamabi Masanori.(1971) "Various issues of legal provision competition (1)", as cited in *Kanagawa Law Review*, Vol. 7, No. 2.

[54] Vgl., H.Jescheck/T.Weigend,*Lehrbuch des Strafrechts.Allgemeiner Teil*, 5.Aufl.,Duncker & Humblot, 1996, S.549;日山火正则:"法条竞合の诸问题(2)"，载《神奈川法学》第7卷

that "since the legislator has made the special law independent, it should be strictly in accordance with the law and cannot be chosen by the judiciary at will",[55] "the concept of legal concurrence implies that the priority of application of a special article is unassailable as long as there is a special relationship, without any question of the weight of the special article",[56] then we can solve the related problems of the specific provisions of criminal law by denying the special relationship and admitting the ideal concurrence.

"The theory of quantity of crime and the theory of concurrence are discussions that provides the basis for sentencing after the judgment stage of the wrongdoing and culpability of an act in substantive law"[57] "The theory of concurrence (*Konkurrenzlehre*) is the suture between the theory of criminal act (*Lehre von der Straftat*) and the theory of illegal consequences (*Lehre von der Unrechtsfolgen*)."[58] So, the theory of quantity of crime, or the theory of concurrence, is all about the problem of sentencing. Or, "the correct sentencing is ultimately the purpose of the whole theory of concurrence".[59] Accordingly, it is a directional deviation to study the issues of quantity of crimes or concurrence purely from formal logic without considering the requirement of fitting punishment with crime.

The benchmark for sentencing is culpability, or culpable wrongdoing.[60] If the content of wrongdoing (degree) provided in article A is adequately capable of including the content of wrongdoing (degree) provided in article B, then only article A needs to be applied, and not article B. If the content of wrongdoing of article A cannot embrace the content of wrongdoing of law B, when C's act has both the content of wrongdoing of article A and the content of wrongdoing of article B, the application of either law will not provide an adequate evaluation of the content of

---

(1971年)第2号。(参见张明楷:《论影响责任刑的情节》，载《清华法学》2015年第2期) See Yamabi Masanori.(1971) "Various issues of legal provision competition (1)", as cited in *Kanagawa Law Review*, Vol. 7, No. 2. (See Zhang Mingkai. (2015) On the Circumstances Affecting the Sentence for Culpability, as cited in *Tsinghua Law Journal*, No. 2.).

[55] 陈兴良:"法条竞合的学术演进——一个学术史的考察"，载《法律科学》2011年第4期。See Chen Xingliang. (2011) "Academic Evolution of the Concurrence of Legal Provisions: An Academic Historical Investigation", as cited in *Legal Science*, No. 4.

[56] 周光权:"法条竞合的特别关系研究"，载《中国法学》2010年第3期。Zhou Guangquan. (2010) "A Study on the Special Relationship in Concurrence of Legal Provisions", as cited in *China Legal Science*, No. 3.

[57] 日只木诚:"罪数论·竞合论"，载日山口厚、甲斐克则编:《21世纪日中刑事法の重要课题》，成文堂2014年版，第73页。Tadaki Makoto.(2014) "Theory of multiple offenses and concurrence", as cited in Yamaguchi Atsushi & Kai Katsunori ed., *Key Issues in Japanese and Chinese Criminal Law in the 21st Century*, Seibundo Publishing Co., 73.

[58] 德约翰内斯·韦塞尔斯:《德国刑法总论》，李昌珂译，法律出版社2008年版，第458页。Johannes Wessels, trans. Li Changke, (2008) *Strafrecht Allgemeiner Teil*, Law Press, 458.

[59] 德Ingeborg Puppe:"基于构成要件结果同一性所形成不同构成要件实现之想象竞合"，陈志辉译，载《东吴法律学报》第17卷第3期。Ingeborg Puppe, trans. Chen Zhihui, *Idealkonkurrenz verschiedener Tatbestandsverwirklichungen kraft Identitat der tatbestandsmasigen Erfolge*, as cited in *Soochow Law Review*, Vol.17, No.3.

[60] 参见张明楷:《责任刑与预防刑》，北京大学出版社2015年版，第239页以下。See Zhang Mingkai. (2015) *Responsibility and Prevention in Sentencing*, Peking University Press, 1–239.

C's act. In this case, it shall be considered as an ideal concurrence. In Germany, "as long as the application of a penalty statutory can be exhausted all evaluations for the content of wrongdoing of an act (criminal facts), it belongs to the legal concurrence; when it is necessary to apply several penalty statutory for evaluation, it is the ideal concurrence (concurrence of ideas)."[61] Professor C. Roxin also clearly pointed out that "the identification of special relations is not always a purely logical. It is not uncommon to have to adopt a complementary consideration of skopos theory of the degree of wrongdoing upon the constitutive element of the excluded party."[62] In Japan, when the theory of criminal law distinguishes the legal concurrence from the ideal concurrence, it also adequately considers the weight of the described punishment and judges whether the application of an article can adequately evaluate the content of wrongdoing of acts. For example, Paragraph 1, Article 223 of *Japanese Criminal Law* provides for the following: "A person who, intimidates another through a threat to his or her life, body, freedom, reputation or property, or causes the other to perform an act which the other person has no obligation to perform by use of assault, or hinders the other from exercising his or her rights, shall be punished by imprisonment with hard labor for not more than three years." Article 193 of *Japanese Criminal Law* provides that "when a public officer abuses his or her authority and causes another to perform an act which the person has no obligation to perform, or hinders another from exercising such person's right, he or she shall be punished by imprisonment with hard labor or imprisonment for not more than two years." Since the abuse of authority includes the use of authority to threaten, so from the perspective of logical relationship, there is special relationship between the two articles (Article 193 is a special article). However, since the described punishment of the crime of abuse of authority of the public officer is lighter than that of the crime of coercion, the application of only one article cannot adequately evaluate the content of wrongdoing of the act. Therefore, the dominant ideology of *Japanese Criminal Law* holds that "when a public officer uses violence or coercion to commit abuses of authority, he shall establish an ideal concurrence between the crime of abuse of authority and the crime of coercion."[63] For another example, Article 195 of *Japanese Criminal Law* stipulates the crime of atrocities, insults and abuses of special public officers.[64] The atrocities, insults and abuses include all acts that cause

---

[61] 日只木诚:"念的竞合における明示机能"，载《研修》2011年4月号(总第754号)。Tadaki Makoto.(2011) "The expressive function in conceptual concurrence", as cited in Kenshuu, No. 754.

[62] C. Roxin, *Strafrecht Allgemeiner Teil, Band II*, C.H.Beck, 2003, S.850.

[63] 日山中敬一:《刑法各论》，成文堂2009年版，第766页。另参见日团藤重光:《刑法纲要(各论)》，创文社1990年版，第125页;日大塚仁:《刑法概说(各论)》，有斐阁2005年增补版，第622页;日大谷实:《刑法讲义各论》，成文堂2013年新版，第631页。Yamanaka, Keiichi. (2009) *Specific Provisions of Criminal Law*, Seibundō, 766. See also Dando, Shigemitsu. (1990) Kōyō: *Outline of Criminal Law: Specific Provisions*, Sōbunsha, p. 125; Ōtsuka, Hitoshi. (2005) Gaisetsu: Keihō (Kakuron) *Introduction to Criminal Law: Specific Provisions*) ed., Yūhikaku, 622; Ōya, Minoru. (2013) *Lectures on the Specific Provisions of Criminal Law* ed., Seibundō, 631.

[64] Special public officers are those who perform or assist in the execution of trials, prosecutions or police duties.

physical and mental pain to the victim, and also encompass the forced indecency and rape.[65] In this sense, the crimes of atrocities, insults and abuses of special public officers has special relationship with the crime of forced indecency and the crime of rape (the former is special article). However, the described punishment of the crimes of atrocities, insults and abuses of special public officers is lighter than the described punishment of the crimes of forced indecency and the crime of rape, and the application of any one of articles cannot adequately evaluate the content of wrongdoing of the act, so the dominant ideology and precedents of Japanese criminal law hold that a special public officers who commits an act of forced indecency or rape in the performance of his or her duties shall establish ideal concurrence, not legal concurrence.[66]

In summary, the aforementioned identity of legal interests focuses on the evaluation of the nature of wrongdoing of the act, but does not adequately address the evaluation of the degree of wrongdoing. An adequate evaluation of the nature of the wrongdoing is not the same as an adequate evaluation of the degree of wrongdoing. However, the adequate evaluation of the degree of wrongdoing is of great importance. First, the purpose of criminal law is to protect the legal interests, and the essence of crime is to infringe on the legal interests. There is not only the question of whether the act infringes on the legal interest is identical or not, but also the question of the difference in severity. It is obviously inappropriate to evaluate a serious infringement of legal interest A as a minor infringement of legal interest A, and vice

---

[65] 日大谷实:《刑法讲义各论》，成文堂2013年新版，第633页;日山中敬一:《刑法各论》，成文堂2009年版，第768页;日山口厚:《刑法各论》，有斐阁2010年版，第609页;大审院1915年6月1日判决，载《大审院刑事判决录》(第21辑)，第717页。Ohya Minoru.(2007) *Lectures on Criminal Law(New Edition)*, Seibundo Publishing Co, 663. Yamanaka, Keiichi. (2009) *Specific Provisions of Criminal Law*, Seibundō, 768; Yamaguchi, Atsushi. (2010) *Specific Provisions of Criminal Law*, Yūhikaku, 609; Great Court of Judicature, Judgment of June 1, 1915, *Great Court of Judicature Criminal Reporter*, *Vol. 21*, 717.

See Yamaguchi Atsushi.(2010) *Special Part of Criminal Law*. Yuhikaku Press, 609. Great Court of Judicature, judgment of June 1, 1915, as cited in *Criminal Case Reports of the Great Court of Judicature* (Vol. 21), 717.

[66] 参见日团藤重光:《刑法纲要(各论)》，创文社1990年版，第128页;日大塚仁:《刑法概说(各论)》，有斐阁2005年增补版，第624页;日大谷实:《刑法讲义各论》，成文堂2013年新版，第634页;日山中敬一:《刑法各论》，成文堂2009年版，第768页;日西田典之:《刑法各论》，弘文堂2012年版，第486页;日前田雅英:《刑法各论讲义》，东京大学出版会2015年版，第481页;日山口厚:《刑法各论》，有斐阁2010年版，第609页;大阪地方裁判所1993年3月25日判决，载《判例タイムズ》第831号，第246页。Dando, Shigemitsu. (1990) *Kōyō: Keihō (Kakuron)* (*Outline of Criminal Law: Specific Provisions*), Sōbunsha, 128; Ōtsuka, Hitoshi. (2005) *Gaisetsu: Keihō (Kakuron)* (*Introduction to Criminal Law: Specific Provisions*) (rev. ed.), Yūhikaku, p. 624; Ōya, Minoru. (2013) *Kōgi Kakuron: Keihō (Lectures on the Specific Provisions of Criminal Law)* (new ed.), Seibundō, 634; Yamanaka, Keiichi. (2009) *Kakuron: Keihō* (Specific Provisions of Criminal Law), Seibundō, 768; Nishida, Noriyuki. (2012) *Kakuron: Keihō* (Specific Provisions of Criminal Law), Kōbundō, 486; Maeda, Masahide. (2015) *Kakuron Kōgi: Keihō* (Lectures on the Specific Provisions of Criminal Law), University of Tokyo Press, 481; Yamaguchi, Atsushi. (2010) *Kakuron: Keihō* (Specific Provisions of Criminal Law), Yūhikaku, 609; Osaka Chiho Saibansho [Osaka District Court], Judgment of March 25, 1993, *Hanrei Taimuzu* [Judgments Times], No. 831, 246.

versa. For example, to evaluate a particularly large amount of theft as a large amount of theft is clearly inconsistent with the purpose of protecting the legal interests of criminal law and the nature of the crime. Second, an important reason for the difference in described punishment under the specific provisions of criminal law is the difference in the content (degree) of wrongdoing. Therefore, an inadequate evaluation will lead to the wrong choice of described punishment, thus leading to the deviation of sentencing and certainly violating the principle of fitting punishment with crime. Only the adequate evaluation of the content of wrongdoing of the act can ensure the correct choice of the described punishment and the appropriate sentence. Third, as mentioned above, although the criminal law is the norm of adjudication, but undoubtedly has the role of behavior regulation. Only by adequately evaluating the content of wrongdoing of the act, can the behavior regulation play its proper role. For example, before the implementation of *Amendment (IX) to the Criminal Law of the People's Republic of China*, when the actor prostitutes girls under the age of 14 and causes the death, the content of wrongdoing of causing the death will not be evaluated if only the crime of prostituting girls under the age of 14 established. Under this condition, the Accused and the general people will assume that the act of prostituting girls under the age of 14 causes the death will not increase the penalty. This is obviously not conducive to the function of the criminal law in regulating behavior, nor is it conducive to achieving the special and general preventive purposes of the penalty.

Therefore, even if the legal interests been infringed are same or the nature of the wrongdoing is same, if the application of an article cannot adequately evaluate the content of wrongdoing of the act, an ideal concurrence must be identified (see later discussion). This is because, "by creating an ideal concurrence, it is possible to adequately evaluate in the judgment the actor's attitude towards the infringement of legal interests (the express function of adequately)... An act must be judged under a proper and all-embracing view of the law".[67]

Conversely, where the identity standard of legal interests is met, a special relation of legal concurrence can be identified only if the application of one article also adequately evaluates the content of wrongdoing of the act and if there is an inclusive relationship between the articles. Thus, the distinction between legal concurrence and ideal concurrence is not fixed, but depends on whether the application of one article can adequately evaluate the content of wrongdoing of the act. In other words, when article A and article B are legal concurrence in the general case, it does not preclude as an ideal concurrence in the special case (where the application of one article does not adequately evaluate the content of wrongdoing of the act).

Drawing on the basic views of German and Japanese criminal law doctrine and jurisprudence, and in the light of the specific provisions of our criminal law, the main types of situations that usually fall into the legal concurrence but are ideal

[67] H.Jescheck/T.Weigend,*Lehrbuch des Strafrechts.Allgemeiner Teil,* 5.Aufl., Duncker & Humblot, 1996, S.718.

concurrence under special circumstances (or in contrast to other circumstances) are as follows:

1. When the accomplished felony A and the misdemeanor B are legal concurrence, the attempted felony A and the misdemeanor B may be an ideal concurrence.

For example, in Germany, although the crime of robbery is a special article of the crime of theft, when an act constitutes both attempted robbery and accomplished theft, it is no longer a legal concurrence, but an ideal concurrence.[68] Because in this case, if only attempted robbery is identified, there is no evaluation of the content of wrongdoing of accomplished theft; and if only accomplished theft is evaluated, there is no evaluation of the content of wrongdoing of attempted robbery. Therefore, the ideal concurrence must be used to evaluate the fact of this crime. For another example, although the jurisprudence of the German Federal Supreme Court holds that killing and injury are supplement relations in legal concurrence,[69] according to the "single theory" as a general rule, the intent to kill must also include the intent to injury the body, and the physical injury is a necessary state for the occurrence of death, so the act of killing adequately includes the act of injury, and there is a special relationship between the crime of homicide and the crime of injury.[70] Professor C. Roxin also argued that the two shall belong to the special relationship because conceptually killing is necessarily accompanied by the transitional stage of injury. However, Professor C. Roxin also pointed out that regardless of the relationship between the two, "an ideal concurrence may exist when the punishment for the crime of homicide cannot adequately encompass the content of wrongdoing of the case in the case of the crime of homicide and multiple forms of the crime of injury."[71] In other words, if a finding of the crime of homicide results in a lighter punishment and thus the content of wrongdoing of the particular injury cannot be evaluated, it must not be treated as a legal concurrence, but rather as an ideal concurrence, and sentenced as a special accomplished injury.

Such a situation also exists in China's criminal law. For example, A prepared the tools for intruding into others' houses to rob, and found no one inside the residence after intentionally invading the house with the intent of robbery, so he stole the property worth 10,000 Yuan. Although the crime of robbery is a special article of the crime of theft, if only the crime of robbery is identified, there is no evaluation of the content of wrongdoing of A's accomplished theft; if only the accomplished theft is identified, there is no evaluation of the content of wrongdoing of the preparation for robbery. Only if it is identified to be an ideal concurrence, it can be

---

[68] Vgl.,C.Roxin, *Strafrecht Allgemeiner Teil, Band II*, C.H.Beck, 2003, S.851;H.Jescheck/T. Weigend, *Lehrbuch des Strafrechts.Allgemeiner Teil*, 5.Aufl., Duncker & Humblot, 1996, S.720.

[69] BGHSt 16,123. In fact, the supplementary relationship and the special relationship are only from different observation angles.(参见柯耀程:《刑法竞合论》，中国人民大学出版社2008年版，第142页)See Ke Yaocheng. (2008) *On Concurrence of Criminal Law*, China Renmin University of Press, 142.

[70] Vgl.Volkey Krey, *Strafrecht Besonderer Teil, Band 1*,11.Aufl.,Kohlhammwer, 1998.S.114ff.

[71] Vgl.,C.Roxin, *Strafrecht Allgemeiner Teil, Band II*, C.H.Beck, 2003, S.856.

adequately evaluated and achieve the express function of ideal concurrence. For another example, in general, the crime of intentional homicide is the special article of the crime of intentional injury, so, in general, the intentional killing (whether it is attempted or accomplished) shall be applied the special article of the crime of intentional homicide. However, when the actor commits an act of killing with special cruelty that causes serious injury and serious disability, the actor will be sentenced lighter or mitigated punishment if he is then identified guilty of attempted intentional homicide under the special article. However, such a penalty cannot adequately evaluate the content of wrongdoing of actor "commits an act of killing with special cruelty that causes serious injury and serious disability", so it should be considered as ideal concurrence and inflicted punishment with one heavier crime. In other words, it can be identified that the act has committed several crimes, and it shall apply the described punishment of "shall be sentenced to fixed-term imprisonment of not less than 10 years, life imprisonment or death" for the crime of intentional injury, and no longer apply the lenient punishment for attempted crimes. Only in this way can the principle of fitting punishment with crime can be adapted.[72] Perhaps some people think that Paragraph 2, Article 234 of *Chinese Criminal Law* has the expression "except as otherwise specifically provided in this Law", and the above view of this article violates this provision. In fact, the phrase "except as otherwise specifically provided in this Law" shall be in respect of legal concurrence, but in the case of ideal concurrence the punishment with one heavier crimes shall be inflicted.

2. When the crime B and the basic provisions of crime A are legal concurrence, the crime B and articles (or parts of) of aggravating punishment of crime A may be ideal concurrence.

For example, Paragraph 3, Article 151 of *Chinese Criminal Law* stipulates that "Whoever smuggles rare plants or products made thereof or other goods or articles whose import and export are prohibited by the state shall be sentenced to imprisonment of not more than 5 years or limited incarceration and a fine or be sentenced to a fine only; or if the circumstances are serious, shall be sentenced to imprisonment of not less than 5 years and a fine." Paragraph 1, Article 153 stipulates that "Whoever smuggles goods or articles other than those as mentioned in Articles 151, 152 and 347 shall be punished in light of the graveness of the crime according to the following provisions: (1) Whoever smuggles goods or articles to evade a relatively large amount of tax payable, or smuggles again after having been given administrative punishment twice for smuggling within a year, shall be sentenced to imprisonment of not more than 3 years or limited incarceration and a fine of not less than the

[72] Some people may think that the principal of fitting punishment with crime can be realized if the above-mentioned acts can be regarded as attempted intentional homicide without the lighter or mitigated punishment. However, in the case of the same statutory punishment, there is not the lenient punishment for the crime of intentional injury, and the case of intentional homicide with the lenient punishment, of course, it should be recognized as the former, otherwise there will be no adequate evaluation of the content of wrongdoing.

evaded amount of tax payable but not more than five times the evaded amount of tax payable. (2) Whoever smuggles goods or articles to evade a huge amount of tax payable or with any other serious circumstance shall be sentenced to imprisonment of not less than 3 years but not more than 10 years and a fine of not less than the evaded amount of tax payable but not more than five times the evaded amount of tax payable. (3) Whoever smuggles goods or articles to evade an especially huge amount of tax payable or with any other especially serious circumstance shall be sentenced to imprisonment of not less than 10 years or life imprisonment and a fine of not less than the evaded amount of tax payable but not more than five times the evaded amount of tax payable or a forfeiture of property." If Article 151 is used as a benchmark, Article 153 can be considered as a supplementary article; if Article 153 is used as a benchmark, then Article 151 is a special article. It is certain that Paragraph 3 of Article 151 is a special article for the legal concurrence if whoever smuggles rare plants or products made thereof to evade a relatively large or a huge amount of tax payable. However, whoever smuggles rare plants or products made thereof to evade an especially huge amount of tax payable, if it is still considered as a special article and is identified to be the crime of smuggling goods and articles whose import and export are prohibited by the State, the content of wrongdoing of 'evade an especially huge amount of tax payable' cannot be adequately evaluated. Therefore, it must be identified as an ideal concurrence, thus can evaluate both the content of wrongdoing of 'smuggling goods and articles whose import and export are prohibited by the State' and the content of wrongdoing of 'evade an especially huge amount of tax payable'.

Further, Article 198 of *Chinese Criminal Law* provides that "Fraudulent insurance activities falling under any one of the following circumstances shall, for cases involving relatively large amounts be punished with imprisonment of less than five years or limited incarceration, with a fine of over 10,000 Yuan but less than 100,000 Yuan; for cases involving large amounts, or of a serious nature, with imprisonment of over five years but less than 10 years, with a fine of over 20,000 Yuan but less than 200,000 Yuan; for cases involving extraordinarily large amounts, or of a heavily serious nature, with imprisonment of over 10 years, with a fine of over 20,000 Yuan but less than 200,000 Yuan, or with forfeiture of property". Article 266 provides that "Those defrauding relatively large amounts of public or private money and property are to be sentenced to 3 years or fewer in prison or put under limited incarceration or surveillance, in addition to fines; or are to be fined. Those defrauding large amounts of money and property or having involvement in other serious cases are to be sentenced to three to 10 years in prison, in addition to fines." Those defrauding extraordinarily large amounts of money and property or involving in especially serious cases are to be sentenced to 10 years or more in prison or given life sentences, in addition to fines or confiscation of property.' If scholars insist that the crime of insurance fraud is a special article of general fraud,[73] it can only be recognized as

[73] Strictly speaking, both are ideal concurrence instead of regulatory concurrence [参见吕英杰:"刑法法条竞合理论的比较研究"，载陈兴良主编:《刑事法评论》(第23卷)，北京大学出版社2008年版，第483页]See Lü Yingjie. (2008) "A Comparative Study on the Theory of Legal

the special relationship between the two when the amount of insurance fraud is within the relatively large or large amounts under general fraud. For on such occasions, the application of the special article recognized as the crime of insurance fraud may also adequately evaluate the content of infringement of the insurance order and property by the act. However, if whoever defrauding insurance has reached extraordinarily large amounts of money and property (such as 20,000,000 Yuan) under the general fraud, and he or she should be given life sentences, then the insurance fraud and general fraud is an ideal concurrence. Because in this occasion, if the special relationship is still recognized and the crime of insurance fraud is identified by applying the special article, the applicable described punishment is "sentenced to 10 years or more in prison", can only evaluate the content of the infringement of 'the insurance order' and 'extraordinarily large amounts of money and property', but cannot adequately evaluate the content of the infringement of 'extraordinarily large amounts of money and property'. Therefore, it must be considered as an ideal concurrence, and the act is identified to be guilty of both crimes and punished by the described punishment for one heavier crime (the crime of general fraud). Likewise, "If cases are governed by other stipulations of this law, those stipulations shall apply" in Article 266 of *Chinese Criminal Law* is only in terms of legal concurrence. For example, in the case of defrauding insurance relatively large amounts of money and property, it shall belong to "If cases are governed by other stipulations of this law" and therefore punishable as the crime of insurance fraud.

Also, if scholars insist that the original article of prostituting girls under the age of 14 is a special article for the crime of adultery with girls under the age of 14,[74] then, under the substantive standard of the inclusiveness of the wrongdoing, this special relationship exists only between the act of prostituting girls under the age of 14 and the usual adultery with girls under the age of 14 (Paragraph 2 of Article 236 of *Chinese Criminal Law*).[75] For example, when the actor commits the act of prostituting girls under the age of 14 on one occasion, the crime of prostituting girls under the age of 14 based on the special article may also achieve the principle of "fitting punishment with crime". However, when the actor prostituted girls under the age of 14 and causing serious injury or death to a young girl, it must be considered as an ideal concurrence between the crime of prostituting girls under the age of 14, and the crime of adultery with girls under the age of 14 causing serious injury or death[76]; when the actor has prostituted more than three girls under the age of 14, it must be considered as an ideal concurrence between the crime of prostituting girls

---

Concurrence of Provisions in Criminal Law", as cited in Chen Xingliang ed. *Criminal Law Review* (Vol. 23), Peking University Press, 483.

[74] As mentioned earlier, I believs that the two are ideal concurrence, for the two do not meet the standard for the identity of legal interests, they are not the regulatory concurrence.

[75] 参见劳东燕:"强奸罪与嫖宿幼女罪的关系新论"，载《清华法学》2011年第2期。See Lao Dongyan. (2011) "A New Theory on the Relationship between the Crime of Rape and the Crime of Whoring with an Underage Girl", as cited in *Tsinghua University Law Journal*, No. 2.

[76] It is not an ideal concurrence between prostituting girls under the age of 14 and negligence causes serious injury, negligence causes death.

under the age of 14 and the act of "adultery with many girls under the age of 14". Only in this way can the nature and content of the wrongdoing of the act be adequately evaluated.

If, for example, scholars insist that the crime of theft and the crime of illegally felling trees are in a special relationship of legal concurrence,[77] then, under the substantive standard of the inclusiveness of wrongdoing, this special relationship is limited to situations where the value of the property stolen by illegally felling trees (the degree of wrongdoing) does not exceed imprisonment of 15 years. In other words, when the degree of property infringement caused by illegally felling trees requires a life sentence, it is an ideal concurrence with the crime of theft. This is because, if only the special relationship of legal concurrence is identified, the content of wrongdoing of significant property infringement is not adequately evaluated, and the content of infringement on forest resources will not been evaluated if only the crime of theft is identified. Therefore, only if the crime is identified to be an ideal concurrence will there be a adequate evaluation of the nature and content of wrongdoing of the act.

The cross-examination that may be encountered here is on what basis can it be said that the application of one article does not adequately evaluate the content of wrongdoing? Will leaving it up to the interpreter lead to arbitrariness in conviction and sentencing? The answer is actually quite simple: it is not only easy but not arbitrary to determine whether the application of one article adequately evaluates the content of wrongdoing of the act in the light of described punishment and sentencing norms (sentencing practice). For one thing, the severity of the described punishment depends primarily on the culpable content of wrongdoing, not simply on the objective wrongdoing or type of culpability. While the degree of necessity of general prevention also affects the described punishment, the general prevention and culpability are closely linked. For example, the described punishment for the crime of theft is higher than that for intentional destruction of property, on the face, because the former has the purpose of illegal possession, but in essence because the purpose of illegal possession (especially the intent of utilization) makes the general necessity of prevention greater, that is, the average person is prone to steal other people's property based on the intent of utilization; whereas the crime of intentional destruction of property is not predicated on the purpose of illegal possession, and the average person does not readily destroy other people's property, so the necessity of general prevention is small. Therefore, the size of the necessity of general prevention actually means that there is a serious culpable content of wrongdoing. On the other hand, because there is a certain range of described punishment, the judgment of the content of wrongdoing can be further refined according to the sentencing norms at the time of the implementation of sentencing normalization. For example, the relationship between the aforementioned insurance fraud and the crime of fraud. The maximum punishment for the crime of fraud is life imprisonment, and the

[77] As mentioned above, judging from the identity of legal interests, it is more appropriate to determine the two as an ideal concurrence.

maximum punishment for the crime of insurance fraud is the imprisonment of 15 years. Therefore, the key is how much property defrauded by the actor will be worth to be sentenced to life imprisonment. If, from 2016, judicial practice only imposes a life sentence for defrauding property worth more than 30 million Yuan, then for the defrauding insurance under 30 million Yuan, an identification of the crime of insurance fraud may still adequately evaluate the content of wrongdoing of the act. Once the defrauding insurance worth more than 30 million Yuan, it should be considered that identifying the act as insurance fraud alone will not adequately evaluate the degree of wrongdoing of the act against property, and therefore, it needs to be identified as an ideal concurrence and the punishment with one heavier crimes (crime of fraud) shall be inflicted. Further, if from 2016, the judicial practice imposes a life sentence for theft property worth more than three million Yuan, then, when the value of illegally felling trees is less than two million Yuan, it is identified that the crime of illegally felling trees can still adequately evaluate the content of wrongdoing of the act. Once the value exceeds 2 million Yuan, it should be considered that the crime of illegally felling trees alone will not be able to adequately evaluate the degree of the content of wrongdoing of the act. Therefore, it needs to be considered as ideal concurrence and the punishment with one heavier crimes (crime of theft) shall be inflicted. It is clear that a slight comparison between described punishment and sentencing norms (sentencing practice) in this matter can lead to reasonable conclusions without leading to arbitrariness in conviction and sentencing.

3. The aggregated consequential offense (*Erfolgsqualifikation*) is a legal concurrence with the basic offense, but an ideal concurrence with the crime committed by the aggravated result.

The most typical special relation can be seen between the aggregated consequential offense and the basic offense.[78] For example, robbery causing death is a special relationship with general robbery. When the actor causes death by robbery, the special article of robbery causing death must be applied, and the basic article may not be applied to identify general robbery. However, in terms of the relationship to intentional homicide and negligent homicide, robbery causing death, the crime of intentional homicide and the crime of negligent homicide are ideal concurrence.

The German Federal Court hold that "there is an ideal concurrence between the crime of murder and the crime of robbery causing death, so that the death intentionally caused is the result of the robbery, whereby a particularly significant and dangerous robbery can be explicitly (expressly) stated in the conviction".[79] That is, in the case of robbery where the purpose is achieved by means of killing, it should be

[78] Vgl.,C.Roxin,*Strafrecht Allgemeiner Teil, Band II*, C.H.Beck,2003,S.849ff;日平野龙一:《刑法总论II》，有斐阁1975年版，第410页。See Hirano Ryuuichi.(1975) General Theory of Criminal Law II, Yuhikaku Press, 410.

[79] BGHSt 27 6667,转引自日只木诚:"观念的竞合における明示机能"，载《研修》2011年4月号(总第754号)。As cited in Tadaki, Makoto. (2011) *The Declaratory Function in Concurrence of Imaginaries*, as cited in *Japanese Judicial Training*, No. 754 (April 2011).

identified to be an ideal concurrence with intentional robbery causing death, not a legal concurrence. This view is also generally accepted by German theory of criminal law. For example, Professor H. Jescheck and Professor T. Weigend pointed out that "if the basic constitutive elements of the aggregated consequential offense are not lacking and the aggravated result can be achieved not only by negligence but also by intent, it must be recognized that there is an ideal concurrence between the aggregated consequential offense and this intentional or negligent constitutive elements. This is because only by adopting such an approach can it be shown whether the aggravated result in a specific case is caused by intention or negligence."[80]

In China, the intentional robbery causing death is considered as an ideal concurrence between robbery causing death and intentional homicide, which not only can perform the above-mentioned express function, but also facilitates the rationalization of sentencing when the basic offense is attempted. For example, the actor planned to kill another person and then obtained the property, but after killed another person, he or she automatically abandoned the act of obtaining the property for fear of punishment, or failed to obtain the property for reasons other than his or her will. In this case, if the crime of robbery (causing death) is identified, there is the question of whether the abandonment of crime and criminal attempt are applicable in the first place, and if they are, it will obviously lead to unfitting punishment with crime. If the crime of robbery (causing death) is identified to be an ideal concurrence with the crime of intentional homicide, the accomplished crime of intentional homicide can be punished, thus ensuring the reasonableness of the sentence.

The question arises as to whether there is a repetitive evaluation by identifying the above situations as an ideal concurrence. The answer is no. On the one hand, the above-mentioned evaluation is aimed first and foremost at achieving the express function of ideal concurrence, thus contributing to the realization of the purpose of special and general prevention, rather than to subject the actor to be double punished. On the other hand, in the case of ideal concurrence, the act is only identified to have committed several crimes, not punished as such, and only a maximum described punishment shall be applied. Therefore, there is no repetitive evaluation against the actor.

In addition, there is a legal concurrence between the aggregated consequential offense and the basic offense. However, a formal aggregated result without an aggravated described punishment in the criminal law is an ideal concurrence. For example, before the implementation of *Amendment (IX)*, the kidnapping causing death was the aggregated consequential offense of the crime of kidnapping, so there was a special relationship between kidnapping causing death and the general kidnapping. However, *Amendment (IX)* does not stipulate the kidnapping causing death is the aggregated consequential offense. Thus, on the occasion of the kidnapping causing death, the actor cannot establish the crime of kidnapping solely, but must be considered as an ideal concurrence between the crime of kidnapping and the crime

[80] H.Jescheck/T.Weigend, *Lehrbuch des Strafrechts.Allgemeiner Teil*, 5.Aufl., Duncker & Humblot, 1996, S.723.

of negligent homicide, and then punished according to the described punishment of the crime of kidnapping.

In summary, the distinction between a special relationship and an ideal concurrence is relative and not fixed. The next question to be discussed is whether there is a legal concurrence in cases where there is a crossed relationship between articles.

For example, Article 224 of *Japanese Criminal Law* states that "A person who kidnaps a minor by force or enticement shall be punished by imprisonment with hard labor for not less than 3 months but not more than seven years." Article 225 states that "A person who kidnaps another by force or enticement for the purpose of profit, indecency, marriage or threat to the life or body shall be punished by imprisonment with hard labor for not less than 1 year but not more than 10 years." According to Professor Yamaguchi Atsushi, in terms of a person who kidnaps a minor by force or enticement for the purpose of profit and indecency, the relationship between the crime of kidnaps a minor by force or enticement and the crime of force or enticement for the purpose of profit is crossed, and the principle that article of serious punishment is prior to article of light punishment shall be applied.[81] However, the general doctrine in Japan and the theory of concurrence in Germany do not recognize the crossed relationship of legal concurrence. This is because, in the occasion of the above-mentioned crossed relationship, if only one article of serious punishment is applied, the content of wrongdoing of the act is not adequately evaluated and the express function of ideal concurrence cannot be performed. For example, when the actor kidnaps a minor by force or enticement for the purpose of profit and indecency, if only Article 224 is applied, the purpose of wrongdoing is not evaluated; if only Article 225 is applied, the content of 'kidnaps a minor by force or enticement' is not evaluated. Only if it is identified to be an ideal concurrence, and if it is made clear in the judgment that the act violates both Article 224 and Article 225, can the adequate evaluation of the content of wrongdoing be achieved. It is easy to see that by giving weight to the express function of ideal concurrence, it is denied that the crossed relationship shall belong to legal concurrence.

Also, some scholars in China have pointed out that a crossed relationship at extension shall be established when the actor posed as state organ personnel to cheat and bluff and fraudulently obtained property. Accordingly, Article 266 and Article 279 have a crossed relationship, which is a crossed relationship of legal concurrence, and the applicable principle is law of serious punishment is prior to law of light punishment.[82] However, (1) the crime of cheating and bluffing does not identify the property as a protected legal interest, and thus does not take 'obtained property' as an element, and "cheating and bluffing" does not have an object, but is merely a synonym of "posed as state organ personnel". Whoever poses as state organ personnel shall establish "to cheat and bluff". In other words, in practice, "pose as state organ personnel to cheat and bluff" is only a fact of the case, not a

---

[81] 参见日山口厚:《刑法总论》，有斐阁2007年版，第368页。See Yamaguchi Atsushi. (2007) *General Part of Criminal Law.* Yuhikaku Press, 368.

[82] 陈兴良:《规范刑法学》(上册)，中国人民大学出版社2008年版，第277~279页。Chen Xingliang. (2008) *Normative Criminal Law 1*, China Renmin University Press, 277~279.

constitutive element of Article 279. Therefore, there is no crossed relationship between the two aforementioned articles; (2) even if it is admitted that there is a crossed relationship between the two, it is not a legal concurrence. The reason is that if only the crime of cheating and bluffing is applied according to Article 279, there is no evaluation of the content of the illegal infringement of property; if only the crime of fraud is applied according to Article 266, there is no evaluation of the content of the public credit of state organs. Only if it is identified to be ideal concurrence, and expressly stated in the judgment that one serious described punishment shall be applied and the act is guilty of the above two crimes, can the content of wrongdoing of the act be adequately evaluated; (3) the view that the crime of fraud and the crime of cheating and bluffing are legal concurrence, and the view that the law of serious punishment is prior to law of light punishment, is obviously inconsistent with the provision of Article 266 "if cases are governed by other stipulations of this law, those stipulations shall apply". In other words, if the act of posing as state organ personnel to cheat and bluff and fraudulently obtained property is identified as the crime of fraud (law of serious punishment), it violates the provisions of Article 266. Thus, scholars who hold the above-mentioned view point out that "It is possible to interpret 'if cases are governed by other stipulations of this law, those stipulations shall apply' as a provision of the principle of legal application of the legal concurrence of special law and common law for the crime of fraud, and it does not apply to the legal concurrence of the selective relationship in the crime of fraud. The principle that 'law of serious punishment is prior to law of light punishment' can be applied straightforwardly to legal concurrence of the selective relationship."[83] The basis for such an interpretation, however, is in doubt. In fact, instead of such an interpretation, it will be better to recognize that the act of posing as state organ personnel to cheat and bluff and fraudulently obtained property is an ideal concurrence. This will allow for an adequate evaluation of the different legal interests infringed by the act, achieve the express function of ideal concurrence, and maintain the harmonization of penalties, without violating the provisions of Article 266.

Also, when the family member abused by the actor is a minor under guardianship, an identification of legal concurrence will either apply Article 260 alone that been evaluated as the crime of abuse, thus the content of wrongdoing of 'abuse a specific subject, a minor under guardianship' is not evaluated, or apply Paragraph 1 of Article 260 alone that been evaluated as the crime of abuse person under guardianship, thus the content of wrongdoing of 'abuse family member' is not evaluated. The content of wrongdoing of the act can only be adequately evaluated if it is identified to be an ideal concurrence.

In summary, Only if the express function of ideal concurrence is taken into account and if there is a crossed relationship between the specific provisions of the

[83] 陈兴良:《判例刑法学》(上卷)，中国人民大学出版社2009年版，第510页。陈兴良教授认为交叉(交互)竞合的两个法条之间存在择一关系。Chen Xingliang. (2009) *Case Studies in Criminal Law* (Vol. 1), China Renmin University of Press, 510. Professor. Chen Xingliang contends that an alternative relationship exists between the two legal provisions involved in intersective (or interactive) concurrence.

criminal law, the legal concurrence cannot be recognized, but only as ideal concurrence.

11.5 Brief Conclusion

In short, "an act shall constitute an ideal concurrence if it violates several criminal law provisions that cannot be excluded by legal concurrence between them".[84] And whether it can be excluded according to the legal concurrence is not simply a matter of whether there is an inclusive and crossed relationship between several articles, but must also consider whether the application of one article adequately evaluates the nature and the content (degree) of wrongdoing of the act. Only if the application of one article can adequately evaluate all contents of wrongdoing of the act, it may belong to legal concurrence. If not, it should be considered an ideal concurrence. The viewpoint of this article makes the distinction between legal concurrence and ideal concurrence not fixed, but does not lead to the arbitrariness of the distinction; the viewpoint of this article leads to the reduction of legal concurrence and the increase of ideal concurrence, but not for the purpose of doctrine of severe punishment, but for the purpose of realizing the fairness and justice of criminal law and the special and general preventive purposes of penalties.

"The possibility of applying the principle of law of serious punishment is prior to law of light punishment in special relationships of legal concurrence has always been a central concern of our criminal law scholarship on the doctrine of legal concurrence, and the debate has lasted for 25 years and still shows no signs of subsiding."[85] From a legislative point of view, it is clear that this ongoing debate is the result of the legislator's indiscriminate efforts to impose "special articles" which stipulates unbalanced described punishment. Although there should not be a debate between formal and substantive interpretation, there is indeed a debate between formal and substantive interpretation in the treatment of "special articles" which stipulates unbalanced described punishment. The interpreter who holds the theory of formal interpretation focuses on the logical relationship between the articles, but does not weigh whether the articles are in harmony with each other, does not consider whether the sentence of each case is in line with the principle of fitting punishment with crime, or puts the problem on the legislator; the interpreter who holds the theory of substantive interpretation believes that the legal concurrence is not a mere logical relationship, but to implement fairness and justice, the rationalization of sentencing in the legal concurrence and the specific case. This is because "a

[84] 德冈特·施特拉腾韦特、洛塔尔·库伦:《刑法总论I——犯罪论》，杨萌译，法律出版社2006年版，第442页。Giinter Stratenwerth & Lothar Kuhlen, trans. Yang Meng, (2006) *Strafrecht Allgemeiner Teil I: Die Straftat*, Law Press, 442.

[85] 陈兴良:"法条竞合的学术演进——一个学术史的考察"，载《法律科学》2011年第4期。See Chen Xingliang. (2011) "Academic Evolution of the Concurrence of Legal Provisions: An Academic Historical Investigation", as cited in *Legal Science*, No. 4.

substantial inconsistency between a crime and the corresponding penalty set for it will be contrary to the general sense of justice."[86] Similarly, a substantial inconsistency between a sentence and the crime for which it was imposed will be contrary to the general sense of justice. This article is clearly a product of the theory of substantive interpretation, aimed at achieving fair justice in criminal law and achieving special and general prevention of punishment. Of course, this article is unlikely to quell the debate in this regard; rather, it may make it more heated (or, rather, this article may be subject to more criticism).

It shall also like to repeat that our criminal law doctrine not only uses a single formal standard to distinguish between legal concurrence and ideal concurrences, but also leaves the protected legal interests of the articles and creates an inclusive or crossed relationship between the articles by envisaging specific facts, which ends up in incorporating a large number of ideal concurrences into the special relationship of legal concurrence. Many scholars, while treating the German and Japanese principle of dealing with the special relationship of legal concurrence (i.e. the special article is prior to general article) as an iron rule, have failed to identify the special relationship in accordance with the German and Japanese criminal law doctrine,[87] resulting in the scope of the special relationship encompassing the German and Japanese absorbing relationship and ideal concurrence. Similarly, although our theory of criminal law and judicial practice have accepted the concept of ideal concurrence originated from Germany, they have ignored the most important express function of ideal concurrence, which is most emphasized by German theory of criminal law and judicial practice, resulting in the crossed relationship originally belonging to ideal concurrence becomes the legal concurrence. This is a phenomenon worth reflecting on.

The author has always opposed the practice of broadly defining the scope of legal concurrence and adhering to the principle of special article is prior to general article without regard to the reasonableness of the conclusions. In other words, in order to reach a reasonable conclusion, realize the concept of justice in criminal law, and achieve the purpose of special and general prevention, either the principle of article of serious punishment is prior to article of light punishment should be applied in a limited manner, or the scope of legal concurrence should be limited to exclude the situations requiring the application of article of serious punishment from the special relationship. The author previously favored the principle of article of serious punishment is prior to article of light punishment should be applied in a limited manner,

---

[86] 美E.博登海默:《法理学:法律哲学与法律方法》，邓正来译，中国政法大学出版社1999年版，第287页。Edgar Bodenheimer, trans. Deng Zhenglai, (1999) *Jurisprudence*, China University of Political Science and Law Press, 287.

[87] For example, in the theory of concurrence of Germany, special relationships are limited to three situations: aggravating or mitigating (privilege) constitutive element, combinative crime and the existence of aggravated principal offender.(Vgl.,C.Roxin,*Strafrecht Allgemeiner Teil, Band II*, C.H.Beck,2003,S.848ff). In Japan, the special relationships exist only in basic types and aggravated types, basic types and mitigated types.(参见日山口厚:《刑法总论》，有斐阁2007年版，第367页See Yamaguchi Atsushi.(2007) *General Part of Criminal Law*. Yuhikaku Press, 367).

which is the former path; the re-distinction between legal concurrence and ideal concurrence proposed in this article[88] is the latter path. Although the former and latter paths are different, the conclusions on specific cases are exactly the same, so it can be said that they all go the same way.

References

"Academic Evolution of the Concurrence of Legal Provisions: An Academic Historical Investigation", as cited in Legal Science, No. 4.

Anthony Lewis, trans. Xv Shuang, (2010) *Freedom for the Thought That We Hate: A Biography of the First Amendment*, China Law Press & Seibundo Publishing Co., 3.

Arthur Kaufmann, trans. Liu Xingyi, (2000) *Rechtsphilosophie*, Wu-Nan Book Inc. 119. BGHSt 16,123.

C. Roxin, *Strafrecht Allgemeiner Teil, Band II*, C.H.Beck, 2003, S.850.

Cai Daotong. (2015) "On the Application of the Principle That the Special Provision Prevails over the General Provision", as cited in *Jurist*, No. 5.

Che Hao. (2010) "On the Relationship between the Crime of Rape and the Crime of Whoring with an Underage Girl", as cited in *Chinese Journal of Law*, No. 2;

Chen Hongbing. (2012) "On the Unnecessity of Strictly Distinguishing Legal Concurrence and Ideal Concurrence: An Advocacy of the Grand Concurrence Theory", as cited in *Tsinghua University Law Journal*, No. 1.

Chen Xingliang ed. (2011a) *General Interpretation of Criminal Law*, People's Court Press, 1-703. Zhang Mingkai. (2011) Criminal Law, Law Press China, 432-906

Chen Xingliang, Gong Peihua & Li Qilu. (1993) *On Concurrence of Legal Provisions*, Fudan University Press, 1-22;

Chen Xingliang. (2006) *"On Concurrence of Criminal Law"*, as cited in *Studies in Law and Business,* No. 2;

Chen Xingliang. (2008) *Normative Criminal Law 1*, China Renmin University Press, 277-279

Chen Xingliang. (2009) *Case Studies in Criminal Law* (vol. 1), China Renmin University of Press, 510.

Chen Xingliang. (2011b) "Academic Evolution of the Concurrence of Legal Provisions: An Academic Historical Investigation", as cited in *Legal Science*, No. 4;

Chen Xingliang. (2011c) "From the Theory of Quantity of Offenses to the Theory of Concurrence: An Academic Historical Investigation", as cited in *Modern Law Journal*, No. 3.

Edgar Bodenheimer, trans. Deng Zhenglai, (1999) *Jurisprudence*, China University of Political Science and Law Press, 287.

Feng Yadong. (1984) "On the Selection of Heavier Punishment after Concurrence of Legal Provisions", as cited in *Journal of Law*, No. 4.

Gao Mingxuan & Ma Kechang eds. (2011) *Criminal Law*, Peking University Press & Higher Education Press, 186;

Giinter Stratenwerth & Lothar Kuhlen, trans. Yang Meng, (2006) *Strafrecht Allgemeiner Teil I: Die Straftat*, Law Press, 436, 442, 445–446.

Great Court of Judicature, judgment of June 1, 1915, as cited in *Criminal Case Reports of the Great Court of Judicature* (Vol. 21), 717.

[88] The viewpoint of this article is based on the systematic reading of the German and Japanese literature on the regulatory concurrence and the ideal concurrence. It is basically a reference and quote to the relevant theories from Germany and Japan, but it can properly handle the relevant provisions of the criminal law of China.

H. Jescheck/T. Weigend, *Lehrbuch des Strafrechts. Allgemeiner Teil*, 5.Aufl., Duncker & Humblot, 1996,S.718,S.720,S.723.

Hirano Ryuuichi. (2015) "Case law and legal doctrines in the interpretation of criminal law", trans., Li Hong, as cited in *Journal of the National Prosecutors College*, No. 1.

Ida Makoto. (2008) *Handout of Criminal Law·General Rules*, Yuhikaku Press, 523, 524, 532.

Ingeborg Puppe, trans. Chen Zhihui, Idealkonkurrenz verschiedener Tatbestandsverwirklichungen kraft Identitat der tatbestandsmasigen Erfolge, as cited in Soochow Law Review, Vol. 17, No. 3.

Ingeborg Puppe, trans. Chen Zhihui, Idealkonkurrenz verschiedener Tatbestandsverwirklichungen kraft Identitat der tatbestandsmasigen Erfolge, as cited in Soochow Law Review, Vol.17, No.3.

Jescheck/T. Weigend, Lehrbuch des Strafrechts.Allgemeiner Teil, 5.Aufl., Duncker & Humblot, 1996, S.732.

Johannes Wessels, trans. Li Changke, (2008) *Strafrecht Allgemeiner Teil*, Law Press, 458. *Kanagawa Law Review*, Vol. 7, No. 1.

Karl Larenz, trans. Chen Aie, (2003) *Methoden lehreder Rechtswissenschaft*, The Commercial Press, 20.

Liu Mingxiang. (2012) "A New Argument on the Application of Legal Provisions to the Act of Whoring with an Underage Girl", as cited in *Journal of Law,* No. 12;

Machino Saku. (1991) "Theory of legal provision competition", as cited in Naitou Ken et al, ed., A Collection of Congratulatory Essays by Mr. Hirano Ryuuichi in His Seventies (Vol. 1), Yuhikaku Press, 1-420.

Maeda Masahide. (2006) *Handouts of General Rules of Criminal Law*, University of Tokyo Press, 392, 399, 555.

Ohya Minoru. (2007) *Lectures on Criminal Law(New Edition)*, Seibundo Publishing Co, 663

Ono Seiichirou. (1948) *Handouts of Crime*, Yuhikaku Press, 266.

Ono Seiichirou. (1953) *Theory of Criminal Composition Requirements*, Yuhikaku Press, 402.

R. Maurach, *Drutsches Strafrecht, Allgemeiner Teil*, 3.Aufl., Karlsruhe, 1965, S.636f.

Rudolf von Jhering, trans. Li Juntao, (2010) *Ist Die Jurisprudenz Eine Wissenschaft?*, Law Press & Seibundo Publishing Co., 81.

See Chen Xingliang. (2007) *Lectures on Criminal Law*, Renmin University of China Press, 372;

See Chen Xingliang. (2011) "Academic Evolution of the Concurrence of Legal Provisions: An Academic Historical Investigation", as cited in *Legal Science*, No. 4.

See Ding Huimin. (2013) *On Legal Concurrence of Provisions in Criminal Law*, Doctoral Dissertation, as cited in Tsinghua University, 1-107.

See Hirano Ryuuichi. (1975) General Theory of Criminal Law II, Yuhikaku Press, 410

See Ke Yaocheng. (2008) *On Concurrence of Criminal Law*, China Renmin University of Press, 142

See Lao Dongyan. (2011) "A New Theory on the Relationship between the Crime of Rape and the Crime of Whoring with an Underage Girl", as cited in *Tsinghua University Law Journal*, No. 2.

See Lü Yingjie. (2008a) "A Comparative Study on the Theory of Legal Concurrence of Provisions in Criminal Law", as cited in Chen Xingliang ed. *Criminal Law Review* (Vol. 23), Peking University Press, 483.

See Lü Yingjie. (2008b) "A Comparative Study on the Theory of Legal Concurrence of Provisions in Criminal Law", as cited in Chen Xingliang ed. *Criminal Law Review* (Vol. 23), Peking University Press, 483.

See Nishida Noriyuki. (2012) *Essays on Criminal Law*, Koubundou Publishers Inc., 331.

See Tadaki Makoto. (2009) *Study on the theory of multiple crimes (revised edition),* Seibundo Publishing Co., 1-187.

See Yamabi Masanori. (1971a) "The nature of legal provision competition", as cited in *Hogaku*, No. 4;

See Yamabi Masanori. (1971b) "Various issues of legal provision competition (1)", as cited in *Kanagawa Law Review*, Vol. 7, No. 1.

See Yamabi Masanori. (1971c) "Various issues of legal provision competition (1)", as cited in

See Yamabi Masanori. (1971d) "Various issues of legal provision competition (1)", as cited in *Kanagawa Law Review*, Vol. 7, No. 2.

SeeYamaguchiAtsushi.(2007) *General Part of Criminal Law*. Yuhikaku Press, 366,367,368,423,609.
See Zhang Mingkai. (2015a) "On the Implementation of the Principle of Definiteness in Criminal Justice", as cited in *Jilin University Journal Social Sciences Edition*, No. 4.
See Zhang Mingkai. (2015b) *Responsibility and Prevention in Sentencing*, Peking University Press, 1-239
Suzuki Shigetsugu. (2011) *General Theory of Criminal Law*, Seibundo Publishing Co., 275;
Tadaki Makoto. (2011) "The expressive function in conceptual concurrence", as cited in *Kenshuu*, No. 754.
Tadaki Makoto. (2014) "Theory of multiple offenses and concurrence", as cited in Yamaguchi Atsushi & Kai Katsunori ed., *Key Issues in Japanese and Chinese Criminal Law in the 21st Century*, Seibundo Publishing Co., 73.
Vgl., H.Jescheck/T. Weigend, *Lehrbuch des Strafrechts.Allgemeiner Teil*, 5.Aufl., Duncker & Humblot, 1996, S.549;
Vgl., C. Roxin, *Strafrecht Allgemeiner Teil, Band II*, C.H.Beck, 2003, S.848ff,849f f,858f,831,822,848,851,856;
Vgl.Volkey Krey, *Strafrecht Besonderer Teil, Band 1*,11.Aufl., Kohlhammwer, 1998.S.114ff.
Wang Qiang. (2012) "The Special Relationship in Concurrence of Legal Provisions and Its Handling", as cited in *Chinese Journal of Law*, No. 1.
Wang Zuofu ed. (2009) *Criminal Law*, China Renmin University of Press, 170, 171.
Wu Zhenxing. (1996) *On Forms of Imputation*, China Procuratorate Press, 173;
Xiao Kaiquan. (1984) "Heavier Punishment Cannot Be Selected after Concurrence of Legal Provisions: A Rejoinder to Comrade Feng Yadong", as cited in *Journal of Law*, No. 8;
Yamaguchi Atsushi. (2007) *General Rules of Criminal Law*, Yuhikaku Press, 365、379;
Zhou Guangquan. (2010a) "A Study on the Special Relationship in Concurrence of Legal Provisions", as cited in *China Legal Science*, No. 3; Che Hao. (2010) "On the Relationship between the Crime of Rape and the Crime of Whoring with an Underage Girl", a cited in *Chinese Journal of Law*, No. 2.
Zhou Guangquan. (2010b) "A Study on the Special Relationship in Concurrence of Legal Provisions", as cited in *China Legal Science*, No. 3;
Zhou Guangquan. (2011) *General Part of Criminal Law*, China Renmin University of Press, 296

MIX
Papier aus verantwortungsvollen Quellen
Paper from responsible sources
FSC® C105338

If you have any concerns about our products,
you can contact us on
ProductSafety@springernature.com

In case Publisher is established outside the EU,
the EU authorized representative is:
Springer Nature Customer Service Center GmbH
Europaplatz 3, 69115 Heidelberg, Germany

Printed by Libri Plureos GmbH
in Hamburg, Germany